COLLECTED POEMS

SRI AUROBINDO

COLLECTED POEMS

SRI AUROBINDO ASHRAM
PONDICHERRY

First Edition 1972
Sixth Impression 1999

(SC) ISBN 81-7058-016-1
(HC) ISBN 81-7058-333-0

© Sri Aurobindo Ashram Trust 1972
Published by Sri Aurobindo Ashram Publication Department
Printed at Sri Aurobindo Ashram Press, Pondicherry 605 002
PRINTED IN INDIA

Contents

I. SHORT POEMS 1890-1900

Songs to Myrtilla	1890-92	1
Perfect thy motion	...	7
Phaethon	1890-92	7
To a Hero-Worshipper	September 1891	8
Estelle	1890-92	9
O Coil, Coil	1890-92	10
Hic Jacet	1890-92	11
Lines on Ireland	1896	12
Charles Stewart Parnell	1891	15
Night by the Sea	1890-92	16
A Thing Seen	...	19
The Lover's Complaint	1890-92	20
Love in Sorrow	1890-92	22
The Island Grave	1890-92	24
Bankim Chandra Chatterjee	...	25
Saraswati with the Lotus	1894	26
Goethe	1890-92	26
The Lost Deliverer	1890-92	26
Madhusudan Dutt	...	27
Envoi	1890-92	28
The Spring Child	1900	29
Since I have seen your face	...	30
Euphrosyne	...	31
The Nightingale	...	31
Song	...	32
Epigram	...	32
The Three Cries of Deiphobus	...	33
Epitaph	...	33
A Doubt	...	33
Perigune Prologuises	...	34

SHORT POEMS 1895-1908

Invitation	1908-09 (Alipore Jail)	39
Who	1908-09	40
Reminiscence	...	41
A Vision of Science	...	42
Immortal Love	...	44
To the Sea	...	45
The Sea at Night	...	46
Evening	...	46

CONTENTS

Revelation	...	47
A Tree	...	47
A Child's Imagination	...	48
Miracles	...	48
The Vedantin's Prayer	...	49
On the Mountains	...	50
Rebirth	...	51
Seasons	...	52
The Triumph-Song of Trishuncou	...	53
The Fear of Death	...	54
Life and Death	...	54
In the Moonlight	...	55
Parabrahman	...	62
God	...	63

SHORT POEMS 1902-1930

The Mother of Dreams	1908-09	67
The Birth of Sin	...	69
Epiphany	...	73
To R.	...	75
The Rakshasas	...	77
Kama	...	80
Kamadeva	...	82
The Mahatmas	...	83
The Meditations of Mandavya	12-4-1913	86
Hell and Heaven	...	93
Life	...	95

SHORT POEMS 1930-1950

A God's Labour	31-7-1935, 1-1-1936	99
Bride of the Fire	11-11-1935	103
The Blue Bird	11-11-1935	104
The Mother of God	1945	105
The Island Sun	3/13-10-1939	106
Silence is all	14-1-1946	107
Is this the end	3-6-1945	108
Who art thou that camest	22-3-1944	109
One Day	1938-39	109
The Dwarf Napoleon	16-10-1939	110
The Children of Wotan	August 1940	112
Despair on the Staircase	October 1939	113
Surrealist	...	113

CONTENTS

SHORT POEMS – FRAGMENTS

Morcundeya	...	117
A voice arose	...	117
I walked beside the waters	25-4-1934	118
Urvasie	...	119
The Cosmic Man	25-9-1938	120

II. SONNETS – EARLY PERIOD

To the Cuckoo	...	123
Transiit, Non Periit	...	123
O face that I have loved	...	124
I cannot equal	...	124
O letter dull and cold	...	125
My life is wasted	...	125
Because thy flame is spent	...	126
Thou didst mistake	...	126
Rose, I have loved	...	127
I have a hundred lives	...	127
Still there is something	...	128
I have a doubt	...	128
To weep because a glorious sun	...	129
What is this talk	...	129

SONNETS 1930-1950

Transformation	...	133
The Other Earths	...	133
Nirvana	...	134
Man the Thinking Animal	...	134
Contrasts	...	135
The Silver Call	...	135
Evolution	...	136
The Call of the Impossible	...	136
Evolution	...	137
Man the Mediator	...	137
The Infinitesimal Infinite	...	138
Discoveries of Science	...	138
The Ways of the Spirit	...	139
Science and the Unknowable	...	139
The Yogi on the Whirlpool	1936	140
The Kingdom Within	14-3-1936	140
Now I have borne	2-2-1938	141
Electron	15-7-1938	141
The Indwelling Universal	15-7-1938	142
Bliss of Identity	25-7-1938, 21-3-1944	142

CONTENTS

THE WITNESS SPIRIT	26-7-1938, 21-3-1944	143
THE HIDDEN PLAN	26-7-1938, 18/21-3-1944	143
THE PILGRIM OF THE NIGHT	26-7-1938, 18-3-44	144
COSMIC CONSCIOUSNESS	26-7-1938, 21-3-44(?)	144
LIBERATION	27-7-1938, 22-3-44	145
THE INCONSCIENT	27-7-1938, 21-3-44	145
LIFE-UNITY	8-8-1938, 22-3-1944	146
THE GOLDEN LIGHT	8-8-1938, 22-3-1944	146
THE INFINITE ADVENTURE	11-9-1939	147
THE GREATER PLAN	12-9-1939	147
THE UNIVERSAL INCARNATION	13-9-1939	148
THE GODHEAD	13-9-1939	148
THE STONE GODDESS	13-9-1939	149
THE COSMIC DANCE	15-9-1939	149
KRISHNA	15-9-1939	150
SHIVA	16-9-1939	150
MAN THE ENIGMA	17-9-1939	151
THE WORD OF THE SILENCE	18/19-9-1939	151
THE SELF'S INFINITY	18/19-9-1939	152
THE DUAL BEING	19-9-1939	152
LILA	20-9-1939	153
SURRENDER	20-9-1939	153
THE DIVINE WORKER	20-9-1939	154
THE GUEST	21-9-1939	154
THE INNER SOVEREIGN	22-9-1939	155
CREATION	24-9-1939	155
A DREAM OF SURREAL SCIENCE	25-9-1939	156
IN THE BATTLE	25-9-1939	156
THE LITTLE EGO	26-9-1939	157
THE MIRACLE OF BIRTH	27-9-1939	157
THE BLISS OF BRAHMAN	29-9-1939	158
MOMENTS	29-9-1939	158
THE BODY	2-10-1939	159
LIBERATION	2/3-10-1939	159
LIGHT	3/4-10-1939	160
THE UNSEEN INFINITE	4-10-1939	160
"I"	15-10-1939	161
THE COSMIC SPIRIT	15-10-1939	161
SELF	15-10-1939	162
OMNIPRESENCE	17-10-1939	162
THE INCONSCIENT FOUNDATION	18-10-1939	163
ADWAITA	19-10-1939	163
THE HILL-TOP TEMPLE	21-10-1939	164
THE DIVINE HEARING	24-10-1939	164

CONTENTS

BECAUSE THOU ART	25-10-1939	165
DIVINE SIGHT	26-10-1939	165
DIVINE SENSE	1-11-1939	166
THE IRON DICTATORS	14-11-1939	166
FORM	16-11-1939	167
IMMORTALITY	8-2-1940	167
MAN THE DESPOT OF CONTRARIES	29-7-1940	168
THE ONE SELF	...	168
THE INNER FIELDS	14-3-1947	169

III. LONGER POEMS

THE VIGIL OF THALIARD	August 1891-April 1892	173
URVASIE	...	189
LOVE AND DEATH	June, July 1899	231
KHALED OF THE SEA	...	261
BAJI PRABHOU	...	281
THE RISHI	...	297
CHITRANGADA	...	315
ULOUPIE	...	325
THE TALE OF NALA	...	335

IV. ON QUANTITATIVE METRE ... 341

V. ILION

ILION	...	391
AHANA	...	523
THE DESCENT OF AHANA	1910-15	537
AN ANSWER TO A CRITICISM	24-12-1942	551

VI. POEMS IN NEW METRES

OCEAN ONENESS	1942	557
TRANCE OF WAITING	...	558
FLAME-WIND	1942	559
THE RIVER	1942	560
THE DREAM BOAT	1942	561
THE WITNESS AND THE WHEEL	...	562
DESCENT	...	563
THE LOST BOAT	...	564
RENEWAL	...	565
SOUL'S SCENE	...	566
ASCENT: 1. THE SILENCE 2. BEYOND THE SILENCE	...	567
THE TIGER AND THE DEER	...	569
SOUL IN THE IGNORANCE	...	570
JOURNEY'S END	...	570

CONTENTS

THE BIRD OF FIRE	15-10-1933	571
TRANCE	15-10-1933	572
SHIVA, THE INCONSCIENT CREATOR	6-11-1933	573
THE LIFE HEAVENS	15-11-1933	574
JIVANMUKTA	13-4-1934	576
IN HORIS AETERNUM	19-4-1932	577
NOTES	...	578
THOUGHT THE PARACLETE	31-12-1934	582
MOON OF TWO HEMISPHERES	...	583
ROSE OF GOD	31-12-1934	584
NOTES	...	585
MUSA SPIRITUS	31-7-1935	589
KRISHNA	...	590
THE WORLD GAME	...	591
SYMBOL MOON	...	593
O PALL OF BLACK NIGHT	...	594
A STRONG SON OF LIGHTNING	...	595
AN IMAGE	...	595
HAIL TO THE FALLEN	...	596
IN A MOUNTING AS OF SEA-TIDES	...	597
THE DEATH OF A GOD	...	598
SOUL, MY SOUL	...	599

FRAGMENTS

IN THE SILENCE OF MIDNIGHT	...	603
SEER DEEP-HEARTED	...	603
DEATH AND THE TRAVELLER FIRE	...	604
TORN ARE THE WALLS	...	605
THE FIRE-KING AND THE MESSENGER	...	606
SILVER FOAM	...	607
VAST-WINGED THE WIND	...	608
TIRESIAS	...	608
OH YE POWERS	...	609
GOD TO THY GREATNESS	...	609

VII. METRICAL EXPERIMENTS 1934-1939 613

INDEX OF TITLES ... 619

INDEX OF FIRST LINES ... 625

I

SHORT POEMS

1890-1900

The poems dated 1890-92 were written by Sri Aurobindo between the age of eighteen and twenty in England.

Songs to Myrtilla

Glaucus

Sweet is the night, sweet and cool
As to parched lips a running pool;
Sweet when the flowers have fallen asleep
And only moonlit rivulets creep
Like glow-worms in the dim and whispering wood,
To commune with the quiet heart and solitude.
When earth is full of whispers, when
No daily voice is heard of men,
But higher audience brings
The footsteps of invisible things,
When o'er the glimmering tree-tops bowed
The night is leaning on a luminous cloud,
And always a melodious breeze
Sings secret in the weird and charmed trees,
Pleasant 'tis then heart-overawed to lie
Alone with that clear moonlight and that listening sky.

Æthon

But day is sweeter; morning bright
Has put the stars out ere the light,
And from their dewy cushions rise
Sweet flowers half-opening their eyes.
O pleasant then to feel as if new-born
The sweet, unripe and virgin air, the air of morn.
And pleasant are her melodies,
Rustle of winds, rustle of trees,
Birds' voices in the eaves,
Birds' voices in the green melodious leaves;
The herdsman's flute among his flocks,
Sweet water hurrying from reluctant rocks,
And all sweet hours and all sweet showers
And all sweet sounds that please the noonday flowers.
Morning has pleasure, noon has golden peace
And afternoon repose and eve the heart's increase.

All things are subject to sweet pleasure,
But three things keep her richest measure.

The breeze that visits heaven
And knows the planets seven,
The green spring with its flowery truth
Creative and the luminous heart of youth.
To all fair flowers and vernal
The wind makes melody diurnal.
On Ocean all night long
He rests, a voice of song.
The blue sea dances like a girl
With sapphire and with pearl
Crowning her locks. Sunshine and dew
Each morn delicious life renew.
The year is but a masque of flowers,
Of light and song and honied showers.
In the soft springtide comes the bird
Of heaven whose speech is one sweet word,
One word of sweet and magic power to bring
Green branches back and ruddy lights of spring.
Summer has pleasant comrades, happy meetings
Of lily and rose and from the trees divinest greetings.

    GLAUCUS

For who in April shall remember
The certain end of drear November?
No flowers then live, no flowers
Make sweet those wretched hours;
From dead or grieving branches spun
Unwilling leaves lapse wearily one by one;
The heart is then in pain
With the unhappy sound of rain.
No secret boughs prolong
A green retreat of song;
Summer is dead and rich repose
And springtide and the rose,
And woods and all sweet things make moan;
The weeping earth is turned to stone.
The lovers of her former face,
Shapes of beauty, melody, grace,
Where are they? Butterfly and bird
No more are seen, no songs are heard.

They see her beauty spent, her splendours done;
They seek a younger earth, a surer sun.
When youth has quenched its soft and magic light,
Delightful things remain but dead is their delight.

Æthon

Ah! for a little hour put by
Dim Hades and his pageantry.
Forget the future, leave the past,
The little hour thy life shall last.
Learn rather from the violet's days
Soft-blooming in retired ways
Or dewy bell, the maid undrest
With creamy childhood in her breast,
Fierce foxglove and the briony
And sapphire thyme, the work-room of the bee.
Behold in emerald fire
The spotted lizard crawl
Upon the sun-kissed wall
And coil in tangled brake
The green and sliding snake
Under the red-rose-briar.
Nay, hither see
Lured by thy rose of lips the bee
To woo thy petals open, O sweet,
His flowery murmur here repeat,
Forsaking all the joys of thyme.
Stain not thy perfumed prime
With care for autumn's pale decay,
But live like these thy sunny day.
So when thy tender bloom must fall,
Then shalt thou be as one who tasted all
Life's honey and must now depart
A broken prodigal from pleasure's mart,
A leaf with whom each golden sunbeam sinned,
A dewy leaf and kissed by every wandering wind.

Glaucus

How various are thy children, earth!
Behold the rose her lovely birth,

What fires from the bud proceed,
As if the vernal air did bleed.
Breezes and sunbeams, bees and dews
Her lords and lovers she indues,
And these her crimson pleasures prove;
Her life is but a bath of love;
The wide world perfumes when she sighs
And, burning all the winds, of love she dies.
The lily liveth pure,
Yet has she lovers, friends,
And each her bliss intends;
The bees besides her treasure
Besiege of pollened pleasure,
Nor long her gates endure.
The snowdrop cold
Has vowed the saintly state to hold
And far from green spring's amorous guilds
Her snowy hermitage she builds.
Cowslip attends her vernal duty
And stops the heart with beauty.
The crocus asks no vernal thing,
But all the lovely lights of spring
Are with rich honeysuckle boon
And praise her through one summer moon.
Thus the sweet children of the earth
Fulfil their natural selves and various birth.
For one is proud and one sweet months approve
Diana's saint, but most are bondmaidens of Love.

Love's feet were on the sea
When he dawned on me.
His wings were purple-grained and slow;
His voice was very sweet and very low;
His rose-lit cheeks, his eyes' pale bloom
Were sorrow's anteroom;
His wings did cause melodious moan;
His mouth was like a rose o'erblown;
The cypress-garland of renown
Did make his shadowy crown.
Fair as the spring he gave

And sadder than a winter's wave
And sweet as sunless asphodel,
My shining lily, Florimel,
My heart's enhaloed moon,
My winter's warmth, my summer's shady boon.

ÆTHON
Not from the mighty sea
Love visited me.
I found as in a jewelled box
Love, rose-red, sleeping with imprisoned locks;
And I have ever known him wild
And merry as a child,
As roses red, as roses sweet,
The west wind in his feet,
Tulip-girdled, kind and bold,
With heartsease in his curls of gold,
Since in the silver mist
Bright Cymothea's lips I kissed,
Whose laughter dances like a gleam
Of sunlight on a hidden stream
That through a wooded way
Runs suddenly into the perfect day.
But what were Cymothea, placed
Where like a silver star Myrtilla blooms?
Such light as cressets cast
In long and sun-lit rooms.
Thy presence is to her
As oak to juniper,
Thy beauty as the gorgeous rose
To privet by the lane that blows,
Gold-crownèd blooms to mere fresh grass,
Eternal ivy to brief blooms that pass.

GLAUCUS
But Florimel beside thee, sweet,
Pales like a candle in the brilliant noon.
Snowdrops are thy feet,
Thy waist a crescent moon,
And like a silver wand

Thy body slight doth stand
Or like a silver beech aspire.
Thine arms are walls for white caresses,
Thy mouth a tale of crimson kisses,
Thine eyes two amorous treasuries of fire.
To what shall poet liken thee?
Art thou a goddess of the sea
Purple-tressed and laughter-lipped
From thy choric sisters slipped
To wander on the flowery land?
Or art thou siren on the treacherous sand
Summer-voiced to charm the ear
Of the wind-vext mariner?
Ah! but what are these to thee,
Brighter gem than knows the sea,
Lovelier girl than sees the stream
Naked, Naiad of a dream,
Whiter Dryad than men see
Dancing round the lone oak-tree,
Flower and most enchanting birth
Of ten ages of the earth!
The Graces in thy body move
And in thy lips the ruby hue of Love.

Perfect thy motion

Perfect thy motion ever within me,
    Master of mind.
Grey of the brain, flash of the lightning,
    Brilliant and blind,
These thou linkest, the world to mould,
Writing the thought in a scroll of gold
    Violet-lined.

Tablet of brain thou hast made for thy writing,
    Master divine.
Calmly thou writest or full of thy grandeur
    Flushed as with wine,
Then with a laugh thou erasest the scroll,
Bringing another, like waves that roll
    And sink supine.

Phaethon

Ye weeping poplars by the shelvy slope
    From murmurous lawns down-dropping to the stream
    On whom the dusk air like a sombre dream
Broods and a twilight ignorant of hope,
    Say what compulsion drear has bid you seam
Your mossy sides with drop on eloquent drop
That in warm rillets from your eyes elope?

Is it for the too patient sure decay
    Pale-gilded Autumn, aesthete of the years,
    A gorgeous death, a fading glory wears
That thus along the tufted, downy way
    Creep slothfully this ooze of amber tears
And thus with tearful gusts your branches sway
Sighing a requiem to your emerald day?

To a Hero-Worshipper

I

My life is then a wasted ereme,
    My song but idle wind
    Because you merely find
In all this woven wealth of rhyme
Harsh figures with harsh music wound,
    The uncouth voice of gorgeous birds,
A ruby carcanet of sound,
    A cloud of lovely words?

I am, you say, no magic-rod,
    No cry oracular,
    No swart and ominous star,
No Sinai-thunder voicing God,
I have no burden to my song,
    No smouldering word instinct with fire,
No spell to chase triumphant wrong,
    No spirit-sweet desire.

Mine is not Byron's lightning spear,
    Nor Wordsworth's lucid strain
    Nor Shelley's lyric pain,
Nor Keats', the poet without peer.
I by the Indian waters vast
Did glimpse the magic of the past,
And on the oaten-pipe I play
Warped echoes of an earlier day.

II

My friend, when first my spirit woke,
    I trod the scented maze
    Of Fancy's myriad ways,
I studied Nature like a book

Men rack for meanings; yet I find
No rubric in the scarlet rose,
    No moral in the murmuring wind,
No message in the snows.

For me the daisy shines a star,
    The crocus flames a spire,
    A horn of golden fire,
Narcissus glows a silver bar:
Cowslips, the golden breath of God,
    I deem the poet's heritage,
And lilies silvering the sod
    Breathe fragrance from his page.

No herald of the Sun am I,
    But in a moon-lit veil
    A russet nightingale
Who pours sweet song, he knows not why,
    Who pours like a wine a gurgling note
    Paining with sound his swarthy throat,
Who pours sweet song, he recks not why,
Nor hushes ever lest he die.

Estelle

    Why do thy lucid eyes survey,
Estelle, their sisters in the milky way?
    The blue heavens cannot see
    Thy beauty nor the planets praise.
Blindly they walk their old accustomed ways.
    Turn hither for felicity.
    My body's earth thy vernal power declares,
    My spirit is a heaven of thousand stars,
And all these lights are thine and open doors on thee.

O Coil, Coil

O coïl, honied envoy of the spring,
Cease thy too happy voice, grief's record, cease:
For I recall that day of vernal trees,
The soft asoca's bloom, the laden winds
And green felicity of leaves, the hush,
The sense of Nature living in the woods.
Only the river rippled, only hummed
The languid murmuring bee, far-borne and slow,
Emparadised in odours, only used
The ringdove his divine heart-moving speech;
But sweetest to my pleased and singing heart
Thy voice, O coïl, in the peepel tree.

O me! for pleasure turned to bitterest tears!
O me! for the swift joy, too great to live,
That only bloomed one hour! O wondrous day,
That crowned the bliss of those delicious years.
The vernal radiance of my lover's lips
Was shut like a red rose upon my mouth,
His voice was richer than the murmuring leaves,
His love around me than the summer air.
Five hours entangled in the coïl's cry
Lay my beloved twixt my happy breasts.
O voice of tears! O sweetness uttering death!
O lost ere yet that happy cry was still!

O tireless voice of spring! Again I lie
In odorous gloom of trees; unseen and near
The windlark gurgles in the golden leaves,
The woodworm spins in shrillness on the bough:
Thou by the waters wailing to thy love,
O chocrobacque! have comfort, since to thee
The dawn brings sweetest recompense of tears
And she thou lovest hears thy pain. But I
Am desolate in the heart of fruitful months,
Am widowed in the sight of happy things,
Uttering my moan to the unhousèd winds,
O coïl, coïl, to the winds and thee.

Hic Jacet
Glasnevin Cemetery

    Patriots, behold your guerdon. This man found
Erin, his mother, bleeding, chastised, bound,
Naked to imputation, poor, denied,
While alien masters held her house of pride.
And now behold her! Terrible and fair
With the eternal ivy in her hair,
Armed with the clamorous thunder, how she stands
Like Pallas' self, the Gorgon in her hands.
True that her puissance will be easily past,
The vision ended; she herself has cast
Her fate behind her: yet the work not vain
Since that which once has been may be again,
And she this image yet recover, fired
With godlike workings, brain and hands inspired,
So stand, the blush of battle on her cheek,
Voice made armipotent, deeds that loudly speak,
Like some dread Sphinx, half patent to the eye,
Half veiled in formidable secrecy.
And he who raised her from her forlorn life
Loosening the fountains of that mighty strife,
Where sits he? On what high foreshadowing throne
Guarded by grateful hearts? Beneath this stone
He lies: this guerdon only Ireland gave,
A broken heart and an unhonoured grave.

Lines on Ireland
1896

After six hundred years did Fate intend
Her perfect perseverance thus should end?
So many years she strove, so many years,
Enduring toil, enduring bitter tears,
She waged religious war, with sword and song
Insurgent against Fate and numbers, strong
To inflict as to sustain; her weak estate
Could not conceal the goddess in her gait;
Goddess her mood. Therefore that light was she
In whom races of weaker destiny
Their beauteous image of rebellion saw;
Treason could not unnerve, violence o'erawe —
A mirror to enslavèd nations, never
O'ercome, though in the field defeated ever.
O mutability of human merit!
How changed, how fallen from her ancient spirit!
She that was Ireland, Ireland now no more,
In beggar's weeds behold at England's door
Neglected sues or at the best returned
With hollow promise, happy if not spurned
Perforce, she that had yesterday disdained
Less than her mighty purpose to have gained.
Had few short change of seasons puissance then,
O nurse and mother of heroic men,
Thy genius to outwear, thy strength well-placed
And old traditionary courage, waste
Thy vehement nature? Nay, not time, but thou
These ancient praises strov'st to disavow.
For 'tis not foreign force, nor weight of wars,
Nor treason, nor surprise, nor opposite stars,
Not all these have enslaved nor can, whate'er
Vulgar opinion bruit, nor years impair,
Ruin discourage, nor disease abate
A nation. Men are fathers of their fate;
They dig the prison, they the crown command.
Yet thine own self a little understand,
Unhappy country, and be wise at length.

An outward weakness doing deeds of strength
Amazed the nations, but a power within
Directed, like effective spirit unseen
Behind the mask of trivial forms, a source
And fund of tranquil and collected force.
This was the sense that made thee royal, blessed
With sanction from on high and that impressed
Which could thyself transfigure and infuse
Thine action with such pride as kings do use.
But thou to thine own self disloyal, hast
Renounced the help divine, turning thy past
To idle legends and fierce tales of blood,
Mere violent wrath with no proposèd good.
Therefore effective wisdom, skill to bend
All human things to one predestined end
Renounce thee. Honest purpose, labour true,
These dwell not with the self-appointed crew
Who, having conquered by death's aid, abuse
The public ear, — for seldom men refuse
Credence, when mediocrity multiplied
Equals itself with genius — fools! whose pride
Absurd the gods permit a little space
To please their souls with laughter, then replace
In the loud limbo of futilities.
How fallen art thou being ruled by these!
Ignoble hearts, courageous to effect
Their country's ruin; such the heavens reject
For their high agencies and leave exempt
Of force, mere mouths and vessels of contempt.
They of thy famous past and nature real
Uncareful, have denied thy rich ideal
For private gains, the burden would not brook
Of that sustaining genius, when it took
A form of visible power, since it demanded
All meaner passions for its sake disbanded.
As once against the loud Euphratic host
The lax Ionians of the Asian coast
Drew out their numbers, but not long enduring
Rigorous hard-hearted toil to the alluring
Cool shadow of the olives green withdrew;

Freedom's preparators though well they knew
Labour exact, discipline, pains well nerved
In the severe unpitying sun, yet swerved
From their ordeal; Ireland so deceiving
The world's great hope, her temples large relieving
Of the too heavy laurel, rather chose
Misery, civil battle, triumphant foes
Than rational order and divine control.
Therefore her brighter fate and nobler soul
Glasnevin with that hardly-honoured bier
Received. But the immortal mind austere,
By man rejected, of eternal praise
Has won its meed and sits with heavenly bays,
Not variable breath of favour, crowned
On high. And grieves it not, spirit renowned,
Mortal ingratitude though now forgiven,
Grieves it not, even on the hills of heaven,
After so many mighty toils, defeats
So many, cold repulse and vernal heats
Of hope, iron endurance throned apart
In lonely strength within thy godlike heart,
Obloquy faced, health lost, the goal nigh won,
To see at last thy strenuous work undone?
So falls it ever when a race condemned
To strict and lasting bondage, have contemned
Their great deliverer, self and ease preferring
To labour's crown, by their own vileness erring.
Thus the uncounselled Israelites of old,
Binding their mightiest, for their own ease sold,
Who else had won them glorious liberty
To his Philistian foes, as thine did thee.
Thou likewise, had thy puissant soul endured
Within its ruined house to stay immured,
With parallel disaster and o'erthrow
Hadst daunted and their conjured strength laid low.
But time was adverse. Thus too Heracles
In exile closed by the Olynthian seas,
Not seeing Thebes nor Dirce any more,
His friendless eyelids on an alien shore.
Yet not unbidden of heaven the men renowned

Have laboured, though no fruit apparent crowned
Nor praise contemporary touched with leaf
Of civic favour, who for joy or grief
To thronèd injustice never bowed the head.
They triumph from the houses of the dead.
Thou too, high spirit, mighty genius, glass
Of patriots, into others' deeds shalt pass
With force and tranquil fortitude thy dower,
An inspiration and a fount of power.
Nor to thy country only nor thy day
Art thou a name and a possession, stay
Of loftiest natures, but where'er and when
In time's full ripeness and the date of men
Alien oppression maddened has the wise, —
For ever thus preparing Nemesis
In ruling nations unjust power has borne
Insolence, injustice, madness, outrage, scorn,
Its natural children, then, by high disdain
And brave example pushed to meet their pain,
The pupils of thy greatness shall appear,
Souls regal to the mould divine most near,
And reign, or rise on throne-intending wings,
Making thee father to a line of kings.

Charles Stewart Parnell
1891

O pale and guiding light, now star unsphered,
Deliverer lately hailed, since by our lords
Most feared, most hated, hated because feared,
Who smot'st them with an edge surpassing swords!
Thou too wert then a child of tragic earth,
Since vainly filled thy luminous doom of birth.

Night by the Sea

Love, a moment drop thy hands;
Night within my soul expands.
Veil thy beauties milk-rose-fair
In that dark and showering hair.
Coral kisses ravish not
When the soul is tinged with thought;
Burning looks are then forbid.
Let each shyly-parted lid
Hover like a settling dove
O'er those deep-blue wells of Love.
Darkness brightens; silvering flee
Pomps of foam the driven sea.

In this garden's dim repose
Lighted with the burning rose,
Soft narcissi's golden camp
Glimmering or with rosier lamp
Censered honeysuckle guessed
By the fragrance of her breast, —
Here where summer's hands have crowned
Silence in the fields of sound,
Here felicity should be.
Hearken, Edith, to the sea.

What a voice of grief intrudes
On these happy solitudes!
To the wind that with him dwells
Ocean, old historian, tells
All the dreadful heart of tears
Hidden in the pleasant years.
Summer's children, what do ye
By the stern and cheerless sea?

Not we first nor we alone
Heard the mighty Ocean moan
By this treasure-house of flowers
In the sweet ambiguous hours.
Many a girl's lips ruby-red

With their vernal honey fed
Happy mouths, and soft cheeks flushed
With Love's rosy sunlight blushed.
Ruddy lips of many a boy
Blithe discovered hills of joy
Ruby-guided through a kiss
To the sweet highways of bliss.
Here they saw the evening still
Coming slowly from the hill
And the patient stars arise
To their outposts in the skies;
Heard the ocean shoreward urge
The speed and thunder of his surge,
Singing heard as though a bee
Noontide waters on the sea.
These no longer. For our rose
In her place they wreathed once, blows,
And thy glorious garland, sweet,
Kissed not once those wandering feet.
All the lights of spring are ended,
To the wintry haven wended.
Beauty's boons and nectarous leisure,
Lips, the honeycombs of pleasure,
Cheeks enrosed, Love's natal soil,
Breasts, the ardent conqueror's spoil,
Spring rejects; a lovelier child
His brittle fancies has beguiled.
O her name that to repeat
Than the Dorian muse more sweet
Could the white hand more relume
Writing and refresh the bloom
Of lips that used such syllables then,
Dies unloved by later men.
Are we more than summer flowers?
Shall a longer date be ours,
Rose and springtime, youth and we
By the everlasting sea?

Are they blown as legends tell
In the smoke and gurge of hell?

Writhe they in relucent gyres
O'er a circle sad of fires?
In what lightless groves must they
Or unmurmuring alleys stray?
Fields no sunlight visits, streams
Where no happy lotus gleams?
Yet, where'er their steps below,
Memories sweet for comrades go.
Lethe's waters had their will,
But the soul remembers still.
Beauty pays her boon of breath
To thy narrow credit, Death,
Leaving a brief perfume; we
Perish also by the sea.

We shall lose, ah me! too soon
Lose the clear and silent moon,
The serenities of night
And the deeper evening light.
We shall know not when the morn
In the widening East is born,
Never feel the west-wind stir,
Spring's delightful messenger,
Never under branches lain
Dally with the sweet-lipped rain,
Watch the moments of the tree,
Nor know the sounds that tread the sea.

With thy kisses chase this gloom: —
Thoughts, the children of the tomb.
Kiss me, Edith. Soon the night
Comes and hides the happy light.
Nature's vernal darlings dead
From new founts of life are fed.
Dawn relumes the immortal skies.
Ah! what boon for earth-closed eyes?
Love's sweet debts are standing, sweet;
Honied payment to complete
Haste — a million is to pay —
Lest too soon the allotted day

End and we oblivious keep
Darkness and eternal sleep.
See! the moon from heaven falls.
In thy bosom's snow-white walls
Softly and supremely housed
Shut my heart up; keep it closed
Like a rose of Indian grain,
Like that rose against the rain,
Closed to all that life applauds,
Nature's perishable gauds,
And the airs that burdened be
With such thoughts as shake the sea.

A Thing Seen

She in her garden, near the high grey wall,
Sleeping; a silver-bodied birch-tree tall
That held its garments o'er her wide and green
Building a parapet of shade between,
Forbidding the amorous sun to look on her.
No fold of gracious raiment was astir.
The wind walked softly; silent moved a cloud
Listening; of all the tree no leaf was loud,
But guarded a divine expectant hush
Thrilled by the silence of a hidden thrush.

The Lover's Complaint

O plaintive, murmuring reed, begin thy strain;
    Unloose that heavenly tongue,
    Interpreter divine of pain;
Utter thy voice, the sister of my song.
Thee in the silver waters growing,
Arcadian Pan, strange whispers blowing
Into thy delicate stops, did teach
A language lovelier than speech.

O plaintive, murmuring reed, begin thy strain;
    O plaintive, murmuring reed.
    Nisa to Mopsus is decreed,
The moonwhite Nisa to a swarthy swain.
What love-gift now shall Hope not bring?
Election dwells no more with beauty's king.
The wild weed now has wed the rose,
Now ivy on the bramble grows;
Too happy lover, fill the lamp of bliss!
Too happy lover, drunk with Nisa's kiss!
For thee pale Cynthia leaves her golden car,
For thee from Tempe stoops the white and evening star.

O plaintive, murmuring reed, renew thy strain;
    O solace anguish yet again.
    I thought Love soft as velvet sleep,
Sweeter than dews nocturnal breezes weep,
Cool as water in a murmuring pass
And shy as violets in the vernal grass,
But hard as Nisa's heart is he
And salt as the unharvestable sea.

O plaintive, murmuring reed, renew thy strain.
    One morn she came; her mouth
    Breathing the odours of the south,
With happy eyes and heaving bosom fain.
She asked for fruit long-stored in autumn's hold.
These gave I; from the branch dislodged I threw
Sweet-hearted apples in their age of gold

And pears divine for taste and hue.
And one I saw, should all the rest excel;
But error led my plucking hand astray
And with a sudden sweet dismay
My heart into her apron fell.

O plaintive, murmuring reed, renew thy strain.
    My bleeding heart awhile
    She kept and bloomed upon its pain,
Then slighted as a broken thing and vile.
Now Mopsus in his unblest arms,
Mopsus enfolds her heavenlier charms,
Mopsus to whom the Muse averse
Refused her gracious secrets to rehearse.

O plaintive, murmuring reed, breathe yet thy strain.
    Ye glades, your bliss I grudge you not,
    Nor would I that my grief profane
Your sacred summer with intruding thought.
Yet since I will no more behold
Your glorious beauty stained with gold
From shadows of her hair, nor by some well
Made naked of their sylvan dress
The breasts, the limbs I never shall possess,
Therefore, O mother Arethuse, farewell.

For me no place abides
By the green verge of thy belovèd tides.
To Lethe let my footsteps go
And wailing waters in the realms below,
Where happier song is none than moaning pain
Nor any lovelier Syrinx than the weed.
Child of the lisping waters, hush thy strain,
O murmuring, plaintive reed.

Love in Sorrow

Do you remember, Love, that sunset pale
    When from near meadows sad with mist the breeze
Sighed like a feverous soul and with soft wail
    The ghostly river sobbed among the trees?
I think that Nature heard our misery
Weep to itself and wept for sympathy.

For we were strangers then; we knew not Fate
    In ambush by the solitary stream
Nor did our sorrows hope to find a mate,
    Much less of love or friendship dared we dream.
Rather we thought that loneliness and we
Were wed in marble perpetuity.

For there was none who loved me, no, not one.
    Alas, what was there that a man should love?
For I was misery's last and frailest son
    And even my mother bade me homeless rove.
And I had wronged my youth and nobler powers
By weak attempts, small failures, wasted hours.

Therefore I laid my cheek on the chill grass
    And murmured, "I am overborne with grief
And joy to richer natures hopes to pass.
    Oh me! my life is like an aspen leaf
That shakes but will not fall. My thoughts are blind
And life so bitter that death seems almost kind.

"How am I weary of the days' increase,
    Of the moon's brightness and the splendid stars,
The sun that dies not. I would be at peace,
    Nor blind my soul with images, nor force
My lips to mirth whose later taste is death,
Nor with vain utterance load my weary breath."

Thus murmured I aloud nor deemed I spoke
    To human ears, but you were hidden, sweet,
Behind the willows when my plaining broke

Upon your lonely muse. Ah, kindly feet
That brushed the grass in tender haste to bind
Another's wounds, you were less wise than kind.

You said, "My brother, lift your forlorn eyes;
    I am your sister more than you unblest."
I looked upon your face, the book of sighs
    And index to incurable unrest.
I rose and kissed you, sweet. Your lips were warm
And drew my heart out like a witch's charm.

We parted where the sacred spires arose
    In silent power above the silent street.
I saw you mid the rose-trees, O white rose,
    Linger a moment, then the dusk defeat
My eyes, and, listening, heard your footsteps fade
On the sad leaves of the autumnal glade.

And were you happy, sweet? In me I know —
    For either in my blood the autumn sang
His own pale requiem or that new sweet glow
    Failed in the light of bitter knowledge — rang
A voice that said, "Behold the loves too pure
To live, the joy that never shall endure."

This too I know, nor is my hope so bright
    But that it sees its autumn cold and sere
Attending with a pale and solemn light
    Beyond the gardens of the vernal year.
Yet will I not my weary heart constrain
But take you, sweet, and sweet surcease from pain.

The Island Grave

    Ocean is there and evening; the slow moan
        Of the blue waves that like a shaken robe
    Two heard together once, one hears alone.

        Now gliding white and hushed towards our globe
    Keen January with cold eyes and clear
        And snowdrops pendent in each frosty lobe

    Ushers the firstborn of the radiant year.
        Haply his feet that grind the breaking mould,
    May brush the dead grass on thy secret bier,

        Haply his joyless fingers wan and cold
    Caress the ruined masses of thy hair,
        Pale child of winter, dead ere youth was old.

    Art thou so desolate in that bitter air
        That even his breath feels warm upon thy face?
    Ah, till the daffodil is born, forbear,

        And I will meet thee in that lonely place.
    Then the grey dawn shall end my hateful days
        And death admit me to the silent ways.

Bankim Chandra Chatterji

How hast thou lost, O month of honey and flowers,
The voice that was thy soul! Creative showers,
The cuckoo's daylong cry and moan of bees,
Zephyrs and streams and softly-blossoming trees
And murmuring laughter and heart-easing tears
And tender thoughts and great and the compeers
Of lily and jasmine and melodious birds,
All these thy children into lovely words
He changed at will and made soul-moving books
From hearts of men and women's honied looks.
O master of delicious words! the bloom
Of chompuk and the breath of king-perfume
Have made each musical sentence with the noise
Of women's ornaments and sweet household joys
And laughter tender as the voice of leaves
Playing with vernal winds. The eye receives
That reads these lines an image of delight,
A world with shapes of spring and summer, noon and night;
All nature in a page, no pleasing show
But men more real than the friends we know.
O plains, O hills, O rivers of sweet Bengal,
O land of love and flowers, the spring-bird's call
And southern wind are sweet among your trees:
Your poet's words are sweeter far than these.
Your heart was this man's heart. Subtly he knew
The beauty and divinity in you.
His nature kingly was and as a god
In large serenity and light he trod
His daily way, yet beauty, like soft flowers
Wreathing a hero's sword, ruled all his hours.
Thus moving in these iron times and drear,
Barren of bliss and robbed of golden cheer,
He sowed the desert with ruddy-hearted rose,
The sweetest voice that ever spoke in prose.

Saraswati with the Lotus
BANKIM CHANDRA CHATTERJI. OBIIT 1894

    Thy tears fall fast, O mother, on its bloom,
    O white-armed mother, like honey fall thy tears;
    Yet even their sweetness can no more relume
    The golden light, the fragrance heaven rears,
    The fragrance and the light for ever shed
    Upon his lips immortal who is dead.

Goethe

    A perfect face amid barbarian faces,
    A perfect voice of sweet and serious rhyme,
    Traveller with calm, inimitable paces,
    Critic with judgment absolute to all time,
    A complete strength when men were maimed and weak,
    German obscured the spirit of a Greek.

The Lost Deliverer

    Pythian he came; repressed beneath his heel
    The hydra of the world with bruisèd head.
    Vainly, since Fate's immeasurable wheel
    Could parley with a straw. A weakling sped
    The bullet when to custom's usual night
    We fell because a woman's faith was light.

Madhusudan Dutt

Poet, who first with skill inspired did teach
Greatness to our divine Bengali speech, —
Divine, but rather with delightful moan
Spring's golden mother makes when twin-alone
She lies with golden Love and heaven's birds
Call hymeneal with enchanting words
Over their passionate faces, rather these
Than with the calm and grandiose melodies
(Such calm as consciousness of godhead owns)
The high gods speak upon their ivory thrones
Sitting in council high, — till taught by thee
Fragrance and noise of the world-shaking sea.
Thus do they praise thee who amazed espy
Thy winged epic and hear the arrows cry
And journeyings of alarmèd gods; and due
The praise, since with great verse and numbers new
Thou mad'st her godlike who was only fair.
And yet my heart more perfectly ensnare
Thy soft impassioned flutes and more thy Muse
To wander in the honied months doth choose
Than courts of kings, with Sita in the grove
Of happy blossoms, (O musical voice of love
Murmuring sweet words with sweeter sobs between!)
With Shoorpa in the Vindhyan forests green
Laying her wonderful heart upon the sod
Made holy by the well-loved feet that trod
Its vocal shades; and more unearthly bright
Thy jewelled songs made of relucent light
Wherein the birds of spring and summer and all flowers
And murmuring waters flow, her widowed hours
Making melodious who divinely loved.
No human hands such notes ambrosial moved;
These accents are not of the imperfect earth;
Rather the god was voiceful in their birth,
The god himself of the enchanting flute,
The god himself took up thy pen and wrote.

Envoi

> Ite hinc, Camenae, vos quoque ite jam, sane
> Dulces Camenae, nam fatebimur verum
> Dulces fuistis, et tamen meas chartas
> Revisitote sed pudenter et raro.

Pale poems, weak and few, who vainly use
Your wings towards the unattainable spheres,
Offspring of the divine Hellenic Muse,
Poor maimèd children born of six disastrous years!

Not as your mother's is your wounded grace,
Since not to me with equal love returned
The hope which drew me to that serene face
Wherein no unreposeful light of effort burned.

Depart and live for seasons many or few
If live you may, but stay not here to pain
My heart with hopeless passion and renew
Visions of beauty that my lips shall ne'er attain.

For in Sicilian olive-groves no more
Or seldom must my footprints now be seen,
Nor tread Athenian lanes, nor yet explore
Parnassus or thy voiceful shores, O Hippocrene.

Me from her lotus heaven Saraswati
Has called to regions of eternal snow
And Ganges pacing to the southern sea,
Ganges upon whose shores the flowers of Eden blow.

The Spring Child
ON BASANTI'S BIRTHDAY - JYESTHA 1900

Of Spring is her name for whose bud and blooming
    We praise today the Giver, —
Of Spring, and its sweetness clings about her
For her face is Spring and Spring's without her,
    As loth to leave her.

See, it is summer; the brilliant sunlight
    Lies hard on stream and plain,
And all things wither with heats diurnal;
But she! how vanished things and vernal
    In her remain.

And almost indeed we repine and marvel
    To watch her bloom and grow;
For half we had thought our sweet bud could never
Bloom out, but must surely remain for ever
    The child we know.

But now though summer must come and autumn
    In God's high governing
Yet I deem that her soul with soft insistence
Shall guard through all change the sweet existence
    And charm of Spring.

O dear child soul, our loved and cherished,
    For this thy days had birth,
Like some tender flower on some grey stone portal
To sweeten and flush with childhood immortal
    The ageing earth.

There are flowers in God's garden of prouder blooming
    Brilliant and bold and bright,
The tulip and rose are fierier and brighter,
But this has a softer hue, a whiter
    And milder light.

Long be thy days in rain and sunshine,
    Often thy spring relume,
Gladdening thy mother's heart with thy beauty,
Flowerlike doing thy gentle duty
    To be loved and bloom.

❈

Since I have seen your face

Since I have seen your face at the window, sweet
Love, you have thrown a spell on my heart, my feet.
My heart to your face, my feet to your window still
Bear me by force as if by an alien will.

O witch of beauty, O Circe with innocent eyes,
You have suddenly caught me fast in a net of sighs.
I look at the sunlight, I see your laughing face;
When I purchase a flower, it is you in your radiant grace.

I have tried to save my soul alive from your snare,
I will strive no more; let it flutter and perish there.
I too will snare your body alive, O my dove,
And teach you all the torture and sweetness of love.

When you have looked from the window out on the trampling city,
Did you think to take my heart and pay me with pity?
But you looked at one who has ever mocked at sin
And gambled with life to lose her all or win.

I will pluck you forth like a fluttering bird from her nest.
You shall lie on Love's strong knees, in his white warm breast,
Afraid, with delighted lids that will not close.
You shall grow white one moment, the next a rose.

Euphrosyne

Child of the infant years, Euphrosyne,
Bird of my boyhood, youth's blithe deity!
If I have hymned thee not with lyric phrase,
Preferring Eros or Aglaia's praise,
Frown not, thou lovely spirit, leave me not.
Man worships the ungrasped. His vagrant thought
Still busy with the illimitable void
Lives all the time by little things upbuoyed
Which he contemns; the wife unsung remains
Sharing his pleasures, taking half his pains,
While to dream faces mounts the poet's song.
Yet she makes not their lyric light her wrong,
Knowing her homely eyes his sorrow's star
Smiles at the eclipsing brow untouched by care.
Content with human love lightly she yields
The immortal fancy its Elysian fields.

The Nightingale
An Impression

Hark in the trees the low-voiced nightingale
Has slain the silence with a jubilant cry;
How clear in the hushed night, yet voluble
And various as sweet water wavering by,
    That murmurs in a channel small
    Beneath a low grey wall,
    Then sings amid the fitful rye.
    O sweet grave Siren of the night,
        Astarte's eremite,
Thou feedest every leaf with solemn glee,
Lo, the night-winds sigh happier, being chid by thee.

Song

O lady Venus, shine on me,
O rose-crowned goddess from thy seas
Radiant among the Cyclades!
O rose-crowned, puissant like the sea.

And bring thy Graces three,
The swift companions of thy mirthful mind,
Bring thy sweet rogue with thee,
Thy careless archer, beautiful and blind.

A woman's royal heart
Bid him to wound and bind her who is free;
Bind her for me!
Nor for the sweet bright crimson blood may start
In little rillets from the little heart
Spare her thy sport to be,
Goddess, she spared not me.

❃

Epigram

If thou wouldst traverse Time with vagrant feet
Nor make the poles thy limit, fill not then
Thy wallet with the fancy's cloying sweet
    Which is no stay to heaven-aspiring men,
But follow wisdom since alone the wise
Can walk through fire with unblinking eyes.

The Three Cries of Deiphobus

Awake, awake, O sleeping men of Troy,
That sleep and know not in the grasp of Hell
I perish in the treacherous lonely night
To foes betrayed, environed and undone.

O Trojans, will ye sleep until the doom
Have slipped its leash and bark upon your doors?
Not long will ye, unless in Pluto's realm,
Have slumber, since forsaken among foes
I drink the bitter cup of lonely death
Unheeded and from helping faces far.

O Trojans, Trojans, yet again I call!
Swift help we need, or Ilion's days are done.

Epitaph

Moulded of twilight and the vesper star
Midnight in her with noon made quiet war; —
Moulded twixt life and death, Love came between;
Then the night fell; twilight faded, the star had been.

A Doubt

Many boons the new years make us
    But the old world's gifts were three,
Dove of Cypris, wine of Bacchus,
    Pan's sweet pipe in Sicily.

Love, wine, song, the core of living
    Sweetest, oldest, musicalest.
If at end of forward striving
    These, Life's first, proved also best?

Perigune Prologuises

    Cool may you find the youngling grass, my herd,
    Cool with delicious dew, while I here dream
    And listen to the sweet and garrulous bird
    That matches its cool note with Thea's stream.
    Boon Zephyr now with waist ungirdled runs,
    And you, O luminous nurslings, wider blow,
    O nurslings of light rain and vernal suns,
    When bounteous winds about the garden go.
    Apt to my soul art thou, blithe honeyed moon,
    O lovely mother of the rose-red June.
    Zephyr that all things soothes, enhances all,
    Dwells with thee softly, the near cuckoo drawn
    To farther groves with sweet inviting call
    And dewy buds upon the blossoming lawn.
    But ah, today some happy soft unrest
    Aspires and pants in my unquiet breast,
    As if some light were from the day withdrawn,
    As if the flitting Zephyr knew a lovelier word
    Than it had spoken yet, and flower and bird
    Kept still some grace that yet is left to bloom,
    Had still a note I never yet have heard,
    That, blossoming, would the wide air more illume,
    That, spoken, would advance the sweet Spring's bounds
    With large serener lights and joy of exquisite sounds.

    Nor have I any in whose ears to tell
    This gracious grief and so by words have peace,
    Save the cold hyacinth in the breezy dell
    And the sweet cuckoo in the sunlit trees
    Since the sharp autumn days when with increase
    Of rosy-lighted cheeks attained the ground
    Weary of waiting and by wasps hung round
    The bough's fair hangings and Thea fell with these,
    My mother, with twelve matron summers crowned.
    Four times since then the visits of green spring
    Have blessed the hillsides with fresh blossoming
    And four times has the winter chilled the brooks,
    Since sole I dwell with my rude father, cheered

By no low-worded speech or sunny looks.
Yet are we rich enough, fruitful our herd
And yields us brimming pails and store we still
Numberless baskets with white cheese and fill
Our cave with fruits for winter, and since wide-feared
My father Sinnis, none have care our wealth to spoil.
Therefore I pass sweet days with easy toil,
Nor other care have much but milk the kine
And call them out to graze in soft sunshine
And stall them when the evening-star grows large.
All else is pleasure, budded wreaths to twine
And please my soul beside my hornèd charge
And bathe in the delicious brook that speeds,
Iris and water-lily capped and green with reeds.

Nor need we flocks for clothing nor the shears;
For when the echoes in the mountain rocks
Mimic the groaning wain that moving peers
Between thick trees or under granite blocks,
Our needs my father takes, nor any yet
Scaped him who breaks the wrestler as these twines
Of bloom I break, so he with little sweat,
And tears the women with dividing pines.
Therefore thin gleaming robes and ruddy wines
We garner, flickering swords in jewelled case
And burning jewels and the beautiful gold
Whereof bright plenty now our caverns hold
And ornaments of utter exquisiteness.
But if these brilliants of their pleasure fail,
The lily blooms from vale to scented vale
And crocus lifts in Spring its golden fire.
Our midnight hears the warbling nightingale,
The cuckoo calls as he would never tire;
Along our hills we pluck the purple grapes,
And in the night a million stars arise
To watch us with their ancient friendly eyes.
Such flowering ease I have and earth's sweet shapes;
And riches, and the green and hivèd springs.
Ah then what longing wakes for new and lovelier things!

SHORT POEMS
1895 - 1908

Invitation

With wind and the weather beating round me
    Up to the hill and the moorland I go.
Who will come with me? Who will climb with me?
    Wade through the brook and tramp through the snow?

Not in the petty circle of cities
    Cramped by your doors and your walls I dwell;
Over me God is blue in the welkin,
    Against me the wind and the storm rebel.

I sport with solitude here in my regions,
    Of misadventure have made me a friend.
Who would live largely? Who would live freely?
    Here to the wind-swept uplands ascend.

I am the lord of tempest and mountain,
    I am the Spirit of freedom and pride.
Stark must he be and a kinsman to danger
    Who shares my kingdom and walks at my side.

Who

In the blue of the sky, in the green of the forest,
    Whose is the hand that has painted the glow?
When the winds were asleep in the womb of the ether,
    Who was it roused them and bade them to blow?

He is lost in the heart, in the cavern of Nature,
    He is found in the brain where He builds up the thought:
In the pattern and bloom of the flowers He is woven,
    In the luminous net of the stars He is caught.

In the strength of a man, in the beauty of woman,
    In the laugh of a boy, in the blush of a girl;
The hand that sent Jupiter spinning through heaven,
    Spends all its cunning to fashion a curl.

These are His works and His veils and His shadows;
    But where is He then? by what name is He known?
Is He Brahma or Vishnu? a man or a woman?
    Bodied or bodiless? twin or alone?

We have love for a boy who is dark and resplendent,
    A woman is lord of us, naked and fierce.
We have seen Him a-muse on the snow of the mountains,
    We have watched Him at work in the heart of the spheres.

We will tell the whole world of His ways and His cunning:
    He has rapture of torture and passion and pain;
He delights in our sorrow and drives us to weeping,
    Then lures with His joy and His beauty again.

All music is only the sound of His laughter,
    All beauty the smile of His passionate bliss;
Our lives are His heart-beats, our rapture the bridal
    Of Radha and Krishna, our love is their kiss.

He is strength that is loud in the blare of the trumpets,
    And He rides in the car and He strikes in the spears;
He slays without stint and is full of compassion;
    He wars for the world and its ultimate years.

In the sweep of the worlds, in the surge of the ages,
    Ineffable, mighty, majestic and pure,
Beyond the last pinnacle seized by the thinker
    He is throned in His seats that for ever endure.

The Master of man and his infinite Lover,
    He is close to our hearts, had we vision to see;
We are blind with our pride and the pomp of our passions,
    We are bound in our thoughts where we hold ourselves free.

It is He in the sun who is ageless and deathless,
    And into the midnight His shadow is thrown;
When darkness was blind and engulfed within darkness,
    He was seated within it immense and alone.

❈

Reminiscence

My soul arose at dawn and, listening, heard
One voice abroad, a solitary bird,
A song not master of its note, a cry
That persevered into eternity.
My soul leaned out into the dawn to hear
In the world's solitude its winged compeer
And, hearkening what the Angel had to say,
Saw lustre in midnight and a secret day
Was opened to it. It beheld the stars
Born from a thought and knew how being prepares.
Then I remembered how I woke from sleep
And made the skies, built earth, formed Ocean deep.

A Vision of Science

I dreamed that in myself the world I saw,
Wherein three Angels strove for mastery. Law
Was one, clear vision and denial cold,
Yet in her limits strong, presumptuous, bold;
The second with enthusiasm bright,
Flame in her heart but round her brows the night,
Faded as this advanced. She could not bear
That searching gaze, nor the strong chilling air
These thoughts created, nourishing our parts
Of mind, but petrifying human hearts.
Science was one, the other gave her name,
Religion. But a third behind them came,
Veiled, vague, remote, and had as yet no right
Upon the world, but lived in her own light.
Wide were the victories of the Angel proud
Who conquered now and in her praise were loud
The nations. Few even yet to the other clove, —
And some were souls of night and some were souls of love.
But this was confident and throned. Her heralds ranged
Claiming that night was dead and all things changed;
For all things opened, all seemed clear, seemed bright —
Save the vast ranges that they left in night.
However, the light they shed upon the earth
Was great indeed, a firm and mighty birth.
A century's progress lived before my eyes.
Delivered from amazement and surprise,
Man's spirit measuring his worlds around
The laws of sight divined and laws of sound.
Light was not hidden from its searching gaze,
Nor matter could deny her myriad maze
To the cold enquiry; for the far came near,
The small loomed large, the intricate grew clear.
Measuring and probing the strong Angel strode,
Dissolving and combining, till she trod
Firmly among the stars, could weigh their forms,
Foretold the earthquakes, analysed the storms.
Doubt seemed to end and wonder's reign was closed.
The stony pages of the earth disclosed

Their unremembered secrets. Horses of steam
Were bitted and the lightnings made a team
To draw our chariots. Heaven was scaled at last
And the loud seas subdued. Distance resigned
Its strong obstructions to the mastering mind.
So moved that spirit trampling; then it laid
Its hand at last upon itself, how this was made
Wondering, and sought to class and sought to trace
Mind by its forms, the wearer by the dress.
Then the other arose and met that spirit robust,
Who laboured; she now grew a shade who must
Fade wholly away, yet to her fellow cried,
"I pass, for thou hast laboured well and wide.
Thou thinkest term and end for thee are not;
But though thy pride is great, thou hast forgot
The Sphinx that waits for man beside the way.
All questions thou mayst answer, but one day
Her question shall await thee. That reply,
As all we must; for they, who cannot, die.
She slays them and their mangled bodies lie
Upon the highways of eternity.
Therefore, if thou wouldst live, know first this thing,
Who thou art in this dungeon labouring."
And Science confidently, "Nothing am I but earth,
Tissue and nerve and from the seed a birth,
A mould, a plasm, a gas, a little that is much.
In these grey cells that quiver to each touch
The secret lies of man; they are the thing called I.
Matter insists and matter makes reply.
Shakespeare was this; this force in Jesus yearned
And conquered by the cross; this only learned
The secret of the suns that blaze afar;
This was Napoleon's giant mind of war."
I heard and marvelled in myself to see
The infinite deny infinity.
Yet the weird paradox seemed justified;
Even mysticism shrank out-mystified.
But the third Angel came and touched my eyes;
I saw the mornings of the future rise,
I heard the voices of an age unborn

That comes behind us and our pallid morn,
And from the heart of an approaching light
One said to man, "Know thyself infinite,
Who shalt do mightier miracles than these,
Infinite, moving mid infinities."
Then from our hills the ancient answer pealed,
"For Thou, O Splendour, art myself concealed,
And the grey cell contains me not, the star
I outmeasure and am older than the elements are.
Whether on earth or far beyond the sun,
I, stumbling, clouded, am the Eternal One."

❋

Immortal Love

If I had wooed thee for thy colour rare,
    Cherished the rose in thee
Or wealth of Nature's brilliants in thy hair,
    O woman fair,
  My love might cease to be.

Or, had I sought thee for thy virtuous youth
    And tender yearning speech,
Thy swift compassion and deliberate truth,
    O heart of ruth,
  Time might pursue, might reach.

But I have loved thee for thyself indeed
    And with myself have snared;
Immortal to immortal I made speed.
    Change I exceed
  And am for Time prepared.

To the Sea

     O grey wild sea,
Thou hast a message, thunderer, for me.
    Their huge wide backs
Thy monstrous billows raise, abysmal cracks
     Dug deep between.
One pale boat flutters over them, hardly seen.
    I hear thy roar
Call me, "Why dost thou linger on the shore
     With fearful eyes
Watching my tops visit their foam-washed skies?
    This trivial boat
Dares my vast battering billows and can float.
    Death if it find,
Are there not many thousands left behind?
    Dare my wide roar,
Nor cling like cowards to the easy shore.
    Come down and know
What rapture lives in danger and o'erthrow."
    Yes, thou great sea,
I am more mighty and outbillow thee.
    On thy tops I rise;
'Tis an excuse to dally with the skies.
     I sink below
The bottom of the clamorous world to know.
    On the safe land
To linger is to lose what God has planned
    For man's wide soul,
Who set eternal godhead for its goal.
    Therefore he arrayed
Danger and difficulty like seas and made
     Pain and defeat,
And put His giant snares around our feet.
    The cloud He informs
With thunder and assails us with His storms,
    That man may grow
King over pain and victor of o'erthrow
    Matching his great

Unconquerable soul with adverse Fate.
   Take me, be
My way to climb the heavens, thou rude great sea.
   I will seize thy mane,
O lion, I will tame thee and disdain;
   Or else below
Into thy salt abysmal caverns go,
   Receive thy weight
Upon me and be stubborn as my Fate.
   I come, O Sea,
To measure my enormous self with thee.

The Sea at Night

The grey sea creeps half-visible, half-hushed,
And grasps with its innumerable hands
These silent walls. I see beyond a rough
Glimmering infinity, I feel the wash
And hear the sibilation of the waves
That whisper to each other as they push
To shoreward side by side, — long lines and dim
Of movement flecked with quivering spots of foam,
The quiet welter of a shifting world.

Evening

A golden evening, when the thoughtful sun
   Rejects its usual pomp in going, trees
That bend down to their green companion
   And fruitful mother, vaguely whispering, — these
And a wide silent sea. Such hour is nearest God, —
Like rich old age when the long ways have all been trod.

Revelation

Someone leaping from the rocks
Past me ran with wind-blown locks
Like a startled bright surmise
Visible to mortal eyes, —
Just a cheek of frightened rose
That with sudden beauty glows,
Just a footstep like the wind
And a hurried glance behind,
And then nothing, — as a thought
Escapes the mind ere it is caught.
Someone of the heavenly rout
From behind the veil ran out.

❋

A Tree

A tree beside the sandy river-beach
    Holds up its topmost boughs
Like fingers towards the skies they cannot reach,
    Earth-bound, heaven-amorous.

This is the soul of man. Body and brain
Hungry for earth our heavenly flight detain.

A Child's Imagination

O thou golden image,
    Miniature of bliss,
Speaking sweetly, speaking meetly!
    Every word deserves a kiss.

Strange, remote and splendid
    Childhood's fancy pure
Thrills to thoughts we cannot fathom,
    Quick felicities obscure.

When the eyes grow solemn
    Laughter fades away,
Nature of her mighty childhood
    Recollects the Titan play;

Woodlands touched by sunlight
    Where the elves abode,
Giant meetings, Titan greetings,
    Fancies of a youthful God.

These are coming on thee
    In thy secret thought;
God remembers in thy bosom
    All the wonders that He wrought.

Miracles

Snow in June may break from Nature,
    Ice through August last,
The random rose may increase stature
    In December's blast;

But this at least can never be,
O thou mortal ecstasy,
That one should live, even in pain,
Visited by thy disdain.

The Vedantin's Prayer

Spirit Supreme
    Who musest in the silence of the heart,
Eternal gleam,

Thou only Art!
    Ah, wherefore with this darkness am I veiled,
My sunlit part

By clouds assailed?
    Why am I thus disfigured by desire,
Distracted, haled,

Scorched by the fire
    Of fitful passions, from thy peace out-thrust
Into the gyre

Of every gust?
    Betrayed to grief, o'ertaken with dismay,
Surprised by lust?

Let not my grey
    Blood-clotted past repel thy sovereign ruth,
Nor even delay,

O lonely Truth!
    Nor let the specious gods who ape Thee still
Deceive my youth.

These clamours still;
    For I would hear the eternal voice and know
The eternal Will.

This brilliant show
    Cumbering the threshold of eternity
Dispel, — bestow

The undimmed eye,
    The heart grown young and clear. Rebuke, O Lord,
These hopes that cry

So deafeningly,
    Remove my sullied centuries, restore
My purity.

O hidden door
    Of Knowledge, open! Strength, fulfil thyself!
Love, outpour!

※

On the Mountains

Immense retreats of silence and of gloom,
    Hills of a sterile grandeur, rocks that sublime
In bareness seek the blue sky's infinite room
    With their coeval snows untouched by Time!

I seek your solemn spaces! Let me at last
    Forgotten of thought through days immemorable
Voiceless and needless keep your refuge vast,
    Growing into the peace in which I dwell.

For like that Soul unmade you seem to brood
    Who sees all things emerge but none creates,
Watching the ages from His solitude,
    Lone, unconcerned, remote. You to all Fates

Offer an unmoved[1] heart and therefore abide,
    Who seek not, act not, strive not nor rebel.
Like you, who are may grow like Him, as wide,[2]
    Mere, uncreative, imperturbable.

[1] unchanged [2] To be like you, grow like Him, silent, wide,

Rebirth

Not soon is God's delight in us completed,
    Nor with one life we end;
Termlessly in us are our spirits seated
    And termless joy intend.

Our souls and heaven are of an equal stature
    And have a dateless birth;
The unending seed, the infinite mould of Nature,
    They were not made on earth,

Nor to the earth do they bequeath their ashes,
    But in themselves they last.
An endless future brims beneath thy lashes,
    Child of an endless past.

Old memories come to us, old dreams invade us,
    Lost people we have known,
Fictions and pictures; but their frames evade us, —
    They stand out bare, alone.

Yet all we dream and hope are memories treasured,
    Are forecasts we misspell,
But of what life or scene he who has measured
    The boundless heavens can tell.

Time is a strong convention; future and present
    Were living in the past;
They are one image that our wills complaisant
    Into three schemes have cast.

Our past that we forget, is with us deathless,
    Our births and later end
Already accomplished. To a summit breathless
    Sometimes our souls ascend,

Whence the mind comes back helped; for there emerges
    The ocean vast of Time
Spread out before us with its infinite surges,
    Its symphonies sublime;

And even from this veil of mind the spirit
    Looks out sometimes and sees
The bygone aeons that our lives inherit,
    The unborn centuries:

It sees wave-trampled realms expel the Ocean, —
    From the vague depths uphurled
Where now Himaloy stands, the flood's huge motion
    Sees measuring half the world;

Or else the web behind us is unravelled
    And on its threads we gaze, —
Past motions of the stars, scenes long since travelled
    In Time's far-backward days.

❋

Seasons

Day and night begin, you tell me,
    When the sun may choose to set or rise.
Well, it may be; but for me their changing
    Is determined only by her eyes.

Summer, spring, the fruitless winter
    Hinge, you say, upon the heavenly sun?
Oh, but I have known a yearlong winter!
    Spring was by her careless smiles begun.

The Triumph-Song of Trishuncou

I shall not die.
    Although this body, when the spirit tires
    Of its cramped residence, shall feed the fires,
My house consumes, not I.

Leaving that case
    I find out ample and ethereal room.
    My spirit shall avoid the hungry tomb,
Deceiving death's embrace.

Night shall contain
    The sun in its cold depths; Time too must cease;
    The stars that labour shall have their release.
I cease not, I remain.

Ere the first seeds
    Were sown on earth, I was already old,
    And when now unborn planets shall grow cold
My history proceeds.

I am the light
    In stars, the strength of lions and the joy
    Of mornings; I am man and maid and boy,
Protean, infinite.

I am a tree
    That stands out singly from the infinite blue;
    I am the quiet falling of the dew
And am the unmeasured sea.

I hold the sky
    Together and upbear the teeming earth.
    I was the eternal thinker at my birth
And shall be, though I die.

The Fear of Death

Death wanders through our lives at will, sweet Death
Is busy with each intake of our breath.
Why do you fear her? Lo, her laughing face
All rosy with the light of jocund grace!
A kind and lovely maiden culling flowers
In a sweet garden fresh with vernal showers,
This is the thing you fear, young portress bright
Who opens to our souls the worlds of light.
Is it because the twisted stem must feel
Pain when the tenderest hands its glory steal?
Is it because the flowerless stalk droops dull
And ghastly now that was so beautiful?
Or is it the opening portal's horrid jar
That shakes you, feeble souls of courage bare?
Death is but changing of our robes to wait
In wedding garments at the Eternal's gate.

❋

Life and Death

Life, death, — death, life; the words have led for ages
    Our thought and consciousness and firmly seemed
Two opposites; but now long-hidden pages
    Are opened, liberating truths undreamed.
Life only is, or death is life disguised, —
Life a short death until by life we are surprised.

In the Moonlight

If now must pause the bullocks' jingling tune,
    Here let it be beneath the dreaming trees
    Supine and huge that hang upon the breeze,
Here in the wide eye of the silent moon.

How living a stillness reigns! The night's hushed rules
    All things obey but three, the slow wind's sigh
    Among the leaves, the cricket's ceaseless cry,
The frog's harsh discord in the ringing pools.

Yet they but seem the silence to increase
    And dreadful wideness of the inhuman night.
    The whole hushed world immeasurable might
Be watching round this single spot of peace.

So boundless is the darkness and so rife
    With thoughts of infinite reach that it creates
    A dangerous sense of space and abrogates
The wholesome littleness of human life.

The common round that each of us must tread
    Now seems a thing unreal; we forget
    The heavy yoke the world on us has set,
The slave's vain labour earning tasteless bread.

Space hedges us and Time our hearts o'ertakes;
    Our bounded senses and our boundless thought
    Strive through the centuries and are slowly brought
Back to the source whence their divergence wakes.

The source that none have traced, since none can know
    Whether from Heaven the eternal waters well
    Through Nature's matted locks, as Ganges fell,
Or from some dismal nether darkness flow.

Two genii in the dubious heart of man,
    Two great unhappy foes together bound
    Wrestle and strive to win unhampered ground;
They strive for ever since the race began.

One from his body like a bridge of fire
    Mounts upward azure-winged with eager eyes;
    One in his brain deep-mansioned labouring lies
And clamps to earth the spirit's high desire.

Here in this moonlight with strange visions rife
    I seem to see their vast peripheries
    Without me in the sombre mighty trees,
And, hark! their silence turns the wheels of life.

These are the middle and the first. Are they
    The last too? Has the duel then no close?
    Shall neither vanquish of the eternal foes,
Nor even at length this moonlight turn to day?

Our age has made an idol of the brain,
    The last adored a purer presence; yet
    In Asia like a dove immaculate
He lurks deep-brooding in the hearts of men.

But Europe comes to us bright-eyed and shrill.
    "A far delusion was that mounting fire,
    An impulse baulked and an unjust desire;
It fades as we ascend the human hill."

She cries to us to labour in the light
    Of common things, grow beautiful and wise
    On strong material food, nor vex our eyes
With straining after visionary delight.

Ah, beautiful and wise, but to what end?
    Europe knows not, nor any of her schools
    Who scorn the higher thought for dreams of fools;
Riches and joy and power meanwhile are gained.

Gained and then lost! For Death the heavy grip
    Shall loosen, Death shall cloud the laughing eye,
    And he who broke the nations soon shall lie
More helpless than a little child asleep.

And after? Nay, for death is end and term.
  A fiery dragon through the centuries curled,
  He feeds upon the glories of the world
And the vast mammoth dies before the worm.

Stars run their cycle and are quenched; the suns
  Born from the night are to the night returned,
  When the cold tenebrous spaces have inurned
The listless phantoms of the Shining Ones.

From two dead worlds a burning world arose
  Of which the late putrescent fruit is man;
  From chill dark space his roll of life began
And shall again in icy quiet close.

Our lives are but a transitory breath:
  Mean pismires in the sad and dying age
  Of a once glorious planet, on the edge
Of bitter pain we wait eternal death.

Watering the ages with our sweat and blood
  We pant towards some vague ideal state
  And by the effort fiercer ills create,
Working by lasting evil transient good.

Insults and servitude we bear perforce;
  With profitable crimes our souls we rack,
  Vexing ourselves lest earth our seed should lack
Who needs us not in her perpetual course;

Then down into the earth descend and sleep
  For ever, and the lives for which we toiled
  Forget us, who when they their turn have moiled,
Themselves forgotten into silence creep.

Why is it all, the labour and the din,
  And wherefore do we plague our souls and vex
  Our bodies or with doubts our days perplex?
Death levels soon the virtue with the sin.

If Death be end and close the useless strife,
    Strive not at all, but take what ease you may
    And make a golden glory of the day,
Exhaust the little honey of your life.

Fear not to take her beauty to your heart
    Whom you so utterly desire; you do
    No hurt to any, for the inner you
So cherished is a dream that shall depart.

The wine of life is sweet; let no man stint
    His longing or refuse one passionate hope.
    Why should we cabin in such infinite scope,
Restrict the issue of such golden mint?

Society forbids? It for our sakes
    Was fashioned; if it seek to fence around
    Our joys and pleasures in such narrow bound,
It gives us little for the much it takes.

Nor need we hearken to the gospel vain
    That bids men curb themselves to help mankind.
    We lose our little chance of bliss, then blind
And silent lie for ever. Whose the gain?

What helps it us if so mankind be served?
    Ourselves are blotted out from joy and light,
    Having no profit of the sunshine bright,
While others reap the fruit our toils deserved.

O this new god who has replaced the old!
    He dies to-day, he dies to-morrow, dies
    At last for ever, and the last sunrise
Shall have forgotten him extinct and cold.

But virtue to itself is joy enough?
    Yet if to us sin taste diviner? why
    Should we not herd in Epicurus' sty
Whom Nature made not of a Stoic stuff?

For Nature being all, desire must reign.
    It is too sweet and strong for us to slay
    Upon a nameless altar, saying nay
To honied urgings for no purpose plain.

A strange unreal gospel Science brings, —
    Being animals to act as angels might;
    Mortals we must put forth immortal might
And flutter in the void celestial wings.

"Ephemeral creatures, for the future live,"
    She bids us, "gather in for unborn men
    Knowledge and joy, and forfeit, nor complain,
The present which alone is yours to give."

Man's immortality she first denies
    And then assumes what she rejects, made blind
    By sudden knowledge, the majestic Mind
Within her smiling at her sophistries.

Not so shall Truth extend her flight sublime,
    Pass from the poor beginnings she has made
    And with the splendour of her wings displayed
Range through the boundaries of Space and Time.

Clamp her not down to her material finds!
    She shall go further. She shall not reject
    The light within, nor shall the dialect
Of unprogressive pedants bar men's minds.

We seek the Truth and will not pause nor fear.
    Truth we will have and not the sophist's pleas;
    Animals, we will take our grosser ease,
Or, spirits, heaven's celestial music hear.

The intellect is not all; a guide within
    Awaits our question. He it was informed
    The reason He surpasses; and unformed
Presages of His mightiness begin.

Nor mind submerged, nor self subliminal,
    But the great Force that makes the planets wheel
    Through ether and the sun in flames reveal
His godhead, is in us perpetual.

That Force in us is body, that is mind,
    And what is higher than the mind is He.
    This was the secret Science could not see;
Aware of death, to life her eyes were blind.

Through chemistry she seeks the source of life,
    Nor knows the mighty laws that she has found
    Are Nature's bye-laws merely, meant to ground
A grandiose freedom building peace by strife.

The organ for the thing itself she takes,
    The brain for mind, the body for the soul,
    Nor has she patience to explore the whole,
But like a child a hasty period makes.

"It is enough," she says, "I have explored
    The whole of being; nothing now remains
    But to put details in and count my gains."
So she deceives herself, denies her Lord.

Therefore He manifests Himself; once more
    The wonders of the secret world within
    Wrapped yet with an uncertain mist begin
To look from that thick curtain out; the door

Opens. Her days are numbered, and not long
    Shall she be suffered to belittle thus
    Man and restrain from his tempestuous
Uprising that immortal spirit strong.

He rises now; for God has taken birth.
    The revolutions that pervade the world
    Are faint beginnings and the discus hurled
Of Vishnu speeds down to enring the earth.

The old shall perish; it shall pass away,
    Expunged, annihilated, blotted out;
    And all the iron bands that ring about
Man's wide expansion shall at last give way.

Freedom, God, Immortality, the three
    Are one and shall be realised at length;
    Love, Wisdom, Justice, Joy and utter Strength
Gather into a pure felicity.

It comes at last, the day foreseen of old,
    What John in Patmos saw, what Shelley dreamed,
    Vision and vain imagination deemed,
The City of Delight, the Age of Gold.

The Iron Age is ended. Only now
    The last fierce spasm of the dying past
    Shall shake the nations, and when that has passed,
Earth washed of ills shall raise a fairer brow.

This is man's progress; for the Iron Age
    Prepares the Age of Gold. What we call sin,
    Is but man's leavings as from deep within
The Pilot guides him in his pilgrimage.

He leaves behind the ill with strife and pain,
    Because it clings and constantly returns,
    And in the fire of suffering fiercely burns
More sweetness to deserve, more strength to gain.

He rises to the good with Titan wings:
    And this the reason of his high unease,
    Because he came from the infinities
To build immortally with mortal things;

The body with increasing soul to fill,
    Extend Heaven's claim upon the toiling earth
    And climb from death to a diviner birth
Grasped and supported by immortal Will.

Parabrahman

These wanderings of the suns, these stars at play
    In the due measure that they chose of old,
Nor only these, but all the immense array
    Of objects that long Time, far Space can hold,

Are divine moments. They are thoughts that form,
    They are vision in the Self of things august
And therefore grandly real. Rule and norm
    Are processes that they themselves adjust.

The Self of things is not their outward view,
    A Force within decides. That Force is He;
His movement is the shape of things we knew,
    Movement of Thought is Space and Time. A free

And sovereign master of His world within,
    He is not bound by what He does or makes,
He is not bound by virtue or by sin,
    Awake who sleeps and when He sleeps awakes.

He is not bound by waking or by sleep;
    He is not bound by anything at all.
Laws are that He may conquer them. To creep
    Or soar is at His will, to rise or fall.

One from of old possessed Himself above
    Who was not anyone nor had a form,
Nor yet was formless. Neither hate nor love
    Could limit His perfection, peace nor storm.

He is, we cannot say; for Nothing too
    Is His conception of Himself unguessed.
He dawns upon us and we would pursue,
    But who has found Him or what arms possessed?

He is not anything, yet all is He;
    He is not all but far exceeds that scope.
Both Time and Timelessness sink in that sea:
    Time is a wave and Space a wandering drop.

Within Himself He shadowed Being forth,
    Which is a younger birth, a veil He chose
To half-conceal Him, Knowledge, nothing worth
    Save to have glimpses of its mighty cause,

And high Delight, a spirit infinite,
    That is the fountain of this glorious world,
Delight that labours in its opposite,
    Faints in the rose and on the rack is curled.

This was the triune playground that He made
    And One there sports awhile. He plucks His flowers
And by His bees is stung; He is dismayed,
    Flees from Himself or has His sullen hours.

The Almighty One knew labour, failure, strife;
    Knowledge forgot divined itself again:
He made an eager death and called it life,
    He stung Himself with bliss and called it pain.

God

Thou who pervadest all the worlds below,
    Yet sitst above,
Master of all who work and rule and know,
    Servant of Love!

Thou who disdainest not the worm to be
    Nor even the clod,
Therefore we know by that humility
    That thou art God.

SHORT POEMS
1902 - 1930

The Mother of Dreams

Goddess supreme, Mother of Dream, by thy ivory doors when thou standest,
Who are they then that come down unto men in thy visions that troop,
group upon group, down the path of the shadows slanting?
Dream after dream, they flash and they gleam with the flame of the stars
still around them;
Shadows at thy side in a darkness ride where the wild fires dance, stars glow
and glance and the random meteor glistens;
There are voices that cry to their kin who reply; voices sweet, at the heart
they beat and ravish the soul as it listens.
What then are these lands and these golden sands and these seas more
radiant than earth can imagine?
Who are those that pace by the purple waves that race to the cliff-bound
floor of thy jasper shore under skies in which mystery muses,
Lapped in moonlight not of our night or plunged in sunshine that is not
diurnal?
Who are they coming thy Oceans roaming with sails whose strands are not
made by hands, an unearthly wind advances?
Why do they join in a mystic line with those on the sands linking hands in
strange and stately dances?
Thou in the air, with a flame in thy hair, the whirl of thy wonders watching,
Holdest the night in thy ancient right, Mother divine, hyacinthine, with a
girdle of beauty defended.
Sworded with fire, attracting desire, thy tenebrous kingdom thou keepest,
Starry-sweet, with the moon at thy feet, now hidden now seen the clouds
between in the gloom and the drift of thy tresses.
Only to those whom thy fancy chose, O thou heart-free, is it given to see
thy witchcraft and feel thy caresses.
Open the gate where thy children wait in their world of a beauty undarkened.
High-throned on a cloud, victorious, proud I have espied Maghavan ride
when the armies of wind are behind him;
Food has been given for my tasting from heaven and fruit of immortal
sweetness;
I have drunk wine of the kingdoms divine and have heard the change of
music strange from a lyre which our hands cannot master;

Doors have swung wide in the chambers of pride where the Gods reside and
       the Apsaras dance in their circles faster and faster.
For thou art she whom we first can see when we pass the bounds of the
                                                                mortal,
There at the gates of the heavenly states thou hast planted thy wand enchanted
                              over the head of the Yogin waving.
From thee are the dream and the shadows that seem and the fugitive lights
                                                         that delude us;
Thine is the shade in which visions are made; sped by thy hands from
              celestial lands come the souls that rejoice for ever.
Into thy dream-worlds we pass or look in thy magic glass, then beyond thee
       we climb out of Space and Time to the peak of divine endeavour.

❋

The Birth of Sin

Lucifer, Sirioth

> LUCIFER
>
> What mighty and ineffable desire
> Impels thee, Sirioth? Thy accustomed calm
> Is potently subverted and the eyes
> That were a god's in sweet tranquillity,
> Confess a human warmth, a troubled glow.
>
> SIRIOTH
>
> Lucifer, son of Morning, Angel! thou
> Art mightiest of the architects of fate.
> To thee is given with thy magic gaze
> Compelling mortals as thou leanst sublime
> From heaven's lucent walls, to sway the world.
> Is thy felicity of lesser date,
> Prince of the patient and untiring gods,
> The gods who work? Dost thou not ever feel
> Angelic weariness usurp the place
> Where the great flame and the august desire
> Were wont to urge thee on? To me it seems
> That our eternity is far too long
> For service and there is a word, a thought,
> More godlike.
>
> LUCIFER
>   Sirioth, I will speak the word.
> Is it not Power?
>
> SIRIOTH
>   No, Lucifer, 'tis Love.
>
> LUCIFER
>
> Love? It was love that for a trillion years
> Gave me the instinct and immense demand
> For service, for activity. It fades.
> Another and more giant passion comes
> Striding upon me. I behold the world
> Immeasurably vast, I see the heavens

Full of an azure joy and majesty,
I see the teeming millions of the stars.
Sirioth, how came the Master of the world
To be the master? Did He seize control
Pushing some ancient weaker sovereign down
From sway immemorable? Did He come
By peaceful ways, permission or inheritance,
To what He is today? Or if indeed
He is for ever and for ever rules,
Are there no bounds to His immense domain,
No obscure corner of unbounded space
Forgotten by His fate, that I may seize
And make myself an empire as august,
Enjoy a like eternity of rule?

    SIRIOTH

Angel, these thoughts are mighty as thyself.
But wilt thou then rebel? If He be great
To conquer and to punish, what of thee?
Eternity of dreadful poignant pain
May be thy fate and not eternal rule.

    LUCIFER

Better than still to serve desirelessly,
Pursued by a compulsion dull and fierce,
Looking through all vast time for one brief hour
Of rest, of respite, but instead to find
Iron necessity and pant in vain
For space, for room, for freedom.

    SIRIOTH

                      Thou intendest?

    LUCIFER

Sirioth, I do not yet intend; I feel.

    SIRIOTH

For me the sense of active force within
Set me to work, as the stars move, the sun
Resistless flames through space, the stormwind runs.

But I have felt a touch as sweet as spring,
And I have heard a music of delight
Maddening the heart with the sweet honied stabs
Of delicate intolerable joy.
Where, where is One to feel the answering bliss?
Lucifer, thou from love beganst thy toil.
What love?

  LUCIFER
    Desire august to help, to serve.

  SIRIOTH
That is not mine. To embrace, to melt and mix
Two beings into one, to roll the spirit
Tumbling into a surge of common joy, —
'Tis this I seek.

  LUCIFER
    Will He permit?

  SIRIOTH
      A bar
I feel, a prohibition. Someone used
A word I could not grasp and called it sin.

  LUCIFER
The word is new, even as these things are.

  SIRIOTH
I know not who he was. He laughed and said,
"Sin, sin is born into the world, revolt
And change, in Sirioth and in Lucifer,
The evening and the morning star. Rejoice,
O world!" And I beheld as in a dream
Leaping from out thy brain and into mine
A woman beautiful, of grandiose mien,
Yet terrible, alarming and instinct
With nameless menace. And the world was full
With clashing and with cries. It seemed to me
Angels and Gods and men strove violently

To touch her robe, to occupy the place
Her beautiful and ominous feet had trod,
Crying, "Daughter of Lucifer, be ours,
O sweet, adorable and mighty Sin!"
Therefore I came to thee.

    LUCIFER
                        Sirioth, await
Her birth, if she must be. For this I know,
Necessity rules all the infinite world,
And even He perhaps submits unknown
To a compulsion. When the time is ripe,
We will consult once more what we shall do.

Epiphany

Majestic, mild, immortally august,
In silence throned, to just and to unjust
One Lord of deep unutterable love,
I saw Him, Shiva, like a brooding dove
Close-winged upon her nest. The outcaste came,
The sinners gathered round that tender Flame,
The demons, by the other sterner gods
Rejected from their luminous abodes,
Gathered around the Refuge of the lost,
Soft-smiling on that wild and grisly host.
All who were refugeless, wretched, unloved,
The wicked and the good together moved
Naturally to Him, the asylum sweet,
And found their heaven at their Master's feet.
The vision changed and in His place there stood
A Terror red as lightning or as blood;
His fierce right hand a javelin advanced
And, as He shook it, earthquake reeling danced
Across the hemisphere, ruin and plague
Rained out of heaven, disasters swift and vague
Threatened, a marching multitude of ills.
His foot strode forward to oppress the hills,
And at the vision of His burning eyes
The hearts of men grew faint with dread surmise
Of sin and punishment; their cry was loud,
"O Master of the stormwind and the cloud,
Spare, Rudra, spare. Show us that other form
Auspicious, not incarnate wrath and storm."

The God of Wrath, the God of Love are one,
Nor least He loves when most He smites. Alone
Who rises above fear and plays with grief,
Defeat and death, inherits full relief
From blindness and beholds the single Form,
Love masking Terror, Peace supporting storm.
The Friend of Man helps him with Life and Death,
Until he knows. Then freed from mortal breath
He feels the joy of the immortal play;
Grief, pain, resentment, terror pass away.
He too grows Rudra fierce, august and dire,
And Shiva, sweet fulfiller of desire.

To R.

On Her Birthday

The repetition of thy gracious years
    Brings back once more thy natal morn.
Upon the crest of youth thy life appears, —
    A wave upborne.

Amid the hundreds thronging Ocean's floor
    A wave upon the crowded sea
With regular rhythm pushing towards the shore
    Our life must be.

The power that moves it is the Ocean's force
    Invincible, eternal, free,
And by that impulse it pursues its course
    Inevitably.

We, too, by the Eternal Might are led
    To whatsoever goal He wills.
Our helm He grasps, our generous sail outspread
    His strong breath fills.

Exulting in the grace and strength of youth
    Pursue the Ocean's distant bound,
Trusting the Pilot's voice, the Master's ruth
    That rings us round.

Rejoice and fear not for the waves that swell,
    The storms that thunder, winds that sweep;
Always our Captain holds the rudder well,
    He does not sleep.

If in the trough of the enormous sea
    Thou canst not find the sky for spray,
Fear never, for our Sun is there with thee
    By night and day.

Even those who sink in the victorious flood,
    Where do they sink? Into His breast.
He who to some gives victory, joy and good,
    To some gives rest.

But thou, look to the radiant days that wait
    Beyond the driving rain and storm.
I have seen the vision of a happier fate
    Brightening thy form.

Confident of His grace, expect His will;
    Let Him lead; though hidden be the bourne,
See Him in all that happens; that fulfil
    For which thou wert born.

The Rakshasas

(The Rakshasa, the violent kinetic Ego, establishes his claim to mastery of the world replacing the animal Soul, — to be followed by controlled and intellectualised but unregenerated Ego, the Asura. Each such type and level of consciousness sees the Divine in its own image and its level in Nature is sustained by a differing form of the World-Mother.)

"Glory and greatness and the joy of life,
Strength, pride, victorious force, whatever man
Desires, whatever the wild beast enjoys,
Bodies of women and the lives of men —
I claim to be my kingdom. I have force
My title to substantiate, I seek
No crown unearned, no lordship undeserved.
Ask what austerity Thou wilt, Maker of man,
Expense of blood or labour or long years
Spent in tremendous meditation, lives
Upon Thy altar spent of brutes or men;
Or if with gold Thy favour purchasable,
I may command rich offerings to glut
Thy triumphs and Thy priests. I have a heart,
A hand for any mighty sacrifice,
A fiery patience in my vehement mood;
I will submit. But ask not this of me,
Meek silence and a pale imprisoned soul
Made colourless of its humanity,
Ask not the heart that quakes, the hand that spares,
What strength can give, not weakness, that demand.
O Rudra! O eternal Mahadev!
Thou too art fierce and mighty, wrathful, bold,
Snuffing Thy winds for blood of sacrifice
And angrily Thou rul'st a prostrate world.
O Rakshasa Almighty, look on me,
Ravan, the lord of all Thy Rakshasas,
Give me Thy high command to smite Thy foes;
But most I would afflict, chase and destroy
Thy devotees who traduce Thee, making Thee
A God of Love, a God too sweet to rule.
I have the knowledge, what Thou art I know

And know myself, for Thou and I are one."
So prayed the Lord of Lanka, and in heaven
Sri Krishna smiled, the Friend of all mankind,
And asked, "O masters of the knowledge, Seers
Who help me by your thoughts to help mankind,
Hearken what Ravan cries against the stars
Demanding earth for heritage. Advise,
Shall he then have it?" And a cry arose,
"He would root out the Brahmin from the earth,
Impose his dreadful Yoga on mankind
And make the violent heart, the iron hand
Sovereign of all." Sri Krishna made reply,
"From out Myself he went to do My will.
He has not lied, he has the knowledge. He
And I are one. How then shall I refuse?
Does it not say, the Veda that you know,
'When one knows That, then whatso he desires,
It shall be his'?" And Atri sage replied,
"Let him then rule a season and be slain."
And He who reigns, "Something you know, O Seers.
Not all my purpose. It is long decreed,
The Rakshasa shall rule the peopled earth.
He takes the brute into himself for man
Yielding it offerings, while with grandiose thoughts
And violent aspirations he controls;
He purifies the demon in the race
Slaying in wrath, not cruelty. Awhile
He puts the Vanara out of the world,
Accustoming to grandeur all mankind;
The Ifrit[1] he rejects. Were he denied
His period, man could not progress. But since
He sees himself as Me, not Me in him,
And takes the life and body for the whole,
He cannot last. Therefore is Atri's word
Accepted." And before the Rakshasa,
Out of the terror of the sacrifice,
Naked and dark, with a blood-dripping sword
And dreadful eyes that seemed to burn the world,
Kali the Rakshasi in flames arose.

[1] The Ifrit, the Djinn, is the demoniac element in Nature.

"Demand a boon," she cried, and all the gods
Trembled. "Give me the earth for my delight,
Her gods to be my slaves", the Rakshasa cried,
"Of strength and pride." "So let it be,"
She answered. "Shall it be eternal then?"
Ravan demanded and she thundered, "No,
For neither thou nor I are best nor last.
The Asuri shall arise to fill my place,
The Asura thy children shall dethrone.
An aeon thou hast taken to evolve,
An aeon thou shalt rule. But since thy wish
I have denied, ask yet another boon."
"Let this be mine then, when at last I sink,
Nor brute nor demon, man nor Titan's hand,
Nor any lesser creature shall o'erthrow,
But only God himself compel my fall."
And Kali answered, smiling terribly,
"It is decreed," and laughing loud she passed.
Then Ravan from his sacrifice arose.

Kama

(According to one idea Desire is the creator and sustainer of things, — Desire and Ignorance. By losing desire one passes beyond the Ignorance, as by passing beyond Ignorance one loses desire; then the created world is surpassed and the soul enters into the Divine Reality. Kama here speaks as Desire the Creator, an outgoing power from the Bliss of the Divine Reality to which, abandoning desire, one returns, *ānandam brahmano vidvān*, possessing the bliss of the Brahman.)

    O desolations vast, O seas of space
    Unpeopled, realms of an unfertile light,
    Grow multitudinous with living forms,
    Enamoured of desire! I send My breath
    Into the heart of being and the storm
    Of sweet attraction shall break up its calm
    With quivering passionate intensity,
    And silence change to a melodious cry,
    And all the world be rose. Out of my heart
    Suns shall flame up into the pitiless void
    And the stars wheel in magic dances round
    Weaving the web of mortal life. For I
    Am love, am passion. I create the world.
    I am the only Brahma. My desire
    Takes many forms; I change and wheel and race
    And with me runs creation. I preserve,
    For I am love. I weary of myself,
    And the world circles back into the Vast.
    Delight and laughter walking hand in hand
    Go with me, and I play with grief and pain.
    I am the dance of Krishna, I the dance
    Of Kali, Might and Majesty are mine.
    And I can make the heart a child at play,
    The soul of things a woman full of bliss.
    Hunger and Thirst, arise and make the world!
    Delight, go down and give it strength to live!
    O ether, change! O breath of things, grow full
    Of the perpetual whirl! Break out, O fire,
    In seas of magic colour, infinite waves
    Of rainbow light! Thou liquid element,

Be sap, be taste in all created things
To please the senses. Thou, O solid earth,
Enter into all life, support the worlds.
I send forth joy to cheer the hearts of men,
I send forth law to harmonise and rule.
And when these things are done, when men have learned
My beauty, My desirability, My bliss,
I will conceal myself from their desire
And make this rule of the eternal chase,
"They who abandon Me, shall to all time
Clasp and possess; they who pursue, shall lose."

Kamadeva

When in the heart of the valleys and hid by the roses
    The sweet Love lies,
Has he wings to rise to his heavens or in the closes
    Lives and dies?

On the peaks of the radiant mountains if we should meet him
    Proud and free,
Will he not frown on the valleys? Would it befit him
    Chained to be?

Will you then speak of the one as a slave and a wanton,
    The other too bare?
But God is the only slave and the only monarch
    We declare.

It is God who is Love and a boy and a slave for our passion
    He was made to serve;
It is God who is free and proud and the limitless tyrant
    Our souls deserve.

The Mahatmas

KUTHUMI

(This poem is purely a play of the imaginative, a poetic reconstruction of the central idea only of Mahatmahood.)

    The seven mountains and the seven seas
Surround me. Over me the eightfold Sun
Blazing with various colours — green and blue,
Scarlet and rose, violet and gold and white,
And the dark disk that rides in the mortal cave —
Looks down on me in flame. Below spread wide
The worlds of the immortals, tier on tier
Like a great mountain climbing to the skies,
And on their summit Shiva dwells. Of old
My doings were familiar with the earth,
The mortals over whom I hold control
Were then my fellows. But I followed not
The usual path, the common thoughts of men.
A thirst of knowledge and a sense of power,
A passion of divine beneficence
Pursued me through a hundred lives. I rose
From birth to birth, until I reached the peak
Of human knowledge, then in Bharat born,
I, Kuthumi, the Kshatriya, the adept,
The mighty Yogin of Dwaipayan's school,
To Vyasa came, our great original sage.
He looked upon me with the eyes that see
And smiled august and awful. "Kuthumi,"
He cried, "now gather back what thou hast earned
In many lives, remember all thy past,
Cease from thy round of human births, resume
The eightfold powers that make a man as God.
Then come again and learn thy grandiose work,
For thou art of the souls to death denied."
I went into the mountains by the sea
That thunders pitilessly from night to morn,
And sung to by that rude relentless sound
Amidst the cries of beasts, the howl of winds,

Surrounded by the gnashing demon hordes,
I did the Hathayoga in three days,
Which men with anguish through ten lives effect,
Not that now practised by earth's feeble race,
But that which Ravan knew in Lanka, Dhruv
Fulfilled, Hiranyakashipu performed,
The Yoga of the old Lemurian Kings.
I felt the strength of Titans in my veins,
The joy of Gods, the pride of Siddhas. Tall
And mighty like a striding God I came
To Vyasa; but he shook his dense piled locks,
Denying me; "Thou art not pure," he cried.
I went in anger to Himaloy's peaks
And on the highest in the breathless snow
Sat dumb for many years. Then knowledge came
Streaming upon me and the hills around
Shook with the feet of the descending power.
I did the Rajayoga in three days,
Which men with care and accuracy minute
Ceaselessly follow for an age in vain —
Not Kali's Rajayoga, but the means
Of perfect knowledge, purity and force
Bali the Titan learned and gave to men,
The Yoga of the old Atlantic Kings.
I came to Vyasa, shining like a sun.
He smiled and said, "Now seek the world's Great Soul,
Sri Krishna, where he lives on earth concealed,
Give up to him all that thou know'st and hast;
For thou art he, elect from mortal men
To guard the knowledge, yet an easy task
While the third age preserves man's godlike form.
But when thou seest the iron Kali come
And he from Dwarca leaves the Earth, know then
The time of trial, help endangered men,
Preserve the knowledge that preserves the world,
Until Sri Krishna utterly returns.
Then art thou from thy mighty work released
Into the worlds of bliss for endless years
To rest, until another aeon comes,
When of the seven Rishis thou art one."

I sent my knowledge forth across the land.
It found him not in Bharat's princely halls,
In quiet asrams, nor in temples pure,
Nor where the wealthy traffickers resort —
Brahmin nor Kshatriya body housed the Lord,
Vaisya nor Sudra nor outcaste. At length
To a bare hut on a wild mountain's verge
Led by the star I came. A hermit mad
Of the wild Abhirs, who sat dumbed or laughed
And ran and leaped and danced upon the hills
But told the reason of his joy to none,
In him I saw the Lord, behind the man
Perceived the spirit that contains the world.
I fell before him, but he leapt and ran
And smote me with his foot and out of me
All knowledge, all desire, all strength was gone
Into its source. I sat an infant child.
He laughed aloud and said, "Take back thy gifts,
O beggar!" and went leaping down the slope.
Then full of light and strength and bliss I soared
Beyond the spheres, above the mighty Gods
And left my human body on the snows.
And others gathered to me, more or less
In puissance to assist, but mine the charge
By Vishnu given. I gather knowledge here,
Then to my human frame awhile descend
And walk mid men, choosing my instruments,
Testing, rejecting and confirming souls —
Vessels of the Spirit; for the golden age
In Kali comes, the iron lined with gold,
The Yoga shall be given back to men,
The sects shall cease, the grim debates die out
And atheism perish from the Earth,
Blasted with knowledge; love and brotherhood
And wisdom repossess Sri Krishna's world.

The Meditations of Mandavya

ONE

O joy of gaining all the soul's desire!
O stranger joy of the defeat and loss!
O heart that yearnest to uplift the world!
O fiercer heart that bendest o'er its pain
And drinkst the savour! I will love thee, O Love,
Naked or veiled or dreadfully disguised;
Not only when thou flatterest my heart
But when thou tearst it! Thy sweet pity I love
And mother's care for creatures, for the joys
I love thee that the lives of things possess,
And love thee for the torment of our pains;
Nor cry, as some, against thy will, nor say,
Thou art not. Easy is the love that lasts
Only with favours in the shopman heart!
Who, tortured, takes and gives the kiss, he loves.

*

Blue-winged like turquoise, crimson-throated, beaked,
Enormous, fluttering over the garden wall
Thou cam'st to me; some moments on a bough
Wast perched, then flewst away, leaving my heart
Enchanted. It was as if thou saidst, "Behold, my love,
How beautiful I am! To show thee this,
I came, my beauty. Now I flee away
Since thou hast seen and lov'st." So dealst thou always,
Luring and fleeing; but our hearts pursue.

*

While on a terrace hushed I walked at night,
He came and stung my foot. My soul surprised
Rejoiced in lover's contact; but the mind
Thought of a scorpion and was snared by forms.
Still, still my soul remembered its delight

Denying mind, and midst the body's pain,
I laughed contented.

                *

All is attained, attained! The pain is dead,
The striving. O thou joy that since this world
Began, wast waiting for me in thy lair.
O Wild Beast of the ways! Thou tearst my soul
With rapture, O thou fierce delightful God.
O cruelly divine! O pity fierce!
O timeless rapture of the nights that pass
Embraced! O terror pure of Thy caress!
Humanity, acceptable I find
Thy ages that have wept out sweat and blood,
Since all was made to give its utter price
To one wild moment of thy hidden God.
Let the whole world end now, since all for which
It was created is fulfilled at last
And I am swallowed up in thee, O God.

            TWO

Who made of Nature here a tyrant? Who
Condemned us to be slaves? It was not God.
Nay, we ourselves chose our own servitude
And we ourselves have forged and heaped our chains
On our own members. God only watched the while
And mocked us sweetly at our childish task.
Then if He seized us helpless in our bonds,
Then if He played with us despite our cries
And answered with His dreadful laugh our wrath,
Ours was the fault who chose the bondage first,
Ours is the folly whom His play affrights
While all the time He tells us, "It is nought."
And now we say we never can be free,
For Nature binds us, for the fire must burn,
The water drown and death must seize his prey,
And grief and torture do their will with us

And sin be like a lion with the world,
Because 'tis Nature. Man's not infinite,
The proof is with us every day, they cry,
And God Himself's a huge machine at last.
Yet over us all the while Thought's lightning plays
And all the while within us works His love.
Now more than when the play began, He laughs.

*

Now I believe that it is possible
To manage the arising clouds, to silence
The thunder when it roars and put our rein
Upon the lightnings. Only first within
The god we must coerce who wallows here
In love with his subjection and confined
By his own servants, wantonly enslaved
To every lure and every tempting bond.
And therefore man loves power, but power o'ercome,
Force that accepts its limits. Wherefore then
A limit? Why not dare the whole embrace,
The vast attraction? Let us risk extinction then
If by that venture immortality
And high omnipotence come near our grasp.
'Tis not the little rippling wayward seas,
Nor all huge ocean tumbled by its storms
That can be our exemplar. The vault of heaven
Is not a true similitude for man
Whose space outgyres thought's last horizon. Something
There is in us fears not the night beyond,
But breathless sails, unanchored, without helm,
Where all the senses end. Our naked soul
Can journey to the farther unshaped void
Where nothing is except ourselves, arrive, hold on,
Not shake, not ask return. Who accepts at last
His limit save the beast and plant and clod?
O to be perfect here, to exceed all bounds,
To feel the world a toy between our hands!
Yet now enough that I have seized one current
Of the tremendous Force that moves the world.

I know, O God, the day shall dawn at last
When man shall rise from playing with the mud
And taking in his hands the sun and stars
Remould appearance, law and process old.
Then, pain and discord vanished from the world,
Shall the dead wilderness accept the rose
And the hushed desert babble of its rills;
Man once more seem the image true of God.

*

I will not faint, O God. There is the thirst,
And thirst supposes water somewhere. Yes,
But in this life we may not ever find;
Old nature sits a phantom by the way,
Old passions may forbid, old doubts return.
Then are there other lives here or beyond
To satisfy us? I will persist, O Lord.

THREE

What is this Love that I have never found?
I have imagined in the skies a God
And seen Him in the stirring of the leaves
And heard Him in the purling of the brooks
And feared Him in the lightning's flashing tusk
And missed Him in the mute eternal night
And woke to Him in the returning Dawns.
And now I say there is no God at all,
But only a dumb Void that belches forth
Numberless larvae and phantasmal shapes
Into a void less happy than itself
Because this feels. O if this dream were true,
This iron, brute, gigantic helpless toy
They call a world, this thing that turns and turns
And shrieks and bleeds and cannot stop, this victim
Broken and living yet on its iron wheel,
And if a Will created this, what name
Shall best blaspheme against that tyrant God?

Let all men seek it out and hurl it up
Against Him with one cry, if yet perchance
Complete denial may destroy His life
With happy end to His unhappy world.
For where in all these stars is any sign of Love?
It is not here, but that which seems like Love
Is a sleek cruel cheat that soon unmasks,
Sent here to make the final suffering worse, —
Not Love, but Death disguised that strokes its food!
And all good in the world is only that,
A death that eats and eating is devoured,
This is the brutal image of the world.

*

Lo, I have cursed Thee, lo, I have denied
Thy love, Thy being. Strike me with Thy rod,
Convince me that Thou art. O leave it not
To Thy dumb messengers that have no heart,
No wrath in the attack, no angered love,
No exultation in the blow that falls,
The cry that answers. Let me feel a Heart,
Even though an evil one, that throbs and is
Against our tears, our pressure and our search.
Beware, for I will send my soul across the earth
And all men turn against Thee at my word.
There is no sign, there comes not any voice.
And yet, alas! I know He will return
And He will soothe my wounds and charm my heart;
I shall again forgive, again shall love,
Again shall suffer, be again deceived.
And where is any end, O Heaven, O Earth?
But there is never any end when one has loved.

*

A sudden silence and a sudden sound,
The sound above and in another world,
The silence here and from the two a thought.
Perhaps the heart of God for ever sings

And worlds come throbbing out from every note;
Perhaps His soul sits ever calm and still
And listens to the music rapturously,
Himself adoring, by Himself adored.
So were the singer and the hearer one
Eternally. The anthem buoyant rides
For ever on the seas of Space and Time
And worships the white Bliss from which 'twas born;
The ineffable Delight leans silent down
And clasps the creatures of its mystic cry
For ever and for ever — without end.

*

Who art thou that pursuest my desire
Like a wild beast behind the jungle's screen
And throw'st a dread upon its fiercest fire,
A shadow on its flowering joy and green?
Thou madest and deniest me my need,
Thou jealous Lover and devouring Greed!

*

Who spoke of God? There is a hungry Beast
In ambush for the world who all devours,
Yet is his hunger sated not the least.
He tears our beauty, strength and happiest hours,
And eats our flesh and drinks our blood and tears,
Ranging as in a thicket through the years.

*

Dost thou desire my last vain hope? Take it, rejoice!
Wilt thou exact my dying bliss? Tear it and end!
But give me this at least, dying, to hear thy voice,
By thee as foeman slain if never clasped as friend.

*

Foeman or friend, lover or slayer, only thee
I need and feel, O personal eternity.

*

If what thou gavest, thou must needs again exact,
Cancel thy forms, deny thy own accomplished fact,
With what wilt thou replace them? Is thy void
Embraceable by arms? Or can the soul upbuoyed
Rest on a shoreless emptiness without a name?
Can Love find rapture by renouncing all his flame?
Thou hast forgotten or our nature is misled,
Lur'st thou to utter[1] life beyond the silence dead?

*

Not sound, nor silence, neither world nor void,
But the unthinkable, absolute, unalloyed
One, multitudinous, nameless, yet a Name,
Innumerably other, yet the same.
Immeasurable ecstasy where Time
And Space have fainted in a swoon sublime!

*

Of silence I have tired, from the profounder Night
I come rejected. All the immensities overhead
Are given to my fierce upwinging soul at last
Rapt into high impossible ranges huge outspread.
Unnumbered voices thrill the silent waiting Vast,
A million flames converge into the rayless Light.

---

[1] silent

Hell and Heaven

In the silence of the night-time,
    In the grey and formless eve
When the thought is plagued with loveless
    Memories that it cannot leave,

When the dawn makes sudden beauty
    Of a peevish clouded sky,
And the rain is sobbing slowly
    And the wind makes weird reply,

Always comes her face before me
    And her voice is in my ear,
Beautiful and sad and cruel
    With the azure eyes austere.

Cloudy figure once so luminous
    With the light and life within
When the soul came rippling outwards
    And the red lips laughed at sin,

Com'st thou with that marble visage
    From what world instinct with pain
Where we pay the price of passion
    By a law our hearts disdain?

Cast it from thee, O thou goddess!
    Earning with a smile release
From these sad imaginations,
    Rise into celestial peace.

Travel from the loveless places
    That our mortal fears create,
Where thy natural heavens claim thee
    And the gods, thy brothers, wait.

Then descend to me grown radiant,
    Lighting up terrestrial ground
With the feet that brighten heaven
    When the mighty dance goes round

And the high Gods beating measure
   Tread the maze that keeps the stars
Circling in their luminous orbits
   Through the eternal thoroughfares.

All below is but confusion
   Of desires that strive and cry,
Some forbidden, some achieving
   Anguish after ecstasy.

But above our radiant station
   Is from which by doubt we fell,
Reaching only after Heaven
   And achieving only Hell.

Let the heart be king and master,
   Let the brain exult and toil,
Disbelieve in good and evil,
   God with Nature reconcile.

Therefore, O rebellious sweetness,
   Thou tookst arms for joy and love.
There achieve them! Take possession
   Of our radiant seats above.

Life

Mystic Miracle, daughter of Delight,
    Life, thou ecstasy,
Let the radius of thy flight
    Be eternity.

On thy wings thou bearest high
    Glory and disdain,
Godhead and mortality,
    Ecstasy and pain.

Take me in thy wild embrace
    Without weak reserve
Body dire and unveiled face;
    Faint not, Life, nor swerve.

All thy bliss I would explore,
    All thy tyranny.
Cruel like the lion's roar,
    Sweet like springtide be.

Like a Titan I would take,
    Like a God enjoy,
Like a man contend and make,
    Revel like a boy.

More I will not ask of thee,
    Nor my fate would choose;
King or conquered let me be,
    Live or lose.

Even in rags I am a god;
    Fallen, I am divine;
High I triumph when down-trod,
    Long I live when slain.

SHORT POEMS
1930-1950

A God's Labour

I have gathered my dreams in a silver air
    Between the gold and the blue
And wrapped them softly and left them there,
    My jewelled dreams of you.

I had hoped to build a rainbow bridge
    Marrying the soil to the sky
And sow in this dancing planet midge
    The moods of infinity.

But too bright were our heavens, too far away,
    Too frail their ethereal stuff;
Too splendid and sudden our light could not stay;
    The roots were not deep enough.

He who would bring the heavens here
    Must descend himself into clay
And the burden of earthly nature bear
    And tread the dolorous way.

Coercing my godhead I have come down
    Here on the sordid earth,
Ignorant, labouring, human grown
    Twixt the gates of death and birth.

I have been digging deep and long
    Mid a horror of filth and mire
A bed for the golden river's song,
    A home for the deathless fire.

I have laboured and suffered in Matter's night
    To bring the fire to man;
But the hate of hell and human spite
    Are my meed since the world began.

For man's mind is the dupe of his animal self;
    Hoping its lusts to win,
He harbours within him a grisly Elf
    Enamoured of sorrow and sin.

The grey Elf shudders from heaven's flame
    And from all things glad and pure;
Only by pleasure and passion and pain
    His drama can endure.

All around is darkness and strife;
    For the lamps that men call suns
Are but halfway gleams on this stumbling life
    Cast by the Undying Ones.

Man lights his little torches of hope
    That lead to a failing edge;
A fragment of Truth is his widest scope,
    An inn his pilgrimage.

The Truth of truths men fear and deny,
    The Light of lights they refuse;
To ignorant gods they lift their cry
    Or a demon altar choose.

All that was found must again be sought,
    Each enemy slain revives,
Each battle for ever is fought and refought
    Through vistas of fruitless lives.

My gaping wounds are a thousand and one
    And the Titan kings assail,
But I cannot rest till my task is done
    And wrought the eternal will.

How they mock and sneer, both devils and men!
    "Thy hope is Chimera's head
Painting the sky with its fiery stain;
    Thou shalt fall and thy work lie dead.

"Who art thou that babblest of heavenly ease
    And joy and golden room
To us who are waifs on inconscient seas
    And bound to life's iron doom?

"This earth is ours, a field of Night
  For our petty flickering fires.
How shall it brook the sacred Light
  Or suffer a god's desires?

"Come, let us slay him and end his course!
  Then shall our hearts have release
From the burden and call of his glory and force
  And the curb of his wide white peace."

But the god is there in my mortal breast
  Who wrestles with error and fate
And tramples a road through mire and waste
  For the nameless Immaculate.

A voice cried, "Go where none have gone!
  Dig deeper, deeper yet
Till thou reach the grim foundation stone
  And knock at the keyless gate."

I saw that a falsehood was planted deep
  At the very root of things
Where the grey Sphinx guards God's riddle sleep
  On the Dragon's outspread wings.

I left the surface gods of mind
  And life's unsatisfied seas
And plunged through the body's alleys blind
  To the nether mysteries.

I have delved through the dumb Earth's dreadful heart
  And heard her black mass' bell.
I have seen the source whence her agonies part
  And the inner reason of hell.

Above me the dragon murmurs moan
  And the goblin voices flit;
I have pierced the Void where Thought was born,
  I have walked in the bottomless pit.

On a desperate stair my feet have trod
    Armoured with boundless peace,
Bringing the fires of the splendour of God
    Into the human abyss.

He who I am was with me still;
    All veils are breaking now.
I have heard His voice and borne His will
    On my vast untroubled brow.

The gulf twixt the depths and the heights is bridged
    And the golden waters pour
Down the sapphire mountain rainbow-ridged
    And glimmer from shore to shore.

Heaven's fire is lit in the breast of the earth
    And the undying suns here burn;
Through a wonder cleft in the bounds of birth
    The incarnate spirits yearn

Like flames to the kingdoms of Truth and Bliss:
    Down a gold-red stair-way wend
The radiant children of Paradise
    Clarioning darkness's end.

A little more and the new life's doors
    Shall be carved in silver light
With its aureate roof and mosaic floors
    In a great world bare and bright.

I shall leave my dreams in their argent air,
    For in a raiment of gold and blue
There shall move on the earth embodied and fair
    The living truth of you.

Bride of the Fire

Bride of the Fire, clasp me now close, —
    Bride of the Fire!
I have shed the bloom of the earthly rose,
    I have slain desire.

Beauty of the Light, surround my life, —
    Beauty of the Light!
I have sacrificed longing and parted from grief,
    I can bear thy delight.

Image of ecstasy, thrill and enlace, —
    Image of bliss!
I would see only thy marvellous face,
    Feel only thy kiss.

Voice of Infinity, sound in my heart, —
    Call of the One!
Stamp there thy radiance, never to part,
    O living Sun.

The Blue Bird

I am the bird of God in His blue;
    Divinely high and clear
I sing the notes of the sweet and the true
    For the god's and the seraph's ear.

I rise like a fire from the mortal's earth
    Into a griefless sky
And drop in the suffering soil of his birth
    Fire-seeds of ecstasy.

My pinions soar beyond Time and Space
    Into unfading Light;
I bring the bliss of the Eternal's face
    And the boon of the Spirit's sight.

I measure the worlds with my ruby eyes;
    I have perched on Wisdom's tree
Thronged with the blossoms of Paradise
    By the streams of Eternity.

Nothing is hid from my burning heart;
    My mind is shoreless and still;
My song is rapture's mystic art,
    My flight immortal will.

The Mother of God

A conscious and eternal Power is here
Behind unhappiness and mortal birth
And the error of Thought and blundering trudge of Time.
The Mother of God, his sister and his spouse,
Daughter of his wisdom, of his might[1] the mate,
She has leapt from the Transcendent's secret breast
To build her rainbow worlds of mind and life.
Between the superconscient absolute Light
And the Inconscient's vast unthinking toil
In the rolling and routine of Matter's sleep
And the somnambulist motion of the stars
She forces on the cold unwilling Void
Her adventure of life, the passionate dreams of her lust.
Amid the work of darker Powers she is here
To heal the evils and mistakes of Space
And change the tragedy of the ignorant world
Into a Divine Comedy of joy
And the laughter and the rapture of God's bliss.
The Mother of God is master of our souls;
We are the partners of his birth in Time,
Inheritors we share his eternity.

---

[1] strength

The Island Sun

I have sailed the golden ocean
    And crossed the silver bar;
I have reached the Sun of knowledge
    The earth-self's midnight star.

Its fields of flaming vision,
    Its mountains of bare might,
Its peaks of fiery rapture,
    Its air of absolute light,

Its seas of self-oblivion,
    Its vales of Titan rest,
Became my soul's dominion,
    Its Island of the Blest.

Alone with God and silence,
    Timeless it lived in Time;
Life was His fugue of music,
    Thought was Truth's ardent rhyme.

The Light was still around me
    When I came back to earth
Bringing the Immortal's knowledge
    Into man's cave of birth.

Silence is all

1

Silence is all, say the sages.
Silence watches the work of the ages;
In the book of Silence the cosmic Scribe has written his cosmic pages;
Silence is all, say the sages.

2

What then of the word, O speaker?
What then of the thought, O thinker?
Thought is the wine of the soul and the word is the beaker;
Life is the banquet-table — the soul of the sage is the drinker.

3

What of the wine, O mortal?
I am drunk with the wine as I sit at Wisdom's portal,
Waiting for the Light beyond thought and the Word immortal.
Long I sit in vain at Wisdom's portal.

4

How shalt thou know the Word when it comes, O seeker?
How shalt thou know the Light when it breaks, O witness?
I shall hear the voice of the God within me and grow wiser and meeker;
I shall be the tree that takes in the light as its food, I shall drink its
                                                                     nectar of sweetness.

Is this the end

Is this the end of all that we have been,
    And all we did or dreamed, —
A name unremembered and a form undone, —
    Is this the end?

A body rotting under a slab of stone
    Or turned to ash in fire,
A mind dissolved, lost its forgotten thoughts, —
    Is this the end?

Our little hours that were and are no more,
    Our passions once so high
Being mocked by the still earth and calm sunshine, —
    Is this the end?

Our yearnings for the human Godward climb
    Passing to other hearts
Deceived, while smiles towards death and hell the world, —
    Is this the end?

Fallen is the harp; shattered it lies and mute;
    Is the unseen player dead?
Because the tree is felled where the bird sang,
    Must the song too hush?

One in the mind who planned and willed and thought,
    Worked to reshape earth's fate,
One in the heart who loved and yearned and hoped,
    Does he too end?

The Immortal in the mortal is his Name;
    An artist Godhead here
Ever remoulds himself in diviner shapes,
    Unwilling to cease

Till all is done for which the stars were made,
    Till the heart discovers God
And the soul knows itself. And even then
    There is no end.

Who art thou that camest

Who art thou that camest
  Bearing the occult Name,
Wings of regal darkness
  Eyes of an unborn flame?

Like the august uprising
  Of a forgotten sun
Out of the caverned midnight
  Fire-trails of wonder run.

Captured the heart renouncing
  Tautness of passion-worn strings
Allows the wide-wayed sweetness
  Of free supernal things.

❊

One Day

THE LITTLE MORE

One day, and all the half-dead is done,
One day, and all the unborn begun;
A little path and the great goal,
A touch that brings the divine whole.

Hill after hill was climbed and now,
Behold, the last tremendous brow
And the great rock that none has trod:
A step, and all is sky and God.

The Dwarf Napoleon

HITLER, OCTOBER 1939

Behold, by Maya's fantasy of will
A violent miracle takes sudden birth,
The real grows one with the incredible.
In the control of her magician wand
The small achieves things great, the base things grand.
This puny creature would bestride the earth
Even as the immense colossus of the past.
Napoleon's mind was swift and bold and vast,
His heart was calm and stormy like the sea,
His will dynamic in its grip and clasp.
His eye could hold a world within its grasp
And see the great and small things sovereignly.
A movement of enormous[1] depth and scope
He seized and gave cohesion[2] to its hope.
Far other this creature of a nether clay,
Void of all grandeur, like a gnome at play,
Iron and mud his nature's mingled stuff,
A little limited visionary brain
Cunning and skilful in its narrow vein,
A sentimental egoist poor and rough,
Whose heart was never sweet and fresh and young,
A headlong spirit driven by hopes and fears,
Intense neurotic with his shouts and tears,
Violent and cruel, devil, child and brute,
This screaming orator with his strident tongue,
The prophet of a scanty fixed idea,
Plays now the leader of our human march;
His might shall build the future's triumph arch.
Now is the world for his eating a ripe fruit.
His shadow falls from London to Korea.
Cities and nations crumble in his course.
A terror holds the peoples in its grip:
World-destiny waits upon that foaming lip.
A Titan Power supports[3] this pigmy man,

[1] gigantic [2] coherence [3] upholds

The crude dwarf instrument of a[1] mighty Force.
Hater of the free spirit's joy and light,
Made only of strength and skill and giant might,
A Will to trample humanity into clay
And unify earth beneath one iron sway,
Insists upon its fierce enormous plan.
Trampling man's mind and will into one mould
Docile and facile in a dreadful hold,
It cries its demon slogans to the crowd;
But if its[2] tenebrous empire were allowed,
Its mastery would prepare the dismal hour
When the Inconscient shall regain its right,
And man who emerged as Nature's conscious power,
Shall sink into the deep original night
Sharing like all her forms that went before
The doom of the mammoth and the dinosaur.
It is the shadow of the Titan's robe
That looms across the panic-stricken globe.
In his high villa on the fatal hill
Alone he listens to that sovereign Voice,
Dictator of his action's sudden choice,
The tiger leap of a demoniac skill.
Too small and human for that dreadful Guest,
An energy his body cannot invest[3], —
A tortured channel, not a happy vessel,
Drives him to think and act and cry and wrestle.
Thus driven he must stride on conquering all,
Threatening and clamouring, brutal, invincible,
Perhaps to meet[4] upon his storm-swept road
A greater devil — or thunderstroke of God.

---

[1] his [2] that [3] house [4] Until he meets

The Children of Wotan (1940)

"Where is the end of your armoured march, O children of Wotan?
Earth shudders with fear at your tread, the death-flame laughs in your eyes."
"We have seen the sign of Thor and the hammer of new creation,
A seed of blood on the soil, a flower of blood in the skies.
We march to make of earth a hell and call it heaven.
The heart of mankind we have smitten with the whip of the sorrows seven;
The Mother of God lies bleeding in our black and gold sunrise."

"I hear the cry of a broken world, O children of Wotan."
"Question the volcano when it burns, chide the fire and bitumen!
Suffering is the food of our strength and torture the bliss of our entrails.
We are pitiless, mighty and glad, the gods fear our laughter inhuman.
Our hearts are heroic and hard; we wear the belt of Orion:
Our will has the edge of the thunderbolt, our acts the claws of the lion.
We rejoice in the pain we create as a man in the kiss of a woman."

"Have you seen your fate in the scales of God, O children of Wotan,
And the tail of the Dragon lashing the foam in far-off seas?"
"We mock at God, we have silenced the mutter of priests at his altar.
Our leader is master of Fate, medium of her mysteries.
We have made the mind a cypher, we have strangled Thought with a cord;
Dead now are pity and honour, strength only is Nature's lord.
We build a new world-order; our bombs shout Wotan's peace.

"We are the javelins of Destiny, we are the children of Wotan,
We are the human Titans, the supermen dreamed by the sage.
A cross of the beast and demoniac with the godhead of power and will,
We are born in humanity's sunset, to the Night is our pilgrimage.
On the bodies of perishing nations, mid the cry of the cataclysm coming,
To a presto of bomb and shell and the aeroplanes' fatal humming,
We march, lit by Truth's death-pyre, to the world's satanic age."

Despair on the Staircase

Mute stands she, lonely on the topmost stair,
An image of magnificent despair;
The grandeur of a sorrowful surmise
Wakes in the largeness of her glorious eyes.
In her beauty's dumb significant pose I find
The tragedy of her mysterious mind.
Yet is she stately, grandiose, full of grace.
A musing mask is her immobile face.
Her tail is up like an unconquered flag,
Its dignity knows not the right to wag.
An animal creature wonderfully human,
A charm and miracle of fur-footed Brahman,
Whether she is spirit, woman or a cat,
Is now the problem I am wondering at.

❊

Surrealist

I have heard a foghorn shouting at a sheep,
And oh the sweet sound made me laugh and weep
But alas,[1] the sheep was on the hither shore
Of the little less and the ever-never more.
I sprang on its back; it jumped into the sea.
I was near to the edges of eternity.
Then suddenly the foghorn blared again.
There was no sheep — it had perished of ear pain.
I took a boat and steered to the Afar
Hoping to colonise the polar star.

[1] ah,

But in the boat there was a dangerous goose
Whom some eternal idiot had let loose.
To this wild animal I said not "Bo!"
But it was not because I did not know.
Full soon I was on shore with dreadful squeals
And the fierce biped cackling at my heels.
Alarmed I ran into a lion's den
And after me ran three thousand armoured men.
The lion bolted through his own backdoor
And set up a morose dissatisfied roar.
At this my courage rose; I grew quite brave
And shoved myself into a tiger's cave.
The tiger snarled; I thought it best instead
To don my pyjamas and go to bed.
But the tiger had a strained objecting face,
So I turned my eyes away from his grimace.
At night the beast began my back to claw
And growled out that I was his brother-in-law.
I rose and thought it best to go away
To a doctor's house: besides 'twas nearly day.
The doctor shook his head and cried "For a back
Pepper and salt are the remedy, alack."
But I objected to his condiments
And thought the doctor had but little sense.
Then I returned to my own little cot
For really things were now extremely hot.
Then *fierily* the world cracked *Nazily* down
And I looked about to find my dressing gown.
I was awake (I had tumbled on the floor).
A shark was hammering away at my front-door.

SHORT POEMS
Fragments

Morcundeya

O will of God that stirrest and the Void
Is peopled, men have called thee force, upbuoyed
Upon whose wings the stars borne round and round
Need not one hour of rest; light, form and sound
Are marks of thy eternal movement. We
See what thou choosest, but 'tis thou we see.

I Morcundeya whom the worlds release,
The Seer, — but it is God alone that sees ! —
Soar up above the bonds that hold below
Man to his littleness, lost in the show
Perennial which the senses round him build;
I find them out and am no more beguiled.
But ere I rise, ere I become the vast
And luminous Infinite and from the past
And future utterly released forget
These beings who themselves their bonds create,
Once I will speak and what I see declare.
The rest is God. There's silence everywhere.

My eyes within were opened and I saw.

A voice arose

(Alexandrines)

A voice arose that was so sweet and terrible
It thrilled the heart with love and pain, as if all hell
Tuned with all heaven in one inextricable note.
Born from abysmal depths on highest heights to float,
It carried all sorrow that the souls of creatures share,
Yet hinted every rapture that the gods can bear.
O Sun of God who camst into my blackest Night
To sound and know its gulfs and bring the immortal light.

I walked beside the waters

(Alexandrines)

I walked beside the waters of a world of light
On a gold ridge guarding two seas of high-rayed night.
One was divinely topped with a pale bluish moon
And swam as in a happy deep spiritual swoon
More conscious than earth's waking; the other's wide delight
Billowed towards an ardent orb of diamond white.
But where I stood, there joined in a bright marvellous haze
The miracled moons with the long ridge's golden blaze.
I knew not if two wakings or two mighty sleeps
Mixed the great diamond fires and the pale pregnant deeps,
But all my glad expanding soul flowed satisfied
Around me and became the mystery of their tide.
As one who finds his own eternal self, content,
Needing naught else beneath the spirit's firmament,
It knew not Space, it heard no more Time's running feet,
Termless, fulfilled, lost richly in itself, complete.
And so it might have lain for ever. But there came
A dire intrusion wrapped in married cloud and flame,
Across the blue-white moon-hush of my magic seas
A sudden sweeping of immense peripheries
Of darkness ringing lambent lustres; shadowy-vast
A nameless dread, a Power incalculable passed
Whose feet were death, whose wings were immortality;
Its changing mind was time, its heart eternity.
All opposites were there, unreconciled, uneased,
Struggling for victory, by victory unappeased.
All things it bore, even that which brings undying peace,
But secret, veiled, waiting for some supreme release.
I saw the spirit of the cosmic Ignorance;
I felt its power besiege my gloried fields of trance.

Urvasie

Pururavus from converse held with Gods
On unseen crest of Nature high, occult,
Traversed the tumult of the flame-tossed seas
That cast their fire between the spirit's poles.
Alone like a bright star twixt earth and heaven,
He reached the crossways of infinity.[1]
A Soul to our apparent life reborn
Out of the vastness of the original Self,
Journeying in dim momentous solitude
Led by the flickering of uncertain suns,
He essayed the fringe of Night's tremendous home.
Before him lay the subtle realm of light
Our organed sense conceals, the light that gleams
Across the sealless musings of the seer,
A slumberless wide eye upon our scene.
Attracted[2] to earth's darkly pregnant dream
He tarried not on these mysterious shores
But still descended the divine abyss
To new adventure in the eternal Night,
Transgressed the wonder-line of things beyond
Abruptly into mortal space and time.
A universe appeared of difficult birth,
The labour of eclipsed and ignorant gods,
An immortality of chance and change.
Bridging the gulf between antagonist planes
He saw the circles of Heaven's rash advance,
Sun upon sun, God's sentinels in the void;
Life's radiant and immeasurable camp
Blazed in the order of the aeonic Will.
But with the menace of the dragon depths
The old blind vigilant Nescience stretched afar
Hungering in serpent dumb infinitude,
And her dark shade besieged the luminaries.
Silence and Death opposed the invading Fire.
And even before he broke into our pale
There came on him a breath from tarnished worlds.

---

[1] eternity. [2] But destined

Averse from an obscure material touch
The images of the supernal realms[1]
That he had left sank from the front of thought
And held their session in the heart's dumb cave.
The glory and grace, the light, the sacred life
Receded as behind a burning door:
Subliminal beneath the lid of mind
The grandeur and the passion and the calm.
His mind became a beat of memory.
Sight, hearing changed towards our diminished scale;
The little views grew great, the great grew small.
As yet some largeness was of inmost things
And he remembered in the formless sense
Proud kingdoms of intense and beautiful life
And love left free to do his absolute will
And dreams at once commuted into power.
Affronting many starfields of our space
And shortening ever the vast lens of Time
He met a smaller movement of desire
Prisoned in the orbit of a few pale globes
And knew in front our little solar belt
Hung casually among the giant stars.
Then[2] earth received him mid her living forms.
Her deep inconscient motions packed and mute,
Her darknesses more wise than her small lights
Oppressed again his young divinity.

The Cosmic Man

I look across the world and no horizon walls my gaze;
I see Paris and Tokio and New York,
I see the bombs bursting on Barcelona and on Canton streets.
Man's numberless misdeeds and rare good deeds take place within my
                                                                                     single self.
I am the beast he slays, the bird he feeds and saves.
The thoughts of unknown minds exalt me with their thrill,
I carry the sorrow of millions in my lonely breast.

[1] fields   [2] Our

II

SONNETS
Early Period

To the Cuckoo

Sounds of the wakening world, the year's increase,
Passage of wind and all his dewy powers
With breath and laughter of new-bathèd flowers
And that deep light of heaven above the trees
Awake mid leaves that muse in golden peace
Sweet noise of birds, but most in heavenly showers
The cuckoo's voice pervades the lucid hours,
Is priest and summoner of these melodies.
The spent and weary streams refresh their youth
At that creative rain and barren groves
Regain their face of flowers; in thee the ruth
Of Nature wakening her dead children moves.
But chiefly to renew thou hast the art
Fresh childhood in the obscured human heart.

Transiit, Non Periit

(My grandfather, Rajnarayan Bose, died September 1899)

Not in annihilation lost, nor given
To darkness art thou fled from us and light,
O strong and sentient spirit; no mere heaven
Of ancient joys, no silence eremite
Received thee; but the omnipresent Thought
Of which thou wast a part and earthly hour,
Took back its gift. Into that splendour caught
Thou hast not lost thy special brightness. Power
Remains with thee and the old genial force
Unseen for blinding light, not darkly lurks:
As when a sacred river in its course
Dives into ocean, there its strength abides
Not less because with vastness wed and works
Unnoticed in the grandeur of the tides.

O face that I have loved

O face that I have loved until no face
Beneath the quiet heavens such glory wear,
They say you are not beautiful, – no snare
Of twilight in the changing mysticness
Or deep enhaloed secrecy of hair,
Soft largeness in the eyes I dare not kiss!
Unreal all your bosom's dreadful bliss.
Too narrow are your brows they say to bear
The temple of vast beauty in its span
Or chaste cold bosom to house fierily
Beauty that maddens all the heart of man.
I know not; this I know that utterly
My soul is by some magic curls surprised,
Some glances have my heart immortalized.

I cannot equal

I cannot equal those most absolute eyes,
Although they rule my being, with the stars,
Nor floral rich comparisons devise
To detail sweetness that your body wears.
Nor in the heavens hints of you I find,
Nor dim suggestions in this thoughtful eve;
The moonlight of your darker grace is blind
Who can with such pale delicacies deceive
A naked burning heart. Only one place
Satisfies me of you, where the feet
That I shall never clasp, with beauty press
The barren earth in one place only sweet,
One face in the wide world alone divine,
The only one that never can be mine.

O letter dull and cold

O letter dull and cold, how can she read
Gladly these lifeless lines, no fire that prove,
When others even their passionate hearts exceed
Caressing her sweet name with words of love?
O me that I could force this barrier, turn
My heart to syllables, make all desire
One burning word, then would my letters yearn
With some reflection of that hidden fire.
Ah if I could, what then? This fiery pit
Within for human eyes was never meant.
All hearts would view with horror or with hate
A picture not of earthly lineament.
Yourself even, sweet, would start with terror back
As at the hissing of a sudden snake.

My life is wasted

My life is wasted like a lamp ablaze
Within a solitary house unused,
My life is wasted and by Love men praise
For sweet and kind. How often have I mused
What lovely thing were love and much repined
At my cold bosom moved not by that flame.
'Tis kindled; lo, my dreadful being twined
Round one whom to myself I dare not name.
I cannot quench the fire I did not light
And he that lit it will not; I cannot even
Drive out the guest I never did invite;
Although the soul he dwells with loses heaven.
I burn and know not why; I sink to hell
Fruitlessly and am forbidden to rebel.

Because thy flame is spent

Because thy flame is spent, shall mine grow less,
O bud, O wonder of the opening rose?
Why both my soul and Love it would disgrace
If I could trade in love, begin and close
My long account of passion, like a book
Of merchant's credit, given to be repaid,
Or not returned, struck off with lowering look
Like a bad debt uncritically made.
What thou couldst give, thou gav'st me, one sweet smile
Worth all the sunlight that the years contain,
One month of months when thy sweet spirit a while
Fluttered o'er mine half-thinking to remain.
What I could give, I gave thee, to my last breath
Immortal love, immovable by death.

Thou didst mistake

Thou didst mistake, thy spirit's infant flight
Opening its lovely wings upon the sun
Paused o'er the first strong bloom that met thy sight
Thinking perhaps it was the only one.
But all this fragrant garden was beyond.
Winds came to thee with hints of honey, and day
Disclosed a brighter hope than this unsunned
Thought-sheltered heart and called thee far away.
Thou didst mistake. Must I then rage, grow ill
With tortured vanity and think it love,
Miscall with brutal names my lady's will
Fouling thy snow-white image, O my dove?
Is not thy kiss enough, though only one,
For all eternity to live upon?

Rose, I have loved

Rose, I have loved thy beauty, as I love
The dress that thou hast worn, the transient grass,
O'er which thy happy careless footsteps move,
The yet-thrilled waysides that have watched[1] thee pass.
Soul, I have loved thy sweetness as men love
The necessary air they crave to breathe,
The sunlight lavished from the skies above,
And firmness of the earth their steps beneath.
But were that beauty all, my love might cease
Like love of weaker spirits; were't thy charm
And grace of soul, mine might with age decrease
Or find in Death a silence and a term,
But rooted to the unnameable in thee
Shall triumph and transcend eternity.

I have a hundred lives

I have a hundred lives before me yet
To grasp thee in, O spirit ethereal,
Be sure I will with heart insatiate
Pursue thee like a hunter through them all.
Thou yet shalt turn back on the eternal way
And with awakened vision watch me come
Smiling a little at errors past and lay
Thy eager hand in mine, its proper home.
Meanwhile made happy by thy happiness
I shall approach thee in things and people dear
And in thy spirit's motions half-possess
Loving what thou hast loved, shall feel thee near;
Until I lay my hands on thee indeed
Somewhere among the stars, as 'twas decreed.

---

[1] seen

Still there is something

Still there is something that I lack in thee
And yet must find. There is a broad abyss
Between possession and true sovereignty
Which thou must bridge with a diviner kiss.
I questioned all the beauty of other girls
Thinking thou hadst it not to give indeed.
But not Giannina's breasts nor Pippa's curls
Contained it; thou alone canst meet my need.
Deniest thou some secret of thy soul
To me who claim thee all? Nay, can it be
Thy bosom's joys escape from my control?
Forbid it Heaven Hell should yawn for thee.
Deny it now! Let not sweet love begun
End in red blood and awful justice done.

I have a doubt

I have a doubt, I have a doubt which kills.
Tell me, O torturing beauty, O divine
Witchcraft, O soul escaped from heaven's hills
Yet fed upon strange food of utter sin.
Why dost thou torture me? Hast thou no fear?
My love was ever like my hate a sword
To search the heart and kill however dear
The joy that would not own me for its lord.
Yet must I still believe that thou art true
If thou wilt say it and smile. Knowest thou not then
I have purchased with my passion all of you
And wilt thou keep one nook for other men?
Deny it now! Let not sweet love begun
End in red blood and awful justice done.

To weep because a glorious sun

    To weep because a glorious sun has set
    Which the next morn shall gild the east again,
    To mourn that mighty strengths must yield to fate
    Which by that fall a double force attain,
    To shrink from pain without whose friendly strife
    Joy could not be, to make a terror of death
    Who smiling beckons us to farther life
    And is a bridge for the persistent breath;
    Despair and anguish and the tragic grief
    Of dry set eyes, or such disastrous tears
    As rend[1] the heart, though meant for its relief,
    And all man's ghastly company of fears
    Are born of folly that believes the span
    Of life the limit of immortal man.

What is this talk

    What is this talk of slayer and of slain?
    Swords are not sharp to slay nor floods assuage
    This flaming soul. Mortality and pain
    Are mere conventions of a mightier stage.
    As when a hero by his doom pursued
    Falls like a pillar of the huge world uptorn
    Shaking the hearts of men and awe-imbued,
    Silent the audience sits of joy forlorn.
    Meanwhile behind the stage the actor sighs
    Deep-lunged relief, puts by what he has been
    And talks with friends that waited or from the flies
    Watches the quiet of the closing scene.
    Even so the unwounded spirits of the slain
    Beyond our vision passing live again.

---

[1] tear

SONNETS
1930 - 1950

Transformation

My breath runs in a subtle rhythmic stream;
   It fills my members with a might divine:
     I have drunk the Infinite like a giant's wine.
Time is my drama or my pageant dream.
Now are my illumined cells joy's flaming scheme
   And changed my thrilled and branching nerves to fine
     Channels of rapture opal and hyaline
For the influx of the Unknown and the Supreme.

I am no more a vassal of the flesh,
   A slave to Nature and her leaden rule;
     I am caught no more in the senses' narrow mesh.
My soul unhorizoned widens to measureless sight,
   My body is God's happy living tool,
     My spirit a vast sun of deathless light.

The Other Earths

An irised multitude of hills and seas,
   And glint of brooks in the green wilderness,
And trackless stars, and miracled symphonies
   Of hues that float in ethers shadowless,

A dance of fire-flies in the fretted gloom,
   In a pale midnight the moon's silver flare,
Fire-importunities of scarlet bloom
   And bright suddenness of wings in a golden air,

Strange bird and animal forms like memories cast
   On the rapt silence of unearthly woods,
Calm faces of the gods on backgrounds vast
   Bringing the marvel of the infinitudes,

Through glimmering veils of wonder and delight
World after world bursts on the awakened sight.

Nirvana

All is abolished but the mute Alone.
    The mind from thought released, the heart from grief
    Grow inexistent now beyond belief;
There is no I, no Nature, known-unknown.
The city, a shadow picture without tone,
    Floats, quivers unreal; forms without relief
    Flow, a cinema's vacant shapes; like a reef
Foundering in shoreless gulfs the world is done.

Only the illimitable Permanent
    Is here. A Peace stupendous, featureless, still,
        Replaces all,⁄– what once was I, in It
A silent unnamed emptiness content
    Either to fade in the Unknowable
        Or thrill with the luminous seas of the Infinite.

Man the Thinking Animal

A trifling unit in a boundless plan
    Amidst the enormous insignificance
    Of the unpeopled cosmos' fire-whirl dance,
Earth, as by accident, engendered man:

A creature of his own grey ignorance,
    A mind half shadow and half gleam, a breath
    That wrestles, captive in a world of death,
To live some lame brief years. Yet his advance,

Attempt of a divinity within,
    A consciousness in the inconscient Night,
    To realise its own supernal Light,
Confronts the ruthless forces of the Unseen.

Aspiring to godhead from insensible clay
He travels slow-footed towards the eternal day.

Contrasts

What opposites are here! A trivial life
    Specks the huge dream of Death called Matter; intense
    In its struggle of weakness towards omnipotence,
A thinking mind starts from the unthinking strife

In the order of the electric elements.
    Immortal life breathed in that monstrous death,
    A mystery of knowledge wore as sheath
Matter's mute nescience. Its enveloped sense

Or dumb somnambulist will obscurely reigns
    Driving the atoms in their cosmic course
    Whose huge unhearing movement serves perforce
The works of a strange blind omniscience.

The world's deep contrasts are but figures spun
Draping the unanimity of the One.

The Silver Call

There is a godhead of unrealised things
    To which Time's splendid gains are hoarded dross;
A cry seems near, a rustle of silver wings
    Calling to heavenly joy by earthly loss.

All eye has seen and all the ear has heard
    Is a pale illusion by some greater voice
And mightier vision; no sweet sound or word,
    No passion of hues that make the heart rejoice

Can equal those diviner ecstasies.
    A Mind beyond our mind has sole the ken
Of those yet unimagined harmonies,
    The fate and privilege of unborn men.

As rain-thrashed mire the marvel of the rose,
Earth waits that distant marvel to disclose.

Evolution

    I passed into a lucent still abode
        And saw as in a mirror crystalline
        An ancient Force ascending serpentine
    The unhasting spirals of the aeonic road.
    Earth was a cradle for the arriving god
        And man but a half-dark half-luminous sign
        Of the transition of the veiled Divine
    From Matter's sleep and the tormented load

    Of ignorant life and death to the Spirit's light.
        Mind liberated swam Light's ocean vast,
            And life escaped from its grey tortured line;
    I saw Matter illumining its parent Night.
        The soul could feel into infinity cast
            Timeless God-bliss the heart incarnadine.

The Call of the Impossible

    A godhead moves us to unrealised things.
        Asleep in the wide folds of destiny,
    A world guarded by Silence' rustling wings
        Shelters their fine impossibility:

    But parting quiver the cerulean gates;
        Strange splendours look into our dreaming eyes;
    We bear proud deities and magnificent fates;
        Faces and hands come near from Paradise.

    What shines above, waits darkling here in us:
        Bliss unattained our future's birthright is,
    Beauty of our dim souls grows amorous,
        We are the heirs of infinite widenesses.

    The impossible is our mask of things to be,
    Mortal the door to immortality.

Evolution

All is not finished in the unseen decree;
　　A Mind beyond our mind demands our ken,
　A life of unimagined harmony
　　Awaits, concealed, the grasp of unborn men.

The crude beginnings of the lifeless earth,
　　The mindless stirrings of the plant and tree
　Prepared our thought; thought for a godlike birth
　　Broadens the mould of our mortality.

A might no human will nor force can gain,
　　A knowledge seated in eternity,
　A bliss beyond our struggle and our pain
　　Are the high pinnacles of our destiny.

O Thou who climbest to mind from the dull stone,
Face now the miracled summits still unwon.

Man the Mediator

A dumb Inconscient drew life's stumbling maze,
　　A night of all things, packed and infinite:
　It made our consciousness a torch that plays
　　Between the Abyss and a supernal Light.

Our mind was framed a lens of segment sight
　　Piecing out inch by inch the world's huge mass,
　And reason a small hard theodolite
　　Measuring unreally the measureless ways.

Yet is the dark Inconscient whence came all
　　The self-same Power that shines on high unwon:
　Our Night shall be a sky purpureal,
　　Our torch transmute to a vast godhead's sun.

Rooted in mire heavenward man's nature grows, –
His soul the dim bud of God's flaming rose.

The Infinitesimal Infinite

Out of a still Immensity we came!
  These million universes were to it
The poor light-bubbles of a trivial game,
  A fragile glimmer in the Infinite.

It could not find its soul in all that vast:
  It drew itself into a little speck
Infinitesimal, ignobly cast
  Out of earth's mud and slime strangely awake, –

A tiny plasm upon a casual globe
  In the small system of a dwarflike sun,
A little life wearing the flesh for robe,
  A little mind winged through wide space to run!

It lived, it knew, it saw its self sublime,
Deathless, outmeasuring Space, outlasting Time.

Discoveries of Science

I saw the electric stream on which is run
  The world, turned motes and spark-whirls of a Light,
A Fire of which the nebula and sun
  Are glints and flame-drops, scattered eremite;

And veiled by viewless Light worked other Powers,
  An Air of movement endless, unbegun,
Expanding and contracting in Time's hours
  And the intangible ether of the One.

The surface finds, the screen-phenomenon,
  Are Nature's offered ransom, while behind,
Her occult mysteries lie safe, unknown,
  From the crude handling of the empiric Mind.

Our truths discovered are but dust and trace
Of the eternal Energy in her race.

The Ways of the Spirit

How shall ascending Nature touch her goal?
    Not through man's stumbling peering[1] intellect
    And its carved figures rigid and erect,
But the far subtler vision of his soul.

An algebra of mind, a scheme of sense,
    A symbol language without depths or wings,
    A power to handle deftly outward things
Are his scant earnings of intelligence.

The Spirit keeps for him its ampler ways,
    A sense that takes the world into our being,
    A close illumined touch and intimate seeing,
Wide Thought that is a god's ensphering gaze,

A tranquil heart in sympathy with all,
Its will vast-visioned, poised, imperial.

Science and the Unknowable

Man's science builds its abstracts cold and brief
    And cuts to formulas the living whole.
    It is a brain and hand without a soul,
An eye that tests the outward carved relief,

Blind to the depths, the occult roots unshown.
    The visible hides its base in the unseen;
    The invisible guards the truth its symbols mean
In a yet deeper invisible's unknown.

The objects we would prove are not their form.
    Each is a mass of forces veiled as[2] shape
    Whose ends we seize, but the inner lines escape
In a fathomless consciousness above mind's norm.

Mind's peering gaze meets only abysses still,
Infinite, wayless, mute, unknowable.

    [1] tardy   [2] thrown in

The Yogi on the Whirlpool

On a dire whirlpool in the hurrying river,
    A life-stilled statue naked, bronze, severe,
        He kept the posture of a deathless seer
Unshaken by the mad water's leap and shiver.
Thought could not think in him, flesh could not quiver;
        The feet of Time could not adventure here;
    Only some unknown Power nude and austere,
Only a Silence mighty to deliver.

His spirit world-wide and companionless
    Seated above the torrent of the days
        On the deep eddy that our being forms,
Silent, sustained the huge creation's stress,
    Unchanged supporting Nature's rounds and norms,
        Immobile background of the cosmic race.

The Kingdom Within

There is a kingdom of the spirit's ease.
    It is not in this helpless swirl of thought,
    Foam from the world-sea or spray-whispers caught,
With which we build mind's shifting symmetries,
Nor in life's stuff of passionate unease,
    Nor the heart's unsure emotions frailly wrought
    Nor trivial clipped sense-joys soon led to nought
Nor in this body's solid transiences.

Wider behind than the vast universe
    Our spirit scans the drama and the stir,
        A peace, a light, an ecstasy, a power
Waiting at the end of blindness and the curse
    That veils it from its ignorant minister
        The grandeur of its free eternal hour.

Now I have borne

Now I have borne Thy presence and Thy light,
    Eternity assumes me and I am
    A vastness of tranquillity and flame,
My heart a deep Atlantic of delight.
My life is a moving moment of Thy might
    Carrying Thy vision's sacred oriflamme
    Inscribed with the white glory of Thy name
In the unborn silence of the Infinite.

My body is a jar of radiant peace,
    The days a line across my timelessness,
        My mind is made a voiceless breadth of Thee,
A lyre of muteness and a luminous sea;
    Yet in each cell I feel Thy fire embrace,
        A brazier of the seven ecstasies.

Electron

The electron on which forms and worlds are built,
    Leaped into being, a particle of God.
A spark from the eternal Energy spilt,
    It is the Infinite's blind minute abode.

In that small flaming chariot Shiva rides.
    The One devised innumerably to be;
His oneness in invisible forms he hides,
    Time's tiny temples to[1] eternity.

Atom and molecule in their unseen plan
    Buttress an edifice of strange onenesses,
Crystal and plant, insect and beast and man, –
    Man on whom the World-Unity shall seize,

Widening his soul-spark to an epiphany
Of the timeless vastness of Infinity.

[1] of

The Indwelling Universal

I contain the wide world in my soul's embrace:
    In me Arcturus and Belphegor burn.
    To whatsoever living form I turn
I see my own body with another face.

All eyes that look on me are my sole eyes;
    The one heart that beats within all breasts is mine.
    The world's happiness flows through me like wine,
Its million sorrows are my agonies.

Yet all its acts are only waves that pass
    Upon my surface; inly for ever still,
    Unborn I sit, timeless, intangible;
All things are shadows in my tranquil glass.

My vast transcendence holds the cosmic whirl;
I am hid in it as in the sea a pearl.

Bliss of Identity

All Nature is taught in radiant ways to move,
    All beings are in myself embraced.
O fiery boundless Heart of joy and love,
    How art thou beating in a mortal's breast!

It is Thy rapture flaming through my nerves
    And all my cells and atoms thrill with Thee;
My body Thy vessel is and only serves
    As a living wine-cup of Thy ecstasy.

I am a centre of Thy golden light
    And I its vast and vague circumference;
Thou art my soul great, luminous and white
    And Thine my mind and will and glowing sense.

Thy spirit's infinite breath I feel in me;
My life is a throb of Thy eternity.

The Witness Spirit

I dwell in the spirit's calm nothing can move
    And watch the actions of Thy vast world-force,
Its mighty wings that through infinity move
    And the Time-gallopings of the deathless Horse.

This mute stupendous Energy that whirls
    The stars and nebulae in its long train,
Like a huge Serpent through my being curls
    With its diamond hood of joy and fangs of pain.

It rises from the dim inconscient deep
    Upcoiling through the minds and hearts of men,
Then touches on some height of luminous sleep
    The bliss and splendour of the eternal plane.

All this I bear in me, untouched and still
Assenting to Thy all-wise inscrutable will.

The Hidden Plan

However long Night's hour, I will not dream
    That the small ego and the person's mask
Are all that God reveals in our life-scheme,
    The last result of Nature's cosmic task.

A greater Presence in her bosom works;
    Long it prepares its far epiphany:
Even in the stone and beast the godhead lurks,
    A bright Persona of eternity.

It shall burst out from the limit traced by Mind
    And make a witness of the prescient heart;
It shall reveal even in this inert blind
    Nature, long veiled in each inconscient part,

Fulfilling the occult magnificent plan,
The world-wide and immortal spirit in man.

The Pilgrim of the Night

I made an assignation with the Night;
    In the abyss was fixed our rendezvous:
In my breast carrying God's deathless light
    I came her dark and dangerous heart to woo.

I left the glory of the illumined Mind
    And the calm rapture of the divinised soul
And travelled through a vastness dim and blind
    To the grey shore where her ignorant waters roll.

I walk by the chill wave through the dull slime
    And still that weary journeying knows no end;
Lost is the lustrous godhead beyond Time,
    There comes no voice of the celestial Friend,

And yet I know my footprints' track shall be
A pathway towards Immortality.

Cosmic Consciousness

I have wrapped the wide world in my wider self
    And Time and Space my spirit's seeing are.
I am the god and demon, ghost and elf,
    I am the wind's speed and the blazing star.

All Nature is the nursling of my care,
    I am the struggle and the eternal rest;
The world's joy thrilling runs through me, I bear
    The sorrow of millions in my lonely breast.

I have learned a close identity with all,
    Yet am by nothing bound that I become;
Carrying in me the universe's call
    I mount to my imperishable home.

I pass beyond Time and life on measureless wings,
Yet still am one with born and unborn things.

Liberation

I have thrown from me the whirling dance of mind
    And stand now in the spirit's silence free;
Timeless and deathless beyond creature-kind,
    The centre of my own eternity.

I have escaped and the small self is dead;
    I am immortal, alone, ineffable;
I have gone out from the universe I made,
    And have grown nameless and immeasurable.

My mind is hushed in a wide and endless light,
    My heart a solitude of delight and peace,
My sense unsnared by touch and sound and sight,
    My body a point in white infinities.

I am the one Being's sole immobile Bliss:
No one I am, I who am all that is.

The Inconscient

Out of a seeming void and dark-winged sleep
    Of dim inconscient infinity
A Power arose from the insentient deep,
    A flame-whirl of magician Energy.

Some huge somnambulist Intelligence
    Devising without thought process and plan
Arrayed the burning stars' magnificence,
    The living bodies of beasts and the brain of man.

What stark Necessity or ordered Chance
    Became alive to know the cosmic whole?
What magic of numbers, what mechanic dance
    Developed consciousness, assumed a soul?

The darkness was the Omnipotent's abode,
Hood of omniscience, a blind mask of God.

Life-Unity

I housed within my heart the life of things,
    All hearts athrob in the world I felt as mine;
I shared the joy that in creation sings
    And drank its sorrow like a poignant wine.

I have felt the anger in another's breast,
    All passions poured through my world-self their waves;
One love I shared in a million bosoms expressed.
    I am the beast man slays, the beast he saves.

I spread life's burning wings of rapture and pain;
    Black fire and gold fire strove towards one bliss:
I rose by them towards a supernal plane
    Of power and love and deathless ecstasies.

A deep spiritual calm no touch can sway
Upholds the mystery of this Passion-play.

The Golden Light

Thy golden Light came down into my brain
    And the grey rooms of mind sun-touched became
A bright reply to Wisdom's occult plane,
    A calm illumination and a flame.

Thy golden Light came down into my throat,
    And all my speech is now a tune divine,
A paean-song of Thee my single note;
    My words are drunk with the Immortal's wine.

Thy golden Light came down into my heart
    Smiting my life with Thy eternity;
Now has it grown a temple where Thou art
    And all its passions point towards only Thee.

Thy golden Light came down into my feet;
My earth is now Thy playfield and Thy seat.

The Infinite Adventure

On the waters of a nameless Infinite
   My skiff is launched; I have left the human shore.
   All fades behind me and I see before
The unknown abyss and one pale pointing light.
An unseen Hand controls my rudder. Night
   Walls up the sea in a black corridor, –
   An inconscient Hunger's lion plaint and roar
Or the ocean sleep of a dead Eremite.

I feel the greatness of the Power I seek
   Surround me; below me are its[1] giant deeps,
   Beyond, the invisible height no soul has trod.
I shall be merged in the Lonely and Unique
   And wake into a sudden blaze of God,
   The marvel and rapture of the Apocalypse.

The Greater Plan

I am held no more by life's alluring cry,
   Her joy and grief, her charm, her laughter's lute.
   Hushed are the magic moments of the flute,
And form and colour and brief ecstasy.
I would hear, in my spirit's wideness solitary,
   The Voice that speaks when mortal lips are mute:
   I seek the wonder of things absolute
Born from the silence of Eternity.

There is a need within the soul of man
   The splendours of the surface never sate;
   For life and mind and their glory and debate
Are the slow prelude of a vaster theme,
   A sketch confused of a supernal plan,
   A preface to the epic of the Supreme.

[1] the

The Universal Incarnation

There is a wisdom like a brooding Sun,
    A Bliss in the heart's crypt grown fiery white,
The heart of a world in which all hearts are one,
    A Silence on the mountains of delight,

A Calm that cradles Fate upon its knees;
    A wide Compassion leans to embrace earth's pain;
A Witness dwells within our secrecies,
    The incarnate Godhead in the body of man.

Our mind is a glimmering curtain of that Ray,
    Our strength a parody of the Immortal's power,
Our joy a dreamer on the Eternal's way
    Hunting the fugitive[1] beauty of an hour.

Only on the heart's veiled door the word of flame
Is written, the secret and tremendous Name.

The Godhead

I sat behind the dance of Danger's hooves
    In the shouting street that seemed a futurist's whim,
And suddenly felt, exceeding Nature's grooves,
    In me, enveloping me the body of Him.

Above my head a mighty head was seen,
    A face with the calm of immortality
And an omnipotent gaze that held the scene
    In the vast circle of its sovereignty.

His hair was mingled with the sun and breeze;
    The world was in His heart and He was I:
I housed in me the Everlasting's peace,
    The strength of One whose substance cannot die.

The moment passed and all was as before;
Only that[2] deathless memory I bore.

[1] unseizable   [2] its

The Stone Goddess

In a town of gods, housed in a little shrine,
   From sculptured limbs the Godhead looked at me, —
A living Presence deathless and divine,
   A Form that harboured all infinity.

The great World-Mother and her mighty will
   Inhabited the earth's abysmal sleep,
Voiceless, omnipotent, inscrutable,
   Mute in the desert and the sky and deep.

Now veiled with mind she dwells and speaks no word,
   Voiceless, inscrutable, omniscient,
Hiding until our soul has seen, has heard
   The secret of her strange embodiment,

One in the worshipper and the immobile shape,
A beauty and mystery flesh or stone can drape.

The Cosmic Dance

DANCE OF KRISHNA, DANCE OF KALI

Two measures are there of the cosmic dance.
   Always we hear the tread of Kali's feet
Measuring in rhythms of pain and grief and chance
   Life's game of hazard terrible and sweet.

The ordeal of the veiled Initiate,
   The hero soul at play with Death's embrace,
Wrestler in the dread gymnasium of Fate
   And sacrifice a lonely path to Grace,

Man's sorrows made a key to the Mysteries,
   Truth's narrow road out of Time's wastes of dream,
The soul's seven doors from Matter's tomb to rise,
   Are the common motives of her tragic theme.

But when shall Krishna's dance through Nature move,
His mask of sweetness, laughter, rapture, love?

Krishna

    At last I find a meaning of soul's birth
        Into this universe terrible and sweet,
    I who have felt the hungry heart of earth
        Aspiring beyond heaven to Krishna's feet.

    I have seen the beauty of immortal eyes,
        And heard the passion of the Lover's flute,
    And known a deathless ecstasy's surprise
        And sorrow in my heart for ever mute.

    Nearer and nearer now the music draws,
        Life shudders with a strange felicity;
    All Nature is a wide enamoured pause
        Hoping her lord to touch, to clasp, to be.

    For this one moment lived the ages past;
    The world now throbs fulfilled in me at last.

Shiva

    On the white summit of eternity
        A single Soul of bare infinities,
        Guarded he keeps by a fire-screen of peace
    His mystic loneliness of nude ecstasy.
    But, touched by an immense delight to be,
        He looks across unending depths and sees
        Musing amid the inconscient silences
    The Mighty Mother's dumb felicity.

    Half now awake she rises to his glance;
        Then, moved to circling by her heart-beats' will,
            The rhythmic worlds describe that passion-dance.
    Life springs in her and Mind is born; her face
        She lifts to Him who is Herself, until
            The Spirit leaps into the Spirit's embrace.

Man the Enigma

A deep enigma is the soul of man.
    His conscious life obeys the Inconscient's rule,
    His need of joy is learned in sorrow's school,
His heart is a chaos and an empyrean.
His subtle Ignorance borrows Wisdom's plan;
    His mind is the Infinite's sharp and narrow tool.
    He wades through mud to reach the Wonderful,
And does what Matter must or Spirit can.

All powers in his living's soil take root
    And claim from him their place and struggling right:
    His ignorant creature mind crawling towards light
Is Nature's fool and Godhead's candidate,
    A demigod and a demon and a brute,
    The slave and the creator of his fate.

The Word of the Silence

A bare impersonal hush is now my mind,
    A world of sight clear and inimitable,
A volume of silence by a Godhead signed,
    A greatness pure of thought, virgin of will.

Once on its pages Ignorance could write
    In a scribble of intellect the blind guess of Time
And cast gleam-messages of ephemeral light,
    A food for souls that wander on Nature's rim.

But now I listen to a greater Word
    Born from the mute unseen omniscient Ray:
The Voice that only Silence' ear has heard
    Leaps missioned from an eternal glory of Day.

All turns from a wideness and unbroken peace
To a tumult of joy in a sea of wide release.

The Self's Infinity

    I have become what before Time I was.
        A secret touch has quieted thought and sense:
    All things by the agent Mind created pass
        Into a void and mute magnificence.

    My life is a silence grasped by timeless hands;
        The world is drowned in an immortal gaze.
    Naked my spirit from its vestures stands;
        I am alone with my own self for space.

    My heart is a centre of infinity,
        My body a dot in the soul's vast expanse.
    All being's huge abyss wakes under me,
        Once screened in a gigantic Ignorance.

    A momentless immensity pure and bare,
    I stretch to an eternal everywhere.

The Dual Being

    There are two beings in my single self.
        A Godhead watches Nature from behind
    At play in front with a brilliant surface elf,
        A time-born creature with a human mind.

    Tranquil and boundless like a sea or sky,
        The Godhead knows himself Eternity's son.
    Radiant his mind and vast, his heart as free;
        His will is a sceptre of dominion.

    The smaller self by Nature's passions driven,
        Thoughtful and erring learns his human task;
    All must be known and to that Greatness given
        His mind and life, the mirror and the mask.

    As with the figure of a symbol dance
    The screened Omniscient plays at Ignorance.

Lila

In us is the thousandfold Spirit who is one,
    An eternal thinker calm and great and wise,
A seer whose eye is an all-regarding sun,
    A poet of the cosmic mysteries.

A critic Witness pieces everything
    And binds the fragments in his brilliant sheaf;
A World-adventurer borne on Destiny's wing
    Gambles with death and triumph, joy and grief.

A king of greatness and a slave of love,
    Host of the stars and guest in Nature's inn,
A high spectator spirit throned above,
    A pawn of passion in the game divine,

One who has made in sport the suns and seas
Mirrors in our being his immense caprice.

Surrender

O Thou of whom I am the instrument,
    O secret Spirit and Nature housed in me,
Let all my mortal being now be blent
    In Thy still glory of divinity.

I have given my mind to be dug Thy channel mind,
    I have offered up my will to be Thy will:
Let nothing of myself be left behind
    In our union mystic and unutterable.

My heart shall throb with the world-beats of Thy love,
    My body become Thy engine for earth-use;
In my nerves and veins Thy rapture's streams shall move;
    My thoughts shall be hounds of Light for Thy power to loose.

Keep[1] only my soul to adore eternally
And meet Thee in each form and soul of Thee.

    [1] Leave

The Divine Worker

I face earth's happenings with an equal soul;
    In all are heard Thy steps: Thy unseen feet
Tread Destiny's pathways in my front. Life's whole
    Tremendous theorem is Thou complete.

No danger can perturb my spirit's calm:
    My acts are Thine; I do Thy works and pass;
Failure is cradled on Thy deathless arm,
    Victory is Thy passage mirrored in Fortune's glass.

In this rude combat with the fate of man
    Thy smile within my heart makes all my strength;
Thy Force in me labours at its grandiose plan,
    Indifferent to the Time-snake's crawling length.

No power can slay my soul; it lives in Thee.
Thy presence is my immortality.

The Guest

I have discovered my deep deathless being:
    Masked by my front of mind, immense, serene,
It meets the world with an Immortal's seeing,
    A god-spectator of the human scene.

No pain and sorrow of the heart and flesh
    Can tread that pure and voiceless sanctuary.
Danger and fear, Fate's hounds, slipping their leash
    Rend body and nerve, – the timeless Spirit is free.

Awake, God's ray and witness in my breast,
    In the undying substance of my soul,
Flamelike, inscrutable the almighty Guest.
    Death nearer comes and Destiny takes her toll;

He hears the blows that shatter Nature's house:
Calm sits he, formidable, luminous.

The Inner Sovereign

Now more and more the Epiphany within
    Affirms on Nature's soil His sovereign rights.
My mind has left its prison-camp of brain;
    It pours, a luminous sea from spirit heights.

A tranquil splendour, waits my Force of Life,
    Couched in my heart, to do what He shall bid,
Poising wide wings like a great hippogriff
    On which the gods of the empyrean ride.

My senses change into gold gates of bliss;
    An ecstasy thrills through touch and sound and sight
Flooding the blind material sheath's dull ease:
    My darkness answers to His call of light.

Nature in me one day like Him shall sit,
Victorious, calm, immortal, infinite.

Creation

Since Thou hadst all eternity to amuse,
    O sculptor of the living shapes of earth,
    O dramatist of death and life and birth,
World-artist revelling in forms and hues,

Hast Thou shaped[1] the marvel of the whirling spheres,
    A scientist passing Nature through his tubes
    And played with numbers, measures, theorems, cubes,
O mathematician Mind that never errs,

Building a universe from Thy theories?
    Protean is Thy spirit of delight,
    Craftsman minute and architect of might,
World-adept of a thousand mysteries.

Or forged[2] some deep Necessity, not Thy whim,
Fate and Inconscience and the net of Time?

[1] made   [2] built

A Dream of Surreal Science

    One dreamed and saw a gland write Hamlet, drink
        At the Mermaid, capture immortality;
    A committee of hormones on the Aegean's brink
        Composed the Iliad and the Odyssey.

    A thyroid, meditating almost nude
        Under the Bo-tree, saw the eternal Light
    And, rising from its mighty solitude,
        Spoke of the Wheel and eightfold Path all right.

    A brain by a disordered stomach driven
        Thundered through Europe, conquered, ruled and fell,
    From St. Helena went, perhaps, to Heaven.
        Thus wagged on the surreal world, until

    A scientist played with atoms and blew out
    The universe before God had time to shout.

In the Battle

    Often, in the slow ages' wide retreat
        On Life's long bridge through Time's enormous sea,
    I have accepted death and borne defeat
        If by my fall some gain were clutched for Thee.

    To this world's inconscient Power Thou hast given[1] the right
        To oppose the shining passage of my soul:
    She levies on each step the tax of Night.
        Doom, her unjust accountant, keeps the roll.

    Around my way the Titan forces press;
        This earth is theirs, they hold the days in fee,
    I am full of wounds and the fight merciless:
        Is it not yet Thy hour of victory?

    Even as Thou wilt! What still to Fate Thou owest,
    O Ancient of the worlds, Thou knowest, Thou knowest.

    [1] gav'st

The Little Ego

This puppet ego the World-Mother made,
    This little profiteer of Nature's works,
Her trust in his life-tenancy betrayed,
    Makes claim on claim, all debt to her he shirks.

Each movement of our life our ego fills;
    Inwoven in each thread of being's weft,
When most we vaunt our selflessness, it steals
    A sordid part; no corner void is left.

One way lies free, our heart and soul to give,
    Our body and mind to Thee and every cell,
And steeped in Thy world-infinity to live.
    Then lost in light, shall fade the ignoble spell.

Nature, of her rebellion quit, shall be
A breath of the spirit's vast serenity.

The Miracle of Birth

I saw my soul a traveller through Time;
    From life to life the cosmic ways it trod,
Obscure in the depths and on the heights sublime,
    Evolving from the worm into the god.

A spark of the eternal Fire, it came
    To build a house in Matter for the Unborn.
The inconscient sunless Night received the flame,
    In the brute seed of things dumb and forlorn

Life stirred and Thought outlined a gleaming shape
    Till on the stark inanimate earth could move,
Born to somnambulist Nature in her sleep,
    A thinking creature who can hope and love.

Still by slow steps the miracle goes on,
The Immortal's gradual birth mid mire and stone.

The Bliss of Brahman

I am swallowed in a foam-white sea of bliss,
    I am a curving wave of God's delight,
      A shapeless flow of happy passionate light,
A whirlpool of the streams of Paradise.
I am a cup of His felicities,
    A thunderblast of His golden ecstasy's might,
      A fire of joy upon creation's height;
I am His rapture's wonderful abyss.

I am drunken with the glory of the Lord,
    I am vanquished by the beauty of the Unborn;
      I have looked, alive, upon the Eternal's face.
My mind is cloven by His radiant sword,
    My heart by His beatific touch is torn,
      My life is a meteor-dust of His flaming Grace.

Moments

If perfect moments on the peak of things,
    These tops of knowledge, greatness, ecstasy,
      Are only moments, this too enough might be.
I have put on the rapid flaming wings
Of souls whom the Ignorance black-robed Nature brings
    And the frail littleness of mortality
      Can bind not always. A high sovereignty
Makes them awhile creation's radiant kings.

These momentary upliftings of the soul
    Prepare the spirit's glorious permanence.
      The peace of God, a mighty transience,
Is now my spirit's boundless atmosphere.
    All parts are gathered into a timeless whole;
      All moments blaze in an eternal year.

The Body

This body which was once my universe,
  Is now a pittance carried by the soul, –
Its Titan's motion bears this scanty purse,
  Pacing through vastness to a vaster goal.

Too small was it to meet the giant need
  That only infinitude can satisfy:
He keeps it still, for in the folds is hid
  His secret passport to eternity.

In his front an endless Time and Space deploy
  The landscape of their golden happenings;
His heart is filled with sweet and violent joy,
  His mind is upon great and distant things.

How grown with all the world conterminous
Is the little dweller in this narrow house!

Liberation

My mind, my soul grow larger than all Space;
  Time founders in that vastness glad and nude:
The body fades, an outline, a dim trace,
  A memory in the spirit's solitude.

This universe is a vanishing circumstance
  In the glory of a white infinity
Beautiful and bare for the Immortal's dance,
  House-room of my immense felicity.

In the thrilled happy giant void within
  Thought lost in light and passion drowned in bliss,
Changing into a stillness hyaline,
  Obey the edict of the Eternal's peace.

Life's now the Ineffable's dominion;
Nature is ended and the spirit alone.

Light

Light, endless Light! darkness has room no more,
    Life's ignorant gulfs give up their secrecy:
The huge inconscient depths unplumbed before
    Lie glimmering in vast expectancy.

Light, timeless Light immutable and apart!
    The holy sealed mysterious doors unclose.
Light, burning Light from the Infinite's diamond heart
    Quivers in my heart where blooms the deathless rose.

Light in its rapture leaping through the nerves!
    Light, brooding Light! each smitten passionate cell
In a mute blaze of ecstasy preserves
    A living sense of the Imperishable.

I move in an ocean of stupendous Light
Joining my depths to His eternal height.

The Unseen Infinite

Arisen to voiceless unattainable peaks
    I meet no end, for all is boundless He,
An absolute joy the wide-winged spirit seeks,
    A Might, a Presence, an Eternity.

In the inconscient dreadful dumb Abyss
    Are heard the heart-beats of the Infinite.
The insensible midnight veils His trance of bliss,
    A fathomless sealed astonishment of Light.

In His ray that dazzles our vision everywhere,
    Our half-closed eyes seek fragments of the One:
Only the eyes of Immortality dare
    To look unblinded on that living Sun.

Yet are our souls the Immortal's selves within,
Comrades and powers and children of the Unseen.

"I"

This strutting "I" of human self and pride
    Is a puppet built by Nature for her use,
And dances as her strong compulsions bid,
    Forcefully feeble, brilliantly obtuse.

Our thinking is her leap of fluttering mind,
    We hear and see by her constructed sense:
Our force is hers; her colours have combined
    Our fly-upon-the-wheel magnificence.

He sits within who turns on her machine
    These beings, portions of his mystery,
Many dwarf beams of his great calm sunshine,
    A reflex of his sole infinity.

One mighty Self of cosmic act and thought
Employs this figure of a unit nought.

The Cosmic Spirit

I am a single Self all Nature fills.
    Immeasurable, unmoved the Witness sits:
He is the silence brooding on her hills,
    The circling motion of her cosmic mights.

I have broken the limits of embodied mind
    And am no more the figure of a soul.
The burning galaxies are in me outlined;
    The universe is my stupendous whole.

My life is the life of village and continent,
    I am earth's agony and her throbs of bliss;
I share all creatures' sorrow and content
    And feel the passage of every stab and kiss.

Impassive, I bear each act and thought and mood;
Time traverses my hushed infinitude.

Self

He said, "I am egoless, spiritual, free,"
Then swore because his dinner was not ready.
I asked him why. He said, "It is not me,
But the belly's hungry god who gets unsteady."

I asked him why. He said, "It is his play.
I am unmoved within, desireless, pure.
I care not what may happen day by day."
I questioned him, "Are you so very sure?"

He answered, "I can understand your doubt.
But to be free is all. It does not matter
How you may kick and howl and rage and shout,
Making a row over your daily platter.

"To be aware of self is liberty.
Self I have got and, having self, am free."

Omnipresence

He is in me, round me, facing everywhere.
    Self-walled in ego to exclude His right,
I stand upon its boundaries and stare
    Into the frontiers of the Infinite.

Each finite thing I see is a façade;
    From its windows looks at me the Illimitable.
In vain was my prison of separate body made;
    His occult presence burns in every cell.

He has become my substance and my breath;
    He is my anguish and my ecstasy.
My birth is His eternity's sign, my death
    A passage of His immortality.

My dumb abysses are His screened abode;
In my heart's chamber lives the unworshipped God.

The Inconscient Foundation

My soul regards[1] its veiled subconscient base;
    All the dead obstinate symbols of the past,
The hereditary moulds, the stamps of race
    Are upheld[2] to sight, the old imprints effaced.

In a downpour of supernal light it reads
    The black Inconscient's enigmatic script –
Recorded in a hundred shadowy screeds
    An inert world's obscure enormous drift;

All flames, is torn and burned and cast away.
    Here slept the tables of the Ignorance,
There the dumb dragon edicts of her sway,
    The scriptures of Necessity and Chance.

Pure is the huge foundation now[3] and nude,
A boundless mirror of God's infinitude.

Adwaita

I walked on the high-wayed Seat of Solomon
    Where Shankaracharya's tiny temple stands
Facing Infinity from Time's edge, alone
    On the bare ridge ending earth's vain romance.

Around me was a formless solitude:
    All had become one strange Unnamable,
An unborn sole Reality world-nude,
    Topless and fathomless, for ever still.

A Silence that was Being's only word,
    The unknown beginning and the voiceless end
Abolishing all things moment-seen or heard,
    On an incommunicable summit reigned,

A lonely Calm and void unchanging Peace
On the dumb crest of Nature's mysteries.

[1] My mind beholds   [2] held up   [3] left

The Hill-top Temple

After unnumbered steps of a hill-stair
    I saw upon earth's head brilliant with sun
    The immobile Goddess in her house of stone
In a loneliness of meditating air.
Wise were the human hands that set her there
    Above the world and Time's dominion;
    The Soul of all that lives, calm, pure, alone,
Revealed its boundless self mystic and bare.

Our body is an epitome of some Vast
    That masks its presence by our humanness.
        In us the secret Spirit can indite
A page and summary of the Infinite,
    A nodus of Eternity expressed
        Live in an image and a sculptured face.

The Divine Hearing

All sounds, all voices have become Thy voice,
    Music and thunder and the cry of birds,
Life babbling of her sorrows and her joys,
    Cadence of human speech and murmured words,

The laughter of the sea's enormous mirth,
    The winged plane purring through the silent air,
The auto's trumpet-song of speed to earth,
    The machine's reluctant drone, the siren's blare

Blowing upon the windy horn of Space
    A call of distance and of mystery,
Memories of sunlit lands and ocean ways,
    All now are wonder-tones and themes of Thee.

A secret harmony smites through the blind heart
And all grows beautiful because Thou art.

Because Thou art

Because Thou art All-beauty and All-bliss,
    My soul blind and enamoured yearns for Thee;
It bears Thy mystic touch in all that is
    And thrills with the burden of that ecstasy.

Behind all eyes I meet Thy secret gaze
    And in each voice I hear Thy magic tune:
Thy sweetness hunts my heart through Nature's ways;
    Nowhere it beats now from Thy snare immune.

It loves Thy body in all living things;
    Thy joy is there in every leaf and stone:
The moments bring Thee on their fiery wings;
    Sight's endless artistry is Thou alone.

Time voyages with Thee upon its prow –
And all the future's passionate hope is Thou.

Divine Sight

Each sight is now immortal with Thy bliss:
    My soul through the rapt eyes has come to see;
A veil is rent and they no more can miss
    The miracle of Thy world-epiphany.

Into an ecstasy of vision caught
    Each natural object is of Thee a part,
A rapture-symbol from Thy substance wrought,
    A poem shaped in Beauty's living heart,

A master-work of colour and design,
    A mighty sweetness borne on grandeur's wings;
A burdened wonder of significant line
    Reveals itself in even commonest things.

All forms are Thy dream-dialect of delight,
O Absolute, O vivid Infinite.

Divine Sense

Surely I take no more an earthly food
    But eat the fruits and plants of Paradise!
For Thou hast changed my sense's habitude
    From mortal pleasure to divine surprise.

Hearing and sight are now an ecstasy,
    And all the fragrances of earth disclose
A sweetness matching in intensity
    Odour of the crimson marvel of the rose.

In every contact's deep invading thrill,
    That lasts as if its source were infinite,
I feel Thy touch; Thy bliss imperishable
    Is crowded into that moment of delight.

The body burns with Thy rapture's sacred fire,
Pure, passionate, holy, virgin of desire.

The Iron Dictators

I looked for Thee alone, but met my glance
    The iron dreadful Four who rule our breath,
Masters of falsehood, Kings of ignorance,
    High sovereign Lords of suffering and death.

Whence came these formidable autarchies,
    From what inconscient blind Infinity, –
Cold propagandists of a million lies,
    Dictators of a world of agony?

Or was it Thou who bor'st the fourfold mask?
    Enveloping Thy timeless heart in Time,
Thou hast bound the spirit to its cosmic task,
    To find Thee veiled in this tremendous mime.

Thou, only Thou, canst raise the invincible siege,
O Light, O deathless Joy, O rapturous Peace!

Form

O worshipper of the formless Infinite,
    Reject not form, what dwells in it[1] is He.
    Each finite is that deep Infinity
Enshrining His veiled soul of pure delight.
Form in its heart of silence recondite
    Hides the significance of His mystery,
    Form is the wonder-house of eternity,
A cavern of the deathless Eremite.

There is a beauty in the depths of God,
    There is a miracle of the Marvellous
        That builds the universe for its abode.
Bursting into shape and colour like a rose,
    The One, in His glory multitudinous,
        Compels the great world-petals to unclose.

Immortality

I have drunk deep of God's own liberty
    From which an occult sovereignty derives:
    Hidden in an earthly garment that survives,
I am the worldless being vast and free.
A moment stamped with that supremacy
    Has rescued me from cosmic hooks and gyves;
    Abolishing death and time my nature lives
In the deep heart of immortality.

God's contract signed with Ignorance is torn;
    Time has become the Eternal's endless year,
        My soul's wide self of living infinite Space[2]
Outlines its body luminous and unborn
    Behind the earth-robe; under the earth-mask grows clear
        The mould of an imperishable face.

---

[1] what lives in form
[2] My soul, the living self of infinite Space,

Man the Despot of Contraries

I am greater than the greatness of the seas,
    A swift tornado of God-energy:
A helpless flower that quivers in the breeze,
    I am weaker than the reed one breaks with ease.

I harbour all the wisdom of the wise
    In my nature of stupendous Ignorance;
On a flame of righteousness I fix my eyes
    While I wallow in sweet sin and join hell's dance.

My mind is brilliant like a full-orbed moon,
    Its darkness is the caverned troglodyte's.
I gather long Time's wealth and squander soon;
    I am an epitome of opposites.

I with repeated life death's sleep surprise;
I am a transience of the eternities.

The One Self

All are deceived, do what the One Power dictates,
    Yet each thinks his own will his nature moves;
The hater knows not 'tis himself he hates,
    The lover knows not 'tis himself he loves.

In all is one being many bodies bear;
    Here Krishna flutes upon the forest mood,
Here Shiva sits ash-smeared, with matted hair.
    But Shiva and Krishna are the single God.

In us too Krishna seeks for love and joy,
    In us too Shiva struggles with the world's grief.
One Self in all of us endures annoy,
    Cries in his pain and asks his fate's relief.

My rival's downfall is my own disgrace;
I look on my enemy and see Krishna's face.

The Inner Fields

There is a brighter ether than this blue
    Pretence of an enveloping heavenly vault,
    Royaler investiture than this massed assault[1]
Of emerald rapture pearled with tears of dew.
Immortal spaces of caerulean hue
    Are in our reach and fields without this fault
    Of drab brown earth and streams that never halt
In their deep murmur which white flowers strew

Floating like stars upon a strip of sky.
    This world behind is made of truer stuff
        Than the manufactured tissue of earth's grace.
There we can walk and see the gods go by
    And sip from Hebe's cup nectar enough
        To make for us heavenly limbs and deathless face.

---

[1] A deeper greenness than this laughing assault

III
LONGER POEMS

THE VIGIL OF THALIARD
August 1891 - April 1892

The Vigil of Thaliard

1

Where Time a sleeping dervish is
Or printed legend of Romance
Mid lilies and mid gold-roses
    Of mediaeval France,
Where Life, a princely servitor
    Mid alien faces cast,
Still wears in memory of her
    The trappings of the Past,
Sweet Lily's child, that golden grape
    Girl prince of Avelion,
Thaliard by early plucking hap
    Star-reaching Prince's son,
Kept vigil by the impious pool
Beyond the misty moaning sea
To win from warlock's weird misrule
    His soul's sweet liberty.

2

For if throughout the monstrous night
Unblest by ave or by creed
By witchèd water Christian wight
    Do finger bead by bead
His scarlet rosary of sins
    And leave his soul ajar,
What hour the sleepy Evening pins
    Her bodice with a star,
Until, the pitchy veil withdrawn
    That swathes the looming[1] dune,
The crowing trumpeter of dawn
    Blows addio to the moon,
The awful record of his soul
Shall by God's finger blotted be,
And o'er his drownèd past shall roll
    Forgiveness like a sea.

[1] yellow

3

The warden of the starry waste
Who walks with orange-coloured lamp
And weird eyes nursing fire, paced
    Night's silver-tented camp.
The rose-lipped golden-footed day,
    A flower by maiden culled,
Beneath star-blossomed arras lay
    In Evening's[1] bosom lulled.
The water seemed a damson crust
    With golden sugar poured,
Or mirror caked with purple dust
    In lady's closet stored.
The hour like a weary snake
Coiled slowly gliding serpentine
Or drowsy nun perforce awake
    To pace a pillared shrine.

4

The roses shuddered in their sleep,
The lilies drooped their silver fires,
The reeds upon the humming steep
    Bowed low their tapering spires;
For tho' no sob pulsed in the air,
    No agony of wind,
Down Heaven's moonlight-painted stair
    Trod angels who had sinned.
Fireflies drizzled in the dark
    Like drops of burning rain,
The glow-worm was a crawling spark,
    The pool a purple stain;
The stars were grains of blazing sand,
A haunted soul the shadowy lea,
In forest-featured Broceliande
    Beyond the echoing sea.

[1] twilit

5

Sir Thaliard by the phantom edge
Heard rustling feet behind the trees
And the weird water lapped the sedge
      With wistful symphonies:
Sometimes a thrill of voices broke
      In runic tongues of old,
Sometimes pale fingers seemed to stroke
      His curls of crisping gold:
Thin laughter sobbed he knew not where
      Till God's own candles paled,
Or else out in the moonless air
      A golden infant wailed.
Now in the moon's enchanted wake
Wild shadows ran a giant race,
And now the golden glassing lake
      Was blotted with a face.

6

But when the naked moon rose clear
Above the ruins of the day,
Childe Thaliard saw a glinting spear
      Across the milky way.
And when the white moon's sliding feet
      One rank of stars had passed,
Upon him smote the windy beat
      And terror of a blast.
The tempest rippled thro' the leaves,
      New wine of evening sucked,
And at the water-lily sheaves
      With nervous fingers plucked.
And in its wind-white arms it bore
A helmeted[1] and sceptred thing,
The semblance of a man, that wore
      The glory of a king.

---

[1] diademed

7

An argent cincture studded thick
With opal and the blushing stone
Fine wrought of texture Arabic
    About his middle shone:
And in its buckled girth did sit,
    A fierce and cloudy star,
Of temper fine as poet's wit
    The Orient scimitar.
Morocco gave his wrathful dart,
    The spring of widowed tears,
Tempered in Afric's sultry heart
    Or famous far Algiers.
His barb was hued like cedar's core
In Aramaic[1] mountains born,
Wild as the sea on storm-vexed shore
    And fronted as the morn.

8

Upon his kingly head the crown
Was eloquent of Iran's gold
Dropping fine threads of glory down
    Upon the turban's fold.
His eyes were drops of smelted ore
    That in a foundry chase:
His lips a cruel promise wore,
    A marble pride his face.
As shows thro' gold caparison
    Laburnum dusky-stemmed,
Thro' silks in Persian harem spun
    His gorgeous body gleamed.
Or as a lithe and tropic snake
That from some fine mosaic glares
Or spotted panther by a lake
    Beneath the Indian stars.

[1] Aramean

9

This Orient vision burning bright
Snapped close his bridle silver-lined
Between the moonlight and the night,
    The water and the wind.
His cry sang like a stormy shower
    Upon a thundering sea:
"O Thaliard, Thaliard, Britain's flower,
    Wilt break a lance with me?
The golden scythe of Mahomet
    Gleams crescent on my shield,
My harvest upon thine is set,
    A cross in argent field.
Prince-errant, prop of battle styled
And flawless glass of chivalry,
O Thaliard, Thaliard, golden childe,
    Wilt break a lance with me?"

10

As trailing thunder dies in heaven
Thro' silence trailed his latest word,
And fire like the bearded levin
    Beneath his eyelids stirred.
Childe Thaliard saw the burning stars
    Vermilion grown like blood,
Thrice drew the serpent cross of Mars,
    Thrice clamoured where he stood.
But Thaliard saw a milk-white star
    Grow large against the moon,
Quelled by whose candid flames, afar
    Mars' ruby paled in a swoon.
"Not here," he faltered like the wind,
"Not here where murmurs poison sleep,
When haunted memories grown half blind
    Their ghastly vigils keep."

11

"Not here, when drifts past happy shores
From mortal vision far withdrawn
With lustrous sails and dripping oars
    The hull that brings the dawn.
Seek me, but in the cloudy time
    When ruin blazons forth
In sanguine hues the vaporous clime
    And champaigns of the North."
As wine that from the bubbling lips
    Of some fine beaker falls,
This honeyed utterance largely slips
    Like murmurs in vast halls.
The wimpled moon bent down her ear,
And in the granaries of light
The seedling splendours thrilled to hear,
    And all the east grew bright.

12

The phantom like a burning page
Was furrowed with the ploughs of wrath,
And thro' his wintry orbs white rage
    Rolled like the dead sea-froth.
His lance poised slanting like a ray
    Of ominous sunlight fell,
Astarte in the milky way
    Saw death half-risen from hell:
And soon the cold hooves of his horse
    On shivering lilies trod,
Till, yellow anguish borrowing force,
    Childe Thaliard cried on God.
The phantom, withering thro' the bars
Of Being like transitory sound,
Left but the murmur of the stars,
    Left but the hush profound.

13

And now the naked wanton moon
Shed languorous glances on the lake
Whose ripples sobbing from their swoon
    Grew golden for her sake:
The amorous stars were faint with love;
    Earth's awning seemed so light
That Hesper like a flying dove
    Would tremble into sight.
When Thaliard saw in drooping skies
    Large drops of beauty burn,
A white-winged chorus did arise,
    The prayers that purely yearn.
But Thaliard saw the curling deep
With foamy moon-tints blaze and break,
Till the slack spirit longed to steep
    Rich fancies in the lake.

14

The penitent chorus of his prayers
Were mingled with voluptuous speech
Of daedal images and airs
    Luxurious wrapping each:
A blue papyrus-leaf designed
    With fretted curls of fire,
A purple page with coronet lined
    Or labyrinthine spire:
The fiery-coloured bee of night
    With folded purple wing,
Or solitary chrysolite
    Shut in an emerald ring:
The vellum binding of a book,
A scented volume spiced with Ind,
A magic purse by Genie shook
    To loose a murmuring wind.

15

But hark! a wailing anguish woke
The silence with a fiery sting:
The foaming gulfs of clamour broke
    Around a fallen king:
A distant moan of battle high
    Above a phantom land,
And heron-weird a woman's cry
    Went shrilling down the strand.
While terror with a vulture's force
    Was plucking at his throat,
He heard the shrill hooves of a horse
    Prick echoes less remote.
And like old accents Night may lend
On lips long hushed in endless sleep,
The voice of a familiar friend
    Came shuddering from the deep.

16

"Thaliard, awake; the smiling morn
Forgets the cloud of yesterday:
The sceptre from thy house is torn,
    Thy glory washed away.
Amid the reeling battle trod,
    As a poppy in the mill,
With white face lifted up to God,
    Thy sire lies very still.
Pendragon's spear has stung him dead,
    He sleeps among the slain;
The glorious princes heap his bed,
    Like lilies in a plain.
Thy brothers Galert and Gyneth
Like toppling mountains whelmed I saw
Beneath the shadowy winds of death
    In the rushing tide of war.

17

"Thy sister, fawn-eyed Guendolen,
Haled captive from thy tottering hall,
Lies helpless in the dragon's den
    Luxurious Gawain's thrall.
His kisses tremble on her mouth
    Like moonbeams on a rose,
For she is water to his drouth,
    He sunlight to her snows:
Her flowering body to his love
    A pleasance-garden sweet;
Her spirit, meeker than a dove,
    Fawns blindly at his feet.
And with the pelting words of shame,
Like delicate pigments bleared by storm,
The gorgeous colouring of thy name
    Is losing gloss and form.

18

"The night-wind in thy yawning dome
Has made her nest alive with song,
The humming wasps of Aeolus roam,
    Low-flying in a throng:
The thunder like a flying stork
    Clangs hoarsely but aloof,
And lightning with his vermil fork
    Has written on thy roof.
The lion lodges in thy gate,
    The werewolf is thy guest,
The night-owl, like a sombre fate,
    Wails weirdly without rest.
Thy deeds are grown a haunting rhyme,
A fragment breaking from the past,
An atom, which the meteor, Time,
    In his fiery flight has cast."

19

With sobs of shuddering agony bled
The silence as with stinging whips,
But Thaliard felt slim fingers laid
      Upon his writhen lips.
The soul's redoubts flung each to each
      A ringing challenge round,
To clench the ruby gates of speech
      On the corridors of sound.
In dancing dithyrambs thro' each vein
      A dizzy echo sang,
While on the anvil of his brain
      The steely syllables rang:
And from the avenues of the heart
Thro' which the river of being pours,
The torpid life with a sudden start
      Recoiled upon its doors.

20

The voice was now a violin
Shrill-winding, now a startled bat,
And now as linnet's warble thin,
      Now wailful as a gnat,
But gathered volume as of yore
      Until with refluent tide,
Like Ocean ebbing from her shore,
      The murmur ebbed and died.
Like beauty losing maidenhood
      Astarte debonair
Undid the crocus-coloured snood
      That bound her glimmering hair.
And up the ladder of the moon,
As white smoke curls upon a glass,
He saw with flakes of glory strewn
      A radiant figure pass.

21

Again the stealthy minutes crept
On tiptoe to the breathless hour
And loud suspense her riot kept
    Till budding doom should flower.
The yellow moon, whom Heaven once more
    From silver cowl did shake,
With golden letters scribbled o'er
    The purple-written lake.
But when to Heaven's polished breast
    Her rounded amulet clung
Below in the blue palimpsest
    A slit, a chasm sprung.
A meteor from the purple brink,
A vivid star no eye may lose,
A pictured bowl of nectarous drink,
    An apparition rose.

22

And in the bridal pomp of hell
Walked beauty hand in hand with sin,
And Thought, the glorious infidel,
    A helmèd Paladin;
When shuttering under cloudy bars
    Astarte's radiant eye,
God sowed with multitudinous stars
    His peacock in the sky,
The diamonds perished from the deep,
    The moon-tints from the edge,
The wrinkled water smoothed in sleep
    His locks of ruffled sedge.
Imagination, like a sponge
Wrung very pure of beauty, wept,
As from his pores with a tired plunge
    His flakes of fancy leaped.

23

Astarte from her cloudy chair
Paced with her troop of star-sweet girls;
Unfilleted her glorious hair
    Hung loose in cowslip curls.
And like the flower-song of a bee
    On April's daffodil skirt,
A whisper from the smiling sea
    In her crocus gown did flirt.
The waters quivering to her wiles
    Among the rushes whipped,
As thro' the network of her smiles
    Her visible murmur slipped.
But when they wooed her to repeat
Her primrose-painted pilgrimage,
She dipped the white palms of her feet
    In beds of bubbling sedge.

24

Her body lapped in cloth of gold
A wave disguised in moonlight seemed,
Whose every curve and curious fold
    With opal facets gleamed.
Her nestling mass of rounded curls
    Were soft as velvet cloths
Once fingered by Arabian girls
    Or piled in Syrian booths.
She was an ebon-framèd lyre
    Where wind-waked murmurs dance,
A tinted statue of Desire
    In studios of Romance.
Her glowing cheeks just ripe with youth,
The purple passion of her eyes,
Half seemed a splendid mock at truth,
    A brilliant mesh of lies.

25

Below with balmy sobs that drank
The must of life thro' thirsty lips,
Her painèd bosom heaved and sank
    Like Ocean-cradled ships.
And as bee-blossoms sapphire-looped,
    The humming waves that kiss,
Her creamy forehead almost drooped
    Burthened with too much bliss.
The artist Grace who limned her fair
    With moist and liberal brush
Painted a glory in her hair
    And mixed a gorgeous blush
To tint her cheeks with a flowery bloom,
To touch her lips with scarlet fire, —
An empire's beauty in small room,
    A vision of desire.

26

A fairy witch by painful charms
Had burgeoned this refulgent flower,
Embraced by wild and wanton arms
    In weird and midnight hour.
She on the amber milk of bees
    By magic mother nursed,
In laurel-sheltered libraries
    Cons rudiments accurst,
The most familiar things of hell
    The mightiest names inherits,
And learns what iron syllable
    Compels reluctant spirits.
A perilous thorn on fire with bloom,
A poppied spell, an empress snake,
She rose, the alchemist of doom,
    The Lady of the Lake.

(Incomplete)

URVASIE

Urvasie

CANTO I

Pururavus from Titan conflict ceased
Turned worldwards, through illimitable space
Had travelled like a star 'twixt earth and heaven
Slowly and brightly. Late our mortal air
He breathed; for downward now the hooves divine
Trampling out fire with sound before them went,
And the great earth rushed up towards him, green.
With the first line of dawn he touched the peaks,
Nor paused upon those savage heights, but reached
Inferior summits subject to the rain,
And rested. Looking northwards thence he saw
The giant snows upclimbing to the sky,
And felt the mighty silence. In his ear
The noise of a retreating battle was,
Wide crash of wheels and hard impetuous blare
Of trumpets and the sullen march of hosts.
Therefore with joy he drank into his soul
The virgin silence inaccessible
Of mountains and divined his mother's breasts.
But as he listened to the hush, a thought
Came to him from the spring and he turned round
And gazed into the quiet maiden East,
Watching that birth of day, as if a line
Of some great poem out of dimness grew,
Slowly unfolding into perfect speech.
The grey lucidity and pearliness
Bloomed more and more, and over earth chaste again
The freshness of the primal dawn returned,
Life coming with a virginal sharp strength,
Renewed as from the streams of Paradise.
Nearer it drew now to him and he saw
Out of the widening glory move a face
Of dawn, a body fresh from mystery,
Enveloped with a prophecy of light
More rich than perfect splendours. It was she,
The golden virgin, Usha, mother of life,

Yet virgin. In a silence sweet she came,
Unveiled, soft-smiling, like a bride, rose-cheeked,
Her bosom full of flowers, the morning wind
Stirring her hair and all about her gold.
Nor sole she came. Behind her faces laughed
Delicious, girls of heaven whose beauties ease
The labour of the battle-weary Gods;
They in the golden dawn of things sprang gold,
From youth of the immortal Ocean born,
They youthful and immortal, and the waves
Were in their feet and in their voices fresh
As foam, and Ocean in their souls was love.
Laughing they ran among the clouds, their hair
And raiment all a tempest in the breeze.
The sky grew glorious with them and their feet
A restless loveliness and glad eyes full
Of morning and divine faces bent back
For the imperious kisses of the wind.
So danced they numberless as dew-drops gleam,
Menaca, Misracayshie, Mullica,
Rumbha, Nelabha, Shela, Nolinie,
Lolita, Lavonya and Tilottama, —
Many delightful names; among them she.
And seeing her Pururavus the king
Shuddered as of felicity afraid,
And all the wide heart of Pururavus
Moved like the sea — when with a coming wind
Great Ocean lifts in far expectancy
Waiting to feel the shock, so was he moved
By expectation of her face. For this
Was secret in its own divinity
Like a high sun of splendour, or half seen
All troubled with her hair. Yet Paradise
Breathed from her limbs and tresses wonderful,
With odours and with dreams. Then for a space
Voiceless the great king stood and, troubled, watched
That lovely advent, laughter and delight
Gaining upon the world. At last he sighed
And the vague passion broke from him in speech
Heard by the solitude. "O thou strong god,

Who art thou graspest me with hands of fire,
Making my soul all colour? Surely I thought
The hills would move and the eternal stars
Deviate from their rounds immutable,
Never Pururavus; yet lo! I fall.
My soul whirls alien and I hear amazed
The galloping of uncontrollable steeds.
Men said of me: 'The King Pururavus
Grows more than man; he lifts to azure heaven
In vast equality his spirit sublime',
Why sink I now towards attractive earth?
And thou, who art thou, mystery! golden wonder!
Moving enchantress! Wast thou not a part
Of soft auspicious evenings I have loved?
Have I not seen thy beauty on the clouds?
In moonlight and in starlight and in fire?
Some flower whose brightness was a trouble? a face
Whose memory like a picture lived with me?
A thought I had, but lost? O was thy voice
A vernal repetition in some grove,
Telling of lilies clustered o'er with bees
And quiet waters open to the moon?
Surely in some past life I loved thy name,
And syllable by syllable now strive
Its sweetness to recall. It seems the grace
Of visible things, of hushed and lonely snows
And burning great inexorable noons,
And towns and valleys and the mountain winds.
All beauty of earthliness is in thee, all
Luxurious experience of the soul.
O comest thou because I left thy charm
Aiming at purity, oh comest thou,
Goddess, to avenge thyself with beauty? Come!
Unveil thyself from light! limit thyself,
O infinite grace, that I may find, may clasp.
For surely in my heart I know thou bearest
A name that naturally weds with mine,
And I perceive our union magically
Inevitable as a perfect verse
Of Veda. Set thy feet upon my heart,

O Goddess! woman, to my bosom move!
I am Pururavus, O Urvasie."
As when a man to the grey face of dawn
Awaking from an unremembered dream,
Repines at life awhile and buffets back
The wave of old familiar thoughts, and hating
His usual happiness and usual cares
Strives to recall a dream's felicity; —
Long strives in vain and rolls his painful thought
Through many alien ways, when sudden comes
A flash, another, and the vision burns
Like lightning in the brain, so leaped that name
Into the musing of the troubled king.
Joyous he cried aloud and lashed his steeds:
They, rearing, leaped from Himalaya high
And trampled with their hooves the southern wind.
But now a cry broke from the lovely crowd
Of fear and tremulous astonishment;
And they huddled together like doves dismayed
Who see the inevitable talons near
And rush of cruel wings. 'Twas not from him,
For him they saw not yet, but from the north
A fear was on them, and Pururavus
Heard a low roar as of a distant cloud.
He turned half-wrathful. In the far north-west
Heaven stood thick, concentrated in gloom,
Darkness in darkness hidden; for the cloud
Rose firmament on sullen firmament,
As if all brightness to entomb. Across
Great thundrous whispers rolled, and lightning quivered
From edge to edge, a savage pallor. Down
The south wind dropped appalled. Then for a while
Stood pregnant with the thunderbolt and wearing
Rain like a colour, the monumental cloud
Sublime and voiceless. Long the heart was stilled
And the ear waited listening. Suddenly
From motionless battalions as outride
A speed disperse of horsemen, from that mass
Of livid menace went a frail light cloud
Rushing through heaven, and behind it streamed

The downpour all in wet and greenish lines.
Swift rushed the splendid anarchy admired,
And reached, and broke, and with a roar of rain
And tumult on the wings of wind and clasp
Of the o'erwhelmed horizons and with bursts
Of thunder breaking all the body with sound
And lightning 'twixt the eyes intolerable,
Like heaven's vast eagle all that blackness swept
Down over the inferior snowless heights
And swallowed up the dawn. Pururavus,
Lost in the streaming tumult, stood amazed:
But as he watched, he was aware of locks
Flying and a wild face and terrible
And fierce familiar eyes. Again he looked
And knew him in a hundred battles crossed,
The giant Cayshie. It seemed but yesterday
That over the waves of fight their angry eyes
Had met. He in the dim disguise of rain,
All swift with storm, came passionate and huge,
Filling the regions with himself. Immense
He stooped upon the brides of heaven. They
Like flowers in a gust scattered and blown
Fled every way; but he upon that beauty
Magical sprang and seized and lifted up,
As the storm lifts a lily, and arrow-like
Up towards the snow-bound heights in rising cloud
Rushed with the goddess to the trembling East.
But with more formidable speed and fast
Storming through heaven King Pururavus
Hurled after him. The giant turned and knew
The sound of those victorious wheels and light
In a man's face more dangerous to evil
Than all the shining Gods. He stood, he raised
One dreadful arm that stretched across the heavens,
And shook his baffling lance on high. But vast,
But magnified by speed came threatening on
With echoing hooves and battle in its wheels
The chariot of the King Pururavus
Bearing a formidable charioteer,
Pururavus. The fiend paused, he rolled his eyes

Full of defiance, passion and despair
Upon the swooning goddess in his arms
And that avenger. Violence and fear
Poised him a moment on a wave of fate
This way to death cadent, that way to shame.
Then groaning in his great tumultuous breast
He dropped upon the snow heaven's ravished flower
And fled, a blackness in the East. New sky
Replenished from the sullen cloud dawned out;
The great pure azure rose in sunlight wide.
Nor King Pururavus pursued but checked
His rushing chariot on the quiet snow
And sprang towards her and knelt down and trembled.
Perfect she lay amid her tresses wide,
Like a mishandled lily luminous,
As she had fallen. From the lucid robe
One shoulder gleamed and golden breast left bare,
Divinely lifting, one gold arm was flung.
A warm rich splendour exquisitely outlined
Against the dazzling whiteness, and her face
Was as a fallen moon among the snows.
And King Pururavus, beholding glowed
Through all his limbs and maddened with a love
He feared and cherished. Overawed and hushed,
Hardly even breathing, long he knelt, a greatness
Made stone with sudden dread and passion. Love
With fiery attempt plucked him all down to her,
But fear forbade his lips the perfect curls.
At length he raised her still unkissed and laid
In his bright chariot, next himself ascended
And resting on one arm with fearful joy
Her drooping head, with the other ruled the car; —
With one arm ruled, but his eyes were for her
Studying her fallen lids and to heart-beats
Guessing the sweetness of the soul concealed.
And soon she moved. Those wonderful wide orbs
Dawned into his, quietly, as if in muse.
A lovely slow surprise crept into them
Afterwards; last, something far lovelier,
Which was herself, and was delight, and love.

As when a child falls asleep unawares
At a closed window on a stormy day,
Looking into the weary rain, and long
Sleeps, and wakes quietly into a life
Of ancient moonlight, first the thoughtfulness
Of that felicitous world to which the soul
Is visitor in sleep, keeps her sublime
Discurtained eyes; human dismay comes next,
Slowly; last, sudden, they brighten and grow wide
With recognition of an altered world,
Delighted: so woke Urvasie to love.

But, hardly now that luminous inner dawn
Bridged joy between their eyes, laughter broke in
And the returning world; for Menaca,
Standing a lily in the snows, laughed back
Those irresistible wheels and spoke like song; —
She tremulous and glad from bygone fear;
But all those flower-like came, increasing light,
Their bosoms quick and panting, bright, like waves
That under sunshine lift remembering storm.
And before all Menaca tremulously
Smiling: "Whither, O King Pururavus,
Bear'st thou thy victory? Wilt thou set her
A golden triumph in thy halls? But she
Is other than thy marble caryatids
And austere doors, purity colourless.
Read not too much thy glory in her eyes.
Will not that hueless inner stream yet serve
Where thou wast wont to know thy perfect deeds?
But give her back, give us our sister back,
And in return take all thyself with thee."
So with flushed cheeks and smiling Menaca.
And great Pururavus set down the nymph
In her bright sister's arms and stood awhile
Stormily calm in vast incertitude,
Quivering. Then divine Tilottama:
"O King, O mortal mightier than the Gods!
For Gods change not their strength, but are of old
And as of old, and man, though less than these,

May yet proceed to greater, self-evolved.
Man, by experience of passion purged,
His myriad faculty perfecting, widens
His nature as it rises till it grows
With God conterminous. For one who tames
His hot tremulousness of soul unblest
And feels around him like an atmosphere
A quiet perfectness of joy and peace,
He, like the sunflower sole of all the year,
Images the divine to which he tends:
So thou, sole among men. And thou today
Hast a high deed perfected, saved from death
The great Gods of the solar world the first,
And saved with them the stars; but her today
Without whom all that world would grow to shade
Or grow to fire, but each way cease to live.
And thou shalt gather strange rewards, O King,
Hurting thyself with good, and lose thy life
To have the life of all the solar world,
Draw infinite gain out of more infinite loss,
And, for the lowest, endless fame. Today
Retire nor pluck the slowly-ripening fates;
Since who anticipates the patient Gods,
Finds his crown ashes and his empire grief.
So choose blind Titans in their violent souls
Unseeing, forfeiting the beautiful world
For momentary splendours." She was silent,
And he replied no word, but gathering
His reins swept from the golden group. His car
Through those mute Himalayan doors of earth
And all that silent life before our life
Solitary and great and merciless,
Went groaning down the wind. He, the sole living,
Over the dead deep-plunging precipices
Passed bright and small in a wide dazzling world
Illimitable, where eye flags and ear
Listening feels inhuman loneliness.
He tended towards Gungotri's solemn peaks
And savage glaciers and the caverns pure
Whence Ganges leaps, our mother, virgin-cold.

But ere he plunged into the human vales
And kindlier grandeurs, King Pururavus
Looked back upon a gust of his great heart,
And saw her. On a separate peak, divine,
In blowing raiment and a glory of hair
She stood and watched him go with serious eyes
And a soft wonder in them and a light.
One hand was in her streaming folds, one shaded
Her eyes as if the vision that she saw
Were brighter even than deathless eyes endure.
Over her shoulder pressed a laughing crowd
Of luminous faces. And Pururavus
Staggered as smitten, and shaking wide his reins
Rushed like a star into the infinite air;
So curving downwards on precipitate wheels,
His spirit all a storm, came with the wind
Far-sounding into Ila's peaceful town.

Canto II

But from the dawn and mountains Urvasie
Went marvelling and glad, not as of old
A careless beam; for an august constraint,
Unfelt before, ruled her extravagant grace
And wayward beauty; and familiar things
Grew strange to her, and to her eyes came mists
Of mortal vision. Love was with her there,
But not of Paradise nor that great guest
Perpetual who makes his golden couch
Between the Opsara's ever-heaving breasts.
For this was rapturous, troubled, self-absorbed,
A gracious human presence which she loved,
And wondered at, and hid deep in her heart.
And whether in the immortal's dance she moved,
A billow, or her fingers like sunbeams
Brightened the harps of heaven, or going out
With the white dawn to bathe in Swerga's streams,
Or in the woods of Eden wandering,
Or happy sitting under peaceful boughs
In a great golden evening, all she did,
Celestial occupations, all she thought
And all she was, though still the same, had changed.
There was a happy trouble in her ways
And movements; her felicitous lashes drooped
With a burden; and all her daily acts
Were as a statue imitating life,
Not single-hearted like the sovran Gods.
Now as the days of heaven went by in quiet
And there was peaceful summer 'mid the Gods,
In Swerga song increased and dances swayed
In multitudinous beauty, jasmine-crowned;
And often in high Indra's hall the spirits
Immortal met to watch the shows divine
Of action and celestial theatre.
For not of earth alone are delicate arts
And noble imitations, but in heaven
Have their rich prototypes. So on that day
Before a divine audience there was staged

The Choice of Luxmie. Urvasie enacted,
The goddess, Ocean's child, and Menaca
Was Varunie, and other girls of heaven
Assembled the august desiring Gods.
Full strangely sweet those delicate mimics were;
Moonbeam faces imitated the strength
And silence of great spirits battle-worn,
And little hands the awful muniments
Of empire grasped and powers that shake the world.
Then with a golden wave of arm sublime
Menaca towards the warlike consistory,
Under half-drooping lashes indicating
Where calm eternal Vishnu like a cloud
Sat discus-armed, said to her sister bright:
"Daughter of Ocean, sister, for whom heaven
Is passionate, thou hast reviewed the powers
Eternal and their dreadful beauty scanned,
And heard their blissful names. Say, unafraid
Before these listening faces, whom thou lovest
Above all Gods and more than earth and more
Than joy of Swerga's streams?" And Urvasie,
Musing with wide unseeing eyes, replied
In a far voice: "The King Pururavus."
Then, as a wind among the leaves, there swept
A gust of laughter through the assembled Gods,
A happy summer sound. But not in mirth
Bharuth, the mighty dramatist of heaven,
Passionate to see his smooth work marred and spell
Broken of scenic fancies finely-touched:
"Since thou hast brought the breath of mortal air
Into the pure solemnities of heaven,
And since thou givest up to other ends
Than the one need for which God made thee form,
Thy being and hast here transferred from earth
Human failure from the divided soul,
Marring my great creation, Urvasie,
I curse thee to possess thy heart's desire.
Exiled from Swerga's streams and golden groves
Thou, by terrestrial Ganges or on sad
Majestic mountains or in troubled towns,

Enjoy thy love, but hope not here to breathe
Felicity in regions built for peace
Of who, erect in their own nature, keep
Living by fated toils the glorious world."
He ceased and there was silence of the Gods.
Then Indra answered, smiling, though ill-pleased:
"Bharuth, not well nor by the fates allowed
To exile without limit from the skies
Who of the skies is part. Her wilt thou banish
From the felicity of grove and stream,
Making our Eden empty of her smiles?
But what felicity in stream or grove
And she not secret there? And hast thou taxed
Her passion, yet in passion would'st deface
The beautiful world because thy work is vain?"
Bharuth replied, the high poet severe:
"Irrevocable is the doom pronounced
Once by my lips. Fates too are born of song.
But if of limit thou speakest and the term
By nature fixed to the divorce of her
From the felicity in which she moves,
Nature that fixed the limit, still effects
Inevitably its fated ends. For Fate,
The dim great presence, is but nature made
Irrevocable in its fruits. Let her
To the pure banks of sacred Ganges wend.
There she may keep her exile, from of old
Intended for perfection of the earth
Through her sweet change. Heaven too shall flash and grow
Fairer with her returning feet though changed, —
Though changed, yet lovelier from beneficence.
For she will come soft with maternal cheeks
And flushed from nuptial arms and human-blest
With touches of the warm delightful earth."
He said and Urvasie from the dumb place
And thoughtful presence of the Gods departed
Into the breezy noon of Swerga. Under
Green well-known boughs laden with nameless fruit
And over blissful swards and perfect flowers
And through the wandering alleys she arrived

To heavenly Ganges where it streams o'er stones;
There from the banks of summer downward stepped,
One little golden hand gathering her dress
Above her naked knees, and, lovely, passed
Through the divine pellucid river on
To Swerga's portals, pausing on the slope
Which goes toward the world. There she looked down
With yearning eyes far into endless space.
Behind her stood the green felicitous peaks
And trembling tops of woods and pulse of blue
With those calm cloudless summits quivering.
All heaven was behind her, but she sent
No look to those eternal seats of joy.
She down the sunbeams gazed where mountains rose
In snow, the bleak and mighty hills of earth,
And virgin forests vast, great infant streams
And cities young in the heroic dawn
Of history and insurgent human art
Titanic on the old stupendous hills.
Towards these she gazed down under eyelids glad.
And to her gazing came Tilottama,
Bright out of heaven, and clasped her quiet hand
And murmured softly, "Sister, let us go."
Then they went down into the waiting world,
The golden women, and through gorges mute
Past Budricayshwur in the silent snow
Came silent to Pururavus Urvasie.

For not in Ilian streets Pururavus
Sojourned, nor in the happy throng of men,
But with the infinite and the lonely hills.
For he grew weary of walls and luminous carved
Imperial pillars bearing up huge weight
Of architectural stone, and the long street,
And thoughtful temple wide, and sharp cymbals
Protecting the august pure place with sound;
The battled tramp of men, sessions of kings,
The lightning from sharp weapons, jubilant crash
Of chariots, and the Veda's mighty chant;
The bright booths of the merchants, the loud looms

And the smith's hammer clanging music out,
And stalwart men driving the patient plow
Indomitable in fierce breath of noon.
Of these he now grew weary and the blaze
Of kingship, its immense and iron toils,
With one hand shielding in the people's ease,
With one hand smiting back the tireless foe,
And difficulty of equal justice cold,
And kind beneficent works harmonious kept
With terrible control; the father's face,
The man's heart, the steeled intellect of power
Insolubly one; and after sleepless nights
Labouring greatly for a great reward,
Frequent failure and vigorous success,
And sweet reward of voices filial grown.
These that were once his life, he loved no more.
They held not his desire nor were alive,
But pale magnificent ghosts out of the past
With sad obsession closing him from warm
Life and the future in far sunlight gold.
For in his heart and in his musing eyes
There was a light on the cold snows, a blush
Upon the virgin quiet of the East
And storm and slowly-lifting lids. Therefore
He left the city Ilian and plains
Whence with a mighty motion eastward flows
Ganges, heroical and young, a swift
Mother of strenuous nations, nor yet reaches
Her musing age in ardent deep Bengal.
He journeyed to the cold north and the hills
Austere, past Budricayshwur ever north,
Till, in the sixth month of his pilgrimage
Uneasy, to a silent place he came
Within a heaped enormous region piled
With prone far-drifting hills, huge peaks o'erwhelmed
Under the vast illimitable snows, —
Snow on ravine, and snow on cliff, and snow
Sweeping in strenuous outlines to heaven,
With distant gleaming vales and turbulent rocks,

Giant precipices black-hewn and bold
Daring the universal whiteness; last,
A mystic gorge into some secret world.
He in that region waste and wonderful
Sojourned, and morning-star and evening-star
Shone over him and faded, and immense
Darkness wrapped the hushed mountain solitudes
And moonlight's brilliant muse and the cold stars
And day upon the summits brightening.
But ere day grew the hero nympholept
Climbed the immortal summits towards the dawn
And came with falling evening down and lay
Watching the marvellous sky, but called not sleep
That beat her gentle wings over his eyes,
Nor food he needed who was grown a god.
And in the seventh month of his waiting long
Summit or cliff he climbed no more, but added
To the surrounding hush sat motionless,
Gazing towards the dim unfathomed gorge.
Six days he sat and on the seventh they came
Through the dumb gorge, a breath of heaven, a stir,
Then Eden's girls stepping with moonbeam feet
Over the barren rocks and dazzling snows,
That grew less dazzling, their tresses half unbound
And delicate raiment girdled enchantingly.
Silent the perfect presences of heaven
Came towards him and stood a little away,
Like flowers waiting for a sunbeam. He
Stirred not, but without voice, in vision merged,
Sat, as one sleeping momently expects
The end of a dear dream he sees, and knows
It is a dream, and quietly resigned
Waits for the fragile bliss to break or fade.
Then nearer drew divine Tilottama
And stood before his silence statuesque,
Holding her sister's hand; for she hung back,
Not as an earthly maiden, cheeks suffused,
Lids drooping, but as men from patience called
Before supreme felicity hang back,

A little awed, a little doubtful, fearing
To enter radiant Paradise, so bright
It seems; thus she and quailed before her bliss.
But her sister, extending one bright arm:
"Pururavus, thou hast conquered and I bring
No dream into thy life, but Urvasie."
And at that name the strong Pururavus
Rose swaying to his feet like one struck blind;
Or when a great thought flashes through his brain,
A poet starts up and almost cries aloud
As at a voice, — so he arose and heard.
And slowly said divine Tilottama:
"Yet, son of Ila, one is man and other
The Opsaras of heaven, daughters of the sea,
Unlimited in being, Ocean-like.
They not to one lord yield nor in one face
Limit the universe, but like sweet air,
Water unowned and beautiful common light
In unrestrained surrender remain pure.
In patient paths of Nature upon earth
And over all the toiling stars we fill
With sacred passion large high-venturing spirits
And visit them with bliss; so are they moved
To immense creative anguish, glad if through
Heart-breaking toil once in bare seasons dawn
Our golden breasts between their hands or rush
Our passionate presence on them like a wave.
In heaven bright-limbed with bodily embrace
We clasp the Gods, and clasp the souls of men,
And know with winds and flowers liberty.
But what hast thou with us or winds or flowers?
O thou who wast so white, wilt thou not keep
Thy pure and lonely eminence and move
For ever towards morning like a star?
Or as thy earthly Ganges rolling down
Between the homes and passionate deeds of men,
And bearing many boats and white with oars,
From all that life quite separate, only lives
Towards Ocean, so thou doest human work,

Making a mighty nation, doing high
And necessary deeds, but, all untouched
By action, livest in thy soul apart
And to the immortal zenith climbest pure."
But he, blind as from dazzling dreams, said low:
"One I thought spoke far-off of purity
And whiteness and the human soul in God.
These things were with me once, but now I see
The Spring a golden child and shaken fields.
All beautiful things draw near and come to me.
I dream upon a woman's glorious breasts,
And watch the dew-drop and am glad with birds,
And love the perfect coilings of the snake,
And cry with fire in the burning trees,
And am a wave towards desired shores.
I move to these and move towards her bosom
And mystic eyes where all these are one dream.
And what shall God profit me or his glory,
Who love one small face more than all his worlds?"
He woke with his own voice. His words that first
Dreamed like a languid wave, sudden were foam;
And he beheld her standing and his look
Grew strong; he yearned towards her like a wave,
And she received him in her eyes as earth
Receives the rain. Then bright Tilottama
Cried in a shining glory over them:
"O happy lover and O fortunate loved,
Who make love heavenlier by loss! Ah yet,
The Gods give no irrecoverable gifts,
Nor unconditioned, O Pururavus,
Is highest bliss even to most favoured men.
And thy deep joy must tremble o'er her with soul
On guard, all overshadowed by a fear.
For one year thou shalt know her on the peaks,
In solitary vastnesses of hills
And regions snow-besieged; and for one year
In the green forests populous and free
Life in sunlight and by delightful streams
Thou shalt enjoy her; and for one year where

The busy tramp of men goes ceaseless by,
Subduing her to lovely human cares:
And so long after as one law observed
Save her to thee, O King; for never man
With Opsara may dwell and both be known:
Either a rapture she invisible
Or he a mystic body and mystic soul.
Reveal not then thy being naked to hers,
O virgin Ila's son, nor suffer ever
Light round thy body naked to her eyes,
Lest day dawn not on thy felicity,
Sole among men." She left them, shining up
Into the sunlight, and was lost in noon.
And King Pururavus stood for a space,
Like the entrancèd calm before great winds
And thunder. Then through all his limbs there flashed
Youth and the beauty and the warmth of earth
And joy of her left lonely to his will.
He moved, he came towards her. She, a leaf
Before a gust among the nearing trees,
Cowered. But, all a sea of mighty joy
Rushing and swallowing up the golden sand,
With a great cry and glad Pururavus
Seized her and caught her to his bosom thrilled,
Clinging and shuddering. All her wonderful hair
Loosened and the wind seized and bore it streaming
Over the shoulder of Pururavus
And on his cheek a softness. She, o'erborne,
Panting, with inarticulate murmurs lay,
Like a slim tree half seen through driving hail,
Her naked arms clasping his neck, her cheek
And golden throat averted, and wide trouble
In her large eyes bewildered with their bliss.
Amid her wind-blown hair their faces met.
With her sweet limbs all his, feeling her breasts
Tumultuous up against his beating heart,
He kissed the glorious mouth of heaven's desire.
So clung they as two shipwrecked in a surge.
Then strong Pururavus, with godlike eyes

Mastering hers, cried tremulous: "O beloved,
O miser of thy rich and happy voice,
One word, one word to tell me that thou lovest."
And Urvasie, all broken on his bosom,
Her godhead in his passion lost, moaned out
From her imprisoned breasts, "My lord, my love!"

Canto III

So was a goddess won to mortal arms;
And for twelve months he held her on the peaks,
In solitary vastnesses of hills
And regions snow-besieged. There in dim gorge
And tenebrous ravine and on wide snows
Clothed with deserted space, o'er precipices
With the far eagles wheeling under them,
Or where large glaciers watch, or under cliffs
O'er-murmured by the streaming waterfalls,
And later in the pleasant lower hills,
He of her beauty world-desired took joy:
And all earth's silent sublime spaces passed
Into his blood and grew a part of thought.
Twelve months in the green forests populous,
Life in sunlight and by delightful streams
He increased rapture. The green tremulous groves,
And solitary rivers white with birds,
And watered hollow's gleam, and sunny boughs
Gorgeous with peacocks or illumining
Bright bosom of doves, in forests, musing day
Or the great night with roar of many beasts, —
All these were Eden round the glorious pair.
And in their third flower-haunted spring of love
A child was born from golden Urvasie.
But when the goddess from maternal pangs
Woke to the child's sweet face and strange tumult
Of new delight and felt the little hands
Erring about her breasts, passionate she cried:
"How long shall we in woods, Pururavus,
Waste the glad days of cheerful human life?
What pleasure is in soulless woods and waves?
But I would go into the homes of men,
Hear the great sound of cities, watch the eager
Faces tending to hall and mart, and talk
With the bright girls of earth, and kiss the eyes
Of little children, feel smooth floors of stone
Under my feet and the restraint of walls,
And eat earth's food from vessels made and drink

Earth's water cool from jars, and know all joy
And labour of that blithe and busy world."
She said, and he with a slight happy smile
Consented. So to sacred Ganges they
Came and the virgin's city Ilian.
But when they neared the mighty destined walls,
His virgin-mother from her temple pure
Saw him, and a wild blare of conchs arose.
Rejoicing to the lion-gates they streamed,
The people of Pururavus, a glad
Throng indistinguishable, traders and priests,
Merchants of many gains and craftsmen fine
Oblivious of their daily toils; the carver
Flinging his tool away and hammerless
The giant smith laughing through his vast beard.
And little children ran, all over flowers,
And girls like dawn with a delightful noise
Of anklets, matrons and old men divine,
And half a godhead with great glances came
The large-eyed poets of the Vedic chant;
Before them, all that multitude divided
Honouring them. In gleaming armour came,
And bearing dreadful bows, with sound of swords,
High lords of sacrifice and aged chiefs
War-weary and great heroes with mighty tread.
All these to a high noise of trumpets came.
They with a wide sound going up to heaven
Welcomed their king, and a soft shower of blooms
Fell on him as from warlike fields returned.
Much all they marvelled at his heavenly bride
And worshipped her, half-awed. And young girls came,
Daughters of warriors, to great houses wed,
Sweet faces of delightful laughter, came
And took into their glad embrace and kissed,
Enamoured of her smiling mouth, and praised
Aloud her beauty. With flowers then they bound
Her soft immortal wrists, and through the gates,
Labouring in vain to bend great bows, waving
Far-glancing steel, and up the bridal streets
Captive the girlish phalanx, bright with swords,

After the old heroic fashion led.
They amid trumpets and the vast acclaim
Of a glad people brought the child of Gods
To her terrestrial home; through the strong doors
They lifted, and upon an earthly floor,
Loosening, let from the gleaming limbs slide down
Her heavenly vesture; next they brought and flung
About her sweet insufferable grace
Mortal habiliments, a clinging robe.
Over her hair the wifely veil was drawn.
Thus was the love of all the world confined
To one man's home. And O too fortunate
Mortal, who could with those auguster joys
Mingle our little happy human pains,
Subduing a fair goddess from her skies
To gentle ordinary things, sweet service
And household tasks making her beautiful,
And trivial daily words, and kisses kind,
And all the meaning dear of wife and home!
Human with earth dwelt golden Urvasie,
And bore to King Pururavus a race
Of glorious children, each a shining god.
She loved that great and simple life of old,
Its marble outlines, strong joys and clear air
Around the soul, loved and made roseate.
The sacred city felt a finer life
Within it; burning inspirations breathed
From hallowed poets; and architects to grace
And fancy their immense conceptions toned;
Numberless heroes emulously drove forth
And in strong joyous battle rolling back
The dark barbarian borders, flashed through fields,
Brilliant, and sages in their souls saw God.
And from the city of Pururavus
High influences went; Indus and Ganges
And all the golden intermediate lands
Grew with them and a perfect impulse felt.
Seven years the earth rejoiced in Urvasie.

But in their fortunate heavens the high Gods

Dwelt infelicitous, losing the old
Rapture inexplicable and thrill beneath
Their ancient calm. Therefore not long enduring,
They in colossal council marble, said
To that bright sister whom she had loved best,
"Menaca!" crying "how long shall one man
Divide from heaven its most perfect bliss?
Go down and bring her back, our bright one back,
And we shall love again our luminous halls."
She heard and went, with her ethereal robe
Murmuring about her, to the gates divine,
And looked into the world, and saw the far
Titanic Ilian city like a stone
Sunlit upon the small and distant earth.
Down from heaven's peaks the daughter of the sea
Went flashing and upon a breathless eve
Came to the city of Pururavus,
Air blazing far behind her till she paused.
She over the palace of Pururavus
Stood in shadow. Within the lights yet were;
Still sat the princes and young poets sang
On harps heroical of Urvasie
And strong Pururavus, of Urvasie
The light and lovely spirit golden-limbed,
Son of a virgin strong Pururavus.
"O earth made heaven to Pururavus!
O heaven left earth without sweet Urvasie!
"Rejoice possessing, O Pururavus!
Be glad who art possessed, O Urvasie!
"Behold the parents of the sacrifice!
When they have met, then they together rush
And in their arms the beautiful fire is born.
"Behold the children of the earth and sky!
When they met, then they loved, O then they clasped,
And from their clasp a lovely presence grew.
"A holy virgin's son we hear of thee
Without a father born, Pururavus,
Without a mother lovely Urvasie.
"Hast thou not brought the sacrifice from heaven,
The unquenched, unkindled fire, Pururavus?

Hast thou not brought delightful Urvasie?
"The fires of sacrifice mount ever up:
To their lost heavens they naturally aspire.
Their tops are weighted with a human prayer.
"The soul of love mounts also towards the sky;
Thence came the spark but hardly shall return;
Its wings are weighted with too fierce a fire.
"Rejoice in the warm earth, O lovely pair,
The green strong earth that gave Pururavus.
"Rejoice in the blithe earth, O lovely pair,
The happy earth all flushed with Urvasie.
"As lightning takes the heart with pleasant dread,
So love is of the strong Pururavus.
"As breathes sweet fragrance from the flower oppressed,
So love from thy bruised bosom, Urvasie."
So sang they and the heart rejoiced. Then rose
The princes and went down the long white street,
Each to his home. Soon every sound had faded;
Heaven and a few bright stars possessed the world.
But in a silent place dim with the west
On that last night of the sweet passionate earth,
The goddess with the mortal hero lay.
For over them victorious love still showered
His arrows marble-dinting, not flower-tipped
As our brief fading fires, — naked and large
As heaven the monumental loves of old.
On their rich bed they lay, and the two rams
That once the subtle bright Gundhurvas gave
To Urvasie, were near; they were ever
With her and cherished; hardly even she loved
The tender faces of her children more
Than these choice from flocks heavenly: only these
Remained to her of unforgotten skies.
So lay they under those fierce shafts of love,
And in the arms of strong Pururavus
Once more were those beloved limbs embraced,
Once more, if never once again on earth.
Before he slept, the lord of Urvasie
Clasped her to him and wooed from her tired lips
One kiss, nor in its passion felt farewell.

But the night darkened over the vague town,
And clouds came gradual up, and through the clouds
In thunderless great flashes stealing came
The subtle-souled Gundhurvas from the peaks
Of distant Paradise. Thunder rolled out,
And through the walls, in a fierce rush of light,
Entered the thieves of heaven and stole the rams,
And fled with the same lightning. Shuddering
The exile of the skies awoke and knew
Her loss, and with a lamentable cry
Turned to her lord. "Arise, Pururavus!"
She wept, "they take from me my snow-white joys."
And starting from his sleep Pururavus,
In that waking when memory is far
And nature of a man unquestioned rules,
Heard of oppression and a space forgot
Fate and his weak tenure of mighty bliss,
Restored to the great nature of a king.
Wrathful he leaped up and on one swift stride
Reached to his bow. Before 'twas grasped he shuddered,
His soul all smitten with a rushing fear,
Alarmed he turned towards her. Suddenly wide
The whole room stood in splendour manifest,
All lightning, and heroically vast,
In gesture kingly like a statue stayed,
Rose glorious, all a grace of naked limbs,
The hero beautiful, Pururavus,
In that fierce light. Intenser than by day
He for one brilliant moment clear beheld
All the familiar place, the fretted huge
Images on the columns, the high-reared
Walls massively erect and silent floor,
And on the floor the gracious fallen dress
That never should embrace her perfect form,
Lying a glimmer, and each noble curve
Of the strong couch, and delicately distinct
The golden body and the flower-like face:
Beside her with a lovely smile that other,
One small hand pressing back the shining curls
Blown with her speed over her. Then all faded.

Thunder crashed through the heavens jubilant.
For a long while he stood with beating heart
Half-conscious of its loss, and as if waiting
Another flash, into the dimness gazed
For those loved outlines that were far away.
Then with a quiet smile he went and placed
Where she had lain such a short while ago
Both hands, expecting her sweet breasts, but found
Her place all empty to him. Silently
He lay down whispering to his own heart:
"She has arisen and her shining dress
Put round her and gone into the cool alcove
To fetch sweet water for the heavenly rams,
And she will stay awhile perhaps to look
And muse upon the night, and then come back,
And give them drink, and silently lie down
Beside me. I shall see her when it dawns."
And so he slept. But the grey dawn came in
And raised his lashes. He stretched out his arms
To find her. Then he knew he was alone.

Even so he would not dwell with his despair.
"She is but gone," he said, "for a little gone
Into the infinite silences afar
To see her golden sisters and revisit
The streams she knew and those unearthly skies.
But she will soon come back, — even if her heart
Would let her linger, mine would draw her back; —
Come soon and talk to me of all she left,
And clasp her children, and resume sweet goings
And happy daily tasks and rooms she loved."
So, steadfast, he continued kingly toils
Among a people greatly-destined, giving
In sacred sessions and assemblies calm
Counsels far-seeing, magnanimous decrees
Bronze against Time, and from the judgment seat
Unblamed sentence or reconcilement large.
And perfect trinity of holy fires
He kindled for desirable rain, and went
To concourse of strong men or pleasant crowds,

Or triumphed in great games armipotent.
Yet behind all his moments there was void.
And as when one puts from him desperately
The thought of an inevitable fate,
Blinding himself with present pleasures, often
At a slight sound, a knocking at the door,
A chance word terrible, or even uncalled
His heart grows sick with sudden fear, and ghastly
The face of that dread future through the window
Looks at him; mute he sits then shuddering:
So to Pururavus in session holy,
Or warlike concourse, or alone, speaking,
Or sitting, often a swift dreadful fear
Made his life naked like a lightning flash;
Then his whole being shook and his strong frame,
As with a fever, and his eyes gazed blind;
Soon with great breaths he repossessed his soul.
Long he endured thus, but when shocks of fear
And brilliant passage of remorseless suns
And wakeful nights wrestling with memory
Invisibly had worn his heart, he then
Going as one desperate, void of thought or aim,
Into that silent place dim with the west,
Saw there her dress empty of her, and bed
Forlorn, and the cold floor where she had lain
At noon and made life sweet to him with her voice.
Sometimes as in an upland reservoir
Built by the hands of early Aryan kings,
Its banks in secret fretted long go down,
Suddenly down with resonant collapse,
Then with a formidable sound the flood
Descends, heard over all the echoing hills,
And marble cities are o'erwhelmed; so sank
The courage of the strong Pururavus,
By memory and anguish overcome
And thoughts of bliss intolerable. Tears
Came from him; the unvanquished hero lay
With outstretched arms and wept. Henceforth his life
Was with that room. If he appeared in high
Session, warlike concourse or pleasant crowd,

Men looked on him as on the silent dead.
Nor did he linger, but from little stay
Would silently return and in hushed rooms
Watch with the little relics left of her,
Things he had hardly borne to see before,
Now clasped them often, often kissed, sometimes
Spoke to them as to sweet and living friends,
And often over his sleeping children hung.
Nor did he count the days, nor weep again,
But looked into the dawn with tearless eyes.
And all the people mourned for their great king,
Silently watching him, and many murmured:
"This is not he, the King Pururavus,
Hero august, who his impetuous soul
Ruled like a calm and skilful charioteer,
And was the virgin Ila's son, our king.
Would that the enemy's war-cry now might rush
Against our gates and all the air be sound.
Surely he would arise and lift his bow,
And his swift chariot hurling through the gates
Advance upon them like a sea, and triumph,
And be himself among the rushing wheels."
So they would murmur grieving. But the king
When the bright months brought round a lustier earth,
Felt over his numbed soul some touch of flowers,
And rose a little from his grief, and lifted
His eyes against the stars. Then he said low:
"I was not wont so quickly to despair.
O hast thou left me and art lost in light,
Cruel, between the shining hemispheres?
Yet even there I will pursue my joy.
Though all the great immortals jealously
Encompass round with shields thy golden limbs,
I may clash through them yet, or my strong patience
Will pluck my love down from her distant stars.
Still am I Ila's son, Pururavus,
That passionless pure strength though lost, though fallen
From the armed splendid soul which once I was."
So saying he to the hall of session strode,
Mightily like a king, a marble place

With wide Titanic arches imminent,
And from the brooding pillars seized a shell
And blew upon it. Like a storm the sound
Through Pratisthana's streets was blown. Forth came
From lintel proud and happy threshold low
The people pouring out. Majestic chiefs
And strong war-leaders and old famous men
And mighty poets first; behind them streamed
The Ilian people like driving rain, and filled
With faces the immeasurable hall.
And over them the beautiful great king
Rose bright; anticipations wonderful
Of immortality flashed through his eyes
And round his brow's august circumference.
"My people whom I made, I go from you;
And what shall I say to you, Ilian people,
Who know my glory and know my grief? Now I
Endure no more the desolate wide rooms
And gardens empty of her. I will depart
And find her under imperishable trees
Or secret beside streams. But since I go
And leave my work behind and a young nation
With destiny like an uncertain dawn
Over it — Ayus her son, I give you. He
By beauty and strength incomparable shall rule.
Lo, I have planted earth with deeds and made
The widest heavens my monument, have brought
From Paradise the sempiternal fire
And warred in heaven among the warring Gods.
O People, you have shared my famous actions
Done in a few great years of earthly life,
The battles I fought, edifications vast,
And perfect institutes that I have framed.
High things we have done together, O my people.
But now I go to claim back from the Gods
Her they have taken from me, my dear reward."
He spoke and all the nation listened, dumb.
Then was brought forth the bud of Urvasie,
With Vedic verse intoned and Ganges pure
Was crowned a king, and empire on his curls

Established. But Pururavus went forth,
Through ranks of silent people and gleaming arms,
With the last cloud of sunset up the fields
And darkening meadows. And from Ila's rock,
And from the temple of Ila virginal,
A rushing splendour wonderfully arose
And shone all round the great departing king.
He in that light turned and saw under him
The mighty city, luminous and vast,
Colossally up-piled towards the heavens,
Temple and street and palace, and the sea
Of sorrowing faces and sad grieving eyes;
A moment saw, and disappeared from light
Into forest. Then a loud wail arose
From Pratisthana, as if barbarous hordes
Were in the streets and all its temples huge
Rising towards heaven in disastrous fire,
But he unlistening into darkness went.

Canto IV

Through darkness and immense dim night he went
Mid phantom outlines of approaching trees,
And all the day in green leaves, till he came
To peopled forests and sweet clamorous streams
And marvellous shining meadows where he lived
With Uravasie his love in seasons old.
These like domestic faces waiting were.
He knew each wind-blown tree, each different field;
And could distinguish all the sounding rivers
Each by its own voice and peculiar flow.
Here were the happy shades where they had lain
Inarmed and murmuring, here half-lustrous groves
Still voiceful with a sacred sound at noon,
And these the rivers from her beauty bright.
There straying in field and forest he to each
Familiar spot so full of her would speak,
Pausing by banks and memorable trees.
"O sacred fig-tree, under thee she paused
Musing amid her tresses, and her eyes
Were sweet and grave. And, O delicious shade,
Thou hast experienced brightness from her feet,
O cool and dark green shelterer, perfect place!
And lo! the boughs all ruinous towards earth
With blossoms. Here she lay, her arms thrown back,
Smiling up to me, and the flowers rained
Upon her lips and eyes and bosom bare.
And here a secret opening where she stood
Waiting in narrow twilight; round her all
Was green and secret with a mystic, dewy
Half invitation into emerald worlds.
O river, from thee she moved towards the glade
Breathing and wet and fresh as if a flower
All bare from rain. And thou, great holy glade,
Sawest her face maternal o'er her child."
Then ceasing he would wait and listen, half
Expecting her. But all was silent; only
Perhaps a bird darted bright-winged away,
Or a grey snake slipped through the brilliant leaves.

Thus wandering, thus in every mindful place
Renewing old forgotten scenes that rose,
Gleam after gleam, upon his mind, as stars
Return at night; thus drawing from his heart
Where they lay covered, old sweet incidents
To live before his eyes; thus calling back
Uncertain moods, brief moments of her face,
And transient postures strangely beautiful,
Pleasures, and little happy mists of tears
Heart-freeing, he, materializing dreams,
Upon her very body almost seized.
Always a sense of imperfection slipped
Between him and that passionate success.
Therefore he murmured at last unsatisfied:
"She is not here; though every mystic glade
And sunbright pasture breathe alone of her
And quiver as with her presence, I find not
Her very limbs, her very face; yet dreamed
That here infallibly I should restrain
Her fugitive feet or hold her by the robe.
O once she was the luminous soul of these,
And in her body lived the summer and spring
And seed and blossoming, ripening and fall,
Hiding of Beauty in the wood and glen,
And flashing out into the sunlit fields
All flowers and laughter. All the happy moods
And all the beautiful amorous ways of earth
She was; but they now seem only her dress
Left by her. Therefore, O ye seaward rivers,
O forests, since ye have deceived my hope,
I go from you to dazzling cruel ravines
And find her on inclement mountains pure."

Then northward blown upon a storm of hope
The hero self-discrowned, Pururavus,
Went swiftly up the burning plains and through
The portals of the old Saivaalic hills
To the inferior heights, nor lingered long,
Though pulsing with fierce memories, though thrilled
With shocks of a great passion touching earth;

But plunged o'er difficult gorge and prone ravine
And rivers thundering between dim walls,
Driven by immense desire, until he came
To dreadful silence of the peaks and trod
Regions as vast and lonely as his love.
Then with a confident sublime appeal
He to the listening summits stretched his hands:
"O desolate strong Himalaya, great
Thy peaks alone with heaven and dreadful hush
In which the Soul of all the world is felt
Meditating creation! Thou, O mountain,
My bridal chamber wast. On thee we lay
With summits towards the moon or with near stars
Watching us in some wild inhuman vale,
Thy silence over us like a coverlid
Or a far avalanche for bridal song.
Lo, she is fled into your silences!
I come to you, O mountains, with a heart
Desolate like you, like you snow-swept, and stretch
Towards your solemn summits kindred hands.
Give back to me, O mountains, give her back."
He ceased and Himalaya bent towards him, white.
The mountains seemed to recognize a soul
Immense as they, reaching as they to heaven
And capable of infinite solitude.
Long he, in meditation deep immersed,
Strove to dissolve his soul among the hills
Into the thought of Urvasie. The snow
Stole down from heaven and touched his cheek and hair,
The storm-blast from the peaks leaped down and smote
But woke him not, and the white drops in vain
Froze in his locks or crusted all his garb.
For he lived only with his passionate heart.
But as the months with slow unnoticed tread
Passed o'er the hills nor brought sweet change of spring
Nor autumn wet with dew, a voice at last
Moved from far heavens, other than our sky.
And he arose as one impelled and came
Past the supreme great ridges northward, came
Into the wonderful land far up the world

Dim-looming, where the Northern Kurus dwell,
The ancients of the world, invisible,
Among forgotten mists. Through mists he moved
Feeling a sense of unseen cities, hearing
No sound, nor seeing face, but conscious ever
Of an immense traditional life
Throbbing round him and dreams historical.
For as he went, old kingly memories surged,
And with vast forward faces driving came
Origins and stabilities and empires,
Huge passionate creations, impulses
National realizing themselves in stone.
Lastly with rolling of the mists afar
He saw beneath him the primeval rocks
Plunge down into the valley, and upsoar
To light wide thoughtful domes and measureless
Ramparts, and mid them in a glory walk
The ancients of the world with eyes august.
Next towards the sun he looked and saw enthroned
Upon the summit one whose regal hair
Crowned her, and purple in waves down to her feet
Flowed, Indira, the goddess, Ocean's child,
Giver of empire who all beauty keeps
Between her hands, all glory, all wealth, all power.
Severe and beautiful she leaned her face.
"What passion, Ilian Pururavus,
Has led thee here to my great capital
And ancient men in the forgotten mists,
The fathers of the Aryan race? Of glory
Enamoured hast thou come, or for thy people
Empire soliciting? But other beauty
Is on thy brow and light no longer mine.
Yet not for self wast thou of virgin born,
Perfect, and the aerial paths of gods
Permitted to thy steps; nor for themselves,
But to the voice of Vedic litanies,
Sacredly placed are the dread crowns of Kings
For bright felicities and cruel toils.
And thou, O Ilian Pururavus,
For passion dost thou leave thy strenuous grandeurs,

A nation's destinies, and hast not feared
The sad inferior Ganges lapsing down
With mournful rumour through the shades of Hell?"
Then with calm eyes the hero Ilian:
"O Goddess, patroness of Aryasthan,
Lover of banyan and of lotus, I
Not from the fear of Hell or hope of Heaven
Do good or ill. Reigning I reigned o'er self,
And with a kingly soul did kingly deeds.
Now driven by a termless wide desire
I wander over snow and countries vague."
And like a viol Luxmie answered him:
"Sprung of the moon, thy grandsire's fault in thee
Yet lives; but since thy love is singly great,
Doubtless thou shalt possess thy whole desire.
Yet hast thou maimed the future and discrowned
The Aryan people; for though Ila's sons,
In Hustina, the city of elephants,
And Indraprustha, future towns, shall rule
Drawing my peoples to one sceptre, at last
Their power by excess of beauty falls, —
Thy sin, Pururavus — of beauty and love:
And this the land divine to impure grasp
Yields of barbarians from the outer shores."
She ceased and the oblivious mists rolled down.
But the strong hero uncrowned, Pururavus,
Eastward, all dreaming with his great desire,
Wandered as when a man in sleep arises,
And goes into the night, and under stars
Through the black spaces moves, nor knows his feet
Nor where they guide him, but dread unseen power
Walks by him and leads his unerring steps
To some weird forest or gaunt mountain-side;
There he awakes, a horror in his soul,
And shudders alien amid places strange.
So wandered, driven by an unknown power,
Pururavus. Over hushed dreadful hills
And snows more breathless to the quiet banks
Of a wide lake mid rocks and bending woods
He came, and saw calm mountains over it,

And knew in his awed heart the hill of God,
Coilas, and Mainaac with its summits gold.
Awed he in heart, yet with a quicker stride
He moved and eyes of silent joy, like one
Who coming from long travel, sees the old
Village and children's faces at the doors.
In a wild faery place where mountain streams
Glimmer from the dim rocks and meet the lake
Amid a wrestle of tangled trees and heaped
Moss-grown disordered stones, and all the water
Is hidden with its lotuses and sways
Shimmering between leaves or strains through bloom,
She sat, the mother of the Aryans, white
With a sublime pallor beneath her hair.
Musing, with wide creative brows, she sat
In a slight lovely dress fastened with flowers,
All heaped with her large tresses. Golden swans
Preened in the waters by her dipping feet.
One hand propped her fair marble cheek, the other
The mystic lotus hardly held. Seeing her
Pururavus bent to her and adored.
And she looked up and musing towards him
Said low: "O son, I knew thy steps afar.
Of me thou wast; for as I suffered rapture,
Invaded by the sea of images
Breaking upon me from all winds, and saw
Indus and Ganges with prophetic mind,
A virginal impulse gleamed from my bosom
And on the earth took beauty and form. I saw
Thee from that glory issue and rejoiced.
But now thou comest quite discrowned. From me,
O son, thou hadst the impulse beautiful
That made thy soul all colour. For I strive
Towards the insufferable heights and flash
With haloes of that sacred light intense.
But lo! the spring and all its flowers, and lo!
How bright the Soma juice. What golden joys,
What living passions, what immortal tears!
I lift the veil that hides the Immortal — Ah!
My lids faint. Ah! the veil was lovelier.

My flowers wither in that height, my swan
Spreads not his wings felicitous so far.
O one day I shall turn from the great verse
And marble aspiration to sing sweetly
Of lovers and the pomps of wealth and wine
And warm delights and warm desires and earth.
O mine own son, Pururavus, I fall
By thy vast failure from my dazzling skies."
And Ila's son made answer, "O white-armed,
O mother of the Aryans, of my life
Creatress! fates colossal overrule.
But lo! I wander like a wave, nor find
Limit to the desire that wastes my soul."
Then with a sweet immortal smile the mother
Gave to him in the hollow of her hand
Wonderful water of the lake. He drank,
And understood infinity, and saw
Time like a snake coiling among the stars;
And earth he saw, and mortal nights and days
Grew to him moments, and his limbs became
Undying and his thoughts as marble endured.
Then to the hero deified the goddess,
"O strong immortal, now pursue thy joy:
Yet first rise up the peaks of Coilas; there
The Mighty Mother sits, whose sovran voice
Shall ratify to thee thy future fair,"
Said and caressed his brow with lips divine.
And bright Pururavus rose up the hill
Towards the breathless summit. Thence, enshrined
In deep concealing glories, came a voice,
And clearer he discerned as one whose eyes,
Long cognizant of darkness, coming forth,
Grow gradually habituated to light,
The calm compassionate face, the heaven-wide brow,
And the robust great limbs that bear the world.
Prophetical and deep her voice came down:
"Thou then hast failed, bright soul; but God blames not
Nor punishes. Impartially he deals
To every strenuous spirit its chosen reward.
And since no work, however maimed, no smallest

Energy added to the mighty sum
Of action fails of its exact result,
Empire shall in thy line and forceful brain
Persist, the boundless impulse towards rule
Of grandiose souls perpetually recur,
And minds immense and personalities
With battle and with passion and with storm
Shall burn through Aryan history, the speech
Of ages. In thy line the Spirit Supreme
Shall bound existence with one human form;
In Mathura and ocean Dwarca Man
Earthly perfectibility of soul
Example: son of thy line and eulogist,
The vast clear poet of the golden verse,
Whose song shall be as wide as is the world.
But all by huge self-will or violence marred
Of passionate uncontrol; if pure, their work
By touch of later turbulent hands unsphered
Or fames by legend stained. Upon my heights
Breathing God's air, strong as the sky and pure,
Dwell only Ixvaacou's children; destined theirs
Heaven's perfect praise, earth's sole unequalled song.
But thou, O Ila's son, take up thy joy.
For thee in sweet Gundhurva world eternal
Rapture and clasp unloosed of Urvasie,
Till the long night when God asleep shall fall."

Ceased the great voice and strong Pururavus
Glad of his high reward, however dearly
Purchased, purchased with infinite downfall,
With footing now divine went up the world.
Mid regions sweet and peaks of milk-white snow
And lovely corners and delicious lakes,
He saw a road all sunlight and the gates
Of the Gundhurvas' home. O never ship
From Ocean into Ocean erring knew
Such joy through all its patient sails at sight
Of final haven near as the tried heart
Of earth's successful son at that fair goal.
Towards the gates he hastened, and one bright

With angel face who at those portals stood
Cried down, "We wait for thee, Pururavus."
Then to his hearing musical, the hinges
Called; he beheld the subtle faces look
Down on him and the crowd of luminous forms,
And entered to immortal sound of lyres.
Up through the streets a silver cry went on
Before him of high instruments. From all
The winds the marvellous musicians pressed
To welcome that immortal lover. One
Whose pure limned brows aerial wore by right
Faery authority, stood from the crowd.
"O Ila's son, far-famed Pururavus,
Destined to joys by mortals all unhoped!
Move to thy sacred glories as a star
Into its destined place, shine over us
Here greatest as upon thy greener earth."
They through the thrilling regions musical
Led him and marvelled at him and praised with song
His fair sublimity of form and brow
And warlike limbs and grace heroical.
He heeded not, for all his soul was straining
With expectation of a near delight.
His eyes that sought her ever, beheld a wall
Of mighty trees and, where they arched to part,
Those two of all their sisters brightest rise,
One blithe as is a happy brook, the other
With her grave smile; and each took a strong hand
In her soft clasp, and led him to a place
Distinct mid faery-leaved ethereal trees
And magic banks and sweet low curves of hills,
And over all the sunlight like a charm.
There by a sounding river downward thrown
From under low green-curtaining boughs was she.
Mute she arose and with wide quiet eyes
Came towards him. In their immortal looks
Was a deep feeling too august for joy,
The sense that all eternity must follow
One perfect moment. Then that comrade bright
With slow grave smile, "O after absence wide

Who meet and shall not sunder any more.
Till slumber of the Supreme, strong be your souls
To bear unchanging rapture; strong you were
By patience to compel unwilling Gods."
And they were left alone in that clear world.
Then all his soul towards her leaning, took
Pururavus into his clasp and felt,
Seriously glad, the golden bosom on his
Of Urvasie, his love; so pressing back
The longed-for sacred face, lingering he kissed.
Then Love in his sweet heavens was satisfied.
But far below through silent mighty space
The green and strenuous earth abandoned rolled.

LOVE AND DEATH
1899

Love and Death

In woodlands of the bright and early world,
When love was to himself yet new and warm
And stainless, played like morning with a flower
Ruru with his young bride Priyumvada.
Fresh-cheeked and dew-eyed white Priyumvada
Opened her budded heart of crimson bloom
To love, to Ruru; Ruru, a happy flood
Of passion round a lotus dancing thrilled,
Blinded with his soul's waves Priyumvada.
To him the earth was a bed for this sole flower,
To her all the world was filled with his embrace.
Wet with new rains the morning earth, released
From her fierce centuries and burning suns,
Lavished her breath in greenness; poignant flowers
Thronged all her eager breast, and her young arms
Cradled a childlike bounding life that played
And would not cease, nor ever weary grew
Of her bright promise; for all was joy and breeze
And perfume, colour and bloom and ardent rays
Of living, and delight desired the world.
Then Earth was quick and pregnant tamelessly;
A free and unwalled race possessed her plains
Whose hearts uncramped by bonds, whose unspoiled thoughts
At once replied to light. Foisoned the fields;
Lonely and rich the forests and the swaying
Of those unnumbered tops affected men
With thoughts to their vast music kin. Undammed
The virgin rivers moved towards the sea,
And mountains yet unseen and peoples vague
Winged young imagination like an eagle
To strange beauty remote. And Ruru felt
The sweetness of the early earth as sap
All through him, and short life an aeon made
By boundless possibility, and love,
Sweetest of all unfathomable love,
A glory untired. As a bright bird comes flying
From airy extravagance to his own home,
And breasts his mate, and feels her all his goal,

So from boon sunlight and the fresh chill wave
Which swirled and lapped between the slumbering fields,
From forest pools and wanderings mid leaves
Through emerald ever-new discoveries,
Mysterious hillsides ranged and buoyant-swift
Races with our wild brothers in the meads,
Came Ruru back to the white-bosomed girl,
Strong-winged to pleasure. She all fresh and new
Rose to him, and he plunged into her charm.
For neither to her honey and poignancy
Artlessly interchanged, nor any limit
To the sweet physical delight of her
He found. Her eyes like deep and infinite wells
Lured his attracted soul, and her touch thrilled
Not lightly, though so light; the joy prolonged
And sweetness of the lingering of her lips
Was every time a nectar of surprise
To her lover; her smooth-gleaming shoulder bared
In darkness of her hair showed jasmine-bright,
While her kissed bosom by rich tumults stirred
Was a moved sea that rocked beneath his heart,
Then when her lips had made him blind, soft siege
Of all her unseen body to his rule
Betrayed the ravishing realm of her white limbs,
An empire for the glory of a God.
He knew not whether he loved most her smile,
Her causeless tears or little angers swift,
Whether held wet against him from the bath
Among her kindred lotuses, her cheeks
Soft to his lips and dangerous happy breasts
That vanquished all his strength with their desire,
Meeting his absence with her sudden face,
Or when the leaf-hid bird at night complained
Near their wreathed arbour on the moonlit lake,
Sobbing delight out from her heart of bliss,
Or in his clasp of rapture laughing low
Of his close bosom bridal-glad and pleased
With passion and this fiery play of love,
Or breaking off like one who thinks of grief,
Wonderful melancholy in her eyes

Grown liquid and with wayward sorrow large.
Thus he in her found a warm world of sweets,
And lived of ecstasy secure, nor deemed
Any new hour could match that early bliss.
But Love has joys for spirits born divine
More bleeding-lovely than his thornless rose.
That day he had left, while yet the east was dark,
Rising, her bosom and into the river
Swam out, exulting in the sting and swift
Sharp-edged desire around his limbs, and sprang
Wet to the bank, and streamed into the wood.
As a young horse upon the pastures glad
Feels greensward and the wind along his mane
And arches as he goes his neck, so went
In an immense delight of youth the boy
And shook his locks, joy-crested. Boundlessly
He revelled in swift air of life, a creature
Of wide and vigorous morning. Far he strayed
Tempting for flower and fruit branches in heaven,
And plucked, and flung away, and brighter chose,
Seeking comparisons for her bloom; and followed
New streams, and touched new trees, and felt slow beauty
And leafy secret change; for the damp leaves,
Grey-green at first, grew pallid with the light
And warmed with consciousness of sunshine near;
Then the whole daylight wandered in, and made
Hard tracts of splendour, and enriched all hues.
But when a happy sheltered heat he felt
And heard contented voice of living things
Harmonious with the noon, he turned and swiftly
Went homeward yearning to Priyumvada,
And near his home emerging from green leaves
He laughed towards the sun: "O father Sun,"
He cried, "how good it is to live, to love!
Surely our joy shall never end, nor we
Grow old, but like bright rivers or pure winds
Sweetly continue, or revive with flowers,
Or live at least as long as senseless trees."
He dreamed, and said with a soft smile: "Lo, she!
And she will turn from me with angry tears

Her delicate face more beautiful than storm
Or rainy moonlight. I will follow her,
And soothe her heart with sovereign flatteries;
Or rather all tyranny exhaust and taste
The beauty of her anger like a fruit,
Vexing her soul with helplessness; then soften
Easily with quiet undenied demand
Of heart insisting upon heart; or else
Will reinvest her beauty bright with flowers,
Or with my hands her little feet persuade.
Then will her face be like a sudden dawn,
And flower compelled into reluctant smiles."
He had not ceased when he beheld her. She,
Tearing a jasmine bloom with waiting hands,
Stood drooping, petulant, but heard at once
His footsteps and before she was aware,
A sudden smile of exquisite delight
Leaped to her mouth, and a great blush of joy
Surprised her cheeks. She for a moment stood
Beautiful with her love before she died;
And he laughed towards her. With a pitiful cry
She paled; moaning, her stricken limbs collapsed.
But petrified, in awful dumb surprise,
He gazed; then waking with a bound was by her,
All panic expectation. As he came,
He saw a brilliant flash of coils evade
The sunlight, and with hateful gorgeous hood
Darted into green safety, hissing, death.
Voiceless he sank beside her and stretched out
His arms and desperately touched her face,
As if to attract her soul to live, and sought
Beseeching with his hands her bosom. O, she
Was warm, and cruel hope pierced him; but pale
As jasmines fading on a girl's sweet breast
Her cheek was, and forgot its perfect rose.
Her eyes that clung to sunlight yet, with pain
Were large and feebly round his neck her arms
She lifted and, desiring his pale cheek
Against her bosom, sobbed out piteously,
"Ah, Love!" and stopped heart-broken; then, "O Love!

Alas the green dear home that I must leave
So early! I was so glad of love and kisses,
And thought that centuries would not exhaust
The deep embrace. And I have had so little
Of joy and the wild day and throbbing night,
Laughter, and tenderness, and strife and tears.
I have not numbered half the brilliant birds
In one green forest, nor am familiar grown
With sunrise and the progress of the eves,
Nor have with plaintive cries of birds made friends,
Cuckoo and rainlark and love-speak-to-me.
I have not learned the names of half the flowers
Around me; so few trees know me by my name;
Nor have I seen the stars so very often
That I should die. I feel a dreadful hand
Drawing me from the touch of thy warm limbs
Into some cold vague mist, and all black night
Descends towards me. I no more am thine,
But go I know not where, and see pale shapes
And gloomy countries and that terrible stream.
O Love, O Love, they take me from thee far,
And whether we shall find each other ever
In the wide dreadful territory of death,
I know not. Or thou wilt forget me quite,
And life compel thee into other arms.
Ah, come with me! I cannot bear to wander
In that cold cruel country all alone,
Helpless and terrified, or sob by streams
Denied sweet sunlight and by thee unloved."
Slower her voice came now, and over her cheek
Death paused; then, sobbing like a little child
Too early from her bounding pleasures called,
The lovely discontented spirit stole
From her warm body white. Over her leaned
Ruru, and waited for dead lips to move.
Still in the greenwood lay Priyumvada,
And Ruru rose not from her, but with eyes
Emptied of glory hung above his dead,
Only, without a word, without a tear.
Then the crowned wives of the great forest came,

They who had fed her from maternal breasts,
And grieved over the lovely body cold,
And bore it from him; nor did he entreat
One last look nor one kiss, nor yet denied
What he had loved so well. They the dead girl
Into some distant greenness bore away.

But Ruru, while the stillness of the place
Remembered her, sat without voice. He heard
Through the great silence that was now his soul,
The forest sounds, a squirrel's leap through leaves,
The cheeping of a bird just overhead,
A peacock with his melancholy cry
Complaining far away, and tossings dim
And slight unnoticeable stir of trees.
But all these were to him like distant things
And he alone in his heart's void. And yet
No thought he had of her so lately lost,
Rather far pictures, trivial incidents
Of that old life before her delicate face
Had lived for him, dumbly distinct like thoughts
Of men that die, kept with long pomps his mind
Excluding the dead girl. So still he was,
The birds flashed by him with their swift small wings,
Fanning him. Then he moved, then rigorous
Memory through all his body shuddering
Awoke, and he looked up and knew the place,
And recognised greenness immutable,
And saw old trees and the same flowers still bloom.
He felt the bright indifference of earth
And all the lonely uselessness of pain.
Then lifting up the beauty of his brow
He spoke, with sorrow pale: "O grim cold Death!
But I will not like ordinary men
Satiate thee with cries, and falsely woo thee,
And make my grief thy theatre, who lie
Prostrate beneath thy thunderbolts and make
Night witness of their moans, shuddering and crying
When sudden memories pierce them like swords,
And often starting up as at a thought

Intolerable, pace a little, then
Sink down exhausted by brief agony.
O secrecy terrific, darkness vast,
At which we shudder! Somewhere, I know not where,
Somehow, I know not how, I shall confront
Thy gloom, tremendous spirit, and seize with hands
And prove what thou art and what man." He said,
And slowly to the forests wandered. There
Long months he travelled between grief and grief,
Reliving thoughts of her with every pace,
Measuring vast pain in his immortal mind.
And his heart cried in him as when a fire
Roars through wide forests and the branches cry
Burning towards heaven in torture glorious.
So burned, immense, his grief within him; he raised
His young pure face all solemnised with pain,
Voiceless. Then Fate was shaken, and the Gods
Grieved for him, of his silence grown afraid.
Therefore from peaks divine came flashing down
Immortal Agni and to the Uswuttha-tree,
Cried in the Voice that slays the world: "O tree
That liftest thy enormous branches able
To shelter armies, more than armies now
Shelter, be famous, house a brilliant God.
For the grief grows in Ruru's breast up-piled,
As wrestles with its anguished barricades
In silence an impending flood, and Gods
Immortal grow afraid. For earth alarmed
Shudders to bear the curse lest her young life
Pale with eclipse and all-creating love
Be to mere pain condemned. Divert the wrath
Into thy boughs, Uswuttha — thou shalt be
My throne — glorious, though in eternal pangs,
Yet worth much pain to harbour divine fire."
So ended the young pure destroyer's voice,
And the dumb god consented silently.
In the same noon came Ruru; his mind had paused,
Lured for a moment by soft wandering gleams
Into forgetfulness of grief; for thoughts
Gentle and near-eyed whispering memories

So sweetly came, his blind heart dreamed she lived.
Slow the Uswuttha-tree bent down its leaves,
And smote his cheek, and touched his heavy hair.
And Ruru turned illumined. For a moment,
One blissful moment he had felt 'twas she.
So had she often stolen up and touched
His curls with her enamoured fingers small,
Lingering, while the wind smote him with her hair
And her quick breath came to him like spring. Then he,
Turning, as one surprised with heaven, saw
Ready to his swift passionate grasp her bosom
And body sweet expecting his embrace.
Oh, now saw her not, but the guilty tree
Shrinking; then grief back with a double crown
Arose and stained his face with agony.
Nor silence he endured, but the dumb force
Ascetic and inherited, by sires
Fierce-musing earned, from the boy's bosom blazed.
"O Uswuttha-tree, wantonly who hast mocked
My anguish with the wind, but thou no more
Have joy of the cool wind nor green delight,
But live thy guilty leaves in fire, so long
As Aryan wheels by thy doomed shadow vast
Thunder to war, nor bless with cool wide waves
Lyric Saruswathi nations impure."
He spoke, and the vast tree groaned through its leaves,
Recognising its fate; then smouldered; lines
Of living fire rushed up the girth and hissed
Serpentine in the unconsuming leaves;
Last, all Hutashan in his chariot armed
Sprang on the boughs and blazed into the sky,
And wailing all the great tormented creature
Stood wide in agony; one half was green
And earthly, the other a weird brilliance
Filled with the speed and cry of endless flame.
But he, with the fierce rushing-out of power
Shaken and that strong grasp of anguish, flung
His hands out to the sun; "Priyumvada!"
He cried, and at that well-loved sound there dawned
With overwhelming sweetness miserable

Upon his mind the old delightful times
When he had called her by her liquid name,
Where the voice loved to linger. He remembered
The chompuc bushes where she turned away
Half-angered, and his speaking of her name
Masterfully as to a lovely slave
Rebellious who has erred; at that the slow
Yielding of her small head, and after a little
Her sliding towards him and beautiful
Propitiating body as she sank down
With timid graspings deprecatingly
In prostrate warm surrender, her flushed cheeks
Upon his feet and little touches soft;
Or her long name uttered beseechingly,
And the swift leap of all her body to him,
And eyes of large repentance, and the weight
Of her wild bosom and lips unsatisfied;
Or hourly call for little trivial needs,
Or sweet unneeded wanton summoning,
Daily appeal that never staled nor lost
Its sudden music, and her lovely speed,
Sedulous occupation left, quick-breathing,
With great glad eyes and eager parted lips;
Or in deep quiet moments murmuring
That name like a religion in her ear,
And her calm look compelled to ecstasy;
Or to the river luring her, or breathed
Over her dainty slumber, or secret sweet
Bridal outpantings of her broken name.
All these as rush unintermitting waves
Upon a swimmer overborne, broke on him
Relentless, things too happy to be endured,
Till faint with the recalled felicity
Low he moaned out: "O pale Priyumvada!
O dead fair flower! yet living to my grief!
But I could only slay the innocent tree,
Powerless when power should have been. Not such
Was Bhrigu from whose sacred strength I spring,
Nor Bhrigu's son, my father, when he blazed
Out from Puloma's side, and burning, blind,

Fell like a tree the ravisher unjust.
But I degenerate from such sires. O Death
That showest not thy face beneath the stars,
But comest masked, and on our dear ones seizing
Fearest to wrestle equally with love!
Nor from thy gloomy house any come back
To tell thy way. But O, if any strength
In lover's constancy to torture dwell
Earthward to force a helping god and such
Ascetic force be born of lover's pain,
Let my dumb pangs be heard. Whoe'er thou art,
O thou bright enemy of Death descend
And lead me to that portal dim. For I
Have burned in fires cruel as the fire
And lain upon a sharper couch than swords."
He ceased, and heaven thrilled, and the far blue
Quivered as with invisible downward wings.

But Ruru passioned on, and came with eve
To secret grass and a green opening moist
In a cool lustre. Leaned upon a tree
That bathed in faery air and saw the sky
Through branches, and a single parrot loud
Screamed from its top, there stood a golden boy,
Half-naked, with bright limbs all beautiful —
Delicate they were, in sweetness absolute:
For every gleam and every soft strong curve
Magically compelled the eye, and smote
The heart to weakness. In his hands he swung
A bow — not such as human archers use:
For the string moved and murmured like many bees,
And nameless fragrance made the casual air
A peril. He on Ruru that fair face
Turned, and his steps with lovely gesture chained.
"Who art thou here, in forests wandering,
And thy young exquisite face is solemnised
With pain? Luxuriously the Gods have tortured
Thy heart to see such dreadful glorious beauty
Agonize in thy lips and brilliant eyes:
As tyrants in the fierceness of others' pangs

Joy and feel strong, clothing with brilliant fire,
Tyrants in Titan lands. Needs must her mouth
Have been pure honey and her bosom a charm,
Whom thou desirest seeing not the green
And common lovely sounds hast quite forgot."
And Ruru, mastered by the God, replied:
"I know thee by thy cruel beauty bright,
Kama, who makest many worlds one fire.
Ah, wherefore wilt thou ask of her to increase
The passion and regret? Thou knowest, great love!
Thy nymph her mother, if thou truly art he
And not a dream of my disastrous soul."
But with the thrilled eternal smile that makes
The spring, the lover of Rathi golden-limbed
Replied to Ruru, "Mortal, I am he;
I am that Madan who inform the stars
With lustre and on life's wide canvas fill
Pictures of light and shade, of joy and tears,
Make ordinary moments wonderful
And common speech a charm: knit life to life
With interfusions of opposing souls
And sudden meetings and slow sorceries:
Wing the boy bridegroom to that panting breast,
Smite Gods with mortal faces, dreadfully
Among great beautiful kings and watched by eyes
That burn, force on the virgin's fainting limbs
And drive her to the one face never seen,
The one breast meant eternally for her.
By me come wedded sweets, by me the wife's
Busy delight and passionate obedience,
And loving eager service never sated,
And happy lips, and worshipping soft eyes:
And mine the husband's hungry arms and use
Unwearying of old tender words and ways,
Joy of her hair, and silent pleasure felt
Of nearness to one dear familiar shape.
Nor only these, but many affections bright
And soft glad things cluster around my name.
I plant fraternal tender yearnings, make
The sister's sweet attractiveness and leap

Of heart towards imperious kindred blood,
And the young mother's passionate deep look,
Earth's high similitude of One not earth,
Teach filial heart-beats strong. These are my gifts
For which men praise me, these my glories calm:
But fiercer shafts I can, wild storms blown down
Shaking fixed minds and melting marble natures,
Tears and dumb bitterness and pain unpitied,
Racked thirsting jealousy and kind hearts made stone:
And in undisciplined huge souls I sow
Dire vengeance and impossible cruelties,
Cold lusts that linger and fierce fickleness,
The loves close kin to hate, brute violence
And mad insatiable longings pale,
And passion blind as death and deaf as swords.
O mortal, all deep-souled desires and all
Yearnings immense are mine, so much I can."
So as he spoke, his face grew wonderful
With vast suggestion, his human-seeming limbs
Brightened with a soft splendour: luminous hints
Of the concealed divinity transpired.
But soon with a slight discontented frown:
"So much I can, as even the great Gods learn.
Only with death I wrestle in vain, until
My passionate godhead all becomes a doubt.
Mortal, I am the light in stars, of flowers
The bloom, the nameless fragrance that pervades
Creation: but behind me, older than me,
He comes with night and cold tremendous shade.
Hard is the way to him, most hard to find,
Harder to tread, for perishable feet
Almost impossible. Yet, O fair youth,
If thou must needs go down, and thou art strong
In passion and in constancy, nor easy
The soul to slay that has survived such grief —
Steel then thyself to venture, armed by Love.
Yet listen first what heavy trade they drive
Who would win back their dead to human arms."
So much the God; but swift, with eager eyes
And panting bosom and glorious flushed face,

The lover: "O great Love! O beautiful Love!
But if by strength is possible, of body
Or mind, battle of spirit of moving speech,
Sweet speech that makes even cruelty grow kind,
Or yearning melody — for I have heard
That when Saruswathi in heaven her harp
Has smitten, the cruel sweetness terrible
Coils taking no denial through the soul,
And tears burst from the hearts of Gods — then I,
Making great music, or with perfect words,
Will strive, or staying him with desperate hands
Match human strength 'gainst formidable Death.
But if with price, ah God! what easier! Tears
Dreadful, innumerable I will absolve,
Or pay with anguish through the centuries,
Soul's agony and torture physical,
So her small hands about my face at last
I feel, close real hair sting me with life,
And palpable breathing bosom on me press."
Then with a lenient smile the mighty God:
"O ignorant fond lover, not with tears
Shalt thou persuade immitigable Death.
He will not pity all thy pangs: nor know
His stony eyes with music to grow kind,
Nor lovely words accepts. And how wilt thou
Wrestle with that grim shadow, who canst not save
One bloom from fading? A sole thing the Gods
Demand from all men living, sacrifice:
Nor without this shall any crown be grasped.
Yet many sacrifices are there, oxen,
And prayers, and Soma wine, and pious flowers,
Blood and the fierce expense of mind, and pure
Incense of perfect actions, perfect thoughts,
Or liberality wide as the sun's,
Or ruthless labour or disastrous tears,
Exile or death or pain more hard than death,
Absence, a desert, from the faces loved;
Even sin may be a sumptuous sacrifice
Acceptable for unholy fruits. But none
Of these the inexorable shadow asks:

Alone of gods Death loves not gifts: he visits
The pure heart as the stained. Lo, the just man
Bowed helpless over his dead, nor all his virtues
Shall quicken that cold bosom: near him the wild
Marred face and passionate and will not leave
Kissing dead lips that shall not chide him more.
Life the pale ghost requires: with half thy life
Thou mayst protract the thread too early cut
Of that delightful spirit — half sweet life.
O Ruru, lo, thy frail precarious days,
And yet how sweet they are! simply to breathe
How warm and sweet! And ordinary things
How exquisite, thou then shalt learn when lost,
How luminous the daylight was, mere sleep
How soft and friendly clasping tired limbs,
And the deliciousness of common food.
And things indifferent thou then shalt want,
Regret rejected beauty, brightnesses
Bestowed in vain. Wilt thou yield up, O lover,
Half thy sweet portion of this light and gladness,
Thy little insufficient share, and vainly
Give to another? She is not thyself:
Thou dost not feel the gladness in her bosom,
Nor with the torture of thy body will she
Throb and cry out: at most with tender looks
And pitiful attempt to feel move near thee,
And weep how far she is from what she loves.
Men live like stars that see each other in heaven,
But one knows not the pleasure and the grief
The others feel: he lonely rapture has,
Or bears his incommunicable pain.
O Ruru, there are many beautiful faces,
But one thyself. Think then how thou shalt mourn
When thou hast shortened joy and feelst at last
The shadow that thou hadst for such sweet store."
He ceased with a strange doubtful look. But swift
Came back the lover's voice, like passionate rain.
"O idle words! For what is mere sunlight?
Who would live on into extreme old age,
Burden the impatient world, a weary old man,

And look back on a selfish time ill-spent
Exacting out of prodigal great life
Small separate pleasures like an usurer,
And no rich sacrifice and no large act
Finding oneself in others, nor the sweet
Expense of Nature in her passionate gusts
Of love and giving, first of the soul's needs?
Who is so coldly wise, and does not feel
How wasted were our grandiose human days
In prudent personal unshared delights?
Why dost thou mock me, friend of all the stars?
How canst thou be love's god and know not this,
That love burns down the body's barriers cold
And laughs at difference — playing with it merely
To make joy sweeter? O too deeply I know,
The lover is not different from the loved,
Nor is their silence dumb to each other. He
Contains her heart and feels her body in his,
He flushes with her heat, chills with her cold.
And when she dies, oh! when she dies, oh me,
The emptiness, the maim! the life no life,
The sweet and passionate oneness lost! And if
By shortening of great grief won back, O price
Easy! O glad briefness, aeons may envy!
For we shall live not fearing death, nor feel
As others yearning over the loved at night
When the lamp flickers, sudden chills of dread
Terrible; nor at short absence agonise,
Wrestling with mad imagination. Us
Serenely when the darkening shadow comes,
One common sob shall end and soul clasp soul,
Leaving the body in a long dim kiss.
Then in the joys of heaven we shall consort,
Amid the gladness often touching hands
To make bliss sure; or in the ghastly stream
If we must anguish, yet it shall not part
Our passionate limbs inextricably locked
By one strong agony, but we shall feel
Hell's pain half joy through sweet companionship.
God Love, I weary of words. O wing me rather

To her, my eloquent princess of the spring,
In whatsoever wintry shores she roam."
He ceased with eager forward eyes; once more
A light of beauty immortal through the limbs
Gleaming of the boy-god and soft sweet face,
Glorifying him, flushed, and he replied:
"Go then, O thou dear youth, and bear this flower
In thy hand warily. For thou shalt come
To that high meeting of the Ganges pure
With vague and violent Ocean. There arise
And loudly appeal my brother, the wild sea."
He spoke and stretched out his immortal hand,
And Ruru's met it. All his young limbs yearned
With dreadful rapture shuddering through them. He
Felt in his fingers subtle uncertain bloom,
A quivering magnificence, half fire,
Whose petals changed like flame, and from them breathed
Dangerous attraction and alarmed delight,
As at a peril near. He raised his eyes,
But the green place was empty of the God.
Only the faery tree looked up at heaven
Through branches, and with recent pleasure shook.
Then over fading earth the night was lord.

But from Shatudru and Bipasha, streams
Once holy, and loved Iravathi and swift
Clear Chandrabhaga and Bitosta's toil
For man, went Ruru to bright sumptuous lands
By Aryan fathers not yet paced, but wild,
But virgin to our fruitful human toil,
Where nature lay reclined in dumb delight
Alone with woodlands and the voiceless hills.
He with the widening yellow Ganges came,
Amazed, to trackless countries where few tribes,
Kirath and Poundrian, warred, worshipping trees
And the great serpent. But robust wild earth,
But forests with their splendid life of beasts
Savage mastered those strong inhabitants.
Thither came Ruru. In a thin soft eve
Ganges spread far her multitudinous waves,

A glimmering restlessness with voices large,
And from the forests of that half-seen bank
A boat came heaving over it, white-winged,
With a sole silent helmsman marble-pale.
Then Ruru by his side stepped in; they went
Down the mysterious river and beheld
The great banks widen out of sight. The world
Was water and the skies to water plunged.
All night with a dim motion gliding down
He felt the dark against his eyelids; felt,
As in a dream more real than daylight,
The helmsman with his dumb and marble face
Near him and moving wideness all around,
And that continual gliding dimly on,
As one who on a shoreless water sails
For ever to a port he shall not win.
But when the darkness paled, he heard a moan
Of mightier waves and had the wide great sense
Of Ocean and the depths below our feet.
But the boat stopped; the pilot lifted on him
His marble gaze coeval with the stars.
Then in the white-winged boat the boy arose
And saw around him the vast sea all grey
And heaving in the pallid dawning light.
Loud Ruru cried across the murmur: "Hear me,
O inarticulate grey Ocean, hear.
If any cadence in thy infinite
Rumour was caught from lover's moan, O Sea,
Open thy abysses to my mortal tread.
For I would travel to the despairing shades,
The spheres of suffering where entangled dwell
Souls unreleased and the untimely dead
Who weep remembering. Thither, O guide me,
No despicable wayfarer, but Ruru,
But son of a great Rishi, from all men
On earth selected for peculiar pangs,
Special disaster. Lo, this petalled fire,
How freshly it blooms and lasts with my great pain!"
He held the flower out subtly glimmering.
And like a living thing the huge sea trembled,

Then rose, calling, and filled the sight with waves,
Converging all its giant crests; towards him
Innumerable waters loomed and heaven
Threatened. Horizon on horizon moved
Dreadfully swift; then with a prone wide sound
All Ocean hollowing drew him swiftly in,
Curving with monstrous menace over him.
He down the gulf where the loud waves collapsed
Descending, saw with floating hair arise
The daughters of the sea in pale green light,
A million mystic breasts suddenly bare,
And came beneath the flood and stunned beheld
A mute stupendous march of waters race
To reach some viewless pit beneath the world.
Ganges he saw, as men predestined rush
Upon a fearful doom foreseen, so ran,
Alarmed, with anguished speed, the river vast.
Veiled to his eyes the triple goddess rose.
She with a sound of waters cried to him,
A thousand voices moaning with one pain:
"Lover, who fearedst not sunlight to leave,
With me thou mayst behold that helpless spirit
Lost in the gloom, if still thy burning bosom
Have courage to endure great Nature's night
In the dire lands where I, a goddess, mourn
Hurting my heart with my own cruelty."
She darkened to the ominous descent,
Unwilling, and her once so human waves
Sent forth a cry not meant for living ears.
And Ruru chilled; but terrible strong love
Was like a fiery finger in his breast
Pointing him on; so he through horror went
Conducted by inexorable sound.
For monstrous voices to his ear were close,
And bodiless terrors with their dimness seized him
In an obscurity phantasmal. Thus
With agony of soul to the grey waste
He came, glad of the pain of passage over,
As men who through the storms of anguish strive
Into abiding tranquil dreariness

And draw sad breath assured; to the grey waste,
Hopeless Patala, the immutable
Country, where neither sun nor rain arrives,
Nor happy labour of the human plough
Fruitfully turns the soil, but in vague sands
And indeterminable strange rocks and caverns
That into silent blackness huge recede,
Dwell the great serpent and his hosts, writhed forms,
Sinuous, abhorred, through many horrible leagues
Coiling in a half darkness. Shapes he saw,
And heard the hiss and knew the lambent light
Loathsome, but passed compelling his strong soul.
At last through those six tired hopeless worlds,
Too hopeless far for grief, pale he arrived
Into a nether air by anguish moved,
And heard before him cries that pierced the heart,
Human, not to be borne, and issued shaken
By the great river accursed. Maddened it ran,
Anguished, importunate, and in its waves
The drifting ghosts their agony endured.
There Ruru saw pale faces float of kings
And grandiose victors and revered high priests
And famous women. Now rose from the wave
A golden shuddering arm and now a face.
Torn piteous sides were seen and breasts that quailed.
Over them moaned the penal waters on,
And had no joy of their fierce cruelty.
Then Ruru, his young cheeks with pity wan,
Half moaned: "O miserable race of men,
With violent and passionate souls you come
Foredoomed upon the earth and live brief days
In fear and anguish, catching at stray beams
Of sunlight, little fragrances of flowers;
Then from your spacious earth in a great horror
Descend into this night, and here too soon
Must expiate your few inadequate joys.
O bargain hard! Death helps us not. He leads
Alarmed, all shivering from his chill embrace,
The naked spirit here. Oh my sweet flower,
Art thou too whelmed in this fierce wailing flood?

Ah me! But I will haste and deeply plunge
Into its hopeless pools and either bring
Thy old warm beauty back beneath the stars,
Or find thee out and clasp thy tortured bosom
And kiss thy sweet wrung lips and hush thy cries.
Love shall draw half thy pain into my limbs;
Then we shall triumph glad of agony."
He ceased and one replied close by his ear:
"O thou who troublest with thy living eyes
Established death, pass on. She whom thou seekest
Rolls not in the accursèd tide. For late
I saw her mid those pale inhabitants
Whom bodily anguish visits not, but thoughts
Sorrowful and dumb memories absolve,
And martyrdom of scourged hearts quivering."
He turned and saw astride the dolorous flood
A mighty bridge paved with mosaic fire,
All restless, and a woman clothed in flame,
With hands calamitous that held a sword,
Stood of the quaking passage sentinel.
Magnificent and dire her burning face.
"Pass on," she said once more, "O Bhrigu's son;
The flower protects thee from my hands." She stretched
One arm towards him and with violence
Majestic over the horrid arch compelled.
Unhurt, though shaking from her touch, alone
He stood upon an inner bank with strange
Black dreary mosses covered and perceived
A dim and level plain without one flower.
Over it paced a multitude immense
With gentle faces occupied by pain;
Strong men were there and grieving mothers, girls
With early beauty in their limbs and young
Sad children of their childlike faces robbed.
Naked they paced with falling hair and gaze
Drooping upon their bosoms, weak as flowers
That die for want of rain unmurmuring.
Always a silence was upon the place.
But Ruru came among them. Suddenly
One felt him there and looked, and as a wind

Moves over a still field of patient corn,
And the ears stir and shudder and look up
And bend innumerably flowing, so
All those dumb spirits stirred and through them passed
One shuddering motion of raised faces; then
They streamed towards him without sound and caught
With desperate hands his robe or touched his hair
Or strove to feel upon them living breath.
Pale girls and quiet children came and knelt
And with large sorrowful eyes into his looked.
Yet with their silent passion the cold hush
Moved not; but Ruru's human heart half burst
With burden of so many sorrows; tears
Welled from him; he with anguish understood
That terrible and wordless sympathy
Of dead souls for the living. Then he turned
His eyes and scanned their lovely faces strange
For that one face and found it not. He paled,
And spoke vain words into the listless air:
"O spirits once joyous, miserable race,
Happier if the old gladness were forgot!
My soul yearns with your sorrow. Yet ah! reveal
If dwell my love in your sad nation lost.
Well may you know her, O wan beautiful spirits!
But she most beautiful of all that died,
By sweetness recognisable. Her name
The sunshine knew." Speaking his tears made way:
But they with dumb lips only looked at him,
A vague and empty mourning in their eyes.
He murmured low: "Ah, folly! were she here,
Would she not first have felt me, first have raised
Her lids and run to me, leaned back her face
Of silent sorrow on my breast and looked
With the old altered eyes into my own
And striven to make my anguish understand?
Oh joy, had she been here! for though her lips
Of their old excellent music quite were robbed,
Yet her dumb passion would have spoken to me;
We should have understood each other and walked
Silently hand in hand, almost content."

He said and passed through those untimely dead.
Speechless they followed him with clinging eyes.
Then to a solemn building weird he came
With grave colossal pillars round. One dome
Roofed the whole brooding edifice, like cloud,
And at the door strange shapes were pacing, armed.
Then from their fear the sweet and mournful dead
Drew back, returning to their wordless grief.
But Ruru to the perilous doorway strode,
And those disastrous shapes upon him raised
Their bows and aimed; but he held out Love's flower,
And with stern faces checked they let him pass.
He entered and beheld a silent hall
Dim and unbounded; moving then like one
Who up a dismal stair seeks ever light,
Attained a dais brilliant doubtfully
With flaming pediment and round it coiled
Python and Naga monstrous, Joruthcaru,
Tuxuc and Vasuki himself, immense,
Magic Carcotaca all flecked with fire;
And many other prone destroying shapes
Coiled. On the wondrous dais rose a throne,
And he its pedestal whose lotus hood
With ominous beauty crowns his horrible
Sleek folds, great Mahapudma; high displayed
He bears the throne of Death. There sat supreme
With those compassionate and lethal eyes,
Who many names, who many natures holds;
Yama, the strong pure Hades sad and subtle,
Dharma, who keeps the laws of old untouched,
Critanta, who ends all things and at last
Himself shall end. On either side of him
The four-eyed dogs mysterious rested prone,
Watchful, with huge heads on their paws advanced;
And emanations of the godhead dim
Moved near him, shadowy or serpentine,
Vast Time and cold irreparable Death.
Then Ruru came and bowed before the throne;
And swaying all those figures stirred as shapes
Upon a tapestry moved by the wind,

And the sad voice was heard: "What breathing man
Bows at the throne of Hades? By what force,
Spiritual or communicated, troubles
His living beauty the dead grace of Hell?"
And one replied who seemed a neighbouring voice:
"He has the blood of Gods and Titans old.
An Apsara his mother liquid-orbed
Bore to the youthful Chyavan's strong embrace
This passionate face of earth with Eden touched.
Chyavan was Bhrigu's child, Puloma bore,
The Titaness, — Bhrigu, great Brahma's son.
Love gave the flower that helps by anguish; therefore
He chilled not with the breath of Hades, nor
The cry of the infernal stream made stone."
But at the name of Love all hell was moved.
Death's throne half faded into twilight; hissed
The phantoms serpentine as if in pain,
And the dogs raised their dreadful heads. Then spoke
Yama: "And what needs Love in this pale realm,
The warm great Love? All worlds his breath confounds,
Mars solemn order and old steadfastness.
But not in Hell his legates come and go;
His vernal jurisdiction to bare Hell
Extends not. This last world resists his power
Youthful, anarchic. Here will he enlarge
Tumult and wanton joys?" The voice replied:
"Menaca momentary on the earth,
Heaven's Apsara by the fleeting hours beguiled
Played in the happy hidden glens; there bowed
To yoke of swift terrestrial joys she bore,
Immortal, to that fair Gundhurva king
A mortal blossom of delight. That bloom
Young Ruru found and plucked, but her too soon
Thy fatal hooded snake on earth surprised,
And he through gloom now travels armed by Love."
But then all Hades swaying towards him cried:
"O mortal, O misled! But sacrifice
Is stronger, nor may law of Hell or Heaven
Its fierce effectual action supersede.
Thy dead I yield. Yet thou bethink thee, mortal,

Not as a tedious evil nor to be
Lightly rejected gave the gods old age,
But tranquil, but august, but making easy
The steep ascent to God. Therefore must Time
Still batter down the glory and form of youth
And animal magnificent strong ease,
To warn the earthward man that he is spirit
Dallying with transience, nor by death he ends,
Nor to the dumb warm mother's arms is bound,
But called unborn into the unborn skies.
For body fades with the increasing soul
And wideness of its limit grown intolerant
Replaces life's impetuous joys by peace.
Youth, manhood, ripeness, age, four seasons
Twixt its return and pale departing life
Describes, O mortal, — youth that forward bends
Midst hopes, delights and dreamings; manhood deepens
To passions, toils and thoughts profound; but ripeness
For large reflective gathering-up of these,
As on a lonely slope whence men look back
Down towards the cities and the human fields
Where they too worked and laughed and loved; next age,
Wonderful age with those approaching skies.
That boon wilt thou renounce? Wherefore? To bring
For a few years — how miserably few! —
Her sunward who must after all return.
Ah, son of Rishis, cease. Lo, I remit
Hell's grasp, not oft-relinquished, and send back
Thy beautiful life unborrowed to the stars.
Or thou must render to the immutable
Total all thy fruit-bearing years; then she
Reblossoms." But the Shadow antagonist:
"Let him be shown the glory he would renounce."
And over the flaming pediment there moved,
As on a frieze a march of sculptures, carved
By Phidias for the Virgin strong and pure,
Most perfect once of all things seen in earth
Or Heaven, in Athens on the Acropolis,
But now dismembered, now disrupt! or as
In Buddhist cavern or Orissan temple,

Large aspirations architectural,
Warrior and dancing-girl, adept and king,
And conquering pomps and daily peaceful groups
Dream delicately on, softening with beauty
Great Bhuvanayshwar, the Almighty's house,
With sculptural suggestion so were limned
Scenes future on a pediment of fire.
There Ruru saw himself divine with age,
A Rishi to whom infinity is close,
Rejoicing in some green song-haunted glade
Or boundless mountain-top where most we feel
Wideness, not by small happy things disturbed.
Around him, as around an ancient tree
Its seedlings, forms august or flame-like rose;
They grew beneath his hands and were his work;
Great kings were there whom time remembers, fertile
Deep minds and poets with their chanting lips
Whose words were seed of vast philosophies —
These worshipped; above this earth's half-day he saw
Amazed the dawn of that mysterious Face
And all the universe in beauty merge.
Mad the boy thrilled upwards, then spent ebbed back.
Over his mind, as birds across the sky
Sweep and are gone, the vision of those fields
And drooping faces came; almost he heard
The burdened river with human anguish wail.
Then with a sudden fury gathering
His soul he hurled out of it half its life,
And fell, like lightning, prone. Triumphant rose
The Shadow chill and deepened giant night.
Only the dais flickered in the gloom,
And those snake-eyes of cruel fire subdued.
But suddenly a bloom, a fragrance. Hell
Shuddered with bliss: resentful, overborne,
The world-besetting Terror faded back
Like one grown weak by desperate victory,
And a voice cried in Ruru's tired soul:
"Arise! the strife is over, easy now
The horror that thou hast to face, the burden
Now shared." And with a sudden burst like spring

Life woke in the strong lover over-tired.
He rose and left dim Death. Twelve times he crossed
Boithorini, the river dolorous,
Twelve times resisted Hell and hurried down
Into the ominous pit where plunges black
The vast stream thundering, saw, led puissantly
From night to unimaginable night, —
As men oppressed in dreams, who cannot wake,
But measure penal visions, — punishments
Whose sight pollutes, unheard-of tortures, pangs
Monstrous, intolerable mute agonies,
Twisted unmoving attitudes of pain,
Like thoughts inhuman in statuary. A fierce
And iron voicelessness had grasped those worlds.
No horror of cries expressed their endless pain,
No saving struggle, no breathings of the soul.
And in the last hell irremediable
Where Ganges clots into that fatal pool,
Appalled he saw her; pallid, listless, bare —
O other than that earthly warmth and grace
In which the happy roses deepened and dimmed
With come-and-go of swift enamoured blood!
Dumb drooped she; round her shapes of anger armed
Stood dark like thunder-clouds. But Ruru sprang
Upon them, burning with the admitted God.
They from his touch like ineffectual fears
Vanished; then sole with her, trembling he cried
The old glad name and crying bent to her
And touched, and at the touch the silent knots
Of Hell were broken and its sombre dream
Of dreadful stately pains at once dispersed.
Then as from one whom a surpassing joy
Has conquered, all the bright surrounding world
Streams swiftly into distance, and he feels
His daily senses slipping from his grasp,
So that unbearable enormous world
Went rolling mighty shades, like the wet mist
From men on mountain-tops; and sleep outstretched
Rising its soft arms towards him and his thoughts,
As on a bed, sank to ascending void.

But when he woke, he heard the koïl insist
On sweetness and the voice of happy things
Content with sunlight. The warm sense was round him
Of old essential earth, known hues and custom
Familiar tranquillising body and mind,
As in its natural wave a lotus feels.
He looked and saw all grass and dense green trees,
And sunshine and a single grasshopper
Near him repeated fierily its note.
Thrilling he felt beneath his bosom her;
Oh, warm and breathing were those rescued limbs
Against the greenness, vivid, palpable, white,
With great black hair and real and her cheek's
Old softness and her mouth a dewy rose.
For many moments comforting his soul
With all her jasmine body sun-ensnared
He fed his longing eyes and, half in doubt,
With touches satisfied himself of her.
Hesitating he kissed her eyelids. Sighing
With a slight sob she woke and earthly large
Her eyes looked upward into his. She stretched
Her arms up, yearning, and their souls embraced;
Then twixt brief sobbing laughter and blissful tears,
Clinging with all her limbs to him, "O love,
The green green world! the warm sunlight!" and ceased,
Finding no words; but the earth breathed round them,
Glad of her children, and the koïl's voice
Persisted in the morning of the world.

A LETTER OF THE AUTHOR
ON
LOVE AND DEATH

The story of Ruru and Pramadvura — I have substituted a name [Priyumvada] more manageable to the English tongue — her death in the forest by the snake and restoration at the price of half her husband's life is told in the Mahabharata. It is a companion legend to the story of Savitri but not being told with any poetic skill or beauty has remained generally unknown. I have attempted in this poem to bring it out of its obscurity. For full success, however, it should have had a more faithfully Hindu colouring, but it was written a score of years ago [1899] when I had not penetrated to the heart of the Indian idea and its traditions, and the shadow of the Greek underworld and Tartarus with the sentiment of life and love and death which hangs about them has got into the legendary framework of the Indian Patala and hells. The central idea of the narrative alone is in the Mahabharata; the meeting with Kama and the descent into Hell were additions necessitated by the poverty of incident in the original story.

KHALED OF THE SEA

An Arabic Romance

An early work, conceived in twelve cantos with a Prologue and Epilogue, found unrevised and incomplete.

Prologue
- Alnuman and the Peri

Canto 1
- The Story of Alnuman and the Emir

Canto 2
- The Companions of Alnuman 1

Canto 3
- The Companions of Alnuman 2

Canto 4
- The Companions of Alnuman 3

Canto 5
- The First Quest of the Sapphire Crown

Canto 6
- The Quest of the Golden Snake

Canto 7
- The Quest of the Marble Queen

Canto 8
- The Quest of the Snowbird

Canto 9
- The Second Quest of the Sapphire Crown

Canto 10
- The Journey of the Green Oasis

Canto 11
- The Journey of the Irremeable Ocean

Canto 12
- The Journey of the Land without Pity

Epilogue
- The Arabian and the Caliph.

Prologue
Alnuman and the Peri

    In Bagdad by Euphrates, Asia's river,
    Euphrates that through deserts must deliver
    The voices which of human daybreaks are
    Into the dim mysterious surge afar,
    The Arabian dwelt; after long travel he
    Regions deserted, wastes of silent sea,
    Wide Ocean ignorant of ships and lands
    Never made glad by toil of mortal hands,
    For he had seen the Indian mountains bare
    Save of hard snow and the unbreathed huge air
    And swum through giant waters and had heard
    In those unhuman forests beast and bird,
    The peacock's cry and tiger's hoarse appeal
    Calling to God for prey, marked the vast wheel
    Of monstrous birds shadowing whole countries; he
    From Singhal through the long infinity
    Of southern floods had steered his shuddering ship
    Where unknown winds their lonely tumult keep
    And he had lived with strong and pitiless men,
    Nations unhumanised by joy and pain,
    And he had tasted grain not sown by man
    And drunk strange milk in weird Mazinderan.
    Silent he was, as one whom thoughts attend,
    Distant whom stiller hearts than ours befriend
    He lived with memories only; no sweet voice
    Made the mute echoes of his life rejoice;
    No lovely face of children brought the dawn
    Into his home; but silent, calm, withdrawn,
    He watched the ways of men with godlike eyes
    Released from trammelling affinities,[1]
    Yet was he young and many women strove
    Vainly to win his marble mind to love.
    One day when wind had fled to the cool north
    And the strong earth was blind with summer, forth
    The Arabian rode from great Bagdad and turned
    Into the desert. All around him burned

[1] Large as from commerce with infinities,

The imprisoned spirit of fire; above his head
The sky was like a tyranny outspread,
The sun a fire in those heavens, and fire
The sands beneath; the air burning desire
And breathless, a plumb weight of flame; yet rode
The Arabian unfeeling like a god.
Three hours he rode and now no more was seen
Bagdad, the imperial city, nor aught green,
But the illimitable sands around
Extend, a silent world waiting for sound,
When in the distance he descried a grace
Of motion beautiful in that dead place.
Wondering he turned, but suddenly the horse
Pricked up his slender ears, swerved from the course
And pawing stood the unwilling air, nor heard
The guiding voice nor the familiar word.
Whinnying with wrath he smote the desert sand
And mocked the rein and raged at the command.
Then raised the man his face and saw above
No cloud with the stark face of heaven strove,
A single blaze of light from pole to pole.
Smiling the Arabian spoke unto his soul.
"Here too then are you strong, O influences
That trouble the earth and air and the strong seas!
Therefore I will not stay your gathering wings
Who watch me from the air, you living things,
But go to find whatever peril or wonder
Wait me of life above the earth or under.
Strange will it be if quiet Bagdad yield
More terror or more sweetness than in field
Has stayed me yet or in untravelled flood
Or mountain or the tiger-throated wood."
So saying he grasped the strong and shaken mane
And set swift footing on that fiery plain.
At once the beast as if by sorcery
Strangely compelled, calmed his impetuous eye:
His angry tremor ceased and bounding wrath
Following unbidden in the Arabian's path.
But he with silent toil the sands untried
Vanquishing through that luminous world and wide

Went a slow shadow, till his feet untired
The fruit of all his labour long acquired.
Before a mile complete he was aware
Of a strange shape of beauty sitting there
On a sole boulder in the level wild,
Maiden, a marvellous bloom, a naked child;
All like a lily from her leaves escaped
The golden summer kissed her close and wrapped
In soft revealing sunshine, — a sweet bareness,
A creature made of flowers and choicest fairness;
And all her limbs were like a luminous dream,
So wonderfully white they burn and gleam,
Her shoulder ivory richly bathed in gold,
Her sides a snowy wonder to behold,
Marble made amorous; her body fair
Seemed one with the divine, translucent air,
A light within the light, a glorious treasure,
A thing to hold, to press, to slay with pleasure.
The girl was not alone, but with her watched
Two shapes of beauty and of terror hatched,
A strong, fierce snake, round her sweet middle twined,
A tigress at her lovely feet reclined.
Dreaming on those tremendous sands she waited
And often with that splendour miscreated
Played thoughtfully; about her wondrous knees
Binding the brilliant death or would increase
The whiteness of her limbs with its fierce hues
Or twine it in her tresses flowing loose.
Below that other restless evil played,
The fierce, sleek terror on the sands outspread.
First of the wonderful three rose with a bound
Waking the desert from its sleep with sound
The tigress, but the Arabian strode more near
As one who had forgotten how to fear
And frowning like a god with kingly look
He threatened the preparing death and shook
His javelin in the sun. Back crouched the fiend
Amazed nor could the steely light attend
Nor that unconquerable glance; yet lowered
To find her dreadful violence overpowered

By any smaller thing than death; and he
Heeded no more crouched limb nor stealthy eye.
He on that flowerlike shape a moment gazed
As one by strange felicity amazed,
Who, long grown sorrow's friend his whole life grieves,
Blest beyond expectation, scarce believes
That joy is in his heart, so gazed, so laid
At last upon the white and gleaming maid
The question of his hands. O soft and real
The nakedness he grasped, no marble ideal
Born of the blazing light and infinite air,
A breathing woman with lovely limbs and bare.
Then with a strong melodious voice he cried
And all his cheek was flushed with kingly[1] pride.
"Thou then art mine, after long labour mine,
O earthly body and O soul divine,
After long labour and thy sounding home
Hast left and caverns where thy sisters roam,
O dweller where the austral tempest raves!
O daughter of the wild and beautiful waves!
O breasts of beauty! O shoulder! my delight!
O luminously near! O woman white!
At length I grasp thee then and snared at length
The ivory swiftness of thy feet and strength
Of this immortal body shaped for kings,
O memory of sweet and dreadful things!
Ah, welcome to the streets that human tread
Makes musical and joy of human bread
Broken between dry hands and to the sight
Of the untroubled narrow rivers, light
Of lamps and warmth of kindled fires and man.
Fairer shall be thy feet on greensward than
On ocean rocks and O! more bright thy beauty
For human passion and for womanly duty
And softer in my bosom shalt thou sleep
Than lulled by the sublime and monstrous deep.
Much have I laboured; the resplendent face
Of summer I have hated, as the days
Went by and no delightful brook was found

[1] royal

Sprinkling with earth's cool love the ruthless ground,
And in my throat there was a desert's thirst
And on my tongue a fire: I have cursed
The spring and all its flowers; the wrathful cry
Of the wild waters and their cruelty
I have endured, labouring with sail and oar
Through the mad tempest for some human shore
And fought with winds and seen vast Hell aflame
Down in the nether flood till I became
Blind with the sight of those abysmal graves
And deaf with the eternal sound of waves
And all my heart was broken alone to be
Day after day with the unending sea.
And much on land I have laboured without moan
Or weakening tears making my heart a stone.
But thou art come and I shall hear no more
By inexorable rocks the Ocean roar,
Nor pine in dungeons far from pity or aid.
But in far other prison, seaborn maid,
Thy limbs shall minister to my delight
Even as an ordinary woman's might
And I shall hear thy voice around my heart
Like a cool rivulet and shall not start
To see thee ivory gleaming and all night
Shall feel thee in my arms, O darling white —
With after-joys that spring from these; the face
Of childish loveliness shall light my days,
About my doors the feet of children tread
And little heads with jonquils garlanded,
That often to sweetness win war-hardened eyes
And hearts grown iron their soft masteries
Compel and the light touch of little hands
Bend sworded fingers to their sweet commands.
O bright felicity, labour's dear end,
Into my arms, into my heart descend."
So as he spoke, the silent desert air
Lived with his gladness, and the maiden there
Listened with downcast lids and a soft flush
Upon her like the coming of a blush.
But when he finished and the air was mute,

She laughed with happy lips most like a flute
Or voice of cuckoo in an Indian grove
Waking the heart to vague delightful love.
And with divine eyes gleaming where strange mirth
A smiling mischief was, the living girth
Of her delicious waist she suddenly
Unbound and by the middle lifting high
Betwixt them shook. Hissed the fierce snake and raised
Its jewelled hood for spotted radiance praised,
Its jewelled hood to the dread leap intended;
Sad limit of noble life, had that descended.
Since short were his breath and evil, who that pang
Experienced; but before the serpent sprang,
Wrathful, the Arabian seized the glittering neck
And twines of bronze burning with many a fleck
Of coloured fire. His angry grasp to quell
Vainly the formidable folds rebel:
Not all that gordian force and slippery strength
Of coils availed. Inanimate at length
The immense destroyer on the Arabian's wrist
Hung in a ruin loose; and to resist
The wrath of love none now might intervene,
Nor she deny him. Yet with tranquil mien
Smiling she sat and swept with noble gesture
Her hair back that had fallen a purple investure
Over her glowing grace. Strong arms he cast
Around her naked loveliness and fast
Showered kisses on her limbs whose marble white
Grew woman with a soft and rosy light
In each kissed place. "Deemedst thou then," he cried,
"Bright fugitive, lovely wanderer with the tide,
By shaking death before death-practised eyes
My crown to wrest of strenuous enterprise,
Thyself, thyself and beauty? O too sweet
To touch our hard earth with thy faultless feet!
Yet on hard earth must dwell. For with the ground
Thy dreadful guardians who have fenced thee round
Are equalled, and thyself, sweet, though thou shame
The winds with swiftness or like mounting flame

Strive all thy days in my imprisoning arms
Couldst burn thyself no exit. With alarms
Menace and shapes of death; call on the flood
For thy deliverance on these sands to intrude
And lead thee to its jealous waters rude;
But hands that have flung back the swallowing sea
Shall stay and chastise and habituate thee
To yield sweet service due, being my slave
Bought with hard pains from the reluctant wave,
With pain ineffable bought and deep despair
And passion of impracticable care."
So saying he seized his lovely prize and grasping
Her fair soft arm in one hand, the other clasping
Her smooth desirèd thighs, from that rude seat,
The grey sun-blistered boulder most unmeet
To bear her snow-white radiance, lifted. She
As to his horse he bore her mightily,
A little strove in his strong arms, but round
Her lithe, reluctant limbs closer he bound
His despot hands and on the saddle set,
Never with such sweet rider burdened yet.
Then to his seat he sprang and musical
His cry in that vast silence, wherewithal
He urged his horse, which delicately went
Arching its neck with joy and proud content.
Great were the Arabian's labours; many seas
He had passed and borne impossible miseries
And battled with impracticable ills
O'er uncrossed rivers and forbidden hills,
Till nature fainted. Yet too little was this
To merit all the heaven now made his.
For she, earth's wonder, hard to grasp as fire,
She whom all ocean's secret depths admire,
Laid her delicious cheek to his and flung
Sweet, bare arms on his neck and round him clung:
Her snowy side was of his being a part;
Her naked breast burdened his throbbing heart,
And all her hair streamed over him and the whiteness
Of her was in his eyes and her soft brightness

A joy beneath his hands to his embrace
And he was clothed with her as in a dress.
Round them the strong recovered coils were rolled
Of the great snake and with imperious fold
Compelled their limbs together, and by their side
Pacing the tigress checked her dangerous stride.
So rode they like a vision. All the time
She murmured accents as of linkèd rhyme
Musical, in a language like the sea,
Accents of undulating melody.
For sometimes it was like a happy noon
Murmuring with waves and sometimes like the swoon
Of calm, a silence heard, or rich by noise
Of rivers pouring with their seaward voice
And leaping laughters and sometimes was wild
And passionate as the sobbing of a child.
But often it was like the cold salt spray
On a health-reddened cheek and glad with day
And life and sad with the far-moaning call
Of wind upon the waters funeral.
Not on the lips of man might fashioned be
A language of such wild variety.
Now of that magic tongue no separate word
Was of Alnuman understood or heard,
And yet he knew that of the caves she spoke
Where never earthly light of sunshine woke,
And of unfathomed things beneath the floods
And peopled depths and Ocean solitudes
And mighty creatures of the main and light
Of jewels making a subluminous night
Lower than even the dead may sink; and walls
Of coral and in what majestic halls
The naked sea-born sisters link their dance;
How sometimes on the shores their white limbs glance
In the mysterious moonlight; how they come
To river banks far from their secret home;
And last she spoke of mighty Love that reaches
Resistless arms beyond the long sea-beaches
And mocks the barriers of the storm, and how

Pearls unattainable a human brow
Have decked and man, the child of misery,
Been mated with the sisters of the sea.
So on she murmured like a ceaseless song
Making the weary sands a rapture; long
The patient desert round them waits; nor soon
The sun toiled through the endless afternoon:
But they paced always like a marvellous dream,
And dreamlike in the eyes of man might seem
Such magic vision (had human eyes been found
In the sole desert void of sign or bound), —
The horse that feared its dread companion not,
The kingly man with brow of reaching thought
And danger-hardened strength; fair as the morn,
The radiant girl upon his saddle borne,
Naked, a vision not of earth; the fell
Serpent that twined about them, terrible
With burning hues, and the fierce tigress there
Following with noiseless step the godlike pair.
Nor when to Bagdad and its street they came,
Did any eye behold. Only a name
Was in the ears of the grim warders. Straight
Like engines blind of some overmastering fate
They rose, the mighty bolts they drew; loud jarred
The doors unhearing with deaf iron barred
And groaned upon their road; then backward swung
Whirling and kissed again with clamorous tongue;
Nor in the streets was any step of man,
Before loud wheels no swift torchbearers ran
Setting the night on fire; bright and rare
The garlanded high-shuttered windows, where
Men revelled and sound into the shadows cast:
All else was night and silence where they passed.
So is the beautiful sea-stranger gone
To her new home, who now no more must run
Upon the bounding waves, nor feel the sun.
On wind-blown limbs, destined a mortal's bride.
So is the strong Arabian deified
In bliss. Moreover from the wondrous night

When with those small beloved feet grew bright
His lonely house, wealth like a sea swept through
Its doors and as a dwelling of gods it grew
In beauty and in brightness. All that thrives
Costly or fragrant upon earth or lives
Of riches in the hoarding ocean lost
And all bright things with gold or gems embossed
By Indian or by Syrian art refined
And all rich cloths and silks with jewels lined
Regal Bokhara weaves or Samarcand,
Increased and gathered to Alnuman's hand
And girls of glorious limb and feature he
Bought for his slaves, of rose and ivory,
Sweet Persians with the honey-hiding mouth
And passionate Arab girls and strong-limbed youth
Of Tartar maidens for his harem doors.
For now not vainly the fair child implores
Of Shaikh or of Emir his love for boon,
But with high marriage-rites some prosperous moon
At last has brought into the marble pride
Of that great house for envy edified.
So in Bagdad the Arabian dwelt nor seemed
Other his life than theirs who never dreamed
Beyond earth's ken, nor made in sun and breeze
Their spirits great with shock of the strong seas,
Nor fortified their hearts with pains sublime
Nor wrestled with the bounds of space and time.
Like common men he lived to whom the ray
Of a new sun but brings another day
Unmeaning, who in their own selves confined
Know not the grandeur which the mightier mind
Inherits when it makes the destinies rude
The chisel by which its marble mass and crude
With God's or hero's likeness is indued.
Yet this was also rumoured that within
The sheath of that calm life he sojourned in
An edge of flaming rapture was, that things
Beyond all transitory imaginings
Came to him secret and vast pleasures more

Than frail humanity had dared to feel before.
Since too much joy man's heart can hardly bear
And all too weak man's narrow senses were
For raptures that eternal spirits attain
In sensuous heavens ignorant of pain.
Yet even such raptures mortal man's could be
Wed with the child of the unbounded sea.

Canto I

The Story of Almaimun[1] and the Emir's Daughter

Now in great Bagdad of the Abbasside
The wanderer rests, to peace at last allied,
Whom storm so long had tossed to storm, and grace
Of love dwelt with him and the nobleness
Of hearts made golden by felicity,
Which is earth's preferable alchemy.
The other is from pain the metal wrought,
Anguish and wrestling in the coils of thought.
These strengthen, these the mind as marble hard
Make and as marble pure, which has not feared
To scourge itself with insight; but the stress
Of joy heightened to self-forgetfulness
Is sweeter and to sweeter uses tends.
With such felicity were crowned the friends
And lovers of Almaimun and increase
In the glad strength that grows from boundless peace.
And each as to her orb the sunflower burns
His spirit to his spirit's image turns.
Such puissance great well-poisèd natures prove
To mould to their own likeness all they love.
But where is she who lit his doubtful morn,
Whose sweet imagined shape each hour new-born
Brightened but to illumine, kindled each
Stray look with godhead and her daily speech
A far ethereal music made, for whom
He sought the wild waves and the peopled gloom
Of the unseen? Must only she make moan?
She in the crowded chambers is alone
And closes eyes kept dry by anguished pride
To wake in tears that hardly will be dried.
Happy the heart and more than earthly blest
That for those hands was meant where 'tis possessed
That to no alien house at the end has come
But winging goes as to its natural home.
The evening bird with no more simple flight

[1] Name changed in MS. on this page.

Reaches its one unfailing nest at night.
The heart which Fate not always here perverse
With the one possible home out of an universe,
Makes simply happy there secure shall dwell,
Feeling that to be there is only well
And equal happy whether queenly chair
Her portion or she kneel loose-girdled there
And serve him as a slave. Alike 'tis heaven,
Rule or obedience to the one heart given.
So did not bright Zuleikha deem when she
The temple was of his idolatry.
Impatient of divine subjection, all
Love's wealth was to her grace imperial
Purple and diadems and earth's noblest gift
But vantage her disdainful pride to lift.
She was an Emir's daughter and her sire
Clothed her in jewels and sublime attire,
From silver dishes fed and emerald
And in a world of delicate air installed
So that her nature with these costly things
Being burdened raised in vain its heavenward wings.
From Koraish and the Abbasside he drew
His stern extraction. Yet what brighter grew
About his formidable name accursed
Was a white fire of riches and the thirst
Of poor men gazing with a bitter stealth
On that impossibility of wealth.
"Abdullah, the Emir", so men would say
Drawing their rags about them, "has display
Of gold and silver and the sunlight fades
At noon in his wide treasury and the shades
Of midnight are more luminous there than birth
Of day upon the ordinary earth.
He has rich garments, would the naked clothe
From Bagdad to the sea, were he not loth;
The leavings of his menials far exceed
In Khorassan the labourer's sharpened need,
And since by thee this fair display was planned,
O God, yet from the beggar's outstretched hand
He guards his boundless trust ignobly well,

Just Lord, display to him the fires of Hell."
And here another pressing from his eye
His children's pining looks, made sad reply:
"Richer his wealth than widest chambers hold,
Not in the weary heaps of ingots told
Entirely, nor the cloths Damascus yields,
Nor what the seas give up, nor what the fields.
He gathers ever with exhaustless hands:
His camels heave across the endless sands.
Through Balkh when to Caboul or Candahar
The wains go groaning or the evening star
Watches the pomp of the wide caravan
Intend to provinces Arabian,
Half is Abdullah the Emir's: and he
Gets spices of the south and porphyry;
His are the Chinese silks, the Indian work
Saved hardly from the horsehooves of the Turk;
From Balsora the ships that o'er the bar
Reel into Ocean's grasp, Abdullah's are;
Yemen's far ports are with his ventures full;
Muscat transmits him horses, arms and wool.
The desert rider hopes no richer prize
To handle than Abdullah's merchandize;
With joy the Malayan sea-robber hails
His argosy and for his western sails
The Moorish pirates all the horizon scan
Upon the far Mediterranean.
Yet though his losses make the desert great
And Ocean a new treasury create
From his sole rapine, yet untouched endure
His riches by that vast expenditure.
He takes but to increase his piles of gold,
He gives but to recover hundredfold.
Thereby the poor increase. Wherefore I trust,
When Azrael shall smite his limbs to dust
And he upon that dolorous bridge is led
Which, lord and peasant, all must one day tread,
The bitter sword that spans the nether hell,
He may be evened with the infidel."
And one might answer mid these wretched men

Who quiet was from constancy to pain:
"Curse him not either lest the Kazi find
And God loose not the chains that he shall bind."
For he indeed was mighty in the town,
A man acceptable in his renown.
The Mullahs to his will interpreted
Their books and the law's lightning from his head
Glanced on the rash accuser; for his word
Was Hédoya before the Kazi heard.
But whence the fountain of his wealth might flow
Well did the sad and toiling peasant know.
For he as governor in Khorassan
Had held the balance betwixt man and man
And justified his rule benevolent
By rape and torture for their own good meant,
The fallen roof-tree and the broken door
And rents wrung from the miserable poor.
And now hemmed in with lustrous things and proud,
Each day a pomp, each night with music loud,
He blazed, however his eye a darkness cast
And pleasure by his sense external passed.
Yet joy he had over his gathered gold
And in that one sweet maiden joy untold.
Daughter of Noureddin the Barmecide
Was she who bore this brightness, but when died
Jaafar and all his house fell like a tower
Loosened in the mutation of an hour,
Abdullah found his foe an outlawed man,
Proscribed, a heretic and Persian
And slew him with the sword juridical
Between his golden house and Allah's wall.

(Incomplete)

BAJI PRABHOU
Author's Note

This poem is founded on the historical incident of the heroic self-sacrifice of Baji Prabhou Deshpande, who to cover Shivaji's retreat, held the pass of Rangana for two hours with a small company of men against twelve thousand Moguls. Beyond the single fact of this great exploit there has been no attempt to preserve historical accuracy.

Baji Prabhou

A noon of Deccan with its tyrant glare
Oppressed the earth; the hills stood deep in haze,
And sweltering athirst the fields glared up
Longing for water in the courses parched
Of streams long dead. Nature and man alike,
Imprisoned by a bronze and brilliant sky,
Sought an escape from that wide trance of heat.
Nor on rare herdsman only or patient hind
Tilling the earth or tending sleeplessly
The well-eared grain that burden fell. It hung
Upon the Mogul horsemen as they rode
With lances at the charge, the surf of steel
About them and behind, as they recoiled
Or circled, where the footmen ran and fired,
And fired again and ran; "For now at last,"
They deemed, "the war is over, now at last
The panther of the hills is beaten back
Right to his lair, the rebel crew to death
Is hunted, and an end is made at last."
Therefore they stayed not for the choking dust,
The slaying heat, the thirst of wounds and fight,
The stumbling stark fatigue, but onward pressed
With glowing eyes. Far otherwise the foe,
Panting and sore oppressed and racked with thirst
And blinded with the blazing earth who reeled
Backward to Raigurh, moistening with their blood
Their mother, and felt their own beloved hills
A nightmare hell of death and heat, the sky
A mute and smiling witness of their dire
Anguish, — abandoned now of God and man,
Who for their country and their race had striven, —
In vain, it seemed. At morning when the sun
Was yet below the verge, the Bhonsle sprang
At a high mountain fortress, hoping so
To clutch the whole wide land into his grasp;
But from the North and East the Moguls poured,
Swords numberless and hooves that shook the hills
And barking of a hundred guns. These bore

The hero backward. Silently with set
And quiet faces grim drew fighting back
The strong Mahrattas to their hills; only
Their rear sometimes with shouted slogan leaped
At the pursuer's throat, or on some rise
Or covered vantage stayed the Mogul flood
A moment. Ever foremost where men fought,
Was Baji Prabhou seen, like a wild wave
Of onset or a cliff against the surge.
At last they reached a tiger-throated gorge
Upon the way to Raigurh. Narrowing there
The hills draw close, and their forbidding cliffs
Threaten the prone incline. The Bhonsle paused,
His fiery glance travelled in one swift gyre
Hill, gorge and valley and with speed returned
Mightily like an eagle on the wing
To a dark youth beside him, Malsure
The younger, with his bright and burning eyes,
Who wordless rode quivering, as on the leash;
His fierce heart hungered for the rear, where Death
Was singing mid the laughter of the swords.
"Ride, Suryaji," the Chieftain cried, his look
Inward, intent, "and swiftly from the rear
Summon the Prabhou." Turning at the word
Suryaji's hooves sped down the rock-strewn slope
Into the trenchant valley's death. Swiftly,
Though burdened with a nation's fate, the ridge
They reached, where in stern silence fought and fell,
Their iron hearts broken with desperate toil,
The Southron rear, and to the Prabhou gave
The summons of the Chief: "Ride, Baji, ride,
The Bhonsle names thee, Baji." And Baji spoke
No word, but stormed with loose and streaming rein
To the high frowning gorge and silent paused
Before the leader. "Baji, more than once
In battle thou hast stood, a living shield,
Between me and the foe. But more today,
O Baji, save than any single life, —
Thy nation's destiny. Thou seest this gorge
Narrow and fell and gleaming like the throat

Of some huge tiger, with its rocky fangs
Agrin for food: and though the lower slope
Descends too gently, yet with roots and stones
It is hampered, and the higher prone descent
Impregnably forbids assault; too steep
The sides for any to ascend and shoot
From vantage. Here might lion-hearted men,
Though few, delay a host. Baji, I speed
To Raigurh and in two brief hours return.
Say with what force thy iron heart can hold
The passage till I come. Thou seest our strength,
How it has melted like the Afghan's ice
Into a pool of blood." And while he paused
Who had been chosen, spoke an iron man
With iron brows who rode behind the Chief,
Tanaji Malsure, that living sword:
"Not for this little purpose was there need
To call the Prabhou from his toil. Enough,
Give me five hundred men; I hold the pass
Till thy return." But Shivaji kept still
His great and tranquil look upon the face
Of Baji Prabhou. Then, all black with wrath,
Wrinkling his fierce hard eyes, the Malsure:
"What ponders then the hero? Such a man
Of men, he needs not like us petty swords
A force behind him, but alone will hold
All Rajasthan and Agra and Cabool
From rise to set." And Baji answered him:
"Tanaji Malsure, not in this living net
Of flesh and nerve, nor in the flickering mind
Is a man's manhood seated. God within
Rules us, who in the Brahmin and the dog
Can, if He will, show equal godhead. Not
By men is mightiness achieved; Baji
Or Malsure is but a name, a robe,
And covers One alone. We but employ
Bhavani's strength, who in an arm of flesh
Is mighty as in the thunder and the storm.
I ask for fifty swords." And Malsure:
"Well, Baji, I will build thee such a pyre

As man had never yet, when we return;
For all the Deccan brightening shall cry out,
Baji the Prabhou burns!" And with a smile
The Prabhou answered: "Me thou shalt not burn.
For this five feet or more of bone and flesh,
Whether pure flame or jackals of the hills
Be fattened with its rags, may well concern
Others, not Baji Prabhou." And the Chief
With a high calmness in his shining look,
"We part, O friend, but meet again we must,
When from our tasks released we both shall run
Like children to our Mother's clasp." He took
From his wide brow the princely turban sown
With aigrette diamond-crowned and on the head
Of Baji set the gleaming sign, then clasped
His friend and, followed by the streaming host
That gathered from the rear, to farther hills
Rode clattering. By the Mogul van approached
Baji and his Mahrattas sole remained
Watched by the mountains in the silent gorge.

Small respite had the slender band who held
Fate constant with that brittle hoop of steel;
For like the crest of an arriving wave
The Moslem van appeared, though slow and tired,
Yet resolute to break such barrier faint,
And forced themselves to run: — nor long availed;
For with a single cry the muskets spoke,
Once and again and always, as they neared,
And, like a wave arrested, for a while
The assailants paused and like a wave collapsed
Spent backward in a cloud of broken spray,
Retreating. Yielding up, the dangerous gorge
Saw only on the gnarled and stumbling rise
The dead and wounded heaped. But from the rear
The main tremendous onset of the North
Came in a dark and undulating surge
Regardless of the check, — a mingled mass,
Pathan and Mogul and the Rajput clans,
All clamorous with the brazen throats of war

And spitting smoke and fire. The bullets rang
Upon the rocks, but in their place unhurt,
Sheltered by tree and rock, the silent grim
Defenders waited, till on root and stone
The confident high-voiced triumphant surge
Began to break, to stumble, then to pause,
Confusion in its narrowed front. At once
The muskets clamoured out, the bullets sped,
Deadly though few; again and yet again,
And some of the impetuous faltered back
And some in wrath pressed on; and while they swayed
Poised between flight and onset, blast on blast
The volleyed death invisible hailed in
Upon uncertain ranks. The leaders fell,
The forward by the bullets chosen out,
Prone or supine or leaning like sick men
O'er trees and rocks, distressed the whole advance
With prohibition by the silent slain.
So the great onset failed. And now withdrawn
The generals consulted, and at last
In slow and ordered ranks the foot came on,
An iron resolution in their tread,
Hushed and deliberate. Far in the van,
Tall and large-limbed, a formidable array,
The Pathan infantry; a chosen force,
Lower in crest, strong-framed, the Rajputs marched;
The chivalry of Agra led the rear.
Then Baji first broke silence, "Lo, the surge!
That was but spray of death we first repelled.
Chosen of Shivaji, Bhavani's swords,
For you the gods prepare. We die indeed,
But let us die with the high-voiced assent
Of Heaven to our country's claim enforced
To freedom." As he spoke, the Mogul lines
Entered the menacing wide-throated gorge,
Carefully walking, but not long that care
Endured, for where they entered, there they fell.
Others behind in silence stern advanced.
They came, they died; still on the previous dead
New dead fell thickening. Yet by paces slow

The lines advanced with labour infinite
And merciless expense of valiant men.
For even as the slopes were filled and held,
Still the velocity and lethal range
Increased of the Mahratta bullets; dead
Rather than living held the conquered slope, —
The living who, half-broken, paused. Abridged,
Yet wide, the interval opposed advance,
Daunting those resolute natures; eyes once bold
With gloomy hesitation reckoned up
The dread equivalent in human lives
Of cubits and of yards, and hardly hoped
One could survive the endless unacquired
Country between. But from the Southron wall
The muskets did not hesitate, but urged
Refusal stern; the bullets did not pause,
Nor calculate expense. Active they thronged
Humming like bees and stung strong lives to death
Making a holiday of carnage. Then
The heads that planned pushed swiftly to the front
The centre yet unhurt, where Rajasthan,
Playmate of death, had sent her hero sons.
They with a rapid royal reckless pace
Came striding over the perilous fire-swept ground,
Nor answered uselessly the bullets thick
Nor paused to judge, but o'er the increasing dead
Leaping and striding, shouting, sword in hand,
Rushed onward with immortal courage high
In mortal forms, and held the lower slope.
But now the higher incline, short but steep,
Baffled their speed, and as they clambered up,
Compact and fiery, like the rapid breath
Of Agra's hot simoom, the sheeted flame
Belched bullets. Down they fell with huge collapse,
And, rolling, with their shock drove back the few
Who still attempted. Banned advance, retreat
Threatening disgrace and slaughter, for a while
Like a bound sacrifice the Rajputs stood
Diminishing each moment. Then a lord
High-crested of the Rathore clan stood out

From the perplexed assailants, with his sword
Beckoning the thousands on against the few.
And him the bullets could not touch; he stood
Defended for a moment by his lease
Not yet exhausted. And a mighty shout
Rose from behind, and in a violent flood
The Rajputs flung themselves on the incline
Like clambering lions. Many hands received
The dead as they descended, flinging back
Those mournful obstacles, and with a rush
The lead surmounted and on level ground
Stood sword in hand; yet only for a while, —
For grim and straight the slogan of the South
Leaped with the fifty swords to thrust them back,
Baji the Prabhou leading. Thrice they came,
Three times prevailed, three times the Southron charge
Repelled them; till at last the Rathore lord,
As one appointed, led the advancing death,
Nor waited to assure his desperate hold,
But hurled himself on Baji; those behind
Bore forward those in front. From right and left
Mahratta muskets rang their music out
And withered the attack that, still dissolved,
Still formed again from the insistent rear
And would not end. So was the fatal gorge
Filled with the clamour of the close-locked fight.
Sword rang on sword, the slogan shout, the cry
Of guns, the hiss of bullets filled the air,
And murderous strife heaped up the scanty space,
Rajput and strong Mahratta breathing hard
In desperate battle. But far off the hosts
Of Agra stood arrested, confident,
Waiting the end. Far otherwise it came
Than they expected. For, as in the front
The Rathore stood on the disputed verge
And ever threw fresh strength into the scale
With that inspiring gesture, Baji came
Towards him singling out the lofty crest,
The princely form: and, as the waves divide
Before a driving keel, the battle so

Before him parted, till he neared, he slew.
Avoiding sword, avoiding lifted arm
The blade surprised the Rajput's throat, and down
As falls an upright poplar, with his hands
Outspread, dying, he clutched Mahratta ground.
Loud rose the slogan as he fell. Amazed,
The eager hosts of Agra saw reel back
The Rajput battle, desperate victory
Turned suddenly into entire defeat,
Not headlong, but with strong discouragement,
Sullen, convinced, rejecting the emprise.
As they retired, the brilliant Pathan van
Assumed the attempt. "Exhaust," the generals cried,
"Exhaust the stubborn mountaineers; for now
Fatigued with difficult effort and success
They hardly stand, weary, unstrung, inert.
Scatter this fringe, and we march on and seize
Raigurh and Shivaji." Meanwhile, they too
Not idle, covered by the rocks and trees,
Straining for vantage, pausing on each ledge,
Seizing each bush, each jutting promontory,
Some iron muscles, climbing, of the south
Lurked on the gorge's gloomy walls unseen.
On came the Pathans running rapidly,
But as the nearmost left the rocky curve
Where lurked the ambush, loud from stone and tree
The silence spoke; sideways, in front, behind
Death clamoured, and tall figures strewed the ground
Like trees in a cyclone. Appalled the rest
Broke this way and broke that, and some cried, "On!"
Some shouted, "Back!" for those who led, fell fast.
So the advance dissolved, divided, — the more
In haste towards the plains, greeted with death
Even while they ran; but others forward, full
Of panic courage, drove towards the foe
They could not reach, — so hot a blast and fell
Stayed their unsteady valour, their retreat
So swift and obstinate a question galled,
Few through the hail survived. With gloom their chiefs
Beheld the rout and drawing back their hosts

In dubious council met, whether to leave
That gorge of slaughter unredeemed or yet
Demand the price of so immense a loss.

But to the Prabhou came with anxious eyes
The Captain of the band. "Baji," he cried,
"The bullets fail; all the great store we had
Of shot and powder by unsparing use
Is spent, is ended." And Baji Prabhou turned.
One look he cast upon the fallen men
Discernible by their attire, and saw
His ranks not greatly thinned, one look below
Upon the hundreds strewing thick the gorge,
And grimly smiled; then where the sun in fire
Descending stooped, towards the vesper verge
He gazed and cried: "Make iron of your souls.
Yet if Bhavani wills, strength and the sword
Can stay our nation's future from o'erthrow
Till victory with Shivaji return."
And so they waited without word or sound,
And over them the silent afternoon
Waited; the hush terrestrial was profound.
Except the mountains and the fallen men
No sight, no voice, no movement was abroad,
Only a few black-winged slow-circling birds
That wandered in the sky, only the wind
That now arose and almost noiselessly
Questioned the silence of the wooded sides,
Only the occasional groan that marked the pang
By some departing spirit on its frame
Inflicted. And from time to time the gaze
Of Baji sought the ever-sinking sun.
Men fixed their eyes on him and in his firm
Expression lived. So the slow minutes passed.
But when the sun dipped very low, a stir
Was felt far off, and all men grasped the hilt
Tighter and put a strain upon their hearts.
Resolved at last the stream of Mogul war
Came once more pouring, not the broken rout
Of Pathans, not discouraged Rajput swords,

But Agra's chivalry glancing with gold
And scimitars inlaid and coloured robes.
Swiftly they came expecting the assault
Fire-winged of bullets and the lethal rain,
But silence met them and to their intent
So ominous it seemed, awhile they paused,
Fearing some ruse, though for much death prepared,
Yet careful of prevention. Reassured,
Onward with a high shout they charged the slope.
No bullet sped, no musket spoke; unhurt
They crossed the open space, unhurt they climbed
The rise; but even as their hands surprised
The shrubs that fringed the vantage, swords unseen
Hacked at their fingers, through the bushes thrust
Lances from warriors unexposed bore through
Their bosoms. From behind the nearest lines
Pressed on to share their fate, and still the sea
Of men bore onward till with violent strain
They reached the perilous crest; there for a while
A slaughter grim went on and all the verge
Was heaped and walled and thickly fortified
With splendid bodies. But as they were piled,
The raging hosts behind tore down their dead
And mounted, till at last the force prevailed
Of obstinate numbers and upon a crest
Swarming with foemen fought 'gainst desperate odds
The Southron few. Small was the space for fight,
And meeting strength with skill and force with soul
The strong and agile keepers of the hills
Prevailed against the city-dwelling hosts,
With covert and the swiftly stabbing blades
O'erpowering all the feints of Agra's schools.
So fought they for a while; then suddenly
Upon the Prabhou all the Goddess came.
Loud like a lion hungry on the hills
He shouted, and his stature seemed to increase
Striding upon the foe. Rapid his sword
Like lightning playing with a cloud made void
The crest before him, on his either side
The swordsmen of the South with swift assault

Preventing the reply, till like a bank
Of some wild river the assault collapsed
Over the stumbling edge and down the rise,
And once again the desperate moment passed.
The relics of the murderous strife remained,
Corpses and jewels, broidery and gold.
But not for this would they accept defeat.
Once more they came and almost held. Then wrath
Rose in the Prabhou and he raised himself
In soul to make an end; but even then
A stillness fell upon his mood and all
That godlike impulse faded from his heart,
And passing out of him a mighty form
Stood visible, Titanic, scarlet-clad,
Dark as a thunder-cloud, with streaming hair
Obscuring heaven, and in her sovran grasp
The sword, the flower, the boon, the bleeding head, —
Bhavani. Then she vanished; the daylight
Was ordinary in a common world.
And Baji knew the goddess formidable
Who watches over India till the end.
Even then a sword found out his shoulder, sharp
A Mogul lance ran griding through his arm.
Fiercely around him gathered in a knot
The mountaineers; but Baji, with a groan,
"Moro Deshpande, to the other side
Hasten of the black gorge and bring me word.
Rides any from the West, or canst thou hear
The Raigurh trumpets blow? I know my hour
Is ended; let me know my work is done."
He spoke and shouted high the slogan loud.
Desperate, he laboured in his human strength
To push the Mogul from the gorge's end
With slow compulsion. By his side fell fast
Mahratta and Mogul and on his limbs
The swords drank blood, a single redness grew
His body, yet he fought. Then at his side
Ghastly with wounds and in his fiery eyes
Death and rejoicing a dire figure stood,
Moro Deshpande. "Baji, I have seen

The Raigurh lances; Baji, I have heard
The trumpets." Conquering with his cry the din
He spoke, then dead upon a Mogul corpse
Fell prone. And Baji with a gruesome hand
Wiping the blood from his fierce staring eyes
Saw round him only fifteen men erect
Of all his fifty. But in front, behind,
On either side the Mogul held the gorge.
Groaning, once more the grim Mahratta turned
And like a bull with lowered horns that runs,
Charged the exultant foe behind. With him
The desperate survivors hacking ran,
And as a knife cuts instantly its way
Through water, so the yielding Mogul wall
Was cleft and closed behind. Eight men alone
Stood in the gorge's narrow end, not one
Unwounded. There where hardly three abreast
Have room to stand, they faced again the foe;
And from this latest hold Baji beheld
Mounting the farther incline, rank on rank,
A mass of horsemen; galloped far in front
Some forty horse, and on a turbaned head
Bright in the glory of the sinking sun
A jewelled aigrette blazed. And Baji looked
Over the wide and yawning field of space
And seemed to see a fort upon a ridge,
Raigurh; then turned and sought again the war.
So for few minutes desperately they strove.
Man after man of the Mahrattas fell
Till only three were left. Then suddenly
Baji stood still and sank upon the ground.
Quenched was the fiery gaze, nerveless the arm:
Baji lay dead in the unconquered gorge.
But ere he fell, upon the rocks behind
The horse-hooves rang and, as the latest left
Of the half hundred died, the bullets thronged
Through the too narrow mouth and hurled those down
Who entered. Clamorous, exultant blared
The Southron trumpets, but with stricken hearts
The swords of Agra back recoiled; fatal

Upon their serried unprotected mass
In hundreds from the verge the bullets rained,
And in a quick disordered stream, appalled,
The Mogul rout began. Sure-footed, swift
The hostile strength pursued, Suryaji first
Shouting aloud and singing to the hills
A song of Ramdas as he smote and slew.
But Shivaji by Baji's empty frame
Stood silent and his gaze was motionless
Upon the dead. Tanaji Malsure
Stood by him and observed the breathless corpse,
Then slowly said, "Thirty and three the gates
By which thou enterest heaven, thou fortunate soul,
Thou valiant heart. So when my hour arrives,
May I too clasp my death, saving the land
Or winning some great fortress for my lord."
But Shivaji beside the dead beheld
A dim and mighty cloud that held a sword
And in its other hand, where once the head
Depended bleeding, raised the turban bright
From Baji's brows, still glittering with its gems,
And placed it on the chief's. But as it rose
Blood-stained with the heroic sacrifice,
Round the aigrette he saw a golden crown.

THE RISHI

The Rishi

(King Manu in the former ages of the world, when the Arctic continent still subsisted, seeks knowledge from the Rishi of the Pole, who after long baffling him with conflicting side-lights of the knowledge, reveals to him what it chiefly concerns man to know.)

    MANU

Rishi who trance-held on the mountains old
    Art slumbering, void
Of sense or motion, for in the spirit's hold
    Of unalloyed
Immortal bliss thou dreamst protected! Deep
    Let my voice glide
Into thy dumb retreat and break that sleep
    Abysmal. Hear!
The frozen snows that heap thy giant bed
    Ice-cold and clear,
The chill and desert heavens above thee spread
    Vast, austere,
Are not so sharp but that thy warm limbs brook
    Their bitter breath,
Are not so wide as thy immense outlook
    On life and death:
Their vacancy thy silent mind and bright
    Outmeasureth.
But ours are blindly active and thy light
    We have forgone.

    RISHI

Who art thou, warrior armèd gloriously
    Like the sun?
Thy gait is as an empire and thine eye
    Dominion.

    MANU

King Manu, of the Aryan peoples lord,
    Greets thee, Sage.

RISHI

I know thee, King, earth to whose sleepless sword
    Was heritage.
The high Sun's distant glories gave thee forth
    On being's edge:
Where the slow skies of the auroral North
    Lead in the morn
And flaming dawns for ever on heaven's verge
    Wheel and turn,
Thundering remote the clamorous Arctic surge
    Saw thee born.
There 'twas thy lot these later Fates to build,
    This race of man
New-fashion. O Watcher with the mountains wild,
    The icy plain,
Thee I too, asleep, have watched, both when the Pole
    Was brightening wan
And when like a wild beast the darkness stole
    Prowling and slow
Alarming with its silent march the soul.
    O King, I know
Thy purpose; for the vacant ages roll
    Since man below
Conversed with God in friendship. Thou, reborn
    For men perplexed,
Seekest in this dim aeon and forlorn
    With evils vexed
The vanished light. For like this Arctic land
    Death has annexed
To sleep, our being's summits cold and grand
    Where God abides,
Repel the tread of thought. I too, O King,
    In winds and tides
Have sought Him, and in armies thundering,
    And where Death strides
Over whole nations. Action, thought and peace
    Were questioned, sleep,
And waking, but I had no joy of these,
    Nor ponderings deep,

And pity was not sweet enough, nor good
    My will could keep.
Often I found Him for a moment, stood
    Astonished, then
It fell from me. I could not hold the bliss,
    The force for men,
My brothers. Beauty ceased my heart to please,
    Brightness in vain
Recalled the vision of the light that glows
    Suns behind:
I hated the rich fragrance of the rose;
    Weary and blind,
I tired of the suns and stars; then came
    With broken mind
To heal me of the rash devouring flame,
    The dull disease,
And sojourned with this mountain's summits bleak,
    These frozen seas.
King, the blind dazzling snows have made me meek,
    Cooled my unease.
Pride could not follow, nor the restless will
    Come and go;
My mind within grew holy, calm and still
    Like the snow.

    MANU

O thou who wast with chariots formidable
    And with the bow!
Voiceless and white the cold unchanging hill,
    Has it then
A mightier presence, deeper mysteries
    Than human men?
The warm low hum of crowds, towns, villages,
    The sun and rain,
The village maidens to the water bound,
    The happy herds,
The fluting of the shepherd lads, the sound
    Myriad of birds,
Speak these not clearer to the heart, convey
    More subtle words?

Here is but great dumb night, an awful day
    Inert and dead.

RISHI

The many's voices fill the listening ear,
    Distract the head:
The One is silence; on the snows we hear
    Silence tread.

MANU

What hast thou garnered from the crags that lour,
    The icy field?

RISHI

O King, I spurned this body's death; a Power
    There was, concealed,
That raised me. Rescued from the pleasant bars
    Our longings build,
My wingèd soul went up above the stars
    Questing for God.

MANU

Oh, didst thou meet Him then? in what bright field
    Upon thy road?

RISHI

I asked the heavenly wanderers as they wheeled
    For His abode.

MANU

Could glorious Saturn and his rings of hue
    Direct thy flight?

RISHI

Sun could not tell, nor any planet knew
    Its source of light,
Nor could I glean that knowledge though I paced
    The worlds beyond
And into outer nothingness have gazed.
    Time's narrow sound

I crossed, the termless flood where on the Snake
    One slumbers throned,
Attempted. But the ages from Him break
    Blindly and Space
Forgets its origin. Then I returned
    Where luminous blaze
Deathless and ageless in their ease unearned
    The ethereal race.

    MANU

Did the gods tell thee? Has Varuna seen
    The high God's face?

    RISHI

How shall they tell of Him who marvel at sin
    And smile at grief?

    MANU

Did He not send His blissful Angels down
    For thy relief?

    RISHI

The Angels know Him not, who fear His frown,
    Have fixed belief.

    MANU

Is there no heaven of eternal light
    Where He is found?

    RISHI

The heavens of the Three have beings bright
    Their portals round,
And I have journeyed to those regions blest,
    Those hills renowned.
In Vishnu's house where wide Love builds his nest,
    My feet have stood.

    MANU

Is he not That, the blue-winged Dove of peace,
    Father of Good?

RISHI

Nor Brahma, though the suns and hills and seas
    Are called his brood.

MANU

Is God a dream then? are the heavenly coasts
    Visions vain?

RISHI

I came to Shiva's roof; the flitting ghosts
    Compelled me in.

MANU

Is He then God whom the forsaken seek,
    Things of sin?

RISHI

He sat on being's summit grand, a peak
    Immense of fire.

MANU

Knows He the secret of release from tears
    And from desire?

RISHI

His voice is the last murmur silence hears,
    Tranquil and dire.

MANU

The silence calls us then and shall enclose?

RISHI

    Our true abode
Is here and in the pleasant house He chose
    To harbour God.

MANU

In vain thou hast travelled the unwonted stars
    And the void hast trod!

RISHI

King, not in vain. I knew the tedious bars
  That I had fled,
To be His arms whom I have sought; I saw
  How earth was made
Out of His being; I perceived the Law,
  The Truth, the Vast,
From which we came and which we are; I heard
  The ages past
Whisper their history, and I knew the Word
  That forth was cast
Into the unformed potency of things
  To build the suns.
Through endless Space and on Time's iron wings
  A rhythm runs
Our lives pursue, and till the strain's complete
  That now so moans
And falters, we upon this greenness meet,
  That measure tread.

MANU

Is earth His seat? this body His poor hold
  Infirmly made?

RISHI

I flung off matter like a robe grown old;
  Matter was dead.

MANU

Sages have told of vital force behind:
  It is God then?

RISHI

The vital spirits move but as a wind
  Within men.

MANU

Mind then is lord that like a sovereign sways
  Delight and pain?

RISHI

Mind is His wax to write and, written, rase
　　Form and name.

MANU

Is thought not He who has immortal eyes
　　Time cannot dim?

RISHI

Higher, O King, the still voice bade me rise
　　Than thought's clear dream.
Deep in the luminous secrecy, the mute
　　Profound of things,
Where murmurs never sound of harp or lute
　　And no voice sings,
Light is not, nor our darkness, nor these bright
　　Thunderings,
In the deep steady voiceless core of white
　　And burning bliss,
The sweet vast centre and the cave divine
　　Called Paradise,
He dwells within us all who dwells not in
　　Aught that is.

MANU

Rishi, thy thoughts are like the blazing sun
　　Eye cannot face.
How shall our souls on that bright awful One
　　Hope even to gaze
Who lights the world from His eternity
　　With a few rays?

RISHI

Dare on thyself to look, thyself art He,
　　O Aryan, then.
There is no thou nor I, beasts of the field,
　　Nor birds, nor men,
But flickerings on a many-sided shield
　　Pass and remain,

And this is winged and that with poisonous tongue
    Hissing coils.
We love ourselves and hate ourselves, are wrung
    With woes and toils
To slay ourselves or from ourselves to win
    Shadowy spoils.
And through it all, the rumour and the din,
    Voices roam,
Voices of harps, voices of rolling seas,
    That rarely come
And to our inborn old affinities
    Call us home.
Shadows upon the many-sided Mind
    Arrive and go,
Shadows that shadows see; the vain pomps wind
    Above, below,
While in their hearts the single mighty God
    Whom none can know,
Guiding the mimic squadrons with His nod
    Watches it all —
Like transient shapes that sweep with half-guessed truth
    A luminous wall.

MANU

Alas! is life then vain? Our gorgeous youth
    Lithe and tall,
Our sweet fair women with their tender eyes
    Outshining stars,
The mighty meditations of the wise,
    The grandiose wars,
The blood, the fiery strife, the clenched dead hands,
    The circle sparse,
The various labour in a hundred lands,
    Are all these shows
To please some audience cold? as in a vase
    Lily and rose,
Mixed snow and crimson, for a moment blaze
    Till someone throws
The withered petals in some outer dust,
    Heeding not, —

The virtuous man made one with the unjust,
    Is this our lot?

RISHI

O King, sight is not vain, nor any sound.
    Weeds that float
Upon a puddle and the majestic round
    Of the suns
Are thoughts eternal, — what man loves to laud
    And what he shuns;
Through glorious things and base the wheel of God
    For ever runs.
O King, no thought is vain; our very dreams
    Substantial are;
The light we see in fancy, yonder gleams
    In the star.

MANU

Rishi, are we both dreams and real? the near
    Even as the far?

RISHI

Dreams are we not, O King, but see dreams, fear
    Therefore and strive.
Like poets in a wondrous world of thought
    Always we live,
Whose shapes from out ourselves to being brought
    Abide and thrive.
The poet from his vast and labouring mind
    Brings brilliant out
A living world; forth into space they wind,
    The shining rout,
And hate and love, and laugh and weep, enjoy,
    Fight and shout,
King, lord and beggar, tender girl and boy,
    Foemen, friends;
So to His creatures God's poetic mind
    A substance lends.
The Poet with dazzling inspiration blind,
    Until it ends,

Forgets Himself and lives in what He forms;
    For ever His soul
Through chaos like a wind creating storms,
    Till the stars roll
Through ordered space and the green lands arise,
    The snowy Pole,
Ocean and this great heaven full of eyes,
    And sweet sounds heard,
Man with his wondrous soul of hate and love,
    And beast and bird, —
Yes, He creates the worlds and heaven above
    With a single word;
And these things being Himself are real, yet
    Are they like dreams,
For He awakes to self He could forget
    In what He seems.
Yet, King, deem nothing vain: through many veils
    This Spirit gleams.
The dreams of God are truths and He prevails.
    Then all His time
Cherish thyself, O King, and cherish men,
    Anchored in Him.

    MANU

Upon the silence of the sapphire main
    Waves that sublime
Rise at His word and when that fiat's stilled
    Are hushed again,
So is it, Rishi, with the Spirit concealed,
    Things and men?

    RISHI

Hear then the Truth. Behind this visible world
    The eyes see plain,
Another stands, and in its folds are curled
    Our waking dreams.
Dream is more real, which, while here we wake,
    Unreal seems.
From that our mortal life and thoughts we take.
    Its fugitive gleams

Are here made firm and solid; there they float
    In a magic haze,
Melody swelling note on absolute note,
    A lyric maze,
Beauty on beauty heaped pell-mell to chain
    The enchanted gaze,
Thought upon mighty thought with grandiose strain
    Weaving the stars.
This is that world of dream from which our race
    Came; by these bars
Of body now enchained, with laggard pace,
    Borne down with cares,
A little of that rapture to express
    We labour hard,
A little of that beauty, music, thought
    With toil prepared;
And if a single strain is clearly caught,
    Then our reward
Is great on earth, and in the world that floats
    Lingering awhile
We hear the fullness and the jarring notes
    Reconcile, —
Then travel forwards. So we slowly rise,
    And every mile
Of our long journey mark with eager eyes;
    So we progress
With gurge of revolution and recoil,
    Slaughter and stress
Of anguish because without fruit we toil,
    Without success;
Even as a ship upon the stormy flood
    With fluttering sails
Labours towards the shore; the angry mood
    Of Ocean swells,
Calms come and favouring winds, but yet afar
    The harbour pales
In evening mists and Ocean threatens war:
    Such is our life.
Of this be sure, the mighty game goes on,
    The glorious strife,

Until the goal predestined has been won.
    Not on the cliff
To be shattered has our ship set forth of old,
    Nor in the surge
To founder. Therefore, King, be royal, bold,
    And through the urge
Of winds, the reboant thunders and the close
    Tempestuous gurge
Press on for ever laughing at the blows
    Of wind and wave.
The haven must be reached; we rise from pyre,
    We rise from grave,
We mould our future by our past desire,
    We break, we save,
We find the music that we could not find,
    The thought think out
We could not then perfect, and from the mind
    That brilliant rout
Of wonders marshal into living forms.
    End then thy doubt;
Grieve not for wounds, nor fear the violent storms,
    For grief and pain
Are errors of the clouded soul; behind
    They do not stain
The living spirit who to these is blind.
    Torture, disdain,
Defeat and sorrow give him strength and joy:
    'Twas for delight
He sought existence, and if pains alloy,
    'Tis here in night
Which we call day. The Yogin knows, O King,
    Who in his might
Travels beyond the mind's imagining,
    The worlds of dream.
For even they are shadows, even they
    Are not, — they seem.
Behind them is a mighty blissful day
    From which they stream.
The heavens of a million creeds are these:
    Peopled they teem

By creatures full of joy and radiant ease.
    There is the mint
From which we are the final issue, types
    Which here we print
In dual letters. There no torture grips,
    Joy cannot stint
Her streams, — beneath a more than mortal sun
    Through golden air
The spirits of the deathless regions run.
    But we must dare
To still the mind into a perfect sleep
    And leave this lair
Of gross material flesh which we would keep
    Always, before
The guardians of felicity will ope
    The golden door.
That is our home and that the secret hope
    Our hearts explore.
To bring those heavens down upon the earth
    We all descend,
And fragments of it in the human birth
    We can command.
Perfect millenniums are sometimes, until
    In the sweet end
All secret heaven upon earth we spill,
    Then rise above
Taking mankind with us to the abode
    Of rapturous Love,
The bright epiphany whom we name God,
    Towards whom we drove
In spite of weakness, evil, grief and pain.
    He stands behind
The worlds of Sleep; He is and shall remain
    When they grow blind
To individual joys; for even these
    Are shadows, King,
And gloriously into that lustre cease
    From which they spring.
We are but sparks of that most perfect fire,
    Waves of that sea:

From Him we come, to Him we go, desire
    Eternally,
And so long as He wills, our separate birth
    Is and shall be.
Shrink not from life, O Aryan, but with mirth
    And joy receive
His good and evil, sin and virtue, till
    He bids thee leave.
But while thou livest, perfectly fulfil
    Thy part, conceive
Earth as thy stage, thyself the actor strong,
    The drama His.
Work, but the fruits to God alone belong,
    Who only is.
Work, love and know, — so shall thy spirit win
    Immortal bliss.
Love men, love God. Fear not to love, O King,
    Fear not to enjoy;
For Death's a passage, grief a fancied thing
    Fools to annoy.
From self escape and find in love alone
    A higher joy.

    MANU

O Rishi, I have wide dominion,
    The earth obeys
And heaven opens far beyond the sun
    Her golden gaze.
But Him I seek, the still and perfect One, —
    The Sun, not rays.

    RISHI

Seek Him upon the earth. For thee He set
    In the huge press
Of many worlds to build a mighty state
    For man's success,
Who seeks his goal. Perfect thy human might,
    Perfect the race.
For thou art He, O King. Only the night
    Is on thy soul

By thy own will. Remove it and recover
> The serene whole
Thou art indeed, then raise up man the lover
> To God the goal.

CHITRANGADA
A Fragment

Chitrangada

In Manipur upon her orient hills
Chitrangada beheld intending dawn
Gaze coldly in. She understood the call.
The silence and imperfect pallor passed
Into her heart and in herself she grew
Prescient of grey realities. Rising,
She gazed afraid into the opening world.
Then Urjoon, felt his mighty clasp a void
Empty of her he loved and, through the grey
Unwilling darkness that disclosed her face,
Sought out Chitrangada. "Why dost thou stand
In the grey light, like one from joy cast down?
O thou whose bliss is sure. Leave that grey space,
Come hither." So she came and leaning down,
With that strange sorrow in her eyes, replied:
"Great, doubtless, is thy love, thy very sleep
Impatient of this brief divorce. And yet
How easily that void will soon be filled!
For thou wilt run thy splendid fiery race
Through cities and through regions like a star.
Men's worship, women's hearts inevitably
Will turn to follow, as the planets move
Unbidden round the sun. Thou wilt accept them,
Careless in thy heroic strength and beauty,
And smile securely kind, even as a god
Might draw an earthly maiden to his arms
And marry his immortal mouth to hers.
Then will thy destiny seize thee, thou wilt pass
Like a great light in heaven and leave behind
Only a memory of force and fire.
No lesser occupation can forever
Keep thee, O hero, whose terrestrial birth
Heaven fostered with her seed, — for what but this
To fill thy soul with battle, and august
Misfortunes and majestic harms embrace
And joys to their own natures mated. Last,
Empire shall meet thee on some mighty field
Disputing thee with death. Thou art not ours

More than the wind that lingers for a while
To touch our hair, then passes to its home."
And Urjoon silently caressing her,
"Muse not again, beloved Chitrangada,
Alone beside the window looking out
On the half-formed aspect and shape of things
Before sunlight was made. For God still keeps
Near to a paler world the hour ere dawn
And one who looks out from the happy, warm
And mortal limit of mankind that live
Enhoused, defended by companionship
With walls and limitations, is outdrawn
To dateless memories he cannot grasp
And infinite yearnings without form, until
The sense of an original vastness grows,
Empty of joyous detail, desolate,
In labour of a wide unfinished world.
Look not into that solemn silence! Rather
Protect thyself with joy, take in my arms
Refuge from the grey summons and defend
Thy soul until God rises with the sun.
Friendly to mortals is the living sun's
Great brilliant light, friendly the cheerful noise
Of earth arising to her various tasks
And myriad hopes. But this grey hour was born
For the ascetic in his silent cave
And for the dying man whose heart released
Loosens its vibrant strings." She answered him,
"Near to the quiet truth of things we stand
In this grey moment. Neither happy light
Nor joyful sound deceives the listening heart,
Nor Night inarms, the Mother brooding vast,
To comfort us with sleep. It helps me not
To bind thee for a moment to my joy.
The impulse of thy mighty life will come
Upon thee like a wind and drive thee forth
To toil and battle and disastrous deeds
And all the giant anguish that preserves
Our world. Thou as resistlessly wast born

To these things as the leopard's leap to strength
And beauty and fierceness, as resistlessly
As women are to love, — even though they know
Pain for the end, yet, knowing, still must love.
Ah, quickly pass! Why shouldst thou linger here
Vainly? How will it serve God's purpose in thee
To tarry soothing for her transient hour
Merely a woman's heart, meanwhile perhaps
Lose some great moment of thy life which once
Neglected never can return." She paused
And great Urjoon made answer, deeply moved:
"Has my clasp slackened or hast thou perceived
A waning passion in my kiss? Much more
My soul needs thee than on that fated day
When through Bengal of the enormous streams
With careless horse-hooves hurrying to the East
I came, a wandering prince, companioned only
By courage and my sword; nor knew such flowers
Were by the wayside waiting to be plucked
As these dark tresses and sweet body small
Of white Chitrangada. Dost thou remember?
O fair young sovereign ruling with pure eyes
And little fearless hand fragile and mild
This strong and savage nation! Didst thou know?
Didst thou expect me in thy soul? Assuredly
Thy heart's first flutterings recognised their lord.
And never with such gladness mountain queen
Exchanged tremendous seat and austere powers,
Her noble ancient right, for only leave
To lay her head upon my feet and wear
My kisses, not the crown. Content with love
All else thou gavest. Now thou speakest sadly,
Too like a mind matured by thought and pain."
And she with passion cried: "Do I remember?
Yes, I remember. What other thing can I
Remember, till forgetfulness arrives?
O endless moments, O rain-haunted nights,
When thou art far! And O intolerable,
The grey, austere discomfortable dawn

To which I shall awake alone! And yet
This year of thee is mine until the end.
The gods demand the rest. With all myself
I loved thee, not as other women do,
Piecemeal, reluctantly, but my whole heart
And being like a sudden spring broke forth
To flowers and greenness at my sungod's touch,
Ceding existence at thy feet. Therefore
I praise my father's wise and prescient love
That kept me from the world for thee, unsought
Amid the rugged mountains and fenced in
With barbarous inhospitable laws.
Around the dying man the torches flared
From pillar to weird pillar; and one discerned
In fitful redness on the shadowy walls
Stone visages of grim un-Aryan gods.
The marble pallor of my father's face
Looked strange to me in that unsteady glare,
As if an alien's; and dream-fantasies
Those figures seemed of Manipurian lords
Strange-weaponed, rude, with faces fierce and gnarled,
Like those they worship. Unafraid I stood
With grave and wide-orbed gaze contemplating
Their rugged pomp and the wild majesty
Of that last scene around my dying sire.
About me stood a circle fierce and strong,
Men high like rough gnarled trees or firm squat towers;
A human fortress in its savage strength
Enringed my future with bright jealous spears.
To them he entrusted me, calling each name,
And made their hearts my steps to mount a throne:
Each name was made a link in a great chain,
A turretted gate inwalling my rule,
Each heart a house of trust, a seal of fealty.
So were their thoughts conciliated; so
Their stern allegiance was secured. He spoke,
And, though of outward strength deprived, his voice
Rang clear yet as when over trumpets heard
It guided battle. 'Warriors of my East,
Take now this small white-bosomed queen of yours,

Surround her with the cincture of your force
And guard her from the thieves of destiny
Who prowl around the house of human life
To impoverish the meanings of the gods.
For I am ended and the shadow falls.
She is the stem from which your kings shall grow
Perpetual. Guard her well lest Fate deceived
Permit unworthier to usurp her days
Than the unconquerable seed of gods.
Oppose, oppose all alien entry here,
Whether by force or guile the stranger comes,
To clutch Nature's forbidden golden fruit.
Serry your bucklers close to overwhelm
The invader, seal your deaf and pitiless ears
To the guest's appeal, the suppliant call. He sole,
Darling of Fate and Heaven, shall break through all
Despising danger's threat and spurning death,
To grasp this prize, whether Ixvacou's clan
Yield a new Rama or the Bhoja hear
And raven for her beauty, — Vrishny-born,
Or else some lion's whelp of those who lair
In Hustina the proud, coveting two worlds,
Leaping from conquered earth to climb to Heaven,
Life's pride doubling with the soul's ethereal crown'.
He closed his eyes against the earthly air,
The last silence fell on him: he spoke no more
Save the great name until his spirit passed.
Then the grim lords forgot their savage calm.
A cry arose, 'Our queen!' and I was caught
From breast to breast of wild affection; all
Crowded upon me kissing feet and hands,
Recording silent oaths of love. Secure,
Alone in this wild, faithful barbarous world,
I ruled by weakness over rugged hearts,
A little queen adored, — until at length
Thou camest. Rumour and wide-mouthed alarm
Running before thy chariot-wheels thou cam'st,
Defeat and death, thy envoys and a cry:
O Manipurians, Manipurians, arm!
Some god incensed invades you, — surely a god

Incensed and fatal, for his bowstring huge
Sounds like the crack of breaking worlds and thick
His arrows as the sleet descends of doom
When the great Serpent wakes in wrath. Behind
That cry the crash of hostile advent came,
Thy chariot caked with mire and blood, its roof
Bristling and shattered from the fight, thy steeds
White with the spume of leagues, though yet they neighed
Lusting for speed and battle, and in the car
Thy grandiose form o'ertowering common mould,
While victory shone from eyes where thunder couched
Above his parent lightning. Swift to arms
My warriors sprang, dismayed but faithful, swift
Around me grew a hedge of steel. Enraged,
Thy coursers shod with wind rushed foaming on
And in with crash and rumour stormed the car
To that wide stone-paved hall; there loudly paused,
While thunderous challenge of the stamping hooves
Claimed all the place. Clanging thou leapedst down,
Urjoon, Gandiva in thy threatening grasp.
Then I beheld thy face, then rose, then stretched
My arms out, pausing not to think what god
Compelled me from my throne. But war came in
Between me and those sudden eyes. One bold
Beyond his savage peers stood questioning forth:
'Who art thou that with challenge insolent
Intruding, from what land of deathless gods
Stormest with disallowed exulting wheels
In white Chitrangada's domain? To death
Men hasten not so quickly, Aryan lord.'
Hero, thy look was calm, yet formidable,
Replying, by thy anger undisturbed:
'To death I haste indeed, but not to mine.
Nor think that Doom has claimed me for her own
Because I sole confront you. For my name
Ask the pale thousands whose swift-footed fear
Hardly escaped my single onset; ask
Your famous chieftains cold on hill or moor
Upon my fatal route. Yet not for war
I sought this region nor by death equipped,

Inhospitable people who deny
The human bond, but as a man to men
Alone I came and without need of fear,
If fear indeed were mine to feel. Nor trumpets blared
My coming nor battalions steel enforced,
Who claimed but what the common bond allows."

ULOUPIE

Uloupie

Canto I

Under the high and gloomy eastern hills
The portals of Patala are and there
The Bhogavathie with her sinuous waves
Rises, a river alien to the sun,
And often to its strange and gleaming sands
Uloupie came, weary of those dim shades
And great disastrous caverns neighbouring Hell,
Avid of sunlight. Through the grasses long
She glided and her fierce and gorgeous hood
Gleamed with a perilous beauty and a light
Above the green spikes of the grass; often
In the slow sinuous waters she was spied
Swimming, with mystic dusky hair and cheeks
That had no rose, — one shoulder's dipping glow
Through water and one white breast hardly seen.
But as she swam she looked towards the west
Dreaming of daily sunlight and of flowers
That need soft rain and of the night with stars,
A friendly darkness and the season's change
In beautiful Aryavertha far away,
The country of the Gods, and yet sometimes
Vaguely expectant to the southward gazed.

But in her city Monipur mid the eastern hills[1]
Chitrangada awoke and saw the dawn
Presaged in bleakness. From Urjoona's arms
Unclasping her rose-white smooth limbs, she looked
Into the opening world; but all was grey
And formless. Then into her mood there passed
The spirit of the gloomy northern hills
Burdening her breasts with terror and her heart
Was bared to insight, and now it heard the moan
Of waters and remembered pain. The sad

---

[1] Then into heaven dim-featured twilight came
And in her city mid the eastern hills

Prophecies of the pale astrologers
Haunted her with affliction, and she found
Pale hints of absence from the twilight drawn.
But now the hero felt his clasp a void
And on one arm half-rising searched the grey
Unlidded darkness for the face; then spoke
Slowly her name, "How has the unborn day
Called thee, beloved, that thou standest dumb
In the grey light like one whose joy is far?
Come hither." Silently she came and knelt
And laid her quiet cheek upon his breast.
He felt her tears, wondering; and she replied,
"Ah dost thou love me and a moment brief
Of absence troubles even in sleep thy heart
Waking to emptiness? And yet, ah God,
How easily that void will soon be filled!
For thou wilt like a glorious burning move
Through cities and through regions like a star,
Careless in thy heroic strength o'er all
The beautiful country Aryavertha. Women
Will see thy face and strangely, swiftly drawn
Thy masculine attraction feel and bow
Over thy feet. For thou wilt come to them
A careless glory taking women's hearts
As one breaks from a tree the wayside flowers,
And smile sunnily kind even as a god
Might draw a mortal maiden to his arms
And marry his immortal mouth to hers.
Then will thy destiny seize thee, thou wilt pass
Like some great light in heaven, leaving behind
A splendid memory of force and fire.
And thou wilt fill thy soul with battle, august
Misfortunes and tremendous harms embrace,
Experience mighty raptures and at last
Upon some world-renowned far-rumoured field
Empire for ever win or lose, nor all
The while think once of my forgotten face."
She ceased and wept; he said, touching her hair,
"What wast thou musing, O Chitrangada,
Lonely beside the window and thine eyes

Looked out on the half-formed aspect of things
Twixt light and darkness? Do not so again.
For bleak and dreadful is the hour ere dawn
And one who gazes out then from his sweet,
Warm, happy, bounded human room, is touched
With awful memories that he cannot grasp
And mighty sorrows without form, the sense
Of an original vastness desolate,
Bleak labour and a sad unfinished world.
Dwell not with these again, but when thou wakest
And seest the unholy hour pallid gaze
Into thy room, draw closer to my bosom
Waking with kisses and with joy surround
Thy soul until God rises with the sun.
Friendly to mortals is the living sun's
Great brilliant light; but this pale hour was made
For slowly-dying men whose lone chilled souls
Grow near to that greyness and dumb mourners
Unfriended." But Chitrangada replied,
"I looked into the dawn and had a dream
Thou wast gone far from me; too well I knew
That sound of trampling horse-hooves in the north
And victor rumours of thy chariot shook
The hearts of distant things. I sat alone
At this pale window and about me saw
My city and our low familiar hills.
Yet these were but as objects painted in
Upon the eye, and round me I beheld
The gloomy northern mountains with their mists
And sorrowful embracing rains and heard
With melancholy voices rolling down
The waters of a dull, ill-omened stream
Sinuous and eddies alien to the sun.
That thou wilt pass from me I know, nor would
I stay thee, had I power; for if today
I held thy feet, yet as the seasons passed,
The impulse of thy mighty life would come
Upon thee like a wind and drive thee forth
To love and battle and disastrous deeds
And all the giant anguish that preserves

This world. Thou as resistlessly wast born
To these things as the leopard sleek to strength
And beauty and fierceness, as resistlessly
As women are to love; though well they know
Pain for the end, yet knowing still must love.
Ah swiftly pass. Why shouldst thou linger here
Vainly? How will it serve God's purpose in thee
To tarry soothing for such brief while longer
Merely a woman's heart; meanwhile perhaps
Lose some great moment of thy life which once
Neglected never can return." She ceased
And strove to conquer overmastering tears.
He was silent a little, then his eyes
Strained towards the dim-seen fairness of her face,
Saying, "O little loving child, who once
Wast simply glad to love and feel my kiss!
But now thou mournest, art in one night changed.
Thou wast not wont to leave my arms ere dawn
And dream of sorrow. Rather wast thou fain
Of all my bosom and the gazing light
Hardly could force away thy obstinate clasp.
Yet now thou speakst of absence easily.
Is my love faded? Dost thou feel my arms
Looser about thee, my beloved? Nay,
Thou knowest that not less but more I love thee
Than when to eastern Monipura far
I came, a wandering prince companioned only
By courage and my sword and found thee here,
O sweet young sovereign, ruling with pure eyes
And little maiden hand, fragile and mild,
A strong and savage nation. At my call
Unquestioning thou camest, oh, meekly down
Leaving tremendous seat and austere powers,
Contented at my feet to dwell and feel
My kisses on thy hair, and couldst renounce
Thy glorious girdle for my simple arms.
O fair young soul, candid and meek and frank
Thy love was, opening to me fragrantly
Like flowers to the sun, wide-orbed, and yielded
Thy whole self up. Yet now thou speakest sadly

Too like a mind matured by thought and pain."

He ceased, covering her bosom with his hands,
And she trembled, and broke out faltering:
"O endlessness of moments and the long
Pain-haunted nights when thou art far! O me
And the pale dreadful dawn when I shall wake
In the grey hour and feel myself alone
For ever! Yet O my rapture and pride! O prince,
O hero, O strong protagonist of earth!
World-conqueror! and in heaven immortal lips
Burning have kissed thy feet, but I possessed.
God knows that I have loved thee, not with grudging
Piecemeal reluctant cessions of the soul
As ordinary women love, but greatly
With one glad falling at my conqueror's feet
All suddenly and warmly like the spring.
Ah God, thy beauty when it dawned on me
And I obeyed thy bright attraction! felt
Thy face like the great moon that draws the tides!
Facing our armèd senate, bow in hand
Leaned on a pillar with a banner's pomp
Seeming to mingle in thy hair thou stoodst
Expectant, careless, and thy strong gracious face
Was brilliant like a sudden god's. And half
I rose up as one called. But even then
Through all the hushed assembly ran a murmur,
An impulse and a movement and with cries
Round thee my strong barbarian nobles pressed
Offering fierce homage. But I sat alone,
Abandoned, with a wounded sad delight,
Loving thy glory, like a young warrior conquered
In battle by the hero he admires.
Thou tookst me by the hand and ledst me down
From the high dais and the ancient throne:
Faltering I went with meek submissive eyes."
Then strong Urjoona: "Beloved, and was this not
Dearer, a woman's bliss in her one lord
Than ruling all those kings? Dost thou not choose
Rather thy body by my kisses wakened

Than those free virgin and unconscious limbs?
Ah wherefore shouldst thou dream of love cut short
And joy without its sequel? Rather think
That thy young passion shall to matron bloom
Live warmly enriched and beautifully changed
When thou with the hushed wonder of motherhood
Touching thy sweet young eyes holdst up to me
Returning from high battle to thine arms
A creature of our own." And she answered
With a low sob, "Would God that it might be!
But though I loved thee I have known I was
No real part of thy great days; only
A bosom on which thou hast lain ere riding
To battle, a face which thou hast loved and passed.
Hero, take up thy bow! Warrior, arise!
Proceed with thy majestic mission. Thou
From many mighty spirits wast selected
And mayst not for a transient joy renounce
The anguish and the crown. I shall witness
Thy far-off pomps, not utterly alone;
As herdsmen pausing under quiet leaves
Watch the stupendous passage of a host,
Shrill neigh of horses, chariots swift and men
Marching, and hear great conch-shells blown, and look
Into the burning eyes of kings. Some wave
Of thy vast fate perhaps shall roll thee here
Or all is over; in the long round of things
We shall touch hands in the old way, yet changed,
Shall wonder in each other's eyes to find
Strange kindlings and the buried deeps of love."

    She ended, and Urjoona for a moment
Beheld vast Aryavertha as if mapped
Before him, rivers, and heaven-invading hills
And cities ancient as their skies; then turned
And drawing to his bosom Chitrangada
With his calm strength surrounding her replied:
"This may be; yet, O woman, O delight,
Remember to rejoice! Flowers die, beloved,
To live again; therefore hold fast to love,

Hold fast the blooming of thy life in love.
The soul's majestic progress moulding doom
Is with the frailest flower helped that blows
In frankness. Therefore is the woman's part
Nearest divine, who to one motion keeps
And like the fixed immortal planets' round
Is constant to herself in him she loves.
Nor though fate call me hence, have I in vain
Loved thee, young virgin of the hills, and snared
Thy feet with kisses; though my soul from thee
Adventure journeying like a star the void, —
As 'tis our spirit's fate ever to roam
Seeking bright portions of ourself, which found,
The strong heart cherishes until his close.
Relinquish nothing grasped, who yields to fate,
To fate or weakness, misses the great goal; —
So have I planted thee within my heart,
O tender beauty, and shall not lightly lose.
Though years divide us and the slow upgrowth
Of overlaying thoughts submerge the peace,
The sweet and mutual self, yet the old joy
Lives like Valmikie in his mound, the sage
Buried, forgot, yet murmuring the name.
Let us not lose then, O Chitrangada,
One moment's possibility of love
Which being squandered, we shall then regret.
Fate that united once, may when she will
Divorce, but cannot the sweet meaning spoil
Of these warm kisses." He embraced her wholly
Confounding her with bliss; so for that time
The shadow fled and joy forgot his close.

But one pale morn Chitrangada rose wan
And to the stable through the grey hushed place
Descending, with her little deft hands yoked
Urjoona's coursers to the car, — persuading
Thrust in their whinnying mouths the bit, fastened
The traces, harmonised the reins, then led
Into the sad dim court, trampling, his steeds;
And with a strange deep look of love and hate

Caressing said, faint with her unshed tears:
"You brought him here who now shall bear away,
O horses yoked to fate. How often yet
Will you deceive us shaking wide your manes
And trampling over women's hearts with hooves
Thunderous towards battle? Yet your breed perhaps
Shall bring him to my wrinkled age." And now
Urjoona came: his mailed and resonant tread
Rang in her very heart, his corslet blazed
Towards the chill skies and his heroic form
Seemed to consent with the surrounding hills.
But in the marble face and eyes august
The light of his tremendous fate had dawned
Like a great sunrise. Calm her shuddering body
He took into his bosom and with no word,
Under the witnessing, unmovèd heavens
Kissed her pale lips; then to his car he rose,
And now she did not weep, but silently
Took and returned his kiss. So he went forth.
Thundering the great wheels jarred upon the stones
Of the wide court and echoes filled the air
With triumph of warlike sound. Outside,
The city's nobles, waiting, saw the car
Emerge, and bowed down to their king. They spoke
No word, but stood austerely watching still,
A mist over their stern and savage eyes,
His going, as men in darkness watch a light
Carried away that cheered them for an hour,
Then turned back homeward. But Chitrangada
Waited till the last thunders died away
And far off on a hill the warlike flag
Waved in the breeze and dipped below the edge;
Then to her chamber slowly went alone.

THE TALE OF NALA
A Fragment Based on the Mahabharata

The Tale of Nala

Nala, Nishadha's king, paced by a stream
Which ran escaping from solitudes
To flow through gardens in a pleasant land.
Murmuring it came of the green souls of hills
And of the lawns and hamlets it had seen,
The brown-limbed peasants toiling in the sun,
And the tired bullocks in the thirsty fields.
In its bright talk and laughter it recalled
The moonlight and the lapping dangerous tongues,
The sunlight and the skimming wings of birds,
And gurgling jars, and bright bathed limbs of girls
At morning, and its noons and lonely eves.
This memory to the jasmine trees it sang
Which dropped their slow white-petalled kisses down
Upon its haste of curling waves. Far off
A mountain rose, alone and purple vague,
Wide-watching from its large stone-lidded eye
The drowsy noontide earth; vastly outspread
Like Vindhya changed, against the height of heaven
It stood. And on the deep-blue nearness limned
Its shoulder in a mighty indolence
Reclined for giant rest the Titan paused.
The birds were voiceless on the unruffled boughs,
The spotted lizard in a dull-eyed ease
Basked on his sentinel stone, a single kite
Circled above; white-headed over rust
Of brown and gold he stained the azure noon.
Solitary in the spaces of his mind
Among these sights and sounds King Nala paced
Oblivious of the joy of world and kind.
Shrill and dissatisfied the wanderer's cry
Came to his ear; he saw with absent eye
The rapid waters in their ripple run
Nor marked the ruddy sprouting of the leaves,
Nor heard the dove's rare cooing on the trees.
His thoughts were with a face his dreams had seen
Diviner than the jasmine's moon-flaked glow;
He listened to a name his dreams had known

Sweeter than passion of the crooning bird.
The delicate syllables yearning through his mind
Repeated longingly their soft-wreathed call,
As if some far-off bright forgotten queen
From whom his heart had wandered through the world
Were summoning back to her her truant thrall,
Luring it with the music of her name,
Some sovereign magic face of amber pearled,
Some spirit embodied in a moon-gold flame.
But now a look on him he seemed to feel.
The summit self-uplifted to the sky
Mounting the air in act to climb and join
Heaven's sapphire longing with earth's green unease
Drew his far gaze, which scanned as for a thought
The undecipherable charactery
Of mingled rocks and woods; but all was lost
In too much light. Dull glared the giant stones;
The woods, fallen sleepy on their mountain couch,
Had nestled in a coverlet of haze.
Like dim-seen shapes of virgins stoled in blue
Huddling close-limbed the slumberers lay.[1]
Then from some covert bosom's shrouded riches
A revelation came; for like a gleam
Of beauty from some purple-guarded breast
A passionate glint of lovely whiteness stole
Fluttering awhile, then fast towards him fled
Seeking his vision; and its glowing race
Splintered the sapphire with a silvery hue,
And soon a flame-bright flock of swans was seen
Flying like one and breasting with its shock
Of faery speed the vastness of the noon.
Not only with an argent flashing ran
The brilliant cohort on its skiey path,
But shaking from its wild wings a hail of gold.
Heaven's lustrous tunic of transparent air
Regretted the bright ornament as they passed.
They flew not like the snowy cranes, a wreath
Of flowers driven in the rain-tide's breath,

---

[1] Together claspèd in a huddled grace
Sleeping close-limbed the mystic slumberers lay.

When thunder calls them northward, but came fast
Ranked in magnificent and lovely lines
Cleaving the air with splendour. All the pride
And rushing glory of their bosoms and wings
Assailed his eyes with silver and with flame.
Over the Nishadhan gardens flying round
They came down whirring softly. Filling awhile
With gentle clamour from their liquid throats
The region, they disturbed with dipping plumes
The turquoise slumber of the motionless lake
Lulled to unrippling rest by windless noon.
A hundred marvellous shapes in mystic crowd
Covered the water like a living robe.
Now on the stream were spread their glorious breasts.
Each close-ranked by her sweet companion's side
Floating they came and preened above the flood
Their long and stately necks like curving flowers.
The water petted with enamoured waves
Their bosoms and the slow air swooned along
Their wings, their motion set a wordless chant
To flow against the chidings of the stream.
A song from heaven was that gliding grace
And hard to speak their beauty, what silver mass
On mass, what flakes and peacock eyes of gold,
What passion of crimson flecked each pure white breast!
It seemed to his charmed sense that in this form
The loveliness of a diviner world
Had come to him winged. Their beauty to tender greed
Moved him of all that living silver and gold.

*

"For now thy heaven-born pride must learn to range
My gardens of the earth and haunt my streams,
And to my call consent. If thou resist
I will imprison thee in a golden cage
And bind thy beauty with a silver chain."
A laughter beautiful arose from her
Thrilling her throat with bubbling ecstasies,
Sweet, satisfied because he praised her grace.

And with mysterious mild deep-glowing eyes
In long and softly wreathing syllables
The wonder spoke: "Release me, for no birds
Are we, O mortal, but the moon-bosomed nymphs
Who to the trance-heard music of the gods
Sway in the mystic dances of the sky,
Apsaras, daughters of the tumbling seas.
Shaped by thy fancy is my white-winged form."
But Nala to his bright prisoner swan replied:
"And now thou choosest thyself by all thy words,
My divine captive and white-bosomed slave,
Bird of desire or goddess luminous-limbed
To satisfy my pride and my delight
Thou stoopst to me from unattainable heavens.
Thou shalt possess my streams, O white-winged swan,
And dance, O Apsara singing in my halls.
Between the illumined pillars thou shalt glide
When flute and breathing lyre and timbrel call,
Adorning with thy golden rhythmic limbs
The crystalline mosaic of my floors.
What I have seized by force, by force I keep."
Her eyes now smiled on him; against his bosom
She laid in all its tender curving grace
The long white wonder of her neck upraised
In suppliant wreaths and flattering his cheek
With her soft gleaming head sweetly she cried:
"Because thou art bright and beautiful and bold,
So have I come to thee and thou hast seized
Whom if thou hadst set free, thy joy were lost,
So in thy mind from some celestial space
A name and face have come, yet are on earth,
Which if thou hadst not held with yearning's stays,
Thy mortal life would have been given in vain.
Forced by thy musing in the sapphire noon
Out of the mountain's breast to thee I flew."

(Incomplete)

IV

ON QUANTITATIVE METRE
An Essay

On Quantitative Metre

THE REASON OF THE PAST FAILURES

A definitive verdict seems to have been pronounced by the critical mind on the long-continued attempt to introduce quantitative metres into English poetry. It is evident that the attempt has failed, and it can even be affirmed that it was predestined to failure; quantitative metre is something alien to the rhythm of the language. Pure quantity, dependent primarily on the length or brevity of the vowel of the syllable, but partly also on the consonants on which the vowel sustains itself, quantity as it was understood in the ancient classical languages, is in the English tongue small in its incidence, compared with stress and accent, and uncertain in its rules; at any rate, even in the most capable hands it has failed to form a practicable basis of metre. Accentual metre is normal in English poetry, stress metres are possible, but quantitative metres can only be constructed by a *tour de force*; artificial and incapable of normality or of naturalisation, they cannot get a certified right of citizenship. If quantity has to be understood in that and no other sense, this verdict must stand; all attempts made hitherto have been a failure, and not usually a brilliant failure. And yet this does not dispose of the question: an appeal is possible against the sentence of illegitimacy and banishment on the ground that from the very first the problem has been misunderstood and misstated, the methods used either a deviation from the true line or, even when close to it, a misfit; a better statement may lead to a solution that could well be viable.

At the very beginning of these attempts a double thesis was raised; two separate problems were closely associated together which are in their nature distinct, although they can be brought into close relation. There was, first, the problem of the naturalisation of classical metres in English poetry, and there was, mixed up with it, the problem of the free creation of quantitative

English verse in its own right, on its own basis, with its own natural laws, not necessarily identical with those laid down in the ancient tongues. The main attempt then made was not to discover a true English principle of quantitative metre, — what was done was to bring in classical metres built according to the laws of quantity proper to a classical tongue but of doubtful validity in a modern language. Chaucer, influenced by mediaeval French and Italian poetry, had naturalised their metrical inventions by making accentual pitch and inflexion the basis of English metre. This revolution succeeded because he had called to his aid one of the most important elements in the natural rhythm of the language and it was easy for him by that happy choice to establish a perfect harmony between this rhythm and his new art of metrical building. The metrical movement he perfected — for others before him had attempted it — passed easily into the language, because he caught and lifted its native rhythm into a perfect beauty of sound captivating to the ear and moving to the inner witness and listener silent within us — the soul, to whom all art and all life should appeal and minister. This great victory was essential for the free flowering of poetry in the English tongue; the absence of any such *coup d'œil* of genius was one chief reason of its failure to flower as freely in so many human languages, — no creative genius found for them the route which leads to the discovery of a perfect plasticity of word and sound, a perfect expressiveness, a perfect beauty of rhythm. But with the Renaissance came a new impulse, a new influence; an enthusiasm was vividly felt by many for the greatness of structure and achievement of the Greek and Latin tongues—an achievement far surpassing anything done in the mediaeval Romance languages — and a desire arose to bring this greatness of structure and achievement into English poetry. As Chaucer by the success of the accentual structure in verse and his discovery of its true and natural rhythm was able to bring in the grace and fluidity of the Romance tongues, so they too conceived that the best way to achieve their aim was to bring in the greatness of classical harmony and the nobility and beauty of Greek and Latin utterance by naturalising the quantitative metres of Virgil, Ovid, Horace. It was also natural that some of these innovators should conceive that this could be best done by imposing the classical laws of quantity wholesale on the English language.

At the first attempt a difference of view on this very point arose; there was a bifurcation of paths, but neither of these branchings led anywhere near the goal. One led nowhere at all, there was a laborious trudging round in a futile circle; the other turned straight back towards accentual metre and ended in the entire abandonment of the quantitative principle. Spenser in his experiments used all his sovereign capacity to force English verse into an unnatural classical mould, Sidney followed his example. Harvey thought, rightly enough, that an adaptation to the natural rhythm of English was indispensable, but he failed to take more than a first step towards the right path; after him, those who followed his line could not get any farther, — in the end, in place of the attempt at quantitative verse, there was an adaptation of classical metres to the accentual system. Some who still experimented with quantity, feeling the necessity of making their verse normally readable, did this by taking care that their long quantities and stress or accentual pitch, wherever these came in, coincided as far as possible. But the result was not encouraging; it made the verse readable indeed, but stiff beyond measure. Even Tennyson in his lines on Milton, where he attempts this combination, seems to be walking on stilts, — very skilfully and nobly, but still on stilts and not on his own free God-given feet. As for other attempts which followed the Spenserian line of approach, they can best be described in Tennyson's own language —

"Barbarous hexameters, barbarous pentameters"

— and the alcaics, sapphics and galliambics were no better. A metre which cannot be read as normal English is read, in which light syllables are forced to carry a voice-weight which they have no strength to bear and strong stresses are compelled to efface themselves while small insignificant sounds take up their burden, is not a real and natural verse movement; it is an artificial structure which will never find an agreed place in the language.

No make-believe can reconcile us to such rhythms as Sidney's

In wīnd | ōr wā|tēr's | streām dŏ rĕ|quīre tŏ bĕ | wrīt. |

Here two intractable iambic feet followed by a resolutely short syllable are compelled to dance a jig garbed as two spondees followed by a solitary long syllable; so disguised, they pretend to be the first half of a pentameter, — the second half with its faultless and natural metre and rhythm is of itself a condemnation of its predecessor. Neither can one accept Bridges'

Flōwerў dŏ|maīn thĕ flŭsh|īng sōft | crōwdīng | lōvelĭnĕss |

ōf Sprīng |

where length is forced on an inexorable short like the "ing" of "flushing" and "crowding" and a pretence is made that an accentual iamb, "of Spring", can be transformed into a quantitative spondee. Still worse, still more impossible to digest or even to swallow, is his forced hexameter ending,

thĕ sĕ|rēnelў sŏ|lēmn spēlls. |

There two successive accentual trochees and a terminal long syllable are turned by force or by farce into a closing dactyl and spondee. Such are the ungainly antics into which the natural movements of verse have to be compelled in this game of thrusting the laws of quantity of an ancient language upon a modern tongue which has quite another spirit and body. What is possible and natural in a clear-cut ancient language where there is a more even distribution of the voice and both the short and long syllables can get their full sound-value, is impossible or unnatural in the English tongue; for there the alternation of stresses with unstressed short and light sounds is a constant and inescapable feature. That makes all the difference; it turns this kind of verse into a frolic of false quantities. In any case, the method has invariably resulted in failure from Spenser to Bridges; the greatness of some of the poets who have made this too daring and unnatural effort has not been great enough to bring success to an impossible adventure.

There remains the alternative way, the adaptation of classical metres to the accentual mould, of which the accentual hexameter is the not too successful consequence; but this is not a solution of the problem of English quantitative verse. Even if successful, in every field and not only in the treatment of the hexameter, it would have only solved the other quite distinct problem of naturalising Greek and Latin metres in English. But even in this direction success has been either nil or partial and defective. The experiments have always remained experiments; there has been no opening of new paths, no new rhythmic discoveries or triumphant original creations. The writers carry with them very evidently the feeling of being experimenters in an abnormal kind; they achieve an artificial rhythm, their very language has an artificial ring: there is always a stamp of manufacture, not a free outflow of significant sound and harmonious word from the depths of the spirit. A poet trying to naturalise in English the power of the ancient hexameter or to achieve a new form of its greatness or beauty natural to the English tongue must have absorbed its rhythm into his very blood, made it a part of himself, then only could he bring it out from within him as a self-expression of his own being, realised and authentic. If he relies not on this inner inspiration, but solely on his technical ability for the purpose, there will be a failure; yet this is all that has been done. There have been a few exceptions like Swinburne's magnificent sapphics; but these are isolated triumphs, there has been no considerable body of such poems that could stand out in English literature as a new form perfectly accomplished and accepted. This may be perhaps because the attempt was always made as a sort of leisure exercise and no writer of great genius like Spenser, Tennyson or Swinburne has made it a main part of his work; but more probably, there is a deeper cause inherent in the very principle and method of the endeavour.

Two poets, Clough and Longfellow, have ventured on a considerable attempt in this kind and have succeeded in creating something like an English hexameter; but this was only a half accomplishment. The rhythm that was so great, so beautiful or, at the lowest, so strong or so happy in the ancient tongues, the hexameter of Homer and Virgil, the hexameter of Theocritus, the hexameter of Horace and Juvenal becomes in their hands something poor, uncertain of itself and defective. There is here the waddle and squawk of a big water-fowl, not the flight and challenge of the eagle. Longfellow was an admirable literary craftsman in his own limits, the limits of ordinary metre perfectly executed in the ordinary way, but his technique like his poetic inspiration had no subtlety and no power. Yet both subtlety and power, or at the very least one of these greater qualities, are imperatively called for in the creation of a true and efficient English hexameter; it is only a great care and refinement or a great poetic force that can overcome the obstacles. Longfellow had his gift of a certain kind of small perfection on his own level; Clough had energy, some drive of language, often a vigorous if flawed and hasty force of self-expression. It cannot be said that their work in this line was a total failure; the "Bothie of Toberna-Vuolich", "Evangeline" and the "Courtship of Miles Standish" have their place, though not a high place, in English poetry. But the little they achieved was not enough to acclimatise the hexameter permanently in English soil; nor did their work encourage others to do better, on the contrary the imperfection of its success has been a deterrent, not an incentive.

It is probable indeed that the real reason of the failure went much deeper; it lay in the very character of the mould they invented. The accentual hexameter was a makeshift and could not be the true thing; its false plausibility could not be an equivalent for the great authentic rhythms of old, its mechanically regular or common uninspiring beat, sometimes stumbling or broken, is something quite different from the powerful sweep, the divine rush or the assured truth of tread of that greater word-music. The hexameter is a quantitative verse or nothing; losing the element of quantity, it loses also its quality. Admitting that quantity as it is ordinarily understood cannot be the sole basic element in any English metre, yet for the hexameter, perhaps for any classical rhythm, the discovery and management of true quantity is an intimate part of its technique; to neglect or to omit it is to neglect or omit something essential, indispensable. Accentual pitch gives beat, but its beat does not depend on quantity except in so far as the stress ictus creates a genuine length valid for any rhythm which is native to the language. To find out what does constitute true quantity is the first need, only then can there be any solution of the difficulty. Tennyson, like Harvey, missed this necessity; he was content to fuse long syllable and stress and manage carefully his short quantities conceived according to the classical law; this he did admirably, but two or three efforts in this kind of tight-rope acrobatics were as much as he cared to manage. But true quantity in English must be something else; it must be something inherent in the tongue, recognisable everywhere in its rhythm, — not an artifice or convention governing its verse forms alone, but a technique of Nature flowing spontaneously through the very texture of the language as a whole.

METRE AND THE THREE ELEMENTS OF ENGLISH RHYTHM

There are three elements which constitute the general exterior forms of rhythm in the English language, — accent, stress, quantity. Each of them can be made in theory the one essential basis of metre, relegating the other indispensable elements to the position of subordinate factors which help out the rhythm but are not counted in the constitution of the metrical basis. But in practice accent and stress combining with it and aiding it have alone successfully dominated English verse-form; intrinsic quantity has been left to do what it can for itself under their rule. The basis commonly adopted in most English poetry since Chaucer is the accentual rhythm, the flow of accentual pitch and inflexion which is so all-important an element in the intonation of English speech. In any common form of English poetry we find all based on pitch and inflexion; the feet are accentual feet, the metrical "length" or "shortness" of syllables — not their inherent quantity — is determined by natural or willed location of a pitch of accent or some helping inflexion falling on the main supporting syllable of the foot and by the absence of any such pitch or accentual inflexion on those that are subordinate and supported: the main accented syllables are supposed to be metrically long, the subordinate unaccented short, there is no other test or standard. To take a familiar example:

The wáy | was lóng, | the wínd | was cóld, |
The mín|strel wàs | infírm | and óld. |[1]

Here there is a regular iambic beat determined by the persistent accentual high pitch or low pitch falling on the second syllable of the foot. In a stress scansion the second foot of the second line would rank not as an iamb but as a pyrrhic, for it is composed of two short unstressed syllables; but there is the minor accentual inflexion which commonly occurs as a sort of stepping-stone helping the voice across a number of unstressed syllables; that, slight as it is, is sufficient to justify in accentual theory the description of this foot as an iamb. Stress usually coincides with the high accentual pitch and is indispensable as the backbone of the rhythm, but it was not treated until recently either as an independent or as the main factor. Inherent quantity is not at all regarded; long-syllable quantity sometimes coincides with both high pitch and stress, sometimes it stands by itself as a rhythmic element, but that makes no difference to the metre.

The instance given is an example of the iambic verse with an extreme, an almost mechanical regularity of beat; so, for completeness, we may turn to poetry of a freer and larger type.

Full mán|y a gló|rious mór|ning hàve | I séen
Fláttering | the móun|tain-tóps | with sóve|reign éye.

Here there are two glide anapaests in the first line, an initial dactyl in the second, — three departures from the regular iambic beat. Such liberty of variation can always be indulged in in English verse and it is sometimes pushed to much greater lengths — as in the line —

Cóver | her fáce; | my éyes dáz|zle; she | díed yóung |

[1] The sign / indicates the accentual high pitch, the sign \ transitional inflexion, unobtrusive and without stress or with only a half-stress.

where there is only one iamb in the five feet of the line; the other four feet are respectively a trochee, a bacchius, a pyrrhic and a closing spondee. Nevertheless the basic system of the metre or at least some form of its spirit asserts itself even here by a predominant beat on the final syllable of most of the feet: all the variations are different from each other, none predominates so as to oust and supplant the iamb in its possession of the metric base. In Webster's line this forceful irregularity is used with a remarkable skill and freedom; the two first feet are combined in a choriamb to bring out a vehemence of swift and abrupt unexpressed emotion; in the rest intrinsic quantitative longs combine with short-vowel stress lengths to embody a surcharged feeling — still unexpressed — in a strong and burdened movement: all is divided into three brief and packed word-groups to bring out by the subtly potent force of the rhythm the overpowering yet suppressed reactions of the speaker. The language used, however vivid in itself, could not have done as much as it does, if it were deprived of this sound-effect; it would have given the idea by its external indices, but it is the rhythm that brings out the concealed feeling. Each word-group has a separate rhythm, an independent life, yet it is by following each other rapidly in a single whole that the three together achieve a complete force and beauty. If the three clauses of this line were cut up into successive lines in modern free-verse fashion, they would lose most of their beauty; it is the total rhythmic power of these three hammer-strokes that brings to the surface all that underlies the words. But without the aid of the unusual arrangements of stress and quantity it could not have been done.

This shows up the true nature of the accentual system as distinguished from its formal theory. It becomes clear that the supposed longs and shorts constituting its feet are not real quantities, they are not composed of long and short syllables, — on the contrary, a very short sound can be made to bear the weight of the whole foot while longer ones trail after it in dependence on their diminutive leader. What we really have is a system of recurrent strokes or beats intervening at a fixed place in each foot, while the syllables which are not hammered into prominent place by this kind of stroke or beat fill the interspaces. A regular metrical base is thus supplied, but the rhythm can be varied or modulated by departures from the base — from it but always upon it; for these departures, variations or modulations, relieve its regularity which might otherwise become monotonous, but do not replace or frustrate the essential rhythm. If the modulations overlay too much the basic sound-system so as to obliterate it or if they are so ill-managed as to substitute another rhythm for it, then we have a rhythmic mixture; or else there is a break of the metrical movement which can be legitimate only if it is done with set purpose and justified by the success of that purpose.

In all these instances it will be seen that inherent quantity combined with distribution of stress — which is also, as we shall see, a true quantity-builder — plays always the same role; it is used as an accessory or important element of the rhythm, to give variety, subtlety, deeper significance. A longer quotation may illustrate this position and function of stress distribution and distribution of quantity in accentual metre with more amplitude —

> The lun|atic, | the lov|er, and | the poet
> Are of | imag|ina|tion all | compact:
> One sees | more de|vils than | vast hell | can hold,
> That is, | the mad|man; the lov|er, all | as fran|tic,
> Sees Hel|en's beau|ty in | a brow | of Egypt:
> The po|et's eye, | in a | fine fren|zy roll|ing,
> Doth glance | from heav|en to earth, | from earth | to
>   heaven;
> And, as | imagina|tion bo|dies forth
> The forms | of things | unknown, | the po|et's pen
> Turns them | to shapes, | and gives | to air|y no|thing
> A lo|cal ha|bita|tion and | a name.[1]

The first six lines of this passage owe much of their beauty

[1] Here only the stresses are marked, by the sign |, and the long-vowel syllables, by the

to the unusual placing of the stresses and the long-vowelled syllables; in each line the distribution differs and creates a special significant rhythm which deepens and reinforces the outward sense and adds to it that atmosphere of the unexpressed reality of the thing in itself which it is in the power of rhythm, of word-music as of all music, to create. In the first line two pyrrhics separate the two long-vowelled sounds which give emphasis and power to the first and last feet from the narrower short-vowel stressed foot in the middle: this gives a peculiar rhythmic effect which makes the line no longer a mere enumerative statement, it evokes three different rhythmic significances isolating and locating each of the three pure Imaginatives in his own kind. In the second line a swift short movement in its first half slows down to a heavy prolonged movement in its second, a swift run with a long and tangled consequence; here too the expressiveness of the rhythm is evident. In the third line there are no fewer than four long vowels and a single pyrrhic separates two rhythmic movements of an unusual power and amplitude expressive of the enormity of the lunatic's vision and imagination; here too, short-vowel stress and intrinsic-quantity longs are combined no less than three times and it is this accumulation that brings about the effect. In the fifth and sixth lines the separative pyrrhic in the middle serves again a similar purpose. In the fifth, it helps to isolate in contrast two opposites each emphasised by its own significant rhythm. In the sixth line there are again four long vowels and a very expressive combination of short-vowel stressed length with intrinsic long syllables, a spacious amphibrach like a long plunge of a wave at the end; no more expressive rhythm could have been contrived to convey potently the power, the excitement and the amplitude of the poet's vision.[1] Afterwards there follow five lines of a normal iambic movement, but still with a great subtlety of variation of rhythm and distribution of

---

sign – ; the quantitative shorts are left unmarked: the accents need no indication.

[1] A combination of powerful intrinsic longs and equally powerful short-vowel stresses help to create two of the most famous "mighty lines" of Marlowe, —

Was this the face that launched a thousand ships
And burned the topless towers of Ilium?

quantity creating another kind of rhythmic beauty, a beauty of pure harmonious word-music, but this too is the native utterance of the thing seen and conveys by significant sound its natural atmosphere. This passage shows us how much the metrically unrecognised element of intrinsic quantity can tell in poetic rhythm bringing real significations into what would be otherwise only sheer beauty of sound; quantity is one among its most important elements, even though it is not reckoned in the constitution of the metre. It combines with stress distribution to give power and expressive richness to the beat or, as it has been called, the strokes and flicks of accentual verse.

It has been seen that accentual high pitch and stress most frequently coincide;— indeed, many refuse to make any distinction between stress of accent and stress proper. The identity is so close that all the passages cited — and accentual verse generally — can, if we so choose, be scanned by stress instead of accentual inflexion. But that at once brings in a difference: for the lower accentual inflexions have then to be ignored because they do not carry in them anything that can be called a stress, as a result syllables which are treated as long in the conventional scansion because of this slight accentual help have now, since they are unstressed, to be regarded as short. Iambs, so reputed, cease, in this reckoning, to be iambs and become pyrrhics; an iambic pentameter has often to be read in the stress scansion as an imperfectly iambic stress verse because of the frequent modulations, trochee or pyrrhic, anapaest, amphibrach or spondee. But apart from this, there can be a more independent stress principle of metre; for, properly speaking, stress means not accentual high pitch, but weight of voice emphasis; it is a brief hammer-stroke of the voice from above which comes down on a long-vowel or a short-vowel syllable and gives even to the latter a metrical length and power which, when without stress, it does not naturally have. This stroke can thus confer metrical length even on a very short vowel or slightest short syllable, because it drives it firmly in like a nail into the wall, so that other unstressed sounds can hang loosely upon it. This provides a distinctive ground-frame which can be generalised and so made into a metrical base.

There can then be a pure stress scansion and pure stress

metres in their own right without any justification by accent. For in stress metre proper the high accentual pitches are swallowed up into stress; any other rise or fall of accentual inflexion is ignored, — it is allowed to influence the rhythm but it does not determine or affect the basic metrical structure. Accent can in this way disappear altogether as a metrical base; stress replaces it. Here, for example, are lines composed entirely of stress paeons —

I have wandered | in the valleys | of Ecstasy, I | have listened |
to the murmur | and the passion | of its streams, |
I have stood up|on the mountains | of the Splendour, |
I have spun a|round my spirit | like a garment |
the purple of | its skies.

It is evident that here there are accentual inflexions other than those taken up into stress, on one syllable even a low pitch, but because they are not reckoned as stresses, they do not count in the metrical structure of the lines. Or there may be a still freer stress metrification which rejects any scheme of regular feet and refuses to recognise the necessity of a fixed number of syllables either to the foot or the line; it regards only the fall of the stress and is faithful to that measure alone.

A far sail | on the unchangeable monotone | of a slow
slumbering sea. |

The line is divided into three word-groups; the first contains two stresses, the others carry each three stresses, but the beats are distributed at pleasure: sometimes they are close together, sometimes they stand separated by far intervals amid a crowd of short unstressed syllables. Sometimes there is a closely packed movement loosening itself at the end, —

Over its head | like a gold ball the sun | tossed by the gods
in their play. |

Sometimes a loose run gathers itself up in its close into a compact movement:

Here or otherwhere, | poised on the unreachable abrupt |
snow-solitary ascent. |

Or any other movement can be chosen which is best suited to the idea or the feeling of the individual line. Quantity as such is here immaterial for metre building; it is of value only in so far as it coincides with stress and gives it an ampler fullness of metrical length so as to build and sustain more strongly the rhythmic totality of the line and the stanza.

But what then of this third element, quantity? Its importance is evident, but it does not form by itself the backbone of the natural rhythm of the language: quantity in English seems to intervene only as a free element taking its chance part in the general movement or its place assigned at will in the architecture. And yet quantity of some kind, shorts, longs, intermediate sounds, is ubiquitous and there seems to be no reason why it should not regulate metre. Indeed, every system affirms some kind of quantity as its constituent material. Stress metre arranges its rhythms by taking all stressed syllables as long, all unstressed syllables as metrically short; accent affirms similarly its own principle of quantity, though here the word seems to be a misnomer. Can then quantity, properly speaking, pure quantity, stand by itself as the whole basis of a metrical system, as accent and stress have done? Can it similarly leave the other two elements, stress and accent, to influence and vary the rhythm but not allow them to interfere in the building of the metre? Can there be in English poetry a quantitative as well as an accentual or a stress building of verse, natural to the turn of the language, recognised and successful? and must stress or accentual lengths in such a metrical system be excluded from the idea of length? For everything here depends upon what we understand by quantity; if stress lengths are admitted, the problem of quantitative metre loses its difficulty, otherwise it seems insoluble.

The experimenters in pure quantitative verse have excluded

stress from their theory of metrical lengths; they have admitted only intrinsic lengths determined by the vowel of the syllable and positional lengths determined by the number of succeeding consonants. That there is a fundamental falsity in this theory is shown by the fact that their lines cannot be read; or else in order to make them readable, an unnatural weight has to be thrown on sounds that are too slender to bear it; a weird sound-system full of false values is artificially created. But stress is a main, if not the main, feature of English rhythm; a metrical method ignoring it is impracticable. A pure quantitative verse of this manufacture has therefore to be ruled out, both because of its intrinsic artificiality and its unsuccessful result; it has to be abandoned as impossible or as inherently false. Those experimenters who avoid these false values and try to get rid of the difficulty by allowing only those stresses which coincide with intrinsic and positional longs, are on firmer ground and have some chance of arriving at something practicable. But their efforts too are hampered by the classical theory that the support of more than one consonant after a short vowel is sufficient to make short syllables metrically long, a statement which is true of the classical languages but not true of English. This either leads them into the introduction of false quantities which cannot stand the test of natural reading or drives them to oblige their longs and shorts to coincide with accentual or stress longs and shorts. Thus we see quantitative feet come to coincide exactly or predominantly with stress or accentual feet in Harvey's hexameter verse, —

Fāme wĭth ă|būndānce | mākĕth ă | mān thrīce | blēssĕd ănd[1] |
                       hāppў.

In Sidney's line —

 These be her words, but a woman's words to a love that is
                       eager

there happens to be a similar predominant identification of quantity with accent or stress, and it is this that makes the line readable. In reality these are stress hexameters, for in each there

[1] The word *and* here ought by the classicist theory to be long because of its two consonants after the vowel and still longer because it is further supported by the initial *h* of *happy*.

are syllables, as in wŏman's, lŏve, hăppy, which are long by stress only and not by either inherent or positional quantity. But, on the other hand, feet which would be trochees in accentual or stress verse are reckoned here quite artificially as spondees, *abundance*, *woman's*, because of the two-or-more-consonants theory; but the closing syllables of these two words, if listened to by the ear and not measured by the eye, are very clearly short, even though not among the shortest possible, and it is only by a violence of the mind or a convention that they can be reckoned as long and this kind of very slightly loaded trochee promoted to the full dignity of a spondee. Evidently, we must seek elsewhere for a true theory of English quantity and a sound basis for quantitative verse.

A THEORY OF TRUE QUALITY

If we are to get a true theory of quantity, the ear must find it; it cannot be determined by mental fictions or by reading with the eye: the ear too in listening must exercise its own uninfluenced pure hearing if it is not to go astray. So listening, we shall find that intrinsic or inherent quantity and the positional sound-values are not the only factors in metrical length, there is also another factor, the weight-length; it may even be said that all quantity in English is determined by weight, all syllables that bear the weight of the voice are long, all over which the voice passes lightly are short. But the voice-weight on a vowel is determined in three different ways. There is a dwelling of the voice, a horizontal weight-bar laid across the syllable, or there is its rapid passing, an absence of the weight-bar: that difference decides its natural length, it creates the inherent or intrinsic long or short, *lāzĭlў*, *swēetnĕss*. There is again a vertical ictus weight of the voice, the hammer-stroke of stress on the syllable; that of itself makes even a short-vowel syllable metrically long, as in *heávĭlў*, *ărĭdĭtў*, *chánnĕl*,[1] *cănál*; the short-vowel syllables that

[1] The double consonant here, as in other words like *happy*, *tell*, can make no difference even in the classicist theory, because it is a mere matter of spelling and represents a single, not a double sound, — the sound is the same as in *pánĕl*.

have not the lengthening ictus or vertical weight and have not either the horizontal weight of the voice upon them remain light and therefore short. It is evident that these words are respectively a natural dactyl, second paeon, trochee, iamb, yet all their syllables are short, apart from the stress; but what true rhythm or metre could treat as other than long these stressed short-vowel syllables? In the words, nárrātĭve, mán-ēatĕr, brūtălĭtў, cŏntémplātĭve, ĭncárnāte, we see this triple power of length at work within one word, — weight-bar long syllables stressed or unstressed, hammer-stroke-weighted short-vowelled longs, natural unweighted short syllables. It is clear that there can be no true reduction of stressed or unstressed or of intrinsic long or short to a sole one-kind principle; both stress and vowel length work together to make a complex but harmonious system of quantity. But, yet again, there is a third factor of length-determination; there is consonantal weight, a lingering or retardation of the voice compelled by a load of consonants, or there is a free unencumbered light movement. This distinction creates the positionally long syllable, short by its vowel but lengthened by its consonants, strēngth, swĭft, ābstrāct; where there is no such weight or no sufficient weight of consonants buttressing up the short syllable, it remains short, unless lengthened by stress. But we must consider separately how far this third or consonantal element is operative, whether its effect is invariable and absolute as the classicists would have it or only produces its result according to circumstance.

It is evident to the natural ear that stress confers in its own right metrical length on the syllable in which it occurs; even an extreme shortness of the vowel does not take away the lengthening force given. To the ear it stands out that the feet in Webster's line, "mў eȳes dáz|zle" and "she|dīed young," are, quantitatively, bacchius[1] and spondee; the one is not and cannot be a true anapaest, as it would or can be accounted by convention in accen-

---

[1] Unless we consider *my* as long, which is a disputable point; the sound is inherently a long-vowel one, but depressed by the absence of stress or accentual high pitch. In quantitative verse this should not matter; it can retain in spite of the depression its native dignity as a long-vowel syllable.

tual scansion, the other is not and cannot be either iamb or trochee. The stress long naturally combines here with the intrinsic long to make bacchius or spondee, because it has itself a true metrical length which is equivalent to that of the long-vowel syllable, though not identical in nature. This stress length, in any valid theory of quantity, cannot be ignored; its ictus weight and the conveyed force of length which the weight carries with it cannot be whittled down to shortness by any mental decree. In accentual verse its power is usually absorbed by coincidence with accentual high pitch and so it is satisfied and does not need to put in a separate claim; but in quantitative verse too it insists on its right and, if denied, fatally disturbs by its presence the rhythm that tries to disown or ignore it. In true quantitative verse, stress lengths and intrinsic lengths can and must be equally accepted because they both carry weight enough to burden the syllable with an enhanced sound-value. The admission or generalisation of the idea of weight lengths clears up many cobwebs and, because it corresponds with the facts, provides us with a rational system of quantitative verse.

What difficulty remains arises from the theory drawn from the classical languages that a sequence of more than one consonant after a short vowel — whether in the word itself or with the help of an initial consonant or consonants in the word that follows — compensates for the shortness and gives the syllable, inexorably, a value of metrical length. This is palpably untrue, as has been shown by the stumbles of Sidney and Bridges and every other classicist operator in quantitative verse. Let us again consult the ear, not the theorising mind; what is its judgment on this point if we listen, for instance, to these four hexameter lines based on natural and true quantity?

Ōne ănd ŭn|ărmed ĭn thĕ | cār wăs thĕ | drīvĕr; | grēy wăs
          hĕ, | shrūnkĕn,
Wōrn wĭth hĭs | dēcādes. Tŏ | Pērgămă | cīnctŭred wĭth |
          strēngth Cȳclŏ|pēān
Ōld ănd ă|lōne hĕ ăr|rīved, ĭnsĭg|nĭfĭcănt, | fēeblĕst ŏf |
          mōrtăls,

Cārrȳĭng | Fāte ĭn hĭs | hēlplĕss | hānds ănd thĕ | dōōm
ŏf ăn | ēmpīre.

According to the classical theory words and syllables like "and", "of", "in", "the", "he", "ing" should be treated as long since or when two or three consonants come immediately after the vowel within the line. But this is quite false; the "dr" of "driver" does not as a matter of fact make the "the" before it long; the natural shortness of "with" is not abolished by the "h" of the following word "his", or the shortness of "his" by the "d" of "decades". All these small light words are so intrinsically short, so light in their very nature, that nothing, or nothing short of an unavoidable stress, can force quantitative length or weight of sound upon them. Even the short "i"s and short "a" of "insignificant" and the short "e" of "feeblest" retain their insignificance and feebleness in spite of the help of the two consonants occurring after them, — the voice passes too swiftly away for any length to accrue before it has left them; there is no weight, no dwelling or lingering upon them sufficient to give them a greater sound-value. It would be a strange and extravagant prosody that would scan the first line —

Ōne ānd ŭn|ārmed ĭn thĕ | cār wās thē | drīvēr; | grēy
wās hē, | shrūnkĕn,

though it might still scan as a hexameter with antibacchius and molossus twice repeated as modulations in place of the dactyl; but it could not be read aloud in that way, — the ear would immediately contradict the arbitrary dictates of the eye and the inapplicable rigidity of the mental theory.

This is not to deny that an additional consonant or consonants within the word after and before the vowel do give greater length to the syllable as a whole; but this does not necessarily transfer it from the category of shorts to the category of longs. At most, when the weight of consonants is not heavy and decisive, it makes it easier for these midway sounds to figure as lengthened shorts; it helps a trochee to serve as a substitute modulation for a spondee but it does not transform it into a spondee. To take an instance from a hexameter movement —

> Wind in the forests, bees in the grove, — spring's ardent symbol
> Thrilling, the voice of the cuckoo.

Here the word "ardent" easily replaces a dactyl or spondee as a modulation, but it remains trochaic. There is more possibility of treating "forests" here with its three heavy consonants as a spondee, — a possibility, not a necessity invariable in all places, for one could very well write "in the forests of autumn", in spite of the three consonants, as the orthodox close of a dactylic hexameter. Let us try again with yet another example, this time of wholly or fundamentally dactylic hexameters, —

> "Onward from continent sailing to continent, ever from harbour
> Hasting to harbour, a wanderer joining[1] ocean to ocean."

Here the word "continent" clearly does not become a cretic, even when a third consonant follows like the "s" of "sailing", still less when a vowel follows; a slight weight is there, but it is altogether insufficient to hamper the pure dactylic flow of the line.

It is only a sufficient consonant weight that can change the category; but even then the result depends less on the number than on the power and heaviness of the consonants composing the word; the theory that it is the number of consonants that determines metrical length cannot stand always. Thus the word *strength* or the word *stripped* is long wherever it may occur, but *string* with its five consonant sounds is long mainly by the voice ictus falling on it; where that lacks it may remain short by the inherent value of its vowel: *heart-string, hamstring* sound more natural as trochees than as spondees; *hamstringing* carries weight as a dactyl, it is too weak to be a good antibacchius. In these matters it is always the ear that must judge, there can be no rule of thumb or fixed mathematical measure determinable by the eye of the reader; it is the weight or lightness of the syl-

[1] This word is a trochaic modulation, it is not intended to figure as a spondee.

lable, the slowed down or unencumbered rapid passage of the voice, the pressure or slightness of its step in passing that makes the difference, and of that the ear alone can be the true judge or arbiter.

In any case it is only the internal consonants that matter; for it is doubtful whether initial consonants in a word that follows can, even when they are many, radically influence the quantity of a preceding syllable. This rule of backward influence could prevail in the classical tongues because there the voice was more evenly distributed over the words; this evenness gave a chance to the short syllables to have their full sound-value and a slight addition of consonantal sound might overweight them and give them, either internally or in position, a decisive length value. Intrinsic quantity also was not crushed under the weight of stress as in English and turned into a secondary factor, it was and remained a prime factor in the rhythm. There is accentual pitch and inflexion, but it does not take the first place. Thus the first lines of the Aeneid, —

Ármă vír|ŭmquĕ că|nō, Trŏ́|jæ qūī | prímŭs ăb | órīs
Ĭtắlĭ|ām, fắ|tō prŏ́fŭ|gūs, Lā|vĭnắquĕ | vḗnĭt
Lítŏră| —

if they were read like an English line, would become some kind of irregular and formless accentual hexameter, —

Árma | vírumque | cáno, | Trójæ qui | prímus ab | óris
Itáli|am, fáto | prófugus, La|vínaque | vénit
Lítora| —

stress would preside and quantity fall into a subordinate second place. If this did not and could not happen, it was evidently because the accent was an inflexion or pitch of the voice and not stress, not an emphatic pressure.[1] In English stress or voice

---

[1] In the Latin metre accent and quantity coincide in the last two feet but not in the earlier four feet; the Harvey type of hexameter has been criticised for not following this rule, but the

emphasis predominates and there is a very uneven distribution of sound-values in which quantity is partly determined and, where not determined, considerably influenced by stress; it has some difficulty in asserting its full independent value. Moreover the words do not cohere or run into each other as in a Sanskrit line, (this cohesion was the *raison d'être* of the complicated law of Sandhi by which the closing letter of one word so frequently unites with the initial letter of its successor in a conjunct sound); each word in English is independent and has its own metrical value unaffected by the word that follows. In Sanskrit, as in Latin and Greek, the short syllable having already its full natural sound-value is affected by the additional consonant and passes into the category of longs by the force of the consonant weightage, but these conditions are not naturally present in English verse.

There is therefore no good reason, or at least no essential reason, for the admission of a rule allowing or obliging a throwback of influence from a following word upon its predecessor. In accentual or stress metre no such rule prevails, — one never thinks of this element in arranging one's line; there is nothing that compels its adoption in quantitative verse. If these initial consonants created an obstacle to the pace of the voice sufficient to make it linger or pause, then such an effect would be justified, — the closing short syllable of the preceding word would or might be lengthened: but, normally, the obstacle is so slight that it is not felt and the voice takes it in its stride and passes on without any slackening or with only a slight slackening of its pace. The distinctness of each word from another does not, indeed, create any gap or pause, but it is strong enough to preserve for it its independence, its separate self-value in the total rhythm of the line, the word-group or the clause. This does not destroy the value of consonant weight in the sound system; it is evident that a crowding or sparseness of consonants will make a great diffe-

---

writers had no choice, — to do otherwise would have brought in the conflict between stress and quantity which for the reason here stated could not occur in Latin. In the English hexameter accent, stress and quantity have inevitably to fuse together in the main long syllable of the foot; relief from a too insistent beat has to be sought by other natural means or technical devices, modulation, the greater value given to long unstressed syllables, variation of foot-grouping, pause, caesura.

rence to the total rhythm, it will produce a greater or less heaviness or lightness; but that is a rhythmic effect quite distinct from any imperative influence on the metre. A trochee does not become a spondee, a dactyl does not become a cretic because its final syllable is followed by a consonant or even by a group of consonants. There is, then, no sense in dragging in the classical rule where its admission is quite contrary to the natural instinct and practice of the language.

If these considerations are accepted as valid, the way lies open for the construction of true quantitative metre; a sound and realistic theory of it becomes possible. Four rules or sets of rules can be formulated which will sum up the whole base of the theory: —

1. All stressed syllables are metrically long, as are also all long-vowel syllables even without stress.

All short-vowel syllables are metrically short, unless they are lengthened by stress — or else by a sufficient weight of consonants or some other lengthening sound-element; but the mere fact of more than one consonant coming after a short vowel, whether within the word or after it, or both in combination, is not sufficient to confer length upon the syllable. Heaviness caused by a crowding of consonants affects the rhythm of a line or part of a line but does not alter its metrical values.

Each word has its own metrical value which cannot be radically influenced or altered by the word that follows.

2. The English language has many sounds which are doubtful or variable in quantity; these may be sometimes used as short and sometimes as long according to circumstance. Here the ear must be the judge.

3. Quantity within the syllable itself is not so rigidly fixed as in the ancient languages; often position or other circumstances may alter the metrical value of a syllable. A certain latitude has to be conceded in such cases, and there again the ear must be the judge.

4. Quantity metres cannot be as rigid and unalterable in English as in the old classical tongues; for the movement of the language is pliant and flexible and averse to rigidity and monotone. English poetry has always a fundamental metrical basis,

a fixed normality of the feet constituting a line; but it relieves the fixity by the use of modulations substituting, with sometimes a less, sometimes a greater freedom, other feet for the normal. This rule of variation, very occasionally admitted in the classical tongues but natural in English poetry, must be applied or at least permitted in quantitative metres also; otherwise, in poems of some length, their rhythms may become stereotyped in a too rigid sameness and fatigue the ear.

No other rule than these four need be laid down, for the rest must be left to individual choice and skill in technique.

In the basic structure of quantitative verse so arranged the three elements of English rhythm, accent, stress and intrinsic quantity are none of them excluded; all are united or even fused together. Accentual high pitch is taken up into stress; low pitch, not amounting to stress, as also slighter accentual inflexions have their place in the rhythm and the intonation but not in the metre; they are not allowed to determine the metrical quantity of the syllable on which they fall. For, in fact, unless they amount to stress, these voice-inflexions do not confer length of true quantity; the quantity conferred by them in accentual verse is conventional and need not be admitted where the accentual basis is abandoned and the convention is not needed. Stress itself is admitted as a quantitative element because it constitutes, by the weight of the voice which it lays on the syllable, a true metrical length, a strong sound-value. Intrinsic quantity, which is not recognised as a metrical constituent in the traditional verse system, recovers here its legitimate place. As a result quantitative metres can be constructed which, like accentual and stress metres but unlike the abortive constructions of the classicists, can flow naturally in a free movement, a movement native to the language; for they will combine in themselves, without disfiguration or forcing, all the natural elements of the rhythm or sound-movement proper to the English tongue.

It may even be said that all English speech, colloquial, prose or verse, has this as its natural rhythm, preserves these normal sound-values. This universality will be at once evident if we take at will or even take at random any snatch of conversation or any prose passage caught from anywhere or everywhere and test by it this rule of quantity; it will be found that the rule is in all cases applicable.

Ĭ hăve dĕ|cĭdĕd tŏ | stārt tŏm|ŏrrōw. | Ĭt ĭs nō ūse | pŭttĭng off | mȳ gōĭng | ănȳ lōngĕr. |

These sentences set out with a dactylo-trochaic movement and change to less simple feet, ionic a minore, cretic, antibacchius, double trochee. Or if you hear an irate voice shouting —

Gĕt out ŏf thăt | ŏr Ĭ'll kĭck yoŭ, |

and have sufficient leisure and equanimity of mind to analyse the rhythm of this exhortation, you will find yourself in the presence of an excited double iamb followed by a vehement antispast, and can then conscientiously determine the rhythm of your own answer. Or if one takes, as a resting-house between colloquial speech and literary prose, the first advertisement that meets the eye in any daily newspaper, the result will still infallibly illustrate our rule. For example,

Thĭs cŏlŭmn | ĭs ĭntĕndĕd | tŏ gĭve | pŭblĭcĭtȳ | tŏ thĕ ă|mēnĭtĭes | ănd cŏmmĕrcĭal | ĭntĕrēsts | ŏf Bangălōre. | —

where amphibrach, paeons, iamb, tribrach, dactyl, cretic, double iamb are harmoniously blended together by an unconscious master of quantitative rhythm. It can be at once and easily established, by multiplying instances, that the daily talk and writing of English-speaking peoples, though not by any means always poetry, is still, in spite of itself and by an unfelt compulsion, always rhythmic and always quantitative in its rhythm.

If we take similarly passages from literary prose, we shall find the same law of rhythm lifted to a higher level. Shakespeare and the Bible will give us the best and most concentrated examples of this rhythm in prose. Our first quotation, from the New Testament, can indeed be arranged, omitting the superfluous word 'even' before 'Solomon', as a very perfect and harmonious stanza of free quantitative verse.

Cōnsĭdĕr | thĕ lĭlĭĕs | ŏf thĕ fīeld, | hōw thēy grōw; |
Thĕy tōil nŏt, | nēithĕr dŏ | thēy spĭn, |
Yĕt Ī | sāy ŭntŏ yoŭ | thăt Sōlŏmŏn | ĭn āll hĭs | glōrў |
Wăs nŏt ărrāyed | līke ŭntŏ | ōne ŏf thēse. |

Or again, let us take the opening verses of the Sermon on the Mount,

Blēssĕd āre | thĕ pōor | ĭn spĭrĭt; | fŏr thēirs ĭs | thĕ
                                                            kīngdŏm | ŏf hēavĕn. |
Blēssĕd āre | thēy thăt mōurn; | fŏr thēy shăll bĕ |
                                                                    cōmfŏrtĕd. |
Blēssĕd āre | thĕ meek; | fŏr thēy shăll | ĭnhērĭt | thĕ ēarth. |
Blēssĕd āre | thĕ mērcĭfŭl; | fŏr thēy shăll | ŏbtāin mērcў. |
Blēssĕd āre | thĕ pūre ĭn hēart; | fŏr thēy shăll sēe | Gōd. |

Or from St. Paul, —

Thōugh Ī spēak | wĭth thĕ tōngues | ŏf mēn | ănd ŏf āngĕls, |
                                           ănd hāve nŏt | chārĭtў, |
Ī ăm bĕcōme | ăs sōundĭng brāss, | ŏr ă tĭnklĭng | cўmbal. |
Ănd thōugh Ī hăve | thĕ gĭft | ŏf prōphĕcў |
ănd ŭndĕrstānd | āll mўstĕrĭes | ănd āll knōwlĕdge, |
ănd thōugh Ī hăve | āll fāith, | sō thăt Ī coŭld | rĕmōve
                                                                           mōuntāins, |
ănd hāve | nŏt chărĭtў, | Ī ăm nōthĭng. |

If we take Shakespeare's prose in a well-known passage, we shall find the same law of quantitative rhythm automatically arranging his word-movement —

Thĭs gōodlў frāme, | thĕ ēarth, sēems tŏ | mĕ ă stĕrīle |
prōmŏntōry; | thĭs mōst ēxcĕl|lĕnt cănŏpў, | thĕ āir, |
lōok yoŭ, | thĭs brāve ō'erhāng|ĭng fĭrmămēnt, | thĭs

mă̄jēstĭ|că̆l rōōf frēttĕd | wĭth gōldĕn fīre, | — whȳ, ĭt
ăppēārs | tŏ mĕ
nō ōth|ĕr thĭng thăn ă | fōul ănd pēstĭ|lĕnt cōngrĕgā|tīōn ŏf
vāpŏurs. | Whăt ă pīece ŏf | wŏrk ĭs ă măn! | Hōw nōblĕ ĭn |
rēasŏn, | hŏw ĭnfĭnĭte | ĭn făcŭltȳ! | ĭn fōrm, | ĭn
mōvĭng, | hŏw ĕxprēss ănd | ādmĭrăblĕ! | ĭn āctĭon hŏw |
lĭke
ăn āngĕl! | ĭn ăpprĕhēnsīōn | hōw lĭke ă gōd! | thĕ bēautȳ
ŏf |
thĕ wōrld! | thĕ pārăgŏn | ŏf ānĭmāls. Ănd yēt, tŏ mē, |
whāt ĭs thĭs quīnt|ĕssĕnce ŏf dūst?

The measures of this prose rhythm find their units of order in word-groups and not as in poetry in metrical lines; the syllabic combinations which we call feet do not follow here any fixed sequence. In colloquial speech the sequence is arranged by impulse of Nature or by the automatic play of the subconscious mind, in prose either by the instinctive or by the conscious action of an inner ear, by a secret and subtle hearing in our subliminal parts. There is not an arrangement of feet previously set by the mind and fixedly recurrent as in metre. But still the measures of speech are the same and in all these prose passages there is a dominant rhythm, — even sometimes a free recurrence or dominance of certain measures, not laid down or fixed, but easy and natural, — which gives an underlying unity to the whole passage. In the instance taken from Shakespeare a remarkable persistence of four-foot measures, with occasional shorter ones intervening, builds up a grave and massive rhythmic feeling and imparts even a poetic motion to the unified whole.

In free verse the difference of prose movement and poetic rhythm tends to disappear; poetry steps down to or towards the level of rhythmic, sometimes a very poorly rhythmic prose; but it is too often a rhythm which misses its aim at the ear and is not evident though it may exist incommunicably somewhere in the mind of the writer. That indeed is the general modernistic tendency — to step back to the level of prose, sometimes to the colloquial level, both in language and in sound movement; the tendency, the aim even, is to throw away the intensities of poetic rhythm and poetic language and approximate to a prose intonation and to a prose diction; one intensity only is kept in view and that too not always, the intensity of the thought substance. It is the thought substance that is expected to determine its own sound harmonies — as in prose: the thought must not subject itself to a preconceived or set rhythm, it must be free from the metrical straitwaistcoat; or else the metrical mould must be sufficiently irregular, capricious, easily modifiable to give a new freedom and ease of movement to the thought substance.

Our immediate concern, however, is with quantitative metre constructed on the principle of quantity, — though free verse also on that basis has to be taken into consideration as a subordinate possibility. After all, the swing against metre has not justified itself; it goes contrary to a very profound law of speech, contradicts a very strong need of the ear, and the metreless verse it prefers disappoints, by the frequent flatness and inequality which seems natural to it at its ordinary level, the listening consciousness. All creation proceeds on a basis of oneness and sameness with a superstructure of diversity, and there is the highest creation where is the intensest power of basic unity and sameness and on that supporting basis the intensest power of appropriate and governed diversity. In poetic speech metre gives us this intensest power of basic unity and sameness — rhythmic variation gives us this intensest power of expressive diversity. Metre was in the thought of the Vedic poets the reproduction in speech of great creative world-rhythms; it is not a mere formal construction, though it may be made by the mind into even such a lifeless form; but even that lifeless form or convention, when genius and inspiration breathe the force of life into it, becomes again what it was meant to be, it becomes itself and serves its own true and great purpose. There is an intonation of poetry which is different from the flatter and looser intonation of prose, and with it a heightened or gathered intensity of language, a deepened vibrating intensity of rhythm, an intense inspiration in the thought substance. One leaps up with this rhythmic spring or flies upon these wings of rhythmic exaltation to a higher scale of consciousness which expresses things common with an uncommon power both of vision and of utterance and things uncommon with their own native and revealing accent; it expresses them, as no mere prose speech can do, with a certain kind of deep appealing intimacy of truth which poetic rhythm alone gives to expressive form and power of language: the greater this element, the greater is the poetry. The essence of this power can be there without metre, but metre is its spontaneous form, raises it to its acme. The tradition of metre is not a vain and foolish convention followed by the great poets of the past in a primitive ignorance unconscious of their own bondage; it is in spite of its appearance of human convention a law of Nature, an innermost mind-nature, a highest speech-nature.

But it does not immediately follow that the metrical application to poetry of the normal rhythm of the language, discoverable even in its colloquial speech and prose, is imperatively called for or that the construction of quantitative metres in that mould will be a needed or a right procedure. It might be reasoned, on the contrary, that precisely because this is a normal movement for colloquial speech and prose, it must be ill-fitted for poetry; poetic speech is supernormal, above the ordinary level, and its principle of rhythm should be other than that of common language. Moreover, it may be said, the admission of intrinsic rhythmic quantities to a share in determining the metrical basis would in practice only give us an accentual or stress metre with a slight difference, and the difference would be for the worse. For the function which quantity now serves in accentual verse as a powerful free element in the variation of the rhythm, would be sacrificed; quantitative verse would be bound to a rigid beat which would impose on it the character of a monotonous drone or would fix it in a shackled stiffness like the drumming of the early "decasyllabon" or that treadmill movement which has been charged, as an incurable defect, against the English hexameter.

But let us note, first, that there can be no idea of replacing altogether the normal accentual mould of English verse by a quantitative structure; the object can only be to introduce new rhythms which extend and vary the established achievement of

English poetry, to create new moulds, to add a rich and possibly a very spacious modern wing to an old edifice. Even if the new forms are only an improvement on stress metre, a rhythm starting from the same swing of the language, that is no objection; it may still be worth doing if it brings in new tunes, other cadences, fresh subtleties of word-music. As for the objection of a tied-up monotony, caused by the disappearance of the free placing and variation of the pure quantitative elements in metrical rhythm, that need not be the consequence: there are other means of variation which are sufficient to dispel that peril. A free use of modulation, an avoidance of metrical rigidity by other devices natural to the flexibility of the English tongue, a skilful employment of overlapping (*enjambement*), of caesura, of word-grouping are presupposed in any reasonable quantitative system. Even where a very regular movement is necessitated or desirable, the resources of the play of sound, a subtle play of vowellation and of consonant harmonies, rhythmic undertones and overtones ought to cure the alleged deficiency. It is not the nature of the material but the unskilful hand that creates the flaw; for each kind of material has its own limitations and its own possibilities, and the hand of the craftsman is needed to restrict or overcome the limitations, even to take advantage of the natural bounds and bring out the full force of the latent creativeness concealed in the obstructing matter.

The application of the quantitative principle and the discovery of the forms that are possible are the task of the creator, not of the theoretical critic. It is, first and foremost, English quantitative forms that we have to create; the reproduction or new-creation of classical metres in English speech is only a side issue. Here the possibilities are endless, but they fall into two or three categories. First, there can be fixed quantitative metres repeated from line to line without variation except for such modulations as are, in the form chosen, possible or desirable. Secondly, stanza forms can be found, either analogous to those used in accentual verse or else analogous to the Greek arrangement in strophe and antistrophe. Thirdly, one can use a freer quantitative verse in which each line has its own appropriate movement, the feet being variable, but with a predominant single rhythm unifying the whole. Lastly, there can be entirely free quantitative verse, true verse with a poetic rhythm, but not bound by any law of metre. The stanza form is the most suitable to quantitative verse, for here there can be much variety and the danger of rigidity or monotony is non-existent. The use of set stanza metres simple or composite is less obligatory than it was in classical verse; even, each poem can discover its own metrical stanza form most in consonance with its own thought and feeling. The fixed metre unchanging from line to line needs greater skill; modulation is here of great importance. A semi-free quantitative verse also gives considerable scope; it can be planned in a form resembling that of the Greek chorus but without the fixed balance of strophe and antistrophe, or a still looser use can be made of it escaping towards the freedom of modernistic verse.

An unconsciously quantitative free verse may be said to exist already in the writings of Whitman and contemporary modernist poets. In modern free verse the underlying impulse is to get away from the fixed limitations of accentual metre, its set forms and its traditional "poetic" language, and to create forms and a diction more kin to the natural rhythm and turns of the language which we find in common speech and in prose. To throw away the bonds of metre altogether, to approximate not only in the language but in the rhythmic movement to normal speech and to prose tone and prose expression was the method first preferred; a great deal of free verse is nothing but prose cut up into lines to make it look like verse. But in the more skilful treatment by the greater writers there is a labour to arrive at a certain power of rhythm and a sufficient unity of movement. Free verse cannot justify itself unless it makes a thing of beauty of every line and achieves at the same time an underlying rhythmic oneness; this is imperative when the power for form and the uplifting intensity of metrical verse is absent, if this kind of writing is not to be, as it too often is, a failure. In the best poetry of the kind the attempt to achieve this end arrives precisely at a form of free quantitative verse based on the natural rhythm of the language liberated from all metrical convention of regularity, and there is sometimes an approximation to its highest possibilities. But the approximation is not so near as it might have been in the work of one who had the theory before him; for it was not the conscious mind, but the creative ear that was active and compelled this result, helped no doubt by the will to outdo the beauty of accentual metrical rhythm in a freer poetry. In Whitman the attempt at perfection of rhythm is often present and, when he does his best as a rhythmist, it rises to a highstrung acuteness which gives a great beauty of movement to his finest lines; but what he arrives at is a true quantitative free verse.

Cōme, | lŏvelў̆ ănd | sōōthĭng | dēāth, |
Ŭndŭlāte | rōūnd thĕ wōrld, | sĕrēnelў̆ | ărrīvĭng, | ărrīvĭng, |
Ĭn thĕ dāy, | ĭn thĕ nīght, | tŏ āll, | tŏ ēāch, |
Sōōnĕr ŏr | lātĕr, | dēlĭcăte | dēāth. | ....
Ăpprōāch | strōng dĕ|līvĕrĕss, |
Whĕn ĭt ĭs sō, | whĕn thōū hăst | tākĕn thĕm | Ī jōyŏuslў̆ |
sīng thĕ dēād, |
Lōst ĭn thĕ | lōvĭng | flōātĭng | ōcĕăn ŏf thēē, |
Lāved ĭn thĕ | flōōd ŏf thў̄ | blīss, Ŏ dēāth. | ....
Ănd thĕ sīghts | ŏf thĕ ōpĕn | lāndscāpe | ănd thĕ
hīgh-sprĕād | skў̄ ăre fīttĭng, |
Ănd līfe | ănd thĕ fīēlds, | ănd thĕ hūge ănd | thōūghtfŭl
nīght. |

That is comparatively rare in its high beauty; but everywhere the rhythmic trend is the same wherever we look at it, — as in the rhymed freedom of this opening, —

Wēāpŏn | shāpelў̆, | nākĕd, | wān, |
Hēād frŏm thĕ | mōthĕr's | bōwĕls | drāwn, |
Wōōdĕd | flēsh ănd | mētăl bōne, | līmb | ōnlў̆ ōne | ănd
lĭp | ōnlў̆ ōne, |
Grēy-blūē | lēaf bў̄ | rēd-hēāt | grōwn, | hĕlve prŏdūced |
frŏm ă lĭttlĕ | sēēd sōwn, |

Rēstĭng thĕ | grāss ămīd | ănd ŭpōn, |
Tŏ bĕ lēan'd | ănd tŏ lēan ōn. |

Even when he loosens into a laxity nearer to prose, the compact quantitative movement, though much less high-strung, is still there, —

Ī sēē | māle ănd | fēmāle | ēvĕrўwhēre, |
Ī sēē | thĕ sĕrēne | brōthĕrhŏŏd | ŏf phĭlŏsōphs, |
Ī sēē thĕ | cŏnstrūctĭvenĕss | ŏf mў rāce. |

It is only when he lies back or lolls indolently content with spreading himself out in a democratic averageness of rhythm that the intensity of poetic movement fades out; but the free quantitative movement is there even then, though near now to the manner and quality of prose.

The later practicians of free verse have not often the heightened rhythmic movement of Whitman at his best, but still they are striving towards the same kind of thing, and their work apparently and deliberately amorphous receives something like a shape, a balance, a reasoned meaning when scanned as quantitative free verse. We find this in passages of the *Hollow Men, e.g.*

Wē āre thĕ | hōllōw mēn |
Wē āre thĕ | stŭffed mēn |
Lēanĭng tŏ|gēthĕr |
Hēadpīece | fĭlled wĭth strāw. | Ălās! |
Oūr drīed | vōīces, whĕn |
Wĕ whīspĕr | tŏgēthĕr, |
Ăre quĭĕt | ănd mēanĭnglĕss |
Ăs wĭnd | ĭn drȳ grāss |
Ŏr rāts' fēet | ōvĕr | brōkĕn glāss |
Ĭn oūr drȳ | cēllăr. |

Shāpe wĭthōut fōrm, | shāde wĭthōut | cōlŏŭr, |
Părălȳsed fōrce, | gēstŭre wĭth|ōut mōtĭŏn; |

or let us take a passage from Stephen Spender, —

Ŏh cōmrādes, | lĕt nŏt thōse | whō fŏllŏw | āftĕr |
—Thĕ beāutĭfŭl | gĕnĕrātiŏn | thăt shăll sprīng frŏm | ōur
sīdes — |
Lĕt nŏt thĕm | wōndĕr | hōw āftĕr | thĕ fāilŭre ŏf | bănks |
Thĕ fāilŭre | ŏf căthēdrăls | ănd thĕ dĕclāred | ĭnsānĭtȳ |
ŏf ōur rūlĕrs, |
Wĕ lācked | thĕ sprīng-līke | rĕsōurcĕs | ŏf thĕ tīgĕr |
Ōr ŏf plānts | whō strīke ōut | nēw rōots tŏ | gūshing wātĕrs. |
Būt thrōugh | thĕ tōrn dōwn | pōrtiŏns ŏf | ōld făbrĭc | lĕt
thēir ēyes |
Wătch thĕ ăd|mīrĭng dāwn | ĕxplōde | līke ă shēll |
Ărōund ŭs, | dāzĭng ŭs | wĭth ĭts līght | līke snōw. |

There is a rhythm there, but it is not sufficiently gathered up or vivid and it is much more subdued than Eliot's towards the atony and flatness of ordinary prose rhythm. The last lines of the quotation from the *Hollow Men* could be used to describe with a painful accuracy most of this ametric poetry. Some kind of poetic shape is there but no realised and convincing form; shade there is plenty, but colour — except perhaps blacks, browns, greys and silver-greys — is mostly absent; force is there but paralysed or only half-carrying out its intention, gestures with much effort and straining, but no successful motion. In less excellent passages of the free verse writers this atony comes out very evidently; all intensity of poetic rhythm disappears and we plod through arid waste-lands. There is an insistence on formlessness as the basis and each writer tries to shape his own rhythm out of this arhythmic amorphousness, sometimes with a half success, but not always or very often. This is clearly the reason of the failure of free verse and the reason too of several besetting general deficiencies of modernist verse; for even where there is form or metre, it seems ashamed of itself and tries to look as if there were none. It is the reason also of the discouraging inequality of modernist poetry, its failure to achieve any supreme beauty or greatness, any outstanding work which could compare with the masterpieces of other epochs. Inspiration is the source of poetic intensity and, while inspiration comes when it will and not at command, yet it is more tempted to come and can be more sustained when there is a conscious and constant form to receive it, — not necessarily metre in the received sense, — and although the highest breath of inspiration cannot, even so, be continuous, for the human mind is too frail to sustain the supernormal luminous inrush, yet the form sustains quality, keeps it at a higher level than can any license of caprice or freedom of shapelessness. When the form is not there the inspiration, the intensity that gives perfect poetic expression to idea, feeling or vision, keeps more at a distance and has to be dragged in with an effort; its impulse, even if it comes in lines, phrases, passages, afterwards ceases or flags and toils and through long weary pages one feels its persistent absence or unwilling half-presence and the mass of the work remains unsatisfying. What is done may be strong or interesting in substance, but it lacks the immortal shape. Mind is there, a fertile and forceful, sometimes too acute and forceful intelligence, but not life, not a firm lasting body. It is possible that one day the impulse which created free verse may be justified; but, if so, it can only be done when a free form is achieved, a free rhythmic unity. For that end the best work of Whitman would seem to point to a free but finely built quantitative rhythm as the most promising base. But, even at its highest, free verse is not likely to replace metre.

THE PROBLEM OF THE HEXAMETER

It is now possible to transfer our attention to the minor problem of the naturalisation of classical quantitative metres in English poetry; for in the light of this more natural theory of quantity we can hope to find an easier solution. Among these metres the hexameter stands as the central knot of the problem; if that is loosened, the rest follows. But first let us return on past attempts and their failure and find by that study a basis of comparison between the true and the false hexameter. There are here two elements to be considered, the metrical form and the characteristic rhythm; both Clough and Longfellow have failed for the most part to get into their form the true metrical movement and missed too by that failure to get the true inner rhythm, the something more that is the soul of the hexameter. Of the two, Longfellow achieved the smoother half-success — or rather the more plausible failure. He realised that the metre must be predominantly dactylic and maintained a smooth dactylic flow, broken only by the false, because mechanical, use of trochees to vary the continuous dactylic beat. Other modulations could not be used with effect because the accentual system only admits in the hexameter the dactyl, the spondee and the trochee. For all three-syllabled feet are in the accentual hexameter reduced to dactyls. The tribrach gets right of entry by imposing an accentual low pitch on its inherently unaccented and unstressed first syllable, *e.g.*,

And with the | others in haste went hurrying down to the sea-shore.

The anapaest is cooked up into a pseudo-dactyl by a similar device of false accentuation and by the belittling of its long vowel, the antibacchius and cretic by a depression or half suppression of the value of the unstressed long syllable, the second long bar that gives them their musical value; the molossus is shorn of its strength by a similar treatment of all its syllables except the opening long sound. All are disabled from coming out in relief on the dactylic background and so cannot do their work as modulating variants; for that they should enter in their own right as themselves and not as false dactyls and with their full metrical value. Even among the three available feet the trochee gives poor service; for it rarely fits in, — its effect, when it is used mechanically as a device and with no meaningful appropriateness or rhythmic beauty, disturbs the dactylic flow without giving any relief to the dactylic monotone. Dactyl and spondee by themselves, pure and unmodulated, or the dactyl by itself cannot, unhelped and unrelieved, bear successfully the burden of a long poem in accentual metre.

Longfellow treats us to a non-stop flow of even hexameters with few overlappings and insufficient use of pauses; such overlappings as there are are hardly noticeable, so mechanical is their intervention, so entirely uncalled for by rhythmic necessity and unburdened with meaning; the pauses are sometimes well-done but the whole tone of the rhythm is so mechanical that even then they lose their effect and seem almost artificial. The result on the rhythmic whole is disastrous; a smooth even sing-song is the constant note, a movement without nobility or beauty or power or swiftness. Sometimes we come across passages that are adequate and achieve a quiet and subdued beauty —

> Filled was the air with a dreamy and magical light; and the landscape
> Lay as if new-created in all the freshness of childhood.
> Peace seemed to reign upon earth, and the restless heart of the ocean
> Was for a moment consoled. All sounds were in harmony blended.

In such passages, the metre, though accentual, satisfies quantitative demand and so escapes from its deficiencies, but the rhythm is too flatly smooth and still indistinctive; it fails to support and achieve fully by the something more behind the metrical movement the beauty that the words intended, — some charm of delicacy is achieved, but it lacks power, height and depth; here certainly is not the tread of the great Olympian measure. Ordinarily, the note sinks lower and even descends to a very low pitch; we hear, not the roll of the hexameter, but some six-foot dactylic rhythm resembling a sort of measured prose recitative —

> Then he arose from his bed, and heard what the people were saying,
> Joined in the talk at the door, with Stephen and Richard and Gilbert,
> Joined in the morning prayer, and in the reading of Scripture.[1]

---

[1] Note the detestable combination of two flat trochees with a falsified tribrach in the middle of this line. These false movements abound in the accentual hexameter.

And yet even the accentual (or perhaps one should say the stress) hexameter is capable of better things. Clough, aiming at this stronger efficiency, tries to escape from the treadmill motion, the sing-song, the monotone; but he does not altogether get away from it and arrives only at a familiar vigour or a capable but undistinguished movement, or falls into a trotting and stumbling rhythm which is sometimes hardly even a rhythm. In attempting to shun the monotony of the unuplifted dactylic beat, he often totally overlays or half overlays the metrical basis of the hexameter rhythm which must be always a sustained dactylic movement. He perpetrates frequently lines that are wholly trochaic and have only this in common with the hexameter that they walk on six feet; a host of other lines are, if not wholly, yet predominantly trochaic. This, which can sometimes be done in a true hexameter rhythm with a special intonation and a special purpose, is fatal if constantly used as an ordinary action of a machine. Very often the trochees break a line that would otherwise have been adequate; sometimes there is what seems to be a cross between hexameter and pentameter; often he indulges in an anapaestic line, sometimes three at a time, disguised as hexameters by turning an initial pyrrhic into a false trochee. The result tends to be tedious, trivial and disappointing; let us take a sample —

> So they bathed, they read, they roamed in glen and forest
> Far amid blackest pines to the waterfalls they shadow
> Far up the long long glens to the loch and the loch behind it
> Deep under huge red cliffs, a secret, and oft by the starlight
> Ŏr thĕ aur|ŏră, pĕr|chānce, rācĭng | hōme tŏ thĕ |
>   ēight-ŏ-clŏck | mutton;[1] |
> So they bathed and read and roamed in heathery Highland.

This indistinctive paddling has even less of the sound and rhythm of the true hexameter than Longfellow's verses which are at least hexametric in form and surface appearance.

But still there are passages, not numerous enough, in which

---

[1] Note that this, the sole truly dactylic line, with quantitative modulations, is in spite of its deliberate prosaism less unsatisfactory in sound than the rest of the passage.

he loses his fear of the pure dactylic movement and does not replace it or break it with the disturbing intrusion of unmanaged or unassimilated trochees; he arrives then at "accentual" lines, — if they must be so called, but they are really stress lines, — with a firm beat that makes the metrical structure adequate; or he achieves a movement in which the trochees come in with a distinct rhythmic meaning and significant effect or, at the least, make themselves at home in the dactylic rhythm, or he brings in other modulations in a way proper to the quantitative hexameter —

Found amid granite dust on the frosty scalp of the Caïrngorm....
Eying one moment the beauty, the life, ere he flung himself in it,
Drinking in, deep in his soul, the beautiful hue and the
                                              clearness....
Often I find myself saying and know not myself as I say it,
Perish the poor and the weary! what can they better than perish,
Perish in labour for her who is worth the destruction of empires....
Dig in thy deep dark prison, O miner! and finding be thankful,
While thou̅ ārt | ēatĭng blāck | brēad ĭn thĕ | pōĭsŏnŏus | āir ŏf
                                              thў | cāvĕrn,
Far away glitters the gem on the peerless neck of a princess....
Into a granite bason the amber torrent descended.

These lines are metrically and rhythmically adequate; the treatment of the metre is unexceptionable: there is a true form, a good basis and beginning of a genuine hexameter movement; and yet something is lacking, something which ought to be there and is not, and its absence prevents them from being quite effective. It is the rhythm that in spite of its soundness is not altogether alive, does not keep sufficiently alert, has not found the true movement that would give it the full power and speed of the true hexameter. A second fault is that while individual lines are good and many sound even excellent when read by themselves or even two or three at a time, there is no rhythmic harmony of the long passage or paragraph; one has, in the mass, the sense of listening to the same indifferent and undistinguished movement repeated without sufficient meaningful variation and without any harmonious total significance. Above all the large hexameter rhythm, such as we have it in Greek or Latin, has not been found, nor anything that would equal it as a native English harmony fitted for great poetic speech, for great thoughts and feelings, for great action and movement. There is a tameness of sound, a flatness of level, or, even when beauty or energy is there, it is a tenuous beauty, a strength that is content to be low-toned and moderate.

One reason of this deficiency must be that in all this work the hexameter is compelled to express subjects whose triviality brings it down far below its natural pitch of greatness, force or beauty. A pathetically sentimental love story, a rather dull-hued tale of courtship among New England Puritans, the trifling doings and amours and chaff and chat of holiday-making undergraduates, these are not subjects in which either language or rhythm can rise to any great heights or reach out into revealing largenesses; they are obliged to key themselves to commonness and flatness; the language is as often as not confidentially familiar or prosaic, a manner good enough for some other kinds of verse but not entitled to call in the power of the great classical metre. There can be in such an atmosphere no room and no courage to dare to rise into any uplifting grandeur or break out into any extreme of beauty. Both Clough and Longfellow tell their stories well and it is more for the interest of the contents than for the beauty of the poetry that we read them. But the hexameter was made for nobler purposes; it has been the medium of epic or pastoral or it tuned itself to a powerful or forcefully pointed expression of thought and observation; power and beauty are its native character and, even when it turns to satire or to familiar speech, it keeps always one or other or both of these characteristics. There is no sound reason why it should be otherwise in English, why this great metre should be condemned to an inferior level and inferior purpose; if that is done, it fails its user and dissatisfies the reader.

In fact, Clough does once or twice rise above these limitations. Here, following immediately three lines that have been already quoted as good in their limits, come three others that suddenly realise the true hexameter rhythm; there is the life and energy natural to that rhythm, there is the characteristic swiftness, rush, force, which is one of its notes, there is an exact clothing of the thought, feeling or action in its own native movement —

> What! for a mite, or a mote, an impalpable odour of honour
> Armies shall bleed, cities burn, and the soldier red from the storming
> Carry hot rancour and lust into chambers of mothers and daughters!

At another place he rises still higher and suddenly discovers, though only once in a way and apparently without being conscious of his find, the rhythm of the true quantitative hexameter —

> Hē like ă | gōd cāme | lēavĭng hĭs | āmplĕ Ŏ|lȳmpĭăn | chāmbĕr

where the opening antibacchius and spondee followed by bounding and undulating dactyls give a sound-value recognisable as akin to the ancient movement. It would be an epic line if it were not in the mock-heroic style; but, even so, if we met it apart from its context, it would remind us at once of the Homeric rhythms —

> Bē de kat' Oulumpoio karēnōn chōömenos kēr....

If all the poem had been written in that manner or in accordant rhythms, the problem of the English hexameter would have been solved; there would have been no failure or half failure.[1]

We begin to glimpse the conditions of success and may now summarily state them. The hexameter is a dactylic metre and it must remain unequivocally and patently dactylic; there can be no escape from its difficulties by diminishing the dactylic beat:

---

[1] Kingsley's *Andromeda* deserves a mention, for it is the most readable of English hexameter poems; the verse is well-constructed, much better than Clough's; it has not the sing-song tameness of Longfellow, there is rhythm, there is resonance. But though the frame is correct and very presentable, there is nothing or little inside it. Kingsley has the trick of romantic language, romantic imagination and thinking, but he is not an original poet; the poetic value of his work is far inferior to Clough's or Longfellow's, it is not sound and good stuff but romantic tinsel.

rather its full quantitative force has to be brought out, — the more that is done, the more the true rhythm will appear. But this need not bring in any sing-song, treadmill walk or monotone. In Longfellow, in Clough at their ordinary level, it is the low even tone without relief, the repetition of a semi-trochaic jog-trot or a smooth unvarying canter, the beat of tame dactyls, that gives this impression. In Harvey or similar writers it is the constrained artificial treatment of the metre that enforces a treadmill labour. But this is not the true hexameter movement; the true movement is a swift stream or a large flow, an undulating run, the impetuous bounding of a torrent, an ocean surge or a divine gallop of the horses of the sun-god. There must be one underlying sameness as in all metre, but there can and should be at the same time a considerable diversity on the surface. That can be secured by several means, each of which gives plenty of room for rhythmic subtlety and for many turns of sound significance. There is the pause in various places of the line, near the beginning, at the middle or just after it or close to the end; all admit of a considerable variety in the exact placing, modulation, combination of the pause or pauses. There is also the line caesura and the foot caesura. The hexameter line in English may be cut into two or else three equal dactylic parts, or it may be cut anywhere in the middle of a foot and this admits of a number of very effective variations which obviate monotony altogether. For example —

In the dawn-ray lofty and voiceless
Ida climbed with her god-haunted peaks | into diamond lustres,
Ida, first of the hills | with the ranges silent beyond her
Watching the dawn in their giant companies, | as since the ages
First began | they had watched her, | upbearing Time on their
summits ....

"Hero Aeneas, swift be thy stride to the Ilian hill-top.
Dardanid, haste! for the gods are at work; they have risen with
the morning,
Each from his starry couch, and they labour. Doom, we can see it,
Glows on their anvils of destiny, clang we can hear of their
hammers.

Something they forge for us, sitting unknown in the silence
                                                    eternal,
Whether of evil or good it is they who shall choose who are
                                                    masters
Calm, unopposed; they are gods and they work out their iron
                                                    caprices.
Troy is their stage and Argos their background; we are their
                                                    puppets.
Always our voices are prompted to speech for an end that we
                                                    know not,
Always we think that we drive, but are driven. Action and
                                                    impulse,
Yearning and thought are their engines, our will is their shadow
                                                    and helper."

There are many other devices for variation: there is overlapping, — but it must be skilfully managed so as to coincide with perceptible movements of the thought, not used merely as a customary technical device; — there is the constant attention to the right vowellation and consonant harmonies which can give an individual character to each line and are also intimately connected with the rhythmic rendering of significance. Even though the free rhythmic placing of intrinsic long syllables is taken away, since they are now bound down to a metrical use, still much can be done with the distribution of stressed long vowels and stressed short vowels among the six beats; for the predominance of either in a line or passage or their more or less equal distribution in various ways creates different psychologies of sound and dictates large or wide or narrow or subtle motions of both rhythm and feeling. In this opening of a poem —

Dawn in her journey eternal compelling the labour of mortals,
Dawn the beginner of things with the night for their rest or their
                                                    ending,
Pallid and bright-lipped arrived from the mists and the chill of
                                                    the Euxine,

in the first line the stressed long vowels predominate, in the second the stressed short vowels, in the third there is an equal distribution; in each case there is a suiting of the choices of sound to a different shade of movement-sense. In another passage —

> doffing his mantle
> Started to run at the bidding a swift-footed youth of the Trojans,
> First in the race and the battle, Thrasymachus son of Aretes,

we can see that the predominance of short stresses amounting to an almost unbroken succession of natural short-vowel syllables creates a long running swiftness of the rhythm which fits in exactly with the action. All these minutiae are part of the technique and the possibilities of the hexameter and, if they are neglected or ineffectively used, the fault does not lie with the metre. The natural resources of the true quantitative hexameter are so great that even a long series of end-stopped lines would not necessarily create a monotone.

Finally, there is the resource of modulation, and in the quantitative hexameter this can be used with great effect, either sparingly or in abundance, best sparing perhaps in epic or high narrative, abundant in poems of complex thinking and emotion. There is only one possible modulation in place of the spondee and that is the trochee. In the quantitative hexameter the trochee, unless unskilfully used, does not break or hurt the flow; it modifies the total rhythm so as to give it an expressive turn and it can easily make itself a part of the general dactylic streaming. For example —

> High over all that a nation has built and its love and its laughter,
> Lighting a last time homestead and highway, temple and market,
> Looking on men who must | dīe ănd | wōměn | destined to
> sorrow,
> Looking on | bēautў | fīre mŭst lāy | low and the sickle of
> slaughter.

Here the two trochees together — a combination almost always awkward or crippling in the accentual hexameter — and the trochee followed by a cretic fit easily into the movement and create by their unusual and appropriate turn of sound a modulation of the rhythmic feeling. If the third line were written —

Looking on men who must die and on women predestined to sorrow,

the common indistinguishable metrical run would not at all serve the intended meaning, — it would be a statement and would inform the mind but, robbed of the special turn of sound, it would not move. For the dactyl there is a great number of possible modulations; the antibacchius can be used freely, the lighter cretic less freely but still frequently, the first paeon often but not too often; even the lighter molossus can come in to our aid; the tribrach or the anapaest can introduce the first foot of a line or step in after a pause in the middle, but elsewhere they can seldom intervene or only if it is done very carefully. Even the choriamb or the double trochee can be employed in place of the paeon, if the second long syllable of the foot is unstressed and therefore not burdensome. Heavy trisyllables can be allowed only now and then, if the movement demands them. But in fact all modulations must be employed only when there is the rhythmic necessity or for rhythmic significance; if they are used mechanically without reason or at random, it does not help the harmony and often destroys it. Rhythmic necessity intervenes when the special movement needed by the thought, feeling or action must so be brought about, by a modulation of the fixed rhythm or a departure from it;[1] rhythmic significance occurs when the deeper unexpressed soul-sense behind the words is brought out, not by word but by sound, to the surface.

The efficacy of this technique depends on the power of the writer to discover and sustain the true movement of the hexameter, its spirit and character, such as we find it in the ancient epics, pastorals, epistles, satires in which it was used with a su-

[1] Thus even an almost wholly trochaic or a wholly spondaic line can be admitted when it is demanded by the action, *e.g.*,

He from the carven couch upreared his giant stature

or,

Fate-weighed up Troy's slope strode musing strong Aeneas.

preme greatness or a consummate mastery. That movement can be of many kinds; it admits a considerable variation of pace, sometimes swift, sometimes slow, short in its rapidity or long-drawn-out with many rhythmic turns, and there are several possibilities in each kind. Only a considerable poetic genius could bring out the full power and subtleties of its rhythms; but it is essential for even a tolerable success to find and keep up a true length and pitch in the delivery of the lines; the dactylic flow is especially exacting in this respect on the care of the rhythmist. An undulant run is the easiest to maintain, the most simple and natural pace, but it has to be varied by other movements, a long or a brief bounding swiftness, the light rapid run or a slower deliberate running; a large even stream is a second possibility as a basic rhythm, but this needs a Virgilian genius or talent; the surge is the greatest of all, but only the born epic poet could sustain it for a long time, — it suits indeed only the epic or high-pitched narrative, but it can come in from time to time as an occasional high rise from a lower level of rhythmic plenitude. Finally, rhyme can be used for poems of reflective thought or lyrical feeling; but it must not be made the excuse for a melodic monotone. That kind of melodic fixity is permissible in very short dactylic pieces, but the hexameter does not move at ease in a short range: it has fluted in the pastoral grove and walked on the Appian way, but it loves better the free sky and the winds of the ocean; it finds its natural self in the wide plain, on high mountains or in the surge and roll of a long venturous voyage.

If the difficulty of the hexameter can be successfully overcome, no insuperable impossibility need be met in the naturalisation of other classical metres, for the harmonic principle will be the same. All that is necessary is that artificial quantity and the atmosphere of a pastime or an experiment must be abandoned; there must not be the sense of an importation or a construction, the metre must read as if it were a born English rhythm, not a naturalised alien. It would be a mistake to cling to rigid scholarly correctness in the process; these metres must submit to the natural law of English poetry, to movements and liberties which the classical rhythms do not admit, to modulation, to slight facilitating changes of form, to the creation of different models of itself, as there are different models of the sonnet. The Alcaic is the most attractive and manageable of the ancient lyrical metres, but in English even the Alcaic cannot easily be the same in all respects as the original verse form of its creator. The original model can indeed be reproduced; but modulations have to be brought in to help the difficulties experienced by English speech in taking a foreign metre into itself; trochees have very usually to be substituted for the not easily found spondee, an occasional anapaest, a paeon lengthening out the orthodox dactyl should not be excluded; the omission of the first syllable in the opening line of the stanza can be admitted as an occasional license. Otherwise the full harmonic possibilities of this rhythmic measure in its new tongue cannot be richly exploited. The Horatian form in which the two opening lines very commonly end in a cretic doing duty for the theoretic dactyl, is more manageable in English in which a constant dactylic close to the line is not easily handled: this change gives a less melodious, a graver and more sculptural turn to the outlines of the stanza. Finally, to this Horatian form it is possible to give a greater amplitude by admitting a feminine ending in these two lines, the cretic turning into a double trochee. That does not break or destroy the spirit and character of the Alcaic verse; it gives it more largeness and resonance.

Other lyrical forms may be less amenable to change; there is sometimes too close an identity between the body and the spirit. It is so with the Sapphic, an alluring metre but, as experimenters have found, difficult to change and anglicise: here only slight modulations are admissible, the trochee for the spondee, the antibacchius or light cretic for the dactyl. Still others would need the minute and scrupulous art of a goldsmith or the force of a giant to make anything of them; yet they are worth trying, for one never knows whether the difficulty may not be the way to a triumph or a *trouvaille*. In any case the hexameter, half a dozen of the greater or more beautiful lyrical forms and the freedom of the use of quantitative verse for the creation of new original rhythms would be enough to add a wide field to the large and opulent estate of English poetry.

V

ILION

An Epic in Quantitative Hexameters

Contents

ILION

BOOK I
THE BOOK OF THE HERALD
391

BOOK II
THE BOOK OF THE STATESMAN
410

BOOK III
THE BOOK OF THE ASSEMBLY
424

BOOK IV
THE BOOK OF PARTINGS
442

BOOK V
THE BOOK OF ACHILLES
463

BOOK VI
THE BOOK OF THE CHIEFTAINS
472

BOOK VII
THE BOOK OF THE WOMAN
484

BOOK VIII
THE BOOK OF THE GODS
492

BOOK IX
513

Book One

The Book of the Herald

Dawn in her journey eternal compelling the labour of mortals,
Dawn the beginner of things with the night for their rest or their ending,
Pallid and bright-lipped arrived from the mists and the chill of the Euxine.
Earth in the dawn-fire delivered from starry and shadowy vastness
Woke to the wonder of life and its passion and sorrow and beauty,
All on her bosom sustaining, the patient compassionate Mother.
Out of the formless vision of Night with its look on things hidden
Given to the gaze of the azure she lay in her garment of greenness,
Wearing light on her brow. In the dawn-ray lofty and voiceless
Ida climbed with her god-haunted peaks into diamond lustres,
Ida first of the hills with the ranges silent beyond her
Watching the dawn in their giant companies, as since the ages
First began they had watched her, upbearing Time on their summits.
Troas cold on her plain awaited the boon of the sunshine.
There, like a hope through an emerald dream sole-pacing for ever,
Stealing to wideness beyond, crept Simois lame in his currents,
Guiding his argent thread mid the green of the reeds and the grasses.
Headlong, impatient of Space and its boundaries, Time and its slowness,
Xanthus clamoured aloud as he ran to the far-surging waters,
Joining his call to the many-voiced roar of the mighty Aegean,
Answering Ocean's limitless cry like a whelp to its parent.
Forests looked up through their rifts, the ravines grew aware of their shadows.
Closer now gliding glimmered the golden feet of the goddess.
Over the hills and the headlands spreading her garment of splendour,
Fateful she came with her eyes impartial looking on all things,
Bringer to man of the day of his fortune and day of his downfall.
Full of her luminous errand, careless of eve and its weeping,
Fateful she paused unconcerned above Ilion's mysteried greatness,
Domes like shimmering tongues of the crystal flames of the morning,
Opalesque rhythm-line of tower-tops, notes of the lyre of the sun-god.
High over all that a nation had built and its love and its laughter,
Lighting the last time highway and homestead, market and temple,
Looking on men who must die and women destined to sorrow,
Looking on beauty fire must lay low and the sickle of slaughter,
Fateful she lifted the doom-scroll red with the script of the Immortals,
Deep in the invisible air that folds in the race and its morrows

Fixed it, and passed on smiling the smile of the griefless and deathless, —
Dealers of death though death they know not, who in the morning
Scatter the seed of the event for the reaping ready at nightfall.
Over the brooding of plains and the agelong trance of the summits
Out of the sun and its spaces she came, pausing tranquil and fatal,
And, at a distance followed by the golden herds of the sun-god,
Carried the burden of Light and its riddle and danger to Hellas.
  Even as fleets on a chariot divine through the gold streets of ether,
Swiftly when Life fleets, invisibly changing the arc of the soul-drift,
And, with the choice that has chanced or the fate man has called and now
                                                                   suffers
Weighted, the moment travels driving the past towards the future,
Only its face and its feet are seen, not the burden it carries.
Weight of the event and its surface we bear, but the meaning is hidden.
Earth sees not; life's clamour deafens the ear of the spirit:
Man knows not; least knows the messenger chosen for the summons.
Only he listens to the voice of his thoughts, his heart's ignorant whisper,
Whistle of winds in the tree-tops of Time and the rustle of Nature.
Now too the messenger hastened driving the car of the errand:
Even while dawn was a gleam in the east, he had cried to his coursers.
Half yet awake in light's turrets started the scouts of the morning
Hearing the jar of the wheels and the throb of the hooves' exultation,
Hooves of the horses of Greece as they galloped to Phrygian Troya.
Proudly they trampled through Xanthus thwarting the foam of his anger,
Whinnying high as in scorn crossed Simois' tangled currents,
Xanthus' reed-girdled twin, the gentle and sluggard river.
One and unarmed in the car was the driver; grey was he, shrunken,
Worn with his decades. To Pergama cinctured with strength Cyclopean
Old and alone he arrived, insignificant, feeblest of mortals,
Carrying Fate in his helpless hands and the doom of an empire.
Ilion, couchant, saw him arrive from the sea and the darkness.
Heard mid the faint slow stirrings of life in the sleep of the city,
Rapid there neared a running of feet, and the cry of the summons
Beat round the doors that guarded the domes of the splendour of Priam.
"Wardens charged with the night, ye who stand in Laomedon's gateway,
Waken the Ilian kings. Talthybius, herald of Argos,
Parleying stands at the portals of Troy in the grey of the dawning."
High and insistent the call. In the dimness and hush of his chamber
Charioted far in his dreams amid visions of glory and terror,
Scenes of a vivider world, — though blurred and deformed in the brain-cells,

Vague and inconsequent, there full of colour and beauty and greatness, —
Suddenly drawn by the pull of the conscious thread of the earth-bond
And of the needs of Time and the travail assigned in the transience
Warned by his body, Deiphobus, reached in that splendid remoteness,
Touched through the nerve-ways of life that branch to the brain of the
                                                                    dreamer,
Heard the terrestrial call and slumber startled receded
Sliding like dew from the mane of a lion. Reluctant he travelled
Back from the light of the fields beyond death, from the wonderful kingdoms
Where he had wandered a soul among souls in the countries beyond us,
Free from the toil and incertitude, free from the struggle and danger:
Now, compelled, he returned from the respite given to the time-born,
Called to the strife and the wounds of the earth and the burden of daylight.
He from the carven couch upreared his giant stature.
Haste-spurred he laved his eyes and regained earth's memories, haste-spurred
Donning apparel and armour strode through the town of his fathers,
Watched by her gods on his way to his fate, towards Pergama's portals.
    Nine long years had passed and the tenth now was wearily ending,
Years of the wrath of the gods, and the leaguer still threatened the ramparts
Since through a tranquil morn the ships came past Tenedos sailing
And the first Argive fell slain as he leaped on the Phrygian beaches;
Still the assailants attacked, still fought back the stubborn defenders.
When the reward is withheld and endlessly lengthens the labour,
Weary of fruitless toil grows the transient heart of the mortal.
Weary of battle the invaders warring heartless and homeless
Prayed to the gods for release and return to the land of their fathers:
Weary of battle the Phrygians beset in their beautiful city
Prayed to the gods for an end of the danger and mortal encounter.
Long had the high-beached ships forgotten their measureless ocean.
Greece seemed old and strange to her children camped on the beaches,
Old like a life long past one remembers hardly believing
But as a dream that has happened, but as the tale of another.
Time with his tardy touch and Nature changing our substance
Slowly had dimmed the faces loved and the scenes once cherished:
Yet was the dream still dear to them longing for wife and for children,
Longing for hearth and glebe in the far-off valleys of Hellas.
Always like waves that swallow the shingles, lapsing, returning,
Tide of the battle, race of the onset relentlessly thundered
Over the Phrygian corn-fields. Trojan wrestled with Argive,
Caria, Lycia, Thrace and the war-lord mighty Achaia

Joined in the clasp of the fight. Death, panic and wounds and disaster,
Glory of conquest and glory of fall, and the empty hearth-side,
Weeping and fortitude, terror and hope and the pang of remembrance,
Anguish of hearts, the lives of the warriors, the strength of the nations
Thrown were like weights into Destiny's scales, but the balance wavered
Pressed by invisible hands. For not only the mortal fighters,
Heroes half divine whose names are like stars in remoteness,
Triumphed and failed and were winds or were weeds on the dance of the
    surges,
But from the peaks of Olympus and shimmering summits of Ida
Gleaming and clanging the gods of the antique ages descended.
Hidden from human knowledge the brilliant shapes of Immortals
Mingled unseen in the mellay, or sometimes, marvellous, maskless,
Forms of undying beauty and power that made tremble the heart-strings
Parting their deathless secrecy crossed through the borders of vision,
Plain as of old to the demigods out of their glory emerging,
Heard by mortal ears and seen by the eyeballs that perish.
Mighty they came from their spaces of freedom and sorrowless splendour.
Sea-vast, trailing the azure hem of his clamorous waters,
Blue-lidded, maned with the Night, Poseidon smote for the future,
Earth-shaker who with his trident releases the coils of the Dragon,
Freeing the forces unborn that are locked in the caverns of Nature.
Calm and unmoved, upholding the Word that is Fate and the order
Fixed in the sight of a Will foreknowing and silent and changeless,
Hera sent by Zeus and Athene lifting his aegis
Guarded the hidden decree. But for Ilion, loud as the surges,
Ares impetuous called to the fire in men's hearts, and his passion
Woke in the shadowy depths the forms of the Titan and demon;
Dumb and coerced by the grip of the gods in the abyss of the being,
Formidable, veiled they sit in the grey subconscient darkness
Watching the sleep of the snake-haired Erinnys. Miracled, haloed,
Seer and magician and prophet who beholds what the thought cannot witness,
Lifting the godhead within us to more than a human endeavour,
Slayer and saviour, thinker and mystic, leaped from his sun-peaks
Guarding in Ilion the wall of his mysteries Delphic Apollo.
Heaven's strengths divided swayed in the whirl of the Earth-force.
All that is born and destroyed is reborn in the sweep of the ages;
Life like a decimal ever recurring repeats the old figure;
Goal seems there none for the ball that is chased throughout Time by the
    Fate-teams;

Evil once ended renews and no issue comes out of living:
Only an Eye unseen can distinguish the thread of its workings.
Such seemed the rule of the pastime of Fate on the plains of the Troad;
All went backwards and forwards tossed in the swing of the death-game.
Vain was the toil of the heroes, the blood of the mighty was squandered,
Spray as of surf on the cliffs when it moans unappeased, unrequited
Age after fruitless age. Day hunted the steps of the nightfall;
Joy succeeded to grief; defeat only greatened the vanquished,
Victory offered an empty delight without guerdon or profit.
End there was none of the effort and end there was none of the failure.
Triumph and agony changing hands in a desperate measure
Faced and turned as a man and a maiden trampling the grasses
Face and turn and they laugh in their joy of the dance and each other.
These were gods and they trampled lives. But though Time is immortal,
Mortal his works are and ways and the anguish ends like the rapture.
Artists of Nature content with their work in the plan of the transience,
Beautiful, deathless, august, the Olympians turned from the carnage,
Leaving the battle already decided, leaving the heroes
Slain in their minds, Troy burned, Greece left to her glory and downfall.
Into their heavens they rose up mighty like eagles ascending
Fanning the world with their wings. As the great to their luminous mansions
Turn from the cry and the strife, forgetting the wounded and fallen,
Calm they repose from their toil and incline to the joy of the banquet,
Watching the feet of the wine-bearers rosily placed on the marble,
Filling their hearts with ease, so they to their sorrowless ether
Passed from the wounded earth and its air that is ploughed with men's
                                                              anguish;
Calm they reposed and their hearts inclined to the joy and the silence.
Lifted was the burden laid on our wills by their starry presence:
Man was restored to his smallness, the world to its inconscient labour.
Life felt a respite from height, the winds breathed freer delivered;
Light was released from their blaze and the earth was released from their
                                                              greatness.
But their immortal content from the struggle titanic departed.
Vacant the noise of the battle roared like the sea on the shingles;
Wearily hunted the spears their quarry; strength was disheartened;
Silence increased with the march of the months on the tents of the leaguer.
But not alone on the Achaians the steps of the moments fell heavy;
Slowly the shadow deepened on Ilion mighty and scornful:
Dragging her days went by; in the rear of the hearts of her people

Something that knew what they dared not know and the mind would not
                                                                  utter,
Something that smote at her soul of defiance and beauty and laughter,
Darkened the hours. For Doom in her sombre and giant uprising
Neared, assailing the skies: the sense of her lived in all pastimes;
Time was pursued by unease and a terror woke in the midnight:
Even the ramparts felt her, stones that the gods had erected.
Now no longer she dallied and played, but bounded and hastened,
Seeing before her the end and, imagining massacre calmly,
Laughed and admired the flames and rejoiced in the cry of the captives.
Under her, dead to the watching immortals, Deiphobus hastened
Clanging in arms through the streets of the beautiful insolent city,
Brilliant, a gleaming husk but empty and left by the daemon.
Even as a star long extinguished whose light still travels the spaces,
Seen in its form by men, but itself goes phantom-like fleeting
Void and null and dark through the uncaring infinite vastness,
So now he seemed to the sight that sees all things from the Real.
Timeless its vision of Time creates the hour by things coming.
Borne on a force from the past and no more by a power for the future
Mighty and bright was his body, but shadowy the shape of his spirit
Only an eidolon seemed of the being that had lived in him, fleeting
Vague like a phantom seen by the dim Acherontian waters.
    But to the guardian towers that watched over Pergama's gateway
Out of the waking city Deiphobus swiftly arriving
Called, and swinging back the huge gates slowly, reluctant,
Flung Troy wide to the entering Argive. Ilion's portals
Parted admitting her destiny, then with a sullen and iron
Cry they closed. Mute, staring, grey like a wolf descended
Old Talthybius, propping his steps on the staff of his errand;
Feeble his body, but fierce still his glance with the fire within him;
Speechless and brooding he gazed on the hated and coveted city.
Suddenly, seeking heaven with her buildings hewn as for Titans,
Marvellous, rhythmic, a child of the gods with marble for raiment,
Smiting the vision with harmony, splendid and mighty and golden,
Ilion stood up around him entrenched in her giant defences.
Strength was uplifted on strength and grandeur supported by grandeur;
Beauty lay in her lap. Remote, hieratic and changeless,
Filled with her deeds and her dreams her gods looked out on the Argive,
Helpless and dumb with his hate as he gazed on her, they too like mortals
Knowing their centuries past, not knowing the morrow before them.

Dire were his eyes upon Troya the beautiful, his face like a doom-mask:
All Greece gazed in them, hated, admired, grew afraid, grew relentless.
But to the Greek Deiphobus cried and he turned from his passion
Fixing his ominous eyes with the god in them straight on the Trojan:
"Messenger, voice of Achaia, wherefore confronting the daybreak
Comest thou driving thy car from the sleep of the tents that besiege us?
Fateful, I deem, was the thought that, conceived in the silence of midnight,
Raised up thy aged limbs from the couch of their rest in the stillness, —
Thoughts of a mortal but forged by the Will that uses our members
And of its promptings our speech and our acts are the tools and the image.
Oft from the veil and the shadow they leap out like stars in their brightness,
Lights that we think our own, yet they are but tokens and counters,
Signs of the Forces that flow through us serving a Power that is secret.
What in the dawning bringst thou to Troya the mighty and dateless
Now in the ending of Time, when the gods are weary of struggle?
Sends Agamemnon challenge or courtesy, Greek, to the Trojans?"
High like the northwind answered the voice of the doom from Achaia:
"Trojan Deiphobus, daybreak, silence of night and the evening
Sink and arise and even the strong sun rests from his splendour.
Not for the servant is rest nor Time is his, only his death-pyre.
I have not come from the monarch of men or the armoured assembly
Held on the wind-swept marge of the thunder and laughter of ocean.
One in his singleness greater than kings and multitudes sends me.
I am a voice out of Phthia, I am the will of the Hellene.
Peace in my right I bring to you, death in my left hand. Trojan,
Proudly receive them, honour the gifts of the mighty Achilles.
Death accept, if Ate deceives you and Doom is your lover,
Peace if your fate can turn and the god in you chooses to hearken.
Full is my heart and my lips are impatient of speech undelivered.
It was not made for the streets or the market, nor to be uttered
Meanly to common ears, but where counsel and majesty harbour
Far from the crowd in the halls of the great and to wisdom and foresight
Secrecy whispers, there I will speak among Ilion's princes."
"Envoy," answered the Laomedontian, "voice of Achilles,
Vain is the offer of peace that sets out with a threat for its prelude.
Yet will we hear thee. Arise who are fleetest of foot in the gateway, —
Thou, Thrasymachus, haste. Let the domes of the mansion of Ilus
Wake to the bruit of the Hellene challenge. Summon Aeneas."
Even as the word sank back into stillness, doffing his mantle
Started to run at the bidding a swift-footed youth of the Trojans

First in the race and the battle, Thrasymachus son of Aretes.
He in the dawn disappeared into swiftness. Deiphobus slowly,
Measuring Fate with his thoughts in the troubled vasts of his spirit,
Back through the stir of the city returned to the house of his fathers,
Taming his mighty stride to the pace infirm of the Argive.

But with the god in his feet Thrasymachus rapidly running
Came to the halls in the youth of the wonderful city by Ilus
Built for the joy of the eye; for he rested from war and, triumphant,
Reigned adored by the prostrate nations. Now when all ended,
Last of its mortal possessors to walk in its flowering gardens,
Great Anchises lay in that luminous house of the ancients
Soothing his restful age, the far-warring victor Anchises,
High Bucoleon's son and the father of Rome by a goddess;
Lonely and vagrant once in his boyhood divine upon Ida
White Aphrodite ensnared him and she loosed her ambrosial girdle
Seeking a mortal's love. On the threshold Thrasymachus halted
Looking for servant or guard, but felt only a loneness of slumber
Drawing the soul's sight within away from its life and things human;
Soundless, unheeding, the vacant corridors fled into darkness.
He to the shades of the house and the dreams of the echoing rafters
Trusted his high-voiced call, and from chambers still dim in their twilight
Strong Aeneas armoured and mantled, leonine striding,
Came, Anchises' son; for the dawn had not found him reposing,
But in the night he had left his couch and the clasp of Creüsa,
Rising from sleep at the call of his spirit that turned to the waters
Prompted by Fate and his mother who guided him, white Aphrodite.
Still with the impulse of speed Thrasymachus greeted Aeneas:
"Hero Aeneas, swift be thy stride to the Ilian hill-top.
Dardanid, haste! for the gods are at work; they have risen with the morning,
Each from his starry couch, and they labour. Doom, we can see it,
Glows on their anvils of destiny, clang we can hear of their hammers.
Something they forge there sitting unknown in the silence eternal,
Whether of evil or good it is they who shall choose who are masters
Calm, unopposed; they are gods and they work out their iron caprices.
Troy is their stage and Argos their background; we are their puppets.
Always our voices are prompted to speech for an end that we know not,
Always we think that we drive, but are driven. Action and impulse,
Yearning and thought are their engines, our will is their shadow and helper.
Now too, deeming he comes with a purpose framed by a mortal,
Shaft of their will they have shot from the bow of the Grecian leaguer,

Lashing themselves at his steeds, Talthybius sent by Achilles."
"Busy the gods are always, Thrasymachus son of Aretes,
Weaving Fate on their looms, and yesterday, now and tomorrow
Are but the stands they have made with Space and Time for their timber,
Frame but the dance of their shuttle. What eye unamazed by their workings
Ever can pierce where they dwell and uncover their far-stretching purpose?
Silent they toil, they are hid in the clouds, they are wrapped with the midnight.
Yet to Apollo, I pray, the Archer friendly to mortals,
Yet to the rider on Fate I abase myself, wielder of thunder,
Evil and doom to avert from my fatherland. All night Morpheus,
He who with shadowy hands heaps error and truth upon mortals,
Stood at my pillow with images. Dreaming I erred like a phantom
Helpless in Ilion's streets with the fire and the foeman around me.
Red was the smoke as it mounted triumphant the house-top of Priam,
Clang of the arms of the Greeks was in Troya, and thwarting the clangour
Voices were crying and calling me over the violent Ocean
Borne by the winds of the West from a land where Hesperus harbours."
Brooding they ceased, for their thoughts grew heavy upon them and voiceless.
Then, in a farewell brief and unthought and unconscious of meaning,
Parting they turned to their tasks and their lives now close but soon severed:
Destined to perish even before his perishing nation,
Back to his watch at the gate sped Thrasymachus rapidly running;
Large of pace and swift, but with eyes absorbed and unseeing,
Driven like a car of the gods by the whip of his thoughts through the
                                                                    highways,
Turned to his mighty future the hero born of a goddess.
One was he chosen to ascend into greatness through fall and disaster,
Loser of his world by the will of a heaven that seemed ruthless and adverse,
Founder of a newer and greater world by daring adventure.
Now, from the citadel's rise with the townships crowding below it
High towards a pondering of domes and the mystic Palladium climbing,
Fronted with the morning ray and joined by the winds of the ocean,
Fate-weighed up Troy's slope strode musing strong Aeneas.
Under him silent the slumbering roofs of the city of Ilus
Dreamed in the light of the dawn; above watched the citadel, sleepless
Lonely and strong like a goddess white-limbed and bright on a hill-top,
Looking far out at the sea and the foe and the prowling of danger.
Over the brow he mounted and saw the palace of Priam,
Home of the gods of the earth, Laomedon's marvellous vision
Held in the thought that accustomed his will to unearthly achievement

And in the blaze of his spirit compelling heaven with its greatness,
Dreamed by the harp of Apollo, a melody caught into marble.
Out of his mind it arose like an epic canto by canto;
Each of its halls was a strophe, its chambers lines of an epode,
Victor chant of Ilion's destiny. Absent he entered,
Voiceless with thought, the brilliant megaron crowded with paintings,
Paved with a splendour of marble, and saw Deiphobus seated,
Son of the ancient house by the opulent hearth of his fathers,
And at his side like a shadow the grey and ominous Argive.
Happy of light like a lustrous star when it welcomes the morning,
Brilliant, beautiful, glamoured with gold and a fillet of gem-fire,
Paris, plucked from the song and the lyre by the Grecian challenge,
Came with the joy in his face and his eyes that Fate could not alter.
Ever a child of the dawn at play near a turn of the sun-roads,
Facing destiny's look with the careless laugh of a comrade,
He with his vision of delight and beauty brightening the earth-field
Passed through its peril and grief on his way to the ambiguous Shadow.
Last from her chamber of sleep where she lay in the Ilian mansion
Far in the heart of the house with the deep-bosomed daughters of Priam,
Noble and tall and erect in a nimbus of youth and of glory,
Claiming the world and life as a fief of her strength and her courage,
Dawned through a doorway that opened to distant murmurs and laughter,
Capturing the eye like a smile or a sunbeam, Penthesilea.
    She from the threshold cried to the herald, crossing the marble,
Regal and fleet, with her voice that was mighty and dire in its sweetness:
"What with such speed has impelled from the wind-haunted beaches of
                                                                Troas,
Herald, thy car while[1] the sun yet hesitates under the mountains?
Comest thou humbler to Troy, Talthybius, now than thou camest
Once when the streams of my East sang low to my ear, not this Ocean
Loud, and I roamed in my mountains uncalled by the voice of Apollo?
Bringest thou dulcet-eyed peace or, sweeter to Penthesilea,
Challenge of war when the spears fall thick on the shields of the fighters,
Lightly the wheels leap onward chanting the anthem of Ares,
Death is at work in his fields and the heart is enamoured of danger?
What says Odysseus, the baffled Ithacan? what Agamemnon?
Are they then weary of war who were rapid and bold and triumphant,
Now that their gods are reluctant, now victory darts not from heaven
Down from the clouds above Ida directing the luminous legions

[1] though

Armed by Fate, now Pallas forgets, now Poseidon slumbers?
Bronze were their throats to the battle like bugles blaring in chorus;
Mercy they knew not, but shouted and ravened and ran to the slaughter
Eager as hounds when they chase, till a woman met them and stayed them,
Loud my war-shout rang by Scamander. Herald of Argos,
What say the vaunters of Greece to the virgin Penthesilea?"
    High was the Argive's answer confronting the mighty in Troya.
"Princes of Pergama, whelps of the lion who roar for the mellay,
Suffer my speech! It shall ring like a spear on the hearts of the mighty.
Blame not the herald; his voice is an impulse, an echo, a channel
Now for the timbrels of peace and now for the drums of the battle.
And I have come from no cautious strength, from no half-hearted speaker,
But from the Phthian. All know him! Proud is his soul as his fortunes,
Swift as his sword and his spear are the speech and the wrath from his bosom.
I am his envoy, herald am I of the conquering Argives.
Has not one heard in the night when the breezes whisper and shudder,
Dire, the voice of a lion unsatisfied, gnawed by his hunger,
Seeking his prey from the gods? For he prowls through the glens of the mountains,
Errs a dangerous gleam in the woodlands, fatal and silent.
So for a while he endures, for a while he seeks and he suffers
Patient yet in his terrible grace as assured of his banquet;
But he has lacked too long and he lifts his head and to heaven
Roars in his wonder incensed, impatiently. Startled the valleys
Shrink from the dreadful alarum, the cattle gallop to shelter.
Arming the herdsmen cry to each other for comfort and courage."
    So Talthybius spoke, as a harper voicing his prelude
Touches his strings to a varied music, seeks for a concord;
Long his strain he prepares. But one broke in on the speaker, —
Sweet was his voice like a harp's though heard in the front of the onset, —
One of the sons of Fate by the people loved whom he ruined,
Leader in counsel and battle, the Priamid, he in his beauty
Carelessly walking who scattered the seeds of Titanic disaster.
"Surely thou dreamedst at night and awaking thy dreams have not left thee!
Hast thou not woven thy words to intimidate children in Argos
Sitting alarmed in the shadows who listen pale to their nurses?
Greek, thou art standing in Ilion now and thou speak'st to[1] princes.
Use not thy words but thy king's. If friendship their honey-breathed burden,
Friendship we clasp from Achilles, but challenge outpace with our challenge

---
[1] facest her

Meeting the foe ere he moves in his will to the clash of encounter.
Such is the way of the Trojans since Phryx by the Hellespont halting
Seated Troy on her hill with Ocean for comrade and sister."
    Shaking in wrath his filleted head Talthybius answered:
"Princes, ye speak their words who drive you! Thus said Achilles:
Rise,[1] Talthybius, meet in her spaces the car of the morning;
Challenge her coursers divine as they bound through the plains of the
                                                                Troad.
Hasten, let not the day wear gold ere thou stand in her ramparts
Herald charged with my will to a haughty and obstinate nation,
Speak in the palace of Priam the word of the Phthian Achilles.
Freely and not as his vassal who leads, Agamemnon, the Argive,
But as a ruler in Hellas I send thee, king of my nations.
Long I lingered[2] apart from the mellay of gods in the Troad,
Long has my listless spear leaned back on the peace of my tent-side,
Deaf to the talk of the trumpets, the whine of the chariots speeding;
Sole with my heart I have lived, unheeding the Hellene murmur,
Chid when it roared for the hunt the lion-pack of the war-god,
Day after day I walked at dawn and in blush of the sunset,
Far by the call of the seas and alone with the gods and my dreaming,
Leaned to the unsatisfied chant of my heart and the rhythms of Ocean,
Sung to by hopes that were sweet-lipped and vain. Polyxena's brothers
Still are the brood of the Titan Laomedon slain in his greatness,
Engines of God unable to bear all the might that they harbour.
Awe they have chid from their hearts, nor our common humanity binds
                                                                                them,
Stay have they none in the gods who approve, giving calmness to mortals:
But like the Titans of old they have hugged to them grandeur and ruin.
Seek then the race self-doomed and the leaders blinded by heaven —
Not in the agora swept by the winds of debate and the shoutings
Lion-voiced, huge of the people! In Troya's high-crested mansion
Speak out my word to the hero Deiphobus, head of the mellay,
Paris the racer of doom and the stubborn strength of Aeneas.
Herald of Greece, when thy feet shall stand[3] on the gold and the marble,
Rise in the Ilian megaron, curb not the cry of the challenge.
Thus shalt thou say to them stroking the ground with the staff of defiance,
Fronting the tempests of war, the insensate, the gamblers with ruin.[4]
'Princes of Troy, I have sat in your halls, I have slept in your chambers;
Not in the battle alone, as a warrior glad of his foemen,

---

[1] Haste   [2] I have walked   [3] be pressed   [4] downfall

Glad of[1] the strength that mates with his own, in peace we encountered.
Marvelling I sat in the halls of my enemies, close to the bosoms
Scarred by the dints of my sword and the eyes I had seen through the battle,
Ate rejoicing the food of the East at the tables of Priam,
Served by the delicatest hands in the world, by Hecuba's daughter,
Or with our souls reconciled in some careless and rapturous midnight
Drank of the sweetness of Phrygian wine, admired[2] your bodies
Shaped by the gods indeed and my spirit revolted from hatred;
Softening it yearned in its strings to the beauty and joy of its foemen,
Yearned from the death that o'ertakes and the flame that cries and desires
Even at the end to save and even on the verge to deliver
Troy and her wonderful works and her sons and her deep-bosomed
                                                                daughters.
Warned by the gods who reveal to the heart what the mind cannot hearken
Deaf with its thoughts, I offered you friendship, I offered you bridal,
Hellas for comrade, Achilles for brother, the world for enjoyment
Won by my spear. And one heard my call and one turned to my seeking.
Why is it then that the war-cry sinks not to rest by the Xanthus?
We are not voices from Argolis, Lacedaemonian tricksters,
Splendid and subtle and false; we are speakers of truth, we are Hellenes,
Men of the northland faithful in friendship and noble in anger,
Strong like our fathers of old. But you answered my truth with evasion
Hoping to seize what I will not yield and you flattered your people.
Long have I waited for wisdom to dawn on your violent natures.
Lonely I paced o'er the sands by the thousand-throated waters
Praying to Pallas the wise that the doom might turn[3] from your mansions
Buildings delightful, gracious as rhythms, lyrics in marble,
Works of the transient gods; — and I yearned for the end of the war-din
Hoping that Death might relent to the beautiful sons of the Trojans.
Far from the cry of the spears, from the speed and the laughter of axles,
Heavy upon me like iron the intolerable yoke of inaction
Weighed like a load on a runner. The war-cry rose by Scamander;
Xanthus was crossed on a bridge of the fallen, not by Achilles.
Often I stretched out my hand to the spear, for the Trojan beaches
Rang with the voice of Deiphobus shouting and slaying the Argives;
Often my heart like an anxious mother for Greece and her children
Leaped, for the air was full of the leonine roar of Aeneas.
Always the evening fell or the gods protected the Argives.
Then by the moat of the ships, on the hither plain of the Xanthus

---

[1] Loving [2] admiring [3] for the doom to swerve

New was the voice that climbed through the din and sailed on the breezes,
High, insistent, clear, and it shouted an unknown war-cry
Threatening doom to the peoples. A woman had come in to aid you
Regal and insolent, fair as the morning and fell as the northwind,
Freed from the distaff who grasps at the sword and spurns at subjection
Breaking the rule of the gods. She is turbulent, swift in the battle.
Clanging her voice of the swan as a summons to death and disaster,
Fleet-footed, happy and pitiless, laughing she runs to the slaughter;
Strong with the gait that allures she leaps from her car to the slaying,
Dabbles in blood smooth hands like lilies. Europe astonished
Reels from her shock to the Ocean. She is the panic and mellay,
War is her paean, the chariots thunder of Penthesilea.
Doom was her coming, it seems, to the men of the West and their legions;
Ajax sleeps for ever,[1] Meriones lies on the beaches,
One by one they are falling before you, the great in Achaia.
Ever the wounded are borne like the stream of the ants when they forage,
Past my ships, and they hush their moans as they near and in silence
Gaze at the legions inactive accusing the fame of Achilles.
Still have I borne with you, waited a little, looked for a summons,
Longing for bridal torches, not flame on the Ilian housetops,
Blood in the chambers of sweetness, the golden amorous city
Swallowed by doom. Not broken I turned from the wrestle Titanic,
Hopeless, weary of toil in the ebb of my glorious spirit,
But from my stress of compassion for doom of the kindred nations,
But for her sake whom my soul desires, for the daughter of Priam.
And for Polyxena's sake I will speak to you yet as your lover
Once ere the Fury, abrupt from Erebus, deaf to your crying,
Mad with the joy of the massacre, seizes on wealth and on women
Calling to Fire as it strides and Ilion sinks into ashes.
Yield; for your doom is impatient. No longer your helpers hasten,
Legions swift to your call; the yoke of your pride and your splendour
Lies not now on the nations of earth as when Fortune desired you,
Strength was your slave and Troya the lioness hungrily roaring
Threatened the western world from her ramparts built by Apollo.
Gladly released from the thraldom they hated, the insolent shackles
Curbing their manhood the peoples arise and they pray for your ruin;

---

[1] Here, as in some other lines, Ajax is spoken of as having been slain by Penthesilea. Elsewhere in the poem we come across a living Ajax. The discrepancy is explained by the fact that in the Trojan War there were two Ajaxes, the Great and the Small. The latter, called also the Locrian, figures as alive in *Ilion*.

Piled are their altars with gifts; their blessings help the Achaians.
Memnon came, but he sleeps, and the faces swart of his nation
Darken no more like a cloud over thunder and surge of the onset.
Wearily Lycia fights; far fled are the Carian levies.
Thrace retreats to her plains preferring the whistle of storm-winds
Or on the banks of the Strymon to wheel in her Orphean measure,
Not in the revel of swords and fronting the spears of the Hellenes.
Princes of Pergama, open your gates to our Peace who would enter
Life in her gracious clasp and forgetfulness, grave of earth's passions,
Healer of wounds and the past. In a comity equal, Hellenic,
Asia join with Greece, our world from the frozen rivers
Trod by the hooves of the Scythian to farthest undulant Ganges.
Tyndarid Helen yield,[1] the desirable cause of your danger,
Back to Greece that is empty long of her smile and her movements.
Broider with[2] riches her coming, pomp of her slaves and the wagons
Endlessly groaning with gold that arrive with the ransom of nations.
So shall the Fury be pacified, she who exultant from Sparta
Breathed in the sails of the Trojan ravisher helping his oarsmen.
So shall the gods be appeased and the thoughts of their wrath shall be
cancelled,
Justice contented trace back her steps and for brands of the burning
Torches delightful shall break into Troy with[3] the swords of the bridal.
I like a bridegroom will seize on your city and clasp and defend her
Safe from the envy of Argos, from Lacedaemonian hatred,
Safe from the hunger of Crete and the Locrian's violent rapine.
But if you turn from my voice and you hearken only to Ares
Crying for battle within you deluded by Hera and Pallas,
Swiftly fierce death's surges shall close over Troy and her ramparts
Built by the gods shall be stubble and earth to the tread of the Hellene.
For to my tents I return not, I swear it by Zeus and Apollo,
Master of Truth who sits within Delphi fathomless brooding
Sole in the caverns of Nature and hearkens her underground murmur,
Giving my oath to his keeping mute and stern who forgets not.
Not from the panting of Ares' toil to repose, from the wrestle
Locked of hope and death in the ruthless clasp of the mellay
Leaving again the Trojan ramparts unmounted, leaving
Greece unavenged, the Aegean a lake and Europe a province.
Choosing from Hellas exile, from Peleus and Deidamia,
Choosing the field for my chamber of sleep and the battle for hearthside

[1] resign [2] Frame in, Chase in, Equal with, Double with [3] and

I shall go warring on till Asia enslaved to my footsteps
Feels the tread of the God in my sandal pressed on her bosom.
Rest shall I then when the borders of Greece are fringed with the Ganges;
Thus shall the past pay its Titan ransom[1] and, Fate her balance
Changing, a continent ravished suffer the fortune of Helen.
This I have sworn allying my will to Zeus and Ananke.' "
    So was it spoken, the Phthian challenge. Silent the heroes
Looked back amazed on their past and into the night of their future.
Silent their hearts felt a grasp from gods and had hints of the heavens.
Hush was awhile in the room as if Fate were trying her balance
Poised on the thoughts of her mortals. At length with a magical laughter
Sweet as the jangling of bells upon anklets leaping in measure
Answered high[2] to the gods the virgin Penthesilea.
"Long I had heard in my distant realms of the fame of Achilles,
Ignorant still while I played with the ball and ran in the dances
Thinking not ever to war; but I dreamed of the shock of the hero.
So might a poet inland who imagines the rumour of Ocean
Yearn with his lust for its[3] giant upheaval, its[4] dance as of hill-tops,
Toss of the yellow mane and the tawny march and the voices
Lionlike claiming earth as a prey for the clamorous waters.
So have I longed as I came for the cry and the speed of Achilles.
But he has lurked in his ships, he has sulked like a boy that is angry.
Glad am I now of his soul that arises hungry for battle,
Glad, whether victor I live or defeated travel to the shadows.
Once shall my spear have rung on the shield of the Phthian Achilles.
Peace I desire not. I came to a haughty and resolute nation,
Honour and fame they cherish, not life by the gift of a foeman.
Sons of the ancient house on whom Ilion looks as on Titans,
Chiefs whom the world admires, do you fear then the shock of the
                                                                                 Phthian?
Gods, it is said, have decided your doom. Are you less in your greatness?
Are you not gods to reverse their decrees or unshaken to suffer?
Memnon is dead and the Carians leave you? Lycia lingers?
But from the streams of my East I have come to you, Penthesilea."
    "Virgin of Asia," answered Talthybius, "doom of a nation
Brought thee to Troy and her haters Olympian shielded thy coming,
Vainly who feedest men's hearts with a hope that the gods have rejected.
Doom in thy sweet voice utters her counsels robed like a woman."
    Answered the virgin disdainfully, wroth at the words of the Argive:

    [1] the Titan ransom be paid   [2] aloud   [3] the   [4] the

"Hast thou not ended the errand they gave thee, envoy of Hellas?
Not, do I think, as our counsellor cam'st thou elected from Argos,
Nor as a lover to Troy hast thou hastened with amorous footing
Hurting thy heart with her frowardness. Hatred and rapine sent thee,
Greed of the Ilian gold and lust of the Phrygian women.
Voice of Achaian aggression! Doom am I truly; let Gnossus
Witness it, Salamis speak of my fatal arrival and Argos
Silent remember her wounds." But the Argive answered the virgin:
"Hearken then to the words of the Hellene, Penthesilea.
'Virgin to whom earth's strongest are corn in the sweep of thy sickle,
Lioness vain of thy bruit thou besiegest the paths of the battle!
Art thou not satiate yet? hast thou drunk then so little of slaughter?
Death has ascended thy car; he has chosen thy hand for his harvest.
But I have heard of thy pride and disdain, how thou scornest the Argives
And of thy fate thou complainest that ever averse to thy wishes
Cloisters the Phthian and matches with weaklings Penthesilea.
'Not of the Ithacan boar nor the wild-cat littered in Locris
Nor of the sleek-coat Argive wild-bulls sates me the hunting;'
So hast thou said, 'I would bury my spear in the lion of Hellas.'
Blind and infatuate, art thou not beautiful, bright as the lightning?
Were not thy limbs made cunningly by linking sweetness to sweetness?
Is not thy laughter an arrow surprising hearts imprudent?
Charm is the seal of the gods upon woman. Distaff and girdle,
Work of the jar at the well and the hush of our innermost chambers;
These were appointed thee, but thou hast scorned them, O Titaness grasping
Rather the shield and the spear. Thou, obeying thy turbulent nature,
Tramplest o'er laws that are old to the pleasure thy heart has demanded.
Rather bow to the ancient Gods who are seated and constant.
But for thyself thou passest and what hast thou gained for the aeons
Mingled with men in their works and depriving the age of thy beauty?
Fair art thou, woman, but fair with a bitter and opposite sweetness
Clanging in war and when thou matchest thy voice with the shout of
                                                          assemblies.
Not to this end was thy sweetness made and the joy of thy members,
Not to this rhythm Heaven tuned its pipe in thy throat of enchantment
Armoured like men to go warring forth and with hardness and fierceness
Mix in the strife and the hate while the varied meaning of Nature
Perishes hurt in its heart and life is emptied of music.
Long have I marked in your world a madness. Monarchs descending
Court the imperious mob of their slaves and their suppliant gesture

Shameless and venal offends the majestic tradition of ages:
Princes plead in the agora; spurred by the tongue of a coward,
Heroes march to an impious war at a priestly bidding.
Gold is sought by the great with the chaffering heart of the trader.
Asia fails and the Gods are abandoning Ida for Hellas.
Why must thou come here to perish, O noble and exquisite virgin,
Here in a cause not thine, in a quarrel remote from thy beauty,
Leaving a land that is lovely and far to be slain among strangers?
Girl, to thy rivers go back and thy hills where the grapes are aspirant.
Trust not a fate that indulges; for all things, Penthesilea,
Break with excess and he is the wisest who walks by a measure.
Yet, if thou wilt, thou shalt meet me today in the shock of the battle;
There will I give thee the fame thou desirest; captive in Hellas,
Men shall point to thee always, smiling and whispering, saying,
This is the woman who fought with the Greeks, overthrowing their
                                                                                heroes;
This is the slayer of Ajax, this is the slave of Achilles."
    Then with her musical laughter the fearless Penthesilea:
"Well do I hope that Achilles enslaved shall taste of that glory
Or on the Phrygian fields lie slain by the spear of a woman."
But to the herald Achaian the Priamid, leader of Troya:
"Rest in the halls of thy foes and ease thy fatigue and thy winters.
Herald, abide till the people have heard and reply to Achilles.
Not as the kings of the West are Ilion's princes and archons,
Monarchs of men who drive their nations dumb to the battle.
Not in the palace of Priam and not in the halls of the mighty
Whispered councils prevail and the few dispose of the millions;
But with their nation consulting, feeling the hearts of the commons
Ilion's princes march to the war or give peace to their foemen.
Lightning departs from her kings and the thunder returns from her people
Met in the ancient assembly where Ilus founded his columns
And since her famous centuries, names that the ages remember
Leading her, Troya proclaims her decrees to obedient nations."
    Ceasing he cried to the thralls of his house and they tended the Argive.
Brought to a chamber of rest in the luminous peace of the mansion,
Grey he sat and endured the food and the wine of his foemen, —
Chiding his spirit that murmured within him and gazed undelighted,
Vexed with the endless pomps of Laomedon. Far from those glories
Memory winged it back to a sward half-forgotten, a village
Nestling in leaves and low hills watching it crowned with the sunset.

So for his hour he abode in earth's palace of lordliest beauty,
But in its caverns his heart was weary and, hurt by the splendours,
Longed for Greece and the smoke-darkened roof of a cottage in Argos,
Eyes of a woman faded and children crowding the hearthside.
Joyless he rose and eastward expected the sunrise on Ida.

Book Two

The Book of the Statesman

Now from his cycle sleepless and vast round the dance of the earth-globe
Gold Hyperion rose in the wake of the dawn like the eyeball
Flaming of God revealed by his uplifted luminous eyelid.
Troy he beheld and he viewed the transient labour of mortals.
All her marble beauty and pomp were laid bare to the heavens.
Sunlight streamed into Ilion waking the voice of her gardens,
Amorous seized on her ways, lived glad in her plains and her pastures,
Kissed her leaves into brightness of green. As a lover the last time
Yearns to the beauty desired that again shall not wake to his kisses,
So over Ilion, doomed leaned the yearning immense of the sunrise.
She like a wordless marble memory dreaming for ever
Lifted the gaze of her perishable immortality sunwards.
All her human past aspired in the clearness eternal,
Temples of Phryx and Dardanus touched with the gold of the morning,
Columns triumphant of Ilus, domes of their greatness enamoured,
Stones that intended to live; and her citadel climbed up to heaven
White like the soul of the Titan Laomedon claiming his kingdoms,
Watched with alarm by the gods as he came. Her bosom maternal
Thrilled to the steps of her sons and a murmur began in her high-roads.
Life renewed its ways which death and sleep cannot alter,
Life that pursuing her boundless march to a goal which we know not,
Ever her own law obeys, not our hopes, who are slaves of her heart-beats.
Then as now men walked in the round which the gods have decreed them
Eagerly turning their eyes to the lure and the tool and the labour.
Chained is their gaze to the span in front, to the gulfs they are blinded
Meant for their steps. The seller opened his shop and the craftsman
Bent o'er his instruments handling the work he never would finish,
Busy as if their lives were for ever, today in its evening
Sure of tomorrow. The hammers clanged and the voice of the markets
Waking desired its daily rumour. Nor only the craftsman,
Only the hopes of the earth, but the hearts of her votaries kneeling
Came to her marble shrines and upraised to our helpers eternal
Missioned the prayer and the hymn or silent, subtly adoring
Ventured upwards in incense. Loud too the clash of the cymbals
Filled all the temples of Troy with the cry of our souls to the azure.
Prayers breathed in vain and a cry that fell back with Fate for its answer

Children laughed in her doorways; joyous they played, by their mothers
Smiled on still, but their tender bosoms unknowing awaited
Grecian spearpoints sharpened by Fate for their unripe bosoms,
Tasks of the slave in Greece. Like bees round their honey-filled dwellings
Murmuring swarmed to the well-heads the large-eyed daughters of Troya,
Deep-bosomed, limbed like the gods, — glad faces of old that were sentient
Rapturous flowers of the soul, bright bodies that lived under darkness
Heavily[1] massed of their locks like day under night made resplendent,
Daughters divine of the earth in the ages when heaven was our father.
They round Troy's well-heads flowerlike satisfied morn with their beauty
Or in the river baring their knees to the embrace of the coolness
Dipped their white feet in the clutch of his streams, in the haste of Scamander,
Lingering this last time with laughter and talk of the day and the morrow
Leaned to the hurrying flood. All his swiftnesses raced down to meet them
Crowding his channel with dancing billows and turbulent murmurs.
Xanthus primaeval met these waves of our life in its passing
Even as of old he had played with Troy's ancient fair generations
Mingling his deathless voice with the laughter and joy of their ages,
Laughter of dawns that are dead and a joy that the earth has rejected.
Still his whispering trees remembered their bygone voices.
Hast thou forgotten, O river of Troy? Still, still we can hear them
Now, if we listen long in our souls, the bygone voices.
Earth in her fibres remembers, the breezes are stored with our echoes.
Over the stone-hewn steps for their limpid orient waters
Joyous they leaned and they knew not yet of the wells of Mycenae,
Drew not yet from Eurotas the jar for an alien master,
Mixed not Pineus yet with their tears. From the clasp of the current
Now in their groups they arose and dispersed through the streets and the
    byways,
Turned from the freedom of earth to the works and the joy of the hearthside,
Lightly, they rose and returned through the lanes of the wind-haunted city
Swaying with rhythmical steps while the anklets jangled and murmured.
Silent temples saw them passing; you too, O houses,
Built with such hopes by mortal man for his transient lodging;
Fragrant the gardens strewed on dark tresses their white-smiling jasmines
Dropped like a silent boon of purity soft from the branches:
Flowers by the wayside were budding, cries flew winged round the tree-tops.
Bright was the glory of life in Ilion city of Priam.
    Thrice to the city the doom-blast published its solemn alarum,

[1] Nobly

Blast of the trumpets that call to assembly clamoured through Troya
Thrice and were still. From garden and highway, from palace and temple
Turned like a steed to the trumpet, rejoicing in war and ambition,
Gathered alert to the call the democracy hated of heaven.
First in their ranks upbearing their age as Atlas his heavens,
Eagle-crested, with hoary hair like the snow upon Ida,
Ilion's senators paced, Antenor and wide-browed Anchises,
Athamas famous for ships and the war of the waters, Tryas
Still whose name was remembered by Oxus the orient river,
Astyoches and Ucalegon, dateless Pallachus, Aetor,
Aspetus who of the secrets divine knew all and was silent,
Ascanus, Iliones, Alcesiphron, Orus, Aretes.
Next from the citadel came with the voice of the heralds before him
Priam and Priam's sons, Aeneas leonine striding,
Followed[1] by the heart of a nation adoring her Penthesilea.
All that was noble in Troy attended the regal procession
Marching in front and behind and the tramp of their feet was a rhythm
Tuned to the arrogant fortunes of Ilion ruled by incarnate
Demigods, Ilus and Phryx and Dardanus, Tros of the conquests,
Tros and far-ruling Laomedon who to his grandiose[2] labour
Drew down the sons of the skies and was served by the ageless immortals.
Into the agora vast and aspirant besieged by its columns
Bathed and anointed they came like gods in their beauty and grandeur.
Last like the roar of the winds came trampling the surge of the people.
Clamorous led by a force obscure to its ultimate fatal
Session of wrath the violent mighty democracy hastened;
Thousands of ardent lives with the heart yet unslain in their bosoms
Lifted to heaven the voice of man and his far-spreading rumour.
Singing the young men with banners marched in their joyous processions,
Trod in martial measure or dancing with lyrical paces
Chanted the glory of Troy and the wonderful deeds of their fathers.
Into the columned assembly where Ilus had gathered his people,
Thousands on thousands the tramp and the murmur poured; in their
                                                                                     armoured
Glittering tribes they were ranked, an untameable high-hearted nation
Waiting the voice of its chiefs. Some gazed on the greatness of Priam
Ancient, remote from their days, the last of the gods who were passing,
Left like a soul uncompanioned in worlds where his strength shall not
                                                                                       conquer:

[1] Led   [2] soul's strong

Sole like a column gigantic alone on a desolate hill-side
Older than mortals he seemed and mightier. Many in anger
Aimed their hostile looks where calm though by heaven abandoned,
Left to his soul and his lucid mind and its thoughts unavailing,
Head of[1] the age-chilled few whom the might of their hearts had not blinded,
Famous Antenor was seated, the fallen unpopular statesman,
Wisest of speakers in Troy but rejected, stoned and dishonoured.
Silent, aloof from the people he sat, a heart full of ruins.
Low was the rumour that swelled like the hum of the bees in a meadow
When with the thirst of the honey they swarm on the thyme and the linden,
Hundreds humming and flitting till all that place is a murmur.
Then from his seat like a tower arising Priam the monarch
Slowly erect in his vast tranquillity silenced the people:
Lonely, august he stood like one whom death has forgotten,
Reared like a column of might and of silence over the assembly.
So Olympus rises alone with his snows into heaven.
Crowned were his heights by the locks that slept like the mass of the snow-swathe
Clothing his giant shoulders; his eyes of deep meditation,
Eyes that beheld now the end and accepted it like the beginning
Gazed on the throng of the people as on a pomp that is painted:
Slowly he spoke like one who is far from the scenes where he sojourns.
"Leader of Ilion, hero Deiphobus, thou who hast summoned
Troy in her people, arise; say wherefore thou callest us. Evil
Speak thou or good, thou canst speak that only: Necessity fashions
All that the unseen eye has beheld. Speak then to the Trojans;
Say on this dawn of her making what issue of death or of triumph
Fate in his suddenness puts to the unseeing, what summons to perish
Send[2] to this nation men who revolt and gods who are hostile."
    Rising Deiphobus spoke, in stature less than his father,
Less in his build, yet the mightiest man and tallest whom coursers
Bore or his feet to the fight since Ajax fell by the Xanthus.
"People of Ilion, long have you fought with the gods and the Argives
Slaying and slain, but the years persist and the struggle is endless.
Fainting your helpers cease from the battle, the nations forsake you.
Asia weary of strenuous greatness, ease-enamoured
Suffers the foot of the Greek to tread on the beaches of Troas.
Yet have we striven for Troy and for Asia, men who desert us.
Not for ourselves alone have we fought, for our life of a moment!

[1] Leading [2] Cry

Once if the Greeks were triumphant, once if their nations were marshalled
Under some far-seeing chief, Odysseus, Peleus, Achilles,
Not on the banks of Scamander and skirts of the azure Aegean
Fainting would cease the audacious emprise, the Titanic endeavour;
Tigris would flee from their tread and Indus be drunk by their coursers.
Now in these days when each sun goes marvelling down that Troy stands yet
Suffering, smiting, alive, though doomed to all eyes that behold her,
Flinging back Death from her walls and bronze to the shock and the clamour,
Driven by a thought that has risen in the dawn from the tents on the beaches
Grey Talthybius' chariot waits in the Ilian portals,
Far voice of the Hellene demigod challenges timeless Troya.
Thus has he said to us: 'Know you not Doom when she walks in your
    heavens?
Feelst thou not then thy set, O sun who illuminedst Nature?
None can escape the wheel of the gods and its vast revolutions!
Fate demands the joy and pride of the earth for the Argive,
Asia's wealth for the lust of the young barbarian nations.
Sink eclipsed in the circle vast of my radiance; Troya,
Joined to my northern realms deliver the East to the Hellene;
Ilion, to Hellas be yoked; wide Asia, fringe thou Peneus.
Lay down golden Helen, a sacrifice lovely and priceless
Cast by your weakness and fall on immense Necessity's altar;
Yield to the grasp of my longing Polyxena, Hecuba's deep-bosomed daughter,
Her whom my heart desires. Accept from me[1] peace and her healing
Joy of mornings secure and death repulsed from your hearthsides.
Yield these[2] and live, else I leap on you, Fate in front, Hades behind me.
Bound to the gods by an oath I return not again from the battle
Till from high Ida my shadow extends to the Mede and Euphrates.
Let not your victories deceive you, steps that defeat has imagined;
Hear not the voice of your heroes; their fame is a trumpet in Hades:
Only they conquer while yet my horses champ free in their stables.
Earth cannot long resist the man whom Heaven has chosen;
Gods with him walk; his chariot is led; his arm is assisted.'
High rings the Hellene challenge, earth waits for the Ilian answer.
Always man's Fate hangs poised on the flitting breath of a moment;
Called by some word, by some gesture it leaps, then 'tis graven, 'tis granite.
Speak! by what gesture high shall the stern gods recognise Troya?
Sons of the ancients, race of the gods, inviolate city,
Firmer my spear shall I grasp or cast from my hand and for ever?

[1] I bring to you   [2] then

Search in your hearts if your fathers still dwell in them, children of Teucer."
So Deiphobus spoke and the nation heard him in silence,
Awed by the shadow vast of doom, indignant with Fortune.
    Calm from his seat Antenor arose as a wrestler arises,
Tamer of beasts in the cage of the lions, eyeing the monsters
Brilliant, tawny of mane, and he knows if his courage waver,
Falter his eye or his nerve be surprised by the gods that are hostile,
Death will leap on him there in the crowded helpless arena.
Fearless Antenor arose, and a murmur swelled in the meeting
Cruel and threatening, hoarse like the voice of the sea upon boulders;
Hisses thrilled through the roar and one man cried to another,
"Lo, he will speak of peace who has swallowed the gold of Achaia!
Surely the people of Troy are eunuchs who suffer Antenor
Rising unharmed in the agora. Are there not stones in the city?
Surely the steel grows dear in the land when a traitor can flourish."
Calm like a god or a summit Antenor stood in the uproar.
But as he gazed on his soul came memory dimming the vision;
For he beheld his past and the agora crowded and cheering,
Passionate, full of delight while Antenor spoke to the people,
Troy that he loved and his fatherland proud of her eloquent statesman.
Tears to his eyes came thick and he gripped at the staff he was holding.
Mounting his eyes met fully the tumult, mournful and thrilling,
Conquering men's hearts with a note of doom in its sorrowful sweetness.
    "People of Ilion, blood of my blood, O race of Antenor,
Once will I speak though you slay me; for who would shrink from
                                                         destruction
Knowing that soon of his city and nation, his house and his dear ones
All that remains will be a couch of trampled ashes? Athene,
Slain today may I join the victorious souls of our fathers,
Not for the anguish be kept and the irremediable weeping.
Loud yet will I speak the word that the gods have breathed in my spirit,
Strive this last time to save the death-destined. Who are these clamour
'Hear him not, the gold of the Greeks bought his words and his throat is
                                                         accursed?'
Troy whom my counsels made great, hast thou heard this roar of their frenzy
Tearing thy ancient bosom? Is it thy voice heaven-abandoned, my mother?
O my country, O my creatress, earth of my longings!
Earth where our fathers lie in their sacred ashes undying,
Memoried temples shelter the shrines of our gods and the altars
Pure where we worshipped, the beautiful children smile on us passing,

Women divine and the men of our nation! O land where our childhood
Played at a mother's feet mid the trees and the hills of our country,
Hoping our manhood toiled and our youth had its seekings for godhead; —
Thou for our age keepst repose mid the love and the honour of kinsmen,
Silent our relics shall lie with the city guarding our ashes!
Earth who hast fostered our parents, earth who hast given us[1] our offspring,
Soil that created our race where fed from the bosom of Nature
Happy our children shall dwell[2] in the storied homes of their fathers,
Souls that our souls have stamped, sweet forms of ourselves when we perish!
Once even then have they seen thee in their hearts, or dreamed of thee ever
Who from thy spirit revolt and only thy name make an idol
Hating thy faithful sons and the cult of thy ancient ideal!
Wake, O my mother divine, remember thy gods and thy wisdom,
Silence the tongues that degrade thee, prophets profane of thy godhead.
Madmen, to think that a man who has offered his life for his country
Served her with words and deeds and adored with victories and triumphs
Ever could think of enslaving her breast to the heel of a foeman!
Surely Antenor's halls are empty, he begs from the stranger
Leading his sons and his children's sons by the hand in the market,
Showing his rags since his need is so bitter of gold from the Argives!
You who demand a reply when Laocoon lessens Antenor,
Hush then your feeble roar and your ear to the past and the distance
Turn. You fields that are famous for ever, reply for me calling,
Fields of the mighty mown by my sword's edge, Chersonese conquered,
Thrace and her snows where we fought on the frozen streams and were
                                                                        victors
Then when they were unborn who are now your delight and your leaders.
Answer return, you columns of Ilus, here where my counsels
Made Troy mightier guiding her safe through the shocks of her foemen.
Gold! I have heaped it up high, I am rich with the spoils of your haters.
It was your fathers dead who gave me that wealth as my guerdon,
Now my reproach, your fathers who saw not the Greeks round their
                                                                        ramparts:
They were not cooped by an upstart race in the walls of Apollo,
Saw not Hector slain and Troilus dragged by his coursers.
Far[3] over wrathful Jaxartes they rode; the shaken Achaian
Prostrate adored their strength who now shouts at your portals and conquers[4]
Then when Antenor guided Troy, this old man, this traitor,
Not Laocoon, nay, not even Paris nor Hector.

[1] cherished [2] reign [3] Fast [4] gates as your victor

But I have changed, I have grown a niggard of blood and of treasure,
Selfish, chilled as old men seem to the young and the headstrong,
Counselling safety and ease, not the ardour of noble decisions.
Come to my house and behold, my house that was filled once with voices.
Sons whom the high gods envied me crowded the halls that are silent.
Where are they now? They are dead, their voices are silent in Hades,
Fallen slaying the foe in a war between sin and the Furies.
Silent they went to the battle to die unmourned for their country,
Die as they knew in vain. Do I keep now the last ones remaining,
Sparing their blood that my house may endure? Is there any in Troya
Speeds to the front of the mellay outstripping the sons of Antenor?
Let him arise and speak and proclaim it and bid me be silent.
Heavy is this war that you love on my heart and I hold you as madmen
Doomed by the gods, abandoned by Pallas, by Hera afflicted.
Who would not hate to behold his work undone by the foolish?
Who would not weep if he saw Laocoon ruining Troya,
Paris doomed in his beauty, Aeneas slain by his valour?
Still you need to be taught that the high gods see and remember,
Dream that they care not if justice be done on the earth or oppression!
Happy to live, aspire while you violate man and the immortals!
Vainly the sands of Time have been strewn with the ruins of empires,
Signs that the gods have left, but in vain. For they look for a nation,
One that can conquer itself having conquered the world, but they find none.
None has been able to hold all the gods in his bosom unstaggered.
All have grown drunken with force and have gone down to Hell and to Ate.
'All have been thrust from their heights,' say the fools; 'we shall live and
                                                                for ever.
We are the people at last, the children, the favourites; all things
Only to us are permitted.' They too descend to the silence,
Death receives their hopes and the void their stirrings of action.
    "Eviller fate there is none than life too long among mortals.
I have conversed with the great who have gone, I have fought in their
                                                                war-cars;
Tros I have seen, Laomedon's hand has lain[1] on my temples.
Now I behold Laocoon, now our leader[2] is Paris.
First when Phryx by the Hellespont reared to the cry of the Ocean
Hewing her stones as vast as his thoughts his high-seated fortress,
Planned he a lair for a beast of prey, for a pantheress dire-souled
Crouched in the hills for her bound or self-gathered against the avenger?

[1] dwelt [2] greatest

Dardanaus shepherded Asia's coasts and her sapphire-girt islands.
Mild was his rule like the blessing of rain upon fields in the summer.
Gladly the harried coasts reposed confessing the Phrygian,
Caria, Lycia's kings and the Paphlagon, strength of the Mysian;
Minos' Crete recovered the sceptre of old Rhadamanthus.
Ilus and Tros had strength in the fight like a far-striding Titan's:
Troy triumphant following the urge of their souls to the vastness
[Helmeted, crowned like a queen of the gods with the fates for her coursers]*
Rode through the driving sleet of the spears to Indus and Oxus.
Then twice over she conquered the vanquished, with peace as in battle;
There where discord had clashed, sweet Peace sat girded with plenty,
There where tyranny counted her blows came the hands of a father.
Neither was[1] Teucer a soul like your chiefs[2] who refounded this nation.
Such was the antique and noble tradition of Troy in her founders,
Builders of power that endured; but it perishes lost to their offspring,
Trampled, scorned by an arrogant age, by a violent nation.
Strong Anchises trod it down trampling victorious onwards,
Stern as his sword and hard as the silent bronze of his armour.
More than another I praise the man who is mighty and steadfast,
Even as Ida the mountain I praise, a refuge for lions;
But in the council I laud him not, he who a god for his kindred
Lives for the rest without bowels of pity or fellowship, lone-souled,
Scorning the world that he rules, who untamed by the weight of an empire
Holds allies as subjects, subjects as slaves and drives to the battle,
Careless more of their wills than the coursers yoked to his war-car.
Therefore they fought while they feared, but gladly abandon us falling.
Yet had they gathered to Teucer in the evil days of our nation.
Where are they now? Do they gather then to the dreaded Anchises?
Or has Aeneas helped with his counsels hateful to wisdom?
Hateful is this, abhorred of the gods, imagined by Ate
When against subjects murmuring discord and faction appointed
Scatter unblest gold, the heart of a people is poisoned,
Virtue pursued and baseness triumphs tongued like a harlot,
Brother against brother arrayed that the rule may endure of a stranger.
Yes, but it lasts! For its hour. The high gods watch in their silence,
Mute they endure for a while that the doom may be swifter and greater.
Hast thou then lasted, O Troy? Lo, the Greeks at thy gates and Achilles.
Dream, when Virtue departs, that Wisdom will linger, her sister!
Wisdom has turned from your hearts; shall Fortune dwell with the foolish?

* Brackets in the original.   [1] had   [2] chiefs'

Fatal oracles came to you great-tongued, vaunting of empires
Stretched from the risen sun to his rest in the occident waters,
Dreams of a city throned on the hills with her foot on the nations.
Meanwhile the sword was prepared for our breasts and the flame for our
                                              housetops.
Wake, awake, O my people! the fire-brand mounts up your doorsteps;
Gods who deceived to slay, press swords on your children's bosoms.
See, O ye blind, ere death in pale countries open your eyelids!
Hear, O ye deaf, the sounds in your ears and the voices of evening!
Young men who vaunt in your strength! when the voice of this aged
                                                   Antenor
Governed your fathers' youth, all the Orient was joined to our banners.
Macedon leaned to the East and her princes yearned to the victor,
Scythians worshipped in Ilion's shrines, the Phoenician trader
Bartered her tokens, Babylon's wise men paused at our thresholds;
Fair-haired sons of the snows came rapt towards golden Troya
Drawn by the song and the glory. Strymon sang hymns unto Ida,
Hoarse Chaleidice, dim Chersonesus married their waters
Under the o'erarching yoke of Troy twixt the term-posts of Ocean.
Meanwhile far through the world your fortunes led by my counsels
Followed their lure like women snared by a magical tempter:
High was their chant as they paced and it came from continents distant.
Turn now and hear! what voice approaches? what glitter of armies?
Loud upon Trojan beaches the tread and the murmur of Hellas!
Hark! 'tis the Achaian's paean rings o'er the Pergaman waters!
So wake the dreams of Aeneas; reaped is Laocoon's harvest.
Speakers whose counsels persuaded our strength from the labour before us,
Artisans new of your destiny fashioned this far-spreading downfall,
Counsellors blind who scattered your strength to the hooves of the Scythian,
Barren victories, trophies of skin-clad Illyrian pastors.
Who but the fool and improvident, who but the dreamer and madman
Leaves for the far and ungrasped earth's close and provident labour?
Children of earth, our mother gives tokens, she lays down her sign-posts,
Step by step to advance on her bosom, to grow by her seasons,
Order our works by her patience and limit our thought by her spaces.
But you had chiefs who were demigods, souls of an earth-scorning stature,
Minds that saw vaster than life and strengths that God's hour could not
                                                         limit!
These men seized upon Troy as the tool of their giant visions,
Dreaming of Africa's suns and bright Hesperian orchards,

Carthage our mart and our feet on the sunset hills of the Latins.
Ilion's hinds in the dream ploughed Libya, sowed Italy's cornfields,
Troy stretched to Gades; even the gods and the Fates had grown Trojan.
So are the natures of men uplifted by Heaven in its satire.
Scorning the bit of the gods, despisers of justice and measure,
Zeus is denied and adored some shadow huge of their natures
Losing the shape of man in a dream that is splendid and monstrous.
Titans, vaunting they stride and the world resounds with their footsteps;
Titans, clanging they fall and the world is full of their ruin.
Children, you dreamed with them, heard the roar of the Atlantic breakers
Welcome your keels and the Isles of the Blest grew your wonderful gardens;
Lulled in the dream, you saw not the black-drifting march of the storm-rack,
Heard not the galloping wolves of the doom and the howl of their hunger.
Greece in her peril united her jarring clans; you suffered
Patient, preparing the north, the wisdom and silence of Peleus,
Atreus' craft and the Argives gathered to King Agamemnon.
But there were prophecies, Pythian oracles, mutterings from Delphi.
How shall they prosper who haste after auguries, oracles, whispers,
Dreams that walk in the night and voices obscure of the silence?
Touches are these from the gods that bewilder the brain to its ruin.
One sole oracle helps, still armoured in courage and prudence
Patient and heedful to toil at the work that is near in the daylight.
Leave to the night its phantoms, leave to the future its curtain!
Only today Heaven gave to mortal man for his labour.
If thou hadst bowed not thy mane, O Troy, to the child and the dreamer,
Hadst thou been faithful to[1] Wisdom the counsellor seated and ancient,
Then would the hour not have dawned when Paris lingered in Sparta
Led by the goddess fatal and beautiful, white Aphrodite.
Man, shun the impulses dire that spring armed from thy nature's abysms!
Dread the dark rose of the gods, flee the honey that tempts from its petals!
Therefore the black deed was done and the hearth that welcomed was sullied.
Sin-called the Fury uplifted her tresses of gloom o'er the nations
Maddening the earth with the scream of her blood-thirst, bowelless,
                                                      stone-eyed,
Claiming her victims from God and bestriding the hate and the clamour.
Yet midst the stroke and the wail when men's eyes were blind with the
                                                      blood-mist,
Still had the high gods mercy remembering[2] Teucer and Ilus.
Sped by the hand of the Thunderer Discord flaming from Ida

---

[1] If thou hadst kept faith with   [2] recalling

Glared from the ships in her wrath[1] through the camp of the victor
                                                                Achaians, —
Love to the discord added her flowerlike lips of Briseis;
Faltering lids of Polyxena conquered the strength of Pelides.
Vainly those helpers high[2] have opened the gates of salvation!
Vainly the winds of their mercy have breathed on our fevered existence!
Man his passion prefers to the voice that guides from the immortals.[3]
These too[4] were here whom Hera had chosen to ruin this nation:
Charioteers cracking the whips of their speed on the paths of destruction,
Demigods they! they have come down from Heaven glad to that labour;
Filled is[5] the world with the fame of their wheels as they race down to Hades.
O that alone they could reach it! O that pity could soften
Harsh Necessity's dealings, sparing our innocent children,
Saving the Trojan women and aged from bonds and the sword-edge!
These had not sinned whom you slay in your madness! Ruthless, O mortals,
Must you be then to yourselves, when the gods even faltering with pity
Turn from the grief that must come and the agony vast and the weeping?
Say not the road of escape sinks too low for your arrogant treading.
Pride is not for our clay; the earth, not heaven was our mother
And we are even as the ant in our toil and the beast in our dying;
Only who cling to the hands of the gods can rise up from the earth-mire.
Children, lie prone to their scourge, that your hearts may revive in their
                                                                sunshine.
This is our lot! when the anger of heaven has passed then the mortal
Raises his head; soon he heals his heart and forgets he has suffered.
Yet if resurgence from weakness and shame were withheld from the creature,
Every fall without morrow, who then would counsel submission?
But since the height of mortal fortune ascending must stumble,
Fallen, again ascend, since death like birth is our portion,
Ripening, mowed, to be sown again like corn by the farmer,
Let us be patient still with the gods and be clay for their handling.
Dream not defeat I welcome. Think not to Hellas submitting
Death of proud hope I would seal. Not this have I counselled, O nation,
But to be even as your high-crested forefathers, greatest of mortals.
Troya of old enringed by the hooves of Cimmerian armies
Flamed to the heavens from her plains and her smoke-blackened citadel
                                                                sheltered

---

[1] Hundred-eyed } glared from the ships
    Hundred-voiced
[2] Vainly the gods who pity [3] heavens. [4] They still [5] Echoes

Hardly[1] the joyless rest of her sons and the wreck of her greatness.
Courage and wisdom survived in that fall and a stern-eyed prudence
Helped her to live; disguised from her mightiness Troy crouched weeping.
Teucer descended whose genius worked at this kingdom and nation,
Patient, scrupulous, wise, like a craftsman carefully toiling
Over a helmet or over a breastplate, testing it always,
Toiled in the eye of the Masters of all and had heed of its labour.
So in the end they would not release him like souls that are common;
They out of Ida sent into Ilion Pallas Athene;
Secret she came and he went with her into the luminous silence.
Teucer's children after their sire completed his labour.
Now too, O people, front adversity self-gathered, silent.
Veil thyself, leonine mighty Ilion, hiding thy greatness!
Be as thy father Teucer; be as a cavern for lions;
Be as a Fate that crouches! Wordless and stern for your vengeance
Self-gathered work in the night and secrecy shrouding your bosoms.
Let not the dire heavens know of it; let not the foe seize a whisper!
Ripen the hour of your stroke, while your words drip sweeter than honey.
Sure am I, friends, you will turn from death at my voice, you will hear me!
Some day yet I shall gaze on the ruins of haughty Mycenae.
Is this not better than Ilion cast to the sword of her haters,
Is this not happier than Troya captured and wretchedly burning,
Time to await in his stride when the southern and northern Achaians
Gazing with dull distaste now over their severing isthmus
Hate-filled shall move to the shock by the spur of the gods in them driven,
Pelops march upon Attica, Thebes descend on the Spartan?
Then shall the hour now kept in heaven for us ripen to dawning,
Then shall Victory cry to our banners over the Ocean
Calling our sons with her voice immortal. Children of Ilus,
Then shall Troy rise in her strength and stride over Greece up to Gades."
  So Antenor spoke and the mind of the hostile assembly
Moved and swayed with his words like the waters ruled by Poseidon.
Even as the billows rebellious lashed by the whips of the tempest
Curvet and rear their crests like the hooded wrath of a serpent,
Green-eyed under their cowls sublime, — unwilling they journey
Foam-bannered, hoarse-voiced, shepherded, forced by the wind, to the
                                                                margin
Meant for their rest, and can turn not at all, though they rage, on their
                                                                driver,—

[1] Mutely

Last with a sullen applause and consenting lapse into thunder,
Where they were led all the while they sink down huge and astonished,
So in their souls that withstood and obeyed and hated the yielding,
Lashed by his censure, indignant, the Trojans moved towards his purpose:
Sometimes a roar arose, then only, weakened, rarer,
Angry murmurs swelled between sullen stretches of silence;
Last, a reluctant applause broke dull from the throats of the commons.
Silent raged in their hearts Laocoon's following daunted;
Troubled the faction of Paris turned to the face of their leader.
He as yet rose not; careless he sat in his beauty and smiling,
Gazing with brilliant eyes at the sculptured pillars of Ilus.
Doubtful, swayed by Antenor, waited in silence the nation.

BOOK THREE

The Book of the Assembly

But as the nation beset betwixt doom and a shameful surrender
Waited mute for a voice that could lead and a heart to encourage,
Up in the silence deep Laocoon rose up, far-heard, —
Heard by the gods in their calm and heard by men in their passion —
Cloud-haired, clad in mystic red, flamboyant, sombre,
Priam's son Laocoon, fate-darkened seer of Apollo.
As when the soul of the Ocean arises rapt in the dawning
And mid the rocks and the foam uplifting the voice of its musings
Opens the chant of its turbulent harmonies, so rose the far-borne
Voice of Laocoon soaring mid columns of Ilion's glories,
Claiming the earth and the heavens for the field of its confident rumour.
"Trojans, deny your hearts to the easeful flutings of Hades!
Live, O nation!" he thundered forth and Troy's hearts and her pillars
Sent back their fierce response. Restored to her leonine spirits
Ilion rose in her agora filling the heavens with shoutings,
Bearing a name to the throne of Zeus in her mortal defiance.
As when a sullen calm of the heavens discourages living,
Nature and man feel the pain of the lightnings repressed in their bosoms,
Dangerous and dull is the air, then suddenly strong from the anguish
Zeus of the thunders starts into glories releasing his storm-voice,
Earth exults in the kiss of the rain and the life-giving laughters,
So from the silence broke forth the thunder of Troya arising;
Fiercely she turned from prudence and wisdom and turned back to greatness,
Casting her voice to the heavens from the depths of her fathomless spirit.
Raised by those clamours, triumphant once more in this scene of his
                                                                greatness,
Tool of the gods, but he deemed of his strength as a leader in Nature,
Took for his own a voice that was given and dreamed that he fashioned
Fate that fashions us all, Laocoon stood mid the shouting
Leaned on the calm of an ancient pillar. In eyes self-consuming
Kindled the flame of the prophet that blinds at once and illumines;
Quivering thought-besieged lips and shaken locks of the lion,
Lifted his gaze the storm-led enthusiast. Then as the shouting
Tired of itself at last disappeared in the bosom of silence,
Once more he started erect and his voice o'er the hearts of his hearers
Swept like Ocean's impatient cry when it calls from its surges,

Ocean loud with a thought sublime in its measureless marching.
Each man felt his heart like foam in the rushing of waters.
  "Ilion is vanquished then! she abases her grandiose spirit
Mortal found in the end to the gods and the Greeks and Antenor,
And when a barbarous chieftain's menace and insolent mercy
Bring here their pride to insult the columned spirit of Ilus,
Trojans have sat and feared! For a man has arisen and spoken,
One whom the gods in their anger have hired. Since the Argive prevailed not,
Armed, with his strength and his numbers, in Troya they sought for her slayer,
Gathered their wiles in a voice and they chose a man famous and honoured,
Summoned Ate to aid and corrupted the heart of Antenor.
Flute of the breath of the Hell-witch, always he scatters among you
Doubt, affliction and weakness chilling the hearts of the fighters,
Always his voice with its cadenced and subtle possession for evil
Breaks the constant will and maims the impulse heroic.
Therefore while yet her heroes fight and her arms are unconquered,
Troy in your hearts is defeated! The souls of your Fathers have heard you
Dallying, shamefast, with vileness, lured by the call of dishonour.
Such is the power Zeus gave to the wingèd words of a mortal!
Foiled in his will, disowned by the years that stride on for ever,
Yet in the frenzy cold of his greed and his fallen ambition
Doom from heaven he calls down on his countrymen, Trojan abuses
Troy, his country, extolling her enemies, blessing her slayers.
Such are the gods Antenor has made in his heart's own image
That if one evil man have not way for his greed and his longing
Cities are doomed and kings must be slain and a nation must perish!
But from the mind of the free and the brave I will answer thy bodings,
Gold-hungry raven of Troy who croakst from thy nest at her princes.
Only one doom irreparable treads down the soul of a nation,
Only one downfall endures; 'tis the ruin of greatness and virtue,
Mourning when Freedom departs from the life and the heart of a people,
Into her room comes creeping the mind of the slave and it poisons
Manhood and joy and the voice to lying is trained and subjection
Easy feels to the neck of man who is next to the godheads.
Not of the fire am I terrified, not of the sword and its slaying;
Vileness of men appals me, baseness I fear and its voices.
What can man suffer direr or worse than enslaved from a victor
Boons to accept, to take safety and ease from the foe and the stranger,
Fallen from the virtue stern that heaven permits to a mortal?

Death is not keener than this nor the slaughter of friends and our dear ones.
Out and alas! earth's greatest are earth and they fail in the testing,
Conquered by sorrow and doubt, fate's hammerers, fires of her furnace.
God in their souls they renounce and submit to their clay and its
                                                               promptings.
Else could the heart of Troya have recoiled from the loom of the shadow
Cast by Achilles' spear or shrunk at the sound of his car-wheels?
Now he has graven an oath austere in his spirit unpliant
Victor at last to constrain in his stride the walls of Apollo
Burning Troy ere he sleeps. 'Tis the vow of a high-crested nature;
Shall it break ramparted Troy? Yea, the soul of a man too is mighty
More than the stones and the mortar! Troy had a soul once, O Trojans,
Firm as her god-built ramparts. When in the hour of his passion[1],
When Sarpedon fell and Zeus averted his visage,
Xanthus red to the sea ran sobbing with bodies of Trojans,
When in the day of the silence of heaven the far-glancing helmet
Ceased from the ways of the fight, and panic slew with Achilles
Hosts who were left unshepherded pale at the fall of their greatest,
Godlike Troy lived on. Do we speak mid a city's ruins?
Lo! she confronts her heavens as when Tros and Laomedon ruled her.
All now is changed, these mutter and sigh to you, all now is ended;
Strength has renounced you, Fate has finished the thread of her spinning.
Hector is dead, he walks in the shadows; Troilus fights not;
Resting his curls on the asphodel he has forgotten his country;
Strong Sarpedon lies in Bellerophon's city sleeping:
Memnon is slain and the blood of Rhesus has dried on the Troad:
All of the giant Asius sums in a handful of ashes.
Grievous[2] are these things; our hearts still keep all the pain of them
                                                               treasured,
Hard though they grow by use and iron caskets of sorrow.
Hear yet, O fainters in wisdom snared by your pathos,
Know this iron world we live in where Hell casts its shadow.
Blood and grief are the ransom of men for the joys of their transience,
For we are mortals bound in our strength and beset in our labour.
This is our human destiny; every moment of living
Toil and loss have gained in the constant siege of our bodies.
Men must sow earth with their lives[3] and their tears that their country may
                                                               prosper;

[1] (i) in the hour of his uplifting (ii) by the Fates (gods) (spears) overtaken
[2] Wretched/Miserable   [3] hearts

Earth who bore and devours us that life may be born from our remnants
Then shall the Sacrifice reap[1] its fruits when the war-shout is silent,
Nor shall the blood be in vain that our mother has felt on her bosom
Nor shall the seed of the mighty fail when Death is the sower.
Still from the loins of the mother eternal are heroes engendered,
Still Deiphobus shouts in the war-front trampling the Argives,
Strong Aeneas' far-borne voice is heard from our ramparts,
Paris' hands are swift and his feet in the chases of Ares.
Lo, when deserted we fight[2] by Asia's soon-wearied peoples,
Men ingrate who enjoyed the protection and loathed the protector,
Heaven has sent us replacing a continent Penthesilea!
Low has the heart of Achaia sunk since it shook at her war-cry.
Ajax has bit at the dust; it is all he shall have of the Troad;
Tall Meriones lies and measures his portion of booty.
Who is the fighter in Ilion thrills not rejoicing to hearken
Even her name on unwarlike lips, much more in the mellay
Shout of the daughter of battles, armipotent Penthesilea?
If there were none but these only, if hosts came not surging behind them,
Young men burning-eyed to outdare all the deeds of their elders,
Each in his beauty a Troilus, each in his valour a Hector,
Yet were the measures poised in the equal balance of Ares.
Who then compels you, O people unconquered, to sink down abjuring
All that was Troy? For O, if she yield, let her use not for ever
One of her titles! shame not the shade of Teucer and Ilus,
Soil not Tros! Are you awed by the strength of the swift-foot Achilles?
Is it a sweeter lure in the cadenced voice of Antenor?
Or are you weary of Time and the endless roar of the battle?
Wearier still are the Greeks! their eyes look out o'er the waters
Nor with the flight of their spears is the wing of their hopes towards Troya.
Dull are their hearts; they sink from the war-cry and turn from the
                                                           spear-stroke
Sullenly dragging backwards, desiring the paths of the Ocean,
Dreaming of hearths that are far and the children growing to manhood
Who are small infant faces still in the thoughts of their fathers.
Therefore these call you to yield lest they wake and behold in the dawn-light
All Poseidon whitening lean to the west in his waters
Thick with the sails of the Greeks departing beaten to Hellas.
Who is it calls? Antenor the statesman, Antenor the patriot,
Thus who loves his country and worships the soil of his fathers!

[1] gather   [2] fought

Which of you loves like him Troya? which of the children of heroes
Yearns for the touch of a yoke on his neck and desires the aggressor?
If there be any so made by the gods in the nation of Ilus,
Leaving this city which freemen have founded, freemen have dwelt in,
Far on the beach let him make his couch in the tents of Achilles,
Not in this mighty Ilion, not with the lioness fighting,
Guarding the lair of her young and roaring back at her hunters.
We who are souls descended from Ilus and seeds of his making,
Other-hearted shall march from our gates to answer Achilles.
What! shall this ancient Ilion welcome the day of the conquered?
She who was head of the world, shall she live in the guard of the Hellene
Cherished as slave-girls are, who are taken in war, by their captors?
Europe shall walk in our streets with the pride and the gait of the victor?
Greeks shall enter our homes and prey on our mothers and daughters?
This Antenor desires and this Ucalegon favours.
Traitors! whether 'tis cowardice drives or the sceptic of virtue,
Cold-blooded age, or gold insatiably tempts from its coffers
Pleading for safety from foreign hands and the sack and the plunder.
Leave them, my brothers! spare the baffled hypocrites! Failure
Sharpest shall torture their hearts when they know that still you are Trojans.
Silence, O reason of man! for a voice from the gods has been uttered!
Dardanus, hearken the sound divine that comes to you mounting
Out of the solemn ravines from the mystic seat on the tripod!
Phoebus, the master of Truth, has promised the earth to our peoples.
Children of Zeus, rejoice! for the Olympian brows have nodded
Regal over the world. In earth's rhythm of shadow and sunlight
Storm is the dance of the locks of the God assenting to greatness,
Zeus who with secret compulsion orders the ways of our nature;
Veiled in events he lives and working disguised in the mortal
Builds our strength by pain, and an empire is born out of ruins.
Then if the tempest be loud and the thunderbolt leaping incessant
Shatters the roof, if the lintels flame at last and each cornice
Shrieks with pain of the blast, if the very pillars totter,
Keep yet your faith in Zeus, hold fast to the word of Apollo.
Not by a little pain and not by a temperate labour
Trained is the nation chosen by Zeus for a dateless dominion.
Long must it labour rolled in the wrath[1] of the fathomless surges,
Often neighbour with death and ere Ares grow firm to its banners
Feel on the pride of its Capitol tread of the triumphing victor,

[1] foam

Hear the barbarian knock at its gates or the neighbouring foeman
Glad of the transient smile of his fortune suffer insulting; —
They, the nation eternal, brook their taunts who must perish!
Heaviest toils they must bear; they must wrestle with Fate and her Titans,
And when some leader returns from the battle sole of his thousands
Crushed by the hammers of God, yet never despair of their country.
Dread not the ruin, fear not the storm-blast, yield not, O Trojans.
Zeus shall rebuild! Death ends not our days, the fire shall not triumph.
Death? I have faced it. Fire? I have watched it climb in my vision
Over the timeless domes and over the roof-tops of Priam,
But I have looked beyond and have seen the smile of Apollo.
After her glorious centuries, after her world-wide triumphs,
If, near her ramparts outnumbered she fights, by the nations forsaken,
Lonely again on her hill, by her streams, and her meadows and beaches,
Once where she revelled, shake to the tramp of her countless invaders,
Testings are these from the god. For Fate severe like a mother
Teaches our wills by disaster and strikes down the props that would weaken,
Fate and the Thought on high that is wiser than yearnings of mortals.
Troy has arisen before, but from ashes, not shame, not surrender!
(Souls that are true to themselves are immortal; the soulless for ever
Lingers helpless in Hades a shade among shades disappointed.)
Now is the god in my bosom mighty compelling me, Trojans,
Now I release what my spirit has kept and it saw in its vision;
Nor will be silent for gibe of the cynic or sneer of the traitor.
Troy shall triumph! Hear, O ye peoples, the word of Apollo —
Hear it and tremble, O Greece, in thy youth and the dawn of thy future;
Rather forget while thou canst, but the gods in their hour shall remind thee.
Tremble, nations of Asia, false to the greatness within you.
Troy shall surge back on your realms with the sword and the yoke of the
                                                                victor.
Troy shall triumph! Though nations conspire and the gods lead her foemen,
Fate that is born of the spirit is greater than they and will shield her.
Foemen shall help her with war, her defeats shall be victory's moulders.
Walls that restrain shall be rent; she shall rise out of sessions unsettled,
Oceans shall be her walls at the end and the desert her limit;
Indus shall send to her envoys; her eyes shall look northward from Thule.
She shall enring all the coasts with her strength like the kingly Poseidon,
She shall o'ervault all the lands with her rule like the limitless azure."
    Ceasing from speech Laocoon, girt with the shouts of a nation,
Lapsed on his seat like one seized and abandoned and weakened; nor ended

Only in iron applause, but throughout with a stormy approval
Ares broke from the hearts of his people in ominous thunder.
Savage and dire was the sound like a wild beast's tracked out and hunted,
Wounded, yet trusting to tear out the entrails live of its hunters,
Savage and cruel and threatening doom to the foe and opponent.
Yet when the shouting sank at last, Ucalegon rose up
Trembling with age and with wrath and in accents hurried and piping
Faltered a senile fierceness forth on the maddened assembly.
"Ah, it is even so far that you dare, O you children of Priam,
Favourites vile of a people sent mad by the gods, and thou risest,
Dark Laocoon, prating of heroes and spurning for cowards,
Smiting for traitors the aged and wise who were grey when they spawned
                                                                  thee!
Imp of destruction, mane of mischief! Ah, spur us with courage,
Thou who hast never prevailed against even the feeblest Achaian.
Rather twice hast thou raced in the rout to the ramparts for shelter,
Leading the panic, and shrieked as thou ranst to the foeman for mercy
Who were a mile behind thee, O matchless and wonderful racer.
Safely counsel to others the pride and the firmness of heroes,
Thou who wilt not die in the battle! For even swiftest Achilles
Could not o'ertake thee, I ween, nor wind-footed Penthesilea.
Mask of a prophet, heart of a coward, tongue of a trickster,
Timeless Ilion thou alone ruinest, helped by the Furies.
I, Ucalegon, first will rend off the mask from thee, traitor.
For I believe thee suborned by the cynic wiles of Odysseus
And thou conspirest to sack this Troy with the greed of the Cretan."
Hasting unstayed he pursued like a brook that scolds amid pebbles,
Voicing angers shrill; for the people astonished were silent;
Long he pursued not; a shouting broke from that stupor of fury,
Men sprang pale to their feet and hurled out menaces lethal;
All that assembly swayed like a forest swept by the storm-wind.
Obstinate, straining his age-dimmed eyes, Ucalegon, trembling
Worse yet with anger, clamoured feebly back at the people,
Whelmed in their roar. Unheard was his voice like a swimmer in surges
Lost, yet he spoke. But the anger grew in the throats of the people
Lion-voiced, hurting the heart with sound and daunting the nature,
Till from some stalwart hand a javelin whistling and vibrant
Missing the silvered head of the senator rang disappointed
Out on the distant wall of a house by the side of the market.
Not even then would the old man hush or yield to the tempest.

Wagging his hoary beard and shifting his aged eyeballs,
Tossing his hands he stood; but Antenor seized him and Aetor,
Dragged him down on his seat though he strove, and chid him and silenced.
"Cease, O friend; for the gods have won. It were easier piping
High with thy aged treble to alter the rage of the Ocean
Than to o'erbear this people stirred by Laocoon. Leave now
Effort unhelpful, wrap thy days in a mantle of silence;
Give to the gods their will and dry-eyed wait for the ending."
So now the old men ceased from their strife with the gods and with Troya;
Cowed by the storm of the people's wrath they desisted from hoping.
But though the roar long swelled, like the sea when the winds have subsided,
One man yet rose up unafraid and beckoned for silence,
Not of the aged, but ripe in his look and ruddy of visage,
Stalwart and bluff and short-limbed, Halamus son of Antenor.
Forward he stood from the press and the people fell silent and listened,
For he was ever first in the mellay and loved by the fighters.
He with a smile began: "Come, friends, debate is soon ended
If there is right but of lungs and you argue with javelins. Wisdom,
Rather pray for her aid in this dangerous hour of your fortunes.
Not to scalp Laocoon, too much praising his swiftness,
Trojans, I rise; for some are born brave with the spear in the war-car,
Others bold with the tongue, nor equal gifts unto all men
Zeus has decreed who guides his world in a round that is devious
Carried this way and that like a ship that is tossed on the waters.
Why should we rail then at one who is lame by the force of Cronion?
Not by his will is he lame; he would race, if he could, with the swiftest
Yet is the halt man no runner, nor, friends, must you rise up and slay me,
If I should say of this priest, he is neither Sarpedon nor Hector.
Then, if my father whom once you honoured, ancient Antenor,
Hugs to him Argive gold which I see not, his son, in his mansion,
Me too accusest thou, prophet Laocoon? Friends, you have watched me
Sometimes fight; did you see with my house's allies how I gambolled,
Changed, when with sportive spear I was tickling the ribs of my Argives,
Nudges of friendly counsel inviting to entry in Troya?
Men, these are visions of lackbrains; men, these are myths of the market.
Let us have done with them, brothers and friends; hate only the Hellene.
Prophet, I bow to the oracles. Wise are the gods in their silence,
Wise when they speak; but their speech is other than ours and their wisdom
Hard for a mortal mind to hold and not madden or wander;
But for myself I see only the truth as a soldier who battles

Judging the strength of his foes and the chances of iron encounter.
Few are our armies, many the Greeks, and we waste in the combat
Bound to our numbers, — they by the Ocean hemmed from their kinsmen,
We by our fortunes, waves of the gods that are harder to master,
They like a rock that is chipped, but we like a mist that disperses.
Then if Achilles, bound by an oath, bring peace to us, healing,
Bring to us respite, help, though bought at a price, yet full-measured,
Strengths of the North at our side and safety assured from the Achaian
For he is true though a Greek, will you shun this mighty advantage?
Peace at the least we shall have, though gold we lose and much glory;
Peace we will use for our strength to breathe in, our wounds to recover,
Teaching Time to prepare for happier wars in the future.
Pause ere you fling from you life; you are mortals, not gods in your glory.
Not for submission to new ally or to ancient foeman
Peace these desire; for who would exchange wide death for subjection?
Who would submit to a yoke? Or who shall rule Trojans in Troya?
Swords are there still at our sides, there are warriors' hearts in our bosoms.
Peace your senators welcome, not servitude, breathing they ask for.
But if for war you pronounce, if a noble death you have chosen,
That I approve. What fitter end for this warlike nation,
Knowing that empires at last must sink and perish all cities,
Than to preserve to the end posterity's praise and its greatness
Ceasing in clangour of arms and a city's flames for our death-pyre?
Choose then with open eyes what the dread gods offer to Troya.
Hope not now Hector is dead and Sarpedon, Asia inconstant,
We but a handful, Troy can prevail over Greece and Achilles.
Play not with dreams in this hour, but sternly, like men and not children,
Choose with a noble and serious greatness fates fit for Troya.
Stark we will fight till buried we fall under Ilion's ruins,
Or, unappeased, we will curb our strength for the hope of the future."
Not without praise of his friends and assent of the thoughtfuller Trojans,
Halamus spoke and ceased. But now in the Ilian forum
Bright, of the sun-god a ray, and even before he had spoken
Sending the joy of his brilliance into the hearts of his hearers,
Paris arose. Not applauded his rising, but each man towards him
Eagerly turned as if feeling that all before which was spoken
Were but a prelude and this was the note he has waited for always.
Sweet was his voice like a harp's, when it chants of war, and its cadence
Softened with touches of music thoughts that were hard to be suffered,
Sweet like a string that is lightly struck, but it penetrates wholly.

"Calm with the greatness you hold from your sires by the right of
                                                          your nature
I too would have you decide before Heaven in the strength of your spirits
Not to the past and its memories moored like the thoughts of Antenor
Hating the vivid march of the present, nor towards the future
Panting through dreams like my brother Laocoon vexed by Apollo.
Dead is the past; the void has possessed it; its drama is ended,
Finished its music. The future is dim and remote from our knowledge,
Silent it lies on the knees of the gods in their[1] luminous stillness.
But to our gaze God's light is a darkness, His plan is a chaos.
Who shall foretell the event of a battle, the fall of a footstep?
Oracles, visions and prophecies voice but the dreams of the mortal,
And 'tis our spirit within is the Pythoness tortured in Delphi.
Heavenly voices to us are a silence, those colours a whiteness.
Neither the thought of the statesman prevails nor the dream of the prophet,
Whether one cry 'Thus devise and thy heart shall be given its wanting',
Vainly the other 'The heavens have spoken; hear then their message'.
Who can point out the way of the gods and the path of their travel,
Who shall impose on them bounds and an orbit? The winds have their
                                                          treading, —
They can be followed and seized, not the gods when they move towards
                                                          their purpose.
They are not bound by our deeds and our thinkings. Sin exalted
Seizes secure on the thrones of the world for her glorious portion,
Down to the bottomless pit the good man is thrust in his virtue.
Leave to the gods their godhead and, mortal, turn to thy labour;
Take what thou canst from the hour that is thine and be fearless in spirit;
This is the greatness of man and the joy of his stay in the sunlight.
Now whether over the waste of Poseidon the ships of the Argives
Empty and sad shall return or sacred Ilion perish,
Priam be slain and for ever cease this imperial nation,
These things the gods are strong to conceal from the hopings of mortals.
Neither Antenor knows nor Laocoon. Only of one thing
Man can be sure, the will in his heart and his strength in his purpose:
This too is Fate and this too the gods, nor the meanest in Heaven.
Paris keeps what he seized from Time and Fate while unconquered[2]
Life speeds warm through his veins and his heart is assured of the sunlight.
After 'tis cold, none heeds, none hinders. Not for the dead man
Earth and her wars and her cares, her joys and her gracious concessions,

[1] the [2] Paris the Priamid keeps what he seized from Time and Fate while

Whether for ever he sleeps in the chambers of Nature unmindful
Or into wideness wakes like a dreamer called from his visions.
Ilion in flames I choose, not fallen from the heights of her spirit.
Great and free has she lived since they raised her twixt billow and mountain,
Great let her end; let her offer her freedom to fire, not the Hellene.
She was not founded by mortals; gods erected her ramparts,
Lifted her piles to the sky, a seat not for slaves but the mighty.
All men marvelled at Troy; by her deeds and her spirit they knew her
Even from afar as the lion is known by his roar and his preying.
Sole she lived royal and fell, erect in her leonine nature.
So, O her children, still let her live unquelled in her purpose
Either to stand with her[1] feet on the world oppressing the nations
Or in her[1] ashes to lie and her[1] name be forgotten for ever.
Justly your voices approve me, armipotent children of Ilus;
Straight from Zeus is our race and the Thunderer lives in our nature.
Long I have suffered this[2] taunt that Paris was Ilion's ruin
Born on a night of the gods and of Ate, clothed in a body.
Scornful I strode on my path[3] secure of the light in my bosom,
Turned from the muttering voices of envy, their hates who are fallen,
Voices of hate that cling round the wheels of the triumphing victor;
Now if I speak, 'tis the strength in me answers, not to belittle,
That excusing which most I rejoice in and glory for ever,
Tyndaris' rape whom I seized by the will of divine Aphrodite.
Mortal this error that Greece would have slumbered apart in her mountains,
Sunk, by the trumpets of Fate unaroused and the morning within her,
Only were Paris unborn and the world had not gazed upon Helen.
Fools, who say that a spark was the cause of this giant destruction!
War would have stridden on Troy though Helen were still in her Sparta
Tending an Argive loom, not the glorious prize of the Trojans,
Greece would have banded her nations though Paris had drunk not Eurotas,
Coast against coast I set not, nor Ilion opposite Argos.
Phryx accuse who upreared Troy's domes by the azure Aegean,
Curse Poseidon who fringed with Greece the blue of his waters:
Then was this war first decreed and then Agamemnon was fashioned;
Armed he strode forth in the secret Thought that is womb of the future.
Fate and Necessity guided these vessels, captained their armies.
When they stood mailed at her gates, when they cried in the might of their union,
'Troy, renounce thy alliances, draw back humbly from Hellas',

[1] your [2] brooked their [3] way

Should she have hearkened persuading her strength to a shameful compliance,
Ilion queen of the world[1] whose voice was the breath of the storm-gods?
Should she have drawn back her foot as it strode towards the hills of the Latins?
Thrace left bare to her foes, recoiled from Illyrian conquests?
If all this without battle were possible, people of Priam,
Blame then Paris, say then that Helen was cause of the struggle.
But I have sullied the hearth and unsealed the gaze of the Furies,
Heaven I have armed with my sin, I have trampled the gift and the guest-rule,
So was Troy doomed who righteous had triumphed, locked with the Argive.
Fools or hypocrites! Meanest falsehood is this among mortals,
Veils of purity weaving, names misplacing ideal
When our desires we disguise and paint the lusts of our nature.
Men, ye are men in your pride and your strength, be not sophists and tonguesters.
Lie not! say[2] not that nations live by righteousness, justice
Shields them, gods out of heaven look down[3] on the crimes of the mighty!
Known have men what screened itself[4] mouthing these semblances.
                                                              Crouching
Dire like a beast in the green of the thicket, selfishness silent
Crunches the bones of its prey while the priest and the statesman are glozing.
So are the nations soothed and deceived by the clerics of virtue,
Taught to reconcile fear of the gods with their lusts and their passions,
So with a lie on their lips they march to the rapine and slaughter.
Truly the vanquished were guilty! Else would their cities have perished,
Shrieked their ravished virgins, their peasants been hewn in the vineyards?
Truly the victors were tools of the gods and their glorious servants!
Else would the war-cars have ground triumphant their bones whom they hated?
Servants of God are they verily, even as the ape and the tiger.
Does not the wild beast too triumph enjoying the flesh of his captives?
Tell us then what was the sin of the antelope, wherefore they doomed her
Wroth at her many crimes? Come, justify God to his creatures!
Not to her sins was she offered, not to the Furies or justice,
But to the strength of the lion the high gods offered a victim,
Force that is God in the lion's breast with the forest for altar.
What, in the cities stormed and sacked by Achilles in Troas

[1] ways/world ways [2] prate [3] wroth
[4] thing lies screened

Was there no just man slain? Was Brises then a transgressor?
Hearts that were pierced in his walls were they sinners tracked by the Furies?
No, they were pious and just and their altars burned for Apollo,
Reverent flamed up to Pallas who slew them aiding the Argives.
Or if the crime of Paris they shared and his doom has embraced them,
Whom had the island cities offended, stormed by the Locrian,
Wave-kissed homes of peace but given to the sack and the spoiler?
Was then King Atreus just and the house accursed of Pelops,
Tantalus' race, whose deeds men shuddering hear and are silent?
Look! they endure, their pillars are firm, they are regnant and triumph.
Or are Thyestean banquets sweet to the gods in their savour?
Only a woman's heart is pursued in their wrath by the Furies!
No, when the wrestlers meet and embrace in the mighty arena,
Not at their sins and their virtues the high gods look in that trial;
Which is the strongest, which is the subtlest, this they consider.
Nay, there is none in the world to befriend save ourselves and our courage;
Prowess alone in the battle is virtue, skill in the fighting
Only helps, the gods aid only the strong and the valiant.
Put forth your lives in the blow, you shall beat back the banded aggressors.
Neither believe that for justice denied your subjects have left you
Nor that for justice trampled Pallas and Hera abandon.
Two are the angels of God whom men worship, strength and enjoyment.
Into this life which the sunlight bounds and the greenness has cradled,
Armed with strength we have come; as our strength is, so is our joyance.
What but for joyance is birth and what but for joyance is living?
But on this earth that is narrow, this stage that is crowded, increasing
One on another we press. There is hunger for lands and for oxen,
Horses and armour and gold required;[1] possession allures us
Adding always as field to field some fortunate farmer.
Hearts too and minds are our prey; we seize on men's souls and their bodies,
Slaves to our works and desires that our hearts may bask golden in leisure.
One on another we prey and one by another are mighty.
This is the world and we have not made it; if it is evil,
Blame first the gods; but for us, we must live by its laws or we perish.
Power is divine; divinest of all is power over mortals.
Power then the conqueror seeks and power the imperial nation,
Even as luminous, passionless, wonderful, high over all things
Sit in their calmness the gods and oppressing our grief-tortured nations
Stamp their wills on the world. Nor less in our death-besieged natures

[1] desired

Gods are and altitudes. Earth resists, but my soul in me widens
Helped by the toil behind and the agelong effort of Nature.
Even in the worm is a god and it writhes for a form and an outlet.
Workings immortal obscurely struggling, hints of a godhead
Labour to form in this clay a divinity. Hera widens,
Pallas aspires in me, Phoebus in flames goes battling and singing,
Ares and Artemis chase through the fields of my soul in their hunting,
Last in some hour of the Fates a Birth stands released and triumphant;
Poured by its deeds over earth it rejoices fulfilled in its splendour.
Conscious dimly of births unfinished hid in our being
Rest we cannot; a world cries in us for space and for fullness.
Fighting we strive by the spur of the gods who are in us and o'er us,
Stamping our image on man and events to be Zeus or be Ares.
Love and the need of mastery, joy and the longing for greatness
Rage like a fire unquenchable burning the world and creating,
Nor till humanity dies will they sink in the ashes of Nature.
All is injustice of love or all is injustice of battle.
Man over woman, woman o'er man, over lover and foeman
Wrestling we strive to expand in our souls, to be wide, to be joyous.[1]
If thou wouldst only be just, then wherefore at all shouldst thou conquer?
Not to be just, but to rule, though with kindness and high-seated mercy,
Taking the world for our own and our will from our slaves and our subjects,
Smiting the proud and sparing the suppliant, Trojans, is conquest.
Justice was base of thy government? Vainly, O statesman, thou liest.
If thou wert just, thou wouldst free thy slaves and be equal with all men.
Such were a dream of some sage at night when he muses in fancy,
Imaging freely a flawless world where none were afflicted,
No man inferior, all could sublimely equal and brothers
Live in a peace divine like the gods in their luminous regions.
This, O Antenor, were justice known but in words to us mortals.
But for the justice thou vauntest enslaving men to thy purpose,
Setting an iron yoke, nor regarding their need and their nature,
Then to say 'I am just; I slay not save by procedure,
Rob not save by law' is an outrage to Zeus and his creatures.
Terms are these feigned by the intellect making a pact with our yearnings,
Lures of the sophist within us draping our passions with virtue.
When thou art weak, thou art just, when thy subjects are strong and
                                                                     remember.
Therefore, O Trojans, be firm in your will and, though all men abandon,

[1] happy.

Bow not your heads to reproach nor your hearts to the sin of repentance;
For you have done what the gods desired in your breasts and are blameless.
Proudly enjoy the earth that they gave you, enthroning their natures,
Fight with the Greeks and the world and trample down the rebellious,
What you have lost recover, nor yield to the hurricane passing.
You cannot utterly die while the Power lives untired in your bosoms;
When 'tis withdrawn, not a moment of life can be added by virtue.
Faint not for helpers fled! Though your yoke had been mild as a father's
They would have gone as swiftly. Strength men desire in their masters;
All men worship success and in failure and weakness abandon.
Not for his justice they clung to Teucer, but for their safety,
Seeing in Troy a head and by barbarous foemen afflicted.
Faint not, O Trojans, cease not from battle, persist in your labour!
Conquer the Greeks, your allies shall be yours and fresh nations your subjects.
One care only lodge in your hearts, how to fight, how to conquer.
Peace has smiled out of Phthia; a hand comes outstretched from the Hellene.
Who would not join with the godlike? who would not grasp at Achilles?
There is a price for his gifts, it is such as Achilles should ask for,
Never this nation concede.[1] O Antenor's golden phrases
Glorifying rest to the tired and confuting patience and courage,
Garbed with a subtlety lax and the hopes that palliate surrender!
Charmed men applaud the skilful purpose, the dexterous speaker,
This they forget that a Force decides, not the wiles of the statesman.[2]
'Now let us yield,' do you say, 'we will rise when our masters are weakened'?
Nay, then our master's master shall find us an easy possession!
Easily nations bow to a yoke when their virtue relaxes;
Hard is the breaking fetters once worn, for the virtue has perished.
Hope you when custom has shaped men into the mould of a vileness,
Hugging their chains when the weak feel easier trampled than rising
Or though they groan, yet have heart nor strength for the anguish of effort,
Then to cast down whom, armed and strong, you prevailed not[3] opposing?
Easy is lapse into uttermost hell, not easy salvation.
Or have you dreamed that Achilles will save, this son of the gods and the
                                                                                             Ocean?
Naught else can be with the strong and the bold[4] save foeman or master.

    [1] endure.
    [2] After this line come two verses which seem to have been rejected in the manuscript:
        O let us give ourselves bound to the swallowing lust of the Ocean!
          Surely 'twill bear up our sloth on its crests to a harbour of Triumph!
    [3] could hold not / were mastered   [4] mighty

Know you so little the mood of the pursuer? Think you the lion
Only will lick his prey, that his jaws will refrain from the banquet?
Rest from thy bodings, Antenor! Not all the valour of Troya
Perished with Hector, nor with Polydamas vision has left her;
Troy is not eager to slay her soul in a pyre of dishonour.
Still she has children left who remember the mood of their mother.
Helen none shall take from me living, gold not a drachma
Travels from coffers of Priam to Greece. Let another and older
Pay down his wealth if he will and his daughters serve Menelaus.
Rather from Ilion I will go forth with my brothers and kinsmen;
Troy I will leave and her shame and live with my heart and my honour
Refuged with lions in Ida or build in the highlands a city
Or in an isle of the seas or by dark-driven Pontic waters.
Dear are the halls of our childhood, dear are the fields of our fathers,
Yet to the soul that is free no spot on the earth is an exile.
Rather wherever sunlight is bright, flowers bloom and the rivers
Flow in their lucid streams to the Ocean, there is our country.
So will I live in my soul's wide freedom, never in Troya
Shorn of my will and disgraced in my strength and the mock of my rivals.
First had you yielded, shame at least had not stained your surrender.
Strength indulges the weak! But what Hector has fallen refusing,
Men! what through ten loud years we denied with the spear for our answer,
That what Trojan will ever renounce, though his city should perish?
Once having fought we will fight to the end nor that end shall be evil.
Clamour the Argive spears in our walls? Are the ladders erected?
Far on the plain is their flight, on the farther side of the Xanthus.
Where are the deities hostile? Vainly the eyes of the tremblers
See them stalking vast in the ranks of the Greeks and the shoutings
Dire of Poseidon they hear and are blind with the aegis of Pallas.
Who then sustained so long this Troy, if the gods are against her?
Even the hills could not stand save upheld by their concert immortal.
Now not with Tydeus' son, not now with Odysseus and Ajax
Trample the gods in the sound of their chariot-wheels, victory leading:
Argos falls red in her heaps to their scythes; they shelter the Trojans;
Victory unleashed follows and fawns upon Penthesilea.
Ponder no more, O Ilion, city of ancient Priam!
Rise, O beloved of the gods, and go forth in thy strength to the battle.
Not by the dreams of Laocoon strung to the faith that is febrile,
Nor with the tremblings vain and the haunted thoughts of Antenor,
But with a noble and serious strength and an obstinate valour

Suffer the shock of your foes, O nation chosen by Heaven;
Proudly determine on victory, live by disaster unshaken.
Either Fate receive like men, nay, like gods, nay, like Trojans."
So like an army that streams and that marches, speeding and pausing,
Drawing in horn and wing or widened for scouting and forage,
Bridging the floods, avoiding the mountains, threading the valleys,
Fast with their flashing panoply clad in gold and in iron
Moved the array of his thoughts; and throughout delight and approval
Followed their march, in triumph led but like prisoners willing,
Glad and unbound to a land they desire. Triumphant he ended,
Lord of opinion, though by the aged frowned on and censured,
But to this voice of their thoughts the young men vibrated wholly.
Loud like a storm on the ocean mounted the roar of the people.
"Cease from debate," men cried, "arise, O thou warlike Aeneas!
Speak for this nation, launch like a spear at the tents of the Hellene,
Ilion's voice of war!" Then up mid a limitless shouting
Stern and armed from his seat like a war-god helmèd Aeneas
Rose by King Priam approved in this last of Ilion's sessions,
Holding the staff of the senate's authority. "Silence, O commons,
Hear and assent or refuse as your right is, masters of Troya,
Ancient and sovereign people, act that your kings have determined
Sitting in council high, their reply to the strength of Achilles.
'Son of the Aeacids, vain is thy offer; the pride of thy challenge
Rather we choose; it is nearer to Dardanus, King of the Hellenes.
Neither shall Helen be led back, the Tyndarid, weeping to Argos
Nor down the paths of peace revisit her fathers' Eurotas.
Death and the fire may prevail o'er us, never our wills shall surrender
Lowering Priam's heights and darkening Ilion's splendours.
Not of such sires were we born but of kings and of gods, O Larissan.
Not with her gold Troy traffics for safety,[1] but with her spear-points.
Stand with thy oath in the war-front, Achilles; call on thy helpers
Armed to descend from the calm of Olympian heights to thy succour
Hedging thy fame from defeat; for we all desire thee in battle,
Mighty to end thee or tame at last by the floods of the Xanthus.' "
So Aeneas resonant spoke, stern, fronted like Ares,
And with a voice that conquered the earth and invaded the heavens
Loud they approved their doom and fulfilled their impulse immortal.
Last Deiphobus rose in their meeting, head of their mellay:
"Proudly and well have you answered, O nation beloved of Apollo;

[1] seeks out her foemen,

Fearless of death they must walk who would live and be mighty for ever.
Now, for the sun is hastening up the empyrean azure,
Hasten we also. Tasting of food round the call of your captains
Meet in your armèd companies, chariots and hoplites and archers,
Strong be your hearts, let your courage be stern like the sun when it blazes;
Fierce will the shock be today ere he sink blood-red in the waters."
They with a voice as of Oceans meeting rose from their session, —
Filling the streets with her tread Troy strode from her Ilian forum.

Book Four

The Book of Partings

Eagerly, spurred by Ares swift in their souls to the war-cry,
All now pressed to their homes for the food of their strength in the battle;
Ilion turned her thoughts in a proud expectancy seaward
Waiting to hear the sounds that she loved and the cry of the mellay.
Now to their citadel Priam's sons returned with their father,
Now from the gates Talthybius issued grey in his chariot;
But in the halls of Anchises Aeneas not doffing his breastpiece
Hastily ate of the corn of his country, cakes of the millet
Doubled with wild-deer's flesh, from the quiet hands of Creüsa.
She, as he ate, with her calm eyes watching him smiled on her husband:
"Ever thou hastest to battle, O warrior, ever thou fightest
Far in the front of the ranks and thou seekest out Locrian Ajax,
Turnest thy ear to the roar for the dangerous shout of Tydides;
There, once heard, leaving all thou drivest, O stark in thy courage.
Yet am I blest among women who tremble not, left in thy mansion,
Quiet at old Anchises' feet when I see thee in vision
Sole with the shafts hissing round thee and say to my quivering spirit,
'Now he is striking at Ajax, now he has met Diomedes.'
Such are the mighty twain who are ever near to protect thee,
Phoebus, the Thunderer's son, and thy mother, gold Aphrodite;
Such are the fates that demand thee, O destined head of the future.
But though my thoughts for their own are not troubled, always, Aeneas,
Sore is my heart with pity for other Ilian women
Who in this battle are losing their children and well-loved husbands,
Brothers too dear, for the eyes that are wet, for the hearts that are silent.
Will not this war then end that thunders for ever round Troya?"
 But to Creüsa the hero answered, the son of Anchises:
"Surely the gods protect, yet is Death too always mighty.
Most in his shadowy envy he strikes at the brave and the lovely,
Grudging works to abridge their days and to widow the sunlight;
Most, disappointed, he rages against the belovèd of Heaven;
Striking their lives through their hearts he mows down their loves and their
                                                                pleasures.
Truly thou say'st, thou need'st not to fear for my life in the battle;
Ever for thine I fear lest he find thee out in his anger,
Missing my head in the fight, when he comes here crossed in his godhead.

Yet shall Phoebus protect and my mother, gold Aphrodite."
  But to Aeneas answered the tranquil lips of Creüsa:
"So may it be that I go before thee, seeing, Aeneas,
Over my dying eyes thy lips bend down for the parting.
Blissfullest end is this for a woman here mid earth's sorrows;
Afterwards there we hope that the hands shall join which were parted."
  So she spoke, not knowing the gods: but Aeneas departing
Clasped his father's knees, the ancient mighty Anchises:
"Bless me, my father; I go to the battle. Strong with thy blessing
Even today may I hurl down Ajax, slay Diomedes,
And on the morrow gaze on the empty beaches of Troas."
Troubled and joyless, nought replying to warlike Aeneas
Long Anchises sat unmoving, silent, sombre,
Gazing into his soul with eyes that were closed to the sunlight.
"Prosper, Aeneas," slowly he answered him, "son of a goddess,
Prosper, Aeneas; and if for Troy some doom is preparing,
Suffer always the will of the gods with a piety constant.
Only they will what Necessity fashions, impelled by the Silence.
Labour and war she has given to man as the law of his transience.
Work;[1] she shall give thee the crown of thy deeds or their ending appointed,
Whether glorious thou pass or in silent shadows forgotten.
But what thy mother commands perform ever, loading thy vessels.
Who can know what the gods have hid with the mist of our hopings?"
  So[2] from the house of his fathers Aeneas rapidly striding
Came to the city echoing now with the wheels of the chariots,
Clanging with arms and astream with the warlike tramp of her thousands.
Fast through the press he strode and men turning knew Aeneas,
Greatened in heart and went on with loftier thoughts towards battle.
He through the noise and the crowd to Antenor's high-built mansion
Striding came, and he turned to its courts and the bronze of its threshold
Trod which had suffered the feet of so many princes departed.
But as he crossed its brazen square from the hall there came running,
Leaping up light to his feet and laughing with sudden pleasure,
Eurus the youngest son of Polydamas. Clasping the fatal
War-hardened hand with a palm that was smooth as a maiden's or infant's,
"Well art thou come, Aeneas," he said, "and good fortune has sent thee!
Now I shall go to the field; thou wilt speak with my grandsire Antenor,
And he shall hear thee though chid by his heart reluctant. Rejoicing
I shall go forth in thy car or warring by Penthesilea,

[1] Fight; [2] Then

Famous, give to her grasp the spear that shall smite down Achilles."
Smiling answered Aeneas, "Surely will, Eurus, thy prowess
Carry thee far to the front; thou shalt fight with Epeus and slay him.
Who shall say that this hand was not chosen to pierce Menelaus?
But for a while with the bulls should it rather strive, O hero,
Till in the play and the wrestle its softness grow hard[1] for the smiting."
Eagerly Eurus answered, "But they have told me, Aeneas,
This is the last of our fights for today will Penthesilea
Meet Achilles in battle and slay him ending the Argives.
Then shall I never have mixed in this war that is famous for ever.
What shall I say when my hairs are white like the aged Antenor's?
Men will ask, 'And what were thy deeds in the warfare Titanic?
Whom didst thou slay of the Argives, son of Polydamas, venging
Bravely thy father?' Then must I say, 'I lurked in the city.
I was too young and only ascending the Ilian ramparts
Saw the return or the flight, but never the deed and the triumph'?
Friend, if thou take me not forth, I shall die of grief ere the sunset."
Plucking the hand of Aeneas he drew him into the mansion
Vast; and over the floor of the spacious hall they hastened
Laughing, the gracious child and the mighty hero and statesman,
Flower of a present stock and the burdened star of the future.
  Meanwhile girt by his sons and the sons of his sons in his chamber
Cried[2] to the remnants left of his blood the aged Antenor:
"Hearken you who are sprung from my loins and children, their offspring!
None shall again go forth to the fight who is kin to Antenor.
Weighed with my curse he shall go and the spear-points athirst of the Argives
Meet him wroth; he shall die in his sin and his name be forgotten.
Oft have I sent forth my blood to be spilled in vain in the battle
Fighting for Troy and her greatness earned by my toil and my fathers'.
Now all the debt has been paid; she rejects us driven by the immortals.
Much do we owe to the mother who bore us, much to our country;
But at the last our life is ours and the gods' and the future's.
Gather the gold of my house and our kin, O ye sons of Antenor.
Warned by a voice in my soul I will go forth tonight from this city,
Fleeing the doom and bearing my treasures; the ships shall receive them
Gathered, new-keeled by my care and the gods', in the narrow Propontis.
Over God's waters guided, treading the rage of Poseidon,
Bellying out with their sails let them cleave to the untravelled distance
Ocean's crests and resign to their fates the doomed and the evil."

[1] is trained [2] Spoke

So Antenor spoke and his children heard him in silence;
Awed by his voice and the dread of his curse they obeyed, though in sorrow.
Halamus only replied to his father: "Dire are the white hairs
Reverend, loved, of a father, dreadful his curse to his children.
Yet in my heart there is one who cries, 'tis the voice of my country,
She for whose sake I would be in Tartarus tortured for ever.
Pardon me then if thou wilt; if the gods can, then let them pardon.
For I will sleep in the dust of Troy embracing her ashes,
There where Polydamas sleeps and the many comrades I cherished.
So let me go to the darkness remembered or wholly forgotten,
Yet having fought for my country, true in my fall to my nation."
    Then in his aged wrath to Halamus answered Antenor:
"Go then and perish doomed with the doomed and the hated of heaven;
Nor shall the gods forgive thee dying nor shall thy father."
Out from the chamber Halamus strode with grief in his bosom
Wrestling with wrath and he went to his doom nor looked back at his dear
                                                                              ones.
Crossing the hall the son of Antenor and son of Anchises
Met in the paths of their fates where they knotted and crossed for the
                                                                               parting,
One with the curse of the gods and his sire fast wending to Hades,
Fortunate, blessed the other; yet equal their minds were and virtues.
Cypris' son to the Antenorid: "Thee I have sought and thy brothers,
Bough of Antenor; sore is our need today of thy counsels,
Endless our want of their arms that are strong and their hearts that recoil
                                                                                 not
Meeting myriads stark with the spear in unequal battle."
Halamus answered him: "I will go forth to the palace of Priam,
There where Troy yet lives and far from the halls of my fathers;
There will I speak, not here. For my kin they repose in the mansion
Sitting unarmed in their halls while their brothers fall in the battle."
Eurus eagerly answered the hero: "Me rather, therefore,
Take to the fight with you; I will make war on the Greeks for my uncles;
One for all I will fill their place in the shock with the foemen."
    But from his chamber-door Antenor heard and rebuked him:
"Scamp of my heart, thou torment! into thy chamber and rest there,
Bound with cords lest thou cease, thou flutter-brain, scourged into quiet;
So shall thy lust of the fight be healed and our mansion grow tranquil."
Chid by the old man Eurus slunk from the hall discontented,
Yet with a dubious smile like a moonbeam lighting his beauty.

But to Antenor the Dardanid born from the white Aphrodite:
"Late the Antenorids learn to flinch from the spears of the Argives,
Even this boy of their blood has Polydamas' heart and his valour.
Nor should a life that was honoured and noble be stained in its ending.
Nay, then, the mood of a child would shame a grey-headed wisdom,
If for the fault of the people virtue and Troy were forgotten.
For, though the people hear us not, yet are we bound to our nation:
Over the people the gods are; over a man is his country;
This is the deity first adored by the hearths of the noble.
For by our nation's will we are ruled in the home and the battle
And for our nation's weal we offer our lives and our children's.
Not by their own wills led nor their passions men rise to their manhood,
Selfishly seeking their good, but the gods' and the State's and the fathers'."

    Wroth Antenor replied to the warlike son of Anchises:
"Great is the soul in thee housed and stern is thy will, O Aeneas;
Onward it moves undismayed to its goal though a city be ruined.
They too guide thee who deepest see of the unageing immortals,
One with her heart and one in his spirit, Cypris and Phoebus.
Yet might a man not knowing this think as he watched thee, Aeneas,
'Spurring Priam's race to its fall he endangers this city,
Hoping to build a throne out of ruins sole in the Troad.'
I too have gods who warn me and lead, Athene and Hera.
Not as the ways of other mortals are theirs who are guided,
They whose eyes are the gods and they walk by a light that is secret."
    Coldly Aeneas made answer, stirred into wrath by the taunting:
"High wert thou always, nurtured in wisdom, ancient Antenor.
Walk then favoured and led, yet watch lest passion and evil
Feign auguster names and mimic the gait of the deathless."
And with a smile on his lips but wrath in his bosom answered,
Wisest of men but with wisdom of mortals, aged Antenor:
"Led or misled we are mortals and walk by a light that is given;
Most they err who deem themselves most from error excluded.
Nor shalt thou hear in this battle the shout of the men of my lineage
Holding the Greeks as once and driving back Fate from their country.
His alone will be heard for a space while the stern gods are patient
Even now who went forth a victim self-offered to Hades,
Last whom their wills have plucked from the fated house of Antenor."
    They now with wrath in their bosoms sundered for ever and parted.
Forth from the hall of Antenor Aeneas rapidly striding

Passed[1] once more through the city hurrying now with its car-wheels,
Filled with a mightier rumour of war and the march of its thousands,
Till at Troy's upward curve he found the Antenorid crestward
Mounting the steep incline that climbed to the palace of Priam
White in her proud and armèd citadel. Silent, ascending
Hardly their feet had attempted the hill when behind them they hearkened
Sweet-tongued a call and the patter and hurry of light-running sandals;
Turning they beheld with a flush on his cheeks and a light on his lashes
Challenging mutely and pleading the boyish beauty of Eurus.
"Racer to mischief," said Halamus, "couldst thou not sit in thy chamber?
Surely cords and the rod await thee, Eurus, returning."
Answered with laughter the child, "I have broken through ranks of the fighters,
Dived under chariot-wheels to arrive here and I return not.
I too for counsel of battle have come to the palace of Priam."
Burdened with thought they mounted slowly the road of their fathers,
Breasting the Ilian hill where Laomedon's mansion was tented,
They from the crest down gazing saw their country's house-tops
Under their feet and heard the murmur of Troya below them.

    But in the palace of Priam coming and going of house-thralls
Filled all the corridors; smoke from the kitchens curled in its plenty
Rich with savour and breathed from the labouring lungs of Hephaestus.
Far in the halls and the chambers voices travelled and clustered,
Anklets jangling ran and sang back from doorway to doorway,
Mocking with music of speed and its laughters the haste of the happy,
Sound came of arms, there was tread of the great, there were murmurs of women, —
Voices glad of the doomed in Laomedon's marvellous mansion.
Six were the halls of its splendour, a hundred and one were its chambers
Lifted high upon columns that soared like the thoughts of its dwellers,
Thoughts that transcended the earth though they sank down at last into ashes.
So had Apollo dreamed to his lyre; and its tops were a grandeur
Domed, as if seeking to roof men's lives with a hint of the heavens;
Marble his columns rose and with marble his roofs were appointed,
Conquered wealth of the world in its largeness suffered, supporting
Purities of marble, glories of gold. Nor only of matter
Blazed there the brutal pomps, but images mystic or mighty
Crowded ceiling and wall, a work that the gods even admire

[1] Pressed

Hardly believing that forms like these were imagined by mortals
Here upon earth where sight is a blur and the soul lives encumbered.
Scrolls that remembered in gems the thoughts austere of the ancients
Bordered the lines of the stone and the forms of serpent and Naiad
Ran in relief on those walls of pride in the palace of Priam
Mingled with Dryads who tempted and fled and Satyrs who followed,
Sports of the nymphs in the sea and the woods and their meetings with
mortals,
Sessions and battles of Trojan demigods, deaths that were famous,
Wars and loves of men and the deeds of the golden immortals.
Pillars sculptured with gods and with giants soared from bases
Lion-carved or were seated on bulls and bore into grandeur
Amply those halls where they soared, or in[1] lordliness slenderly fashioned,
Dressed in flowers and reeds like virgins standing on Ida,
Guarded the screens of stone and divided alcove and chamber.
Ivory carved and broidered robes and the riches of Indus
Cherished in sandalwood triumphed and teemed in the palace of Priam;
Doors that were carven and fragrant sheltered the joys of its princes.
    Here in a chamber of luminous privacy Paris was arming.
Near him moved Helen, a whiteness divine and intent on her labour
Fastened his cuirass, bound the greaves and settled the hauberk,
Thrilling his limbs with her touch that was heaven to the yearning of mortals,
She with her hands of delight caressing the senseless metal
Pressed her lips to his brilliant armour; she bowed down, she whispered:
"Cuirass, allowed by the gods, protect the beauty of Paris:
Keep for me that for which country was lost and my child and my brothers."
Yearning she bent to his feet, to the sandal-strings of her lover;
Then as she gazed up, changed grew her mood; for the Daemon within her
Rose that had banded Greece and was burning Troy into ashes.
Slowly a smile that was perfect and perilous over her beauty
Dawned like the sunlight on Paradise; strangely she looked on her lover.
So might a goddess have gazed as she played with the love of a mortal
Passing an hour on the earth ere she rose up white to Olympus.
"So art thou winner, Paris, yet and thy spirit ascendant
Leads this Troy where thou wilt, O thou mighty one veiled in thy beauty
First in the dance and the revel, first in the joy of the mellay;
Who would not leave for thy sake and repent it not country and homestead?
Winning thou reignest still over Troy, over Fate, over Helen.
Always so canst thou win? Has Death no claim on thy beauty,

[1] to

Fate no scourge for thy sins? How the years have passed by in a glory,
Years of this heaven of the gods, O ravisher, since from my hearthstone
Seizing thou borest me compelled to thy ships and my joy on the waters.
Troy is enringed with the spears, her children fall and her glories,
Mighty souls of heroes have gone down prone to the darkness;
Thou and I abide! the mothers wail for our pleasure.
Wilt thou then keep me for ever, O son of Priam, in Troya?
Fate was my mother, they say, and Zeus for this hour begot me.
Art thou a god too, O hero, disguised in this robe of the mortal,
Brilliant, careless of death and of sin as if sure of thy rapture?
What then if Fate today were to lay her hand on thee, Paris?"
Calmly he looked on the face of which Greece was enamoured, the body
For whose desire great Troy was a sacrifice, tranquil regarded
Lovely and dire on the lips he loved that smile of a goddess,
Saw the daughter of Zeus in the woman, yet was not shaken.
"Temptress of Argos," he answered, "thou snare for the world to be seized
                                                                            in,
Thou then hop'st to escape! But the gods could not take thee, O Helen,
How then thy will that to mine is a captive, or how, though with battle,
He who has lost thee, unhappy, the Spartan, bright Menelaus?
All things yield to a man and Zeus is himself his accomplice
When like a god he wills without remorse or longing.
Thou on this earth art mine since I claimed thee beheld, not speaking,
But with thy lids that fell thou veiledst thy heart of compliance.
Then in whatever beyond I shall know how to take thee, O Helen,
Even as here upon earth I knew, in heaven as in Sparta;
I on Elysian fields will enjoy thee as now in the Troad."
Silent a moment she lingered like one who is lured by a music
Rapturous, heard by himself alone and his lover in heaven,
Then in her beauty compelling she rose up divine among women.
"Yes, it is good," she cried, "what the gods do and actions of mortals:
Good is the play of the world; it is good, the joy and the torture.
Praised be the hour of the gods when I wedded bright Menelaus!
Praised, more praised the keels that severed the seas towards Helen
Churning the senseless waves that knew not the bliss of their burden!
Praised to the end the hour when I passed through the doors of my husband
Laughing with joy in my heart for the arms that bore and enchained me!
Never can Death undo what life has done for us, Paris.
Nor, whatever betide, can the hour be unlived of our rapture.
This too is good that nations should meet in the shock of the battle,

Heroes be slain and a theme be made for the songs of the poets,
Songs that shall thrill with the name of Helen, the beauty of Paris.
Well is this also that empires should fall for the eyes of a woman,
Well that for Helen Hector ended, Memnon was slaughtered,
Strong Sarpedon fell and Troilus ceased in his boyhood.
Troy for Helen burning, her glory, her empire, her riches,
This is the sign of the gods and the type of things that are mortal.
Thou who art kin to the masters of heaven, unconstrained like thy kindred
High on this ancient stage of the Troad with gods for spectators,
Play till the end thy part, O thou wondrous and beautiful actor:
Fight and slay the Greeks, my countrymen; victor returning
Take for reward of the play, thy delight of Argive Helen.
Force from my bosom a hint of the joy denied to the death-claimed,
Rob in the kiss of my lips a pang from the raptures of heaven."
Clasping him wholly her arms of desire were a girdle of madness,
Cestus divine of the dread Aphrodite. He with her kisses
Flushed like the gods with unearthly wine and rejoiced in his ruin.
    Thus while they conversed now in this hour that was near to their parting
Last upon earth, a fleet-footed slave-girl came to the chamber:
"Paris, thy father and mother desire thee; there in the strangers'
Outer hall Aeneas and Halamus wait for thy coming."
So with the Argive he wended to Priam's ample chamber
Far in Laomedon's house where Troy looked upwards to Ida.
Priam and Hecuba there, the ancient grey-haired rulers
Waiting him sat in their chairs of ivory calm in their greatness;
Hid in her robes at their feet lay Cassandra crouched from her visions.
"Since, O my father," said Paris, "thy thoughts have been with me, thy blessing
Surely shall help me today in my strife with the strength of Achilles.
Surely the gods shall obey in the end the might of our spirits,
[Pallas and Hera, flame-sandalled Artemis, Zeus and Apollo.]*
Ever serve the immortal brightnesses man when he stands up
Firm with his will uplifted a steadfast flame towards the heavens,
Ares works in his heart and Hephaestus burns in his labour."
Priam replied to his son: "Forewilled by the gods, Alexander,
All things happen on earth and yet we must strive who are mortals.
Knowing all vain, yet we strive; for our nature seizing us always
Drives like the flock that is herded and urged towards shambles or pasture.
So have the gods fashioned these tools of their action and pleasure;

    * Brackets in the original.

Failure and grief are their engines no less than the might of the victor;
They in the blow descend and resist in the sobs of the smitten.
Such are their goads that I too must walk in the paths that are common,
Even I who know must send for thee, moved by Cassandra.
Speak, O my child, since Apollo has willed it, once, and be silent."
   But in her raiment hidden Cassandra answered her father:
"No, for my heart has changed since I cried for him, vexed by Apollo.
Why should I speak? For who will believe me in Troy? who believed me
Ever in Troy or the world? Event and disaster approve me
Only, my comrades, not men in their thoughts, not my brothers and kinsmen.
All by their hopes are gladly deceived and grow wroth with the warner,
Half-blind prophets of hope entertained by the gods in the mortal!
Wiser blind, if nothing they saw or only the darkness.
I too once hoped when Apollo pursued me with love in his temple,
Round me already there gleamed the ray of the vision prophetic,
Thrill of that rapture I felt and the joy of the god in his seeing,
Nor did I know that the knowledge of mortals is bound unto blindness.
Either only they walk mid the coloured dreams of the senses
Treading the greenness of earth and deeming the touch of things real,
Or if they see, by the curse of the gods their sight into falsehood
Easily turns and leads them more stumbling astray than the sightless.
So are we either blind in a darkness or dazzled by seeing.
Thus have the gods protected their purpose and baffled the sages;
Over the face of the Truth their shield of gold is extended.
But I deemed otherwise, urged by the Dreadful One, he who sits always
Veiled in us fighting the gods whom he uses. I cried to Apollo:
'Give me thy vision sheer, not such as thou giv'st to thy prophets,
Troubled though luminous; clear be the vision and ruthless to error,
Far-darting god who art veiled by the sun and by death thou art shielded.
Then I shall know that thou lovest.' He gave, alarmed and reluctant,
Driven by Fate and his heart; but I mocked him, I broke from my promise;
Courage fatal helping my heart to its ruin with laughter.
Always now I remember his face that grew tranquil and ruthless,
Hear the voice divine and implacable: 'Since thou deceivest
Even the gods and thou hast not feared to lie to Apollo,
Speak shalt thou henceforth only truth, but none shall believe thee:
Scorned in thy words, rejected yet more for their bitter fulfilment,
Scourged by the gods thou must speak though thy sick heart yearns to be
                                                                silent.
For in this play thou hast dared to play with the masters of heaven,

Girl, it is thou who hast lost; thy voice is mine and thy bosom.'
Since then all I foreknow; therefore anguish is mine for my portion:
Since then all whom I love must perish slain by my loving.
Even of that I denied him, violent force shall bereave me
Grasped mid the flames of my city and shouts of her merciless victors."
But to Cassandra answered gently the voice of her brother:
"Sister of mine, afflicted and seized by the dreadful Apollo,
All whose eyes can pierce that curtain, gaze into dimness;
This they have glimpsed and that they imagine deceived by their natures
Seeing the forms in their hearts of dreadful things and of joyous;
As in the darkness our eyes are deceived by shadows uncertain,
Such is their sight who rend the veil that the dire gods have woven.
Busy our hearts are weaving thoughts and images always;
After their kind they see what here we call truth. So thy nature
Tender and loving, plagued by this war and its fear for thy loved ones,
Sees calamity everywhere; when the event like the vision
Seems, as in every war the beloved must fall and the cherished,
Then the heart cries, 'It has happened as all shall happen I mourn for.'
All that was bright it misses and only seizes on sorrow.
Dear, on the brightness look and if thou must prophesy, tell us
Rather of great Pelides slain by my spear in the onset."
But with a voice of grief the sister answered her brother:
"Yes, he shall fall and his slayer too shall perish and Troy with his slayer."
But in his spirit rejoicing Paris answered Cassandra:
"Let but this word come true; for the rest, the gods shall avert it.
Look once more, O Cassandra, and comfort the heart of thy mother,
See, O seer, my safe return with the spoils of Achilles."
And with a voice of grief the sister answered her brother:
"Thou shalt return for thy hour while Troy yet stands in the sunshine."
But in his spirit exultant Paris seizing the omen,
"Hearst thou, my father, my mother? She who still prophesied evil
Now perceives of our night this dawning. Yet is it grievous,
Since through a heart that we love must be pierced the heart of Achilles,
Fate, with this evil satisfied, turn in the end from Troya.
Bless me, my father, and thou, O Hecuba, mother long patient,
Still forgive that thy children have fallen for Helen and Paris."
Tenderly yearning his mother drew him towards her and murmured:
"All for thy hyacinth curls was forgiven even from childhood
And for thy sunlit looks, O wonder of charm, O Paris.
Paris, my son, though Troy must fall, thy mother forgives thee,

Blessing the gods who have lent thee to me for a while in their sunshine.
Theirs are fate and result, but ours is the joy of our children;
Even the griefs are dear that come from their hands while they love us.
Fight and slay Achilles, the murderer dire of thy brothers;
Venging Hector return, my son, to the clasp of thy mother."
But in his calm august to Paris Priam the monarch:
"Victor so mightst thou come, so gladden the heart of thy mother."
Then to the aged father of Paris Helen the Argive
Bright and immortal and sad like a star that grows near to the dawning
And on its pale companions looks who now fade from its vision:
"Me too pardon and love, my parents, even Helen,
Cause of all bane and all death; but I came from the gods for this ruin
Born as a torch for the burning of empires, cursed with this beauty.
Nor have I known a father's embrace, a mother's caresses,
But to the distant gods I was born and nursed as an alien
Here by earth from fear, not affection, compelled by the thunders.
Two are her monstrous births, from the Furies and from the immortals;
Either touching mortality suffers and bears not the contact.
I have been both, a monster of doom and a portent of beauty."
Slowly Priam the monarch answered to Argive Helen:
"That which thou art the gods have made thee; thou couldst not be other:
That which thou didst, the gods have done; thou couldst not prevent them.
Who here shall blame or whom shall he pardon? Should not my people
Rail at me murmuring, 'Priam has lost what his fathers had gathered;
Cursed is this king by heaven and cursed who are born as his subjects'?
Masked the high gods act; the doer is hid by his working.
Each of us bears his punishment, fruit of a seed that's forgotten;
Each of us curses his neighbour protecting his heart with illusions:
Therefore like children we blame each other and hate and are angry.
Take, my child, the joy of the sunshine won by thy beauty.
I who lodge on this earth as an alien bound by the body,
Wearing my sorrow even as I wear the imperial purple,
Praise yet the gods for my days that have seen thee at last in my ending.
Fitly Troy may cease having gazed on thy beauty, O Helen."
He became silent, he ceased from words. But Paris and Helen
Lightly went forth and gladly; pursuing their footsteps the mother,
Mother once of Troilus, mother once of Hector,
Stood at the door with her death in her eyes, nor returned from her yearning,
But as one after a vanishing sunbeam gazes in prison,
Gazed down the corridors after him, long who had passed from her vision.

Then in the silent chamber Cassandra seized by Apollo
Staggered erect and tossing her snow-white arms of affliction
Cried to the heavens in her pain; for the fierce god tortured her bosom:
"Woe is me, woe for the guile and the bitter gift of Apollo!
Woe, thrice woe, for my birth in Troy and the lineage of Teucer!
So do you deal, O gods, with those who have served you and laboured,
Those who have borne for your sake the evil burden of greatness.
Blessed is he who holds mattock in hand or who bends o'er the furrow
Taking no thought for the good of mankind, with no yearnings for
                                                    knowledge.
Woe unto me for my wisdom which none shall value nor hearken!
Woe unto thee, O King, for thy strength which shall not deliver!
Better the eye that is sealed, more blest is the spirit that's feeble.
Vainly your hopes with iron Necessity struggle, O mortals.
Virtue shall lie in her pangs, for the gods have need of her torture;
Sin shall be scourged, though her deeds were compelled by the gods in their
                                                    anger.
None shall avail in the end, the coward shall die and the hero.
Troy shall fall in her sin and her virtues shall not protect her;
Argos shall grow by her crimes till the gods shall destroy her for ever.
Now have I fruit of thy love, O Loxias, dreadful Apollo.
Woe is me, woe for the flame that approaches the house of my fathers!
Woe is me, woe for the hand of Ajax laid on my tresses!
Woe, thrice woe to him who shall ravish and him who shall cherish!
Woe for the ships that shall bound too swift o'er the azure Aegean!
Woe for thy splendid shambles of hell, O Argive Mycenae!
Woe for the evil spouse and house accursed of Atreus!"
So with her voice of the swan she clanged out doom on the peoples,
Over the palace of Priam and over the armèd nation
Marching resolved to the war in the pride of its centuries conquered,
Centuries slain by a single day of the anger of heaven.
Dim to the thoughts like a vision of Hades the luminous chamber
Grew; in his ivory chair King Priam sat like a shadow
Throned mid the ghosts of departed kings and forgotten empires.
    But in his valiance careless and blithe the Priamid hastened
Seeking the pillared megaron wide where Deiphobus armoured
Waited his coming forth with the warlike chiefs of the Trojans.
Now as he passed by the halls of the women, the chambers that harboured
Daughters and wives of King Priam and wives of his sons and their playmates,
Niches of joy that were peopled with murmurs and sweet-tongued laughters,

Troubled like trees with their birds in a morning of sun and of shadow
Where in some garden of kings one walks with his heart in the sunshine,
Out from her door where she stood for him waiting Polyxena started,
Seized his hand and looked in his face and spoke to her brother.
Then not even the brilliant strength of Paris availed him;
Joyless he turned his face from her eyes of beauty and sorrow.
"So is it come, the hour that I feared, and thou goest, O Paris,
Armed with the strength of Fate to strike at my heart in the battle;
For he is doomed and thou and I, a victim to Hades.
This thou preferrest and neither thy father could move nor thy mother
Burning with Troy in their palace, nor could thy country persuade thee,
Nor dost thou care for thy sister's happiness pierced by thy arrows.
Will she remember it all, my sister Helen, in Argos
Passing tranquil days with her husband, bright Menelaus,
Holding her child on her knees? But we shall lie joyless in Hades."
Paris replied: "O my sister Polyxena, blame me not wholly.
We by the gods are ensnared; for the pitiless white Aphrodite
Doing her will with us both compels this. Helpless our hearts are
And when she drives perforce must love, for death or for gladness:
Weighed in unequal scales she deals them to one or another.
Happy who holding his love can go down into bottomless Hades."
But to her brother replied in her anguish the daughter of Priam:
"Evilly deal with thy days the immortals happy in heaven;
Yes, I accuse the gods and I curse them who heed not our sorrow.
This they have done with me, forcing my heart to the love of a foeman,
One whose terrible hands have been stained with the blood of my brothers,
This now they do, they have taken the two whom I love beyond heaven,
Brother and husband, and drive to the fight to be slain by each other.
Nay, go thou forth; for thou canst not help it, nor I, nor can Helen.
Since I must die as a pageant to satisfy Zeus and his daughter,
Since now my heart must be borne as a victim bleeding to please them,
So let it be, let me deck myself and be bright for the altar."
Into her chamber she turned with her great eyes blind, unregarding;
He for a moment stood, then passed to the megaron slowly;
Dim was the light in his eyes and clouded his glorious beauty.
    Meanwhile armed in the palace of Priam Penthesilea.
Near her her captains silent and mighty stood, from the Orient
Distant clouds of war, Surabdas and iron Surenas,
Pharatus planned like the hills, Somaranes, Valarus, Tauron,
High-crested Sumalus, Arithon, Sambas and Artavoruxes.

There too the princes of Phrygian Troya gathered for counsel
And with them Eurus came, Polydamas' son, who most dearly
Loved was of all the Trojan boys by the glorious virgin.
She from her arming stayed to caress his curls and to chide him:
"Eurus, forgotten of grace, dost thou gad like a stray in the city
Eager to mix with the armoured men and the chariots gliding?
High on the roofs wouldst thou watch the swaying speck that is battle?
Better to aim with the dart or seek with thy kind the palaestra;
So wilt thou sooner be part of this greatness rather than straining
Yearn from afar to the distance that veils the deeds of the mighty."
But with an anxious lure in his smile on her Eurus answered:
"Not that remoteness to see have I come to the palace of Priam
Leaving the house of my fathers, but for the spear and the breast-piece.
Hast thou not promised me, long I shall fight in thy car with Achilles?"
Doubtful he eyed her, a lion's cub at play in his beauty,
And mid the heroes who heard him laughter arose for a moment,
Yet with a sympathy stirred; they remembered the days of their childhood,
Thinking[1] of Troy still mighty, life in its rose-touched dawning
When they had longed for the clash of the fight and the burden of armour.
Glad, with the pride of the lioness watching her cub in the desert, —
Couchant she lies with her paws before her and joys in his gambols,
Over the prey as he frisks and is careless, — answered the virgin:
"Younger than thou in my nation have mounted the steed and the war-car.
Eurus, arm; from under my shield thou shalt gaze at the Phthian,
Reaching my shafts for the cast from the rim of my car in the battle
Handle perhaps the spear that shall smite down the Phthian Achilles.
What sayst thou, Halamus? Were not such prowess a perfect beginning
Worthy Polydamas' son and the warlike house of Antenor?"
Halamus started and smiting his hand on the grief of his bosom
Sombre replied and threatened with Fate the high-hearted virgin.
"Virgin armipotent, wherefore mockst thou thy friend, though unwitting?
Nay, — for the world will know at the end and my death cannot hide it, —
Slain by a father's curse we fight who are kin to Antenor.
Take not the boy in thy car, lest the Furies, Penthesilea,
Aim through the shield and the shielder to wreak the curse of the grandsire.
They will not turn nor repent for thy strength nor his delicate beauty."
Swiftly to Halamus answered the high-crested strength of the virgin:
"Curses leave lightly the lips when the soul of a man is in anger
Even as blessings easily crowd round the head that is cherished.

[1] Thought

Yet have I never seen that a curse has sharpened a spear-point;
Never Death has drawn[1] back from the doomed by the power of a blessing.
Valour and skill and chance are Fate and the gods and the Furies.
Give me the boy; a hero shall come back formed from the onset."
"Do as thou wilt," replied Halamus, "Fate shall guard or shall end him."
Then to the boy delighted and smiling-eyed and exultant
Cried with her voice like the call of heaven's bugles Penthesilea:[2]
"Go, find the spear, gird the sword, don the cuirass, child of the mighty.
Armed when thou standest on the plain of the Xanthus, field of thy fathers,
See that thou fight on this day like the comrade of Penthesilea.
Bud of a hero, gaze unalarmed in the eyes of Achilles."
Light as a hound released he ran to the hall of the armour
Where were the shields of the mighty, the arms of the mansion of Teucer;
There from the house-thralls he wrung the greaves and the cuirass and helmet
Troilus wore, the wonderful boy who, ere ripened his prowess,
Conquered the Greeks and drove to the ships and fought with Achilles.
These on his boyish limbs he donned and ran back exulting
Bearing spears and a sword and rejoiced in the clank on his armour.
    Meanwhile Deiphobus, head of the mellay, moved by Aeneas
Opened the doors of their warlike debate to the strength of the virgin:
"Well do I hope that our courage outwearying every opponent
Triumph shall lift to her ancient seat on the Pergaman turrets;
Clouds from Zeus come and pass; his sunshine eternal survives them.
Yet we are few in the fight and armoured nations besiege us.
Surging on Troy today a numberless foe well-captained
Hardly pushed back in shock after shock with the Myrmidon numbers
Swelled returns; they fight with a hope that broken refashion
Helpful skies and a man now leads them who conquers and slaughters,
One of the sons of the gods and armed by the gods for the struggle.
We unhelped save by Ares stern and the mystic Apollo
And but as mortals striving with stubborn mortal courage,
Hated and scorned and alone in the world by the nations rejected,
Fight with the gods and mankind and Achilles and numbers against us,
Keeping our country from death in this bitter hour of her fortunes.
Therefore have prudence and hardihood severed contending our counsels
Whether far out to fight on the seaward plain with the Argives
Or behind Xanthus the river impetuous friendly to Troya.

---

[1] drew
[2] Cried with her voice like the call of heaven's bugles waking the heroes,
   Blown by the lips of gold-haired Valkyries, Penthesilea:

This my brother approves and the son of Antenor advises,
Prudent masters of war who prepare by defence their aggression.
But for myself from rashness I seek a more far-seeing wisdom,
Not behind vain defences choosing a tardy destruction,
Rather as Zeus with his spear of the lightning and chariot of tempest
Scatters and chases the heavy mass of the clouds through the heavens,
So would I hunt the Greeks through the plains to their lair by the Ocean,
Straight at the throat of my foeman so would I leap in the battle.
Swiftly to smite at the foe is prudence for armies outnumbered."
Then to the Dardanid answered the high-crested Penthesilea:
"There where I find my foe I will fight him, whether by Xanthus
Or at the fosse of the ships where they crouch behind bulwarks for shelter,
Or if they dare by Scamander the higher marching on Troya."
Sternly approved her the Trojan, "So should they fight who would triumph
Meeting the foe ere he moves in his will to the clash of encounter."
But with his careless laughter the brilliant Priamid Paris:
"Joy of the battle, joy of the tempest, joy of the gamble
Mated are in thy blood, O virgin, daughter of Ares,
Thou like the deathless wouldst have us combat, us who are human?
Come, let the gods do their will with us, Ares let lead and his daughter!
Always the blood is wiser and knows what is hid from the thinker.
Life and treasure and fame to cast on the wings of a moment,
Fiercer joy than this the gods have not given to mortals."
Highly to Paris answered the virgin armipotent Penthesilea,
"Paris and Halamus, shafts of the war-god, fear not for Troya.
Not as a vaunt do I speak it, you gods who stern-thoughted watch us,
But in my vision of strength and the soul that is seated within me,
Not while I live and war, shall the host of the Myrmidon fighters
Forcing the currents, lave as once they were wont, in Scamander
Vaunting their victor car-wheels red with the blood of the vanquished.
Then when I lie by some war-god slain on the fields of the Troad,
Fight again if you will behind high-banked fast-flowing Xanthus."
Halamus answered her, "Never so by my will would I battle
Flinging Troy as a stake on the doubtful diceboard of Ares.
But you have willed it and so let it be; yet hearken my counsel.
Massed in the fight let us aim the storm of our spears at one greatness,
Mighty Pelides' head who gives victory still to the Argives.
Easy the Greeks to destroy if Achilles once slain on the Troad,
But if the Peleid lives the fire shall yet finish with Troya.
Join then Orestes' speed to the stubborn might of Aeneas,

Paris' fatal shafts and the missiles of Penthesilea.
Others meanwhile a puissant screen of our bravest and strongest
Fighting shall hold back Pylos and Argolis, Crete and the Locrian.
Thou, Deiphobus, front the bronze-clad stern Diomedes,
I with Polydamas' spear will dare to restrain and discourage
Ajax' feet though they yearn for pursuit and are hungry for swiftness;
Knot of retreat behind let some strong experienced captain
Stand with our younger levies guarding the fords of the Xanthus,
Fortify the wavering line and dawn as fresh strength on the wearied.
Then if the fierce gods prevail we shall perish not driven like cattle
Over the plains, but draw back sternly and slowly to Troya."
Answered the Priamid, "Wise is thy counsel, branch of Antenor.
Chaff are the southern Achaians, only the hardihood Hellene,
Only the savage speed of the Locrian rescues their legions.
Marshal we so the field. Stand, Halamus, covering Xanthus,
Helping our need when the foe press hard on the Ilian fighters.
Paris, my brother, thou with our masses aid the Eoan.
I with Aeneas' single spear am enough for the Argive."
"Gladlier," Halamus cried, "would I fight in the front with the Locrian!
This too let be as you will; for one is the glory and service
Fighting in front or guarding behind the fate of our country."
    So in their thoughts they ordered battle. Meanwhile Eurus
Gleaming returned and the room grew glad with the light of his armour.
Glad were its conscious walls of that vision of boyhood and valour;
Gods of the household sighed and smiled at his courage and beauty,
They who had seen so many pass over their floors and return not
Hasting to battle, the fair and mighty, the curled and the grizzled,
All of them treading one path like the conscious masks of one pageant
Winding past through the glare of a light to the shadows[1] beyond them.
But on her captains proudly smiling Penthesilea
Seized him and cried aloud, her wild and warlike nature
Moved by the mother's heart that the woman loses not ever.
"Who then shall fear for the fate of Troy when such are her children?
Verily, Eurus, yearning has seized me to meet thee in battle
Rather than Locrian Ajax, rather than Phthian Achilles.
There acquiring a deathless fame I would make thee my captive,
Greedy and glad who feel as a lioness eyeing her booty.
Nay, I can never leave thee behind, my delicate Trojan,
But, when this war ends, will bear thee away to the hills of my country

[1] darkness

And, as a robber might, with my captive glad and unwilling
Bring thee a perfect gift to my sisters Ditis and Anna.
Eurus, there in my land thou shalt look on such hills as thy vision
Gazed not on yet, with their craggy tops besieging Cronion,
Sheeted in virgin white and chilling his feet with their vastness.
Thou shalt rejoice in our wooded peaks and our fruit-bearing valleys,
Lakes of Elysium dreaming and wide and rivers of wonder.
All day long thou shalt glide between mystic woodlands in silence
Broken only by call of the birds and the plashing of waters.
There shalt thou see, O Eurus, the childhood of Penthesilea,
There shalt repose in my father's house and walk in the gardens
Green where I played at the ball with my sisters Ditis and Anna."
Musing she ceased, but if any god had touched her with prescience
Bidding her think for the last time now of the haunts of her childhood
Gazing in her soul with a parting love at the thought of her sisters
And of the lovely and distant land where she played through her
                                                           summers,
Brief was the touch; for she changed at once and only of triumph
Dreamed and only yearned in her heart for the shock of Achilles.
   So they passed from the halls of Priam fated and lofty,
Halls where the air seemed sobbing yet with the cry of Cassandra;
Clad in their brilliant armour, bright in their beauty and courage,
Sons of the passing demigods, they to their latest battle
Down the ancestral hill of the Pergamans, moved to the gateway
Loud with an endless march, with a tireless gliding to meet them
All Troy streamed from her streets and her palaces armed for the combat;
Then to the voice of Deiphobus clanging high o'er the rumour
Wide the portals swung that shall close on blood-red evening,
Slow, foreboding, reluctant, and through the yawn of the gateway
Drove with a cry her steeds the virgin Penthesilea
Calling aloud, "O steeds of my east, we drive to Achilles."
Blithe in the car behind her Eurus scouted around him
Scared with his eyes lest Antenor his grandsire should rise in the gateway,
Hardly believing his fate that led him safe through the portals.
After her trampled and crashed the ranks of her orient fighters.
Paris next with his hosts came brilliant, gold on his armour,
Gold on his helm; a mighty bow hung slack on his shoulder,
Propped o'er his arm a spear, as he drove his car through the gateway.
Next Deiphobus drove and the hero strong Aeneas,
Leading their numbers on. Behind them Dus and Polites,

Helenus, Priam's son, Thrasymachus, grizzled Aretes,
Came like the tempest his father, Aiamos, son of the Northwind —
Orus old in the battle[1] and Eumachus, kin to Aeneas,
Who was Creüsa's brother and richest of men in the Troad
After Antenor only and Priam, Ilion's monarch.
Halamus drove and Corecbus[2] led on his Lycian levies.
Who were the last to speed out of Troya of all those legions
Doomed to the sword? for never again from the ancient city
Foot would march or chariots crash in their pride to the Xanthus.
Aetor the old and Tryas the conqueror known by the Oxus,
They in the portals met and their ancient eyes on each other
Looked amazed, admiring on age the harness of battle.
They in the turreted head of the gateway talked and conversed.
"Twenty years have passed, O Tryas, chief of the Trojans,
Since in the battle thy car was seen and the arm of thy prowess
Age has wronged. Why now to the crowded ways of the battle
Move once more thy body infirm and thy eyes that are faded?"
And to Antenor's brother the Teucrian, "Thou too, O Aetor,
Old and weary hast sat in thy halls and desisted from battle.
Now in Troy's portals I meet thee driving forth to the mellay."
Aetor answered, "Which then is better, to wretchedly perish
Crushed by the stones of my falling house or slain like a victim
Dragged through the blood of my kin on the sacred hearth of my fathers,
Or in the battle to cease mid the war-shouting hymn of chariots
Knowing that Troy yet stands in her pride though doomed in her morrows?
So have the young men willed and the old like thee who age not,
Old are thy limbs, but thy heart still young and hot for the war-din."
Tryas replied: "To perish is better for man or for nation
Nobly in battle, nor end disgraced by disease or subjection.
So have I come here to offer this shoulder Laomedon leaned on,
Arms that have fought by the Oxus and conquered the Orient's heroes
Famous in Priam's wars, and a heart that is faithful to Troya.
These I will offer to death on his splendid altar of battle,
Tribute from Ilion. If she must fall, I shall see not her ending."
Aetor replied to Tryas: "Then let us perish together,
Joined by the love of our race who in life were divided in counsel.
All things embrace in death and the strife and the hatred are ended."
Silent together they drove for the last time through Ilion's portals
Out with the rest to the fight towards the sea and the spears of the Argives.

[1] fight [2] Arintheus

Only once from their speed[1] they gazed back silent on Troya
Lifting her marble pride in the golden joy of the morning.
So through the ripening morn the army, crossing Scamander,
Filling the heavens with the dust and the war-cry, marched on the Argives.
Far in front Troy's plain spread wide to the echoing Ocean.

[1] as they drove

Book Five

The Book of Achilles

Meanwhile grey from the Trojan gates Talthybius journeyed,
Spurred by the secret thought of the Fates who change not nor falter.
Simois sighed round his wheels and Xanthus roared at his passing,
Troas' god like a lion wroth and afraid; to meet him
Whistling the ocean breezes came and Ida regarded.
So with his haste in his wheels the herald oceanward driving
Came through the gold of the morn o'er the trampled green of the pastures
Back to the ships and the roar of the sea and the iron-hooped leaguer.
Wide to the left his circle he wrote where the tents of Achilles
Trooped like a flock of the sea-fowl pensive and still on the margin.
He past the outposts rapidly coursed to the fosse[1] of the Argives.
In with a quavering cry to the encampment over the causeway
Bridging the moat of the ships Talthybius drove in his chariot
Out of the wide plains azure-roofed and the silence of Nature
Passing in to the murmur of men and the thick of the leaguer.
There to a thrall of the Hellene he cast his reins and with labour
Down from the high seat climbed of the war-car framed for the mighty.
Then betwixt tent-doors endless, vistaed streets of the canvas,
Slowly the old man toiled with his eager heart, and to meet him
Sauntering forth from his tent at the sound of the driving car-wheels
Strong Automedon came who was charioteer of Achilles.
 "Grey Talthybius, whence art thou coming? From Troya the ancient?
Or from a distant tent was thy speed and the King Agamemnon?
What in their armoured assembly counsel the Kings[2] of the Argives?"
 "Not from the host but from Troy, Automedon, come I with tidings,
Nor have I mixed with the Greeks in their cohorts ranked by the Ocean,
Nor have I stood in their tents who are kings in sceptred Achaia,
But from Achilles sent to Achilles I bring back the message.
Tell me, then, what does Pelides, — whether his strength he reposes
Soothed by the lyre or hearing the chanted deeds of the mighty,
Or does he walk as he loves by the shore of the far-sounding waters?"
 And to the Argive herald grey Automedon answered:
"Now from the meal he rests and Briseis lyres to him singing
One of the Ilian chants of old in the tongue of the Trojans."
 "Early then he has eaten, Automedon, early reposes?"

[1] moat [2] chiefs

"Early the meat was broached on the spits, Talthybius, early
High on the sands or under the tents we have eaten and rested.
None knows the hour of the hunt red, fierce nor the prey he shall leap on,
All are like straining hounds; for Achilles shares not his counsels,
But on the ships, in the tents the talk has run like Peneus;
These upon Troy to be loosed and the hard-fighting wolf-brood of Priam,
These hope starkly with Argos embraced, to have done with the Spartan,
Ending his brilliance in blood, to sport on the sands of the margent
Playing at bowls with the heads of the Cretan and crafty Odysseus.
Welcome were either or both; we shall move in the dances of Ares,
Quicken heart-beats dulled and limbs that are numb with reposing.
War we desire and no longer this ease by the drone of the waters."
    So as they spoke, they beheld far-off the tent of Achilles,
Splendid and spacious even as the hall of a high-crested chieftain,
Lofty, held by a hundred stakes to the Phrygian meadow.
Hung were its sides with memories bronze and trophies of armour,
Sword and spear and helmet and cuirass of fallen heroes
Slain by the hand of mighty Achilles warring with Troya.
Teemed in its canvas rooms the plundered riches of Troas,
Craftsman's work and the wood well-carved and the ivory painted,
Work of bronze and work of gold and the dreams of the artist.
And in those tents of his pride, in the dreadful guard of the Hellene,
Nobler boys and daughters of high-born Phrygians captive,
Borne from the joyless ruins that now were the sites of their childhood,
Served in the land of their sires the will of the Phthian Achilles.
There on a couch reclined in his beauty mighty and golden,
Loved by the Fates and doomed by them, spear of their will against Troya,
Peleus' hero son by the foam-white child of the waters
Dreaming reposed and his death-giving hand hung lax o'er the couch-side.
Near him dark-eyed Briseis, the fatal and beautiful captive,
Sung to the Grecian victor chants of the land of her fathers,
Sang the chant of Ilus, the tale of the glories of Troya.
Trojan boys and maidens sat near the singer and listened
Heart-delighted if with some tears; for easy are mortal
Hearts to be bent by Fate and soon we consent to our fortunes.
But in the doorway Automedon stood with the shadowy Argive
And at the ominous coming the voice of the singer faltered,
Faltering hushed like a thought melodious ceasing in heaven.
    But from his couch the Peleid sprang to action, rejoicing,
Gladly delivered from patience long and he cried to the herald:

"Long hast thou lingered in Ilion, envoy, mute in the chambers
Golden of Priam old; while around thee darkened the counsels
Wavering blindly and fiercely of minds that revolt from compulsion,
Natures at war with the gods and their fortunes. Fain would I fathom
Whatever the thoughts of Deiphobus locked in that nature of iron
Now that he stands confronting his fate in the town of his fathers.
Peace dwells not in thy aspect. Sowst thou a seed then of ruin
Cast from the inflexible heart and the faltering tongue of Aeneas
Or with the golden laugh of the tameless bright Alexander?"
Grey Talthybius answered: "Surely their doom has embraced them
Wrapping her locks round their ears and their eyes, lest they see and escape her,
Kissing their tongue with her fatal lips and dictating its answers.
Dire is the hope of their chiefs and fierce is the will of their commons.
'Son of the Aeacids, spurned is thy offer. The pride of thy challenge
Rather we choose; it is nearer to Dardanus, King of the Hellenes.
Neither shall Helen captive be dragged to the feet of her husband,
Nor down the paths of peace revisit her fathers' Eurotas.
Death and the fire may prevail on us, never our wills shall surrender
Lowering Priam's heights and darkening Ilion's splendours;
Not of such sires were we born, but of kings and of gods. Larissan,
Not with her gold Troy purchases safety but with her spear-point.
Stand with thy oath in the war-front, Achilles, call on thy helpers
Armed to descend from the calm of Olympian heights to thy succour,
Hedging thy fame from defeat; for we all desire thee in battle,
Mighty to end thee or tame at last by the floods of the Xanthus.'
So they reply; they are true to their death, they are constant for ruin.
Humbler answer hope not, O hero, from Penthesilea;
Insolent, warlike, regal and swift as herself is her message:
'Sea of renown and of valour that fillest the world with thy rumour,
Speed of the battle incarnate, mortal image of Ares!
Terror and tawny delight like a lion one hunts or is hunted!
Dread of the world and my target, swift-footed glorious hero!
Thus have I imaged thee, son of Peleus, dreaming in countries
Far from thy knowledge, in mountains that never have rung to thy war-cry.
O, I have longed for thee, warrior! Therefore today by thy message
So was I seized with delight that my heart was hurt with its rapture,
Knowing today I shall gaze with my eyes on that which I imaged
Only in air of the mind or met in the paths of my dreaming.
Thus have I praised thee first with my speech; with my spear I would answer.

Yet for thy haughty scorn who deeming of me as some Hellene
Or as a woman weak of these plains fit but for the distaff,
Promisest capture in war and fame as thy slave-girl in Phthia, —
Surely I think that death today will reply to that promise, —
Now I will give thee my answer and warn thee ere we encounter.
Know me queen of a race that never was conquered in battle!
Know me armed with a spear that never has missed in the combat!
There where my car-wheels run, good fruit gets the husbandman after.
This thou knowest. Ajax has told thee, thy friend, in his dying.
Has not Meriones' spirit come in thy dreams then to warn thee?
Didst thou not number the Argives over ere I came to the battle?
Number them now and measure the warrior Penthesilea.
Such am I then whom thy dreams have seen meek-browed in Larissa,
And in the battle behind me thunder the heroes Eoan,
Ranks whose feeblest can match with the vaunted chiefs of the Argives.
Never yet from the shock have they fled; if they turn from the foeman,
Always 'tis to return like death recircling on mortals.
Yet being such, having such for my armies, this do I promise:
I on the left of the Trojans war with my bright-armed numbers,
Thou on the Argive right come forth, Achilles, and meet me!
If thou canst drive us with rout into Troy, I will own thee for master,
Do thy utmost will and make thee more glorious than gods are,
Serving thy couch in Phthia and drawing the jar from thy rivers.
Nay, if thou hast that strength, then hunt me, O hunter, and seize me,
If 'tis thy hope indeed that the sun can turn back from the Orient,
But if thou canst not, death of myself or thyself thou shalt capture."

    Musing heard and was silent a while the strength of Achilles,
Musing of Fate and the wills of men and the purpose of Heaven,
Then from his thoughts he broke and turned in his soul towards battle.
"Well did I know what reply would come winged from the princes of Troya.
Prone are the hearts of heroes to wrath and to god-given blindness
When from their will they are thrust and harried by Fate and disaster:
Fierceness then is the armour of strength against grief and its yieldings.
So have the gods made man for their purpose, cunningly fashioned.
Once had defiance waked from my depths a Fury far-striding
Flaming for justice and vengeance, nor had it, satisfied, rested,
Sunk to its lair till the insulter died torn or was kneeling for pardon.
Fierce was my heart in my youth and exulted in triumph and slaughter.
Now as I grow in my spirit like to my kin the immortals,
Joy more I find in saving and cherishing than in the carnage.

Greater it seems to my mind to be king over men than their slayer,
Nobler to build and to govern than what the ages have laboured
Putting their godhead forth to create or the high gods have fashioned,
That to destroy in our wrath of a moment. Ripened, more widely
Opens my heart to the valour of man and the beauty of woman,
Works of the world and delight; the cup of my victory sweetens
Not with the joys of hate, but the human pride of the triumph.
Yet was the battle decreed for the means supreme of the mortal
Placed in a world where all things strive from the worm to the Titan.
So will I seize by the onset what peace from my soul would sequester,
So will I woo with the sword and with love the delight of my foeman,
Troy and Polyxena, beauty of Paris and glory of Priam.
This was the ancient wrestling, this was the spirit of warfare
Fit for the demigods. Soon in the city of gold and of marble,
There where Ilus sat and Tros, where Laomedon triumphed,
Peleus' house shall reign, the Hellene sit where the Trojan
Thought himself deathless. Arise, Automedon! Out to the people!
Send forth the cry through the ships and the tents of the Myrmidon nation.
Let not a man be found then lingering when o'er the causeway
Thunder my chariot-wheels, nor let any give back in the battle,
Good if he wills from me, till through the conquered gates of the foeman
Storming we herd in their remnants and press into Troy as with evening
Helios rushing sinks to the sea. But thou, Briseis,
Put by thy lyre, O girl; it shall gladden my heart in my triumph
Victor returned from Troy to listen pleased to thy singing,
Bearing a captive bound to my car-wheels Penthesilea,
Bearing my valour's reward, Polyxena, daughter of Priam,
Won in despite of her city and brothers and spears of her kindred.
So by force it is best to take one's will and be mighty."
Joyful, Automedon ran through the drowsy camp of the Hellenes
Changing the hum of the tents as he raced into shoutings of battle;
For with the giant din of a nation triumphant arising
Hellas sprang from her irksome ease and mounted her war-car;
Donning her armour bright she rejoiced in the trumpet of battle.
    But to the herald grey the Peleid turned and the old man
Shuddered under his gaze and shrank from the voice of the hero:
"Thou to the tents of thy kings, Talthybius, herald of Argos!
Stand in the Argive assembly, voice of the strength of Achilles.
Care not at all though the greatest and fiercest be wroth with thy message.
Deem not thyself, old man, as a body and flesh that is mortal,

Rather as living speech from the iron breast of the Hellene.
Thus shalt thou chide the vanquished chiefs who have fled from a woman
Thus shalt thou speak my will to the brittle and fugitive legions: —
'Now Achilles turns towards Troya and fast-flowing Xanthus,
Now he leaps at the iron zone, the impregnable city.
Two were the Forms of the Gods that o'erhung the sails of Pelides
When with a doubtful word in his soul he came wind-helped from Hellas
Cleaving the Aegean deep towards the pine-crested vision of Ida.
Two are the Fates that stride with the hero counting his exploits.
Over all earthly things the soul that is fearless is master,
Only on death he can reckon not whether it comes in the midnight
Treading the couch of Kings in their pride or speeds in the spear-shaft.
Now will I weigh down that double beam of the Olympian balance
Claiming one of the equal Fates that stand robed for the fighter,
For to my last dire wrestle I go with the Archer of heaven,
And ere the morning gleam have awakened the eagles on Ida,
Troy shall lie prone[1] or earth shall be empty of Phthian Achilles.
But for whatever Fate I accept from the ageless Immortals,
Whether cold Hades dim or Indus waits for my coming
Pouring down vast to the sea with the noise of his numberless waters,
I with Zeus am enough. Your mortal aid I desire not,
Rushing to Troy like the eagle of Zeus when he flies towards the thunders, —
Winged with might, the bird of the spaces, upbuoying his pinions.
Nor shall my spirit look back for the surge of your Danaan fighters,
Tramp of the Argive multitudes helping my lonely courage,
Neither the transient swell of the cry Achaian behind me
Seek, nor the far-spreading voice of Atrides guiding his legions.
Need has he none for a leader who himself is the soul of his action.
Zeus and his Fate and his spear are enough for the Phthian Achilles.
Rest, O wearied hosts; my arm shall win for you Troya,
Quelled when the stern Eoans break and Penthesilea
Lies like a flower in the dust at my feet. Yet if Ares desire you,
Come then and meet him once more mid the cry and the trampling! Assemble
Round the accustomed chiefs, round the old victorious wrestlers
Wearied strengths Deiphobus leaves you or sternest Aeneas.
But when my arm and my Fate have vanquished their gods and Apollo,
Brilliant with blood when we stand amid Ilion's marble splendours,
Then let none seat deaf flame on the glory of Phrygia's marbles
Or with his barbarous rapine shatter the chambers of sweetness

[1] stoop low

Slaying the work of the gods and the beauty the ages have lived for.
For he shall moan in the night remote from the earth and her greenness,
Spurred like a steed to its goal by my spear dug deep in his bosom;
Fast he shall fleet to the waters of wailing, the pleasureless pastures.
Touch not the city Apollo built, where Poseidon has laboured.
Seized and dishelmed and disgirdled of Apollonian ramparts,
Empty of wide-rolling wheels and the tramp of a turbulent people
Troy with her marble domes shall live for our nations in beauty
Hushed mid the trees and the corn and the pictured halls of the ancients,
Watching her image of dreams in the gliding waves of Scamander,
Sacred and still, a city of memory spared by the Grecians.[1]
So shalt thou warn the arrogant hearts of Achaia's chieftains
Lest upon Greece an evil should fall and her princes should perish.
Herald, beware how thou soften my speech in the ears of thy nation
Sparing their pride and their hearts but dooming their lives to the death-
stroke.
Even thy time-touched snows shall not shield thy days from my sword-edge."
  Wroth grew the old man's heart, but he feared Achilles and slowly
Over the margin grey on the shore of the far-sounding Ocean
Silent paced to the tents of the Greeks and the Argive assembly.
There on the sands while the scream of the tide as it dragged at the pebbles
Strove in vain with their droning roar, awaiting their chieftains
Each in his tribe and his people far down the margin Aegean,
Argolis' sons and Epirote spears and the isles and the southron,
Locris' swarms and Messene's pikes and the strength of the Theban,
Hosts bright-armed, bright-eyed, bright-haired, time-hardened to Ares,
Stretched in harsh and brilliant lines with a glitter of spear-points
Far as the eye could toil. All Europe helmeted, armoured
Swarmed upon Asia's coasts disgorged from their ships in their hundreds.
There in the wide-winged tent of the council that peered o'er the margin,
High where the grass and the meadow-bloom failed on the sand-rifted
sward-edge,
Pouring his argent voice Epeus spoke to the princes,
Rapid in battle and speech; and even as boy in a courtyard
Tosses his ball in the air and changes his hands for the seizing,
So he played with his counsel and thought and rejoiced in his swiftness.
But now a nearing Fate he felt and his impulse was silenced.
Stilled were his thoughts by the message that speeds twixt our minds in their
shadows

[1] nobles.

Dumb, unthought, unphrased, to us dark, but the caverns of Nature
Hear its cry when God's moment changing our fate comes visored
Silently into our lives and the spirit too knows, for it watches.
Quiet he fell and all men turned to the face of the herald.
Mute and alone through the ranks of the seated and silent princes
Old Talthybius paced, nor paused till he stood at the midmost
Fronting that council of Kings and nearest to Locrian Ajax
And where Sthenelus sat and where sat the great Diomedes,
Chiefs of the South, but their love was small for the Kings of the Spartans.
There like one close to a refuge he lifted his high-chanting accents.
High was his voice like the wind's when it whistles shrill o'er a forest
Sole of all sounds at night, for the kite is at rest and the tiger
Sleeps from the hunt returned in the deepest hush of the jungle.
"Hearken, O Kings of the world, to the lonely will of the Phthian!
One is the roar of the lion heard by the jungle's hundreds,
One is the voice of the great and the many shall hear it inclining.
Lo, he has shaken his mane for the last great leap upon Troya
And when the eagle's scream shall arise in the dawn over Ida,
Troy shall have fallen or earth shall be empty of Phthian Achilles.
But by whatever Fate he is claimed that waits for the mortal,
Whether the fast-closed hands above have kept for his morrows
Chill of the joyless shades or earth and her wooings of sunlight
Still shall detain his days with the doubtful meed of our virtues,
He and Zeus shall provide, not mortals. Chaff are men's armies
Threshed by the flails of Fate; 'tis the soul of the hero that conquers.
Not on the tramp of the multitudes, not in the cry of the legions
Founds the strong man his strength but the god that he carries within him.
Zeus and his Fate and his spear are enough for the Phthian Achilles.
Prudence of men shall curb no more his god-given impulse.
He has no need of thy voice, O Atreus, guiding the legions,
He is the leader, he is the soul of magnificent emprise.
Rest, O ye sons of the Greeks,[1] the Phthian shall conquer for Hellas!
Rest! expose not your hearts to the war-cry of Penthesilea.
Yet if the strength in you thirsts for the war-din, if Ares is hungry,
Meet him stark in the mellay surging Deiphobus' coursers,
Guiding Aeneas' spear; recover the souls of your fathers.
Bronze must his heart be who looks in the eyes of the implacable war-god!
But when his Fate has conquered their gods and slaughtered their heroes,
And in this marble Ilion bowed[2] to the tread of her foemen

[1] O Greeks in your tents, [2] forced

Watched by the ancient domes you stand by the timeless turrets,
Then let no chieftain crowned[1] for offering lift against Troya,
Counselled of Ate, torch of the burning, hand of the plunder
Groping for gold but finding death in her opulent chambers.
For he shall moan in the night regretting the earth and her greenness,
Spurred by the spear in his arrogant breast like a steed to the gorges:
Fast he shall fleet to the flowerless meadows, the sorrowful pastures.
Touch not the city Apollo built, where Poseidon laboured,
Slay not the work of the gods and the glory the ages have lived for.
Mute of the voice of her children, void of the roll of her war-cars
Timeless Troy leave solitary dreaming by ancient Scamander
Sacred and still, a city of memory spared by the Grecians."[2]
So Talthybius spoke and anger silenced the Argives.
Mute was the warlike assembly, silent Achaia's princes.
Wrath and counsel strove in the hush for the voice of the speakers.

[1] garbed [2] Phthian.

BOOK SIX

The Book of The Chieftains

But from their midst uprearing a brow that no crown could ennoble,
Male and kingly of front like a lion conscious of puissance
Rose a form august, the monarch great Agamemnon.
Wroth he rose yet throwing a rein on the voice of his passion,
Governing the beast and the demon within by the god who is mighty.
"Happily for thy life and my fame that thou comst with the aegis of heaven
Shadowing thy hoary brows, thou herald of pride and of insult.
Well is it too for his days who sent thee that other and nobler
Heaven made my heart than his who insults and a voice of the immortals[1]
Cries to my soul forbidding its passions. O hardness of virtue
Thus to be seized and controlled as in fetters by Zeus and Athene.
Free is the peasant to smite in the pastures the mouth that has wronged him,
Chained in his soul is Atrides. Bound by their debt to the fathers,
Curbed by the god in them painfully move the lives of the noble,
Forced to obey the eye that watches within in their bosoms.
Ever since Zeus Cronion turned in our will towards the waters,
Scourged by the heavens in my dearest, wronged by men and their clamours
Griefs untold I have borne in Argos and Aulis and Troas,
Yoked to the sacred toil of the Greeks for their children and country,
Bound by the gods to a task that is heavy, a load that is bitter.
Seeing the faces[2] of foes in the mask of a friend I was silent.
Hateful I hold him who sworn to a cause that is holy and common
Broods upon private wrongs or serving his[3] lonely ambition

[1] *Alternative to lines 4-9:*
   Wroth he rose with a reddened brow as reddens the forehead
   Wide of the heavens with a glory of wrath on the eve of a* tempest.
   "Well is it, herald, that sacred thou comst with the aegis of heaven
   Sheltering thy hoary brows; for thy age should not shield thee nor pardon.†
   Shame to the ancient years and the Argive tongue that can utter
   Words like these into Argive ears from the mouth of a Hellene.
   Well is it too for the length of his days who sent thee, O envoy,
   Voicing‡ his pride, the haughty§ chief of a barbarous nation,
   One who imagines that sole upon earth he is brave and a fighter.
   Well for his days that my strength is restrained by a voice that within me
* some
† *Alternative:* Well is it, herald, that sacred thou comst and protected of heaven,
   Bearing this stab to Achaia nor fearest insulting her princes.
‡ Voice of § insolent
[2] eyes [3] lured by a

Studies to reap his gain from the labour and woe of his fellows.
Mire is the man who hears not the gods when they cry to his bosom.
Grief and wrath I coerced nor carried my heart to its record,
All that has hurt its chords and wounded the wings of my spirit.
Nobler must kings be than natures of earth on whom Zeus lays no burden.
Other is Peleus' son than the race of his Aeacid fathers,
Nor like his sire of the wise-still heart deep-sighted and patient
Bearing the awful ruin of the gods, but hastes to his longings;
Dire is his wrath and pursued by the band of his giant ambitions.
Measure and virtue forsake him as Ate grows in his bosom.
Yet not for tyrant wrong nor to serve as a sword for our passions
Zeus created our strength, but that earth might have help from her children.
Not of our moulding its gifts to our soul nor were formed by our labour.
When did we make them, and where were they forged, in what workshop
                                                          or furnace?[1]
Found in what aeon of Time, that pride should bewilder the mortal?
Bowed to our will are the folk and our prowess dreadful and godlike?
Shadows are these of the gods which the deep heavens cast on our spirits.
Transient we made not ourselves, but at birth from the first we were fashioned
Valiant or fearful and as was our birth by the gods and their thinkings
Formed, so already enacted and fixed by their wills are our fortunes.
What were the strength of Atrides and what were the craft of Odysseus
Save for their triumphing gods? They would fail and be helpless as infants.
Stronger a woman, wiser a child were, favoured by Heaven.
Ceased not Sarpedon slain who was son of Zeus and unconquered?
Not to Achilles he fell, but Fate and the gods were his slayers.
Kings, to the arrogant shaft that was launched, the unbearable insult
Armoured wisdoms oppose, let not Ate seize on your passions.
Be not as common souls, O you who are Greece and her fortunes,
Nor of your spirits of wrath take counsel but of Athene.
Merit the burden laid by Zeus, his demand from your natures
Suffer, O hearts of his seed, O souls who are chosen and mighty,
All forgetting but Greece and her good; resolve what is noble.
I will not speak nor advise, for 'tis known we are rivals and foemen."

    Calmed by his words and his will he sat down mighty and kinglike;
But Menelaus arose, the Spartan, the husband of Helen,
Atreus' younger son from a lesser womb, in his brilliance
Dwarfed by the other's port, yet tall was he, gracile and splendid,
As if a panther might hunt by a lion's side in the forest.

[1] of being?

Smiting his thigh with his firm-clenched hand he spoke mid the Argives:
"Woe to me, shameless, born to my country a cause of affliction,
Since for my sake all wrongs must be borne and all shames be encountered;
And for my sake you have spun through the years down the grooves of
                                                                  disaster
Bearing the shocks of the Trojans and ravaged by Zeus and by Hector,
Slaughtered by Rhesus and Memnon, Sarpedon and Penthesilea;
Or by the Archer pierced, the hostile dreadful Apollo,
Evilly end the days of the Greeks remote from their kindred —
Slain on an alien soil by Asian Xanthus and Ida.
Doomed to the pyre we have toiled for a woman ungracious who left us
Passing serenely my portals to joy in the chambers of Troya.
Here let it cease, O my brother! how much wilt thou bear for this graceless
Child of thy sire, cause still of thy griefs and never of blessing?
Easily Zeus afflicts who trouble their hearts for a woman;
But in our ships that sailed close-fraught with this dolorous Ate
Worse was the bane they bore which King Peleus begot on white Thetis.
Evil ever was sown by the embrace of the gods with a mortal!
Alien a portent is born and a breaker of men and their labours,
One who afflicts with his light or his force mortality's weakness
Stripping for falsehoods their verities, shaking the walls they erected.
Neither without him his fellows can prosper nor will his spirit
Fit in the frame of things earthly but shatters their rhythm and order
Rending the measures just that the wise have decreed for our growing.
So have our mortal plannings broken in this fateful Achilles
And with our blood and our anguish Heaven has fostered his greatness.
It is enough; let the dire gods choose between Greece and their offspring.
Even as he bids us, aloof let our hosts twixt the ships and the Xanthus
Stand from the shock and the cry where Hellene meets with Eoan,
Troy and Phthia locked, Achilles and Penthesilea,
Nor any more than watchers care who line an arena;
Calm like the impartial gods they approve the bravest and swiftest.
So let him fight! The fates shall preserve him he vaunts of or gather,
Even as death shall gather us all for memory's clusters,
All in their day who were great or were little, heroes or cowards.
So shall he slay or be slain, a boon to mankind and his country.
Since if he mow down this flower of bale, this sickle by Hades
Whirled if he break — for the high gods ride on the hiss of his spear-shaft, —
Ours is the gain who shall break rejoicing through obdurate portals
Praising Pallas alone and Hera daughter of Heaven.

But if he sink in this last of his fights, as they say it is fated, —
Nor do I deem that the man has been born in Asia or Hellas
Who in the dreadful field can prevail against Penthesilea, —
If to their tents the Myrmidons fleeing cumber the meadows
Slain by a girl in her speed and leaving the corpse of their leader,
Ours is the gain, we are rid of a shame and a hate and a danger.
True is it, Troy shall exultant live on in the shadow of Ida,
Yet shall our hearts be light because earth is void of Achilles.
And for the rest of the infinite loss, what we hoped, what we suffered,
Let it all go, let the salt floods swallow it, fate and oblivion
Bury it out in the night; let us sail o'er the waves to our country
Leaving Helen in Troy since the gods are the friends of transgressors."
So Menelaus in anger and grief miscounselled the Argives.

    Great Idomeneus next, the haughty king of the Cretans,
Raised his brow of pride in the lofty Argive assembly.
Tall like a pine that stands up on the slope of Thessalian mountains
Overpeering a cascade's edge and is seen from the valleys,
Such he seemed to their eyes who remembered Greece and her waters,
Heard in their souls the torrent's leap and the wind on the hill-top:
"Long[1] have I marvelled at heart[2] to behold in this levy of heroes
Armies so many, chieftains so warlike suffer in silence
Pride of a single man when he thunders and lightens in Troas.
Doubtless the nations that follow his cry are many and valiant,
Doubtless the winds of the north have made him a runner and spearman.
Shall not then force be the king? is not strength the seal of the godhead?
This my soul replies, 'Agamemnon the Atreid only
Choosing for leader and king I have come to the toil and the warfare.
Wisdom and greatness he owns and the wealth and renown of his fathers
But for this whelp of the northlands, nursling of rocks and the sea-cliff,
Who with his bleak and rough-hewn Myrmidons hastes to the carnage,
Leader of wolves to their prey, not the king of a humanised nation.
Not to such head of the cold-drifting mist and the gloom-vigilled Chaos,
Crude to our culture and light and void of our noble fulfilments
Minos shall bend his knee nor Crete, a barbarian's vassal,
Stain her old glories.' Oh, but he boasts of a goddess for mother
Born in the senseless seas mid the erring wastes of the Ocean![3]
Gods we adore enough in the heavens, and if from us Hades
Claim one more of this breed, we can bear that excess to her glories,
Not upon earth these new-born deities huge-passioned, sateless

[1] Oft   [2] O Greeks   [3] White and swift and foam-footed, vast Oceanus' daughter!

Who with their mouth as of Orcus and stride of the ruinous Ocean
Sole would be seen mid her sons and devour all life's joy and its greatness.
Millions must empty their lives that a few men may o'ershadow the nations,
Numberless homes must weep but their hunger of glory is sated!
Troy shall descend to the shadow; gods and men have condemned her,
Weary, hating her fame. Her dreams, her grandeur, her beauty,
All her greatness and deeds that now end in miserable ashes,
Ceasing shall fade and be as a tale that was forged by the poets.
Only a name shall go down from her past and the woe of her ending
Naked to hatred and rapine and punished with rape and with slaughter.
Never again must her marble pride high-crowned on her hill-top
Look forth dominion and menace over the crested Aegean
Shadowing[1] Achaia. Fire shall abolish the fame of her ramparts,
Earth her foundations forget. Shall she stand then affronting the azure?
Dire in our path like a lioness once again must we meet her,
Leap and roar of her led by the spear of Achilles, not Hector!
Asia by Peleus guided[2] shall stride on us after Antenor?
Though one should plan in the night of his thoughts where no eye can pursue him,
Instincts of men discover their foe and like hounds in the darkness
Bay at a danger hid. No silence of servitude trembling
Trains to bondage sons of the race of whom Aeolus father
Storm-voiced was and free, nor like other groupings of mortals
Moulded we were by Zeus, but supremely were sifted and fashioned;
Other are Danaus' sons and other the lofty Achaians:
Chainless like Nature's tribes in their many-voiced colonies founded
They their god-given impulse shall keep and their natures of freedom.
Only themselves shall rule them, only their equal spirits
Bowed to the voice of a law that is just, obeying their leaders
Awed by the gods. So with order and balance and harmony noble
Life shall move golden, free in its steps and just in its measure,
Glad of a manhood complete, by excess and defect untormented.
Freedom is life to the Argive's soul, to Aeolia's peoples.
Dulled by a yoke our nations would perish, or live but as shadows,
Changed into phantoms of men with the name of a Greek for a byword.
Not like the East and her sons is our race, they who bow to a mortal.
Gods there may be in this flesh that suffers and dies; Achaia
Knows them not. Need if he feels of a world to endure and adore him,

---

[1] Lessening / Stunting / Dwarfing [2] prompted

Hearts let him seek that are friends with the dust, overpowered by their
                                                                     heavens,
Here in these Asian vastnesses, here where the heats and the perfumes
Sicken the soul and the sense and a soil of indolent plenty
Breeds like the corn in its multitudes natures accustomed to thraldom.
Here let the northern Achilles seek for his slaves and adorers,
Not in the sea-ringed isles and not in the mountains Achaian.
Ten long years of the shock and the war-cry twixt rampart and ocean
Hurting our hearts we have toiled; shall they reap not their ease in the
                                                                 vengeance?
Troas is strewn[1] with the lives of our friends and with ashes remembered;
Shall not Meriones slain be reckoned in blood and in treasure?
Cretan Idomeneus girt with the strength of his iron retainers
Slaying and burning will stride through the city of music and pleasure,
Babes of her blood borne high on the spears at the head of my column,
Wives of her princes dragged through her streets in its pomp to their passion,
Gold of Troy stream richly past in the gaze of Achilles.
Then let him threaten my days, then let him rally the might of his trumpets,
Yet shall a Cretan spear make search in his heart for his godhead.
Limbs of this god can be pierced; not alone shall I fleet down to Hades."
    After him rose from the throne the Locrian swift-footed Ajax.
"Kings of the Greeks, throw a veil o'er[2] your griefs, lay a curb on your anger.
Moved man's tongue in its wrath looses speech that is hard to be pardoned,
Afterwards stilled we regret, we forgive. If all were resented,
None could live on this earth that is thick with our stumblings. Always
This is the burden of man that he acts from his heart and his passions,
Stung by the goad of the gods he hacks[3] at the ties that are dearest.
Lust was the guide they sent us, wrath was a whip for his coursers,
Madness they made the heart's comrade, repentance they gave for its
                                                                  scourger.
This too our hearts demand that we bear with our friend when he chides us.
Insult forgive from the noble embittered soul of Achilles!
When with the scorn and the wrath of a lover our depths are tormented,
Who shall forbid the cry and who shall measure the anguish?
Sharper the pain that looses the taunt than theirs who endure it.
Rage has wept in my blood as I lived through the flight o'er the pastures,
Shame coils a snake in my back when thought whispers of Penthesilea.
Bright shine his morns if he mows down this hell-bitch armed by the Furies!
But for this shaft of his pity it came from a lesser Pelides,

[1] sown [2] on [3] hews

Not from the slayer of Hector, not from the doom of Sarpedon,
Memnon's mighty o'erthrower, the blood-stained splendid Achilles.
These are the Trojan snares and the fateful smile of a woman!
This thing the soul of a man shall not bear that blood of his labour
Vainly has brought him victory leaving life to the hated;
This is a wound to our race that a Greek should whisper of mercy.
Who can pardon a foe though a god should descend to persuade him?
Justice is first of the gods, but for Pity 'twas spawned by a mortal,
Pity that only disturbs God's measures and false and unrighteous
Holds man back from the joy he might win and troubles his bosom.
Troy has a debt to our hearts; she shall pay it all down to the obol,
Blood of the fall and anguish of flight when the heroes are slaughtered,
Days without joy while we labour and see not the eyes of our parents,
Toil of the war-cry, nights that drag past upon alien beaches,
Helen ravished, Paris triumphant, endless the items
Crowd on a wrath in the memory, kept as in bronze the credit
Stretches out long and blood-stained and savage. Most for the terror
Graved in the hearts of our fathers that still by our youth is remembered,
Hellas waiting and crouching, dreading the spear of the Trojan,
Flattering, sending gifts and pale in her mortal anguish,
Agony long of a race at the mercy of iron invaders,
This shall pay most, the city of pride, the insolent nation,
Pay with her temples charred and her golden mansions in ruins,
Pay with the shrieks of her ravished virgins, the groans of the aged
Burned in their burning homes for our holiday. Music and dancing
Shall be in Troy of another sort than she loved in her greatness,
Merry with conquered gold and insulting the world with her flutings.
All that she boasted of, statue and picture, all shall be shattered;
Out of our shame she chiselled them, rich with our blood they were coloured.
This not the gods from Olympus crowding, this not Achilles,
This not your will, O ye Greeks, shall deny to the Locrian Ajax.
Even though Pallas divine with her aegis counselling mercy
Cumbered my path I would push her aside to leap on my victims.
Learn shall all men on that day how a warrior deals with his foemen."

    Darting flames from his eyes the barbarian sate and there rose up
Frowning Tydeus's son, the Tirynthian, strong Diomedes.
"Ajax Oileus, thy words are foam on the lips of a madman.
Cretan Idomeneus, silence the vaunt that thy strength can fulfil not.
Strong art thou, fearless in battle, but not by thy spear-point, O hero,
Hector fell, nor Sarpedon, nor Troilus leading the war-cry.

These were Achilles' deeds which a god might have done out of heaven.
Him we upbraid who saved, nor would any now who revile him
Still have a living tongue for ingratitude but for the hero.
Much to the man forgive who has saved his race and his country:
Him shall the termless centuries praise when we are forgotten.
Curb then your speech, crush down in your hearts the grief and the choler;
Has not Atrides curbed who is greatest of all in our nations
Wrath in the heart and the words that are winged for our bale from our
                                                                                       bosoms?
For as a load to be borne were these passions given to mortals.
Honour Achilles, conquer Troy by his god-given valour.
Now of our discords and griefs debate not for joy of our foemen!
First over Priam's corpse stand victors in Ilion's ramparts;
Discord then let arise or concord solder our nations."
Rugged words and few as fit for the soul that he harboured
Great Tydides spoke and ceased; and there rose up impatient
Tall mid the spears of the north the hero king Prothoënor,
Prince in Cadmeian Thebes who with Leitus led on his thousands:
"Loudly thou vauntest thy freedom Ionian Minos recalling:
Lord of thy southern isles who gildst with thy tribute Mycenae!
We have not bowed our neck to Pelops' line or at Argos'
Iron heel have not crouched nor clasped like thy time-wearied nations,
Python-befriended, gripped in the coils of an iron protection,
Bondage soothed by a name and destruction masked as a helper.
We are the young and lofty and free-souled sons of the Northland.
Nobly Peleus, the Aeacid, seer of a vaster Achaia,
Pride and his strength and his deeds renouncing for joy of that vision,
Yielded his hoary right to the sapling stock of Atrides.
Noble, we gave to that nobleness freely our grandiose approval.
Not as a foe then, O King, who angered sharpens his arrows,
Fits his wrath and hate to the bow and aims at the heart-strings
But from the Truth that is seated within me compelling my accents,
Taught by my fathers stern not to lie nor to hide what I harbour,
Truth the goddess I speak, nor constrain the voice in my bosom.
Monarch, I own thee first of the Greeks save in valour and counsel,
Brave but less than Achilles, wise but not as Odysseus,
First still in greatness and calm and majesty. Yet, Agamemnon,
Love of thy house and thy tribe disfigures the king in thy nature;
Thou thy brother preferrest, thy friends and thy nation unjustly,
Even as a common man whose heart is untaught by Athene,

Beastlike favours his brood forgetting the law of the noble.
Therefore Ajax grew wroth and Teucer sailing abandoned
Over the angry seas this stern fierce toil of the nations;
Therefore Achilles has turned in his soul and gazed towards the Orient.
Yet are we fixed in our truth like hills in heaven, Atrides;
Greece and her safety and good in our passions strive to remember.
Nor of this stamp was thy brother's speech; such words Lacedaemon
Hearing may praise in her kings; we speak not in Thebes what is shameful.
Shamefuller thoughts have never escaped from lips that were high-born.
We will not send forth earth's greatest to die in a friendless battle,
Nor will forsake the daughter of Zeus and white glory of Hellas,
Helen the golden-haired Tyndarid, left for the joy of our foemen,
Chained to Paris' delight, earth's goddess the slave of the Phrygian,
Though Menelaus the Spartan abandon his wife to the Trojans
And from the field where he lavished the unvalued blood of his people
Flee to a hearth dishonoured. Not the Atreid's sullied grandeurs,
Greece to defend we have toiled through the summers and lingering autumns
Blind with our blood; for our country we bleed, repelling her foemen.
Dear is that loss to our veins and still that expense we would lavish,
Claiming its price from the heavens, though thou sail with thy brother and
cohorts.
Weakling, flee! take thy southern ships, take thy Spartan levies,
Still will the Greeks fight on in the Troad helped by thy absence.
For though the beaches vast grow empty, the tents can be numbered
Standing friendless and few on the huge and hostile champaign,
Always a few will be left whom the threatenings of Fate cannot conquer,
Always earth has sons[1] whose courage waits not on fortune;
Hellas' heart will be firm confronting the threat of the victor,
Sthenelus war and Tydides, Odysseus and Locrian Ajax,
Thebes' unconquered sons and the hero chiefs of the northland.
Stern and persistent as Time or the seas and as deaf to affliction
We will clash on in the fight unsatisfied, fain of the war-cry,
Helped by the gods and our cause through the dawns and the blood-haunted
evenings,
Rising in armour with morn and outstaying the red of the sunset,
Till in her ashes Troy forgets that she lusted for empire
Or in our own honour and valour of Greece are extinguished."
So Prothoënor spoke nor pleased with his words Agamemnon;
But to the northern kings they were summer rain on the visage.

[1] souls are born

Last Laertes' son, the Ithacan, war-wise Odysseus,
Rose up wide-acclaimed; like an oak was he stunted in stature,
Broad-shouldered, firm-necked, lone and sufficient, as on some island
Regnant one peak whose genial streams flow down to the valley,
Dark on its slopes are the olives, the storms butt in vain at its shoulders, —
Such he stood and pressed the earth with his feet like one vanquished,
Striving, but held to his will. So Atlas might seem were he mortal,
Atlas whose vastness free from impatience suffers the heavens,
Suffering spares the earth, the thought-haunted motionless Titan,
Bearer of worlds. In those jarring tribes no man was his hater;
For as the Master of all guides humanity, so this Odysseus
Dealt with men and helped and guided them, careful and selfless,
Crafty, tender and wise, — like the Master who bends o'er his creatures,
Suffers their sins and their errors and guides them screening his guidance;
Each through his nature He leads and the world by the lure of His wisdom.
  "Princes of Argolis, chiefs of the Locrians, spears of the northland,
Warriors vowed to a sacred hate and a vengeance that's holy,
Sateless still is that hate, that vengeance cries for its victims,
Still is the altar unladen, the priest yet waits with the death-knife.
Who while the rites are unfinished, the gods unsatisfied, impious
Turns in his heart to the feuds of the house and his strife with his equals?
None will approve the evil that fell from the younger Atrides;
But it was anger and sorrow that spoke, it was not Menelaus.
Who would return from Troy and arrive with his war-wasted legions
Back to his home in populous city or orcharded island;
There from his ships disembarked look round upon eyes that grow joyless
Seeking a father or husband slain, a brother heart-treasured,
Mothers in tears for their children, and when he is asked, 'O our chieftain,
What dost thou bring back in place of our dead to fill hearts that are empty?'
Who then will say, 'I bring back my shame and the shame of my nation;
Troy yet stands confronting her skies and Helen in Troya?'
Nor for such foil will I go back to Ithaca or to Laertes,
Rather far would I sail in my ships past southern Cythera,
Turning away in silence from waters where on some headland
Gazing south o'er the waves my father waits for my coming,
Leaving Sicily's shores and on through the pillars of Gades.
Far I would sail whence sound of me never should come to Achaia
Out into tossing worlds and weltering reaches of tempest
Dwarfing the swell of the wide-wayed Aegean, — oceans unbounded
Either by cliff or by sandy margin, only the heavens

Ever receding before my keel as it ploughs on for ever
Frail and alone in a world of waves. Even there would I venture
Seeking some island unknown, not return with shame to my fathers.
Well might they wonder how souls like theirs begot us for their offspring.
Fighters[1] war-afflicted, princes[2] banded by heaven,
Wounds and defeat you have borne; bear too their errors who lead you.
Mortals are kings and have hearts; our leaders too have their passions.
Then if they err, yet still obey lest anarchy fostered,
Discord and deaf rebellion that speed like a poison through kingdoms,
Break all this army in pieces while Ate mocking at mortals
Trails to a shameful end this noble[3] essay of the nations.
Who among men has not thoughts that he holds for the wisest, though
                                                                foolish?
Who, though feeble and nought, esteems not his strength o'er his fellow's?
Therefore the wisest and strongest choose out a king and a leader,
Not as a perfect arbiter armed with impossible virtues
Far o'er our heads and our ken like a god high-judging his creatures,
But as a man among men who is valiant, wise and far-seeing,
One of ourselves and the knot of our wills and the sword of our action.
Him they advise and obey and cover his errors with silence.
Not Agamemnon the Atreid, Greeks, we obey in this mortal;
Greece we obey; for she walks in his gait and commands by his gestures.
Evil he works then who loosens this living knot of Achaia,
Falling apart from his nation; who, wed to a solitary virtue,
Deeming he does but right, renounces the yoke of his fellows, —
Errs more than hearts of the mire that in blindness and weakness go
                                                                stumbling.
Man when he spurns his kind, when he equals himself with the deathless,
Even in his virtues sins and, erring, calls up Ate:
For among men we were born, not as wild beasts sole in a fastness.
Oft with a name are misled the passionate hearts of the noble;
Chasing highly some image of good they trample its substance.
Evil is worked, not justice, when into the mould of our thinkings
God we would force and enchain to the throb of our hearts the immortals, —
Justice and Virtue, her sister; for where is justice mid creatures
Perfectly? Even the gods are betrayed by our clay to a semblance.
Evil not good he sows who lifted high o'er his fellows
Dreams by his light or his force to compel this deity earth-born,
Evil though his wisdom exceeded the gathered light of the millions,

[1] Chieftains [2] champions [3] lofty

Evil though his single fate were vaster than Troy and Achaia.
Less is our gain from gods upon earth than from men in our image;
Just is the slow and common march, not a lonely swiftness
Far from our human reach that is vowed to impossible strivings.
Better the stumbling leader of men than inimitable paces.
If he be Peleus' son and his name the Phthian Achilles,
Worse is the bane: lo, the Ilian battlefield red with his errors!
Yet, O ye Greeks, if the heart returns that was loved, though it wandered,
Though with some pride it return and reproaching the friends that it fled
                                                                      from,
Be not less fond than heart-satisfied parents who yearn o'er that coming,
Smile at its pride and accept the wanderer. Happier music
Never has beat on my grief-vexed ears than the steps of Achilles
Turning back to this Greece and the cry of his strength in its rising.
Zeus is awake in this man who his dreadful and world-slaying puissance
Gave in an hour of portentous birth to the single Achilles.
Taken today are Ilion's towers, a dead man is Priam.
Cross not the hero's will in his hour, Agamemnon Atrides,
Cross not the man whom the gods have chosen to work out their purpose
Then when he rises; his hour is his, though thine be all morrows.
First in the chambers of Paris' delight let us stable our horses,
Afterwards bale that is best shall be done persuading Achilles;
Doubt not the gods' decisions, awful, immutable, ruthless.
Flame shall lick Troy's towers and the limbs of her old men and infants.
O not today, not now remember the faults of the hero!
Follow him rather bravely and blindly as children their leader,
Guide your fate through the war-surge loud in the wake of his exploits,
Rise, O ye kings of the Greeks! leave debate for the voices of battle.
Peal forth the war-shout, pour forth the spear-sleet, surge towards Troya.
Ilion falls today; we shall turn in our ships to our children."
So Odysseus spoke and the Achaians heard him applauding;
Ever the pack by the voice of the mighty is seized and attracted!
Then from his seat Agamemnon arising his staff to the herald
Gave and around him arose the Kings of the west and its leaders.
Loud their assembly broke with a stern and martial rumour.

BOOK SEVEN

The Book of the Woman

So to the voice of their best they were bowed and obeyed undebating;
Men whose hearts were burning yet with implacable passion
Felt Odysseus' strength and rose up clay to his counsels.
King Agamemnon rose at his word, the wide-ruling monarch,
Rose at his word the Cretan and Locrian, Thebes and Epirus,
Nestor rose, the time-tired hoary chief of the Pylians.
Round Agamemnon the Atreid Europe surged in her chieftains
Forth from their tent on the shores of the Troad, splendid in armour,
Into the golden blaze of the sun and the race of the sea-winds.
Fierce and clear like a flame to the death-gods bright on its altar
Shone in their eyes the lust of blood and of earth and of pillage;
For in their hearts those fires replaced the passions of discord,
Forging a brittle peace by a common hatred and yearning.
Joyous they were of mood; for their hopes were already in Troya
Sating with massacre, plunder and rape and the groans of their foemen
Death and Hell in our mortal bosoms seated and shrouded;
There they have altars and seats in mankind in this fair-built temple
Made for purer gods; but we turn from tender luminous temptings,
Vainly the divine whispers seek us; the heights are rejected.[1]
Man to his earth drawn always prefers the murmurs of her promptings,
Man, devouring, devoured who is slayer and slain through the ages
Since by the beast he soars held and exceeds not that pedestal's measure.
They now followed close on the steps of the mighty Atrides,
Glued like the forest pack to the war-scarred coat of its leader,
Glued as the pack when wolves follow their prey like Doom that can turn no
Perfect forms and beautiful faces crowded the tent-door,
Brilliant eyes and fierce of souls that remembered the forest,
Wild beasts touched by thought and savages lusting for beauty,
Dire and fierce and formidable chieftains followed Atrides,
Merciless kings of merciless men and the founders of Europe,
Sackers of Troy and sires of the Parthenon, Athens and Caesar.
Here they had come to destroy the ancient perishing cultures;
For, it is said, from the savage we rose and were born to a wild beast.
So when the Eye supreme perceives that we rise up too swiftly,
Drawn towards height but fullness contemning, called by the azure,

[1] man rejects them.

Life when we fail in, poor in our base and forgetting our mother,
Back we are hurled to our roots; we recover our sap from the savage.
So were these sent by Zeus to destroy the old that was grandiose,
Such were those frames of old as the sons of Heaven might have chosen
Who in the dawn of eternity wedded the daughters of Nature,
Cultures touched by the morning star, vast, bold and poetic,
Titans' works and joys, but thrust down from their puissance and pleasure
Fainting now fell from the paces of Time or were left by his ages.
So were these born from Zeus to found the new that should flower
Lucid and slender and perfectly little as fit for this mortal
Ever who sinks back fatigued from immortality's stature;
Man, repelled by the gulfs within him and shrinking from vastness,
Form of the earth accepts and is glad of the lap of his mother.
Safe through the infinite seas could his soul self-piloted voyage
Chasing the dawns and the wondrous horizons, eternity's secrets
Drawn from her luminous gulfs! But he journeys rudderless, helmless,
Driven and led by the breath of God who meets him with tempest,
Hurls at him Night. The earth is safer, warmer its sunbeams;
Death and limits are known; so he clings to them hating the summons.
So might one dwell who has come to take joy in a fair-lighted prison;
Amorous grown of its marble walls and its noble adornments,
Lost to mightier cares and the spaces boundlessly calling,
Lust of the infinite skies he forgets and the kiss of the storm-winds,
So might one live who inured to his days of the field and the farm-yard
Shrinks from the grandiose mountain-tops; shut up in lanes and in hedges
Only his furrows he leads and only orders his gardens,
Only his fleeces weaves and drinks of the yield of his vine-rows:
Lost to his ear is the song of the waterfall, wind in the forests.
Now to our earth we are bent and we study the skies for its image.
That was Greece and its shining, that now is France and its keenness,
That still is Europe though by the Christ-touch troubled and tortured,
Seized by the East but clasping her chains and resisting our freedom.
Then was all founded, on Phrygia's coasts, round Ilion's ramparts,
Then by the spear of Achilles, then in the Trojan death-cry;
Bearers mute of a future world were those armoured Achaians.
So they arrived from Zeus, an army led by the death-god.
So one can see them still who has sight from the gods in the trance-sleep
Out from the tent emerging on Phrygia's coasts in their armour;
Those of the early seed Pelasgian slighter in stature,
Dark-haired, hyacinth-curled from the isles of the sea and the southron

Soft-eyed men with pitiless hearts; bright-haired the Achaians
Hordes of the Arctic Dawn who had fled from the ice and the death-blasts;
Children of conquerors lured to the coasts and the breezes and olives,
Noons of Mediterranean suns and the kiss of the south-wind
Mingled their brilliant force with the plastic warmth of the Hamite.
There they shall rule and their children long till Fate and the Dorian
Break down Hellene doors and trample stern through the passes.
Mixed in a glittering rout on the Ocean beaches one sees them,
Perfect and beautiful figures and fronts, not as now are we mortals
Marred and crushed by our burden long of thought and of labour;
Perfect were these as our race bright-imaged was first by the Thinker
Seen who in golden lustres shapes all the glories we tarnish,
Rich from the moulds of gods and unmarred in their splendour and
                   swiftness
Many and mighty they came o'er the beaches loud of the Aegean,
Roots of an infant world and the morning stars of this Europe,
Great Agamemnon's kingly port and the bright Menelaus,
Tall Idomeneus, Nestor, Odysseus Atlas-shouldered,
Helmeted Ajax, his chin of the beast and his eyes of the dreamer.
Over the sands they dispersed to their armies ranked by the Ocean.
  But from the Argive front Acirrous loosed by Tydides
Parted as hastens a shaft from the string and he sped on intently
Swift where the beaches were bare or threading the gaps of the nations;
Crossing Thebes and Epirus he passed through the Lemnian archers,
Ancient Gnossus' hosts and Meriones' leaderless legions.
Heedless of cry and of laughter and calling over the sea-sands
Swiftly he laboured, wind in his hair and the sea to him crying,
Straight he ran to the Myrmidon hosts and the tents of Achilles.
There he beheld at his tent-door the Phthian gleaming in armour,
Glittering-helmed with the sun that climbed now the cusp of Cronion,
Nobly tall, excelling humanity, planned like Apollo.
Proud at his side like a pillar upreared of snow or of marble,
Golden-haired, hard and white was the boy Neoptolemus, fire-eyed.
New were his feet to the Trojan sands from the ships and from Scyros:
Led to this latest of all his father's fights in the Troad
He for his earliest battle waited, the son of Achilles.
So in her mood had Fate brought them together, the son and the father,
Even as our souls travelling different paths have met in the ages
Each for its work and they cling for an hour to the names of affection,
Then Time's long waves bear them apart for new forms we shall know not,

So these two long severed had met in the shadow of parting.
Often he smote his hand on the thigh-piece for sound of the armour,
Bent his ear to the plains or restless moved like a war-horse
Curbed by his master's will, when he stands new-saddled for battle
Hearing the voice of the trumpets afar and pawing the meadows.
Over the sands Acirrous came to them running and toiling,
Known from far-off for he ran unhelmeted. High on the hero
Sunlike smiled the golden Achilles and into the tent-space
Seized by the hand and brought him and seated. "War-shaft of Troezen,
Whence was thy speed, Acirrous? Com'st thou, O friend, to my tent-side
Spurred by thy eager will or the trusted stern Diomedes?
Or from the Greeks like the voice still loud from a heart that is hollow?
What say the banded princes of Greece to the single Achilles?
Bringst thou flattery pale or an empty and futureless menace?"
But to the strength of Pelides the hero Acirrous answered:
"Response none send[1] the Greeks to thy high-voiced message and challenge;
Only their shout at thy side will reply when thou leapst into Troya.
So have their chieftains willed and the wisdom calm of Odysseus."
But with a haughty scorn made answer the high-crested Hellene:
"Wise is Odysseus, wise are the hearts of Achaia's chieftains.
Ilion's chiefs are enough for their strength and life is too brittle
Hurrying Fate to advance on the spear of the Phthian Achilles."
"Not from the Greeks have I sped to thy tents, their friendship or quarrel
Urged not my feet; but Tiryn's chieftain strong Diomedes
Sent me claiming a word long old that first by his war-car
Young Neoptolemus come from island Scyros should enter
Far-crashing into the fight that has lacked this shoot of Achilles,
Pressing in front with his father's strength in the playground of Ares,
Shouting his father's cry as he clashed to his earliest battle.
So let Achilles' son twin-carred fight close by Tydides,
Seal of the ancient friendship new-sworn twixt your sires in their boyhood
Then when they learned the spear to guide and strove in the wrestle."
So he spoke recalling other times and regretted
And to the Argive's word consented the strength of Pelides.
He on the shoulder white of his son with a gesture of parting
Laid his fateful hand and spoke from his prescient spirit:
"Pyrrhus, go. No mightier guide couldst thou hope into battle
Opening the foemen's ranks than the hero stern Diomedes.
Noble that rugged heart, thy father's friend and his father's.

[1] give / make

Journey through all wide Greece, seek her prytanies, schools and
                                                              palaestras,
Traverse Ocean's rocks and the cities that dream on his margin,
Phocian dales, Aetolia's cliffs and Arcady's pastures,
Never a second man wilt thou find, but alone Diomedes.
Pyrrhus, follow his counsels always losing thy father,
If in this battle I fall and Fate has denied to me Troya.
Pyrrhus, be like thy father in virtue, thou canst not excel him;
Noble be in peace, invincible, brave in the battle,
Stern and calm to thy foe, to the suppliant merciful. Mortal
Favour and wrath as thou walkst heed never, son of Achilles.
Always thy will and the right impose on thy friend and thy foeman.
Count not life nor death, defeat nor triumph, Pyrrhus.
Only thy soul regard and the gods in thy joy or thy labour."
Pyrrhus heard and erect with a stride that was rigid and stately
Forth with Acirrous went from his sire to the joy of the battle.
Little he heeded the word of death that the god in our bosom
Spoke from the lips of Achilles, but deemed at sunset returning,
Slaying Halamus, Paris or dangerous mighty Aeneas,
Proudly to lay at his father's feet the spoils of the foeman.
    But in his lair alone the godlike doomed Pelides
Turned to the door of his tent and was striding forth to the battle,
When from her inner chamber Briseis parting the curtain, —
Long had she stood there spying and waiting her lonely occasion, —
Came and caught and held his hand like a creeper detaining
Vainly a moment the deathward stride of the kings of the forest.
"Tarry awhile, Achilles; not yet have the war-horns clamoured.
Nor have the scouts streamed yet from Xanthus fierily running.
Lose a moment for her who has only thee under heaven.
Nay, had war sounded, thou yet wouldst squander that moment, Achilles,
Hearkening a woman's fears and the voice of a dream in the midnight.
Art thou not gentle, even as terrible, lion of Hellas?
Others have whispered the deeds of thy wrath; we have heard, but not seen it;
Marvelling much at their pallor and awe we have listened and wondered.
Never with thrall or slave-girl or captive saw I thee angered,
Hero, nor any humble heart ever trembled to near thee.
Pardoning rather our many faults and our failures in service
Lightly thou layest thy yoke on us, kind as the clasp of a lover
Sparing the weak as thou breakest the mighty, O godlike Achilles.
Only thy equals have felt all the dread of the death-god within thee;

We have presumed and played with the strength at which nations have
                                                              trembled.
Lo, thou hast leaned thy mane to the clutch of the boys and the maidens."
But to Briseis white-armed made answer smiling Achilles:
"Something surely thou needst, for thou flatterest long, O Briseis.
Tell me, O woman, thy fear or thy dream that my touch may dispel it,
White-armed net of bliss slipped down from the gold Aphrodite."
And to Achilles answered the captive white Briseis:
"Long have they vexed my soul in the tents of the Greeks, O Achilles,
Telling of Thetis thy mother who bore thee in caves of the Ocean
Clasped by a mortal and of her fear from the threats of the Ancients,
Weavers of doom who play with our hopes and smile at our passions
Painting Time with the red of our hearts on the web they have woven,
How on the Ocean's bosom she hid thee in vine-tangled Scyros
Clothed like a girl among girls with the daughters of King Lycomedes, —
Art thou not fairer than woman's beauty, yet great as Apollo? —
Fearing Paris' shafts and the anger of Delian Phoebus.
Now in the night has a vision three times besieged me from heaven.
Over the sea in my dream an argent bow was extended;
Nearing I saw a terror august over moonlit waters,
Cloud and a fear and a face that was young and lovely and hostile.
Then three times I heard arise in the grandiose silence, —
Still was the sky and still was the land and still were the waters, —
Echoing a mighty voice, 'Take back, O King, what thou gavest;
Strength, take thy strong man, sea, take thy wave, till the warfare eternal
Need him again to thunder through Asia's plains to the Ganges.'
That fell silent, but nearer the beautiful Terror approached me,
Clang I heard of the argent bow and I gazed on Apollo.
Shrilly I cried, for 'twas[1] thee that the shaft of the heavens had yearned for,
Thee that it sought like a wild thing in anger straight at its quarry,
Quivering into thy heel. I awoke and found myself trembling,
Held thee safe in my arms, yet hardly believed that thou livest.
Lo, in the night came this dream; on the morn thou arisest for battle."
But to Briseis white-armed made answer the golden Achilles:
"This was a dream indeed, O princess, daughter of Brises!
Will it restrain Achilles from fight, the lion from preying?
Come, thou hast heard of my prowess and knowest what man is Achilles.
Deemst thou so near my end? or does Polyxena vex thee,
Jealousy shaping thy dreams to frighten me back from her capture?"

[1] it was

Passionate, vexed Briseis, smiting his arm with her fingers,
Yet with a smile half-pleased made answer to mighty Achilles:
"Thinkst thou I fear thee at all? I am brave and will chide thee and threaten.
See that thou recklessly throw not, Achilles, thy life into battle
Hurting this body, my world, nor venture sole midst thy foemen,
Leaving thy shielders behind as oft thou art wont in thy war-rage
Lured by thy tempting gods who seek their advantage to slay thee,
Fighting divinely, careless of all but thy spear and thy foeman.
Cover thy limbs with thy shield, speed slowly restraining thy coursers.
Dost thou not know all the terrible void and cold desolation
Once again my life must become if I lose thee, Achilles?
Twice then thus wilt thou smite me, O hero, a desolate woman?
I will not stay behind on an earth that is empty and kingless.
Into the grave I will leap, through the fire I will burn, I will follow
Down into Hades' depths or wherever thy footsteps go clanging,
Hunting thee always, — didst thou not seize me here for thy pleasure? —
Stronger there by my love as thou than I here, O Achilles.
Thou shalt not dally alone with Polyxena safe in the shadows."
But to Briseis answered the hero, mighty Pelides,
Holding her delicate hands like gathered flowers in his bosom,
Pressing her passionate mouth like a rose that trembles with beauty:
"There then follow me even as I would have drawn thee, O woman,
Voice that chimes with my soul and hands that are eager for service,
Beautiful spoil beloved of my foemen, perfect Briseis.
But for the dreams that come to us mortals sleeping or waking,
Shadows are these from our souls and who shall discern what they figure?
Fears from the heart speak voiced like Zeus, take shape as Apollo.
But were they truer than Delphi's cavern voice or Dodona's
Moan that seems wind in his oaks immemorable, how should they alter
Fate that the stern gods have planned from the first when the earth was
                                                              unfashioned,
Shapeless the gyre of the sun? For dream or for oracle adverse
Why should man swerve from the path of his feet? The gods have invented
Only one way for a man through the world, O my slave-girl Briseis,
Valiant to be and noble and truthful and just to the humble.
Only one way for a woman, to love and serve and be faithful.
This observe, thy task in thy destiny noble or fallen;
Time and result are the gods'; with these things be not thou troubled."
So he spoke and kissed her lips and released her and parted.
Out from the tent he strode and into his chariot leaping

Seized the reins and shouted his cry and drove with a far-borne
Sound of wheels mid the clamour of hooves and neigh of the war-steeds
Swift through the line of the tents and forth from the heart of the leaguer.
Over the causeway Troyward thundered the wheels of Achilles.
After him crashing loud with a fierce and resonant rumour
Chieftains impetuous prone to the mellay and swift at the war-cry
Came, who long held from the lust of the spear and the joy of the war-din
Rushed over earth like hawks released through the air; a shouting
Limitless rolled behind, for nations followed each war-cry.
Lords renowned of the northern hills and the plains and the coast-lands,
Many a Dorian, many a Phthian, many a Hellene,
Names now lost to the ear though then reputed immortal!
Night has swallowed them, Zeus has devoured the light of his children;
Drawn are they back to his bosom vast whence they came in their fierceness
Thinking to conquer the earth and dominate Time and his ages.
Nor on their left less thick came numerous even as the sea-sands
Forth from the line of the leaguer that skirted the far-sounding waters,
Ranked behind Tydeus' son and the Spartan, bright Menelaus,
Ithaca's chief and Epeus, Idomeneus lord of the Cretans,
Acamos, Nestor, Neleus' son, and the brave Ephialtus,
Prothous, Meges, Leitus the bold and the king Prothoënor,
Wise Alceste's son and the Lemnian, stern Philoctetes,
These and unnumbered warlike captains marching the Argives.
Last in his spacious car drove shaping the tread of his armies,
Even as a shepherd who follows his flock to the green of the pastures,
Atreus' far-famed son, the monarch great Agamemnon.
They on the plain moved out and gazing far over the pastures
Saw behind Xanthus rolling with dust like a cloud full of thunder,
Ominous, steadily nearing, shouting their war-cry the Trojans.

BOOK EIGHT

The Book of the Gods

So on the earth the seed that was sown of the centuries ripened;
Europe and Asia, met on their borders, clashed in the Troad.
All over earth men wept and bled and laboured, world-wide
Sowing Fate with their deeds and had other fruit than they hoped for.
Out of desires and their passionate griefs and fleeting enjoyments
Weaving a tapestry fit for the gods to admire, who in silence
Joy, by the cloud and the sunbeam veiled, and men know not their movers.
They in the glens of Olympus, they by the waters of Ida
Or in their temples worshipped in vain or with heart-strings of mortals
Sated their vast desire and enjoying the world and each other
Sported free and unscourged; for the earth was their prey and their play-
                                                                  ground.
But from his luminous deep domain, from his estate of azure
Zeus looked forth; he beheld the earth in its flowering greenness
Spread like an emerald dream that the eyes have enthroned in the sunlight,
Heard the symphonies old of the ocean recalling the ages
Lost and dead from its marches salt and unharvested furrows,
Felt in the pregnant hour the unborn hearts of the future.
Troubled kingdoms of men he beheld, the hind in the furrow,
Lords of the glebe and the serf subdued to the yoke of his fortunes,
Slave-girls tending the fire and herdsmen driving the cattle,
Artisans labouring long for a little hire in men's cities,
Labour long and the meagre reward for a toil that is priceless.
Kings in their seats august or marching swift with their armies
Founded ruthlessly brittle empires. Merchant and toiler
Patiently heaped up our transient wealth like the ants in their hillock.
And to preserve it all, to protect this dust that must perish,
Hurting the eternal soul and maiming heaven for some metal
Judges condemned their brothers to chains and to death and to torment,
Criminals scourgers of crime, — for so are these ant-heaps founded, —
Punishing sin by a worse affront to our crucified natures.
All the uncertainty, all the mistaking, all the delusion
Naked were to his gaze; in the moonlit orchards there wandered
Lovers dreaming of love that endures — till the moment of treason;
Helped by the anxious joy of their kindred supported their anguish
Women with travail racked for the child who shall rack them with sorrow.

Hopes that were confident, fates that sprang dire from the seed of a moment,
Yearning that claimed all time for its date and all life for its fuel,
All that we wonder at gazing back when the passion has fallen,
Labour blind and vain expense and sacrifice wasted,
These he beheld with a heart unshaken; to each side he studied
Seas of confused attempt and the strife and the din and the crying.
All things he pierced in us gazing down with his eyelids immortal,
Lids on which sleep dare not settle, the Father of men on his creatures;
Nor by the cloud and the mist was obscured which baffles our eyeballs,
But he distinguished our source and saw to the end of our labour.
He in the animal racked knew the god that is slowly delivered;
Therefore his heart rejoiced. Not alone the mind in its trouble
God beholds, but the spirit behind that has joy of the torture.
Might not our human gaze on the smoke of a furnace, the burning
Red, intolerable, anguish of ore that is fused in the hell-heat,
Shrink and yearn for coolness and peace and condemn all the labour?
Rather look to the purity coming, the steel in its beauty,
Rather rejoice with the master who stands in his gladness accepting
Heat of the glorious god and the fruitful pain of the iron.
Last the eternal gaze was fixed on Troy and the armies
Marching swift to the shock. It beheld the might of Achilles
Helmed and armed, knew all the craft in the brain of Odysseus,
Saw Deiphobus stern in his car and the fates of Aeneas,
Greece of her heroes empty, Troy enringed by her slayers,
Paris a setting star and the beauty of Penthesilea.
These things he saw delighted; the heart that contains all our ages
Blessed our toil and grew full of its fruits, as the Artist eternal
Watched his vehement drama staged twixt the sea and the mountains,
Phrased in the clamour and glitter of arms and closed by the firebrand,
Act itself out in the blood and in passions fierce on the Troad.
Yet as a father his children, who sits in the peace of his study
Hearing the noise of his brood and pleased with their play and their quarrels,
So he beheld our mortal race. Then, turned from the armies,
Into his mind he gazed where Time is reflected and, conscient,
Knew the iron knot of our human fates in their warfare.
Calm he arose and left our earth for his limitless kingdoms.
    Far from this lower blue and high in the death-scorning spaces
Lifted above mortal mind where Time and Space are but figures
Lightly imagined by Thought divine in her luminous stillness,
Zeus has his palace high and there he has stabled his war-car.

Thence he descends to our mortal realms; where the heights of our mountains
Meet with the divine air, he touches and enters our regions.
Now he ascended back to his natural realms and their rapture,
There where all life is bliss and each feeling an ecstasy mastered.
Thence his eagle Thought with its flashing pinions extended
Winged through the world to the gods, and they came at the call, they
                                                                   ascended
Up from their play and their calm and their works through the infinite azure.
Some from our mortal domains in grove or by far-flowing river
Cool from the winds of the earth or quivering with perishable fragrance
Came, or our laughter they bore and the song of the sea in their paces.
Some from the heavens above us arrived, our vital dominions
Whence we draw breath; for there all things have life, the stone like the ilex,
Clay of those realms like the children of men and the brood of the giants.
There Enceladus groans oppressed and draws strength from his anguish
Under a living Aetna and flames that have joy of his entrails.
Fiercely he groans and rejoices expecting the end of his foemen
Hastened by every pang and counts long Time by his writhings.
There in the champaigns unending battle the gods and the giants,
There in eternal groves the lovers have pleasure for ever,
There are the faery climes and there are the wonderful pastures.
Some from a marvellous Paradise hundred-realmed in its musings
Million-ecstasied, climbed like flames that in silence aspire
Windless, erect in a motionless dream, yet ascending for ever.
All grew aware of the will divine and grew near[1] to their Father.
     Grandiose, calm in her gait, imperious, awing the regions,
Hera came in her pride, the spouse of Zeus and his sister.
As at her birth from the foam of the spaces white Aphrodite
Rose in the cloud of her golden hair like the moon in its halo.
Aegis-bearing Athene, shielded and helmeted, answered
Rushing the call and the heavens thrilled with the joy of her footsteps
Dumbly repeating her name, as insulted and trampled by beauty
Thrill might the soul of a lover and cry out the name of its tyrant.
Others there were as mighty; for Artemis, archeress ancient,
Came on her sandals lightning-tasselled. Up the vast incline
Shaking the world with the force of his advent thundered Poseidon;
Space grew full of his stride and his cry. Immortal Apollo
Shone and his silver clang was heard with alarm in our kingdoms.
Ares' impetuous eyes looked forth from a cloud-drift of splendour;

[1] The original which seems scratched out in favour of "grew near" was "were drawn".

Themis' steps appeared and Ananke, the mystic Erinnys;
Nor was Hephaestus' flaming strength from his father divided.
Even the ancient Dis to arrive dim-featured, eternal,
Seemed; but his rays are the shades and his voice is the call of the silence.
    Into the courts divine they crowded, radiant, burning,
Perfect in utter grace and light. The joy of their spirits
Calls to eternal Time and the glories of Space are his answer:
Thence were these bright worlds born and persist by the throb of their
                                                                  heart-beats.
Not in the forms that mortals have seen when assisted they scatter
Mists of this earthly dust from their eyes in their moments of greatness
Shone those unaging Powers; nor as in our centuries radiant
Mortal-seeming bodies they wore when they mixed with our nations.
Then the long youth of the world had not faded still out of our natures,
Flowers and the sunlight were felt and the earth was glad like a mother.
Then for a human delight they were masked in this denser vesture
Earth desires for her bliss, — thin veils, for the god through them glimmered.
Quick were men's days with the throng of the brilliant presences near them:
Gods from the wood and the valley, gods from the obvious wayside,
Gods on the secret hills leaped out from their light on the mortal.
Oft in the haunt and the grove they met with our kind and their touches
Seized and subjected our clay to the greatness of passions supernal,
Grasping the earthly virgin and forcing heaven on this death-dust.
Glorifying human beauty Apollo roamed in our regions
Clymene when he pursued or yearned in vain for Marpessa;
Glorifying earth with a human-seeming face of the beauty
Brought from her heavenly climes Aphrodite mixed with Anchises.
Glimpsed in the wilds were the Satyrs, seen in the woodlands the Graces,
Dryad and Naiad in river and forest, Oreads haunting
Glens and the mountain-glades where they played with the manes of our
                                                                                    lions
Glimmered on death-claimed eyes; for the gods then were near us and
                                                                               clasped us,
Heaven leaned down in love with our clay and yearned to its transience.
But we have coarsened in heart and in mood; we have turned in our natures
Nearer our poorer kindred; leaned to the ant and the ferret.
Sight we have darkened with sense and power we have stifled with labour,
Likened in mood to the things we gaze at and are in our vestures:
Therefore we toil unhelped; we are left to our weakness and blindness.
Not in those veils now they rose to their skies, but like loose-fitting mantles

Dropped in the vestibules huge of their vigorous realms that besiege us
All that reminded of earth; then clothed with raiment of swiftness
Straight they went quivering up in a glory like fire or the storm-blast.
Even those natural vestures of puissance they leave when they enter
Mind's more subtle fields and agree with its limitless regions
Peopled by creatures of bliss and forms more true than earth's shadows,
Mind that pure from this density, throned in her splendours immortal
Looks up at Light and suffers bliss from ineffable kingdoms
Where beyond Mind and its rays is the gleam of a glory supernal:
There our sun cannot shine and our moon has no place for her lustres,
There our lightnings flash not, nor fire of these spaces is suffered.
They with bodies impalpable here to our touch and our seeing,
But for a higher delight, to a brighter sense, with more sweetness
Palpable there and visible, thrilled with a lordlier joyance,
Came to the courts of Zeus and his heavens sang to their footsteps.
Harmonies flowed through the blissful coils of the kingdoms of rapture.
Then by his mighty equals surrounded the Thunderer regnant
Veiled his thought in sound that was heard in their souls as they listened.
Veiled are the high gods always lest there should dawn on the mortal
Light too great from the skies and men to their destiny clear-eyed
Walk unsustained like the gods; then Night and Dawn were defeated
And of their masks the deities robbed would be slaves to their subjects.
    "Children of Immortality, gods who are joyous for ever,
Rapture is ours and eternity measures our lives by his aeons.
For we desireless toil who have joy in the fall as the triumph,
Knowledge eternal possessing we work for an end that is destined
Long already beyond by the Will of which Time is the courser.
Therefore death cannot alter our lives nor pain our enjoyment.
But in the world of mortals twilight is lord of its creatures.
Nothing they perfectly see, but all things seek and imagine,
Out of the clod who have come and would climb from their mire to our
                                                            heavens
Blindly mistaking the throb of their mortal desires for our guidance.
Yet are the heavenly seats not easy even for the chosen:
Rough and remote is that path; that ascent is too hard for the death-bound.
Hard are God's terms and few can meet them of men who are mortal.
Mind resists; their breath is a clog; by their tools they are hampered.
How shall they win in their earth to our skies who are clay and a life-wind,
But that their hearts we invade? Our shocks on their lives come incessant,
Ease discourage and penetrate coarseness; sternness celestial

Forces their souls towards the skies and their bodies by anguish are sifted.
We in the mortal wake an immortal strength by our tortures
And by the flame of our lightnings choose out the vessels of godhead.
This is the nature of earth that to blows she responds and by scourgings
Travails excited; pain is the bed of her blossoms of pleasure.
Earth that was wakened by pain to life and by hunger to thinking
Left to her joys rests inert and content with her gains and her station.
But for the unbearable whips of the gods back soon to her matter
She would go glad and the goal would be missed and the aeons be wasted.
But for the god in their breasts unsatisfied, but for his spurrings
Soon would the hero turn beast and the sage reel back to the savage;
Man from his difficult heights would recoil and be mud in the earth-mud.
This by pain we prevent; we compel his feet to the journey.
But in their minds to impression made subject, by forms of things captured
Blind is the thought and presumptuous the hope and they swerve from our
                                                                    goading;
Blinded are human hearts by desire and fear and possession,
Darkened is knowledge on earth by hope the helper of mortals.
    Now too from earth and her children voices of anger and weeping
Beat at our thrones; 'tis the grief and the wrath of fate-stricken creatures,
Mortals struggling with destiny, hearts that are slaves to their sorrow.
We unmoved by the cry will fulfil our unvarying purpose.
Troy shall fall at last and the ancient ages shall perish.
You who are lovers of Ilion turn from the moans of her people,
Chase from your hearts their prayers, blow back from your nostrils the
                                                                    incense.
Let not one nation resist by its glory the good of the ages.
Twilight thickens over man and he moves to his winter of darkness.
Troy that displaced with her force and her arms the luminous ancients,
Sinks in her turn by the ruder strength of the half-savage Achaians.
They to the Hellene shall yield and the Hellene fall by the Roman.
Rome too shall not endure, but by strengths ill-shaped shall be broken,
Nations formed in the ice and mist, confused and crude-hearted.
So shall the darker and ruder always prevail o'er the brilliant
Till in its turn to a ruder and darker it falls and is shattered.
So shall mankind make speed to destroy what 'twas mighty creating.
Ever since knowledge failed and the ancient ecstasy slackened,
Light has been helper to death and darkness increases the victor.
So shall it last till the fallen ages return to their greatness.
For if the twilight be helped not, night o'er the world cannot darken;

Night forbidden how shall a greater dawn be effected?
Gods of the light who know and resist that the doomed may have succour,
Always then shall desire and passion strive with Ananke?
Conquer the cry of your heart-strings that man too may conquer his sorrow
Stilled in his yearnings. Cease, O ye gods, from the joy of rebellion.
Open the eye of the soul, admit the voice of the Silence."
    So in the courts of Heaven august the Thunderer puissant
Spoke to his sons in their souls and they heard him, mighty in silence.[1]
Then to her brother divine the white-armed passionless Hera:
"Zeus, we remember, thy sons forget, Apollo and Ares."
"Hera, queen of the heavens, they forget not, but choose to be mindless.
This is the greatness of gods that they know and can put back the knowledge;
Doing the work they have chosen they turn not for fruit nor for failure.
Griefless they walk to their goal and strain not their eyes towards the ending.
Light that they have they can lose with a smile, not as souls in the darkness
Clutch at every beam and mistake their one ray for all splendour.
All things are by Time and the Will eternal that moves us.
And for each birth its hour is set in the night or the dawning.
There is an hour for knowledge, an hour to forget and to labour."
    Great Cronion ceased and high in the heavenly silence
Rose in their midst the voice of the loud impetuous Ares
Sounding far in the luminous fields of his soul as with thunder.
"Father, we know and we have not forgotten. This is our godhead,
Still to strive and never to yield to the evil that conquers.
I will not dwell with the Greeks nor aid them save forced by Ananke
And because lives of the great and the blood of the strong are my portion.
This too thou knowest, our nature enjoys in mankind its fulfilment.
War is my nature and greatness and hardness, the necks of the vanquished;
Force is my soul and strength is my bosom; I shout in the battle
Breaking cities like toys and the nations are playthings of Ares:
Hither and thither I shove them and throw down or range on my table.
Constancy most I love, nobility, virtue and courage;
Fugitive hearts I abhor and the nature fickle as sea-foam.
Now if the ancient spirit of Titan battle is over, —
Tros fights no more on the earth, nor now Heracles tramples and struggles,
Bane of the hydra or slaying the Centaurs o'er Pelion driven, —
Now if the earth no more must be shaken by Titan horse-hooves,
Since to a pettier framework all things are fitted consenting,
Yet will I dwell not in Greece nor favour the nurslings of Pallas.

[1] "Silence" was cancelled in the MS. but remained unsubstituted.

I will await the sons of my loins and the teats of the she-wolf,
Consuls browed like the cliffs and plebeians stern of the wolf-brood,
Senates of kings and armies of granite that grow by disaster;
Such be the nation august that is fit for the favour of Ares!
They shall fulfil me and honour my mother, imperial Hera.
Then with an iron march they shall move to their world-wide dominion,
Through the long centuries rule and at last because earth is impatient,
Slowly with haughtiness perish compelled by mortality's transience
Leaving a Roman memory stamped on the ages of weakness."
But to his son far-sounding the Father high of the Immortals:
"So let it be since such is the will in thee, mightiest Ares;
Thou shalt till sunset prevail, O war-god, fighting for Troya."
So he decreed and the soul of the Warrior sternly consented.
He from his seats arose and down on the summits of Ida
Flaming through Space in his cloud in a headlong glory descended,
Prone like a thunderbolt flaming down from the hand of the Father.
Thence in his chariot drawn by living fire and by swiftness,
Thundered down to earth's plains the mighty impetuous Ares.
Far where Deiphobus stern was labouring stark and outnumbered
Smiting the Achaian myriads back on the right of the carnage,
Over the hosts in his car he stood and darkened the Argives.

    But in the courts divine the Thunderer spoke to his children:
"Ares resisting a present Fate for the hope of the future
Gods has gone forth from us. Choose thou thy paths, O my daughter,
More than thy brother assailed by the night that darkens o'er creatures.
Choose the silence in heaven or choose the struggle mid mortals,
Golden joy of the worlds, O thou roseate white Aphrodite."
Then with her starry eyes and bosom of bliss from the Immortals
Glowing and rosy-limbed cried the wonderful white Aphrodite,
Drawing her fingers like flowers through the flowing gold of her tresses,
Calm, discontented, her perfect mouth a rose of resistance
Chidingly budded 'gainst Fate, a charm to their senses enamoured:
"Well do I know thou hast given my world to Hera and Pallas.
What though my temples shall stand in Paphos and island Cythera
And though the Greek be a priest for my thoughts and a lyre for my singing,
Beauty pursuing and light through the figures of grace and of rhythm, —
Forms shall he mould for men's eyes that the earth has forgotten and mourns
                                                            for,
Mould even the workings of Pallas to commune with Paphia's sweetness,
Mould Hephaestus' craft in the gaze of the gold Aphrodite, —

Only my form he pursues that I wear for a mortal enchantment,
He to whom now thou givest the world, the Ionian, the Hellene,
But for my might is unfit which Babylon worshipped and Sidon
Palely received from the past in images faint of the gladness
Once that was known by the children of men when the thrill of their
                                                                    members
Was but the immortal joy of the spirit overflowing in Nature
Wine-cups of God's desire; but their clay from my natural greatness
Falters betrayed to pain, their delight they have turned into ashes.
Nor to my peaks shall he rise and the perfect fruit of my promptings,
There where the senses swoon but the heart is delivered by rapture:
Never my touch can cling to his soul nor reply from his heart-strings.
Once could my godhead surprise all the stars with the seas of its rapture;
Once the world in its orbit danced to a marvellous rhythm.
Men in their limits, gods in their amplitudes answered my calling;
Life was moved by a chant of delight that sang[1] from the spaces
Sung from the Soul of the Vast, His[2] ecstasy clasping His[2] creatures.
Sweetly agreed my fire with their soil and their hearts were as altars.
Pure were its crests; 'twas not dulled with earth, 'twas not lost in the hazes.
Then when the sons of earth and the daughters of heaven together
Met on lone mountain peaks or, linked on wild beach and green meadow,
Twining embraced. For I danced on Taygetus' peaks and o'er Ida
Naked and loosing my golden hair like a nimbus of glory
O'er a deep-ecstasied earth that was drunk with my roses and whiteness.
There was no shrinking nor veil in our old Saturnian kingdoms,
Equal were heaven and earth, twin gods on the lap of Dione.
Now shall my waning greatness perish and pass out of Nature.
For though the Romans, my children, shall grasp at the strength of their
                                                                    mother,
They shall not hold the god, but lose in unsatisfied orgies
Yet what the earth has kept of my joy, my glory, my puissance,
Who shall but drink for a troubled hour in the dusk of the sunset
Dregs of my wine Pandemian missing the Uranian sweetness.
So shall the night descend on the greatness and rapture of living;
Creeds that refuse shall persuade the world to revolt from its mother.
Pallas' adorers shall loathe me and Hera's scorn me for lowness;

[1] There is some uncertainty about this word in relation to the next line which now begins with "Sung" but originally did so with "Out". Originally, "sprang" stood instead of "sang" in the first line.
[2] Its

Beauty shall pass from men's work and delight from their play and their
                                                                  labour;
Earth restored to the Cyclops shall shrink from the gold Aphrodite.
So shall I live diminished, owned but by beasts in the forest,
Birds of the air and the gods in their heavens, but disgraced in the mortal."
Then to the discontented rosy-mouthed Aphrodite
Zeus replied, the Father divine: "O goddess Astarte,
What are these thoughts thou hast suffered to wing from thy rose-mouth
                                                                immortal?
Bees that sting and delight are the words from thy lips, Cytherea.
Art thou not womb of the world and from thee are the throngings of
                                                                creatures?
And didst thou cease the worlds too would cease and the aeons be ended.
Suffer my Greeks; accept who accept thee, O gold Dionaean.
They in the works of their craft and their dreams shall enthrone thee for
                                                                    ever,
Building thee temples in Paphos and Eryx and island Cythera,
Building the fane more enduring and bright of thy golden ideal.
Even if natures of men could renounce thee and God do without thee,
Rose of love and sea of delight, O my child Aphrodite
Still wouldst thou live in the worship they gave thee protected from fading,
Splendidly statured and shrined in men's works and men's thoughts,
                                                                Cytherea."
Pleased and blushing with bliss of her praise and the thought of her
                                                                empire
Answered, as cries a harp in heaven, the gold Aphrodite:
"Father, I know and I spoke but to hear from another my praises.
I am the womb of the world and the cause of this teeming of creatures,
And if discouraged I ceased, God's world would lose heart and perish.
How will you do then without me your works of wisdom and greatness,
Hera, queen of heaven, and thou, O my sister Athene?
Yes, I shall reign and endure though the pride of my workings be conquered.
What though no second Helen find a second Paris,
Lost though the glories of form to the earth, though their confident gladness
Pass from a race misled and forgetting the sap that it sprang from,
They are eternal in man in the worship of beauty and rapture.
Ever while earth is embraced by the sun and hot with his kisses
And while a Will supernal works through the passions of Nature,
Me shall men seek with my light or their darkness, sweetly or crudely,
Cold on the ice of the north or warm with the heats of the southland,

Slowly enduring my touch or with violence rapidly burning.
I am the sweetness of living, I am the touch of the Master.
Love shall die bound to my stake like a victim adorned as for bridal,
Life shall be bathed in my flames and be purified gold or be ashes.
I, Aphrodite, shall move the world for ever and ever.
Yet now since most to me, Father of all, the ages arriving,
Hostile, rebuke my heart and turn from my joy and my sweetness,
I will resist and not yield, nor care what I do, so I conquer.
Often I curbed my mood for your sakes and was gracious and kindly,
Often I lay at Hera's feet and obeyed her commandments
Tranquil and proud or o'ercome by a honeyed and ancient compulsion
Fawned on thy pureness and served thy behests, O my sister Pallas.
Deep was the love that united us, happy the wrestle and clasping;
Love divided, love united, love was our mover.[1]
But since you now overbear and would scourge me and chain and control
                                                                    me,
War I declare on you all, O my Father and brothers and sisters.
Henceforth I do my will as the joy in me prompts or the anger.
Ranging the earth with my beauty and passion and golden enjoyments
All whom I can, I will bind; I will drive at the bliss of my workings,
Whether men's hearts are seized by the joy or seized by the torture.
Most will I plague your men, your worshippers and in my malice
Break up your works with confusion divine, O my mother and sister;
Then shall you fume and resist and be helpless and pine with my torments.
Yet will I never relent but always be sweet and malignant,
Cruel and tyrannous, hurtful and subtle, a charm and a torture.
Thou too, O father Zeus, shalt always be vexed with my doings;
Called in each moment to judge thou shalt chafe at our cry and our quarrels,
Often grope for thy thunderbolt, often frown magisterial
Joining in vain thy awful brows o'er thy turbulent children.
Yet in thy wrath recall my might and my wickedness, Father;
Hurt me not then too much lest the world and thyself too should suffer.
Save, O my Father, life and grace and the charm of the senses;
Love preserve lest the heart of the world grow dulled and forsaken."
Smiling her smile immortal of love and of mirth and of malice
White Aphrodite arose in her loveliness armed for the conflict.
Golden and careless and joyous she went like a wild bird that winging
Flits from bough to bough and resumes its chant interrupted.
Love where her fair feet trod bloomed up like a flower from the spaces;

[1] the master.

Mad round her touches billowed incessantly laughter and rapture.[1]
Rich as a summer fruit and fresh as Spring's blossoms her body
Gleaming and blushing, veiled and bare and with ecstasy smiting
Burned out rosy and white through her happy ambrosial raiment,
Golden-tressed and a charm, her bosom a fragrance and peril.
So was she framed to the gaze as she came from the seats of the Mighty.
So embodied she visits the hearts of men and their dwellings
And in her breathing tenement laughs at the eyes that can see her.
Swift-footed down to the Troad she hastened thrilling the earth-gods.
There with ambrosial secrecy veiled, admiring the heroes
Strong and beautiful, might of the warring and glory of armour,
Over her son Aeneas she stood, his guard in the battle.
    But in the courts divine the Thunderer spoke mid his children:
"Thou for a day and a night and another day and a nightfall,
White Aphrodite, prevail; o'er thee too the night is extended.
She has gone forth who made men like gods in their glory and gladness.
Now in the darkness coming all beauty must wane or be tarnished;
Joy shall fade and mighty Love grow fickle and fretful;
Even as a child that is scared in the night, he shall shake in his chambers.
Yet shall a portion be kept for these, Ares and white Aphrodite.
Thou whom already thy Pythoness bears not, torn by thy advent,
Caverned already who sittest in Delphi knowing thy future,
What wilt thou do with the veil and the night, O burning Apollo?"
Then from the orb of his glory unbearable save to immortals
Bright and austere replied the beautiful mystic Apollo:
"Zeus, I know that I fade; already the night is around me.
Dusk she extends her reign and obscures my lightnings with error.
Therefore my prophets mislead men's hearts to the ruin appointed,
Therefore Cassandra cries in vain to her sire and her brothers.
All I endure I foresee and the strength in me waits for its coming;
All I foresee I approve; for I know what is willed, O Cronion.
Yet is the fierce strength wroth in my breast at the need of approval
And for the human race fierce pity works in my bosom;
Wroth is my splendid heart with the cowering knowledge of mortals,
Wroth are my burning eyes with the purblind vision of reason.
I will go forth from your seats and descend to the night among mortals
There to guard the flame and the mystery; vast in my moments

[1] *Alternatives to this line and the preceding:*
  Thrilled with her feet was the bosom of Space, for her amorous motion
  Floated a flower on the wave of her bliss or swayed like the lightning.

Rare and sublime to sound like a sea against Time and its limits,
Cry like a spirit in pain in the hearts of the priest and the poet,
Cry against limits set and disorder sanities bounded.
Jealous for truth to the end my might shall prevail and for ever
Shatter the moulds that men make to imprison their limitless spirits.
Dire, overpowering the brain I shall speak out my oracles splendid.
Then in their ages of barren light or lucidity fruitful
Whenso the clear gods think they have conquered earth and its mortals,
Hidden God from all eyes, they shall wake from their dream and recoiling
Still they shall find in their paths the fallen and darkened Apollo."
So he spoke, repressing his dreadful might in his bosom,
And from their high seats passed, his soul august and resplendent
Drawn to the anguish of men and the fierce terrestrial labour.
Down he dropped with a roar of light invading the regions,
And in his fierce and burning spirit intense and uplifted
Sure of his luminous truth and careless for weakness of mortals
Flaming oppressed the earth with his dire intolerant beauty.
Over the summits descending that slept in the silence of heaven,
He through the spaces angrily drew towards the tramp and the shouting
Over the speeding of Xanthus and over the pastures of Troya.
Clang of his argent bow was the wrath restrained of the mighty,
Stern was his pace like Fate's; so he came to the warfare of mortals
And behind Paris strong and inactive waited God's moment
Knowing what should arrive, nor disturbed like men by their hopings.
But in the courts of Heaven Zeus to his brother immortal
Turned like a menaced king on his counsellor smiling augustly:
"Seest thou, Poseidon, this sign that great gods revolting have left us,
Follow their hearts and strive with Ananke? Yet though they struggle,
Thou and I will do our will with the world, O earth-shaker."
    Answered to Zeus the besieger of earth, the voice of the waters:
"This is our strength and our right, for we are the kings and the masters.
Too much pity has been and yielding of Heaven to mortals.
I will go down with my chariot drawn by my thunder-maned coursers
Into the battle and thrust down Troy with my hand to the silence,
Even though she cling round the snowy knees of our child Aphrodite
Or with Apollo's sun take refuge from Night and her shadows.
I will not pity her pain, who am ruthless even as my surges.
Brother, thou knowest, O Zeus, that I am a king and a trader;
For on my paths I receive earth's skill and her merchandise gather,
Traffic richly in pearls and bear the swift ships in my bosom.

Blue are my waves and they call men's hearts to wealth and adventure.
Lured by[1] the shifting surges they launch their delight and their treasures
Trusting the toil of years to the perilous moments of Ocean.
Huge man's soul[2] in its petty frame goes wrestling with Nature
Over her vasts and his fragile ships between my horizons
Buffeting death in his solitudes labour through swell and through storm-blast
Bound for each land with her sons and watched for by eyes in each haven.
I from Tyre up to Gades trace on my billows their trade-routes
And on my vast and spuming Atlantic suffer their rudders.
Carthage and Greece are my children, the marts of the world are my
                                                            term-posts.
Who then deserves the earth if not he who enriches and fosters?
But thou hast favoured thy sons, O Zeus; O Hera, earth's sceptres
Still were denied me and kept for strong Ares and brilliant Apollo.
Now all your will shall be done, so you give me the earth for my nations.
Gold shall make men like gods and bind their thoughts into oneness;
Peace I will build with gold and heaven with the pearls of my caverns."
Smiling replied to his brother's craft the mighty Cronion:
"Lord of the boundless seas, Poseidon, soul of the surges,
Well thou knowest that earth shall be seized as a booth for the trader.
Rome nor Greece nor France can drive back Carthage for ever.
Always each birth of the silence attaining the field and the movement
Takes from Time its reign; for it came for its throne and its godhead.
So too shall Mammon take and his sons their hour from the ages.
Yet is the flame and the dust last end of the silk and the iron,
And at their end the king and the prophet shall govern the nations.
Even as Troy, so shall Babylon flame up to heaven for the spoiler
Wailed by the merchant afar as he sees the red glow from the Ocean."
Up from the seats of the Mighty the Earth-shaker rose; his raiment
Round him purple and dominant rippled[3] and murmured and whispered,
Whispered of argosies sunk and the pearls and the Nereids playing,
Murmured of azure solitudes, sounded of storm and the death-wail.
Even as the march of his waters so was the pace of the sea-god
Flowing on endless through Time; with the glittering symbol[4] of empire
Crowned were his fatal brows; in his grasp was the wrath of the trident,
Tripled forces, life-shattering, brutal, imperial, sombre.
Resonant, surging, vast in the pomp of his clamorous greatness
Proud and victorious he came to his home in the far-spuming waters.
Even as a soul from the heights of thought plunges back into living,

[1] on   [2] mind   [3] Originally the word here was: sounded.   [4] shadow

So he plunged like a rock through the foam; for it falls from a mountain
Overpeering the waves in some silence of desolate waters
Left to the wind and the sea-gull where Ocean alone with the ages
Dreams of the calm of the skies or tosses its spray to the wind-gods,
Tosses for ever its foam in the solitude huge of its longings
Far from the homes and the noises of men. So the dark-browed Poseidon
Came to his coral halls and the sapphire stables of Nereus
Ever where champ their bits the harnessed steeds of the Ocean
Watched by foam-white girls in the caverns of still Amphitrite.
There was his chariot yoked by the Tritons, drawn by his coursers
Born of the fleeing sea-spray and shod with the north-wind who journey
Black like the front of the storm and clothed with their manes as with
thunder.
This now rose from its depths to the upper tumults of Ocean
Bearing the awful brows and the mighty form of the sea-god
And from the roar of the surges fast o'er the giant margin
Came remembering the storm and the swiftness wide[1] towards the Troad.
So among men he arrived to the clamorous labours of Ares,
Close by the stern Diomedes stood and frowned o'er the battle.
He for the Trojan slaughter chose for his mace and his sword-edge
Iron Tydeus' son and the adamant heart of young Pyrrhus.
    But in the courts divine the Father high of the immortals
Turned in his heart to the brilliant offspring born of his musings,
She who tranquil observes and judges her father and all things.
"What shall I say to the thought that is calm in thy breasts, O Athene?
Have I not given thee earth for thy portion, throned thee and armoured,
Darkened Cypris' smile, dimmed Hera's son and Latona's?
Swift in thy silent ambition, proud in thy radiant sternness,
Girl, thou shalt rule with the Greek and the Saxon, the Frank and the Roman.
Worker and fighter and builder and thinker, light of the reason,
Men shall leave all temples to crowd in thy courts, O Athene.
Go then and do my will, prepare man's tribes for their fullness."
    But with her high clear smile on him answered the mighty Athene, —
Wisely and soberly, tenderly smiled she chiding her father
Even as a mother might rail at her child when he hides and dissembles:
"Zeus, I see and I am not deceived by thy words in my spirit.
We but build forms for thy thought while thou smilest down high o'er our
toiling;
Even as men are we tools for thee, who are thy children and dear ones.

[1] straight

All this life is thy sport and thou workst like a boy at his engines
Making a toil of the game and a play of the serious labour.
Then to that play thou callest us wearing a sombre visage,
This consulting, that to our wills confiding, O Ruler;
Choosing thy helpers, hastened by those whom thou lurest to oppose thee
Guile thou usest with gods as with mortals, scheming, deceiving,
And at the wrath and the love thou hast prompted laughest in secret.
So we too who are sisters and enemies, lovers and rivals,
Fondled and baffled in turn obey thy will and thy cunning,
I, thy girl of war, and the rosy-white Aphrodite.
Always we served but thy pleasure since our immortal beginnings,
Always each other we helped by our play and our wrestlings and quarrels.
This too I know that I pass preparing the paths of Apollo
And at the end as his sister and slave and bride I must sojourn
Rapt to his courts of mystic light and unbearable brilliance.
Was I not ever condemned since my birth from the toil of thy musings
Seized like a lyre in my body to sob and to laugh out his music,
Shake as a leaf in his fierceness and leap as a flame in his splendours?
So must I dwell overpowered and so must I labour subjected
Robbed of my loneliness pure and coerced in my radiant freedom,
Now whose clearness and pride are the sovereign joy of thy creatures.
Such the reward that thou keepst for my labour obedient always.
Yet I work and I do thy will, for 'tis mine, O my father."
Proud of her ruthless lust of thought and action and battle, —
Swift-footed rose the daughter of Zeus from her sessions immortal:
Breasts of the morning unveiled in a purity awful and candid,
Head of the mighty Dawn, the goddess Pallas Athene!
Strong and rapacious she swooped on the world as her prey and her booty,
Down from the courts of the Mighty descending, darting on Ida.
Dire she descended, a god in her reason, a child in her longings,
Joy and woe to the world that is given to the whims of the child-god
Greedy for rule and play and the minds of men and their doings!
So with her aegis scattering light o'er the heads of the nations
Shining-eyed in her boyish beauty severe and attractive
Came to the fields of the Troad, came to the fateful warfare,
Veiled, the goddess calm and pure in her luminous raiment
Zoned with beauty and strength. Rejoicing, spurring the fighters
Close o'er Odysseus she stood and clear-eyed governed the battle.
    Zeus to Hephaestus next, the Cyclopean toiler
Turned, Hephaestus the strong-souled, priest and king and a bond-slave,

Servant of men in their homes and their workshops, servant of Nature,
He who has built these worlds and kindles the fire for a mortal.
"Thou, my son, art obedient always. Wisdom is with thee,
Therefore thou know'st and obeyest. Submission is wisdom and knowledge;
He who is blind revolts and he who is limited struggles:
Strife is not for the infinite; wisdom observes to accomplish.
Troy and her sons and her works are thy food today, O Hephaestus."
    And to his father the Toiler answered, the silent Seer:
"Yes, I obey thee, my Father, and That which than thou is more mighty;
Even as thou obeyest by rule, so I by my labour.
Now must I heap the furnace, now must I toil at the smithy,
I who have flamed on the altar of sacrifice helping the sages.
I am the Cyclops, the lamester, who once was pure and a high-priest.
Holy the pomp of my flames ascendent from pyre and from altar
Robed men's souls for their heavens and my smoke was a pillar to Nature.
Though I have burned in the sight of the sage and the heart of the hero,
Now is no nobler hymn for my ear than the clanging of metal,
Breath of human greed and the dolorous pant of the engines.
Still I repine not, but toil; for to toil was I yoked by my Maker.
I am your servant, O Gods, and his of whom you are servants."
    But to the Toiler Zeus replied, to the servant of creatures:
"What is the thought thou hast uttered betrayed by thy speech, O
                                            Hephaestus?
True is it earth shall grow as a smithy, the smoke of the furnace
Fill men's eyes and their souls shall be stunned with the clang of the hammers,
Yet in the end there is rest on the peak of a labour accomplished.
Nor shall the might of the thinker be quelled by that iron oppression,
Nor shall the soul of the warrior despair in the darkness triumphant,
For when the night shall be deepest, dawn shall increase on the mountains
And in the heart of the worst the best shall be born by my wisdom.
Pallas thy sister shall guard man's knowledge fighting the earth-smoke.
Thou too art mighty to live through the clamour even as Apollo.
Work then, endure; expect from the Silence an end and thy wages."
So King Hephaestus arose and passed from the courts of his father;
Down upon earth he came with his lame omnipotent motion;
And with uneven steps absorbed and silent the Master
Worked employed mid the wheels of the cars as a smith in his smithy,
But it was death and bale that he forged, not the bronze and the iron.
Stark, like a fire obscured by its smoke, through the spear-casts he laboured
Helping Ajax' war and the Theban and Phocian fighters.

Zeus to his grandiose helper next, who proved and unmoving,
Calm in her greatness waited the mighty command of her husband:
"Hera, sister and spouse, what my will is thou knowest, O consort.
One are our blood and our hearts, nor the thought for the words of the
                                                                speaker
Waits, but each other we know and ourselves and the Vast and the heavens,
Life and all between and all beyond and the ages.
That which Space not knows nor Time, we have known, O my sister.
Therefore our souls are one soul and our minds become mirrors of oneness.
Go then and do my will, O thou mighty one, burning down Troya."
    Silent she rose from the seats of the Blissful, Hera majestic,
And with her flowing garment and mystical zone through the spaces
Haloed came like the moon on an evening of luminous silence
Down upon Ida descending, a snow-white swan on the greenness,
Down upon Ida the mystic haunted by footsteps immortal
Ever since out of the Ocean it rose and lived gazing towards heaven.
There on a peak of the mountains alone with the sea and the azure
Voiceless and mighty she paused[1] like a thought on the summits of being
Clasped by all heaven; the winds at play in her gust-scattered raiment
Sported insulting her gracious strength with their turbulent sweetness,
Played with their mother and queen; but she stood absorbed and unheeding,
Mute, with her sandalled foot for a moment thrilling the grasses,
Dumbly adored by a soul in the mountains, a thought in the rivers,
Roared to loud by her lions. The voice of the cataracts falling
Entered her soul profound and it heard eternity's rumour.
Silent its gaze immense contained the wheeling of aeons.
Huge-winged through Time flew her thought and its grandiose vast
                                                            revolutions
Turned and returned. So musing her timeless creative spirit,
Master of Time its instrument, grieflessly hastening forward
Parted with greatnesses dead and summoned new strengths from their stables;
Maned they came to her call and filled with their pacings the future.
Calm, with the vision satisfied, thrilled by the grandeurs within her,
Down in a billow of whiteness and gold and delicate raiment
Gliding the daughter of Heaven came to the earth that received her
Glad of the tread divine and bright with her more than with sunbeams.
King Agamemnon she found and smiling on Sparta's levies
Mixed unseen with the far-glinting spears of the haughty Mycenae.
    Then to the Mighty who tranquil abode and august in his regions

[1] stood

Zeus, while his gaze over many forms and high-seated godheads
Passed like a swift-fleeing eagle over the peaks and the glaciers
When to his eyrie he flies alone through the vastness and silence:
"Artemis, child of my loins and you, O legioned immortals,
All you have heard. Descend, O ye gods, to your sovereign stations,
Labour rejoicing whose task is joy and your bliss is creation;
Shrink from no act that Necessity asks from your luminous natures.
Thee I have given no part in the years that come, O my daughter,
Huntress swift of the worlds who with purity all things pursuest.
Yet not less is thy portion intended than theirs who o'erpass thee:
Helped are the souls that wait more than strengths soon fulfilled and
                                                                                                             exhausted.
Archeress, brilliance, wait thine hour from the speed of the ages."
    So they departed, Artemis leading lightning-tasselled.
Ancient Themis remained and awful Dis and Ananke.
Then mid these last of the gods who shall stand when all others have perished,
Zeus to the Silence obscure under iron brows of that goddess, —
Griefless, unveiled was her visage, dire and unmoved and eternal:
"Thou and I, O Dis, remain and our sister Ananke.
That which the joyous hearts of our children, radiant heaven-moths
Flitting mid flowers of sense for the honey of thought, have not captured,
That which Poseidon forgets mid the pomp and the roar of his waters,
We three keep in our hearts. By the Light that I watch for unsleeping,
By thy tremendous consent to the silence and darkness, O Hades,
By her delight renounced and the prayers and the worship of mortals
Making herself as an engine of God without bowels or vision, —
Yet in that engine are only heart-beats, yet is her riddle
Only Love that is veiled and pity that suffers and slaughters,
We three are free from ourselves, O Dis, and free from each other.
Do then, O King of the Night, observe then with Time for thy servant
Not my behest, but What she and thou and I are for ever."
    Mute the Darkness sat like a soul unmoved through the aeons,
Then came a voice from the silence of Dis, from the night there came wisdom.
"Yes, I have chosen and that which I chose I endure, O Cronion, —
Though to the courts of the gods I come as a threat and a shadow,
Even though none to their counsels call me, none to their pastime,
None companions me willingly; even thy daughter, my consort,
Trembling whom once from our sister Demeter I plucked like a blossom[1]
Torn from Sicilian[2] fields, while Fate reluctant, consenting,

    [1] flower   [2] Enna's

Bowed her head, lives but by her gasps of the sun and the azure;
Stretched are her hands to the light and she seeks for the clasp of her mother.
I, I am Night and her reign and that of which Night is a symbol.
All to me comes, even thou shalt come to me, brilliant Cronion.
All here exists by me whom all walk fearing and shunning;
He who shuns not, He am I and thou and Ananke.
All things I take to my bosom that Life may be swift in her voyage;
For out of death is Life and not by birth and her motions
And behind Night is light and not in the sun and his splendours.
Troy to the Night I will gather a wreath for my shadows, O grower."
So in his arrogance dire the vast invincible Death-god
Triumphing passed out of heaven with Themis and silent Ananke.
Zeus alone in the spheres of his bliss, in his kingdom of brilliance
Sat divine and alarmed; for even the gods in their heavens
Scarce shall live who have gazed on the unveiled face of Ananke,
Heard the accents dire of the Darkness that waits for the ages.
Awful and dull grew his eyes and mighty and still grew his members,
Back from his nature he drew to the passionless peaks of the spirit,
Throned where it dwells for ever uplifted and silent and changeless
Far beyond living and death, beyond Nature and ending of Nature.
There for a while he dwelt veiled, protected from Dis and his greatness;
Then to the works of the world he returned and the joy of his musings.
Life and the blaze of the mighty soul that he was of God's making
Dawned again in the heavenly eyes and the majestied semblance.
Comforted heaven he beheld, to the green of the earth was attracted.
    But through this Space unreal, but through these worlds that are
                                                               shadows
Went the awful Three. None saw them pass, none felt them.
Only in the heavens was a tread as of death, in the air was a winter,
Earth oppressed moaned long like a woman striving with anguish.
Ida saw them not, but her grim lions cowered in their caverns,
Ceased for a while on her slopes the eternal laughter of fountains.
Over the ancient ramparts of Dardanus' high-roofed city
Darkening her victor domes and her gardens of life and its sweetness
Silent they came. Unseen and unheard was the dreadful arrival.
Troy and her gods dreamed secure in the moment flattered by sunlight.
Dim to the citadel high they arrived and their silence invaded
Pallas' marble shrine where stern and white in her beauty,
Armed on her pedestal, trampling the prostrate image of darkness
Mighty Athene's statue guarded imperial Troya.

Dim and vast they entered in. Then through all the great city
Huge a rushing sound was heard from her gardens and places
And in their musings her seers as they strove with night and with error
And in the fane of Apollo Laocoon torn by his visions
Heard aghast the voice of Troy's deities fleeing from Troya,
Saw the flaming lords of her households drive in a death-rout
Forth from her ancient halls and their noble familiar sessions.
Ghosts of her splendid centuries wailed on the wings of the doom-blast.
Moaning the Dryads fled and his Naiads passed from Scamander
Leaving the world to deities dumb of the clod and the earth-smoke,
And from their tombs and their shrines the shadowy Ancestors faded.
Filled was the air with their troops and the sound of a vast lamentation.
Wailing they went, lamenting mortality's ages of greatness,
Ruthless Ananke's deeds and the mortal conquests of Hades.
Then in the fane Palladian the shuddering priests of Athene
Entered the darkened shrine and saw on the suffering marble
Shattered Athene's mighty statue prostrate as conquered,
But on its pedestal rose o'er the unhurt image of darkness
Awful shapes, a Trinity dim and dire unto mortals.
Dumb they fell down on the earth and the life-breath was slain in their bosoms
And in the noon there was night. And Apollo passed out of Troya.

Book Nine*

Nor could the Trojan fighters break through the walls of their foemen,
Nor could the mighty Pelides slay in his war-rage the Trojans.
Ever he fought surrounded or drew back compelled to his legions;
For to each spear of his strength full twenty hissed round his helmet,
Cried[1] on his shield, attempted his cuirass or leaped at his coursers
Or at Automedon ran like living things in their blood-thirst.
Galled the deathless steeds high-neighing pawed in their anger;
Wrathful Achilles wheeled and threatened seeking a victim.
So might a fire on the high-piled altar of sacrifice blazing
Seek for its tongues an offering fit for the gods, but 'tis answered
Only by spitting rain that a dense cloud sends out of heaven.
Sibilant hiss the drops on the glowing wood and the altar.
Chill a darkness o'erhangs and its brief and envious spirits
Rail at the glorious flame, desiring an end of its brilliance.
Meanwhile behind by the ranks of the fighters sheltered from Hades
Paris loosed his lethal shafts at the head of the Hellene.
Then upon Helenus wrath from the gods who are noble descended,
Seized on the tongue of the prophet and spoke out[2] their thoughts in his
                                                                                accents,
Thoughts by men rejected who follow the beast in their reason,
Only advantage seek, and honour and pride are forgotten:
"Paris, not thus shalt thou slay Achilles but only thy glory.
Dost thou not heed that the women should mock in the streets of our
                                                                                            city
Thee and thy bow and thy numbers, hearing the shame of the Trojans?
Dost thou not fear the gods and their harms? Not so do they combat
Who have the awe of their deeds and follow the way of the mighty."
Paris the Priamid answered his brother: "Helenus, wherefore
Care should I have for fame, or the gods and their punishments, heeding
Breath of men when they praise or condemn me? Victory I ask for,
Joy for my living heart, not a dream and a breath for my ashes.
Work I desire and the wish of my heart and the fruit of my labour.
Nay, let my fame be crushed into mire for the ages to spit at,
But let my country live and her foes be slain on her beaches."
So he spoke and fitted another shaft to the bow-string,
Aimed and loosed the death at the greatness that heaven protected.

    * No title for this book in the MS.
    [1] Rang   [2] fashioned / framed

Always they fought and were locked in a fierce unyielding combat.
But on the Hellene right stood the brothers stark in their courage
Waiting the Eoan horse-hooves that checked at the difficult crossing
Late arrived through field and through pasture. Zethus exultant
Watched their advent stern and encouraged the legions behind him:
"Now is the hour of your highest fame, O ye sons of the Hellenes.
These are the iron squadrons, these are the world-famed fighters.
Here is a swifter than Memnon, here is a greater than Hector.
Who would fight with the war-wearied Trojans, the Lycian remnants,
When there are men in the world like these? O Phthians, we conquer
Asia's best today. And you, O my brothers, with courage
Reap all the good I have won for our lives this morn from Achilles.
Glad let our fame go before us to our mother Arithoa waiting
Lonely in Phthia, desiring death or the eyes of her children.
Soon will our sails pursue their herald Fame, with our glory
Bellying out and the winds. They shall bear o'er the murmurs of Ocean
Heaped up Ilion's wealth and the golden bricks of King Priam
And for the halls of our fathers a famous and noble adornment
Bear the beautiful head of the virgin Penthesilea."
So he cried and the Hellenes shouted, a savage rumour,
Proud of their victories past and incredulous grown of disaster.
   Now from the Xanthus dripping-wheeled came the Eoan war-cars
Rolling thunder-voiced with the tramp of the runners behind them,
Dust like a flag and dire with the battle-cry, full on the Hellenes.
They to the mid-plain arrived where the might of the Hellene brothers
Waited their onset.[1] Zethus first with his cry of the cascade
Hurrying-footed headlong that leaps far down to the valley:
"Curb, but curb thy advance, O Amazon Penthesilea!
These are not Gnossus' ranks and these are not levies from Sparta.
Hellas' spears await thee here and the Myrmidon fighters."
High like the north-wind racing and whistling over the ice-fields,
Death at its side and snow for its breath in the pitiless winter:[2]
"Who art thou biddest to pause the horse-hooves of Penthesilea,
Hellene, thou in thy strength who standest forth from thy shielders?
Turn yet, save thy life; for I deem that thou art not Achilles."
"Zethus the Hellene I am and Cyenus and Pindus, my brothers,
Stand at my either side, and thou passest not farther, Bellona.

[1] coming.
[2] *Alternative to this line and the preceding:*
But like the northwind high and clear answered Penthesilea

Lioness, turn thou back, for thou canst not here be a hunter."
"Zethus and Cyenus and Pindus, little you loved then your mother,
Who in this field that is wide must needs all three perish together
Piled on one altar of death by the spear-shafts of Penthesilea.
Empty for ever your halls shall be, childless the age of your father."
High she rose to the spear-cast, poised like a thunderbolt lifted,
Forward swung to the blow and loosed it hissing and ruthless
Straight at the Hellene shield, and it tore through the bronze and groaning
Butted and pushed through the cuirass and split the breast of the hero.
Round in his car he spun, then putting his hands out before him,
Even as a diver who leaps from the shed of the bath to the current,
Launched out so headlong, struggled, sideward collapsed, then was quiet,
Dead on Trojan earth. But dismay and grief on his brothers
Yet alive now seized, then rage came blinding the eyeballs.
Blindly they hurled, yet attained, for Athene guided the spear-shafts;
Death like a forest beast yet played with the might of the virgin.
One on her shield and one on her cuirass rang, but rejected
Fell back like reeds that are thrown at a boulder by boys on the sea-shore.
She unmoved replied; her shafts in their angry succession
Hardly endured delay between. Like trees the brothers,
Felled, to each side sank prone. So lifeless these strong ones of Hellas
Lay in their couch of the hostile soil reunited in slumber
As in their childhood they lay in Hellas watched by their mother,
Three of them side by side and she dreamed for her darlings their future.
But on the ranks of the Hellenes fear and amazement descended, —
Messengers they from Zeus to discourage the pride and the blood-lust.
Back many yards their foremost recoiled in a god-given terror,
As from a snake a traveller scorned for a bough by the wayside,
But it arises puffing its hood and hisses its hatred.
Forward the henchmen ran and plucked back the spears from the corpses;
Onward the Eoan thousands rolled o'er the ground that was conquered
Trampling the fallen men into earth with the wheels of their war-cars.
    But in her speed like the sea or the storm-wind Penthesilea
Drove towards the ranks of the foe and her spear-shafts hastened before her,
Messengers whistling shrilly to death; she came like a wolf-hound
Called by his master's voice and silently fell on the quarry.
Hyrtamus fell, Admetus was wounded, Charmidas slaughtered;
Cirrhes died, though he faced not the blow while he hastened to shelter.
Itylus, bright and beautiful, went down to night and to Hades.
Back, ever back the Hellenes recoiled from the shock of the Virgin,

Slain by her prowess fierce, alarmed by the might of her helpers.
For at her right Surabdas threatened and iron Surenas,
And at her left hill-shouldered Pharatus slaughtered the Hellenes.
Then in the ranks of the Greeks a shouting arose and the leaders
Cried to their hosts and recalled their unstained fame and their valour
Never so lightly conquered before in the trial[1] of Ares,
And of Achilles they spoke and King Peleus waiting in Phthia,
Listening for Troy overthrown not his hosts overcome by a woman.
And from the right and the left came heroes mighty to succour.
Chiefs of the Dolopes Ar and Aglauron came mid the foremost,
Hillus fair as a drifting moon but fierce as the winter;
Pryas came the Thessalian and Sebes whom Pharsalus honoured,
Victors in countless fights who had stood against Memnon and Hector.
But though their hands were mighty, though fierce their obdurate natures,
Mightier strengths they met and a sterner brood of the war-god.
Light from the hand of the Virgin the spear ran laughing at Sebes,
Crashed through his helmet and left him supine on the pastures of Troya;
Ar to Surabdas fell and the blood-spirting head of Aglauron
Dropped like a fruit from a branch by its weight to the discus of Sambus;
Iron Surenas' mace-head shattered the beauty of Hillus;
Pryas by Pharatus slain lay still and had rest from the war-cry.
Back, ever back reeled the Hellene host with the Virgin pursuing.
Storm-shod the Amazon fought and she slew like a god unresisted.
None now dared to confront her burning eyes; the boldest
Shuddered back from her spear and the cry of her tore at the heart-strings.
Fear, the daughter of Zeus, had gripped at the hearts of the Hellenes.
So as the heroes yielded before her, Penthesilea
Lifted with victory cried to her henchman, Aurus of Ellae,
Who had the foot of the wind and its breath that scants not for running:
"Hasten, hasten, Aurus; race to the right where unwarring
Valarus leads his host; bid him close with the strength of the Hellenes.
Soon will they scatter like chaff on the threshing-floor blown to the beaches.
But when he sees their flight by Sumalus shepherded seaward,
Swift let him turn like the wind in its paths and follow me, pouring
Down, a victorious flood,[2] on the Myrmidon left and Achilles.
Then shall no Hellene again dare embark in ships for the Troad.
Cursed shall its beaches be to their sons and their sons and forever."
So she spoke and Aurus ran by the chariot protected.
Then had all Hellas perished indeed on the beaches of Troas,

[1] onsets [2] All in a victor flood,

But from the Argive's right where she battled Pallas Athene
Saw and was wroth and she missioned her thought to Automedon speeding,
Splendid it came and found him out mid the hiss of the spear-shafts
Guiding, endangered, Achilles' steeds in the thick of the battle.
Shaped like a woman clad in armour and fleeing from battle,
Helmed with the Hellene crest it knocked at the gate of his spirit,
Shaking his hero's heart with the vision that came to his eyeballs;
Silent he stared aghast and turned his ear to the war-din.
"Dost thou not hear to our right, Achilles, these voices of Ares?
High is the sound of Eoan battle, a woman's war-cry
Rings in my ears, but faint and sparse come the shouts of our nation.
Far behind is their call and nearer the ships and the beaches."
Great Pelides heard and groaned in the caves of his spirit:
"It is the doom that I feared and the fatal madness of Zethus;
Slain are the men of my nations or routed by Penthesilea.
Drive, Automedon, drive, lest shame and defeat upon Hellas
Fasten their seal and her heroes flee from the strength of a woman."
And to the steeds divine Automedon called and they hearkened,
Rose as if seeking their old accustomed paths in the heavens,
Then through the ranks that parted they galloped as gallops a dust-cloud
When the cyclone is abroad and the high trees snap by the wayside,
And from the press of the Hellenes into the plain of the Xanthus
Thundering, neighing came with the war-car borne like a dead leaf
Chased by the blast. Then Athene opened the eyes of Achilles,
Eyes that in all of us sleep, yet can see the near and the distant,
Eyes that the gods in their pity have sealed from the giant confusion,
Sealed from the bale and the grief. He saw like one high on a summit
Near him the Eoans holding the plain and out in the distance
Breaking the Hellene strengths. Like a dream in the night he regarded
High-crested Sumalus fight[1], Somaranes swift in the onset,
Bull-shouldered Tauron's blows and the hero Artavoruxes.
But in the centre fiercest the cry and the death and the fleeing.
There were his chieftains ever reforming vainly resistance, —
Even in defeat these were Hellenes and fit to be hosts of Achilles, —
But like a doom on them thundered the war-car of Penthesilea,
Pharatus smote and Surabdas and Sambus and iron Surenas,
Down the leaders fell and the armies reeled towards the Ocean.
Wroth he cried to his coursers and fiercely they heard and they hastened;
Swift like a wind o'er the grasses galloped the car of Achilles.

[1] war,

Echemus followed, Ascanus drove and Drus and Thretaon:
Phoces alone in the dust of the Troad lay there and moved not.
Yet brought not all of them help to their brothers oppressed in the combat;
For from the forefront forth on the knot of the swift-speeding war-cars
High an Eoan chariot came drawn fast by its coursers
Bearing a mighty chieftain, Valarus son of Supaures.
Fire-footed thundered past him the hooves of the heavenly coursers,
Nor to his challenging shout nor his spear the warlike Pelides
Answered at all, but made haste like a flood to the throng and the mellay.
But 'twixt the chariots behind and their leader the mighty Eoan
Drove his dark-maned steeds and stood like a cliff to their onset.
"Great is your haste, O ye Kings of the Greeks! Abide yet and converse.
Scatheless your leader has fled from me borne by the hooves of his coursers.
Ye, abide! For we meet from far lands on this soil of the Trojans.
All of us meet from afar, but not all shall return to their hearth-sides.
Valarus stays you, O Greeks, and this is the point of his greeting."
So as he spoke he launched out his spear as a cloud hurls its storm-flash;
Nor from that fatal hand parted vainly the pitiless envoy,
But of its blood-thirst had right. Riven through and through with the
    death-stroke
Drus fell prone and tore with dying fingers the grasses.
Sobbing his soul fled out to the night and the chill and the silence.
They like leaves that are suddenly stayed by the fall of a wind-gust
Ceased from their headlong speed. And Echemus poising his spear-shaft:
"Sharp are thy greetings, chieftain Eoan. Message for message
Echemus son of Aëtes, one of the mighty in Hellas,
Thus returns. Let Ares judge 'twixt the Greek and the Eastern."
Fast sped the spear but Valarus held forth his shield and rebutted,
Shouting, the deadly point that could pierce not his iron refusal.
"Echemus, shrill thy vaunt has reached me, but unfelt is thy spear-point.
Weak are men's arms, it seems, in Hellas; a boy there Ares
Aims with reeds not spears at pastoral cheeses not iron.
Judge now my strength." Two spears from him ran at the hearts of his
    foemen,
Crouching Thretaon heard the keen death over him whistle;
Ascanus hurt in the shoulder cried out and paused from his war-lust.
Echemus hurled now again and hurled with him stalwart Thretaon.
Strong Thretaon missed, but Echemus' point at the helmet
Bit and fastened as fastens a hound on the ear of the wild boar
Wroth with the cry and the hunt, that gores the pack and his hunters.

Valarus frowning tugged at the heavy steel; yet his right hand
Smote at Echemus. Him he missed but valiant Thretaon
Sat back dead in his seat and the chariot wild with its coursers
Snorting and galloping bore his corpse o'er the plains to the Hellenes.
But while yet Valarus strove with the shaft, obscured and encumbered,
Ascanus sprang down swift from his car and armed with his sword-point
Clove the Eoan's neck as the lightning springs at an oak-trunk
Seized in the stride of the storm and severs that might with its sharpness.
Slain the hero fell; his mighty limbs the spirit
Mightier released to the gods and it rose to the heavens of the noble.
Ascanus gathered the spear-shaft; loud was his shout as exulting
Back he leaped to the car triumphant o'er death and its menace:
"Lie there, Valarus, King of the East, with imperial Troya.
Six rich feet of her soil she gives thee for couch of the nuptials.
Rest then! Talk not again on the way with the heroes of Hellas."
So delivered they hastened glad to the ranks of their brothers.
After them rolled the Eoan war-cars, Arithon leading
Loud with the clamour of hooves and the far-rolling gust of the war-cry;
Wroth at their chieftain's fall they moved to the help of their nation,
Now by the unearthly horses neared and the might of Achilles.
Then from the Hellenes who heard the noise and cry of their coming
Lifted eyes dismayed, but saw the familiar war-car,
Saw the heaven-born steeds and the helm unconquered in battle,
Cry was of other hopefulness. Loud as the outbursting thunder
Rises o'er lower sounds of the storm, o'er the din of the battle
Rose the Hellene shout and rose the name of Achilles.

(The rest of Book Nine is missing)

AHANA
A poem in rhymed quantitative hexameters

Ahana

(Ahana, the Dawn of God, descends on the world where amid the strife and trouble of mortality the Hunters of Joy, the Seekers after Knowledge, the Climbers in the quest of Power are toiling up the slopes or waiting in the valleys. As she stands on the mountains of the East, voices of the Hunters of Joy are the first to greet her.)

Vision delightful alone on the hills whom the silences cover,
Closer yet lean to mortality; human, stoop to thy lover.
Wonderful, gold like a moon in the square of the sun where thou strayest
Glimmers thy face amid crystal purities; mighty thou playest
Sole on the peaks of the world, unafraid of thy loneliness. Glances
Leap from thee down to us, dream-seas and light-falls and magical trances;
Sun-drops flake from thy eyes and the heart's caverns packed are with pleasure
Strange like a song without words or the dance of a measureless measure.
Tread through the edges of dawn, over twilight's grey-lidded margin;
Heal earth's unease with thy feet, O heaven-born delicate virgin.
Children of Time whose spirits came down from eternity, seizing
Joys that escape us, yoked by our hearts to a labour unceasing,
Earth-bound, torn with our longings, our life is a brief incompleteness.
Thou hast the stars to sport with, the winds run like bees to thy sweetness.
Art thou not heaven-bound even as I with the earth? Hast thou ended
All desirable things in a stillness lone and unfriended?
Only is calm so sweet? is our close tranquillity only?
Cold are the rivers of peace and their banks are leafless and lonely.
Heavy is godhead to bear with its mighty sun-burden of lustre.
Art thou not weary of only the stars in their solemn muster,
Sky-hung the chill bare plateaus and peaks where the eagle rejoices
In the inhuman height of his nesting, solitude's voices
Making the heart of the silence lonelier? strong and untiring,
Deaf with the cry of the waterfall, lonely the pine lives aspiring.
Two are the ends of existence, two are the dreams of the Mother:
Heaven unchanging, earth with her time-beats yearn to each other, —
Earth-souls needing the touch of the heavens peace to recapture,
Heaven needing earth's passion to quiver its peace into rapture.
Marry, O lightning eternal, the passion of a moment-born fire!
Out of thy greatness draw close to the breast of our mortal desire!
Is he thy master, Rudra the mighty, Shiva ascetic?
Has he denied thee his world? In his dance that they tell of, ecstatic,

Slaying, creating, calm in the midst of the movement and madness,
Stole there no rhythm of an earthly joy and a mortal sadness?
Wast thou not made in the shape of a woman? Sweetness and beauty
Move like a song of the gods in thy limbs and to love is thy duty
Graved in thy heart as on tablets of fate; joy's delicate blossom
Sleeps in thy lids of delight; all Nature hides in thy bosom
Claiming her children unborn and the food of her love and her laughter.
Is he the first? was there none then before him? shall none come after?
He who denies and his blows beat down on our hearts like a hammer's,
He whose calm is the silent reply to our passion and clamours!
Is not there deity greater here new-born in a noble
Labour and sorrow and struggle than stilled into rapture immobile?
Earth has beatitudes warmer than heaven's that are bare and undying,
Marvels of Time on the crest of the moments to Infinity flying.
Earth has her godheads; the Tritons sway on the toss of the billows,
Emerald locks of the Nereids stream on their foam-crested pillows, —
Dryads peer out from the branches, Naiads glance up from the waters;
High are her flame-points of joy and the gods are ensnared by her daughters.
Artemis calls as she flees through the glades and the breezes pursue her;
Cypris laughs in her isles where the ocean-winds linger to woo her.
Here thou shalt meet amid beauty forgotten the dance of the Graces;
Night shall be haunted for ever with strange and delicate faces.
Music is here of the fife and the flute and the lyre and the timbal,
Wind in the forests, bees in the grove, — spring's ardent symbol
Thrilling, the cry of the cuckoo; the nightingale sings in the branches,
Human laughter is heard and the cattle low in the ranches.
Frankly and sweetly she gives to her children the bliss of her body,
Breath of her lips and the green of her garments, rain-pourings heady
Tossed from her cloud-carried beaker of tempest, oceans and streamlets,
Dawn and the mountain-air, corn-fields and vineyards, pastures and hamlets,
Tangles of sunbeams asleep, mooned dream-depths, twilight's shadows,
Taste and scent and the fruits of her trees and the flowers of her meadows,
Life with a wine-cup of longing under the purple of her tenture,
Death as her gate of escape and rebirth and renewal of venture.
Still must they mutter that all here is vision and passing appearance,
Magic of Maya with falsehood and pain for its only inherence.
One is there only, apart in his greatness, the End and Beginning, —
He who has sent through his soul's wide spaces the universe spinning.
One eternal, Time an illusion, life a brief error!
One eternal, Master of heaven — and of hell and its terror!

Spirit of silence and purity rapt and aloof from creation, —
Dreaming through aeons unreal his splendid and empty formation!
Spirit all-wise in omnipotence shaping a world but to break it, —
Pushed by what mood of a moment, the breath of what fancy to make it?
None is there great but the eternal and lonely, the unique and unmated,
Bliss lives alone with the self-pure, the single, the forever-uncreated.
Truths? or thought's structures bridging the vacancy mute and unsounded
Facing the soul when it turns from the stress of the figures around it?
Solely we see here a world self-made by some indwelling Glory
Building with forms and events its strange and magnificent story.
Yet at the last has not all been solved and unwisdom demolished,
Myth cast out and all dreams of the soul and all worship abolished?
All now is changed, the reverse of the coin has been shown to us; Reason
Waking, detecting the hoax of the spirit, at last has arisen,
Captured the Truth and built round her its bars that she may not skedaddle,
Gallop again with the bit in her teeth and with Fancy in the saddle.
Now have the wise men discovered that all is the craft of a super-
Magic of Chance and a movement of Void and inconscient Stupor.
Chance by a wonderful accident ever her ripples expanding
Out of a gaseous circle of Nothingness, implacably extending
Freak upon freak, repeating rigidly marvels on marvels,
Making a world out of Nothing, started on the arc of her travels.
Nothingness born into feeling and action dies back to Nothing.
Sea of a vague electricity, romping through space-curves and clothing
Strangely the Void with a semblance of Matter, painfully flowered
Into this giant phenomenon universe. Man who has towered
Out of the plasm and struggled by thought to Divinity's level,
Man, this miniature second creator of good and of evil,
He too was only a compost of Matter made living, organic,
Forged as her thinking tool by an Energy blind and mechanic.
Once by an accident queer but quite natural, provable, simple,
Out of blind Space-Nought lashed into life, wearing Mind as its wimple,
Dupe of a figment of consciousness, doped with behaviour and feature,
Matter deluded claimed to be spirit and sentient creature.
All the high dreams man has dreamed and his hopes and his deeds, his soul's
greatness
Are but a food-seeking animal's acts with the mind for their witness, —
Mind a machine for the flickers of thought, Matter's logic unpremissed, —
Are but a singular fireworks, chemistry lacking the chemist,
Matter's nervous display; the heart's passion, the sorrow and burning,

Fire of delight and sweet ecstasy, love and its fathomless yearning,
Boundless spiritual impulses making us one with world-being,
Outbursts of vision opening doors to a limitless seeing,
Gases and glands and the genes and the nerves and the brain-cells have
    done it,
Brooded out drama and epic, structured the climb of the sonnet,
Studied the stars and discovered the brain and the laws of its thinking,
Sculptured the cave-temple, reared the cathedral, infinity drinking
Wrought manufacturing God and the soul for the uplift of Nature, —
Science, philosophy, head of his mystical chemical stature,
Music and painting revealing the godhead in sound and in colour,
Acts of the hero, thoughts of the thinker, search of the scholar,
All the magnificent planning, all the inquiry and wonder
Only a trick of the atom, its marvellous magical blunder.
Who can believe it? Something or someone, a Force or a Spirit
Conscious, creative, wonderful shaped out a world to inherit
Here for the beings born from its vast universal existence, —
Fields of surprise and adventure, vistas of light-haunted distance,
Play-routes of wisdom and vision and struggle and rapture and sorrow,
Sailing in Time through the straits of today to the sea of tomorrow.
Worlds and their wonders, suns and their flamings, earth and her nations,
Voyages endless of Mind through the surge of its fate-tossed creations,
Star upon star throbbing out in the silence of infinite spaces,
Species on species, bodies on bodies, faces on faces,
Souls without number crossing through Time towards eternity, aeons
Crowding on aeons, loving and battle, dirges and paeans,
Thoughts ever leaping, hopes ever yearning, lives ever streaming,
Millions and millions on trek through the days with their doings and
    dreaming,
Herds of the Sun who move on at the cry of the radiant drover, —
Countless, surviving the death of the centuries, lost to recover,
Finished, but only to begin again, who is its tireless creator,
Cause or the force of its driving, its thinker or formless dictator?
Surely no senseless Vacancy made it, surely 'twas fashioned
By an almighty One million-ecstasied, thousand-passioned.
Self-made? then by what self from which thought could arise and emotion,
Waves that well up to the surface, born from what mysteried ocean?
Nature alone is the fountain. But what is she? Is she not only
Figure and name for what none understands, though all feel, or a lonely
Word in which all finds expression, spirit-heights, dumb work of Matter, —

Vague designation filling the gaps of our thought with its clatter?
Power without vision that blunders in man into thinking and sinning?
Rigid vast inexhaustible mystery void of a meaning?
Energy blindly devising, unconsciously ranging in order?
Chance in the march of a cosmic Insanity crossing the border
Out of the eternal silence to thought and its strangeness and splendour?
Consciousness born by an accident until an accident end her?
Nought else is she but the power of the Spirit who dwells in her ever,
Witness and cause of her workings, lord of her pauseless endeavour.
All things she knows, though she seems here unseeing; even in her slumber
Wondrous her works are, design and its magic and magic of number,
Plan of her mighty cosmic geometry, balance of forces,
Universe flung beyond universe, law of the stars and their courses,
Cosmos atomic stretched to the scale of the Infinite's measure.
Mute in the trance of the Eternal she sleeps with the stone and the azure.
Now she awakes; for life has just stirred in her, stretching first blindly
Outward for sense and its pleasure and pain and the gifts of the kindly
Mother of all, for her light and her air and the sap from her flowing,
Pleasure of bloom and inconscient beauty, pleasure of growing.
Then into mind she arises; heart's yearning awakes and reflection
Looks out on struggle and harmony, — conscious, her will of selection
Studies her works and illumines the choice of her way; last, slowly
Inward she turns and stares at the Spirit within her. Holy
Silences brood in her heart and she feels in her ardent recesses
Passions too great for her frame, on her body immortal caresses.
Into the calm of the Greatness beyond her she enters, burning
Now with a light beyond thought's, towards Self and Infinity turning,
Turned to beatitude, turned to eternity, spiritual grandeur,
Power without limit, ecstasy imperishable, shadowless splendour.
Then to her mortals come, flashing, thoughts that are wisdom's fire-kernel;
Leaping her flame-sweeps of might and delight and of vision supernal
Kindle the word and the act, the Divine and humanity fusing,
Illuminations, trance-seeds of silence, flowers of musing, —
Light of our being that yet has to be, its glory and glimmer
Smiting with sunrise the soul of the sage and the heart of the dreamer.
Or is it all but a vain expectation and effort ungrounded,
Wings without body, sight without object, waters unsounded,
Hue of a shimmer that steals through some secret celestial portal,
Glory of a gleam or a dream in an animal brief-lived and mortal?
Are they not radiances native to heaven's more fortunate ether,

Won when we part from this body, this temporal house of a nether
Mystery of life lived in vain? Upon earth is the glory forbidden,
Nature for ever accursed, frustrate, grief-vexed, fate-ridden?
Half of the glory she dreamed of forgotten or lost in earth's darkness,
Half of it mangled and missed as the death-wheels whirl in their starkness,
Cast out from heaven a goddess rebellious with mind for her mirror,
Cursed with desire and self-will and doomed to self-torture and error,
Came she to birth then with God for her enemy? Were we created
He unwilling or sleeping? did someone transgress the fated
Limits he set, outwitting God? In the too hasty vision
Marred of some demiurge filmed there the blur of a fatal misprision,
Making a world that revolves on itself in a circuit of failure,
Aeons of striving, death for a recompense, Time for our tenure?
Out of him rather she came and for him are her cry and her labour;
Deep are her roots in him; topless she climbs, to his greatness a neighbour.
All is himself in her, brooding in darkness, mounting the sun-ways:
Air-flight to him is man's journey with heaven and earth for the runways.
He is the witness and doer, he is the loved and the lover,
He the eternal Truth that we look in ourselves to discover.
All is his travel in Time; it is he who turns history's pages,
Act and event and result are the trail that he leaves through the ages;
Form and idea are his signs and number and sound are his symbols,
Music and singing, the word and its rhythm are Divinity's cymbals,
Thunder and surge are the drums of his marching. Through us, with urges
Self-ward, form-bound, mute, motionless, slowly inevitably emerges
Vast as the cosmos, minute as the atom, the Spirit eternal.
Often the gusts of his force illumining moments diurnal
Flame into speech and idea; transcendences splendid and subtle
Suddenly shoot through the weft of our looms from a magical shuttle;
Hid in our hearts is his glory; the Spirit works in our members.
Silence is he, with our voices he speaks, in our thoughts he remembers.
Deep in our being inhabits the voiceless invisible Teacher;
Powers of his godhead we live; the Creator dwells in the creature.
Out of his Void we arise to a mighty and shining existence,
Out of Inconscience, tearing the black Mask's giant resistance;
Waves of his consciousness well from him into these bodies in Nature,
Forms are put round him; his oneness, divided by mind's nomenclature,
High on the summits of being ponders immobile and single,
Penetrates atom and cell as the tide drenches sand-grain and shingle.
Oneness unknown to us dwells in these millions of figures and faces,

Wars with itself in our battles, loves in our clinging embraces,
Inly the self and the substance of things and their cause and their mover
Veiled in the depths which the foam of our thoughts and our life's billows
                                                                    cover,
Heaves like the sea in its waves; like heaven with its star-fires it gazes
Watching the world and its works. Interned in the finite's mazes,
Still shall he rise to his vast superconscience, we with him climbing;
Truth of man's thought with the truth of God's spirit faultlessly timing,
That which was mortal shall enter immortality's golden precincts,
Hushed breath of ecstasy, honey of lotus-depths where the bee sinks,
Timeless expanses too still for the voice of the hours to inveigle,
Spaces of spirit too vast for the flight of the God-bearing eagle, —
Enter the Splendour that broods now unseen on us, deity invading,
Sight without error, light without shadow, beauty unfading,
Infinite largeness, rapture eternal, love none can sever,
Life, not this death-play, but a power God-driven and blissful for ever.
"No," cry the wise, "for a circle was traced, there was pyloned a limit,
Only we escape through dream's thin passages. None can disclaim it;
All things created are made by their borders, sketched out and coded;
Vain is the passion to divinise manhood, humanise godhead.
None can exceed himself; even to find oneself hard for our search is:
Only we see as in night by a lustre of flickering torches.
To be content with our measure, our space is the law of our living.
All of thyself to thy manhood and Nature and Circumstance giving,
Be what thou must be or be what thou canst be, one hour in an era.
Knowing the truth of thy days, shun the light of ideal and chimera:
Curb heart's impatience, bind thy desires down, pause from self-vexing."
Who is the nomad then? who is the seeker, the gambler risking
All for a dream in a dream, the old and the sure and the stable
Flung as a stake for a prize that was never yet laid on the table?
Always the world is expanding and growing from minute to minute;
Playing the march of the adventure of Time with our lives for her spinet.
Maya or Nature, the wonderful Mother, strikes out surprising
Strains of the Spirit disprisoned; creation heavenward rising
Wrestles with Time and Space and the Unknown to give form to the Formless.
Bliss is her goal, but her road is through whirlwind and death-blast and
                                                                storm-race.
All is a wager and danger, all is a chase and a battle.
Vainly man, crouched in his corner of safety, shrinks from the fatal
Lure of the Infinite. Guided by Powers that surround and precede us

Fearful and faltering steps are our perishing efforts that lead us
On through the rooms of the finite till open the limitless spaces
And we can look into all-seeing eyes and imperishable faces.
But we must pass through the aeons; Space is a bar twixt our ankles,
Time is a weight that we drag and the scar of the centuries rankles:
Caught by the moments, held back from the spirit's timelessness, slowly
Wading in shallows we take not the sea-plunge vastly and wholly.
Hard is the way to the Eternal for the mind-born will of the mortal
Bound by the body and life to the gait of the house-burdened turtle.
Here in this world that knows not its morrow, this reason that stumbles
Onward from error to truth and from truth back to error while crumbles
All that it fashioned, after the passion and travail are ended,
After the sacrifice offered when the will and the strength are expended,
Nothing is done but to have laid down one stone of a road without issue,
Added our quota of evil and good to an ambiguous tissue.
Destiny's lasso, its slip-knot tied by delight and repining,
Draws us through tangles of failure and victory's inextricable twining.
In the hard reckoning made by the grey-robed accountant at even
Pain is the ransom we pay for the smallest foretaste of heaven.
Ignorance darkens, death and inconscience gape to absorb us;
Thick and persistent the Night confronts us, its hunger enormous
Swallowing our work and our lives. Our love and our knowledge squandered
Lie like a treasure refused and trod down on the ways where we wandered;
All we have done is effaced by the thousands behind us arriving.
Trapped in a round fixed for ever circles our thought and our living.
Fiercely the gods in their jealousy strike down the heads that have
                                                             neighboured
Even for a moment their skies; in the sands our achievements are gravured.
Yet survives bliss in the rhythm of our heart-beats, yet is there wonder,
Beauty's immortal delight, and the seals of the mystery sunder.
Honied a thousand whispers come, in the birds, in the breezes,
Moonlight, the voices of streams; with a hundred marvellous faces
Always he lures us to love him, always he draws us to pleasure
Leaving remembrance and anguish behind for our only treasure.
Passionate we seek for him everywhere, yearn for some sign of him, calling,
Scanning the dust for his foot-prints, praying and stumbling and falling;
Nothing is found and no answer comes from the masks that are passing.
Memories linger, lines from the past like a half-faded tracing.
He has passed on into silence wearing his luminous mantle.
Out of the melodied distance a laugh rings pure-toned, infantile,

Sole reminder that he is, last signal recalling his presence.
There is a joy behind suffering; pain digs our road to his pleasure.
All things have bliss for their secret; only our consciousness falters
Fearing to offer itself as a victim on ecstasy's altars.
Is not the world his disguise? when that cloak is tossed back from his shoulders,
Beauty looks out like a sun on the hearts of the ravished beholders.
Mortals, your end is beatitude, rapture eternal his meaning:
Joy, which he most now denies, is his purpose: the hedges, the screening
Were but the rules of his play; his denials came to lure farther.
These too were magic of Maya, smiles of the marvellous Mother.
Oh, but the cruelty! oh, but the empty pain we go rueing!
Edges of opposite sweetness, calls to a closer pursuing.
All that we meet is a symbol and gateway; cryptic intention
Lurks in a common appearance, smiles from a casual mention:
Opposites hide in each other; in the laughter of Nature is danger,
Glory and greatness their embryos form in the womb of her anger.
Why are we terrified? wherefore cry out and draw back from the smiting —
Blows from the hands of a lover to direr exactions exciting,
Fiery points of his play! Was he Rudra only, the mighty?
Whose were the whispers of sweetness, whose were the murmurs of pity?
Something opposes our grasp on the light and the sweetness and power,
Something within us, something without us, trap-door or tower,
Nature's gap in our being — or hinge. That device could we vanquish,
Once could we clasp him and hold, his joy we could never relinquish.
Then we could not be denied, for our might would be single and flawless.
Sons of the Eternal, sovereigns of Nature absolute and lawless,
Termlessly our souls would possess as he now enjoys and possesses,
Termlessly probe the delight of his laughter's lurking recesses,
Chasing its trail to the apex of sweetness and secrecy. Treasured
Close to the beats of Eternity's heart in a greatness unmeasured,
Locked into a miracle and mystery of Light we would live in him, — seated
Deep in his core of beatitude ceaselessly by Nature repeated,
Careless of Time, with no fear of an end, with no need for endeavour
Caught by his ecstasy dwell in a rapture enduring for ever.
What was the garden he built when the stars were first set in their places,
Soul and Nature together mid streams and in cloudless spaces
Naked and innocent? Someone offered a fruit of derision,
Knowledge of good and of evil, cleaving in God a division.
Though he who made all said, "It is good, I have fashioned perfection,"

"No, there is evil," someone whispered, "'tis screened from detection."
Wisest he of the beasts of the field, one cunning and creeping;
"See it," he said, "be wise; you shall be as the gods are, unsleeping,
They who know all." And they ate. The roots of our being were shaken;
Hatred and weeping and wrath at once trampled a world overtaken,
Terror and fleeing and anguish and shame and desires unsated;
Cruelty stalked like a lion; Revenge and her brood were created.
Out to the desert he drove the rebellious. Flaming behind them
Streamed out the sword of his wrath and it followed leaping to find them,
Stabbing at random. The pure and the evil, the strong and the tempted,
All are confounded in punishment; justly is no one exempted.
Virtuous? yes, there are many, but who is there innocent? Toiling
Therefore we seek, but find not that Eden. Planting and spoiling,
"This is the garden," we say, "lo, the trees and this is the river."
Vainly redeemers came, not one has availed to deliver.
Never can Nature go back to her careless and childlike beginning,
Laugh of the babe and the song of the wheel in its delicate spinning,
Smile of the sun upon flowers and earth's beauty, life without labour
Plucking the fruits of the soil and rejoicing in cottage and arbour.
Once we have chosen to be as the gods, we must follow that motion.
Knowledge must grow in us, might like a Titan's, bliss like an ocean,
Calmness and purity born of the spirit's gaze on the Real,
Rapture of his oneness embracing the soul in a clasp hymeneal.
Was it not he once in Brindavan? Woods divine to our yearning,
Memorable always! O flowers, O delight on the tree-tops burning,
Grasses his herds have grazed and crushed by his feet in the dancing,
Yamuna flowing with song, through the greenness always advancing,
You unforgotten remind; for his flute with its sweetness ensnaring
Sounds in our ears in the night and our souls of their teguments baring
Hales us out naked and absolute, out to his woodlands eternal,
Out to his moonlit dances, his dalliance sweet and supernal,
And we go stumbling, maddened and thrilled to his dreadful embraces,
Slaves of his rapture to Brindavan crowded with amorous faces,
Luminous kine in the green glades seated, soft-eyed gazing,
Flowers on the branches distressing us, moonbeams unearthly amazing,
Yamuna flowing before us, laughing low with her voices,
Brindavan arching o'er us where Shyama sports and rejoices.
Inly the miracle trembles repeated; mist-walls are broken
Hiding that country of God and we look on the wonderful token,
Clasp the beautiful body of the Eternal; his flute-call of yearning

Cries in our breast with its blissful anguish for ever returning;
Life flows past us with passionate voices, a heavenly river,
All our being goes back as a bride of his bliss to the Giver.
Even an hour of the soul can unveil the Unborn, the Everlasting,
Gaze on its mighty Companion; the load of mortality casting,
Mind hushes stilled in eternity; waves of the Infinite wander
Thrilling body and soul and its endless felicity squander;
All world-sorrow is finished, the cry of the parting is over;
Ecstasy laughs in our veins, in our heart is the heart of the Lover.
As when a stream from a highland plateau green mid the mountains
Draws through broad lakes of delight the gracious sweep of its fountains,
Life from its heaven of desire comes down to the toil of the earthways;
Streaming through mire it pours still the mystical joy of its birthplace,
Green of its banks and the green of its trees and the hues of the flower.
Something of child-heart beauty, something of greatness and power,
Dwell with it still in its early torrent laughter and brightness,
Call in the youth of its floods and the voice of the wideness and whiteness.
But in its course are set darkness and fall and the spirit's ordeal.
Hating its narrowness, forced by an ardour to see all and be all,
Dashed on the inconscient rocks and straining through mud, over gravel,
Flows, like an ardent prisoner bound to the scenes of his travail,
Life, the river of the Spirit, consenting to anguish and sorrow
If by her heart's toil a loan-light of joy from the heavens she can borrow.
Out of the sun-rays and moon-rays, the winds' wing-glimmer and revel,
Out of the star-fields of wonder, down to earth's danger and evil
Headlong cast with a stridulant thunder, the doom-ways descending,
Shuddering below into sunless depths, across chasms unending,
Baulked of the might of its waters, a thread in a mountainous vastness,
Parcelled and scanted it hurries as of storming a Titan fastness,
Carving the hills with a sullen and lonely gigantic labour.
Hurled into strangling ravines it escapes with a leap and a quaver,
Breaks from the channels of hiding it grooves out and chisels and twistens,
Angry, afraid, white, foaming. A stony and monstrous resistance
Meets it piling up stubborn limits. Afflicted the river
Treasures a scattered sunbeam, moans for a god to deliver,
Longing to lapse through the plain's green felicity, yearning to widen
Joined to the ocean's shoreless eternity far-off and hidden.
High on the cliffs the Great Ones are watching, the Mighty and Deathless,
Soaring and plunging the roadway of the Gods climbs uplifted and breathless;
Ever we hear in the heart of the peril a flute go before us,

Luminous beckoning hands in the distance invite and implore us.
Ignorant, circled with death and the abyss, we have dreamed of a human
Paradise made from the mind of a man, from the heart of a woman,
Dreamed of the Isles of the Blest in a light of perpetual summer,
Dreamed of the joy of an earthly life with no pain for incomer.
Never, we said, can these waters from heaven be lost in the marshes,
Cease in the sands of the desert, die where the simoom parches;
Plains are beyond, there are hamlets and fields where the river rejoices
Pacing once more with a quiet step and with amical voices:
Bright amid woodlands red with the berries and cool with the breezes
Glimmer the leaves; all night long the heart of the nightingale eases
Sweetly its burden of pity and sorrow. There amid flowers
We shall take pleasure in arbours delightful, lengthening the hours,
Time for our servitor waiting our fancy through moments unhasting,
Under the cloudless blue of those skies of tranquillity resting,
Lying on beds of lilies, hearing the bells of the cattle
Tinkle, and drink red wine of life and go forth to the battle,
Fight and unwounded return to our beautiful home by the waters,
Fruit of our joy rear tall strong sons and radiant daughters.
Then shall the Virgins of Light come down to us clad in clear raiment
Woven from sunbeam and moonbeam and lightnings, limitless payment
Bring of our toil and our sorrow, carrying life-giving garlands
Plucked by the fountains of Paradise, bring from imperishable star-lands
Hymn-words of wisdom, visions of beauty, heaven-fruit ruddy,
Wine-cups of ecstasy sending the soul like a stream through the body.
Fate shall not know; if her spies come down to our beautiful valley,
They shall grow drunk with its grapes and wander in woodland and alley.
There leaps the anger of Rudra? there will his lightnings immortal
Circle around with their red eye of cruelty stabbing the portal?
Fearless is there life's play; I shall sport with my dove from his highlands,
Drinking her laughter of bliss like a god in my Grecian islands.
Life in my limbs shall grow deathless, flesh with the God-glory tingle,
Lustre of Paradise, light of the earth-ways marry and mingle.
These are but dreams and the truth shall be greater. Heaven made woman!
Flower of beatitude! living shape of the bliss of the Brahman!
Art thou not she who shall bring into life and time the Eternal?
Body of the summer of the Gods, a sweetness virginal, vernal,
Breathes from thy soul into Nature; Love sits dreaming in thy bosom,
Wisdom gazes from thy eyes, thy breasts of God-rapture are the blossom.
If but the joy of thy feet once could touch our spaces smiting

Earth with a ray from the Unknown, on the world's heart heaven's script
                                                                writing,
All then would change into harmony and beauty, Time's doors shudder
Swinging wide on their hinges into Eternity, other
Voices than earth's would be fire in our speech and make deathless our
                                                                thinking.
One who is hidden in Light would grow visible, multitudes linking,
Lyres of a single ecstasy, throbs of the one heart beating,
Wonderful bodies and souls in the spirit's identity meeting
Even as stars in sky-vastness know their kindred in grandeur.
Yet may it be that although in the hands of our destiny stands sure
Fixed to its hour the Decree of the Advent, still it is fated
Only when kindling earth's bodies a mightier Soul is created.
Far-off the gold and the greatness, the rapture too splendid and dire.
Are not the ages too young? too low in our hearts burns the fire.
Bringest thou only a gleam on the summits, a cry in the distance,
Seen by the eyes that are wakened, heard by a spirit that listens?
Form of the formless All-Beautiful, lodestar of Nature's aspirance,
Music of prelude giving a voice to the ineffable Silence,
First white dawn of the God-Light cast on these creatures that perish,
Word-key of a divine and eternal truth for mortals to cherish,
Come! let thy sweetness and force be a breath in the breast of the future
Making the god-ways alive, immortality's golden-red suture:
Deep in our lives there shall work out a honeyed celestial leaven,
Bliss shall grow native to being and earth be a kin-soil to heaven.
Open the barriers of Time, the world with thy beauty enamour.
Trailing behind thee the purple of thy soul and the dawn-moment's glamour,
Forcing the heart of the Midnight where slumber and secrecy linger,
Guardians of mystery, touching her bosom with thy luminous finger,
Daughter of Heaven, break through to me moonlike, mystic and gleaming;
Tread through the margins of twilight, cross over borders of dreaming.
Vision delightful alone on the peaks whom the silences cover,
Vision of bliss, stoop down to mortality, lean to thy lover.

AHANA

Voice of the sensuous mortal, heart of eternal longing,
Thou who hast lived as in walls, thy soul with thy senses wronging!
But I descend at last. Fickle and terrible, sweet and deceiving,
Poison and nectar one has dispensed to thee, luring thee, leaving.
We two together shall capture the flute and the player relentless.

Son of man, thou hast crowned thy life with the flowers that are scentless,
Chased the delights that wound. But I come and midnight shall sunder.
Lo, I come, and behind me Knowledge descends and with thunder
Filling the spaces Strength, the Angel, bears on his bosom
Joy to thy arms. Thou shalt look on her face like a child's or a blossom,
Innocent, free as in Eden of old, not afraid of her playing,
When thy desires I have seized and devoured like a lioness preying.
Thou shalt not suffer always nor cry to me lured and forsaken:
I have a snare for his footsteps, I have a chain for him taken.
Come then to Brindavan, soul of the joyous; faster and faster
Follow the dance I shall teach thee with Shyama for slave and for master.
Follow the notes of the flute with a soul aware and exulting;
Trample Delight that submits and crouch to a sweetness insulting.
Then shalt thou know what the dance meant, fathom the song and the singer,
Hear behind thunder its rhymes, touched by lightning thrill to his finger,
Brindavan's rustle shalt understand and Yamuna's laughter,
Take thy place in the Ras[1] and thy share of the ecstasy after.

---

[1] The dance-round of Krishna with the cowherdesses in the moonlit groves of Brindavan, type of the dance of Divine Delight with the souls of men liberated in the world of Bliss secret within us.

The Descent of Ahana*

AHANA

Strayed from the roads of Time, far-couched on the void I have slumbered;
Centuries passed me unnoticed, millenniums perished unnumbered.
I, Ahana, slept. In the stream of thy sevenfold Ocean,
Being, how hast thou laboured without me? Whence was thy motion?
Not without me can thy existence be. But I came fleeing; —
Vexed was my soul with joys of sound and weary of seeing;
Into the deeps of my nature I lapsed, I escaped into slumber.
Out of the silence who call me back to the clamour and cumber?
Why should I go with you? What hast thou done in return for my labour,
World? What wage had my soul when its strength was thy neighbour,
Though I have loved all, working and suffering, giving them pleasure?
I have escaped from it all; I have fled the pitiless pressure.
Silence vast and pure, again to thy wideness receive me;
For unto thee I turn back from those who would use me and grieve me.

VOICES

Nay, it is done, to the lash of our cry thou hast started, O Woman.
Lured shalt thou fall from thy empty peace and the silence inhuman.
Joy as thou canst, endure as thou must, but bend to our uses.
Vainly thy heart repines, — thou wast made for this, — vainly refuses.
Wilt thou then crave for a recompense? Other the nature He gave thee,
Scourged and indulged, to obey and to wrestle with strengths that enslave
thee.
Just as thy nature, thy task for the love and the laughter of the ages;
Mighty thou art, but a slave, and the chain and the whip are thy wages.

AHANA

Voices of joy, from the roseate arbour of sense and the places
Thrilled with the song and the scent and peopled with beautiful faces,
Long in your closes of springtime, lured to joyances unsated
Tarried my heart and I walked in your meadows, your chaplets I plaited,
Played in your gardens of ease and, careless of blasts in the distance,
Paced, pursued by the winds, your orchard of autumn's persistence,
Saw on the dance of a ripple your lotus that slumbers and quivers,
Heard your nightingales warbling in covert by moon-gilded rivers.

* The earlier and unrevised version of the poem of which the last portion was considerably revised and enlarged under the title *Ahana*.

But I relinquished your streams and I turned from your moon-beams and
    flowers;
Now I have done with space and my soul is released from the hours.
Freed am I now from the need of joy, the attraction to sorrow,
Who have escaped from my past and forgotten today and tomorrow;
I have grown vacant and mighty, naked and wide as the azure.
Will you now plant in this blast, on this snow your roses of pleasure?
Once was a dwelling here that was made for the dance of the Graces,
But I have hewn down its gardens and ravaged its delicate places,
Driven the revellers out from their pleasance to wander unfriended,
Flung down the walls and over the debris written 'tis ended'.
Now, and I know not yet wherefore, the Mighty One suffers you near Him,
But in their coming the great Gods hesitate seeming to fear Him.
Thought returns to my soul like a stranger. Sweetness and feature
Draw back appalled to their kind from the frozen vasts of my nature.
Turn back, you also, angels of yearning, vessels of sweetness.
Have I not wandered from Time, left ecstasy, outstripped completeness?

    VOICES

Goddess, we moaned upon earth and we wandered exiled from heaven.
Joy from us fled; our hearts to the worm and the arrow were given.
Old delights we remembered, natures of ecstasy keeping,
Hastened from rose to rose, but were turned back wounded and weeping:
Snatches of pleasure we seized; they were haunted and challenged by sorrow.
Marred was our joy of the day by the care and the dread of the morrow.
Star of infinity, we have beheld thee bright and unmoving
Seated above us, in tracts unattained by us, throned beyond loving.
Lonely thou sittest above in the fruitless vasts of the Spirit.
Waitest thou, Goddess, then for a purer world to inherit?
Wilt thou not perfect this rather that sprang too from Wisdom and Power?
Taking the earthly rose canst thou image not Heaven in a flower?
Winging like bees to thy limbs we made haste like flames through the azure,
O we were ploughed with delight, we were pierced as with arrows of pleasure.
Rapture yearned and the Uswins cried to us; Indra arising
Gazed from the heights of his mental realms and the moonbeams surprising
Flowed on him out of the regions immortal; their nectar slowly
Mixed with the scattered roses of dawn and mastered us wholly.
Come, come down to us, Woman divine whom the world unforgetting
Yearns for still; we will draw thee, O star, from thy colourless setting.
Lonely thou sittest above in the fruitless vasts of the Spirit;

Waitest thou, Goddess, then for some younger world to complete or inherit?
Nay, if thou save not this, will another rise from the spaces?
Only the past fulfilled can conjure room to the future that presses.[1]
Goddess, we understand thee not; Woman, we know not thy nature;
This yet we know we have need of thee here in our world of misfeature.
Therefore we call to thee and would compel if our hands could but reach
                                                                    thee.
O, we have means to compel; we have many a sweetness to teach thee
Charming thee back to thy task mid our fields and our sunbeams and flowers,
Weaving a net for thy feet with the snare of the moonlit hours.

    AHANA
Spirits of helpless rapture, spirits of sweetness and playtime,
Thrilled with my honey of night and drunk with my wine of the daytime,
If there were strengths that could seize on the world for their passion and
                                                                    rapture,
If there were souls that could hunt after God as a prey for their capture,
Such might aspire to possess me. I am Ahana the mighty,
I am Ashtaroth, I am the goddess, divine Aphrodite.
You have a thirst full sweet, but earth's vineyards quickly assuage it:
Hearts there must be that outmeasure existence, strengths that besiege it,
Natures fit for my vastness! Return to your haunts, O ye shadows
Beautiful. Not of my will I descend to the bee-haunted meadows,
Rivulets stealing through flowers. Let those who are mighty aspire,
Gods if there are of such greatness, to seize on the world's Desire.

    VOICES
Good, it is spoken. We wait thee, Ahana, where fugitive traces
Came of the hunted prey of the Titans in desert places
Trod by thee once when the world was mighty and violent. Risen,
Hark, they ascend; they are freed by thy call from the seals of their prison.

    AHANA
Rush I can hear as of wings in the void and the march of a nation.
Shapes of old mightiness visit me; movements of ancient elation
Stride and return in my soul, and it turns like an antelope fleeing.
What was the cry that thou drewst from my bosom, Lord of my being?
Lo, their souls are cast on my soul like forms in a mirror!
Hark, they arise, they aspire, they are near, and I shudder with terror,

[1] Is not the past fulfilled that finds room for the future faces?

Quake with delight and attraction. Lord of the worlds, dost thou leave me
Bare for their seizing? Of peace and of strength in a moment bereave me?
Long hast Thou kept me safe in Thy soul, but I lose my defences.
Thought streams fast on me; joy is awake and the strife of the senses.
Ah, they have clutched my feet, my thighs are seized by them! Legions
Mighty around me they stride: I feel them filling the regions.
See'st Thou their hands on my locks? Wilt Thou suffer it, Master of Nature?
I am Thy force and Thy strength; wilt Thou hand me enslaved to Thy
                                                              creature?
Headlong they drag me down to their dreadful worlds far below me.
What will you do with me there, O you mighty Ones? Speak to me, show me
One of your faces, teach me one of your names while you ravish,
Dragging my arms and my knees while you hurry me. Tell me what lavish
Ecstasy, show me what torture immense you seize me for. Quittance
When shall I have from my labour? What term has your tyranny, Titans?
Masters fierce of your worlds who would conquer the higher creation,
What is your will with me, giants of violence, lords of elation?

VOICES

In the beginning of things when nought was abroad but the waters,
Ocean stirred with longing his mighty and deep-bosomed daughters.
Out of that longing gigantic we rose from the voiceless recesses;[1]
Candid, unwarmed, O Ahana, the wide ethereal abysses[2]
Stretched enormous, silent, void of the breath of thy greatness;
We alone peopled, and troubled with rapture their ancient sedateness:[3]
We are the gods who have mapped out Time and measured its spaces;
Raised there our mansions of pride and planted its amorous places.
Trembling like flowers appeared in the void the immense constellations;
Gods grew possessed of their heavens, earth rose with her joy-haunted
                                                              nations.
Calm were we, mighty, magnificent, hunting and seizing
Whatso we willed through the world, in a rapture that thought not of ceasing.[4]
But thou hast turned from us, favouring gods who are slighter, and fairer,
Swift-footed, subtle of mind; but the sword was too great for the bearer,
Heavy the sceptre weighed upon hands not created to bear it.
Cruel and jealous the gods of thy choice were, cunning of spirit,
(Suave were their eyes of beauty that mastered thy heart, O woman!)

[1] heart of the ocean;   [2] spaces empty of motion
[3] Hushed to thy sweetnesses, rapt in the (calm?) of their ancient sedateness:
[4] enjoying and, careless, releasing.

They who to govern our world, made it tarnished, sorrowful, common.
[Mystic and vast our world, but they hoped in their smallness to sum it
Schooled and coerced in themselves and they sank an ignorant plummet
Into infinity, shaping a limited beauty and power,
Confident, figuring Space in an inch and Time in an hour.
Therefore pleasure was troubled and beauty tarnished, madness
Mated with knowledge, the heart of purity sullied with sadness.
Strife began twixt the Infinite deathless within and the measure
Falsely imposed from without on its thought and its force and its pleasure.][1]
We who could help were condemned in their sunless Hells to languish,
Shaking the world with the heave of our limbs, for our breath was an anguish.
There were we cast down, met and repulsed by the speed of their thunder,
Earth piled on us, our Mother; her heart of fire burned under.
Now we escape, we are free; our triumph and bliss are before us,
Earth is our prey and the heavens our hunting ground; stars in their chorus
Chant, wide-wheeling, our paean; the world is awake and rejoices:
Hast thou not heard its trampling of strengths and its rapturous voices?
Is not our might around thee yet? does not our thunder-winged fleetness
Drag thee down yet to the haunts of our strength and the cups of our
                                                             sweetness?
There thou shalt suffer couched on our mountains, over them stretching
All thy defenceless bliss, thy pangs to eternity reaching.
Thou shalt be taken and whelmed in our trampling and bottomless Oceans,
Chained to the rocks of the world and condemned to our giant emotions.
Violent joy thou shalt have of us, raptures and ruthless revulsions
Racking and tearing thee, and each thrill of thy honied convulsions,
We, as it shakes the mountains, we as thou churnst up the waters,
Laughing shall turn to a joy for Delight and her pitiless daughters.
They shall be changed to a strength for the gods and for death-besieged
                                                             natures.
When we have conquered, when thou hast yielded to earth and her creatures,
Boundless, thy strength, O Ahana, delivered, thy sorrowless joyance,
Hope, if thou canst, release from the meed of thy pride and defiance.

AHANA

Gods irresistible, blasts of His violence, fighters eternal,
Churners of Ocean, stormers of Heaven! but limits diurnal
Chafe you and bonds of the Night. I know in my soul I am given,
Racked to your joys as a sacrifice, writhing, to raise you to heaven.

[1] The square brackets are in the original.

Therefore you seize on me, vanquish and carry me swift to my falling.
Fain would I linger, pain resist, to Infinity calling;
But you possess all my limbs, you compel me, giants of evil.
Am I then doomed to your darkness and violence, moonlight and revel?
Hast thou no pity, O Earth,[1] my soul from this death to deliver?
Who are you, luminous movements? Around me you glimmer and quiver.
Visible, not to the eyes, and not audible, only you call me,
Teaching my soul with sound and the joy that shall seize and befall me.[2]
What are you, lords of the brightness vague that aspires, but fulfils not?
For you possess and retire but your yearning quenches not, stills not.
Yet is your touch a pleasure that thrills all my soul with its sweetness:
I am in love with your whispers and snared by your bright incompleteness.
Speak to me, downward falling, and comfort me. Will you not follow
Still to console on the hills of my pain and in Ocean's hollow?[3]

    VOICES

We are the Ancients of Knowledge, Ahana, the Sons of the Morning.
Why dost thou cry to us, Daughter of Bliss, who left us with scorning?
We too dwelt in delight when these were supreme in their spaces;
We too were riven with pain when they fell down prone from their places.
Hast thou forgotten the world as it was ere thou fledst from our nations?
Dost thou remember at all the joy of the ancient creations?
Thrilled were its streams with our intimate bliss and our happy contriving;
Sound was a song and movement the dance of our rhythmical living.
Out of our devious delight came the senses and all their deceptions;
Earth was our ring of bliss and the map of our mighty conceptions.
For we sustained the inert sitting secret in clod and in petal,
And we awoke to a twilight of life in the leaf and the metal.
Active we dreamed in the mind and we ordered our dreams to a measure,
Making an image of pain and shaping an idol of pleasure.
Good we have made by our thoughts and sin by our fear and recoiling;
It was our weakness invented grief, O delight! reconciling
Always the touch that was borne with strength that went out for possessing,
Somewhere, somehow we failed; there was discord, a pang, a regressing.
Goddess, His whispers bewildered us; over us vainly aspirant

---

[1] Is there no help in the world,
[2] You who are visible, not to the eyes, who, not audible, flutter
   Teaching my soul with sound; your name and your progeny utter.
[3] Speak to me, comfort me falling, grapple me, follow
   Down to the hills of my pain and into the Ocean's hollow.

Galloped the throng of His strengths like the steeds of a pitiless tyrant.
Since in the woods of the world we have wandered, thrust from sereneness,
Erring mid pleasures that fled and dangers that coiled in the greenness.
Someone surrounds and possesses our lives whom we cannot discover,
Someone our heart in its hunger pursues with the moans of a lover.
Knowledge faints in its toil, amasses but loses its guerdon;
Strength is a worker blinded and maimed who is chained to his burden,
Love a seeker astray; he finds in a seeming, then misses;
Weariness hampers his feet. Desire with unsatisfied kisses
Clings to each object she lights upon, loving, forsaking, returning:
Earth is filled with her sobs and the cry of her fruitlessly burning.
All things we sounded here. Everything leaves us or fails in the spending;
Strength has its weakness, knowledge its night and joy has its ending.
Is it not thou who shalt rescue us, freeing the Titans, the Graces?
Hast thou not hidden thyself in the mask of a million faces?
Nay, from thyself thou art hidden; thy secret intention thou shunnest
And from the joy thou hast willed like an antelope fleest and runnest.
Thou shalt be forced, O Ahana, to bear enjoyment and knowing
Termlessly. Come, O come from thy whiteness and distance, thou glowing,
Mighty and hundred-ecstasied Woman! Daughter of Heaven,
Usha, descend to thy pastimes below and thy haunts that are given.
She-wolf avid of cruelty, lioness eager for battle,
Tigress that prowlst in the night and leapest out dire on the cattle,
Sarama, dog of the heavens, thou image of grosser enjoying,
Hungry slave of the worlds, incessantly pawing and toying,
Snake of delight and of poison, gambolling beast of the meadows,
Come to thy pastures, Ahana, sport in the sunbeams and shadows.
Naiad swimming through streams and Dryad fleeing through forest
Wild, from the clutch of the Satyr! Ahana, who breakest and restorest!
Oread, mountain Echo, cry to the rocks in thy running!
Nymph in recess and in haunt the pursuit and the melody shunning!
Giantess, cruel and false and grand! Gandharvi that singest
Heavenward, bird exultant through storm and through sapphire who wingest!
Centauress galloping wild through the woods of Himaloy high-crested!
Yakshini brooding o'er treasure down in earth's bowels arrested!
Demoness gnashing thy teeth in the burial-ground! Titaness striding
Restless through worlds for thy rest, the brain and the bosom not ridding
Even one hour of the ferment-waste and the load beyond bearing,
Recklessly slaying the peoples in anger, recklessly sparing,
Spending the strength that is thine to inherit the doom of another!

Goddess of pity who yearnst and who helpest, Durga and Mother!
Brooder in Delphi's caverns, Voice in the groves of Dodona!
Goddess serene of an ancient progeny, Dian, Latona!
Virgin! ascetic frank or remote, Athene the mighty!
Harlot supine to the worlds, insatiate white Aphrodite!
Hundred-named art thou, goddess, a hundred-formed, and thy bosom
Thrills all the world with its breasts, O starlight, O mountain, O blossom!
Rain that descendest kissing our lips and lightning that slayest!
Thou who destroyest to save, to delight who hurtst and dismayest!
Thou art our mother and sister and bride. O girdled with splendour,
Cruel and bright as the sun, O moonlike, mystic and tender!
Thou art the perfect peopling of Space, O Ahana; thou only
Fillest Time with thy forms. Leave then thy eternity lonely,
Come! from thy summits descending arrive to us, Daughter of Heaven,
Usha, Dawn of the world, for our ways to thy footsteps are given.
Strength thou hast built for the floor of the world and delight for its rafter.
Calm are thy depths, O Ahana, above is thy hundred-mouthed laughter.
Rapture can fail not in thee though he rend like a lion preying
Body and soul with his ecstasies vast. These for ever delaying,
Feigning to end, shall renew thyself, never exhausting his blisses,
Joy shall be in thy bosom satisfied never with kisses;
Strength from thy breasts drawing force of the Titans shall unrelaxing
Stride through the worlds at his work. One shall drive him ruthlessly taxing
Sinew and nerve, he shall toil exultantly, helpless to tire,
Borne by unstumbling speed to the soul of a God's desire.
What shall thy roof be, crown of thy building? Knowledge, sublimely,
High on her vaulted arches where thought, half-lost, wings dimly,
Luring the flaming heart above and the soul in its stillness
Pure in a sky beyond sky. Delivered from virtue and vileness,[1]
Vast, uncompelled we shall range once more[2] at peace with our nature,
Reconciled, knowing ourselves. To her pain and the longings that reach her
Come from thy summits, Ahana, come! Our desire unrelenting
Hales thee down from God and He smiles at thee sweetly consenting.
Lo, she is hurried down and the regions live in her tresses.
Worlds, she descends to you! Peoples, she nears with her mighty caresses.
Man in his sojourn, Gods in their going, Titans exultant
Thrill with thy fall, O Ahana, and wait for the godhead resultant.

[1] Luring the flaming heart above and the soul through its shadows,
  Winging wide like a bird through the night and the moonlit meadows,
[2] released and

AHANA

Calm like a goddess, alarmed like a bride is my spirit descending,
Falling, O Gods, to your arms. I know my beginning and ending;
All I have known and I am not astonished; alarmed and attracted
Therefore my soul descends foreknowing the rapture[1] exacted,
Gulf of the joys you would doom me to, torment of infinite striving,
Travail of knowledge. Was I not made for your mightier living?
Gods, I am falling, I am descending, cast down as for ever,
Thrown as a slave at your feet and a tool for your ruthless endeavour.
Yet while I fall, I will threaten you. Hope shall be yours, so it trembles.
I have a bliss that destroys and the death in me wooes and dissembles.
Will you not suffer then my return to my peace beyond telling?
You have accepted death for your pastime, Titans rebelling!
Hope then from pain delight and from death an immortal stature!
Slaves of her instruments, rise to be equals and tyrants of Nature!
Lay not your hands so fiercely upon me! Compel me not, falling![2]
'Tis not a merciful One that you seize. I fall and, arisen,
Earth strides towards me. Gods, my possessors, kingdoms, my prison,
So shall you prosper or die as you use or misuse and deceive me.
Vast, I descend from God. O world and its masters, receive me!

II

AHANA

Lo, on the hills I have paused, on the peaks of the world I have halted
Here in the middle realms of Varuna the world-wide exalted.
Gods, who have drawn me down to the labour and sobs of creation,
First I would speak with the troubled hearts and the twilit nation,
Speak then, I bend my ear to the far terrestrial calling,
Speak, O thou toiling race of humanity, welcome me falling,
Space for whose use in a boundless thought was unrolled and extended;
Time in its cycles waited for man. Though his kingdom is ended,
Here in a speck mid the suns and his life is a throb in the aeons,
Yet, O you Titans and Gods, O Rudras, O strong Aditians,
Man is the centre and knot; he is first, though the last in the ages.
I would remember your cycles, recover your vanished pages;
I have the vials divine, I rain down the honey and manna;
Speak, O thou soul of humanity, knowing me. I am Ahana.

[1] your pleasures [2] A line before or after this seems to be missing.

A Voice

Vision bright, that walkest crowned on the hills far above me,
Vision of bliss, stoop down from thy calm and thy silence to love me.
Only is calm so sweet? Is our end tranquillity only?
Chill are your rivers of peace and their banks are leafless and lonely.
Art thou not sated with sunlight only, cold in its lustre?
Art thou not weary of only the stars in their solemn muster?
Always the hills and the high-hung plateaus, — solitude's voices
Making the silence lonelier! Only the eagle rejoices
In the inhuman height of his nesting, — austerely striving,
Deaf with the cry of the waterfall, only the pine there is thriving.
We have the voice of the cuckoo, the nightingale sings in the branches,
Human laughter leads and the cattle low in the ranches.
Come to our tangled sunbeams, dawn on our twilights and shadows,
Taste with us, scent with us fruits of our trees and flowers of our meadows.
Art thou an angel of God in His heavens that they vaunt of, His sages?
Skies of monotonous calm and His stillness filling the ages?
Is He thy master, Rudra the mighty, Shiva ascetic?
Has He denied thee his worlds? In His dance that they tell of, ecstatic,
Slaying, creating, calm in the midst of his movement and madness?
Was there no place for an earthly joy, for a human sadness?
Did He not make us and thee? O Woman, joy's delicate blossom
Sleeps in thy lids of delight! All Nature laughs in thy bosom
Hiding her children unborn and the food of her love and her laughter.
Is He then first? Was there none before Him? Shall none come after?
We too have gods, — the Tritons rise in the leap of the billows,
Emerald locks of the Nereids stream on their foam-crested pillows,
Dryads sway out from the branches, Naiads glance up through the waters;
Heaven has dances of joy and the gods are ensnared by her daughters.
Artemis calls as she flees through the glades and the breezes pursue her,
Cypris laughs in her isles where the Ocean-winds linger to woo her.
Thou shalt behold in glades forgotten the dance of the Graces,
Night shall be haunted for ever with strange and delicate faces.
Lo, all these peoples and who was it fashioned them? Who is unwilling
Still to have done with it? laughs beyond pain and saves in the killing?
Nature, you say; but is God then her enemy? Was she created,
He unknowing or sleeping? Did someone transgress the fated
Limits He set, outwitting God? Nay, we know it was fashioned
By the Almighty One, million-ecstasied, thousand-passioned.
But He created a discord within it, fashioned a limit?

Fashioned or figured? For He set completeness beyond. To disclaim it,
To be content with our measure, they say, is the law of our living.
Rather to follow always and, baffled, still to go striving.
Yes, it is true that we dash ourselves stark on a barrier appearing,
Fall and are wounded. But He insists who is in us, the fearing —
Conquers the grief. We resist; His temptations leap down compelling;
Virtue cheats us with noble names to a lofty rebelling.
Fiercely His wrath and His jealousy strike down the rebel aspiring,
Thick and persistent His might confronts our eager enquiring;
Yet 'tis His strengths descend crying always, "Rebel, aspire!";
Still through the night He sends rays, to our bosoms a quenchless fire.
Most to our joys He sets limits, most with His pangs He perplexes;
Yet when we faint it is He that spurs. Temptation vexes;
Honied a thousand whispers come, in the birds, in the breezes,
Moonlight, the voice of the streams; from hundreds of beautiful faces
Always He cries to us, "Love me!", always He lures us to pleasure,
Then escapes and leaves anguish behind for our only treasure.
Shall we not say then that joy is greatest, rapture His meaning?
That which He most denies is His purpose? The hedges, the screening,
Are they not all His play? In our end we have rapture for ever
Careless of Time, with no fear of the end, with no need for endeavour.
What was the garden He built when the stars were first set in their places,
Man and woman together mid streams and in cloudless spaces,
Naked and innocent? Someone offered a fruit of derision,
Knowledge of good and evil, cleaving in God a division,
Though He who made all said, "It is good; I have fashioned perfection."
"Nay, there is evil", someone whispered, "'tis screened from detection."
Wisest he of the beasts of the field, one cunning and creeping.
"See it," he said, "be wise. You shall be as the gods are, unsleeping,
They who know all", and they ate. The roots of our being were shaken;
Hatred and weeping and death at once trampled a world overtaken,
Terror and fleeing and wrath and shame and desire unsated;
Cruelty stalked like a lion; Revenge and her brood were created.
Out to the desert He drove the rebellious. Flaming behind them
Streamed out the sword of His wrath; it followed, eager to find them,
Stabbing at random. The pure and the evil, the strong and the tempted,
All are confounded in punishment. Justly is no one exempted.
Virtuous? Yes, there are many; but who is there innocent? Toiling,
Therefore, we seek, but find not that Eden. Planting and spoiling,
"This is the garden," we say, "lo, the trees! and this is the river."

Vainly! Redeemers come, but none yet availed to deliver.
Is it not all His play? Is He Rudra only, the mighty?
Whose are the whispers of sweetness? Whence are the murmurs of pity?
Why are we terrified then, cry out and draw back from the smiting?
Blows of a lover, perhaps, intended for fiercer inciting!
Yes, but the cruelty, yes, but the empty pain we go on rueing!
Edges of sweetness, it may be, call to a swifter pursuing.
Was it not He in Brindavan? O woods divine to our yearning,
Memorable always! O flowers, O delight on the treetops burning!
Grasses His kine have grazed and crushed by His feet in the dancing!
Yamuna flowing with sound, through the greenness always advancing!
You unforgotten remind! For His flute with its sweetness ensnaring
Sounds in our ears in the night and our souls of their teguments baring
Hales them out naked and absolute, out to His woodlands eternal,
Out to His moonlit dances, His dalliance sweet and supernal,
And we go stumbling, maddened and thrilled, to His dreadful embraces,
Slaves of His rapture to Brindavan crowded with amorous faces,
Luminous kine in the green glades seated soft-eyed grazing,
Flowers from the branches distressing us, moonbeams unearthly amazing,
Yamuna flowing before us, laughing low with her voices,
Brindavan arching o'er us where Shyama sports and rejoices.
What though 'tis true that the river of Life through the valley of Peril
Flows! But the diamond shines on the cliffside, jacinth and beryl
Gleam in the crannies, sapphire, smaragdus the roadway bejewel,
Down in the jaws of the savage mountains granite and cruel.
Who has not fathomed once all the voiceless throat of those mountains?
Always the wide-pacing river of Life from its far-off fountains
Flows down mighty and broad, like a warhorse brought from its manger
Arching its neck as it paces grand to the gorges of danger.
Sometimes we hesitate, often start and would turn from the trial,
Vainly; a fierce Inhabitant drives and brooks no denial.
Headlong, o'ercome with a stridulant horror the river descending
Shudders below into sunless depths among chasms unending,
Angry, afraid, white, foaming. A stony and monstrous resistance
Meets it, piling up stubborn limits, an iron insistence.
Yet in the midst of our labour and weeping not utterly lonely
Wander our steps, nor are terror and grief our portion only.
Do we not hear in the heart of the peril a flute go before us?
Are there not beckoning hands of the gods that insist and implore us?
Plains are beyond; there are hamlets and fields where the river rejoices

Pacing once more with a quiet step and amical voices.
There in a woodland red with berries and cool with the breezes, —
Green are the leaves, all night long the heart of the nightingale eases
Sweetly its burden of pity and sorrow, fragrant the flowers, —
There in an arbour delightful I know we shall sport with the Hours,
Lying on beds of lilies, hearing the bells of our cattle
Tinkle, and drink red wine of our life and go forth to the battle
And unwounded return to our beautiful home by the waters,
Pledge of our joys, rear tall strong sons and radiant daughters.
Shall God know? Will His spies come down to our beautiful valley?
They shall grow drunk with its grapes and wander in woodland and alley.
There will His anger follow us, there will His lightnings immortal
Wander around with their red eye of cruelty stabbing the portal?
Yes, I shall fear then His play! I will sport with my dove from His highlands,
Pleased with her laughter of bliss like a god in my Grecian islands.
Daughter of Heaven, break through to me, moonlike, mystic and gleaming.
Come through the margins of twilight, over the borders of dreaming;
Vision bright that walkest crowned on the hills far above me,
Vision of bliss, stoop down! Encircle me, madden me, love me.

AHANA

Voice of the sensuous mortal! heart of eternal longing!
Thou who hast lived as in walls, thy soul with thy senses wronging!
But I descend to thee. Fickle and terrible, sweet and deceiving,
Poison and nectar One has dispensed to thee, luring thee, leaving.
We two together shall capture the flute and the player relentless.
Son of man, thou hast crowned thy life with flowers that are scentless,
Chased the delights that wound. But I come and the darkness shall sunder.
Lo, I come and behind me knowledge descends and with thunder
Filling the spaces Strength the Angel bears on his bosom
Joy to thy arms. Thou shalt look on her face like a child's or a blossom,
Innocent, free as in Eden of old, not afraid of her playing.
Pain was not meant for ever, hearts were not made but for slaying.
Thou shalt not suffer always nor cry to me, lured and forsaken.
I have a snare for His footsteps, I have a chain for Him taken.
Come then to Brindavan, soul of the joyous; faster and faster
Follow the dance I shall teach thee with Shyama for slave and for master, —
Follow the notes of the flute with a soul aware and exulting,
Trample Delight that submits and crouch to a sweetness insulting.
Thou shalt know what the dance meant, fathom the song and the singer,

Hear behind thunder its rhythms, touched by lightning thrill to His finger,
Brindavan's rustle shall understand and Yamuna's laughter,
Take thy place in the Ras and thy share of the ecstasy after.

An Answer to a Criticism*

Milford accepts the rule that two consonants after a short vowel make the short vowel long, even if they are outside the word and come in another word following it. To my mind that is an absurdity. I shall go on pronouncing the *y* of *frosty* as short whether it has two consonants after it or only one or none; it remains *frosty* whether it is a *frosty scalp* or *frosty top* or a frosty anything. In no case have I pronounced it or could I consent to pronounce it as *frostee*. My hexameters are intended to be read naturally as one would read any English sentence. But if you admit a short syllable to be long whenever there are two consonants after it, then Bridges' scansions are perfectly justified. Milford does not accept that conclusion; he says Bridges' scansions are an absurdity. But he bases this on his idea that quantitative length does not count in English verse. It is intonation that makes the metre, he says, high tones or low tones — not longs and shorts, and stress is there of the greatest importance. On that ground he refuses to discuss my idea of weight or dwelling of the voice or admit quantity or anything else but tone as determinative of the metre and declares that there is no such thing as metrical length. Perhaps also that is the reason why he counts *frosty* as a spondee before *scalp*; he thinks that it causes it to be intoned in a different way. I don't see how it does that; for my part, I intone it just the same before *top* as before *scalp*. The ordinary theory is, I believe, that the *sc* of *scalp* acts as a sort of stile (because of the two consonants) which you take time to cross, so that *ty* must be considered as long because of this delay of the voice, while the *t* of *top* is merely a line across the path which gives no trouble. I don't see it like that; at most, *scalp* is a slightly longer word than *top* and that affects perhaps the rhythm of the line but not the metre; it cannot lengthen the preceding syllable so as to turn a trochee into a spondee. Sanskrit quantitation is irrelevant here (it is the same as Latin or Greek in this

---

* Apropos of *Ahana*, an English critic made some comments on the poet's system of "true English Quantity" as set forth in his essay "On Quantitative Metre". Sri Aurobindo examines them in this letter replying to a disciple's queries.

respect), for both Milford and I agree that the classical quantitative conventions are not reproducible in English: we both spew out Bridges' eccentric rhythms.

This answers also your question as to what Milford means by 'fundamental confusion' regarding *aridity*. He refuses to accept the idea of metrical length. But I am concerned with metrical as well as natural vowel quantities. My theory is that natural length in English depends, or can depend, on the dwelling of the voice giving metrical value or weight to the syllable; in quantitative verse one has to take account of all such dwelling or weight of the voice, both weight by ictus (stress) and weight by prolongation of the voice (ordinary syllabic length); the two are different, but for metrical purposes in a quantitative verse can rank as of equal value. I do not say that stress turns a short vowel into a long one.

Milford does not take the trouble to understand my theory — he ignores the importance I give to modulations and treats cretics and antibacchii and molossi as if they were dactyls; he ignores my objection to stressing short insignificant words like *and, with, but, the* — and thinks that I do that everywhere, which would be to ignore my theory. In fact I have scrupulously applied my theory in every detail of my practice. Take, for instance (*Ahana*, p. 523),

Art thou not heaven-bound even as I with the earth? Hast thou ended...

Here *art* is long by natural quantity though unstressed, which disproves Milford's criticism that in practice I never put an unstressed long as the first syllable of a dactyllic foot or spondee, as I should do by my theory. I don't do it often because normally in English rhythm stress bears the foot — a fact to which I have given full emphasis in my theory. That is the reason why I condemn the Bridgesean disregard of stress in the rhythm, — still I do it occasionally whenever it can come in quite naturally.[1] My

---

[1] *E.g.* Opening tribrachs are very frequent in my hexameter. *Cf. Ahana*, p. 524.
Is He then first? Was there none then before Him? Shall none come after?
But Milford thinks I have stressed the first short syllable to make them into dactyls — a thing I abhor. *Cf.* also *Ahana*, p. 530 (initial anapaest):

quantitative system, as I have shown at great length, is based on the natural movement of the English tongue, the same in prose and poetry, not on any artificial theory.

24-12-1942

Ĭn thĕ hārd | reckoning made by the grey-robed accountant at even,
or p. 530 (two anapaests):
   Yĕt sŭrvīves | bliss in the rhythm of our heart-beats, yĕt ĭs thēre | wonder,
or again p. 532:
   Ănd wĕ gō | stumbling, maddened and thrilled to his dreadful embraces,
or in my poem *Ilion* p. 393:
   Ănd thĕ fĭrst | Argive fell slain as he leaped on the Phrygian beaches.
There are even opening amphibrachs here and there. *Cf. Ahana*, p. 527:
   Ĭllūmĭ|nations, trance-seeds of silence, flowers of musing.

VI

POEMS IN NEW METRES

Ocean Oneness*

Silence is round me, wideness ineffable;
White birds on the ocean diving and wandering;
    A soundless sea on a voiceless heaven,
        Azure on azure, is mutely gazing.

Identified with silence and boundlessness
My spirit widens clasping the universe
    Till all that seemed becomes the Real,
        One in a mighty and single vastness.

Someone broods there nameless and bodiless,
Conscious and lonely, deathless and infinite,
    And, sole in a still eternal rapture,
        Gathers all things to his heart for ever.

---

* Alcaics. Modulations are allowed, trochee or iamb in the first foot or a long monosyllable; an occasional anapaest in place of an iamb is permitted; a bacchius can replace a dactyl.

Trance of Waiting*

Lone on my summits of calm I have brooded with voices around me,
    Murmurs of silence that steep mind in a luminous sleep,
  Whispers from things beyond thought in the Secrecy flame-white for ever,
    Unscanned heights that reply seek from the inconscient deep.
Distant below me the ocean of life with its passionate surges
    Pales like a pool that is stirred by the wings of a shadowy bird.
Thought has flown back from its wheelings and stoopings, the nerve-beat of living
    Stills; my spirit at peace bathes in a mighty release.
Wisdom supernal looks down on me, Knowledge mind cannot measure;
    Light that no vision can render garments the silence with splendour.
Filled with a rapturous Presence the crowded spaces of being
    Tremble with the Fire that knows, thrill with the might of repose.
Earth is now girdled with trance and Heaven is put round her for vesture.
    Wings that are brilliant with fate sleep at Eternity's gate.
Time waits, vacant, the lightning that kindles, the Word that transfigures:
    Space is a stillness of God building his earthly abode.
All waits hushed for the fiat to come and the tread of the Eternal;
    Passion of a bliss yet to be sweeps from Infinity's sea.

---

* Elegiacs, with rhyme in the pentameter. A syllable or two introducing the last hemistich of the pentameter is allowed, but this must not be made the rule. This license, impossible in the strict cut of classical metre, comes in naturally in English and is therefore permissible.

Flame-Wind*

    A flame-wind ran from the gold of the east,
    Leaped on my soul with the breath of a sevenfold noon.
        Wings of the angel, gallop of the beast!
    Mind and body on fire, but the heart in swoon.

        O flame, thou bringest the strength of the noon,
    But where are the voices of morn and the stillness of eve?
        Where the pale-blue wine of the moon?
    Mind and life are in flower, but the heart must grieve.

        Gold in the mind and the life-flame's red
    Make of the heavens a splendour, the earth a blaze,
        But the white and rose of the heart are dead.
    Flame-wind, pass! I will wait for Love in the silent ways.

---

* Dactylic tetrameter and pentameter catalectic; an additional foot in the last line; trochee or spondee freely admitted anywhere; first paeon, bacchius, cretic can replace a dactyl. One or two extra syllables are allowed sometimes at the beginning of the line.

The River*

Wild river in thy cataract far-murmured and rash rapids to sea hasting,
Far now is that birth-place mid abrupt mountains and slow dreaming of lone valleys
Where only with blue heavens was rapt converse or green orchards with fruit leaning
Stood imaged in thy waves and, content, listened to thy rhapsody's long murmur.

Vast now in a wide press and a dense hurry and mass movement of thronged waters
Loud-thundering, fast-galloping, might, speed is the stern message of thy spirit,
Proud violence, stark claim and the dire cry of the heart's hunger on God's barriers
Self-hurled, and a void lust of unknown distance, and pace reckless and free grandeur.

Calm yet shall release thee; an immense peace and a large streaming of white silence,
Broad plains shall be thine, greenness surround thee, and wharved cities and life's labour
Long thou wilt befriend, human delight help with the waves' coolness, with ship's furrows
Thrill, — last become, self losing, a sea-motion and joy boundless and blue laughter.

---

* Ionic a majore pentameter catalectic. In one place an epitrite replaces the ionic.

The Dream Boat*

Who was it that came to me in a boat made of dream-fire,
    With his flame brow and his sun-gold body?
Melted was the silence into a sweet secret murmur,
    "Do you come now? is the heart's fire ready?"

Hidden in the recesses of the heart something shuddered,
    It recalled all that the life's joy cherished,
Imaged the felicity it must leave lost for ever,
    And the boat passed and the gold god vanished.

Now within the hollowness of the world's breast inhabits —
    For the love died and the old joy ended —
Void of a felicity that has fled, gone for ever,
    And the gold god and the dream boat come not.

---

* Lines 1, 3 dactyl, second paeon, ionic a minore, amphibrach (or antibacchius)
  — ∪ ∪ | ∪ — ∪ ∪ | ∪ ∪ — — | ∪ — ∪
                                        ∪ — —
Lines 2, 4 two ionics a minore with a closing trochee ∪ ∪ — — | ∪ ∪ — — | — ∪

The Witness and the Wheel*

> Who art thou in the heart comrade of man who sitst
> August, watching his works, watching his joys and griefs,
> Unmoved, careless of pain, careless of death and fate?
> Witness, what hast thou seen watching this great blind world
> Moving helpless in Time, whirled on the Wheel in Space,
> That yet thou with thy vast Will biddest toil our hearts,
> Mystic, — for without thee nothing can last in Time?
> We too, when from the urge ceaseless of Nature turn
> Our souls, far from the breast casting her tool, desire,
> Grow like thee. In the front Nature still drives in vain
> The blind trail of our acts, passions and thoughts and hopes;
> Unmoved, calm, we look on, careless of death and fate,
> Of grief careless and joy, — signs of a surface script
> Without value or sense, steps of an aimless world.
> Something watches behind, Spirit or Self or Soul,
> Viewing Space and its toil, waiting the end of Time.
> Witness, who then art thou, one with thee who am I,
> Nameless, watching the Wheel whirl across Time and Space?

---

* The metre is the little Asclepiad used by Horace in his Ode addressed to Maecenas, two choriambs between an initial spondee and a final iamb. Here modulations are admitted, trochee or iamb for the spondee, occasionally a spondee for the concluding iamb; an epitrite or ionic a minore can replace the choriamb.

Descent*

All my cells thrill swept by a surge of splendour,
Soul and body stir with a mighty rapture,
Light and still more light like an ocean billows
    Over me, round me.

Rigid, stone-like, fixed like a hill or statue,
Vast my body feels and upbears the world's weight;
Dire the large descent of the Godhead enters
    Limbs that are mortal.

Voiceless, thronged, Infinity crowds upon me;
Presses down a glory of power eternal;
Mind and heart grow one with the cosmic wideness;
    Stilled are earth's murmurs.

Swiftly, swiftly crossing the golden spaces
Knowledge leaps, a torrent of rapid lightnings;
Thoughts that left the Ineffable's flaming mansions,
    Blaze in my spirit.

Slow the heart-beats' rhythm like a giant hammer's;
Missioned voices drive to me from God's doorway
Words that live not save upon Nature's summits,
    Ecstasy's chariots.

All the world is changed to a single oneness;
Souls undying, infinite forces, meeting,
Join in God-dance weaving a seamless Nature,
    Rhythm of the Deathless.

Mind and heart and body, one harp of being,
Cry that anthem, finding the notes eternal, —
Light and might and bliss and immortal wisdom
    Clasping for ever.

---

* Sapphics. But the second-foot spondee is very usually replaced by a trochee, the final trochee sometimes by a spondee; a bacchius, cretic or molossus can replace the dactyl. In the fifteenth line elision is used; in a Sapphic line there can be only one dactyl.

The Lost Boat*

At the way's end when the shore raised up its dim line and remote lights from the port glimmered,
Then a cloud darkened the sky's brink and the wind's scream was the shrill laugh of a loosed demon
And the huge passion of storm leaped with its bright stabs and the long crashing of death's thunder;
As if haled by an unseen hand fled the boat lost in the wide homeless forlorn ocean.

Is it Chance smites? is it Fate's irony? dead workings or blind purpose of brute Nature?
Or man's own deeds that return back on his doomed head with a stark justice, a fixed vengeance?
Or a dread Will from behind Life that regards pain and salutes death with a hard laughter?
Is it God's might or a Force rules in this dense jungle of events, deeds and our thought's strivings?

Yet perhaps sank not the bright lives and their glad venturings foiled, drowned in the grey ocean,
But with long wandering they reached an unknown shore and a strange sun and a new azure,
Amid bright splendour of beast glories and birds' music and deep hues, an enriched Nature
And a new life that could draw near to divine meanings and touched close the concealed purpose.

In a chance happening, fate's whims and the blind workings or dead drive of a brute Nature,
In her dire Titan caprice, strength that to death drifts and to doom, hidden a Will labours.
Not with one moment of sharp close or the slow fall of a dim curtain the play ceases:
Yet is there Time to be crossed, lives to be lived out, the unplayed acts of the soul's drama.

---

* Ionic a minore pentameter with an overflow of one short syllable
  ᴗ ᴗ − − | ᴗ ᴗ − − | ᴗ ᴗ − − | ᴗ ᴗ − − | ᴗ ᴗ − − | ᴗ

Renewal*

When the heart tires and the throb stills recalling
    Things that were once and again can be never,
When the bow falls and the drawn string is broken,
    Hands that were clasped, yet for ever are parted,

When the soul passes to new births and bodies,
    Lands never seen and meetings with new faces,
Is the bow raised and the fall'n arrow fitted,
    Acts that were vain rewedded to the Fate-curve?

To the lives sundered can Time bring rejoining,
    Love that was slain be reborn with the body?
In the mind null, from the heart's chords rejected,
    Lost to the sense, but the spirit remembers!

---

* Lines 1, 3 two ionics a minore with a final amphibrach,
    ∪∪−−│∪∪−−│∪−∪.
Lines 2, 4 choriamb, paeon, bacchius (or sometimes antibacchius or amphibrach),
    −∪∪−│∪∪−∪│−−∪
    ∪−∪∪│∪⸗∪

Soul's Scene*

The clouds lain on forlorn spaces of sky, weary and lolling,
Watch grey waves of a lost sea wander sad, reckless and rolling,
    A bare anguish of black beaches made mournful with the breath of
                                                            the Northwind
    And a huddle of melancholy hills in the distance.

The blank hour in some vast mood of a Soul lonely in Nature
On earth's face puts a mask pregnantly carved, cut to misfeature,
    And man's heart and his stilled mind react hushed in a spiritual passion
    Imitating the contours of her desolate waiting.

Impossible she waits long for the sun's gold and the azure,
The sea's song with its slow happy refrain's plashes of pleasure, —
    As man's soul in its depths waits the outbreaking of the light and the
                                                                 godhead
    And the bliss that God felt when he created his image.

---

* Lines 1, 2 three antispasts (or in the first foot a second paeon), amphibrach,
    ◡ — — ◡ | ◡ — — ◡ | ◡ — — ◡ | ◡ — ◡
    ◡ — ◡ ◡ |
Line 3 two antispasts, ionic a majore, second paeon, trochee
    ◡ — — ◡ | ◡ — — ◡ | — — ◡ ◡ | ◡ — ◡ ◡ | — ◡.
Line 4 three paeons, trochee, but the middle paeon can be replaced by an antispast or an ionic a majore; a double iamb once replaces the third paeon.

ASCENT*

The Silence

Into the Silence, into the Silence,
Arise, O Spirit immortal,
Away from the turning Wheel, breaking the magical Circle.
Ascend, single and deathless:
Care no more for the whispers and the shoutings in the darkness,
Pass from the sphere of the grey and the little,
Leaving the cry and the struggle,
Into the Silence for ever.

Vast and immobile, formless and marvellous,
Higher than Heaven, wider than the universe,
In a pure glory of being,
In a bright stillness of self-seeing,
Communing with a boundlessness voiceless and intimate,
Make thy knowledge too high for thought, thy joy too deep for emotion;
At rest in the unchanging Light, mute with the wordless self-vision,
Spirit, pass out of thyself; Soul, escape from the clutch of Nature.
All thou hast seen cast from thee, O Witness.
Turn to the Alone and the Absolute, turn to the Eternal:
Be only eternity, peace and silence,
O world-transcending nameless Oneness,
Spirit immortal.

---

* Free quantitative verse with a predominant dactylic movement.

2

Beyond the Silence

Out from the Silence, out from the Silence,
Carrying with thee the ineffable Substance,
Carrying with thee the splendour and wideness,
Ascend, O Spirit immortal.
Assigning to Time its endless meaning,
Blissful enter into the clasp of the Timeless.
Awake in the living Eternal, taken to the bosom of love of the Infinite,
Live self-found in his endless completeness,
Drowned in his joy and his sweetness,
Thy heart close to the heart of the Godhead for ever.

Vast, God-possessing, embraced by the Wonderful,
Lifted by the All-Beautiful into his infinite beauty,
Love shall envelop thee endless and fathomless,
Joy unimaginable, ecstasy illimitable,
Knowledge omnipotent, Might omniscient,
Light without darkness, Truth that is dateless.
One with the Transcendent, calm, universal,
Single and free, yet innumerably living,
All in thyself and thyself in all dwelling,
Act in the world with thy being beyond it.
Soul, exceed life's boundaries; Spirit, surpass the universe.
Outclimbing the summits of Nature,
Transcending and uplifting the soul of the finite,
Rise with the world in thy bosom,
O Word gathered into the heart of the Ineffable.
One with the Eternal, live in his infinity,
Drowned in the Absolute, found in the Godhead,
Swan of the supreme and spaceless ether wandering winged through
                                                        the universe,
Spirit immortal.

The Tiger and the Deer*

Brilliant, crouching, slouching, what crept through the green heart of the forest,
Gleaming eyes and mighty chest and soft soundless paws of grandeur and murder?
The wind slipped through the leaves as if afraid lest its voice and the noise of its steps perturb the pitiless Splendour,
Hardly daring to breathe. But the great beast crouched and crept, and crept and crouched a last time, noiseless, fatal,
Till suddenly death leaped on the beautiful wild deer as it drank
Unsuspecting from the great pool in the forest's coolness and shadow,
And it fell and, torn, died remembering its mate left sole in the deep woodland, —
Destroyed, the mild harmless beauty by the strong cruel beauty in Nature.
But a day may yet come when the tiger crouches and leaps no more in the dangerous heart of the forest,
As the mammoth shakes no more the plains of Asia;
Still then shall the beautiful wild deer drink from the coolness of great pools in the leaves' shadow.
The mighty perish in their might;
The slain survive the slayer.

---

* Free quantitative verse, left to find out its own line by line rhythm and unity.

Soul in the Ignorance*

Soul in the Ignorance, wake from its stupor.
Flake of the world-fire, spark of Divinity,
Lift up thy mind and thy heart into glory.
Sun in the darkness, recover thy lustre.

One, universal, ensphering creation,
Wheeling no more with inconscient Nature,
Feel thyself God-born, know thyself deathless.
Timeless return to thy immortal existence.

Journey's End**

The day ends lost in a stretch of even,
A long road trod — and the little farther.
　　Now the waste-land, now the silence;
A blank dark wall, and behind it heaven.

---

* Dactylic tetrameter, usually catalectic, with the ordinary modulations.
** Lines 1, 2, 4 epitrite, third paeon, trochee ⌣ — — — | ⌣ ⌣ — ⌣ | — ⌣ . In line 3 two double trochees — ⌣ — ⌣ | — ⌣ — ⌣ |

The Bird of Fire

Gold-white wings a-throb in the vastness, the bird of flame went
    glimmering over a sunfire curve to the haze of the west,
Skimming, a messenger sail, the sapphire-summer waste of a
    soundless wayless burning sea.
Now in the eve of the waning world the colour and splendour re-
    turning drift through a blue-flicker air back to my breast,
Flame and shimmer staining the rapture-white foam-vest of
    the waters of Eternity.

Gold-white wings of the miraculous bird of fire, late and slow
    have you come from the Timeless. Angel, here unto me
Bringst thou for travailing earth a spirit silent and free or
    His crimson passion of love divine, —
White-ray-jar of the spuming rose-red wine drawn from the vats
    brimming with light-blaze, the vats of ecstasy,
Pressed by the sudden and violent feet of the Dancer in Time
    from his sun-grape fruit of a deathless vine?

White-rose-altar the eternal Silence built, make now my nature
    wide, an intimate guest of His solitude,
But golden above it the body of One in her diamond sphere
    with Her halo of star-bloom and passion-ray!
Rich and red is thy breast, O bird, like blood of a soul climbing
    the hard crag-teeth world, wounded and nude,
A ruby of flame-petalled love in the silver-gold altar-vase
    of moon-edged night and rising day.

O Flame who art Time's last boon of the sacrifice, offering-flower
    held by the finite's gods to the Infinite,
O marvel bird with the burning wings of light and the unbarred
    lids that look beyond all space,
One strange leap of thy mystic stress breaking the barriers of mind
    and life, arrives at its luminous term thy flight;
Invading the secret clasp of the Silence and crimson Fire
    thou frontest eyes in a timeless Face.

Trance

    A naked and silver-pointed star
        Floating near the halo of the moon;
    A storm-rack, the pale sky's fringe and bar,
        Over waters stilling into swoon.

    My mind is awake in stirless trance,
        Hushed my heart, a burden of delight;
    Dispelled is the senses' flicker-dance,
        Mute the body aureate with light.

    O star of creation pure and free,
        Halo-moon of ecstasy unknown,
    Storm-breath of the soul-change yet to be,
        Ocean-self enraptured and alone!

Shiva

The Inconscient Creator

A face on the cold dire mountain peaks
  Grand and still; its lines white and austere
Match with the unmeasured snowy streaks
  Cutting heaven, implacable and sheer.

Above it a mountain of matted hair
  Aeon-coiled on that deathless and lone head
In its solitude huge of lifeless air
  Round, above illimitably spread.

A moon-ray on the forehead, blue and pale,
  Stretched afar its finger of still light
Illumining emptiness. Stern and male
  Mask of peace indifferent in might!

But out from some Infinite born now came
  Over giant snows and the still face
A quiver and colour of crimson flame,
  Fire-point in immensities of space.

Light-spear-tips revealed the mighty shape,
  Tore the secret veil of the heart's hold;
In that diamond heart the fires undrape,
  Living core, a brazier of gold.

This was the closed mute and burning source
  Whence were formed the worlds and their star-dance;
Life sprang a self-rapt inconscient Force,
  Love, a blazing seed, from that flame-trance.

The Life Heavens

    A life of intensities wide, immune
        Floats behind the earth and her life-fret,
    A magic of realms mastered by spell and rune,
        Grandiose, blissful, coloured, increate.

    A music there wanders mortal ear
        Hears not, seizing, intimate, remote,
    Wide-winged in soul-spaces, fire-clear,
        Heaping note on enrapturing new note.

    Forms deathless there triumph, hues divine
        Thrill with nets of glory the moved air;
    Each sense is an ecstasy, love the sign
        Of one outblaze of godhead that two share.

    The peace of the senses, the senses' stir
        On one harp are joined mysteries; pain
    Transmuted is ravishment's minister,
        A high note and a fiery refrain.

    All things are a harmony faultless, pure;
        Grief is not nor stain-wound of desire;
    The heart-beats are a cadence bright and sure
        Of Joy's quick steps, too invincible to tire.

    A Will there, a Force, a magician Mind
        Moves, and builds at once its delight-norms,
    The marvels it seeks for surprised, outlined,
        Hued, alive, a cosmos of fair forms.

    Sounds, colours, joy-flamings. Life lies here
        Dreaming, bound to the heavens of its goal,
    In the clasp of a Power that enthrals to sheer
        Bliss and beauty body and rapt soul.

    My spirit sank drowned in the wonder surge:
        Screened, withdrawn was the greatness it had sought;
    Lost was the storm-stress and the warrior urge,
        Lost the titan winging of the thought.

It lay at ease in a sweetness of heaven-sense
    Delivered from grief, with no need left to aspire,
Free, self-dispersed in voluptuous innocence,
    Lulled and borne into roseate cloud-fire.

But suddenly there soared a dateless cry,
    Deep as Night, imperishable as Time;
It seemed Death's dire appeal to Eternity,
    Earth's outcry to the limitless Sublime.

"O high seeker of immortality,
    Is there not, ineffable, a bliss
Too vast for these finite harmonies,
    Too divine for the moment's unsure kiss?

"Arms taking to a voiceless supreme delight,
    Life that meets the Eternal with close breast,
An unwalled mind dissolved in the Infinite,
    Force one with unimaginable rest?

"I, Earth, have a deeper power than Heaven;
    My lonely sorrow surpasses its rose-joys,
A red and bitter seed of the raptures seven;—
    My dumbness fills with echoes of a far Voice.

"By me the last finite, yearning, strives
    To reach the last infinity's unknown,
The Eternal is broken into fleeting lives
    And Godhead pent in the mire and the stone."

Dissolving the kingdoms of happy ease
    Rocked and split and faded their dream-chime.
All vanished; ungrasped eternities
    Sole survived and Timelessness seized Time.

Earth's heart was felt beating below me still,
    Veiled, immense, unthinkable above
My consciousness climbed like a topless hill,
    Crossed seas of Light to epiphanies of Love.

Jivanmukta

There is a silence greater than any known
To earth's dumb spirit, motionless in the soul
    That has become Eternity's foothold,
        Touched by the infinitudes for ever.

A Splendour is here, refused to the earthward sight,
That floods some deep flame-covered all-seeing eye;
    Revealed it wakens when God's stillness
        Heavens the ocean of moveless Nature.

A Power descends no Fate can perturb or vanquish,
Calmer than mountains, wider than marching waters,
    A single might of luminous quiet
        Tirelessly bearing the worlds and ages.

A bliss surrounds with ecstasy everlasting,
An absolute high-seated immortal rapture
    Possesses, sealing love to oneness
        In the grasp of the All-beautiful, All-beloved.

He who from Time's dull motion escapes and thrills
Rapt thoughtless, wordless into the Eternal's breast,
    Unrolls the form and sign of being,
        Seated above in the omniscient Silence.

Although consenting here to a mortal body,
He is the Undying; limit and bond he knows not;
    For him the aeons are a playground,
        Life and its deeds are his splendid shadow.

Only to bring God's forces to waiting Nature,
To help with wide-winged Peace her tormented labour
    And heal with joy her ancient sorrow,
        Casting down light on the inconscient darkness,

He acts and lives. Vain things are mind's smaller motives
To one whose soul enjoys for its high possession
    Infinity and the sempiternal
        All is his guide and beloved and refuge.

In Horis Aeternum

A far sail on the unchangeable monotone of a slow slumbering sea,
A world of power hushed into symbols of hue, silent unendingly;
Over its head like a gold ball the sun tossed by the gods in their play
Follows its curve, — a blazing eye of Time watching the motionless day.

Here or otherwhere, — poised on the unreachable abrupt snow-solitary ascent
Earth aspiring lifts to the illimitable Light, then ceases broken and spent,
Or in the glowing expanse, arid, fiery and austere, of the desert's hungry soul, —
A breath, a cry, a glimmer from Eternity's face, in a fragment the mystic Whole.

Moment-mere, yet with all eternity packed, lone, fixed, intense,
Out of the ring of these hours that dance and die, caught by the spirit in sense,
In the greatness of a man, in music's outspread wings, in a touch, in a smile, in a sound,
Something that waits, something that wanders and settles not, a Nothing that was all and is found.

NOTES

The Bird of Fire and Trance

These two poems are in the nature of metrical experiments. The first is a kind of compromise between the stress system and the foot measure. The stanza is of four lines, alternately of twelve and ten stresses. The second and fourth line in each stanza can be read as a ten-foot line of mixed iambs and anapaests, the first and third, though a similar system subject to replacement of a foot anywhere by a single-syllable half-foot could be applied, are still mainly readable by stresses.

The other poem is an experiment in the use of quantitative foot measures. It is a four-line stanza reading alternately

$$\smile - \smile \;|\; \smile - \smile \;|\; - \smile - \;|$$
$$- - \smile \;|\; \smile - - \;| \qquad |$$
$$\text{and} \; - \smile - \;|\; \smile - \smile \;|\; \simeq \smile - \;|$$

It could indeed be read otherwise, in several ways, but read in the ordinary way it would lose all lyrical quality and the soul of its rhythm.

The Bird of Fire is the living vehicle of the gold fire of the Divine Light and the white fire of the Divine Tapas and the crimson fire of Divine Love — and everything else of the Divine Consciousness.

Shiva — The Inconscient Creator

The quantitative metre of *Trance* is suited only for a very brief lyrical poem. For longer poems I have sought to use it as a base but to liberate it by the introduction of an ample number of modulations which allow a fairly free variation of the rhythm without destroying the consistency of the underlying rhythmic measure. This is achieved in *Shiva* by allowing as the main modulations (1) a paeon anywhere in place of an amphibrach, (2) the substitution of a long for a short syllable either in the first or the last syllable of an amphibrach, at will, (3) the substitution of a dactyl for an initial amphibrach, (4) the substitution of a long instead of short syllable in the middle of the final anapaest, both this and the ultimate syllable to be in that case stressed in reading, *e.g.*,

    deathless | and lóne héad.

The suppression of the full value of long syllables to make them figure as metrical shorts has to be avoided in quantitative metre.

Scan:

    Ă fāce ŏn | thĕ cōld dīre | mōuntaĭn pēaks
      Grānd ănd stĭll; | ĭts līnes whīte | ănd aūstēre
    Mātch wĭth thĕ | ŭnmēasŭred | snōwў strēaks
      Cūttĭng hēavĕn, | ĭmplācă|blĕ ănd shēer.

The Inconscient as the source and author of all material creation is one of the main discoveries of modern psychology, but it agrees with the idea of a famous Vedic hymn. In the Upanishads, Prajna, the Master of Sushupti, is the Ishwara and therefore the original Creator out of a superconscient sleep. The idea of the poem is that this creative Inconscient also is Shiva creating here life in matter out of an apparently inconscient material trance as from above he creates all the worlds (not the material only) from a superconscient trance. The reality is a supreme Consciousness — but that is veiled by the appearance on one side of the superconscient sleep, on the other of the material Inconscience. Here the emphasis is on the latter; the superconscient is only hinted at, not indicated, — it is the Infinity out of which comes the revealing Flame.

THE LIFE HEAVENS

Further modulations have been introduced in this poem —

a greater use is made of tetrasyllabic feet such as paeons, epitrites, di-iambs, ionics and, once only, the antispast — and in a few places the foot of three long syllables (molossus) has been used, and in others a foot extending to five syllables (*e.g.*, Dĕlīvĕred frŏm grīef).

Scan:

Ă līfe ŏf | ĭntēnsĭtīes | wīde, ĭmmūne
　　Flōāts bĕhīnd | thĕ ēarth ănd | hĕr līfe-frēt,
Ă māgĭc ŏf | rēalms māstĕred bў | spēll ănd rūne,
　　Grāndĭōse, blĭss|fŭl, cōlŏured, | ĭncrĕāte.

There were two places in which at the time of writing there did not seem to me to be a satisfactory completeness and the addition of a stanza seemed to be called for — one at the end of the description of the Life Heavens, a stanza which would be a closing global description of the essence of the vital Heavens, the other (less imperatively called for) in the utterance of the Voice. There it is no doubt very condensed, but it cannot be otherwise. I thought, however, that one stanza might be added hinting rather than stating the connection between the two extremes. The connection is between the Divine suppressed in its opposites and the Divine eternal in its own unveiled and undescended nature. The idea is that the other worlds are not evolutionary but typal and each presents in a limited perfection some aspect of the Infinite, but each complete, perfectly satisfied in itself, not asking or aspiring for anything else, for self-exceeding of any kind. That aspiration, on the contrary, is self-imposed on the imperfection of Earth; the very fact of the Divine being there, but suppressed in its phenomenal opposites, compels an effort to arrive at the unveiled Divine — by ascent, but also by a descent of the Divine perfection for evolutionary manifestation here. That is why the Earth declares itself a deeper Power than Heaven because it holds in itself that possibility implied in the presence of the suppressed Divine here, — which does not exist in the perfection of the vital (or even the mental) Heavens.

JIVANMUKTA

Written in Alcaics. These Alcaics are not perhaps very orthodox. I have treated the close of the first two lines not as a dactyl but as a cretic and have taken the liberty in any stanza of turning this into a double trochee. In one closing line I have started the dactylic run with two short preliminary syllables and there is occasionally a dactyl or anapaest in unlawful places; the dactyls too are not all pure dactyls. The object is to bring in by modulations some variety and a more plastic form and easier run than strict orthodoxy could give. But in essence, I think, the alcaic movement remains in spite of these departures.

The subject is the Vedantic ideal of the living liberated man — *jivanmukta* — though perhaps I have given a pull towards my own ideal which the strict Vedantin would consider illegitimate.

IN HORIS AETERNUM

This poem on its technical side aims at finding a halfway house between free verse and regular metrical poetry. It is an attempt to avoid the chaotic amorphousness of free verse and keep to a regular form based on the fixed number of stresses in each line and part of a line while yet there shall be a great plasticity and variety in all the other elements of poetic rhythm, the number of syllables, the management of the feet, if any, the distribution of the stress-beats, the changing modulation of the rhythm. *In Horis Aeternum* was meant as a first essay in this kind, a very simple and elementary model. The line here is cast into three parts, the first containing two stresses, the second and third each admitting three, four such lines rhymed constituting the stanza.

(From Letters of the Author)

Thought the Paraclete

As some bright archangel in vision flies
Plunged in dream-caught spirit immensities,
Past the long green crests of the seas of life,
Past the orange skies of the mystic mind
Flew my thought self-lost in the vasts of God.
Sleepless wide great glimmering wings of wind
Bore the gold-red seeking of feet that trod
Space and Time's mute vanishing ends. The face
Lustred, pale-blue-lined of the hippogriff,
Eremite, sole, daring the bourneless ways,
Over world-bare summits of timeless being
Gleamed; the deep twilights of the world-abyss
Failed below. Sun-realms of supernal seeing,
Crimson-white mooned oceans of pauseless bliss
Drew its vague heart-yearning with voices sweet.
Hungering, large-souled to surprise the unconned
Secrets white-fire-veiled of the last Beyond,
Crossing power-swept silences rapture-stunned,
Climbing high far ethers eternal-sunned,
Thought the great-winged wanderer paraclete
Disappeared slow-singing a flame-word rune.
Self was left, lone, limitless, nude, immune.

Moon of Two Hemispheres

A gold moon-raft floats and swings slowly
And it casts a fire of pale holy blue light
On the dragon tail aglow of the faint night
                       That glimmers far, — swimming,
The illumined shoals of stars skimming,
Overspreading earth and drowning the heart in sight
With the ocean depths and breadths of the Infinite.

A gold moon-ship sails or drifts ever
In our spirit's skies and halts never, blue-keeled,
And it throws its white-blue fire on this grey field,
                       Night's dragon loop, — speeding,
The illumined star-thought sloops leading
To the Dawn, their harbour home, to the Light unsealed,
To the sun-face Infinite, the Untimed revealed.

Rose of God

Rose of God, vermilion stain on the sapphires of heaven,
Rose of Bliss, fire-sweet, seven-tinged with the ecstasies seven!
Leap up in our heart of humanhood, O miracle, O flame,
Passion-flower of the Nameless, bud of the mystical Name.

Rose of God, great wisdom-bloom on the summits of being,
Rose of Light, immaculate core of the ultimate seeing!
Live in the mind of our earthhood; O golden Mystery, flower,
Sun on the head of the Timeless, guest of the marvellous Hour.

Rose of God, damask force of Infinity, red icon of might,
Rose of Power with thy diamond halo piercing the night!
Ablaze in the will of the mortal, design the wonder of thy plan,
Image of Immortality, outbreak of the Godhead in man.

Rose of God, smitten purple with the incarnate divine Desire,
Rose of Life, crowded with petals, colour's lyre!
Transform the body of the mortal like a sweet and magical rhyme;
Bridge our earthhood and heavenhood, make deathless the children
                                                          of Time.

Rose of God, like a blush of rapture on Eternity's face,
Rose of Love, ruby depth of all being, fire-passion of Grace!
Arise from the heart of the yearning that sobs in Nature's abyss:
Make earth the home of the Wonderful and life beatitude's kiss.

NOTES

In some of these poems, as in others of the *Six Poems*,[1] a quantitative metrical system has been used which seems to have puzzled some critics, apparently because it does not follow the laws of quantity obtaining in the ancient classical languages. But those laws are quite alien to the rhythm and sound-structure of the English tongue; the attempt to observe them has always ended in deserved and inevitable failure. Another system has been followed here which is in agreement with the native rhythm of English speech. There what determines the metrical length or brevity of syllables is weight, the weight of the voice emphasis or the dwelling of the voice upon the sound. Where there is that emphasis or that dwelling of the voice, the syllable may be considered metrically long; where both are absent there will be, normally, a recognisable shortness which can only be cured by some aid of consonant weight or other lengthening circumstance. All stressed syllables are metrically long in English and cannot be otherwise however short the vowel may be, for they dominate the verse movement; this is a fact which is ignored in the traditional account of English quantity and which many experimenters in quantitative verse have chosen to disregard with disastrous consequences, — all their genius or skill in metrical technique could not save them from failure. On the other hand, a long-vowel syllable can be regarded as metrically long even if there is no stress upon it. In the quantitative system used in these poems this possibility is converted into a law: metrical length is obligatory for all such natural syllabic longs, while a short-vowel syllable unstressed is normally short for metrical purposes unless it is very heavily weighted with consonants. But the mere occurrence of two or more consonants after a short vowel does not by itself make the syllable long as it necessarily does in Greek, Latin or Sanskrit.

The system may then be reduced to the following rules: —

1. All stressed syllables are regarded as metrically long, as also all syllables supported on a long vowel.

2. All short-vowel syllables not stressed are regarded as

[1] See Bibliography.

short unless they are heavily weighted with consonants. But on this last point no fixed rule can be given; in each case the ear must be the judge.

3. There are a great number of sounds in English which can be regarded according to circumstances either as longs or as shorts. Here too the ear must decide in each case.

4. English quantity metres cannot be as rigid as the metres of ancient tongues. The rhythm of the language demands a certain variability, free or sparing, without which monotony sets in; accordingly, in all English metres modulation is admitted as possible. Even the most regular rhythms do not altogether shut out the substitution of other feet than those fixed in the normal basic arrangement of the line; they admit at least so much as is needed to give the necessary pliancy or variety to the movement. There is sometimes a very free use of such variations; but they ought not to be allowed to break the basic movement or overburden or overlay it. The same rule must apply in quantitative metres; especially in long poems modulations are indispensable.

This system is not only not at discord with the sound-structure of the language, it accords closely with its natural rhythm; it only regulates and intensifies into metrical pitch and tone the cadence that is already there even in prose, even in daily speech. If we take passages from English literature which were written as prose but with some intensity of rhythm, its movement can be at once detected, *e.g.*,

Cŏnsīdĕr | thĕ lĭlĭēs | ŏf thĕ fīeld, | hōw thēy grōw; ‖ thēy tōil nŏt, | nēithĕr dŏ | thēy spīn; ‖ yĕt Ī | sāy ŭntŏ | yoū thăt ēvĕn | Sōlŏmŏn | ĭn āll hĭs | glōrў ‖ wăs nŏt ărrāyed | līke ŭntŏ | ōne ŏf thēse: ‖

or again,

Blēssĕd āre | thĕ meēk; | fŏr thēy shăll | ĭnhĕrĭt | thĕ eārth | ....
Blēssĕd āre | thĕ pūre ĭn heārt; | fŏr thēy shăll seē | Gōd;

or again, from Shakespeare's prose,

Thĭs goōdlў frāme, | thĕ eārth, seēms tŏ | mĕ ă stĕrīle |
               prōmŏntŏrў; |

thĭs mōst ēxcĕl|lĕnt cānŏpў, | thĕ āīr, lōōk yŏu, | thĭs brāve
ō'ĕrhāng|ĭng fīrmămĕnt, | thĭs măjēstĭc|ăl rōōf frēttĕd | wĭth
gōldĕn fīre |

and so on with a constant recurrence of the same quantitative movement all through; or, yet more strikingly,

Hōw ārt thōū | fāllĕn frŏm | Hēavĕn, Ŏ | Lūcĭfĕr, | sōn ŏf thĕ
mōrnĭng!

This last sentence can be read indeed as a very perfect hexameter. The first of these passages could be easily presented as four lines of free quantitative verse, each independent in its arrangement of feet, but all swaying in a single rhythm. Shakespeare's is most wonderfully balanced in a series of differing four-syllabled, with occasional shorter, feet, as if of deliberate purpose, though it is no intention of the mind but the ear of the poet that has constructed this fine design of rhythmic prose. A free quantitative verse in this kind would be perfectly possible.

A more regular quantitative metre can be of two kinds. There could be lines all with the same metrical arrangement following each other without break or else alternating lines with a different arrangement for each, forming a stanza, — as in the practice of accentual metres. But there could also be an arrangement in strophe and antistrophe as in the Greek chorus. In *Thought the Paraclete* the first rule is followed; all the lines are on the same model. The metre of this poem has a certain rhythmic similarity to the Latin hendecasyllable which runs − − | − ᴗ ᴗ | − ᴗ | − ᴗ | ᴗ ≈, *e.g.*

Sōlēs | ōccĭdĕr(e) | ēt rĕ|dīrĕ | pōssūnt,
Nōbĭs | cūm sĕmĕl | ōccĭd|ĭt brĕ|vĭs lūx
Nōx ēst | pērpĕtŭ(a) | ūnă | dōrmī|ēndă.[1]

But here the metre runs − ᴗ | − − | − ᴗ ᴗ | − ᴗ | − − ᴗ ; a trochee

---

[1] Suns may set and come again;
For us, when once our brief light has set,
There is one perpetual night to be slept.
CATULLUS

is transferred from the closing flow of trochees to the beginning of the line, the spondee and dactyl are pushed into the middle, the last syllable of the closing trochee is most often dropped altogether. Classical metres cannot always with success be taken over just as they are into the English rhythm; often some modifications are needed to make them more malleable.

In *Moon of Two Hemispheres* the strophe antistrophe system has been used: the lines of the stanza differ from each other in the nature and order of the feet, no identity or approach to identity is imposed; but each line of the antistrophe follows scrupulously the arrangement of the corresponding line of the strophe. An occasional modulation at most is allowed, *e.g.*, the substitution of a trochee for a spondee. The whole poem, however, in spite of its metrical variations, follows a single general rhythmic movement.

Rose of God, like a previous poem *In Horis Aeternum*, is written in pure stress metre. As stress and high accentual pitch usually coincide, it is possible to scan accentual metre on the stress principle and stress metre also can be so written that it can be scanned as accentual verse; but pure stress metre depends entirely on stress ictus. In ordinary poetry stress and natural syllabic quantity enter in as elements of the rhythm, but are not, *qua* stress and quantity, essential elements of the basic metre: in pure stress metre there is a reversal of these values; quantity and accentual inflexion are subordinate and help to build the rhythm, but stress alone determines the metrical basis. In *Rose of God* each line is composed of six stresses, and the whole poem is built of five stanzas, each containing four such lines; the arrangement of feet varies freely to suit the movement of thought and feeling in each line. Thus,

Róse of | Gód, | damask fórce of | Infinity, | red ícon of | míght,
Róse of | Pówer | with thy diam|ond hálo | píercing | the níght,
Abláze | in the will of | the mórtal, | desígn | the wónder of | thy
plán,
Ímage of | Ímmor|táility, | outbréak of | the Gódhead | in mán.

Musa Spiritus

O word concealed in the upper fire,
    Thou who hast lingered through centuries,
Descend from thy rapt white desire,
    Plunging through gold eternities.

Into the gulfs of our nature leap,
    Voice of the spaces, call of the Light!
Break the seals of Matter's sleep,
    Break the trance of the unseen height.

In the uncertain glow of human mind,
    Its waste of unharmonied thronging thoughts,
Carve thy epic mountain-lined
    Crowded with deep prophetic grots.

Let thy hue-winged lyrics hover like birds
    Over the swirl of the heart's sea.
Touch into sight with thy fire-words
    The blind indwelling deity.

O Muse of the Silence, the wideness make
    In the unplumbed stillness that hears thy voice,
In the vast mute heavens of the spirit awake
    Where thy eagles of Power flame and rejoice.

Out, out with the mind and its candle flares,
    Light, light the suns that never die.
For my ear the cry of the seraph stars
    And the forms of the Gods for my naked eye!

Let the little troubled life-god within
    Cast his veils from the still soul,
His tiger-stripes of virtue and sin,
    His clamour and glamour and thole and dole;

All make tranquil, all make free.
    Let my heart-beats measure the footsteps of God
As He comes from His timeless infinity
    To build in their rapture His burning abode.

Weave from my life His poem of days,
   His calm pure dawns and His noons of force.
My acts for the grooves of His chariot-race,
   My thoughts for the tramp of His great steeds' course!

※

Krishna
CRETICS

O immense Light and thou, O spirit-wide boundless Space,
Whom have you clasped and hid, deathless limbs, gloried face?
Vainly lie Space and Time, "Void are we, there is none."
Vainly strive Self and World crying, "I, I alone."
One is there, Self of self, Soul of Space, Fount of Time,
Heart of hearts, Mind of minds, He alone sits, sublime.
Oh, no void Absolute self-absorbed, splendid, mute,
Hands that clasp hold and red lips that kiss blow the flute.
All He loves, all He moves, all are His, all are He!
Many limbs sate His whims, bear His sweet ecstasy.
Two in One, Two who know difference rich in sense,
Two to clasp, One to be, this His strange mystery.

The World Game

THE ISHWARA TO THE ISHWARI

In god-years yet unmeasured by a man's thought or by the earth's dance or
the moon's spin
    I have guarded the law of the Invisible for the sake of thy smile, O
sweet;
While lives followed innumerable winged lives, as if birds crossing a wide sea,
    I have watched on the path of the centuries for the light of thy running
feet.

The earth's dancing with the sun in his fire-robes, was it not thou circling
my flame-soul?
    The gazings of the moon in its nectar-joy were my look questing for thee
through Space.
The world's haste and the racing of the tense mind and the long gallop of
fleet years
    Were my speed to arrive through the flux of things and to neighbour
at last thy face.

The earth's seeking is mine and the immense scope of the slow aeons my
heart's way;
    For I follow a secret and sublime Will and the steps of thy Mother-might.
In the dim brute and the peering of man's brain and the calm sight in a
god's eyes
    It is I who am questing in Life's broken ways for thy laughter and love
and light.

When Time moved not yet nor Space was unrolled wide, for thy game of
the worlds I gave
    Myself to thy delightful hands of power to govern me and move and
drive;
To earth's dumbness I fell for thy desire's sport weaving my spirit stuff
    In a million pattern-shapes of souls made with me alive.

The worlds are only a playfield of Thou-I and a hued masque of the Two-One,
    I am in thee as thou art in me, O Love; we are closer than heart and
breast;
From thee I leaped forth struck to a spirit spark, I mount back in the soul's
fire;

To our motion the stars whirl in the swing of Time, our oneness is Nature's rest.
When Light first from the unconscious Immense broke[1] to create nebula and sun
'Twas the meeting of our hands through the empty Night that enkindled the fateful blaze;
The huge systems abandoned their inert trance and this green crater of life rose
That we might look on each other form on form from the depths of a living gaze.

The Mind travelled in its ranges tier on tier with its wide-eyed or its rapt thought,
My thought toiling laboured to know all myself in thee to our atoms and widths and deeps,
My all yearned to thy all to be held close, to the heart heart and to self self,
As a sea with a sea joins or limbs with limbs, and as waking's delight with sleep's.

When mind pinnacled is lost in thy Light-Vasts and the man drowns in the god,
Thy Truth shall ungirdle its golden flames and thy diamond whiteness blaze;
My souls lumined shall discover their joy-self, they shall clasp all in the near One,
And the sorrow of the heart shall turn to bliss and thy sweetness possess earth's days.

Then shall Life be thy arms drawing thy own clasped to thy breast's rapture or calm peace,
With thy joy for the spirit's immortal flame and thy peace for its deathless base.
Our eyes meeting the long love shut in deep eyes and our beings held fast and one,
I shall know that the game was well worth the toil[2] whose end is thy divine embrace.

---

[1] burst [2] strife

Symbol Moon

Once again thou hast climbed, O moon, like a white fire on the glimmering edge,
   Floating up, floating up from the haunted verge of a foam-tremulous sea,
Mystic-horned here crossing the grey-hued listless nights and days,
   Spirit-silver craft from the ports of eternity.

Dumbly blithe, shuddering, the air is filled from thy cup of pale mysterious wine:
   Gleam quivers to longing gleam; and the faery torches lit for Night's mysteries, set in her niches stark and deep;
The inconscient gulfs stir and are vaguely thrilled, while their unheard voices cry to the Wonder-light new-seen
   Till descending its ray shall unlock with a wizard rod of fire the dumb recesses of sleep.

Overhead with thy plunging and swaying prow thou fleetest, O ship of the gods,
   Glorifying the clouds with thy halo, but our hearts with a rose-red rapture shed from the secret breasts of love;
Almost thou seemest the very bliss that floats in opaline air over heaven's golden roads,
   Embodied here to capture our human lives like a nectar face of light in the doubtful blue above.

Bright and alone in a white-foam-glinted delicate dim-blue ocean of sky,
   Ever thou runst and thou floatest as a magic drifting bowl
Flung by the hand of a drunken god in the river of Time goes tossing by,
   O icon and chalice of spiritual light whose spots are like Nature's shadow stains on a white and immaculate soul.

How like one frail and hunted thou com'st, O white moon, lonely call from thy deep sky-covert heights,
   A voyager carrying through the myriad-isled archipelago of the spear-pointed questioning stars
The circle of the occult argent Yes of the Invisible to the dim query of the yearning witness lights
   That burn in the dense vault of Matter's waking mind — innumerable, solitary and sparse.

A disk of a greater Ray that shall come, a white-fire rapture and girdling rose
of love,
Timelessly thou driftest, O sliver boat that set out from the far Unknown,
Moon-crystal of silver or gold of some spirit joy spun by Time in his dense
aeonic groove,
A messenger and bearer of an unembodied beauty and unseized bliss
advancing over our life's wan sea—significant, bright and alone.

❋

O pall of black Night

O pall of black Night painted with still gold stars,
Hang now thy folds, close, clinging against earth's bars,
   O dim Night!
Then slumber shall come swinging[1] the unseen
   Gates, and to lands guarded by a screen
   Of strange light
Set free my soul charioted in a swift dream,
From earth slipping into the unknown gleam,
   The Ray white.

---
[1] parting

A strong son of lightning

A strong son of lightning came down to the earth with fire-feet of swiftness,
    splendid;
Light was born in a womb and thunder's force filled a human frame.
The calm speed of heaven, the sweet greatness, pure passion, winged power
    had descended;
All the gods in a mortal body dwelt, bore a single name.

A wide wave of movement stirred all the dim globe in each glad and dreaming
    fold;
Life was cast into grandeur, ocean hands took the wheels of Time.
Man's soul was again a bright charioteer of days hired by gods impetuous
    bold,
Hurled by One on His storm-winged ways, a shaft aimed at heights sublime.

The old tablets clanging fell, ancient slow Nature's dead wall was rent
    asunder,
God renewed himself in a world of young beauty, thought and flame:
Divine voices spoke on men's lips, the heart woke to white dawns of gleaming
    wonder,
Air a robe of splendour, breath a joy, life a godlike game.

An Image

Rushing from Troy like a cloud on the plains the Trojans thundered,
Just as a storm comes thundering, thick with the dust of kingdoms,
Edged with the devious dance of the lightning, so all Troas
Loud with the roar of the chariots, loud with the vaunt and the war-cry,
Rushed from Troywards gleaming with spears and rolled on enormous.
Joyous as ever Paris led them glancing in armour,
Brilliant with gold like a bridegroom, playing with death and the battle
Even as apart in his chamber he played with his beautiful Helen,
Touching her body rejoiced with a low and lyrical laughter,
So he laughed as he smote his foemen. Round him the arrows,
Round him the spears of the Argives sang like the voices of maidens
Trilling the anthem of bridal bliss, the chant hymeneal;
Round him the warriors fell like flowers strewn at a bridal
Red with the beauty of blood.

Hail to the Fallen

Hail to the fallen, the fearless! hail to the conquered, the noble!
I out of ancient India great and unhappy and deathless,
I in a loftiest[1] nation though subject born, salute thee,
Thou too great and unfortunate! All is not given by Nature
Only to Force and the strong and the violent. Courage and wisdom,
Steadfast will and the calm magnificent dream of thy spirit
Crown thee for ever, O Emperor! Fiercely by Destiny broken,
Hurled[2] from thy throne and defeated, forsaken, a wandering exile,
Far from the hills of thy land and thy fallen and vanquished nation,
Yet has thy glory overtopped and the deathless pride of thy laurel
Conquered the conqueror's, Haile Selassie, Lion of Judah.
France for her southern borders fearing spared the aggressor.
England the sea queen, England the fortunate, England the victor
Fled like a dog from the whip of the menace yelping for succour,
Loudly to Frank and to Greek and to Turk and to Yugoslav calling
"Help me! I dare not alone: he will shatter my fleet and my empire."
You did not cower, African people, you did not tremble.
Armed but with rifle and spear you fronted the legions of Caesar.
Statesman wise and beneficent, emperor, patriot, hero,
King of the Sahavas,[3] Haile Selassie, Lion of Judah.

[1] Tentative reading [2] Cast [3] Tentative reading

In a mounting as of sea-tides

In a mounting as of sea-tides, in a rippling as of invisible waters,
On a cry in me my soul is uplifted, in a passion of my nature
My heart climbs up towards thee, O unimaginable Wonder and Resplendence,
In its[1] striving for the caress of thy Light and for the embrace of thy Presence.

If once given were but a touch of thy feet on the thrilled bosom of my longing,
But a glance of thy eyes mingling with mine in the recesses and the silence,
Such a rapture would envelop me, such a fire of transfiguring effulgence,
I could never again be as a man upon this earth, but one immortal.

For my mind would be dissolved in a sun-glory of God-vision and of knowledge,
And my heart would be made suddenly more pure and determined and self-tranquil,
And my nerves and my body would transmute into an ethereal divineness,
A fit vesture for the godhead thou buildest in me, for the immortal thy adorer.

O thou Life of my life and the unseen heart of its ecstasy and its beating,
O Face that was disclosed in the beginning of the worlds and the immenseness,
Let thy Flame-wisdom leap down upon the coilings of our python inconscience,
Let the Love-wine be poured out in Thy chalice, let me be drunk with it for ever.

I shall meet thee in the ocean of thy stillness, in the ether of thy splendour,
Thy Force shall be in my veins like the ichor in the Unaging who are deathless;
My soul shall be as one breath with thy soul and thy infinity around thee,
And shall quiver into the vision of thy beauty and the marvel of thy sweetness.

---

[1] a

The Death of a God

Arise now, tread out the fire!
Scatter the ashes of a God through the stars.
   Forget to hope and aspire.
Let us paint our prison, let us strengthen its bars.

Lo, now he is dead and the greatness that cumbered the world and Time's ways
   Has vanished like a golden shadow thrust out from the anguish of the ages;
The glory and burden, the sunlight and the passion have left our days;
   Once more we can wear the grey livery of Death and gather in his wages.

All that drew back from his splendour, fleeing as ashamed from the light and the beauty and invincible sweetness
Now returns vaunting this darkness and littleness, this fret of life's fever, its cruel and sad incompleteness.
All that is false and wry and little are freed to follow their nature once more.
   Close time's brilliant pages!
Give back to life the old tables; its dull ease, its bowed greyness restore.

Soul, my soul

Soul, my soul, reascend over the edge of life, —
Far, far from the din burn into tranquil skies,
Cross bright ranges of mind measureless, visioned, white;
Thoughts sail down as if ships carrying bales of light,
Truth's form-robes by the Seers woven from spirit-threads,
From wide havens where luminous argosies,
Gold-robed Wisdom's divine traffic and merchandise;
But there pause not but go far beyond
Where thy natural home motionless vast and mute
Waits thy tread; on a throne facing infinity
Thought-nude, void of the world, one with the silence be.
Sole, self-poised and unmoved thou shalt behold below
Hierarchies and domains, godheads and potencies,
Titans, demons and men each in his cosmic role;
Midst all these in the lone centre of forces spun,
Fate there under thy feet turning the wheels of Time,
The World Law thou shalt know[1] mapped in its codes sublime,
Yet thyself shalt remain viewless, eternal, free.

[1] view

FRAGMENTS

In the silence of midnight

In the silence of midnight, in the light of dawn or noontide
I have heard the flutings of the Infinite, I have seen the sun-wings of the
seraphs.
On the boundless solitude of the mountains, on the shoreless roll of ocean
Something is felt of God's vastness, floating touches of the Absolute;
Momentary and immeasurable smiled the sense nature free from its limits, —
A brief glimpse, a hint, it passes but the soul grows deeper, wider:
God has set his mark upon the creature.

In the flash or flutter of flight of bird and insect, in the passion of winged cry
on the treetops;
In the golden feathers of the eagle, in the maned and tawny glory of the lion,
In the voiceless hierophants of Nature with their hieratic script of colour,
Orchid, tulip and narcissus, rose and nenuphar and lotus,
Something of eternal beauty seizes on the soul and nerves and heartstrings...

Seer deep-hearted

Seer deep-hearted, divine King of the secrecies,
Occult fountain of love sprung from the heart of God,
Ways thou knewest no feet ever in time had trod.
Words leaped shining,[1] the flame-billows of wisdom's seas,
Vast in thy soul was a tide washing the coasts of heaven,
Thoughts broke burning and bare crossing the human night,
White star-scripts of the gods born from the presses of Light
Page by page to the dim children of earth were given.

---

[1] flashing

Death and the Traveller Fire

DEATH

Flame that[1] invadest my empire of sorrow wordless and sombre,
  Arrow of azure light, golden-winged barbed with delight,
Who was it aimed thee into my[2] crucified Soul that forever
  Passions and beats in the womb of a universe built for its tomb?

I who am Death and live in the boundless cavern of Nature[3],
  I am Death who cannot die. A Shadow of Eternity, —
Vainly I throb in the stars that err through the void without feature,
  Scintillant forms in a Nought vast without life, without thought.

O these stars[4] that glitter and wander, God has devised them
  Burning nails in my heart, stones of my prisonhouse. God
Architect griefless relentless and mighty built and raised them,
  Clamped with them Time, His road to[5] Nothingness, Death's grim abode.

Fire of God, I passioned for life and have gathered but ashes —
  Life so that Death might die. Yea, was it life that He gave me?
Glow of my darkness, reflex and nerve-beat devoured the[6] devourer,
  Tortured by the flame an obscure will in me kindled to save me.

Life was[7] a sorrowful throb of this Matter teaching it anguish,
  Teaching it hope and desire trod out too soon in the mire,
Life the frail joy that regrets its briefness, life the long sorrow,
  Love the close kinsman to hate and its freedom but bedfellow[8] of Fate.[9]

Then in my anguish I reached out for knowledge, light on my midnight,
  Light on its symbols of dream, strength of the thought to redeem,
Yea, was it light He permitted, this thought that is tangled in darkness?
  Ignorance sees by its own record of sense and of stone.

[1] Fire who [2] the [3] Matter [4] All these worlds [5] towards [6] its [7] is [8] comrade
[9] *Alternative Stanza:*
  Boons for a shortlived sweetness were given me — hours that were tortures,
    Hope more blind than my night, desire for deadly delight,
  Joy that outlasts not its moment, vivid and barren,
    Love a close kinsman to hate, freedom a minister of Fate.

Ignorance building its schemes and its dreams on a basis of error,
  This was the mind I had sought fashioned out of His nought.
Alphabet hieroglyphs of the reflexes life had engendered,
  Spasms of matter caught in a luminous figment of thought.

Lo, is not God but myself, Death's euphemism fictioned immortal,
  Nothing eternalised bare, yet as if one who is None,
Death yet for ever alive, an Inconscient troubled with seemings,
  Matter tormented with life, a Void with its forces at strife?

O by my thought to escape from myself out of thought into Nothing,
  Thus I had hoped to dissolve, rapt in some featureless Bliss,
Rending the illusion I made to be immutable and formless and timeless,
  This dream too now I leave, long not even to cease.

Into numb discontent I have lapsed of a universe barren,
  Goalless, condemned to survive, a spiral of matter in pain,
Now have I known myself as thy boundless finite, thy darkness without end
  Shadowily self-lit, grown content to strive and in vain.

Fire that travellest from immortality, spark of the Timeless,
  Why hast thou come to my night, unbearable Idol of Light,
Ah, from what happier universe straydest thou kindling my torpor?
  Pass, O spirit of Light, now perturb not my vastness of Night.

Torn are the walls

Torn are the walls and the borders carved by a miserly Nature,
  I have burst into limitless kingdoms of sweetness and wonder.
Breaking the fences of Matter's gods and their form and their feature,
  Fall'n are the barriers schemed and the vetoes are shattered asunder.

The Fire-King and the Messenger

THE FIRE-KING

O soul who com'st fire-mantled from the earth
Into the silence of the seven skies,
Art thou an heir of the spiritual birth?
Art thou an ancient guest of Paradise?

THE MESSENGER

I am the Messenger of the human race,
I am the Pioneer from death and night.
I am the nympholept of Beauty's face,
I am the hunter of the immortal Light.

THE FIRE-KING

What wearest thou that wraps thee with its power
Protecting from the Guardians of the Way?
What wanderer born from the eternal Hour?
What fragment of the inconceivable Ray?

THE MESSENGER

It is the fire of an awakened soul
Aspiring from death to reach Eternity,
The wings of sacrifice flaming to their goal,
The burning godhead of humanity.

THE FIRE-KING

What seekst thou here, child of the transient ways?
Wouldst thou be free and still in deathless peace
Or gaze for ever on the Eternal's face
Hushed in an incommunicable release?

THE MESSENGER

I claim for men the peace that shall not fail,
I claim for earth the unsorrowing timeless bliss,
I seek God-strength for souls that suffer in hell,
God-light to fill the ignorant Abyss.

THE FIRE-KING

Ascend no more with thy presumptuous prayer,
But safe return to the forsaken globe,
Wake not heaven's Lightning from its slumber's lair
To clothe thee with the anguish of its robe.

❋

Silver foam

Silver foam in the dim East
    And blood red in the brilliant Western sun.
Silver foam and a birth unseen,
    Blood red and the long death begun.

Vast-winged the wind

Vast-winged the wind ran, violent, black-cowled waves
    O'er-topped with fierce green eyes the deck,
        Huge heads upraised.
Death-hunted, wound-weary, groaned like a whipped beast the ship
    Shrank, cowered, sobbed, each blow like Fate's
        Despairing felt.

❋

Tiresias

Sole in the meadows of Thebes Tiresias sat by the Dirce,
Blind Tiresias lonely and old. The song of the river
Moaned in his ears and the scent of the flowers afflicted his spirit
Wandering naked and chill in the winds of the world and its greyness.
Silent awhile, then he smote on the ground with the stay of his blindness,
Calling "O murmuring waters of Dirce, loved by my childhood,
Waters of murmuring Dirce, flowers that were dear to the lover,
Then was your perfume a sweetness, then were your voices a carol;
Now you are dark to me, scents that hurt; you are dirges, O waters.
      We are weary of sorrow,
Sated with salt of human tears; and the thronèd oppressor
Seems not divine to our eyes, but a worm that stings and is happy —
Groans of the sad oppressed have no tone for our ears any longer.
Death we have taken in horror, the anguish of others afflicts us
And with the pangs of an alien heart are we shaken and troubled.
Lo, I am born by a woman's sobs that come up in the midnight.

Oh ye Powers

Oh ye Powers of the Supreme and of the Mother, the Divine,
I have come to you initiate, a bearer of the sign.
For I carry the name in me that nothing can efface.
I have breathed in an illimitable spiritual Space
And my soul through the unfathomable stillnesses has heard
The god-voices of Knowledge and the marvels of the Word.
It has listened to the secret that was hidden in the night
Of the inconscient infinities foreshadowing His might.
He arose out of the caverns of the darknesses self-enwrapped
And the nebulae were churned up like to foam-froth and were shaped
Till the millions of universes mystical upbuoyed
Were outsprinkled as if stardust on the Dragon of the Void.
I was borne[1] then in the infinitesimal and obscure
As a seed soul in the fire seeds of the energies that endure.
I have learned now to what purpose I have laboured as His spark
In the midnight of Matter[2] like a glow-worm in the dark,
And my spirit was imprisoned in the muteness of a stone,
A soul thoughtless and left[3] voiceless and impuissant and alone.

God to thy greatness

God to thy greatness
Of utter sedateness
Has given a name
That fills it with light
Of His sovereign might.
He has lavished a flame
Of passionate fleetness
On thy stillness and sweetness.
His ecstasies seven,
O daughter of Heaven,
Have seized thy limbs
That were mateless dreams.

---

[1] Tentative reading.   [2] Earth   [3] Tentative reading.

VII

METRICAL EXPERIMENTS

Winged with dangerous deity,
Passion swift and implacable
Arose and, storm-footed
In the dim heart of him,

Ran, insatiate, conquering,
Worlds devouring and hearts of men,
Then perished, broken by
The irresistible

Occult masters of destiny, —
They who sit in the secrecy
And watch unmoved ever
Unto the end of all.

Metrical Scheme:

− ∪ | − ∪ ∪ | − ∪ ∪ |
− ∪ | − ∪ ∪ | − ∪ ∪ |
∪ − | ∪ − | ∪ ∪ |
∪ ∪ ∪ | − ∪ ∪ |

Outspread a Wave burst, a Force leaped from the Unknown,
Vague, wide, some veiled Maker, masked Lighter of the Fire:
    With dire blows the Smith of the World
    Forged strength from hearts of the weak;
    Earth's hate the edge of the axe,
    Smitten by the gods,
Hewn, felled, the Form crashed that touched heaven and its stars.

Metrical Scheme:

− − ∪ | − − ∪ | − − ∪ | ∪ ∪ − |
− − ∪ | − − ∪ | − − ∪ | ∪ ∪ − |
∪ − − ∪ | − ∪ ∪ − |
− − ∪ | − ∪ ∪ − |
− − ∪ | − ∪ ∪ − |
− ∪ | ∪ ∪ − |
− − ∪ | − − ∪ | − − ∪ | ∪ ∪ − |

In a flaming as of spaces
    Curved like spires
An epiphany of faces,
    Long curled fires,
The illumined and tremendous
    Masque drew near,
A god-pageant of the aeons
    Vast, deep-hued,
And the thunder of its paeans,
    Wide-winged, nude
In their harmony stupendous,
    Smote earth's ear.

Metrical Scheme:

$$\smile\smile-\smile\,|\,\smile\smile-\smile\,|$$
$$---\,|$$

O life, thy breath is but a cry to the Light
Immortal, out of which has sprung thy delight,
    Thy grasp.
All things in vain thy hands seize;
Earth's music fails; the notes cease
    Or rasp.
Aloud thou call'st to blind Fate,
"Remove the bar, the gold gate
    Unhasp."
But never yet hast thou the goal of thy race
Attained, nor thrilled to the ineffable Face
    And clasp.

Metrical Scheme:

$$\smile-\,|\,\smile-\,|\,\smile\smile\,|\,\smile-\,|\,\smile\smile-\,|$$
$$\smile-\,|\,\smile-\,|\,\smile\smile\,|\,\smile-\,|\,\smile\smile--\,|$$
$$\smile-\,|$$
$$--\,|\,\smile-\,|\,\smile--\,|$$
$$--\,|\,\smile-\,|\,\smile--\,|$$
$$\smile-\,|$$

To the hill-tops of silence from over the infinite sea,
    Golden he came,
    Armed with the flame,
Looked on the world that his greatness and passion must free.

❋

Oh, but fair was her face as she lolled in her green-tinted robe,
    Emerald trees,
    Sapphire seas,
Sun-ring and moon-ring that glittered and hung in each lobe.

Metrical Scheme:

$$\smile\smile- | \smile\smile- | \smile\smile- | \smile\smile- | \smile\smile- |$$
$$-\smile\smile | - |$$
$$-\smile\smile | - |$$
$$-\smile\smile | -\smile\smile | -\smile\smile | -\smile\smile | - |$$

❋

In the ending of time, in the sinking of space
    What shall survive?
    Hearts once alive,
        Beauty and charm of a face?
Nay, these shall be safe in the breast of the One,
    Man deified,
    World-spirits wide,
        Nothing ends, all but began.

Metrical Scheme:

$$\smile\smile- | \smile\smile- | \smile\smile- | \smile\smile- |$$
$$-\smile\smile | - |$$
$$-\smile\smile | - |$$
$$-\smile\smile | -\smile\smile | - |$$

On the grey street, on the lagging winding waters
One sees far off stealing away to meet the rich drooping purple of the sky,
A stillness falls; a supernatural silence
Lies on the lap of Nature.

The street is man's life, and the waters, earth's sky-dowry,
And this rich span's unreal splendour, symbol hue, sign of sight of the Unseen.
Man's life lies mute, the waters run to the splendour,
The Unseen is this mighty Silence.

Metrical Scheme:

⏑⏑ | −− ‖ ⏑⏑ | −⏑ | −⏑ | −⏑ |
⏑− | −− ‖ −⏑⏑ | −⏑ | −⏑ | −−⏑ | −⏑⏑ | ⏑− |
⏑− | ⏑− ‖ ⏑−⏑ | −⏑⏑ | −⏑ |
−⏑⏑ | −⏑ | −⏑ |
⏑−⏑ | −− ‖ ⏑⏑ | −⏑ | −− | −⏑ |
⏑⏑ | −− ‖ ⏑−⏑ | −⏑ | −⏑ | −−⏑ | −⏑⏑ | ⏑− |
−− | −− ‖ ⏑−⏑ | −⏑⏑ | −⏑ |
⏑⏑ | −⏑⏑ | −⏑ | −⏑ |

❀

In some faint dawn,
In some dim eve,
    Like a gesture of Light,
    Like a dream of delight
Thou comst nearer and nearer to me.

Metrical Scheme:

⏑⏑ | −− |
⏑⏑ | −− |
⏑⏑− | ⏑⏑− |
⏑⏑− | ⏑⏑− |
⏑⏑− | ⏑⏑− | ⏑⏑− |

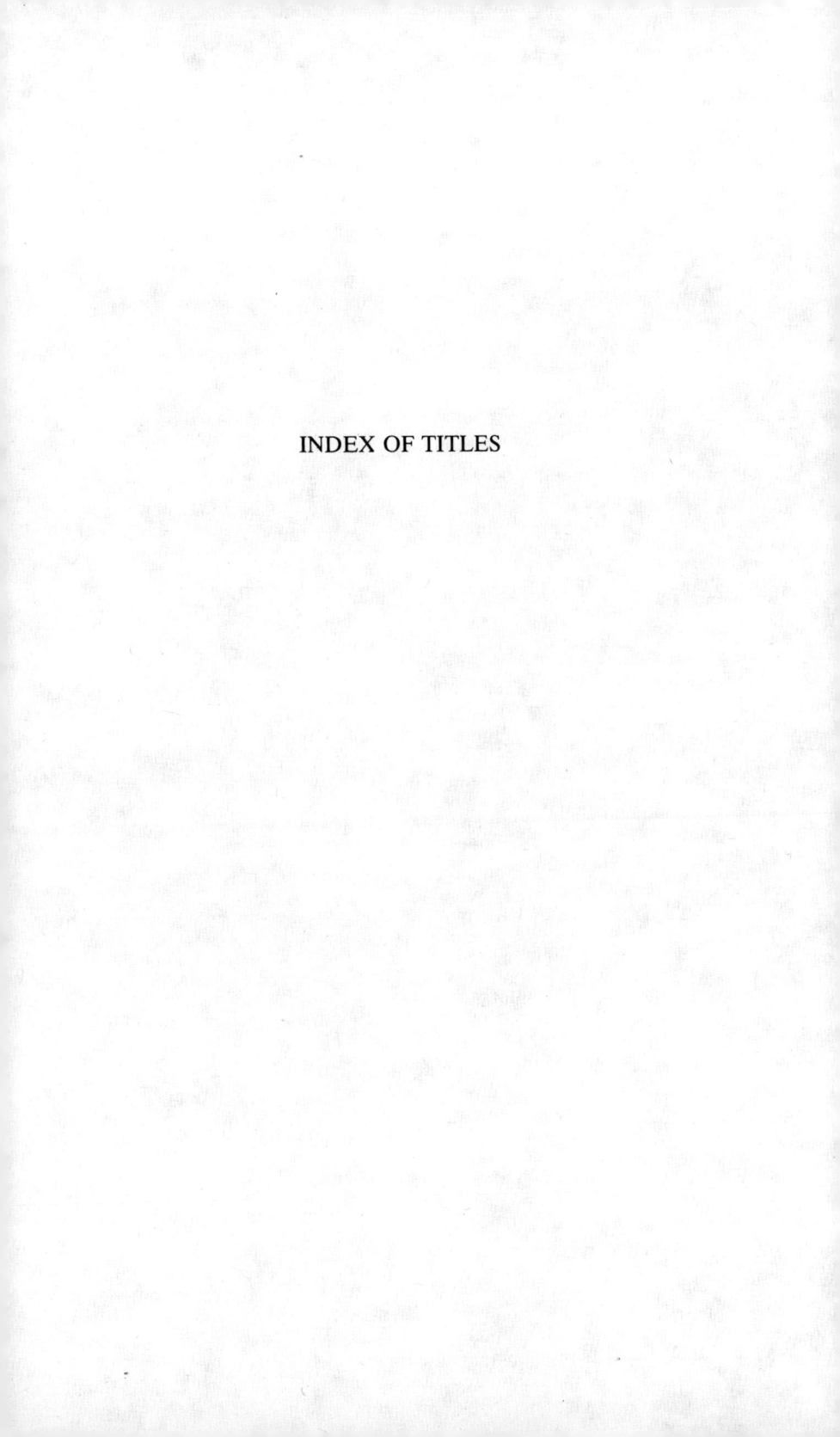

INDEX OF TITLES

INDEX OF TITLES

Adwaita	163
Ahana	523
Ascent: Beyond the Silence	568
Ascent: The Silence	567
Baji Prabhou	281
Bankim Chandra Chatterji	25
Because Thou art ...	165
Because thy flame is spent ...	126
The Bird of Fire	571
The Birth of Sin	69
The Bliss of Brahman	158
Bliss of Identity	142
The Blue Bird	104
The Body	159
Bride of the Fire	103
The Call of the Impossible	136
Charles Stewart Parnell	15
The Children of Wotan (1940)	112
A Child's Imagination	48
Chitrangada	315
Contrasts	135
Cosmic Consciousness	144
The Cosmic Dance	149
The Cosmic Man	120
The Cosmic Spirit	161
Creation	154
Death and the Traveller Fire	604
The Death of a God	598
Descent	563
The Descent of Ahana	537
Despair on the Staircase	113
Discoveries of Science	138
The Divine Hearing	164
Divine Sense	166
Divine Sight	165
The Divine Worker	154
A Doubt	33

The Dream Boat	561
A Dream of Surreal Science	156
The Dual Being	152
The Dwarf Napoleon	110
Electron	141
Envoi	28
Epigram	32
Epiphany	73
Epitaph	33
Estelle	9
Euphrosyne	31
Evening	46
Evolution	136
Evolution	137
The Fear of Death	54
The Fire-King and the Messenger	606
Flame-Wind	559
Form	167
God	63
God to thy greatness ...	609
A God's Labour	99
The Godhead	148
Goethe	26
The Golden Light	146
The Greater Plan	147
The Guest	154
Hail to the Fallen	596
Hell and Heaven	93
Hic Jacet: Glasnevin Cemetery	11
The Hidden Plan	143
The Hill-top Temple	164
"I"	161
I cannot equal ...	124
I have a doubt ...	128
I have a hundred lives ...	127

Title	Page
Ilion	391
An Image	595
Immortality	167
Immortal Love	44
In a flaming as of spaces ...	614
In a mounting as of sea-tides ...	597
The Inconscient	145
The Inconscient Foundation	163
The Indwelling Universal	142
The Infinite Adventure	147
The Infinitesimal Infinite	138
In Horis Aeternum	577
The Inner Fields	169
The Inner Sovereign	155
In some faint dawn ...	616
In the Battle	156
In the ending of time ...	615
In the Moonlight	55
In the silence of midnight ...	603
Invitation	39
The Iron Dictators	166
The Island Grave	24
The Island Sun	106
Is this the end ...	108
I walked beside the waters ...	118
Jivanmukta	576
Journey's End	570
Kama	80
Kamadeva	82
Khaled of the Sea	259
The Kingdom Within	140
Krishna	150
Krishna: Cretics	590
Liberation	145
Liberation	159
Life	95
Life and Death	54
The Life Heavens	574
Life-Unity	146
Light	160
Lila	153
Lines on Ireland: 1896	12
The Little Ego	157
The Lost Boat	564
The Lost Deliverer	26
Love and Death	231
Love in Sorrow	22
The Lover's Complaint	20
Madhusudan Dutt	27
The Mahatmas: Kuthumi	83
Man the Despot of Contraries	168
Man the Enigma	151
Man the Mediator	137
Man the Thinking Animal	134
The Meditations of Mandavya	86
The Miracle of Birth	157
Miracles	48
Moments	158
Moon of Two Hemispheres	583
Morcundeya	117
The Mother of Dreams	67
The Mother of God	105
Musa Spiritus	589
My life is wasted ...	125
Night by the Sea	16
The Nightingale: An Impression	31
Nirvana	134
Now I have borne	141
Ocean Oneness	557
O Coil, Coil	10
O face that I have loved ...	124
Oh, but fair was her face ...	615
Oh ye Powers ...	609
O letter dull and cold ...	125
O life, thy breath ...	614
Omnipresence	162
One Day: The Little More	109
The One Self	168

Index of Titles

On the grey street ...	616
On the Mountains	50
O pall of black Night ...	594
The Other Earths	133
Outspread a Wave burst ...	613
Parabrahman	62
Perfect thy motion ...	7
Perigune Prologuises	34
Phaethon	7
The Pilgrim of the Night	144
The Rakshasas	77
Rebirth	51
Reminiscence	41
Renewal	565
Revelation	47
The Rishi	297
The River	560
Rose, I have loved ...	127
Rose of God	584
Saraswati with the Lotus	26
Science and the Unknowable	139
The Sea at Night	46
Seasons	52
Seer deep-hearted ...	603
Self	162
The Self's Infinity	152
Shiva	150
Shiva: The Inconscient Creator	573
Silence is all ...	107
The Silver Call	135
Silver foam ...	607
Since I have seen your face ...	30
Song	32
Songs to Myrtilla	1
Soul in the Ignorance	570
Soul, my soul ...	599
Soul's Scene	566
The Spring Child	29
Still there is something ...	128

The Stone Goddess	149
A strong son of lightning ...	595
Surrealist	113
Surrender	153
Symbol Moon	593
The Tale of Nala	335
A Thing Seen	19
Thou didst mistake ...	126
Thought the Paraclete	582
The Three Cries of Deiphobus	33
The Tiger and the Deer	569
Tiresias	608
To a Hero-Worshipper	8
To R.: On Her Birthday	75
Torn are the walls ...	605
To the Cuckoo	123
To the hill-tops ...	615
To the Sea	45
To weep because a glorious sun ...	129
Trance	572
Trance of Waiting	558
Transformation	133
Transiit, non Periit	123
A Tree	47
The Triumph-Song of Trishuncou	53
Uloupie	325
The Universal Incarnation	148
The Unseen Infinite	160
Urvasie	119
Urvasie	189
Vast-winged the wind ...	608
The Vedantin's Prayer	49
The Vigil of Thaliard	173
A Vision of Science	42
A voice arose ...	117
The Ways of the Spirit	139
What is this talk ...	129

Who	40	The Witness Spirit	143
Who art thou that camest ...	109	The Word of the Silence	151
Winged with dangerous deity ...	613	The World Game	591
The Witness and the Wheel	562	The Yogi on the Whirlpool	140

INDEX OF FIRST LINES

INDEX OF FIRST LINES

First line	Title	Page
A bare impersonal hush is now my mind	The Word of the Silence	151
A conscious and eternal Power is here	The Mother of God	105
A deep enigma is the soul of man	Man the Enigma	151
A dumb Inconscient drew life's stumbling maze	Man the Mediator	137
A face on the cold dire mountain peaks	Shiva	573
A far sail on the unchangeable monotone of a slow slumbering sea	In Horis Aeternum	577
A flame-wind ran from the gold of the east	Flame-Wind	559
A godhead moves us to unrealised things	The Call of the Impossible	136
After six hundred years did Fate intend	Lines on Ireland	12
After unnumbered steps of a hill-stair	The Hill-top Temple	164
A golden evening, when the thoughtful sun	Evening	46
A gold moon-raft floats and swings slowly	Moon of Two Hemispheres	583
A life of intensities wide, immune	The Life Heavens	574
All are deceived, do what the One Power dictates	The One Self	168
All is abolished but the mute Alone	Nirvana	134
All is not finished in the unseen decree	Evolution	137
All my cells thrill swept by a surge of splendour	Descent	563
All Nature is taught in radiant ways to move	Bliss of Identity	142
All sounds, all voices have become Thy voice	The Divine Hearing	164
A naked and silver-pointed star	Trance	572
An irised multitude of hills and seas	The Other Earths	133
A noon of Deccan with its tyrant glare	Baji Prabhou	281
A perfect face amid barbarian faces	Goethe	26
Arise now, tread out the fire	The Death of a God	598
Arisen to voiceless unattainable peaks	The Unseen Infinite	160
As some bright archangel in vision flies	Thought the Paraclete	582
A strong son of lightning came down...	A Strong Son of Lightning	595
At last I find a meaning of soul's birth	Krishna	150
A tree beside the sandy river-beach	A Tree	47
A trifling unit in a boundless plan	Man the Thinking Animal	134
At the way's end when the shore raised up its dim line...	The Lost Boat	564
A voice arose that was so sweet and terrible	A voice arose	117
Awake, awake, O sleeping men of Troy	The Three Cries of Deiphobus	33
Because Thou art All-beauty and All-bliss	Because Thou art	165
Because thy flame is spent, shall mine grow less	Because thy flame is spent	126
Behold, by Maya's fantasy of will	The Dwarf Napoleon	110
Bride of the Fire, clasp me now close	Bride of the Fire	103
Brilliant, crouching, slouching,...	The Tiger and the Deer	569

Index of First Lines

Child of the infant years, Euphrosyne	*Euphrosyne*	31
Cool may you find the youngling grass, my herd	*Perigune Prologuises*	34
Drawn in her journey eternal compelling the labour of mortals	*Ilion*	391
Day and night begin, you tell me	*Seasons*	52
Death wanders through our lives at will, sweet Death	*The Fear of Death*	54
Do you remember, Love, that sunset pale	*Love in Sorrow*	22
Each sight is now immortal with Thy bliss	*Divine Sight*	165
Flame that invadest my empire of sorrow wordless and sombre	*Death and the Traveller Fire*	604
Glory and greatness and the joy of life	*The Rakshasas*	77
Goddess supreme, Mother of Dream, by thy ivory doors...	*The Mother of Dreams*	67
God to thy greatness	*God to thy greatness*	609
Gold-white wings a-throb in the vastness	*The Bird of Fire*	571
Hail to the fallen, the fearless	*Hail to the fallen*	596
Hark in the trees the low-voiced nightingale	*The Nightingale*	31
He is in me, round me, facing everywhere	*Omnipresence*	162
He said, "I am egoless, spiritual, free"	*Self*	162
However long Night's hour, I will not dream	*The Hidden Plan*	143
How hast thou lost, O month of honey and flowers	*Bankim Chandra Chatterjee*	25
How shall ascending Nature touch her goal	*The Ways of the Spirit*	139
I am a single Self all Nature fills	*The Cosmic Spirit*	161
I am greater than the greatness of the seas	*Man the Despot of Contraries*	168
I am held no more by life's alluring cry	*The Greater Plan*	147
I am swallowed in a foam-white sea of bliss	*The Bliss of Brahman*	158
I am the bird of God in His blue	*The Blue Bird*	104
I cannot equal those most absolute eyes	*I cannot equal*	124
I contain the wide world in my soul's embrace	*The Indwelling Universal*	142
I dreamed that in myself the world I saw	*A Vision of Science*	42
I dwell in the spirit's calm nothing can move	*The Witness Spirit*	143
I face earth's happenings with an equal soul	*The Divine Worker*	154
If I had wooed thee for thy colour rare	*Immortal Love*	44
If now must pause the bullock's jingling tune	*In the Moonlight*	55
If perfect moments on the peak of things	*Moments*	158
If thou wouldst traverse Time with vagrant feet	*Epigram*	32
I have a doubt, I have a doubt that kills	*I have a doubt*	128
I have a hundred lives before me yet	*I have a hundred lives*	127
I have become what before Time I was	*The Self's Infinity*	152
I have discovered my deep deathless being	*The Guest*	154
I have drunk deep of God's own liberty	*Immortality*	167
I have gathered my dreams in a silver air	*A God's Labour*	99
I have heard a foghorn shouting at a sheep	*Surrealist*	113

Index of First Lines

I have sailed the golden ocean	The Island Sun	106
I have thrown from me the whirling dance of mind	Liberation	145
I have wrapped the wide world in my wider self	Cosmic Consciousness	144
I housed within my heart the life of things	Life-Unity	146
I look across the world and no horizon walls my gaze	The Cosmic Man	120
I looked for Thee alone, but met my glance	The Iron Dictators	166
I made an assignation with the Night	The Pilgrim of the Night	144
Immense retreats of silence and of gloom	On the Mountains	50
In a flaming as of spaces	(a fragment)	614
In a mounting as of sea-tides	In a mounting as of sea-tides	597
In a town of gods, housed in a little shrine	The Stone Goddess	149
In Bagdad by Euphrates, Asia's river	Khaled of the Sea	263
In god-years yet unmeasured by a man's thought	The World Game	591
In Manipur upon her orient hills	Chitrangada	315
In some faint dawn	(A fragment)	616
In the blue of the sky, in the green of the forest	Who	40
In the ending of time, in the sinking of space	(a fragment)	615
In the silence of midnight, in the light of dawn or noontide	In the silence of midnight	603
In the silence of the night-time	Hell and Heaven	93
Into the Silence, into the Silence	Ascent – The Silence	567
In us is the thousandfold Spirit who is one	Lila	153
In woodlands of the bright and early world	Love and Death	231
I passed into a lucent still abode	Evolution	136
I sat behind the dance of Danger's hooves	The Godhead	148
I saw my soul a traveller through Time	The Miracle of Birth	157
I saw the electric stream on which is run	Discoveries of Science	138
I shall not die	The Triumph-Song of Trishuncou	53
Is this the end of all that we have been	Is this the end	108
I walked beside the waters of a world of light	I walked beside the waters	118
I walked on the high-wayed Seat of Solomon	Adwaita	163
Life, death, – death, life; the words have led for ages	Life and Death	54
Light, endless Light! darkness has room no more	Light	160
Lone on my summits of calm...	Trance of Waiting	558
Love, a moment drop thy hands	Night by the Sea	16
Majestic, mild, immortally august	Epiphany	73
Man's science builds its abstracts cold and brief	Science and the Unknowable	139

Index of First Lines

Many boons the new years make us	*A Doubt*	33
Moulded of twilight and the vesper star	*Epitaph*	33
Mute stands she, lonely on the topmost stair	*Despair on the Staircase*	113
My breath runs in a subtle rhythmic stream	*Transformation*	133
My life is then a wasted ereme	*To a Hero-Worshipper*	8
My life is wasted like a lamp ablaze	*My life is wasted*	125
My mind, my soul grow larger than all Space	*Liberation*	159
My soul arose at dawn and, listening, heard	*Reminiscence*	41
My soul regards its veiled subconscient base	*The Inconscient Foundation*	163
Mystic Miracle, daughter of Delight	*Life*	95
Nala, Nishadha's king, paced by a stream	*The Tale of Nala*	335
Not in annihilation lost, nor given	*Transiit, non Periit*	123
Not soon is God's delight in us completed	*Rebirth*	51
Now I have borne Thy presence and Thy light	*Now I have borne*	141
Now more and more the Epiphany within	*The Inner Sovereign*	155
Ocean is there and evening; the slow moan	*The Island Grave*	24
O Coil, honied envoy of the spring	*O Coil, Coil*	10
O desolations vast, O seas of space	*Kama*	80
O face that I have loved	*O face that I have loved*	124
Of Spring is her name for whose bud and blooming	*The Spring Child*	29
Often, in the slow ages' wide retreat	*In the Battle*	156
O grey wild sea	*To the Sea*	45
Oh, but fair was her face as she lolled in her green-tinted robe	*(a fragment)*	615
Oh ye Powers of the Supreme and of the Mother, the Divine	*Oh ye Powers*	609
O immense Light and thou, O spirit-wide boundless Space	*Krishna*	590
O joy of gaining all the soul's desire	*The Meditations of Mandavya*	86
O Lady Venus, shine on me	*Song*	32
O letter dull and cold, how can she read	*O letter dull and cold*	125
O life, thy breath is but a cry to the Light	*(a fragment)*	614
On a dire whirlpool in the hurrying river	*The Yogi on the Whirlpool*	140
Once again thou hast climbed, O moon	*Symbol Moon*	593
One day, and all the half-dead is done	*One Day*	109
One dreamed and saw a gland write Hamlet, drink	*A Dream of Surreal Science*	156
On the grey street, on the lagging winding waters	*(a fragment)*	616
On the waters of a nameless Infinite	*The Infinite Adventure*	147
On the white summit of eternity	*Shiva*	150
O pale and guiding light, now star unsphered	*Charls Stewart Parnell*	15

Index of First Lines

First line	Title	Page
O pall of black Night painted with still gold stars	O pall of black Night	594
O plaintive, murmuring reed, begin thy strain	The Lover's Complaint	20
O Soul who com'st fire-mantled from the earth	The Fire-King and the Messenger	606
O thou golden image	A Child's Imagination	48
O Thou of whom I am the instrument	Surrender	153
Our godhead calls us in unrealised things	Our godhead calls us	165
Out from the Silence, out from the Silence	Ascent – Beyond the Silence	568
Out of a seeming void and dark-winged sleep	The Inconscient	145
Out of a still Immensity we came	The Infinitesimal Infinite	138
Outspread a Wave burst, a Force leaped from the Unknown	(a fragment)	613
O Will of God that stirrest and the Void	Morcundeya	117
O word concealed in the upper fire	Musa Spiritus	589
O worshipper of the formless Infinite	Form	167
Pale poems, weak and few, who vainly use	Envoi	28
Patriots, behold your guerdon. This man found	Hic Jacet	11
Perfect thy motion ever within me	Perfect thy motion	7
Poet, who first with skill inspired did teach	Madhusudan Dutt	27
Pururavus from converse held with Gods	Urvasie	119
Pururavus from Titan conflict ceased	Urvasie	189
Pythian he came; repressed beneath his heel	The Lost Deliverer	26
Rishi who trance-held on the mountains old	The Rishi	297
Rose, I have loved thy beauty, as I love	Rose, I have loved	127
Rose of God, vermilion stain on the sapphires of heaven	Rose of God	584
Rushing from Troy like a cloud on the plains...	An Image	595
Seer deep-hearted, divine King of the secrecies	Seer deep-hearted	603
She in her garden, near the high grey wall	A Thing Seen	19
Silence is all, say the sages	Silence is all	107
Silence is round me, wideness ineffable	Ocean Oneness	557
Silver foam in the dim East	Silver foam	607
Since I have seen your face at the window, sweet	Since I have seen your face	30
Since Thou hadst all eternity to amuse	Creation	155
Snow in June may break from Nature	Miracles	48
Sole in the meadows of Thebes Tiresias sat by the Dirce	Tiresias	608
Someone leaping from the rocks	Revelation	47
Soul in the Ignorance, wake from its stupor	Soul in the Ignorance	570
Soul, my soul, reascend over the edge of life	Soul, my soul	599

Index of First Lines

Sounds of the wakening world, the year's increase	To the Cuckoo	123
Spirit Supreme	The Vedantin's Prayer	49
Still there is something that I lack in thee	Still there is something	128
Strayed from the roads of Time...	The Descent of Ahana	537
Surely I take no more an earthly food	Divine Sense	166
Sweet is the night, sweet and cool	Songs to Myrtilla	1
The clouds lain on forlorn spaces of sky, weary and lolling	Soul's Scene	566
The day ends lost in a stretch of even	Journey's End	570
The electron on which forms and worlds are built	Electron	141
The grey sea creeps half-visible, half-hushed	The Sea at Night	46
There are two beings in my single self	The Dual Being	152
There is a brighter ether than this blue	The Inner Fields	169
There is a godhead of unrealised things	The Silver Call	135
There is a kingdom of the spirit's ease	The Kingdom Within	140
There is a silence greater than any known	Jivanmukta	576
There is a wisdom like a brooding Sun	The Universal Incarnation	148
The repetition of thy gracious years	To R.	75
The seven mountains and the seven seas	The Mahatmas	83
These wanderings of the suns, these stars at play	Parabrahman	62
This body which was once my universe	The Body	159
This puppet ego the World-Mother made	The Little Ego	157
This strutting "I" of human self and pride	"I"	161
Thou didst mistake, thy spirit's infant flight	Thou didst mistake	126
Thou who pervadest all the worlds below	God	63
Thy golden Light came down into my brain	The Golden Light	146
Thy tears fall fast, O mother on its bloom	Saraswati with the Lotus	26
Torn are the walls and the borders carved by a miserly Nature	Torn are the walls	605
To the hill-tops of silence from over the infinite sea	(a fragment)	615
To weep because a glorious sun has set	To weep because a glorious sun	129
Two measures are there of the cosmic dance	The Cosmic Dance	149
Under the high and gloomy eastern hills	Uloupie	325
Vast-winged the wind ran, violent, black-cowled waves	Vast-winged the wind	608
Vision delightful alone on the hills...	Ahana	523
What is this talk of slayer and of slain	What is this talk	129
What mighty and ineffable desire	The Birth of Sin	69
What opposites are here! A trivial life	Contrasts	135
When in the heart of the valleys and hid by the roses	Ramadeva	92
When the heart tires and the throb stills recalling	Renewal	565

Where Time a sleeping dervish is	*The Vigil of Thaliard*	173
"Where is the end of your armoured march, O children of Wotan?	*The Children of Wotan (1940)*	112
Who art thou in the heart comrade of man who sitst	*The Witness and the Wheel*	562
Who art thou that camest	*Who art thou that camest*	109
Who was it that came to me in a boat made of dream-fire	*The Dream Boat*	561
Why do thy lucid eyes survey	*Estelle*	9
Wild river in thy cataract far-murmured...	*The River*	560
Winged with dangerous deity	*(a fragment)*	613
With wind and the weather beating round me	*Invitation*	39
Ye weeping poplars by the shelvy slope	*Phaethon*	7